FARTHER TO GO

*Readings and Cases in
African-American Politics*

FARTHER TO GO

*Readings and Cases in
African-American Politics*

FRANKLIN D. GILLIAM, JR.

University of California, Los Angeles

HARCOURT COLLEGE PUBLISHERS

Fort Worth   Philadelphia   San Diego   New York   Orlando   Austin   San Antonio
Toronto   Montreal   London   Sydney   Tokyo

PUBLISHER	Earl McPeek
EXECUTIVE EDITOR	David Tatom
MARKETING STRATEGIST	Laura Brennan
PROJECT MANAGER	Angela Williams Urquhart

Image provided by Photodisc © 2002.

ISBN: 0-15-507232-3

Library of Congress Catalog Card Number: 2001086255

Address for Domestic Orders
Harcourt College Publishers, 6277 Sea Harbor Drive, Orlando, FL 32887-6777
800-782-4479

Address for International Orders
International Customer Service
Harcourt College Publishers, 6277 Sea Harbor Drive, Orlando, FL 32887-6777
407-345-3800
(fax) 407-345-4060
(e-mail) hbintl@harcourtbrace.com

Address for Editorial Correspondence
Harcourt College Publishers, 301 Commerce Street, Suite 3700, Fort Worth, TX 76102

Web Site Address
http://www.harcourtcollege.com

Printed in the United States of America

1 2 3 4 5 6 7 8 9 0   039   9 8 7 6 5 4 3 2 1

Harcourt College Publishers

To Jacquie, Ariel, and Frank III

And

Velma and Frank, Sr.

PREFACE

This book grew out of teaching African-American politics at the graduate and undergraduate level. Throughout the years I became convinced of a few simple things. First, students need a better historical grounding if they are to understand contemporary racial politics. At the very least, for example, they ought to have a strong working knowledge of the civil rights movement. Second, the study of black politics ultimately involves the totality of the black experience. In other words, students need to know something about culture, economics, and social psychology in order to usefully understand the relationship between the black "community" and the political system. Third, students should be exposed to primary documents. In addition to scholarly writings, they need to read significant court cases, speeches, and statutes to discover the real texture of racial politics in America. These three intuitions guide the design of the book.

Although there are excellent texts on African-American politics, the pedagogical concerns raised above require a broader and quite different set of materials.[1] Over the years, and with the input of my students, I developed *Farther to Go* as a course "reader" that is part documentary anthology, part literature review, and part bibliography. The title refers to the notion that the United States has made tremendous strides toward racial equality but clearly has "farther to go." Put differently, African-American inclusion in American political life can be characterized as an ongoing and often volatile process. The primary aim of the book is to account for how we got this far, how much farther we have to go, and how we propose to get there. To do this I selected a blend of primary documents, academic research, and popular essays related to black politics. I provide context for each selection and summarize key themes, ideas, theories, and findings. In addition, I provide footnotes in support of particular points of view or to guide readers to relevant bodies of literature. To the extent that I make judgments it is to distinguish key points or concepts between the readings. I leave it to the instructor and the student to formulate a critical analysis. My role, as I see it, is to provide a broad overview of the African-American political experience.

OUTLINE OF THE BOOK

The book has three parts. The first two parts reflect the significance of history to an understanding of modern black politics. Part I focuses on political history before the 1950s. Chapter 1 examines how the politics of race, as defined by the slavery issue, influenced early American government. Chapter 2 covers black politics from the middle of the 19th century to the middle of the 20th century. In particular, it explores Emancipation, Reconstruction, and Jim Crow. Part II is a study of the civil rights movement. This section posits that the movement had three analytically distinct stages that are identified by an emphasis on a specific political tactic. Chapter 3 looks at litigation over school desegregation as a dominant political strategy. Chapter 4 highlights the approach of nonviolent direct action advocated by Martin Luther King, Jr., and Chapter 5 studies "black power."

The last part of the book investigates the contemporary consequences of the struggle for black political inclusion. The basic argument is that the politics of race in the post-civil rights period is infinitely more complex compared to the 1950s and 1960s. Put differently, there is serious and legitimate disagreement about the appropriate goals and remedies. I examine five dimensions of contemporary black politics. Chapter 6 looks at the current state of racial attitudes. Chapter 7 is about ideology, identity, and black political thought. Chapter 8 examines racial politics in urban centers. Chapter 9 explores national-level politics, and Chapter 10 touches on key public policy debates. In sum, the book looks backward to understand the future. As George Santayana said, "those who cannot remember the past are condemned to repeat it."

SELECTION CRITERIA

The selection of the particular pieces was based on several factors. Some choices were obvious on their face; others are less well known. I also included a mixture of "classics" and works from contemporary authors. I tried to incorporate a range of perspectives and many different political "voices." Moreover, I tried to excerpt, present, and summarize each piece without prejudice. As with any survey, there is bound to be sampling error. Space constraints, the inability to secure certain permissions, and personal taste have surely led to the omission of some essential writings. In addition, the book is confined to the black political experience in America.[2] From time to time, writers make explicit connection to the African Diaspora and to the struggles of oppressed people of color worldwide. Nonetheless, the focus of the book is on the domestic context. Another goal was to offer readings with varying degrees of difficulty. Some items are "quick reads" whereas others require more diligence. I also included works that represent different research traditions. For instance, certain pieces are discursive while others hew to an empirical approach using statistical data. Some are historical while others are topical and current. In sum, the included selections were picked because they dramatize important elements of the African-American political experience.

NOMENCLATURE

I use "African-American" and "black" interchangeably throughout the book because I think both convey important information about people of African descent living in America.[3] On the one hand, the concept of the hyphenated American implicitly accepts the metaphor of the mosaic—separate strands woven together by a common thread. At some level this notion is applicable to the modern American experience as blacks and nonblacks (especially whites) often peacefully coexist in separate enclaves but sharing public spaces. On the other, the fact that skin color is so important for many societies must be noted. Indeed, skin pigmentation is commonly the basis for prejudice and discrimination in many cultures. For example, most black Americans know the immediate sting of prejudgment on the basis of visual racial cues. Being passed up by cabdrivers and indiscriminately stopped by police officers is far too routine for many blacks in contemporary society. In short, using both terms is an attempt to convey the point that the black experience in American politics is multidimensional.

I also use the term "black community" to refer loosely to the common elements of African-American life. This is more out of convenience than any serious belief that there is a singular world view among black Americans.[4] To the contrary, one of the implicit assumptions of the book is that black (political) life, particularly in the post-civil rights era, is nuanced and complex. Nonetheless, the idea of "community" is expressed in the everyday exchanges of recognition between black strangers. In other words, concepts like "brothers" and "sisters," for example, suggest the existence of an imagined black family or nation that is borne out of not only a unique and shared historical legacy, but also from a modern sensibility that even the highest achievements cannot exempt one from racism.

Finally, at some points in the book I refer to "racial" politics instead of black or African-American politics. I have tried to use the term in the context of talking specifically about the African-American political experience. Living in California, however, I am abundantly aware that "racial" politics is about more than the black/white dichotomy. The emergence of Latino and Asian candidates and voters will surely shape the future of the American political process.[5] Nonetheless, African-American politics is fundamentally defined by racial distinctions. That is, the long history of government-sanctioned discrimination against blacks marked phenotype as the basis for political, social, and economic distinctions.

COMMENTS FOR INSTRUCTORS

My hope and expectation is that individual instructors will tailor the material in the book to their own pedagogical goals. I designed the book as a primary text for undergraduate classes in African-American politics. I have also found that it is useful as a supplemental text for introductory graduate courses on race and politics (especially in political science and African-American Studies). Additionally, it can be used to complement courses on intergroup relations, American Studies, Ethnic Studies, and modern political history. I have tried to use accessible language in the headnotes while at the same time paying attention to higher order analytics. In addition, I have included study questions at the end of each chapter.

I realize there is great variation in the background and knowledge level of students who take courses in black politics. With this in mind I have tried to include some materials that cover the "basics" and others that offer more in-depth analysis on particular topics. I have also tried not to take a "point of view." There are some articles consistent with my personal politics and some that cut against the very grain of my core beliefs. My simple goal is to pierce a wide swath through the readings and cases of African-American politics leaving traces that others can follow. Although some chapters are more detailed than others, I do not purport to be an expert on most of the topics presented in the book. What I have tried to do, however, is to bring together a wide range of materials in one place and provide commentary on the context and significance of the various selections.

ACKNOWLEDGMENTS

I would like to thank the many students at the University of California, Los Angeles (UCLA), the University of Wisconsin-Madison, the University of Dar Es Salaam (Tanzania), and Grinnell College who contributed to my thinking about African-American politics. In addition, I am grateful to the thoughtful comments of the following reviewers: James C. Foster, Oregon State University; John A. Garcia, University of Arizona; Jan Leighley, Texas A&M University; and Sharon D. Wright, University of Missouri–Columbia.

I am also grateful to the Department of Political Science and the Center for Communications at UCLA, the support of the National Science Foundation, the Annie E. Casey Foundation, the Ford Foundation, and the W.T. Grant Foundation. I would like to extend special thanks to Jessica Hausman, Elizabeth Frank, and Pam Singh for their tireless work in surveying a vast body of literature. Finally, I would like to thank my wife Jacquie for her love and support

NOTES

1. For example, Lucius J. Barker and Mack H. Jones. *African-Americans and the American political system* 3rd edition (Englewood Cliffs, NJ: Prentice Hall) 1994; Matthew Holden. *The politics of the black "nation."* (New York, Chandler Pub. Co.) 1973; Paula D. McClain and Joseph Stewart, Jr. *Can we all get along?" Racial and ethnic minorities in American politics* (Boulder, Colo.: Westview Press) 1995; Huey L. Perry (ed.) *Race, politics, and governance in the United States* (Gainesville, FLA: University Press of Florida) 1996; Huey L. Perry and Wayne Parent (eds.) *Blacks and the American political system* (Gainesville: University Press of Florida) 1995; Michael B. Preston, Lenneal J. Henderson, Jr., Paul Puryear (eds.) *The new black politics: The search for political power* (New York: Longman) 1982; Theodore Rueter. *The politics of race: African-Americans and the political system.* (Armonk, N.Y.: M. E. Sharpe) 1995. Hanes Walton, Jr. *African-American power and politics: the political context variable.* (New York: Columbia University Press) 1997; Hanes Walton, Jr. and Robert C.

Smith. *American politics and the African American quest for universal freedom* (New York: Longman) 2000.

2. For material on the African Diaspora, see for example, Michael L. Conniff and Thomas J. Davis. *Africans in the Americas: a history of the Black Diaspora* (New York: St. Martin's Press) 1994; Joseph E. Harris (ed.) *Global dimensions of the African Diaspora* 2nd ed. (Washington, D.C.: Howard University Press) 1993; Sidney J. Lemelle and Robin D.G. Kelley. *Imagining home: class, culture, and nationalism in the African Diaspora* (London; New York: Verso) 1994.

3. Karlyn Bowman, "What we call ourselves," *Public Perspective 5* 1994:29–31; Ruth W. Grant and Marion Orr, "Language, race and politics:" From "Black" to "African-American," *Politics and Society* 24:2 1996:137–152.

4. See, Michael C. Dawson. *Behind the mule: Race and class in African-American politics* (Princeton: Princeton University Press) 1994; Patricia Gurin, Shirley Hatchett, and James S. Jackson. *Hope and independence: Blacks' response to party and electoral politics* (New York: Russell Sage Foundation) 1989; Andrea Y. Simpson. *The tie that binds: Identity and political attitudes in the post-civil rights generation* (New York: New York University Press) 1998; Katherine Tate. *From protest to politics: the new black voters in American elections* (Cambridge: Harvard University Press) 1993.

5. Louis DeSipio. *Counting on the Latino vote: Latinos as a new electorate* (Charlottesville, Va.: University of Virginia Press) 1996; Rodolfo O. de la Garza, Louis DeSipio (eds.) *Awash in the mainstream: Latino politics in the 1996 elections* (Boulder, Colo.: Westview Press) 1999; Carol Hardy-Fanta. *Latina politics, Latino politics: gender, culture, and political participation in Boston* (Philadelphia: Temple University Press) 1993. Rodney E. Hero. *Latinos and the U.S. political system: two-tiered pluralism* (Philadelphia: Temple University Press) 1992; *Faces of inequality: social diversity in American politics* (New York: Oxford University Press) 1998; Lisa Lowe. *Immigrant acts: on Asian American cultural politics* (Durham, N.C.: Duke University Press) 1996; Don T. Nakanishi. *The UCLA Asian Pacific American voter registration study* (Los Angeles, Calif.: University of California Los Angeles, Institute for Social Science Research) 1986; *National Asian Pacific American political roster and resource guide*. 6th ed. (Los Angeles, CA: UCLA Asian American Studies Center) 1995; Harry Pachon and Louis DeSipio. *New Americans by choice: political perspectives of Latino immigrants* (Boulder: Westview Press) 1994.; Wayne A. Santoro, "Conventional politics takes center stage: the Latino struggle against English-only laws," *Social Forces* 77: 3(March 1999):887–890; Leland T. Saito. *Race and politics: Asian Americans, Latinos, and whites in a Los Angeles suburb* (Urbana, Ill.: University of Illinois Press) 1998.

CONTENTS

1

THE POLITICAL HISTORY OF RACE

THE PRE-CIVIL WAR PERIOD: 1787–1862

Black politics has deep historical roots in American political life. From the beginning, the "founding fathers" struggled to determine the rules of inclusion (or exclusion, as the case may be) for people of African descent. On the one hand, it was clear that any new constitution could not be ratified if it sought to abolish slavery. On the other hand, the institution of slavery itself was, *prima facie*, incompatible with the principles articulated by the framers of the constitution. The net result was a document that never used the word "slavery" but was nonetheless deeply imbued with racial considerations.

*There are three parts of the original Constitution that bear directly on racial matters. **Article I, section 3**, or the 3/5ths Compromise as it is commonly known, was the result of a compromise between representatives from the Northern and Southern states. The North wanted the slaves to count for taxation purposes whereas the South wanted them to count for representational purposes. Both sides finally agreed to a scheme in which "[R]epresentation and direct taxes shall be apportioned among the several states . . . by adding to the number of free persons . . . three fifths of all other persons." In short, slaves were conceived of as part property, part human. The degradation of American blacks was thus woven into the very fabric of American government.*

This is not to say that all Americans supported slavery. Groups of "free blacks" and any number of "abolition societies" lobbied the delegates at the Constitutional Convention for the abolition of slavery. Even some delegates, such as James Madison, called for an end to the slave trade. Further, European observers were quick to point out the discrepancy between American ideals and "that peculiar institution."

*The slave commerce clause (**Article 2, section 9**) dealt with this tension by stipulating that Congress could not prohibit ". . . the migration or importation of such persons" (the slave trade) before 1808 but at the same time levied a $10/person import tax. While tacitly accepting the institution of slavery, the "founding fathers" also left some "wiggle room" to accommodate the impending abolitionist movement.*

***Article IV, section, 2**, or the "fugitive slave clause," represents the substantive impact of slavery on the lives of most black Americans. There was no discharge from service even if one could escape to a free territory or state. Runaway slaves were to be returned to ". . . the party to whom such service or labor may be due." In essence, there was no way to flee for freedom.*

THE CONSTITUTION OF THE UNITED STATES: ARTICLE 1, SECTION 3; ARTICLE II, SECTION 9; ARTICLE IV, SECTION 2

ARTICLE I

Section 2. [1] The House of Representatives shall be composed of Members chosen every second Year by the People of the several States, and the Electors in each State shall have the Qualifications requisite for Electors of the most numerous Branch of the State Legislature.

[3] Representatives and direct Taxes shall be apportioned among the several States which may be included within this Union, according to their respective Numbers, which shall be determined by adding to the whole Number of free Persons, including those bound to Service for a Term of Years, and excluding Indians not taxed, three fifths of all other Persons. The actual Enumeration shall be made within three Years after the first Meeting of the Congress of the United States, and within every subsequent Term of ten Years, in such Manner as they shall by Law direct. The Number of Representatives shall not exceed one for every thirty Thousand, but each State shall have at Least one Representative; and until such enumeration shall be made, the State of New Hampshire shall be entitled to chuse three, Massachusetts eight, Rhode Island and Providence Plantations one, Connecticut five, New York six, New Jersey four, Pennsylvania eight, Delaware one, Maryland six, Virginia ten, north Carolina five, South Carolina five, and Georgia three.

ARTICLE II

Section 9. [1] The Migration or Importation of Such Persons as any of the States now existing shall think proper to admit, shall not be prohibited by the Congress prior to the Year one thousand eight hundred and eight, but a Tax or duty may be imposed on such Importation, not exceeding ten dollars for each Person.

ARTICLE IV

Section 2. [1] The Citizens of each State shall be entitled to all Privileges and Immunities of Citizens in the several States.

[3] No Person held to Service or Labour in one State, under the Laws thereof, escaping into another, shall, in Consequence of any Law or Regu-

lation therein, be discharges from such Service or Labour, but shall be delivered up on Claim of the Party to whom such Service or Labour may be due.

———————————————— ■ ————————————————

There are at least two plausible ways to interpret the founding fathers' handling of the race issue. Scholars such as John Roche contend that the framers were simply consensus-building politicians motivated by the simple desire to build a national government capable of reconciling competing state, political, and economic interests.[1] From this view, the failure to end slavery or to grant even the barest of citizenship rights to African-Americans was simply part of the bargain to ratify the constitution. In contrast, other scholars interpret the framers as unwilling to reconcile the conflict between democratic values and the institution of slavery to maintain elite hegemony. In his seminal book, *An American Dilemma*, Gunnar Myrdal contends that this "failure" is a direct historical cause of racial cleavage in America. In either case, race has a prominent role in the political history of the United States.[2]

The most obvious manifestation of America's early racial politics was the existence of slavery. Clearly, groups other than people of African descent were denied basic democratic rights.[3] Native Americans, white women, the landless, and a nontrivial number of white indentured servants were also discriminated against overtly. Nonetheless, the institution of slavery was a particular brand of domination reserved for blacks. The scope and extent of forced servitude was of overwhelming proportions.

As John Hope Franklin and Alfred Moss point out in the selection from their book From Slavery to Freedom, *rapid changes brought on by the Industrial Revolution made slavery a core element of southern economic life. This leads some observers to argue that slavery was essentially the result of economic, not racial concerns. As Eugene Genovese points out, however, while "planter capitalism" may have begun as an appendage to British capitalism, it quickly transformed into a ". . . powerful, largely autonomous civilization" with slave-holding as its central mark of distinction. Control of the slave population, therefore, was critical not only to the stability of the southern economy, but to the very nature of southern life.[4]*

As Franklin and Moss describe, southern states quickly moved to adopt a series of restrictive laws (or slave codes) ". . . which covered every aspect of the life of a slave." Additionally, new member states, such as Mississippi (1817) and Alabama (1819), made explicit provisions for the continuation of (black) slavery in their founding constitutions. The denial of fundamental political and human rights to slaves, therefore, destined the slaves to a subordinate position in the social, political, and economic hierarchy. They had no rights to their bodies, their offspring, or their fate. The implementation of the slave codes was achieved through several mechanisms. Slave patrols, whippings, imprisonment, and lynching were common forms of social control. The southern defense of racialized slavery was based on the view that blacks were not fully developed human beings. As such, they needed protection, guidance, and discipline. In contrast, by 1800, the majority of white indentured servants had bought their way out of servitude and received rights of citizenship. In this way, slavery had a special racial cast.

FROM SLAVERY TO FREEDOM
■

John Hope Franklin and Alfred A. Moss, Jr.

Excert from From Slavery to Freedom, *Chapter 8: That Peculiar Institution*

SCOPE AND EXTENT

Plantation slavery, as it developed in the cotton kingdom, was something of an anomaly on the American frontier. Although slavery was almost as old as the permanent settlements in America, not until the 19th century did it occupy so much of the attention and energy of the settlers as to threaten other forms of labor. The frontier had been a place where one could make or lose a fortune largely by one's own labors. The emergence of the great cotton plantation introduced a kind of exploitation of human and natural resources and fostered a type of discipline in rural areas that created what could at best be called a peculiar situation. Indeed, every aspect of agricultural life in the Southern United States underwent a complete transformation as a result of the new economic and social forces let loose by the Industrial Revolution. And what the industrial Revolution did to the capitalistic system, new lands and the prospect of wealth from cotton culture did to the system of slavery. Large-scale operations were the order of the day. The farm became a plantation, which in turn became a rural factory with the impersonality of a large-scale economic organization. The face of the Southern frontier had been changed. Cotton and slavery were the great transforming forces.

One of the most rapidly growing elements in the population was the slaves. In 1790 there had been less than 700,000 slaves. By 1830 there were more than 2 million. The South Atlantic states, from Delaware to Florida, were still ahead in numbers, with 1,300,000, while the states of the lower South, none of which had been in the Union in 1790, now had 604,000 slaves. By the last census before the Civil War, the slave population had grown to 3,953,760! The states of the cotton kingdom had taken the lead, with 1,998,000 slaves within their borders. Virginia was still ahead in the number of slaves in a single state, but Alabama and Mississippi were rabidly gaining ground. As a matter of fact, the slave population of all the states of the lower South was increasing rapidly, while that of the upper South was either increasing very slowly or, as in the case of Maryland, was actually declining. The increase in the slave population to virtually 4 million by 1860 is an eloquent testimony to the extent to which slavery had become entrenched in the Southern states.

The impression should not be conveyed that the whites of the South, numbering about 8 million in 1860, generally enjoyed the fruits of slave labor. There was a remarkable concentration of the slave population in the hands of a relative few. In 1860 there were only 384,884 slave owners. Thus, fully three-fourths of the white people of the South had neither slaves nor an immediate economic interest in the maintenance of slavery or the plantation system.

And yet, the institution came to dominate the political and economic thinking of the entire South and to shape its social pattern for two principal reasons. The great majority of the staple crops were produced on plantations employing slave labor, thus giving the owners an influence out of proportion to their number. Then, there was the hope on the part of most nonslaveholders that they would some day become owners of slaves. Consequently, they took on the habits and patterns of thought of slaveholders before they actually joined that select class.

While slaves were concentrated in areas where the staple crops were produced on a large scale, the bulk of the slave owners were small farmers. It is not too generally known that more than 200,000 owners in 1860 had five slaves or less. Fully 338,000 owners, or 88% of all the owners of slaves in 1860, held fewer than 20 slaves. (One must not be misled by these figures, however, for more than one-half of the slaves were employed as field workers on plantations with holdings of more than 20 slaves, and at least 25% of the slave community lived on plantations where the number of slaves was in excess of 50.) It is fairly generally conceded that from 30 to 60 slaves constituted the most profitable agricultural unit. If that is true, there were fewer plantations in the South that had what might be considered a satisfactory working force than has been generally believed. The concentration of 88% of all slaveholders in the small slave-owning group is significant for several important reasons. In the first place, it emphasizes the fact that the influence of large owners must have been enormous, since they have been successful in impressing posterity with the erroneous conception that plantations on which there were large numbers of slaves were typical. In the second place, it brings out the fact that the majority of slaveholding was carried on by yeomen rather than gentry. Finally, in a study of the institution of slavery, there is a rather strong indication that some distinction should be made between the possession of one or two slaves and the possession of, say, 50 or more.

But it was the tremendous productivity of the large plantations that placed the large slaveholder in a position of great influence. By 1860 Southern states were production 5,387,000 bales of cotton annually. Four state, Mississippi, Alabama, Louisiana, and Georgia, produced more than 3,500,000 bales of this crop. It is no mere accident that these same states were also at the top of the list in the number of large slaveholders. Of the states having slaveholders with more than 20 slaves, Mississippi led, just as it did in productivity of cotton, followed by Alabama, Louisiana, and Georgia.

THE SLAVE CODES

After the colonies secured their independence and established their own governments, they did not neglect the matter of slavery in the laws that they enacted. Where slavery was growing, as in the lower South in the late 18th and early 19th centuries, new and more stringent laws were enacted. All over the South, however, there emerged a body of laws generally regarded as the Slave Codes, which covered every aspect of the life of the slave. There were variations from state to state, but the general point of view expressed in most of them was the same: slaves are not people but property; laws should protect the ownership of such property and should also protect whites against any dangers that might arise from the presence of large numbers of slaves. It was also felt that slaves should be maintained in a position of due subordination in order that the optimum of discipline and work could be achieved.

The regulatory statues were frankly repressive, and whites made no apologies for them. The laws represented merely the reduction to legal phraseology of the philosophy of the South with regard to the institution of slavery. Slaves had not standing in the courts: they could not be a party to a law suit; they could not offer testimony, except against another slave or a free black; and their irresponsibility meant that their oaths were not binding. Thus, they could make no contracts. The ownership of property was generally forbidden them, though some states permitted slaves to have certain types of personal property. A slave could not strike a white person, even in self-defense; but the killing of a slave, however malicious the act, was rarely regarded as murder. The rape of a female slave was regarded as a crime but only because it involved trespassing.

The greater portion of the Slave Codes involved the many restrictions place on slaves to ensure the maximum protection of the white population and to maintain discipline among slaves. These rules were primarily negative. Slaves could not leave the plantation without authorization, and any white person finding them outside without permission could capture them and turn them over to public officials. They could not possess firearms, and in Mississippi they could not beat drums or blow horns. They could not hire themselves out without permission or in any other way conduct themselves as free people. They could not buy or sell goods. Their relationships with whites and free blacks were to be kept at a minimum. They could hot visit the homes of whites or free blacks, and they could not entertain such individuals in their quarters. They were never to assemble unless a white person was present, and they were never to receive, possess, or transmit any incendiary literature calculated to incite insurrections.

Whenever there was an insurrection, or even rumors of one, it was usually the occasion for the enactment of even more stringent laws to control activities and movements of slaves. For example, after the Vesey insurrection of 1822, South Carolina enacted a law requiring the imprisonment of all black seamen during the stay of their vessel in port. The Nat Turner insurrection of 1831 and the simultaneous drive of abolitionists against slavery brought fourth the enactment of many new repressive measures in other parts of the South as well as in Virginia and neighboring states. Long before the end of the slave period the Slave Codes in all the Southern states had become so elaborate that there was hardly need for modification even when new threats arose to shake the foundations of the institution.

One of the devices set up to enforce the Slave Codes and thereby maintain the institution of slavery was the patrol, which has been aptly described as an adaptation of the militia. Counties were usually divided into "beats," or areas of patrol, and free white men were called upon to serve for a stated period of time, one, three, or six months. These patrols were to apprehend slaves out of place and return them to their masters or commit them to jail, to visit slave quarters and search for various kinds of weapons that might be used in an uprising, and to visit assemblies of slaves where disorder might develop or where conspiracy might be planned. This system proved so inconvenient to some citizens that they regularly paid the fines that were imposed for dereliction of duty. A corrupted form of the patrol system was the vigilance committee, which came into existence during the emergencies created by uprisings or rumors of them. At such times, it was not unusual for the committee to disregard all caution and prudence and kill any blacks whom they encountered in their search. Committees like these frequently ended up engaging in nothing except a lynching party.

The most sensational and desperate reaction of slaves to their status was the conspiracy to revolt. To those who could summon the nerve to strike for their freedom in a group, it was what might be termed "carrying the fight to the enemy" in the hope that it would end, once and for all, the degradation of human enslavement. To whites it was a mad, sinister act of desperate savages, in with the devil, who could not appreciate the benign influences of the institution and who would dare shed the blood of their benefactors. Inherent in revolts was bloodshed on both sides. Blacks accepted this as the price of liberty, while whites were panic-stricken at the very thought of it. Even rumors of insurrections struck terror in the hearts of slaveholders and called forth the most vigorous efforts to guard against the dreaded eventuality.

Revolts, or conspiracies to revolt, persisted down to 1865. They began with the institution and did not end until slavery was abolished. It can, therefore, be said that they were a part of the institution, a kind of bitterness that whites had to take along with the sweetness of slavery. As the country was turning to Jeffersonian Republicanism at the beginning of the 19th century, many people believed that a new day had arrived for the common person. Some blacks, however, felt that they would have to force their new day by breaking away from slavery. In Henrico County, Virginia, they resolved to revolt against the institution under the leadership of Gabriel Prosser and Jack Bowler. For months they planned the desperate move, gathering clubs, swords, and the like for the appointed day. On August 30, 1800, over 1,000 slaves met six miles outside of Richmond and began to march on the city, but a violent storm almost routed the insurgents. Two slaves had already informed the whites, and Governor Monroe, acting promptly, called out more than 600 troops and notified every militia commander in the state. In due time scores of slaves were arrested, and 35 were executed. Gabriel Prosser was captured in late September, and after he refused to talk to anyone, he too was executed.

Following the War of 1812 the efforts of slaves to revolt continued. In Virginia in 1815 a white man, George Boxley, decided to attempt to free the slaves. He made elaborate plans, but a slave woman betrayed him and his conspirators. Although Boxley himself escaped, six slaves were hanged and another six were banished. When the revolutions of Latin America and Europe broke out, Americans could not restrain themselves in their praise and support of the fighters for liberty. The South joined in the loud hosannas, while slaves watched the movements for the emancipation of the slaves in Latin America and the Caribbean. Perhaps all these developments had something to do with what was the most elaborate, though not the most effective, conspiracy of the period: the Denmark Vesey insurrection.

Vesey had purchased his freedom in 1800 and for a score of years had made respectable living as a carpenter in Charleston, South Carolina. He was a sensitive, liberty-loving person and was not satisfied in the enjoyment of his own relatively comfortable existence. He believed in equality for everyone and resolved to do something for his slave brothers and sisters. Over a period of several years he carefully plotted his revolt and chose his assistants. Together they made and collected their weapons: 250 pike heads and bayonets and 300 daggers. Vesey also sought assistance from Haiti. He set the second Sunday in July 1822 for the day of the revolt; and when the word leaked out, he moved it up one month, but his assistants, who were scattered for miles around Charleston, did not all get the word. Meanwhile, the whites were well aware of what was going on and began to round up suspects. At least 139 blacks were arrested, 47 of whom were condemned. Even four white men were fined and imprisoned for encouraging them in their work. Estimates of the number of blacks involved in the plot ran as high as 9,000.

The following decade saw the entire South apprehensive over possible uprising. The revival of the antislavery movement and the publication of such incendiary material as David Walker's *Appeal* put the South's nerves on edge. Several revolts were reported on Louisiana plantations in 1829, and in 1830 a number of citizens of North Carolina asked their legislature for and because their slaves had become "almost uncountroulable." The panic of the 1820s culminated in 1831 with the insurrection of Nat Turner. This slave from Southampton County, Virginia, was a mystical, rebellious person who had on one occasion run away and then decided to return to his master. Perhaps he had already begun to feel that he had been selected by some divine power to deliver his people from slavery.

Upon the occasion of the solar eclipse in February 1831, Turner decided that the time had come for him to lead his people out of bondage. He selected the Fourth of July as the day, but when he became ill he postponed the revolt until he saw another sign. On August 13, when the sun turned a "peculiar greenish blue," he called the revolt for August 21. He and his followers began by killing Turner's master, Joseph Travis, and his family. In rapid succession other families fell before the blows of the blacks. Within 24 hours, 60 whites had been killed. The revolt was spreading rapidly when the main group of blacks was met and overpowered by state and federal troops. More than 100 slaves were killed in the encounter, and 13 slaves and 3 free Negroes were immediately hanged. Turner was captured on October 30, and in less than two weeks, on November 11, he was executed.

The South was completely dazed by the Southampton uprising. The situation was grossly exaggerated in many communities. Some reports were that whites had been murdered by the hundreds in Virginia. Small wonder that several states felt it necessary to call special sessions of the legislature to consider the emergency. Most states strengthened their Slave Codes, and citizens literally remained awake nights waiting for slaves to make another break. The uprisings continued. In 1835 several slaves in Monroe County, Georgia, were hanged or shipped to death because of implication in a conspiracy. In the following decade there were several uprisings in Alabama, Louisiana, and Mississippi. In 1853 a serious revolt in New Orleans involving 2,500 slaves was aborted by the informing of a free black. In 1856 the Maroons in Bladen and Robeson counties, North Carolina, "went on the warpath" and terrorized the countryside. Up until and throughout the Civil War, slaves demonstrated their violent antipathy for slavery by continuing to rise against it.

As restrictions mounted, slave revolts became increasingly common. Insurrections led by Gabriel Prosser (1800), Denmark Vesey (1822), and Nat Turner (1831) provided justification for a tightening of the slave codes. Politically, white southerners ". . . took the constitutional position that it was the responsibility of the federal government to protect individual property rights of slaveholders and to guarantee the capture of fugitive slaves."[5] Attacks on slavery, therefore, were not only a threat to southern economic and political interests but were also perceived as an assault on the core of southern culture.

As the size and the influence of northern population grew, however, there was notable concern that the spread of slavery into the western territories would jeopardize white "free labor." Further, the growing presence of abolitionists such as Sojourner Truth, Harriet Tubman, William Lloyd Garrison, Samuel Cornish, David Walker, and Frederick Douglass fueled increasing moral dissatisfaction with the institution of slavery.[6] The seeds for a showdown had been sown. The Missouri Compromise (1820), the Wilmot Proviso (1847), and the Kansas-Nebraska Act (1854) spelled out the fundamental differences between the North and the South and foreshadowed the start of the Civil War. In each case, northern interests sought to increase the number of "free" states admitted to the Union, while southern states sought to extend slavery into the territories under the auspices of federal protection.

The conflict came to a head with the Supreme Court's ruling in Dred Scott v. Sanford *(1857). In perhaps the most important governmental act concerning race in the 19th century, Chief Justice Taney ruled that blacks ". . . had no rights which the white man was bound to respect." The facts of Dred Scot are as follows. Dr. John Anderson left Missouri and went to Illinois for a period of four years to serve as an Army surgeon. He took his slave, Dred Scot, with him. Illinois was a free state, while Missouri was a slave state. Upon his return to Missouri, Scot filed suit for his freedom. Although the Circuit Court ruled in his favor, the Missouri*

Supreme Court reversed the lower court ruling. After some clever legal manuerving, Scot presented his case to the United States Supreme Court in 1856.

The case revolved around two basic issues. First, were blacks to be considered citizens within the meaning of the Constitution? Writing for the majority, Justice Taney concluded that the slavery commerce clause and the fugitive slave clause " . . . point directly and specifically to the Negro race as a separate class of persons, and show clearly that they were not regarded as a portion of the people or citizens of the government then formed." The second issue turned on the question of the scope of congressional authority over the territories. Here Taney ruled that the Missouri Compromise of 1820 was unconstitutional because it violated the protection of property rights as spelled out in the 5th Amendment. Put differently, the Supreme Court ruled that Congress overstepped its authority by prohibiting slavery in certain territories. Far from settling the issue of slavery, the ruling in Dred Scot *brought the issue to a head.*

EXCERPT FROM
DRED SCOTT V. SANFORD(1856)

Mr. Chief Justice Taney, The Opinion of the Court

Dred Scott v. John F. A. Sanford, 19 Howard 393, 400-411, 426-432, 436-437, 452, 454

There are two leading questions presented by the record:

1. Had the Circuit Court of the United States jurisdiction to hear and determine the case between these parties? And

2. If it had jurisdiction, is the judgment it has given erroneous or not?

Although [the government of the United States] . . . is sovereign and supreme in its appropriate sphere of action, yet it does not possess all the powers which usually belong to the sovereignty of a nation. Certain specified powers, enumerated in the Constitution, have been conferred upon it; and neither the legislative, executive, nor judicial departments of the government can lawfully exercise any authority beyond the limits marked out by the Constitution. And in regulating the judicial department, the cases in which the courts of the United States shall have jurisdiction are particularly and specifically enumerated and defined; and they are not authorized to take cognizance of any case which does not come within the description therein specified. Hence, when a plaintiff sues in a court of the Unites States, it is necessary that he should show, in his pleading, that the suit he brings is within the jurisdiction of the court, and that he is entitled to sue there. And if he omits to do this, and should, by any oversight of the Circuit Court, obtain a judgment in his favor, the judgment would be reversed in the appellate court for want of jurisdiction in the court below. The jurisdiction would not be presumed, as in the case of a common-law English or State court, unless the contrary appeared. But the record, when it comes before the appellate court, must show, affirmatively, that the inferior court had authority under the Constitution, to hear and determine the case. And if the plaintiff claims a right to sue in a Circuit Court of the United States, under that provision of the Constitution which gives jurisdiction in controversies between citizens of different States, he must distinctly aver in his pleading that they are citizens of different States; and he cannot maintain his suit without showing that fact in the pleadings. . . .

If, however, the fact of citizenship is averred in the declaration, and the defendant does not deny it, and put it in issue by plea in abatement, he cannot offer evidence at the trial to disprove it, and consequently cannot avail himself of the objection in the appellate court, unless the defect should be apparent in some other part of the record. For if there is no plea in abatement, and the want of jurisdiction does not appear in any other part of the transcript brought up by the writ of error, the undisputed averment of citizenship in the declaration must be taken in this court to be true. In this case, the citizenship is averred, but it is denied by the defendant in the manner required by the rules of pleading, and the fact upon which the denial is based is admitted by the demurrer. And, if the plea and demurrer, and judgment of the court below upon it, are before us upon this record, the question to be decided is, whether the facts stated in the plea are sufficient to show that the plaintiff is not entitled to sue as a citizen in a court of the United States.

We think they are before us. The plea in abatement and the judgment of the court upon it, are a part of the judicial proceedings in the Circuit Court, and are there recorded as such; and a writ of error always brings out to the superior court the whole record of the proceedings in the court below. . . . And this being the case in the present instance, the plea in abatement is necessarily under consideration; and it becomes, therefore, our duty to decide whether the facts stated in the plea are or are not sufficient to show that the plaintiff is not entitled to sue as a citizen in a court of the United States.

This is certainly a very serious question, and on that now for the first time has been brought for decision before this court. But it is brought here by those who have a right to bring it, and it is our duty to met it and decide it.

The question is simply this: Can a negro, whose ancestors were imported into this country, and sold as slaves, become a member of the political community formed and brought into existence by the Constitution of the United States, and as such become entitled to all the rights, and privileges, and immunities, guarantied by the instrument to the citizen? One of which rights is the privilege of suing in a court of the United States in the cases specified in the Constitution.

It will be observed, that the plea applies to that class of persons only whose ancestors were negroes of the African race, and imported into this country, and sold and held as slaves. The only matter in issue before the court, therefore, is, whether the descendants of such slaves, when they shall be emancipated, or who are born of parents who had become free before their birth, are citizens of a State, in the sense in which the word citizen is used in the Constitution of the United States. And this being the only matter in dispute on the pleadings, the court must be understood as speaking in this opinion of that class only, that is, of those persons who are descendants of Africans who were imported into this country, and sold as slaves. . . .

We proceed to examine the case as presented by the pleadings.

The words "people of the United States" and "citizens" are synonymous terms, and mean the same thing. They both describe the political body who, according to our republican institutions, form the sovereignty, and who hold the power and conduct the Government through their representatives. They are what we familiarly call the "sovereign people," and every citizen is one of this people, and a constituent member of this sovereignty. The question before us is, whether the class of persons described in the plea in abatement compose a portion of this people, and are constituent members of this sovereignty? We think they are not, and that they are not included, and were not intended to be included, under the word "citizens" in the Constitution, and can therefore claim none of the rights and privileges which that instrument provides for and secures to citizens of the United States. On the contrary, they were at that time considered as a subordinate and inferior class of beings, who had been subjugated by the dominant race, and whether emancipated or not, yet remained subject to their authority, and had no rights or privileges but such as those who held the power and the Government might choose to grant them.

It is not the province of the court to decide upon the justice or injustice, the policy or impolicy, of these laws. The decision of that questions belonged to the political or law-making power; to those who formed the sovereignty and framed the Constitution. The duty of the court is, to interpret the instrument they have framed, with the best lights we can obtain on the subject, and to administer it as we find it, according to its true intent and meaning when it was adopted.

In discussing this question, we must not confound the rights of citizenship which a State may confer within its own limits, and the rights of citizenship as a member of the Union. It does not by any means follow, because he has all the rights and privileges of a citizen of a State, that he must be a citizen of the United States. He may have all of the rights and privileges of the citizen of a State, and yet not be entitled to the rights and privileges of a citizen in any other State. . . .

It is very clear, therefore, that no State can, by any act or law of its own, passed since the adoption of the Constitution, introduce a new member into the political community created by the Constitution of the United States. It cannot make him a member of this community by making him a member of its own. And for the same reason it cannot introduce any person, or description of persons, who were not intended to be embraced in this new political family, which the Constitution brought into existence, but were intended to be excluded from it.

The question then arises, whether the provisions of the Constitution, in relation to the personal rights and privileges to which the citizen of a State should be entitled, embraced the negro African race, at that time in this country, or who might afterwards be imported, who had then or should afterwards be made free in any State; and to put it in the power of a single State to make him a citizen of the United States, and endue him with the full rights of citizenship in every other State without their consent? Does the Constitution of the United States act upon him whenever he shall be made free under the laws of a State, and raised there to the rank of a citizen, and immediately clothe him with all the privileges of a citizen in every other State, and in its own courts?

In the opinion of the court, the legislation and histories of the times, and the language used in the Declaration of Independence, show, that neither the class of persons who had been imported as slaves, nor their descendants, whether they had become free or not, were then acknowledged as a part of the people, nor intended to be included in the general words used in that memorable instrument.

But there are two clauses in the Constitution which point directly and specifically to the negro race as a separate class of persons, and show clearly that they were not regarded as a portion of the people or citizens of the Government then formed.

One of these clauses reserves to each of the thirteen States the right to import slaves until the year 1808, if it thinks proper. And the importation which it thus sanctions was unquestionably of persons of the race of which we are speaking, as the traffic in slaves in the United Stated had always been confined to them. And by the other provision the States pledge themselves to each other to maintain the right of property of the master, by delivering up to him any slave who may have escaped from his service, and be found within their respective territories. . . .

No one, we presume, supposes that any change in public opinion or feeling, in relation to this unfortunate race, in the civilized nations of Europe or in this country, should induce the court to give to the words of the Constitution a more liberal construction in their favor than they were intended to bear when the instrument was framed and adopted. Such an argument would be altogether inadmissible in any tribunal called on to interpret it. If any of its provisions are deemed unjust, there is a mode described in the instrument itself by which it may be amended; but while it remains unaltered, it must be construed now as it was understood at the time of its adoption. It is not only the same in words, but the same in meaning, and delegates the same powers to the Government, and reserves and secures the same rights and privileges to the citizen; and as long as it continues to exist in its present form, it speaks not only in the same words, but with the same meaning and intent with which it spoke when it came from the hands of its framers, and was voted on and adopted by the people of the United States. Any other rule of construction would abrogate the judicial character of this court, and make it the mere reflex of the popular opinion or passion of the day. This court was not created by the Constitution for such purposes. Higher and graver trusts have been confided to it, and it must not falter in the path of duty.

What the construction was at that time, we think can hardly admit of doubt. We have the language of the Declaration of Independence and of the Articles of Confederation, in addition to the plain words of the Constitution itself; we have the legislation of the different States, before, about the time, and since, the Constitution was adopted; we have the legislation of Congress, from the time of its adoption to a recent period; and we have the constant and uniform action of the Executive Department, all concurring together, and leading to the same result. And if anything in relation to the construction of the Constitution can be regarded as settled, it is that which we now give to the word "citizen" and the word "people."

And upon a full and careful consideration of the subject, the court is of opinion, that, upon the facts stated in the plea in abatement, Dred Scott was not a citizen of Missouri within the meaning of the Constitution of the United States, and not entitled as such to sue in its courts; and, consequently, that the Circuit Court had no jurisdiction of the case, and that the judgment on the plea in abatement is erroneous.

We are aware that doubts are entertained by some of the members of the court, whether the plea in abatement is legally before the court upon this writ of error; but it that plea is regarded as waived, or out of the case upon any other ground, yet the questions as to the jurisdiction of the Circuit Court is presented on the face of the bill of exception itself, taken by the plaintiff at the trial; for he admits that he and his wife were born slaves, but endeavors to make out his title to freedom and citizenship by showing that they were taken by their owner to certain places, hereinafter mentioned, where slavery could not by law exist, and that they thereby became free and upon their return to Missouri became citizens of that State.

Now, if the removal of which he speaks did not give them their freedom, then by his own admission he is still a slave; and whatever opinions may be entertained in favor of the citizenship of a free person of the African race, no one supposes that a slave is a citizen of the State or of the United States. If, therefore, the acts done by his owner did not make them free persons, he is still a slave, and certainly incapable of suing in the character of a citizen.

Now, as we have already said in an earlier part of this opinion, upon a different point, the right of property in a slave is distinctly and expressly affirmed in the Constitution. The right to traffic in it, like an ordinary article of merchandise and property, was guarantied to the citizens of the United States, in every State that might desire it, for twenty years. And the Government in express terms is pledged to protect it in all future time, if the slave escapes from his owner. This is done in plain words—too plain to be misunderstood. And no word can be found in the Constitution which gives Congress a greater power over slave property, or which entitles property of that kind to less protection than property of any other description. The only power conferred is the power coupled with the duty of guarding and protecting the owner in his rights.

Upon these considerations, it is the opinion of the court that the act of Congress which prohibited a citizen from holding and owning property of this kind in the territory of the United States north of the line therein mentioned, is not warranted by the Constitution, and is therefore void; and that neither Dred Scott himself, nor any of his family, were made free by being carried into this territory; even if they had been carried there by the owner, with the intention of becoming a permanent resident.

We have so far examined the case, as it stands under the Constitution of the United States, and the powers thereby delegated to the Federal Government.

But there is another point in the case which depends on State power and State law. And it is contended, on the part of the plaintiff, that he is made free by being taken to Rock Island, in the State of Illinois, independently of his residence in the territory of the United States; and being so made free, he was not again reduced to a state of slavery by being brought back to Missouri.

Our notice of this part of the case will be very brief; for the principle on which it depends was decided in this court, upon much consideration, in the case of Strader et al. *V.* Graham, reported in 10th Howard, 82. In that case, the slaves had been taken from Kentucky to Ohio, with the consent of the owner, and afterwards brought back to Kentucky. And this court held that their *status* or condition, as free or slave, depended upon the laws of Kentucky, when they were brought back into that State, and not of Ohio; and that this court had no jurisdiction to revise the judgment of a State court upon its own laws. This was the point directly before the court, and the decision that this court had not jurisdiction turned upon it, as will be seen by the report of the case.

So in this case. As Scott was a slave when taken into the State of Illinois by his owner, and was there held as such, and brought back in that character, his *status*, as free or slave, depended on the laws of Missouri, and not of Illinois. . . .

Upon the whole, therefore, it is the judgment of this court, that it appears by the record before us that the plaintiff in error is not a citizen of Missouri, in the sense in which that word is used in the Constitution; and that the Circuit Court of the United States, for that reason, had no jurisdiction in that case, and could give no judgment in it. Its judgment for the defendant must, consequently, be reversed, and a mandate issued, directing the suit to be dismissed for want of jurisdiction.

———————————————— ■ ————————————————

The Lincoln-Douglass senatorial debates of 1858 clearly reiterated the fundamental differences between the North and the South. For Douglass, extension of slavery into the western territories was a matter of popular sovereignty—the people of the territories could decide on their own whether to have slavery or not. In stark opposition, Lincoln contended that slavery was "a moral, a social, and a political wrong" and the federal government was obliged to restrict its encroachment into the new territories. Although Lincoln lost the election, he gained political visibility. Moreover, the Republican Party was now poised to be a major player in national politics.

An analysis of the causes of the Civil War is well beyond the scope (and intent) of this book.[7] Suffice it to say the conflict was produced by a complicated weave of political, economic, and social factors. The two regions clearly disagreed about the scope of the federal government and the direction of macroeconomic policy. Slavery, nonetheless, was at the heart of the matter. It animated the debates about the role of the central government, and it was critical to policy differences over tariffs, tax revenues, and infrastructure expenditures.

The violence of John Brown's raid at Harper's Ferry, and more importantly, the election of Abraham Lincoln to the presidency resulted in Southern secession from the Union. Starting with South Carolina in 1860, the 11 states of the Confederacy formed the Confederated States of America and elected Jefferson Davis as their provisional president. Confederate seizure of federal forts, particularly Fort Sumter, prompted Lincoln to mobilize northern militias and directly confront southern troops.

As the war raged, Lincoln's goals began to change. Initially, his primary concern was the preservation of the Union, not the abolition of slavery. It became evident, however, that preserving the Union meant abolishing slavery. Doing away with slavery accomplished several things for Lincoln. It undermined slave labor support of the South's war effort, it prevented Britain and France from recognizing the Confederacy, and it clarified the status of the large number of slaves crossing Union lines.[8]

STUDY QUESTIONS

1. The period between the signing of the Constitution and the Civil War was marked by measures to control and maintain chattel slavery in the South. What were some of the rules implemented during this time period to accomplish said goal? How did African-Americans react to the regulations?

2. Was the Constitution the work of consensus-building politicians or was it the product of a hegemonic group seeking to consolidate and protect its political, social, and economic advantage?

3. Do you believe that Chief Justice Taney correctly interpreted the Constitution in *Dred Scot v. Sanford*? What was the Court's conception of citizenship? Is there any evidence that the political climate of the time influenced the Court's decision?

4. The fugitive slave clause of the Constitution (Article IV, Section 2) acted to restrict the mobility of African slaves and return those who had successfully fled to their owners. Were these attempts to restrict slave freedom successful? What impact did this have on community-building in the African-American community?

NOTES

1. John P. Roche, "The founding fathers: A reform caucus in action," *American Political Science Review* December 1961.

2. Gunnar Myrdal. *An American dilemma: the Negro problem and modern democracy* 2nd ed. (New York; London: Harper & Brothers) 1944.

3. James McGregor Burns. *The vineyard of liberty.* (New York: Knopf) 1982; Sonia R. Jarvis, "Historical overview: African-Americans and the evolution of voting rights," in Ralph C. Gomes and Linda Faye Williams (eds.) *From exclusion to inclusion: The long struggle for African-American political power.* (Westport, CT: Greenwood Press) 1992; Benjamin J. Quarles. *The making of the Negro in America.* (New York: Macmillan) 1964.

4. Eugene D. Genovese. *The political economy of slavery: Studies in the economy and society of the slave South.* (Middletown, Conn.: Wesleyan University Press) 1989.

5. Albert P. Blaustein and Robert L. Zangrando (eds.) *Civil Rights and African-Americans.* (Evanston, ILL: Northwestern University Press) 1991.

6. For example, Frederick Douglass. *Narrative of the life of Frederick Douglass.* (New York: Signet) 1968; Margaret Washington. The narrative of Sojourner Truth. (New York: Vintage) 1993.

7. For example, Kenneth M. Stampp (ed.). *The Causes of the Civil War* 3rd rev. ed. (New York: Simon & Schuster) 1991.

8. LaWanda Cox, *Lincoln and black freedom: A study in presidential leadership* (Columbia, S.C.: University of South Carolina Press) 1994; John L. Thomas, (ed.). *Abraham Lincoln and the American political tradition.* (Amherst: University of Massachusetts Press) 1986.

THE CIVIL WAR, RECONSTRUCTION, AND JIM CROW: 1863–1953

*Shortly after the Union victory at Antietam, Lincoln utilized his war powers authority to seize enemy property and issued the **Emancipation Proclamation** (1863), which ended slavery in the Confederate states but, ironically, protected slavery in the Union states. Slavery did not come to an "official" end until after Lee's surrender at Appomatox and the South had agreed to terms in 1865.*

THE EMANCIPATION PROCLAMATION

". . . I do order and declare that ALL PERSONS HELD AS SLAVES within said designated States and parts of States ARE, AND HENCEFORWARD SHALL BE FREE! . . ."

Whereas, on the twenty-second day of September, in the year of our Lord one thousand eight hundred and sixty-two, a proclamation was issued by the President of the Unites States, containing among other thing the following, to wit:

"That on the First Day of January, in the Year of our Lord One Thousand Eight Hundred and Sixty-three, all persons held as Slaves within any State, or designated part of a State, the people whereof shall there be in rebellion against the United States, shall be then thenceforth and FOREVER FREE, and the Executive Government of the United States, including the Military and Naval authority thereof, will recognize and maintain the freedom of such persons, and will do no act or acts to repress such persons, or any of them, in any effort they make for their actual freedom.

"That the Executive will, on the first day of January aforesaid, by Proclamation, designate the States and parts of States, if any, in which the people therein respectively shall then be in Rebellion against the United States, and the fact that any State, or the people thereof, shall on that day be in good faith represented in the Congress of the United States by Members chosen thereto at elections wherein a majority of the qualified voters of such State shall have participated, shall, in the absence of strong countervailing testimony, be deemed conclusive evidence that such State and the people thereof are not then in Rebellion against the United States."

Now, there, I, Abraham Lincoln, President of the United States by virtue of the power vested in me as Commander-in-Chief of the Army and Navy of the United States, in time of actual armed rebellion against the authority and Government of the United States, and as a fit and necessary war measure for suppressing said Rebellion, do, on this first day of January, in the year of our Lord one thousand eight hundred and sixty-three, and in accordance with my purpose so to do, publicly proclaim for the full period of one hundred days from the date of the first above-mentioned order, and designate, as the States and parts of States wherein the people thereof, respectively, are this day in rebellion against the United States, the following, to wit: Arkansas, Texas, Louisiana—except the Parishes of St. Bernard, Palquemines, Jefferson, St. John, St. Charles, St. James, Ascension, Assumption, Terre Bonne, Lafourch, St. Mary, St. Martin and Orleans, including the City of New Orleans—Mississippi, Alabama, Florida, Georgia, South Carolina, North Carolina, and Virginia—except the forty-eight counties designated as West Virginia, and also the counties of Berkley, Accomac, Northampton, Elizabeth City, York, Princess Ann, and Norfolk, including the cities of Norfolk and Portsmouth—and which excepted parts are, for the present, left precisely as if this Proclamation were not issued.

And by virtue of the power and for the purpose aforesaid, I do order and declare that ALL PERSONS HELD AS SLAVES within said designated States and parts of States ARE, AND HENCEFORWARD SHALL BE FREE! And that the Executive Government of the United States, including the Military and Naval Authorities thereof, will recognize and maintain the freedom of said persons.

And I hereby enjoin upon the people so declared to be free, to abstain from all violence, unless in necessary self-defense; and I recommend to them that in all cases, when allowed, they labor faithfully for reasonable wages.

And I further declare and make known, that such persons, of suitable condition, will be received into the armed service of the United States, to garrison forts, positions, stations, and other places, and to man vessels of all sorts in said service.

And, upon this, sincerely believed to be an act of justice, warranted by the Constitution, upon military necessity, I invoke the considerate judgment of mankind and the gracious favor of Almighty God.

January 1, 1863

———————————————————— ■ ————————————————————

*The **13th Amendment** (1865) effectively eliminated slavery throughout the country and gave Congress the authority to enforce the legislation. Given that the amendment required ratification by 3/4 of the states (which meant at least eight former Confederate states), it represents the first national attempt at broad-scale racial reform. These efforts, not surprisingly, were met with resistance by states of the Old Confederacy. Under the guise of providing social and economic stability, many southern states quickly enacted "black codes" to govern the "status and conduct" of the newly freed slaves. These codes* were restrictive and punitive, and in many ways, returned African-Americans to bondage-like conditions.

In response, Congress passed the Civil Rights Act of 1866 to ensure the rights of freed men and women and to protect them against discrimination. The constitutionality of the act was questionable, thus Congress quickly moved to ratify the **14th Amendment,** which laid out the rights of "due process," "equal protection," and "privileges and immunities" as federal guarantees against state encroachments. Interpretation and implementation of the amendment has been the subject of significant political debate and litigation. As a result, its effectiveness in protecting civil rights has paled in comparison to its effectiveness in protecting property rights. This, of course, was not the original intent of the Reconstruction Congress.

The **15th Amendment** (1870) was the last of the so-called "Civil War Amendments" designed to integrate the newly freed slaves into American life. The purpose was to provide blacks with the right to vote, ". . . The right of citizens of the United States to vote shall not be abridged . . . on account of race, color, or previous condition of servitude." Implementing the 15th Amendment proved to be a most difficult task. Southern political elites designed a wide array of clever electoral devices to deny suffrage to the newly freed slaves. Poll taxes, literacy tests, "grandfather clauses," and stringent residency requirements effectively prevented African-Americans from exercising their right to vote in most southern states. As we will discover, it wasn't until a century later that black voting rights were adequately secured.

THE CONSTITUTION OF THE UNITED STATES: 13TH AMENDMENT (1865); 14TH AMENDMENT (1868); 15TH AMENDMENT (1870)

AMENDMENT XIII (1865)

Section 1. Neither slavery nor involuntary servitude, except as a punishment for crime whereof the party shall have been duly convicted, shall exist within the United States, or any place subject to their jurisdiction.

Section 2. Congress shall have power to enforce this article by appropriate legislation.

AMENDMENT XIV (1868)

Section 1. All persons born or naturalized in the United States, and subject to the jurisdiction thereof, are citizens of the United States and of the State wherein they reside. No State shall make or enforce any law which shall abridge the privileges or immunities of citizens of the United States; nor shall any State deprive any person of life, liberty, or property, without due process of law; nor deny to any person within its jurisdiction the equal protection of the laws.

Section 2. Representatives shall be apportioned among the several States according to their respective numbers, counting the whole number of persons in each State, excluding Indians not taxed. But when the right to vote at any election for the choice of electors for President and Vice President of the United States, Representatives in Congress, the Executive and Judicial officers of a State, or the members of the Legislature thereof, is denied to any of the male inhabitants of such State, being twenty-one years of age, and citizens of the United States, or in any way abridged, except for participation in rebellion, or other crime, the basis or representation therein shall be reduced in the proportion which the number of such male citizens shall bear to the whole number of male citizens shall bear to the whole number of male citizens twenty-one years of age in such State.

Section 5. The Congress shall have power to enforce, by appropriate legislation, the provisions of this article.

AMENDMENT XV (1870)

Section 1. The right of citizens of the United States to vote shall not be denied or abridged by the United States or by any State on account of race, color, or previous condition of servitude.

Section 2. The Congress shall have power to enforce this article by appropriate legislation.

The period between the freeing of the slaves in 1863 and the return of southern white supremacy after the presidential election of 1876 is commonly known as "Reconstruction," so named because the central political question concerned the terms under which Confederate states would return to the Union. Although the conditions of southern re-entry were many, there was a clear directive to abolish slavery. This seemingly simple goal served to alter the course of southern life greatly.

In the following selections from his book, Reconstruction: America's Unfinished Revolution, *Eric Foner describes "the meaning of freedom." Freedom had a profound effect on the everyday lives on the newly freed slaves. It meant they could go where they wished, when they wished, without encumbrance. It provided the opportunity to reunite families, build churches, and generally develop the civic infrastructure. In turn, social development provided the necessary ingredients for political empowerment.*

As Foner indicates, African-Americans engaged in widespread political mobilization even before the passage of the 15th Amendment. From participation in the Union League to slating black candidates, political involvement became the sine qua non of post-Emancipation life. Foner argues that political involvement was also tied to the pursuit of economic interests. In other words, freedom meant a fundamental restructuring of the relationship between plantation owners and black labor. Land redistribution, or the acquisition of "40 acres and a mule," became emblematic of black demands for full participation in the fruits of America. Early black hopes for economic self-sufficiency were soon dashed as organizations like the Freedmen's Bureau sought to stabilize southern agriculture by ensuring the smooth return of blacks to plantation labor.

By 1876, jubilation gave way to sorrow as the highly controversial presidential election ended in a bitter compromise that essentially returned control of the South to white supremacists. Foner maintains that economic depression, a rejection of black empowerment, scandal, and labor problems contributed to the inability of the Republican Party to maintain control over the South.

THE MEANING OF FREEDOM

Eric Foner

Excerpt from Reconstruction: America's Unfinished Revolution, 1863–1877, *Chapter 8*

F reedom came in different ways to different parts of the South. In large areas, slavery had disintegrated long before Lee's surrender, but elsewhere, far from the presence of federal troops, blacks did not learn of its irrevocable end until the spring of 1865. Despite the many disappointments that followed, this generation of blacks would always regard the moment when "de freedom sun shine out" as the great watershed of their lives. Houston H. Holloway, who had been sold three times before he reached the age of twenty in 1865, later recalled with vivid clarity the day emancipation came to his section of Georgia: "I felt like a bird out of a cage. Amen. Amen. Amen. I could hardly ask to feel any better than I did that day. . . . The week passed off in a blaze of glory." Six weeks later Holloway and his wife "received my free born son into the world."[1]

"Freedom," said a black minister, "burned in the black heart long before freedom was born." But what did "freedom" mean? "It is necessary to define that word," Freedmen's Bureau Commissioner O. O. Howard told a black audience in 1865, "for it is most apt to be misunderstood." Howard assumed a straightforward definition existed. But instead of a predetermined category or static concept, "freedom" itself became a terrain of conflict, its substance open to different and sometimes contradictory interpretations, its content changing for whites as well as blacks in the aftermath of the Civil War.[2]

Many Southern whites assumed that blacks confronted the demise of slavery entirely unprepared for the responsibilities of freedom. "The Negroes are to be pitied, . . ." wrote South Carolinian Julius J. Fleming, an educator, minister, and public official. "They do not understand the liberty which has been conferred upon them." In fact, blacks carried out of bondage an understanding of their new condition shaped both by their experience as slaves and by observation of the free society around them. What one planter called their "wild notions of right and freedom" encompassed, first of all, an end to the myriad injustices associated with slavery. Like the Louisiana blacks interviewed by General Banks's agents during the Civil War, many former slaves saw freedom as an end to the separation of families, the abolition of punishment by the lash, and the opportunity to educate their children. Others, like black minister Henry M. Turner, stressed that freedom meant the enjoyment of "our rights in common with other men." "If I cannot do like a white man I am not free," Henry Adams told his former master in 1865. "I see how the poor white people do. I ought to do so too, or else I am a slave."[3]

But underpinning the specific aspirations lay a broader theme: a desire for independence from white control, for autonomy both as individuals and as members of a community itself being transformed as a result of emancipation. Before the war, free blacks had created a network of churches, schools, and mutual benefit societies, while slaves had forged a semiautonomous culture centered on the family and church. With freedom, these institutions were consolidated, expanded, and liberated from white supervision, and new ones—particularly political organizations—joined them as focal points of black life. In stabilizing their families, seizing control of their churches, greatly expanding their schools and benevolent societies, staking a claim to economic independence, and forging a distinctive political culture, blacks during Reconstruction laid the foundation for the modern black community, whose roots lay deep in slavery, but whose structure and values reflected the consequences of emancipation.

FROM SLAVERY TO FREEDOM

Long after the end of the Civil War, the experience of bondage remained deeply etched in blacks' collective memory. As one white writer noted years later, blacks could not be shaken from the conviction "that the white race has barbarously oppressed them." They took particular offense at contentions that American slavery had been unusually benevolent and that "harmonious relations" had existed between master and slave. "All of us know how happy we have been. . . ." declared one black orator. "Have these gentlemen forgotten so soon to what ills we have been subjected?" Fundamentally, however, blacks resented not only the incidents of slavery—the whippings, separations of families, and countless rituals of subordination—but the fact of having been held as slaves at all. During a visit to Richmond, Scottish minister David Macrae was surprised to hear a former slave complain of past mistreatment, while acknowledging he had never been whipped. "How were you cruelly treated then?" asked Macrae. "I was cruelly treated," answered the freedman, "because I was kept in slavery."[4]

In countless ways, the newly freed slaves sought to "throw off the badge of servitude," to overturn the real and symbolic authority whites had exercised over every aspect of their lives. Some took new names that reflected the lofty hopes inspired by emancipation. One Northern teacher in Savannah reported among her black pupils an Alexander Hamilton, a Franklin Pierce, even a General Joe E. Johnston; in Georgetown, South Carolina, former slaves' new names included Deliverance Berlin, Hope Mitchell, Chance

Great, and Thomas Jefferson. Many blacks now demanded to be addressed by whites as Mr. or Mrs. rather than by their first name, as was conventional under slavery.[5]

Blacks relished opportunities to flaunt their liberation from the innumerable regulations, significant and trivial, associated with slavery. Freedmen held mass meetings and religious services unrestrained by white surveillance, acquired dogs, guns, and liquor (all barred to them under slavery), and refused to yield the sidewalks to whites. They dressed as they pleased, black women sometimes wearing gaudy finery, carrying parasols, and replacing the slave kerchief with colorful hats and veils. In the summer of 1865, Charleston saw freedmen occupying "some of the best residences," and promenading on King Street "arrayed in silks and satins of all the colors of the rainbow," while black schoolchildren sang "'John Brown's Body' within ear-shot of Calhoun's tomb." Rural whites complained of "insolence" and "insubordination" among the freedmen, by which they meant any departure from the deference and obedience expected under slavery. On the Bradford plantation in Florida, one untoward incident followed another. First, the family cook told Mrs. Bradford "if she want any dinner she kin cook it herself." Then the former slaves went off to a meeting with Northern soldiers to discuss "our freedom." Told that she and her daughter could not attend, one woman replied "they were now free and if she saw fit to take her daughter into that crowd it was nobody's business." "Never before had I a word of impudence from any of our black folk," recorded 19-year-old Susan Bradford, "but they are not ours any longer."[6]

The presence of black troops among the occupying Union army reinforced the freedmen's assertiveness and inspired constant complaint on the part of whites. Black soldiers acted, in the words of the New York *World*, as "apostles of black equality," spreading among the former slaves ideas of land ownership and civil and political equality. They intervened in plantation disputes and sometimes arrested whites. ("It is very hard . . ." wrote a Confederate veteran, "to see a white man taken under guard by one of those black scoundrels.") Black troops helped construct schools, churches, and orphanages, organized debating societies, and held political gatherings where "freedom songs" were sung and soldiers delivered "speeches of the most inflammatory kind." In Southern cities they demanded the right to travel on segregated streetcars, taunted white passersby with remarks like "We's all equal now," and advised freedmen in cities like Memphis that they need not obey military orders to return to the plantations.[7]

For a variety of reasons, Southern towns and cities experienced an especially large influx of freedmen during and immediately after the Civil War. In the cities, many blacks believed, "freedom was free-er." Here were black social institutions—schools, churches, and fraternal societies—and here too, in spite of inequities in law enforcement, were the army (including black soldiers) and Freedmen's Bureau, offering protection from the violence so pervasive in much of the rural South. "People who get scared at others being beaten go to the cities," said a Georgia black legislator during Reconstruction. Between 1865 and 1870, the black population of the South's ten largest cities doubled, while the number of white residents rose by only 10 percent. Smaller towns, from which blacks had often been excluded as slaves, experienced even more dramatic increases. The black population of Demopolis, Alabama, site of a regional Freedmen's Bureau office, grew from one individual in 1860 to nearly 1,000 ten years later.[8]

Of all the motivations for black mobility, none was more poignant than the effort to reunite families separated during slavery. "In their eyes," wrote a Freedmen's Bureau agent, "the work of emancipation was incomplete until the families which had been dispersed by slavery were reunited." In September 1865, Northern reporter John Dennett encountered a freedman who had walked more than 600 miles from Georgia to North Carolina, searching for his wife and children from whom he had been separated by sale. Another freedman, writing from Texas, asked the aid of the Freedmen's Bureau in locating "my own dearest relatives," providing a long list of sisters, nieces, nephews, uncles, and in-laws, none of whom he had seen since his sale in Virginia 24 years before.

As late as the turn of the century, black newspapers carried advertisements that testified to the human tragedies that formed an everyday part of slavery. A typical plea for help appeared in the Nashville *Colored Tennessean*:

> During the year 1849, Thomas Sample carried away from this city, as his slaves, our daughter, Polly, and son. . . . We will give $100 each for them to any person who will assist them. . . to get to Nashville, or get word to us of their whereabouts.

Usually, such quests ended in failure, and others produced wrenching disappointment when spouses were located who had remarried. But few scenes were as affecting as the reunion of long-separated relatives. "I wish you could see this people as they step from slavery into freedom," a Union officer wrote his wife in May 1865. "Men are taking their wives and children, families which had been for a long time broken up are united and oh! such happiness. I am glad I am here."[9]

Strong family ties, it is clear, had existed under slavery, but had always been vulnerable to disruption. Emancipation allowed blacks to reaffirm and solidify their family connections, and most freedmen seized the opportunity with alacrity. During the Civil War, John Eaton, who, like many whites, believed that slavery had destroyed the sense of family obligation, was astonished by the eagerness with which former slaves in contraband camps legalized their marriage bonds. The same pattern was repeated when the Freedmen's Bureau and state governments made it possible to register and solemnize slave unions. Many families, in addition, adopted the children of deceased relatives and friends, rather than see them apprenticed to white masters or placed in Freedmen's Bureau orphanages. By 1870, a large majority of blacks lived in two-parent family households, a fact that can be gleaned from the manuscript census returns but also "quite incidentally" from the Congressional Ku Klux Klan hearings, which recorded countless instances of victims assaulted in their homes, "the husband and wife in bed, and . . . their little children beside them."[10]

BUILDING THE BLACK COMMUNITY

Second only to the family as a focal point of black life stood the church. And, as in the case of the family, Reconstruction was a time of consolidation and transformation for black religion. With the death of slavery, urban blacks seized control of their own churches, while the "invisible institution" of the rural slave church emerged into the full light of day. The creation of an independent black religious life proved to be a momentous and irreversible consequence of emancipation.

In the aftermath of emancipation, the wholesale withdrawal of blacks from biracial congregations redrew the religious map of the South. Two causes combined to produce the independent black church: the refusal of whites to offer blacks an equal place within their congregations and the black quest for self-determination. The end of slavery does not appear to have altered the views of many white clergymen as to the legitimacy of the peculiar institution or the desirability of preserving unaltered blacks' second-class status within biracial churches. The "whole doctrine" of the scriptural justification for slavery remained intact, declared the General Assembly of the Southern Presbyterian Church in December 1865; as late as the 1890s, Southern ecclesiastics were still denouncing the idea of the inherent sinfulness of slaveholding. While initially urging blacks to remain within their congregations, most white ministers insisted that the old inequalities—separate pews, the white monopoly on church governance—must continue.[11]

The rise of the independent black church provides only the most striking example of the thriving institutional structure blacks created in the aftermath of emancipation. A host of fraternal, benevolent, and mutual-aid societies also sprang into existence. Even before the Civil War, free blacks had formed fraternal organizations, and secret societies of various kinds had existed among the slaves. In early Reconstruction, blacks created literally thousands of such organizations; a partial list includes burial societies, debating clubs, Masonic lodges, fire companies, drama societies, trade associations, temperance clubs, and equal rights leagues. Often spawned in black churches, they quickly took on lives of their own. By the 1870s, over 200 such organizations existed in Memphis, 400 in Richmond, and countless others were scattered across the rural South. Although their activities generally took place away from white observation, they appeared in public in the processions and celebrations that seemed ubiquitous, especially in Southern cities, during Reconstruction. Black parades commemorated special occasions like the ratification of the 15th Amendment, but the largest celebrations were reserved for January 1 (the anniversary of the Emancipation Proclamation) and July 4—days on which Southern whites generally remained indoors.[12]

Perhaps the most striking illustration of the freedmen's quest for self-improvement was their seemingly unquenchable thirst for education. Before the war, every Southern state except Tennessee had prohibited the instruction of slaves, and while many free blacks had attended school and a number of slaves became literate through their own efforts or the aid of sympathetic masters, over 90 percent of the South's adult black population was illiterate in

1860. Access to education for themselves and their children was, for blacks, central to the meaning of freedom, and white contemporaries were astonished by their "avidity for learning." A Mississippi Freedmen's Bureau agent reported in 1865 that when he informed a gathering of 3,000 freedmen that they "were to have the advantages of schools and education, their joy knew no bounds. They fairly jumped and shouted in gladness." The desire for learning led parents to migrate to towns and cities in search of education for their children, and plantation workers to make the establishment of a school-house "an absolute condition" of signing labor contracts. (One 1867 Louisiana contract specified that the planter pay a "5 percent tax" to support black education.) Adults as well as children thronged the schools established during and after the Civil War. A Northern teacher in Florida reported how one 60-year-old woman, "just beginning to spell, seems as if she could not think of any thing but her book, says she spells her lesson all the evening, then she dreams about it, and wakes up thinking about it."[13]

In the severing of ties that had bound black and white families and churches to one another under slavery, the coming together of blacks in an explosion of institution building, and the political and cultural fusion of former free blacks and former slaves, Reconstruction witnessed the birth of the modern black community. All in all, the months following the end of the Civil War were a period of remarkable accomplishment for Southern blacks. Looking back in January 1866, the Philadelphia-born black missionary Jonathan C. Gibbs could only exclaim: "we have progressed a century in a year."[14]

ORIGINS OF BLACK POLITICS

If the goal of autonomy inspired blacks to withdraw from religious and social institutions controlled by whites and to attempt to work out their economic destinies for themselves, in the polity, "freedom" meant inclusion rather than separation. Recognition of their equal rights as citizens quickly emerged as the animating impulse of Reconstruction black politics. In the spring and summer of 1865, blacks organized a seemingly unending series of mass meetings, parades, and petitions demanding civil equality and the suffrage as indispensable corollaries of emancipation. The most extensive mobilization occurred in areas that had been occupied by Union troops during the war, where political activity had begun even before 1865. Union Leagues and similar groups sprang up in low country South Carolina and Georgia, their meetings bringing together Freedmen's Bureau agents, black soldiers, and local freedmen, to demand the vote and the repeal of all laws discriminating against blacks. "By the Declaration of Independence," declared a gathering on St. Helena Island, "we believe these are rights which cannot justly be denied us."[15]

Political mobilization also proceeded apace in Southern cities, where the flourishing network of churches and fraternal societies provided a springboard for organization, and the army and Freedmen's Bureau stood ready to offer protection. In Wilmington, North Carolina, freedmen in 1865 formed an Equal Rights League which, local officials reported, insisted upon "all the social and political rights of white citizens" and demanded that blacks be consulted in the selection of policemen, justices of the peace, and county commissioners. By midsummer, "secret political Radical Associations" had been formed in Virginia's major cities. Richmond blacks first organized politically to protest the army's rounding up of "vagrants" for plantation labor, but soon expanded their demands to include the right to vote and the removal of the "Rebel-controlled" local government. In Norfolk, occupied by the Union Army since 1862, blacks early in 1865 created the Union Monitor Club to press their claim to equal rights, and in May hundreds attempted to vote in a local election. A mass meeting endorsed a militant statement drafted by former fugitive slave Thomas Bayne: "Traitors shall not dictate or prescribe to us the terms or conditions of our citizenship."[16]

Statewide conventions held throughout the South in 1865 and early 1866 offered the most visible evidence of black political organization. Several hundred delegates attended these gatherings, some selected by local meetings occasionally marked by "animated debate," others by churches, fraternal societies, Union Leagues, and black army units, still others simply appointed by themselves. "Some bring credentials," observed North Carolina black leader James H. Harris, "others had as much as they could do to bring themselves, having to escape from their homes stealthily at night" to avoid white reprisal. Although little information survives about the majority of these individuals, certain patterns can be discerned from the fragmentary evidence. The delegates "ranged all colors and apparently all conditions," but urban free mulattoes took the most prominent roles, and former slaves were almost entirely absent from leadership positions. One speaker at the Tennessee gathering doubted it should be called a "Negro convention" at all, since its officers were "all mixed blood," some "as white as the editor of the New York *Herald*." Charleston free blacks, along with six Northern-born newcomers, dominated South Carolina's gathering, and at Louisiana's Republican state convention 19 of the 20 black delegates had been born free. But other groups also came to the fore in 1865. In Mississippi, a state with few free blacks before the war, ex-slave army veterans and their relatives comprised the majority of the delegates. Alabama and Georgia had a heavy representation of black ministers, and all the conventions included numerous skilled artisans. Many of the delegates, especially those born free, were relatively well-to-do, although the very richest blacks held aloof, too linked to whites economically and by kinship to risk taking an active role in politics.

The prominence of free blacks, ministers, artisans, and former soldiers in these early conventions established patterns that would characterize black politics for much of Reconstruction. From among these delegates would emerge such prominent officeholders as Alabama Congressman James T. Rapier and Mississippi Secretary of State James D. Lynch. The most remarkable continuity in black leadership occurred in South Carolina, for among the 52 delegates to the November 1865 convention sat four future Congressmen, 13 legislators, and 12 delegates to the state's 1868 constitutional convention. In general, however, what is striking is how few of these early leaders went on to positions of prominence. Only two of Alabama's 56 delegates (William V. Turner and Holland Thompson) later played significant roles in Reconstruction politics, a pattern repeated in Virginia, North Carolina, Tennessee, Mississippi, Alabama, and Arkansas. In most states, black political mobilization had advanced far more rapicly in cities and in rural areas occupied by federal troops during the war, than in the bulk of plantation counties, where the majority of the former slaves lived. The free blacks of Louisiana and South Carolina who stepped to the fore in 1865 would remain at the helm of black politics throughout Reconstruction; elsewhere, however, a new group of leaders, many of them freedmen from the black belt, would soon supersede those who had taken the lead in 1865.[62] Like their Northern counterparts during the Civil War, Southern blacks proclaimed their identification with the nation's history, destiny, and political system. The very abundance of letters and petitions addressed by black gatherings and ordinary freedmen to officials of the army, Freedmen's Bureau, and state and federal authorities, as well as the decision of a number of conventions to send representatives to Washington to lobby for black rights, revealed a belief that the political order was at least partially open to their influence. "We are Americans," declared a meeting of Norfolk blacks, "we know no other country, we love the land of our birth." Their address reminded white Virginians that in 1619, "our fathers as well as yours were toiling in the plantations on James River" and that a black man, Crispus Attucks, had shed "the first blood" in the American Revolution. And, of course, blacks had fought and died to save the Union. America, resolved another Virginia meeting, was "now our country—made emphatically so by the blood of our brethren." "We stood by the government when it wanted help," a delegate to Mississippi's convention wrote President Johnson. "Now . . . will it stand by us?"[17]

All in all, the most striking characteristic of this initial phase of black political mobilization was its very unevenness. In some states, organization proceeded steadily in 1865 and 1866, in others, such as Mississippi, little activity occurred between an initial flurry in the summer of 1865 and the advent of black suffrage two years later. Large parts of the black belt remained untouched by organized politics, but many blacks were aware of Congressional debates on Reconstruction policy, and quickly employed on their own behalf the Civil Rights Act of 1866. "The negro of today," remarked a correspondent of the New Orleans *Tribune* in September 1866, "is not the same as he was six years ago. . . . He has been told of his rights, which have long been robbed." Only in 1867 would blacks enter the "political nation," but in organization, leadership, and an ideology that drew upon America's republican heritage to demand an equal place as citizens, the seeds that flowered then were planted in the first years of freedom.[18]

VIOLENCE AND EVERYDAY LIFE

The black community's religious, social, and political mobilization was all the more remarkable for occurring in the face of a wave of violence that raged almost unchecked in large parts of the postwar South. Although wartime conflicts between white Unionists and Confederates, as well as the economic destitution that inspired local bands to prey upon the property of others, contributed to the unsettled condition of Southern life, in the vast majority of cases freedmen were the victims and whites the aggressors.

Probably the largest number of violent acts stemmed from disputes arising from black efforts to assert their freedom from control by their former masters. Freedmen were assaulted and murdered for attempting to leave plantations, disputing contract settlements, not laboring in the manner desired by their employers, attempting to buy or rent land, and resisting whippings. One black who refused to be bound and whipped, asserting that "he was a freeman and he would not be tied like a slave," was shot dead by his employer, a prominent Texas lawyer. In parts of Tennessee, a Nashville newspaper reported early in 1867, "regulators . . . are riding about whipping, maiming and killing all Negroes who do not obey the orders of their former masters, just as if slavery existed." In the face of this pervasive violence, local leaders of society and politics remained silent, reluctant to hold other whites responsible for crimes against blacks. A resident of southwestern Alabama wrote the governor of his shock at hearing "men of standing . . . countenance disorder and abuse of negroes" and their refusal to "restrain young men in their violence." John Wesley North, a Northerner who went to Knoxville after the war, in 1866 encountered a mob beating a freedman. When North intervened, the crowd dispersed, "evidently amazed that any person should venture to remonstrate against even the *murder* of a *black man*." A local banker subsequently offered the Yankee this advice: "never in this country . . . interfere in behalf of a nigger."

NOTES

1. George P. Rawick, ed., *The American Slave: A Composite Autobiography* (Westport, Conn., 1972–79), Supplement, Ser. 2, 2:1945; Houston H. Holloway Autobiography, Miscellaneous Manuscript Collections, LC.

2. Quitman *Banner* in Savannah *Daily News and Herald*, July 15, 1867; New Orleans *Tribune*, November 6, 1865.

3. John H. Moore, ed., *The Juhl Letters to the "Charleston Courier"* (Athens, Ga., 1974), 20; Will Martin to Benjamin G. Humphreys, December 5, 1865, Mississippi Governor's Papers, MDAH; Joseph P. Reidy, "Masters and Slaves, Planters and Freedmen: The Transition from Slavery to Freedom in Central Georgia, 1820–1880" (unpub. diss., Northern Illinois University, 1982), 162; 46th Congress, 2d Session, Senate Report 693, pt. 2:191. Most older historical accounts, and some more recent ones, echo the idea that the ex-slaves were completely unprepared for freedom. Walter I. Fleming, *Civil War and Reconstruction in Alabama* (New York, 1905), 270–71; Howard K. Beale, *The Critical Year* (New York, 1930), 188–89; William C. Harris, *Presidential Reconstruction in Mississippi* (Baton Rouge, 1967), 80–81.

4. Z. T. Filmore to History Company Publishers, March 2, 1887, Bancroft Library, University of California, Berkeley; undated manuscript speech, 1865 or 1866, Pinckney S. Pinchback Papers, Howard University; David Macrae, *The Americans at Home* (New York, 1952 [orig. pub. 1870]), 133.

5. Eliza F. Andrews, *The War-Time Journal of a Georgia Girl* (New York, 1908), 347; Sarah A. Jenness to Samuel Hunt, December 30, 1865, *AMA Archives*, Amistad Research Center, Tulane University; George C. Rogers, Jr., *The History of Georgetown County, South Carolina* (Columbia, S.C., 1970), 439–41.

6. Vincent Harding, *There Is a River: The Black Struggle for Freedom in America* (New York, 1981), 278–81; Jacqueline Jones, *Labor of Love, Labor of Sorrow: Black Women, Work and the Family, from Slavery to the Present* (New York, 1985), 69; Joel Williamson, *After Slavery: The Negro in South Carolina During Reconstruction, 1861–1877* (Chapel Hill, 1965), 46–47; Leon F. Litwack, *Been in the Storm So Long: The Aftermath of Slavery* (New York, 1979), 359; Elias H. Dees to Anne Dees, August 12, 1865, Elias H. Deas Papers, USC; Joseph H. Mahaffey, ed., "Carl Schurz's Letters From the South," *GaHQ*, 35 (September 1951), 235; Susan B. Eppes, *Through Some Eventful Years* (Macon, 1926), 279–84, 294–95.

7. New York *World*, September 13, 1865; Ira Berlin et al., eds., *Freedon: A Documentary History of Emancipation 1861–1867* (New York, 1982–), Ser. 2, 733–39; Emile E. Delserier to Marguerite E. Williams, May 6, 1865, Marguerite E. Williams Papers, UNC; Jacob Schirmer Diary, June 1865, SCHS; *Weekly Anglo-African*, August 12, 1865; Charleston *South Carolina Leader*, March 31, 1866; Elizabeth A. Meriweather, *Recollections of 92 Years* (Nashville, 1958), 164–68; Bobby L. Lovett, "Memphis Riots: White Reactions to Blacks in Memphis, May 1865–July 1866," *THQ*, 38 (Spring 1979), 15–17.

8. Litwack, *Been in the Storm*, 310–16; 42d Congress, 2d Session, House Report 22. Georgia, 7 (hereafter cited as KKK Hearings); Herbert A. Thomas, Jr., "Victims of Circumstance; Negroes in a Southern Town, 1865—1880," *Register of the Kentucky Historical Society,* 71 (July 1973), 253; Orville V. Burton, "The Rise and Fall of Afro-American Town Life: Town and Country in Reconstruction Edgefield, South Carolina," in Orville H. Burton and Robert C. McMath, Jr., eds., *Toward a New South? Studies in Post-Civil War Southern Communities,* (Westport, Conn., 1982), 152–53; Peter Kolchin, *First Freedom: The Responses of Alabama's Blacks to Emancipation and Reconstruction* (Westport, Conn., 1972), 10.

9. John W. DeForest, *A Union Officer in the Reconstruction,* edited by James H. Croushore and David M. Potter (New Haven, 1948), 36–37; John R. Dennett, *The South As It Is: 1865–1866,* edited by Henry M. Christman (New York, 1965), 130; Hawkins Wilson to "Chief of the Freedmen's Bureau at Richmond," May 11, 1867, Letters Received, Ser. 3892, Bowling Green Subasst. Comr., RG105, NA [FSSP A-8254]; Lester C. Lamon, *Blacks in Tennessee 1791–1970* (Knoxville, 1981), 43; John E. Bryant to Emma Bryant, May 29, 1865, John E. Bryant Papers, DU.

10. John Eaton, *Grant, Lincoln and the Freedmen* (New York, 1907), 34, 211; Herbert G. Gutman, *The Black Family in Slavery and Freedom, 1750–1925* (New York, 1976), 61–62, 141–42, 225–28, 417–20; KKK Hearings, Georgia, 817.

11. John L. Bell, Jr., "The Presbyterian Church and the Negro in North Carolina During Reconstruction," *NCHR*, 40 (Winter, 1963), 15–27; H. Shelton Smith, *In His Image But . . . : Racism in Southern Religion, 1780–1910* (Durham, 1972), 209–13; W. Harrison Daniel, "Virginia Baptists and the Negro," *VaMHB*, 76 (July 1968), 340–43; *Christian Recorder,* June 3, 1865.

12. Robinson, "Plans," 78; Peter J. Rachleff, *Black Labor in the South: Richmond, Virginia, 1865–1890* (Philadelphia, 1984), 25; Rabinowitz, *Race Relations,* 228–29; *Christian Recorder,* January 27, 1866; Savannah *Freemen's Standard,* February 15, 1868; Jacob Schirmer Diary, July 4, 1871, January 1, 1874.

13. William P. Vaughan, *Schools for All: The Blacks and Public Education in the South, 1865–1877*, (Lexington, Ky., 1974), 1; Joseph Crosfield to Unknown, October 5, 1865 (typed copy), Society of Friends Library, Friends House, London; L. C. Hubbard to R. S. Donaldson, August 5, 1865, H-2 1865, Registered Letters Received, Ser. 2180, Jackson, Ms. Acting Asst. Comr., RG 105, NA [FSSP A-9304]; Whitelaw Reid, *After the War: A Southern Tour* (Cincinnati, 1866), 511; Hartford *Courant*, March 1, 1867; Dorothy Sterling, ed., *We Are Your Sisters: Black Women in the Nineteenth Century* (New York, 1984), 298–99; Richardson, ed., "'We are Truly doing Missionary Work'," 185.

14. Unidentified newspaper clipping, January 22, 1866, Rufus and S. Willard Saxton Papers, Yale University.

15. Salmon P. Chase to Andrew Johnson, May 21, 1865, J. G. Dodge to Johnson, June 20, 1865, Petition, June 1865, to Charles Sumner, Charles Sumner to Johnson, June 30, 1865, Andrew Johnson Papers, LC; *Christian Recorder*, June 10, 1865; Holt, *Black over White*, 12; Herbert Aptheker, "South Carolina Negro Conventions, 1865," *JNH*, (January 1946), 93.

16. Jonathan Dawson, et al. to William W. Holden, July 12, 1865, North Carolina Governor's Papers, NCDAH; *Address. The Members of the Equal Rights League of Wilmington, N. C.*, printed circular, January 1866, AMA Archives; J. K. Van Fleet to Benjamin F. Butler, August 1, 1865, Benjamin F. Butler Papers, LC; Rachleff, *Black Labor*, 13–14, 35; O'Brien, "Reconstruction in Richmond," 274–80; *Equal Suffrage: Address from the Colored Citizens of Norfolk, Va., to the People of the United States* (New Bedford, Mass., 1865), 8–14.

17. Peter D. Klingman, "Rascal or Representative? Joe Oates of Tallahassee and the 'Election' of 1866," *FIHQ*, 51 (July 1972), 52–57; *Equal Suffrage*, 1, 8; Joseph R. Johnson to O. O. Howard, August 4, 1865, Unregistered Letters Received, Ser. 457, D.C. Asst. Comr., RG 105, NA [FSSP A-9851]; J. W. Blackwell to Andrew Johnson, November 24, 1865, Johnson Papers.

18. William C. Harris, *The Day of the Carpetbagger: Republican Reconstruction in Mississippi* (Baton Rouge, 1979), 96; Joseph H. Catching to Benjamin G. Humphreys, August 24, 1866, Mississippi Governor's Papers; New Orleans *Tribune*, September 13, 1866, S. W. Laidler to Thaddeus Stevens, May 7, 1866, Thaddeus Stevens Papers, LC.

A series of Supreme Court decisions known as the "Civil Rights Cases" essentially negated legislation designed to ensure racial equality.[1] Free from federal intervention, southern whites (led by the Redeemers) swiftly moved to undo black gains made during Reconstruction. Throughout the 1880s and 1890s southern states passed an array of legislation designed to oppress and disenfranchise the black population. Economic and political deprivation was oftentimes accompanied by physical terror as mob violence and lynching were the order of the day. This period is generally referred to as the "Jim Crow" era.[2]

The Supreme Court ruling in **Plessy v. Ferguson** *(1896) fully institutionalized southern apartheid and stood as precedence in civil rights law for the next 50 or so years. The issue in question turned on a 1890 Louisiana statute that required railroad companies to provide separate accommodations for whites and blacks, making it a criminal offense to occupy a seat reserved for the other race. Homer Plessy, reportedly 1/8 black, refused to relinquish his seat in the whites only coach in violation of Louisiana law. Plessy argued that the law violated his civil rights provided by the 13th and 14th Amendments. Delivering the opinion for the majority, Justice Brown maintained that the Louisiana was not in violation of the 13th Amendment because it clearly did not ". . . reestablish a state of involuntary servitude." As to the 14th Amendment, the majority opined that its intent was ". . . to enforce the absolute equality between the two races before the law," not to ". . . abolish distinctions based upon color." The Court went on to note that the* *society widely accepted separation of the races in many areas of social life. To the Court, state-or-dered segregation in railroad accommodations was no more "obnoxious" than laws providing for separate schools or prohibiting intermarriage. In a scathing dissent, Justice Harlan argued that "[O]ur Constitution is color-blind, and neither knows nor tolerates classes among citizens." Harlan's words fell on deaf ears as the doctrine of "separate but equal" codified a retrenchment in American racial politics that did not abate until the Brown ruling in 1954.*

PLESSY V. FERGUSON (1896)

JUSTICE BROWN **delivered the opinion of the Court**

Plessy v. Ferguson, 163 U.S. 537, 16 S. Ct. 1138, 41 L. ED. 256

An 1890 Louisiana law required that railway passenger cars have "equal but sepa-rate accommodations for the white, and colored races." Plessy, alleging that he "was seven-eighths Caucasian and one-eighth African blood; that the mixture of colored blood was not discernible in him; and that he was entitled to every right [of] the white race," was arrested for refusing to vacate a seat in a coach for whites.

That it does not conflict with the *13th Amendment* [is] too clear for argu-ment. Slavery implies involuntary servitude,—a state of bondage. . . . This amendment [was] regarded by the statesmen of that day as insufficient to protect the colored race from certain laws [imposing] onerous disabilities and burdens, and curtailing their rights in the pursuit of life, liberty, and property to such an extent that their freedom was of little value; [and] the *14th Amendment* was devised to meet this exigency. . . .

The object of the amendment was undoubtedly to enforce the absolute equality of the two races before the law, but, in the nature of things, it could not have been intended to abolish distinctions based upon color, or to enforce social, as distinguished from political, equality, or a commingling of the two races upon terms unsatisfactory to either. [Laws] requiring their separation, in places where they are liable to be brought into contact [have] been gener-ally, if not universally, recognized as within the competency of the state leg-islatures in the exercise of their police power. The most common instance of this is connected with the establishment of separate schools for white and col-ored children, which have been [upheld] even by courts of states where the political rights of the colored race have been longest and most earnestly en-forced [citing cases from Mass., Ohio, Mo., Cal., La., N.Y., Ind. and Ky.].

Laws forbidding the intermarriage of the two races may be said in a tech-nical sense to interfere with the freedom of contract, and yet have been uni-versally recognized as within the police power of the state. [S]tatutes for the separation of the two races upon public conveyances were held to be consti-tutional in [federal decisions and cases from Pa., Mich., Ill., Tenn. and N.Y. It is suggested] that the same argument that will justify the state legislature in requiring railways to provide separate accommodations for the two races will also authorize them to require separate cars to be provided for people whose hair is of a certain color, or who are aliens, or who belong to certain nationalities, or to enact laws requiring colored people to walk upon one side of the street, and white people upon the other, or requiring white men's houses to be painted white, and colored men's black, or their vehicles or business signs to be of different colors, upon the theory that one side of the street is as good as the other, or that a house or vehicle of one color is as good as one of another color. (The reply to all this is that every exercise of the police power must be reasonable, and extend only to such laws as are enacted in good faith for the promotion of the public good, and not for the annoyance or oppression of a particular class.) [In] determining the question of reasonableness, [the state] is at liberty to act with reference to the established usages, customs, and traditions of the people, and with a view to the promotion of their comfort, and the preservation of the public peace and good order. Gauged by this standard, we cannot say [this law] is unreasonable, or more obnoxious to the 14th amendment than the [acts] requiring separate schools for colored children in the District of Columbia, the constitutionality of which does not seem to have been questioned or the corresponding acts of state legislatures.

We consider the underlying fallacy of the plaintiff's argument to consist in the assumption that the enforced separation of the two races stamps the colored race with a badge of inferiority. If this be so, it is not by reason of anything found in the act, but solely because the colored race chooses to put that construction upon it. [The] argument also assumes that social prejudices may be overcome by legislation, and that equal rights cannot be secured to the negro except by an enforced commingling of the two races. We cannot accept this proposition. If the two races are to meet upon terms of social equality, it must be the result [of] voluntary consent of individuals. . . . Legislation is powerless to eradicate racial instincts, or to abolish distinctions based upon physical differences, and the attempt to do so can only result in accentuating the difficulties of the present situation. . . .

Affirmed.

JUSTICE BREWER did [not] participate in the decision of this case.

JUSTICE HARLAN dissenting.

[No] legislative body or judicial tribunal may have regard to the race of citizens when the civil rights of those citizens are involved. . . .

It was said in argument that the statute of Louisiana does not discriminate against either race, but prescribes a rule applicable alike to white and colored citizens. But [e]very one knows that [it] had its origin in the purpose, not so much to exclude white persons from railroad cars occupied by blacks, as to exclude colored people from coaches occupied by or assigned to white persons. [The] fundamental objection, therefore, to the statute, is that it interferes with the personal freedom of citizens. . . .

The white race deems itself to be the dominant race in this country. And so it is, in prestige, in achievements, in education, in wealth, and in power. So, I doubt not, it will continue to be for all time, if it remains true to its great heritage, and holds fast to the principles of constitutional liberty. But in view of the constitution, in the eye of the law, there is in this country no superior, dominant, ruling class of citizens. There is no caste here. Our constitution is color-blind. . . .

In my opinion, the judgment this day rendered will, in time, prove to be quite as pernicious as the decision made by this tribunal in the *Dred Scott Case* [that] the descendants of Africans who were imported into this country, and sold as slaves, were not included nor intended to be included under the word "citizens" in the constitution; [that,] at the time of the adoption of the constitution, they were "considered as a subordinate and inferior class of beings, who had been subjugated by the dominant race, and, whether emancipated or not, yet remained subject to their authority, and had no rights or privileges but such as those who held the power and the government might choose to grant them." The recent amendments of the constitution, it was supposed, had eradicated these principles from our institutions. [What] can more certainly arouse race hate, what more certainly create and perpetuate a feeling of distrust between these races, than state enactments which, in fact, proceed on the ground that colored citizens are so inferior and degraded that they cannot be allowed to sit in public coaches occupied by white citizens? [The] thin disguise of "equal" accommodations for passengers in railroad coaches will not mislead any one, nor atone for the wrong this day done. . . .

The ascendance of Jim Crow policy was buoyed by the advent of the "age of science." Some of the country's most well-respected scholars articulated an intellectual defense of racial separation. The core premise was that because the "Negro" was inherently inferior, he should never again be allowed to participate in public affairs. Moreover, enforced separation was necessary to insure the "purity" of the white race (i.e., the sanctity of white women). That this philosophy was braced by "scientific" rigor provided legitimacy for one of the most oppressive periods in American race relations. The tragic irony, of course, it that it followed one of the most remarkable eras of African-American progress.

In the following excerpts from Jim Crow's Defense, *I.A. Newby discusses the major scholarly works associated with the rise of "scientific racism" or "eugenics." As Newby notes, evolutionary explanations of racial differences relied on the so-called "race-climate" hypothesis. The basic idea is that ". . . racial characteristics represented adaptations to the physical environment in which evolution had occurred." In turn, scientific racists focused on heredity as the primary engine of intergenerational transmission. Racial inequality persisted, according to this view, because differences were passed on from generation to generation. The development of "primitive" traits in blacks, they contended, was the result of the nature and size of the "Negro" brain. In essence, blacks' "smaller" craniums were directly related to their presumed intellectual deficiencies. If the brain stopped growing at puberty, as scientific racists argued, the Negro could ". . . never escape from mental and consequently moral retardation."*

Racial differences in physical attributes were also taken as evidence of black inferiority. Black features were understood to closely represent those associated with "anthropoid apes." Whereas much was made of physiological differences, scientific racists went on to develop a brand of "racial psychology" to explain social and cultural differences between the races. Thus understood, it was not a far leap to maintain that the races should (and must) abide by strict laws of separation.

Although there is some debate about the extent to which the intellectual defense of segregation contributed to the development of anti-black public policies, it is abundantly clear that the link between science and racism provided the fodder for a public discourse that worked to the disadvantage of African-Americans. Fortunately, as "higher standards" of science were implemented, the dominance of scientific racism began to drown under the weight of more rigorous scholarship. Nonetheless, basic assertions associated with this period of American science still rear their ugly head from time to time and continue to sustain underlying racial stereotypes about African-Americans.[3]

THE CONTRIBUTIONS OF SCIENCE AND SOCIAL SCIENCE

I.A. Newby

Excerpt from Jim Crow's Defense

The theories of scientists are of no more value than those of other men. What we look to them for is facts, and from admitted truth others can argue well or better than they; for they are by no means the best logicians.

—"CAUCASIAN," *ANTHROPOLOGY FOR THE PEOPLE* (1891)

In formulating and discriminating their ideology, anti-Negro writers unconscionably exploited science and social science. Drawing heavily upon the theories and researches, as they interpreted them, of eugenics, genetics, ethnology, biology, psychology, physiology, anthropology, sociology, and geography, they assembled a formidable array of scientific and pseudoscientific evidence to support their cause. Their efforts, moreover, were facilitated by reputable scientists in all disciplines who accepted the contentions that races are unequal and that Negroes are inferior to other basic stocks. Thus fortified by respectable scientific authority, they developed in detail the *"science of race."* They often disagreed among themselves upon details and the implications of basic concepts, but they generally agreed upon fundamentals. In this manner they gave coherence to a body of thought that was in other respects amorphous and disorganized.

. . . [S]cientific racists relied heavily upon the *race-climate hypothesis* to prove that evolution was the source of racial inequality. Few hypotheses received greater attention from racists or were developed in more detail. They arrogated to themselves the theory, long supported by many geographers, that racial characteristics represented adaptations to the physical environment in which evolution had occurred. For racist purposes this idea was as plausible as it was ingenious. The hot and stultifying climate of tropical Africa, its dense and humid jungles, had halted the Negro's evolutionary development at primitive, generalized levels. The invigorating and exacting climate of the north temperate zone, however, had stimulated the Caucasian's development into advanced and specialized channels. The result was a fundamental difference in physical appearance, emotional stability, and mental capability.

. . . Convinced now that evolution was the source of racial inequality, racists turned their attention to *heredity*, the process through which they believed this inequality to be perpetuated. They were convinced that this was the real function of the laws of heredity, and not until the 20th century did they take the trouble to explain fully the scientific mechanisms by which those laws operated. Beginning about 1900 this emphasis on heredity—on genetics and eugenics—formed the most significant new element in racist thought in the 20th century. For the first quarter of the century, indeed, eugenics and genetics constituted the single most important authority of scientific racists. So completely were these sciences permeated by racism that Harvard anthropologist E. A. Hooten complained as late as 1937 that eugenics was little more than "a lay form of ancestor worship" clothed in "Ku Klux Klan regalia."

The sources of *eugenic racism* were two. One, Sir Francis Galton's science of heredity, was discussed earlier. The other, the application of genetics to plant and animal breeding, must also be noted. Long before racists became interested in heredity, the principles of genetics had been known and practiced by American plant and animal breeders, and the results had sometimes been phenomenal. They eliminated undesirable strains and unhealthy characteristics, developing new and heartier breeds of animals as well as plants. Was it not reasonable that an application of similar principles to mankind would create a new race of human thoroughbreds?

Surveying the history and present state of eugenics, Popenoe and Johnson illustrated the remarkable confluence of scientific and racist thought on this subject. Relying upon such authorities as John Moffatt Mecklin's *Democracy and Race Friction* (1921), they endorsed racial segregation as "a social adaptation with survival value." It was necessary because the mental development and group traits of Negroes are more primitive than those of whites. "We feel justified in concluding," they wrote, "that the Negro race differs greatly from the white race, mentally as well as physically, and that in many respects it may be said to be inferior when tested by the requirements of modern civilization and progress, with particular reference to North America." Specifically, "the Negro lacks in his germ plasm excellence of some qualities which the white races possess, and which are essential for success in competition with the civilizations of the white races of the present day." He is, therefore, not only different from the white but in large measure eugenically inferior as well. Thus, "if eugenics is to be thought of solely in terms of the white race, there can be no hesitation about rendering a verdict. We must unhesitatingly condemn miscegenation."

They began with the premise that a direct correlation existed between brain size and mental capacity. From this they inferred that the average Negro brain was significantly smaller than the average white brain, an inference which they substantiated by a multitude of studies on the relative cranial capacity and brain weight of different races. Drawn largely from studies made by Europeans in the nineteenth century, these studies were particularly attractive because they corresponded invariably to the racists' hierarchical ranking of races. According to figures offered by sociologist John Maffatt Mecklin, the cranial capacity of the average Caucasian male was 1,500 to 1,600 cubic centimeters, of the Mongolian 1,500 to 1,580, of the Negro 1,388, of the Australian aborigine 1,245.

Racists explained the physiological deficiencies of the Negro's brain by theorizing that its physical growth halted abruptly at puberty. At this time the sutures of the skull were said to knit firmly together, preventing further enlargement of the brain. Puberty was, of course, an especially inopportune time for the cessation of mental development. Prior to this age brain activity involved only such processes as perception, memory, and motor responses. Not until later did it broaden into abstraction, critical thinking, comprehension of complex and subtle relationships, and "ability to appreciate logical, aesthetic and moral situations." But even though the Negro's mental development ceased at puberty, his animal and sexual development continued unabated. The adult Negro was, thus, physically and sexually mature, but lacking in the restraints of mental maturity. He was a boy with a man's passions but a deadened intellect. He could never escape from mental and consequently moral retardation.

During the first half of the 20th century American blacks endured widespread social, political, and economic deprivation (particularly in the south).[4] Degradation took many forms. For example, blacks were forced to receive food from the back of restaurants, drink from separate water fountains, and ride in the back of the bus. More seriously, southern blacks faced the constant threat of death for even the most minor of perceived transgressions (e.g., looking a white woman in the eye, failing to give a white pedestrian the right of way, addressing a white person in an "impertinent" tone, etc.). And while law in the states of the Old Confederacy enforced this discrimination, it was also practiced by custom in other parts of the country.

The massive changes associated with the First and Second World Wars, coupled with the demise of King Cotton and the rise of industrialization fundamentally altered the context of racial politics. As Doug McAdam points out, large-scale external changes reshuffled political and economic opportunities for American blacks.[5] For example, massive black in-migration from the south to the north significantly altered black (and white) life.[6] In political terms, the influx of blacks to the cities opened the possibility for Democratic overtures to an increasingly urban (and northern) black population. In social terms, black in-migration influenced black family life as rural southern values culled from the slave experience collided with the black northern values.[7] In economic terms, war and mass industrialization provided steady employment that served as a platform for community development. For example, organizations like the National Association for the Advancement of Colored People and the Urban League came to prominence between the wars. In short, the first four decades of the 20th century produced an environment ripe for change.

Much of this activity came to a head in 1942 when civil rights activist and labor organizer A. Phillip Randolph organized the original *March on Washington*. The primary purpose was to protest employment segregation in the federal defense industries. Randolph, who was the president of the influential Brotherhood of Sleeping Car Porters, threatened a mass march on the nation's capitol if President Roosevelt did not protect and expand employment opportunities in the federal government. In the midst of a war effort for democracy abroad, Roosevelt could ill afford a potential public relations nightmare. Randolph called off the march when FDR signed Executive Order #8802 creating the Fair Employment Practices Commission to investigate discrimination in federal hiring in the defense industry. Although the FEPC had little enforcement authority, its creation was a stepping-stone for future black empowerment.

STUDY QUESTIONS

1. How do you think the history of African-Americans in this country would be different if the Reconstruction era had produced a more egalitarian economic system, rather than political system? Put differently, what is the relationship among race, politics, and economics?

2. The Supreme Court ruling in *Plessy v. Ferguson* (1896) clearly defined African-Americans as second-class citizens by affirming the doctrine of "separate but equal." How did the Court justify this decision? How did this ruling influence race-related public policy in the 20th century?

3. What scientific innovations were articulated in defense of racial separation? How did these scholarly opinions help to validate notions of African-American inferiority? What are the implications of scientific racism for the contemporary public discourse on race?

4. What are the key elements of the Civil War Amendments? What governmental mechanisms were designed to enforce blacks' newly acquired constitutional rights? What impact did the Amendments have on race relations in the South?

NOTES

1. Blaustein and Zangrando, pp. 246–281.

2. C. Vann Woodward. *The strange career of Jim Crow.* (New York: Oxford University Press, 3rd edition) 1974.

3. Richard J. Herrnsetin and Charles Murray. *The bell curve: Intelligence and class structure in American life* (New York: The Free Press) 1994.

4. But see Alain Locke (ed.) *The New Negro.* (New York: Macmillan) 1925.

5. Doug McAdam, *Political Process and the Development of Black Insurgency, 1930–1970.* (Chicago: University of Chicago Press) 1982.

6. Stewart E. Tolnay, The great migration and changes in the northern black family, 1940 to 1990. *Social Forces* 75,4 (1997):1213–1239.

7. E. Franklin Frazier. *The Negro family in Chicago.* (Chicago: University of Chicago Press 1932).

The Civil Rights Movement: 1950–1972

The aborted March on Washington foreshadowed growing disenchantment among blacks with their subordinate status. One hundred years had passed since emancipation, and African-Americans were still second-class citizens. Black workers earned about 50 cents on the dollar compared with white workers and owned little property.[1] To the extent that there was a black entrepreneurial class, it was almost exclusively based on services to the black community (e.g., mortuaries, hair salons, and restaurants). Politically, only 27% of the black voting-age electorate was registered to vote nationwide, and the percentage was in the single digits in the South. Black elected officials constituted less than 0.2 of 1% of all elected officials in the United States, and black suffrage was severely limited by law and custom. [2] Socially, the society was segregated in almost all areas of public (and private) life, particularly in the South.[3] Blacks and whites ate, learned, played, and prayed apart. For example, less than 1% of school-aged children attended integrated schools in the South by the early 1950s. Coupled with dramatic changes brought on by the end of the Second World War, the beginning of the Cold War, and widespread economic prosperity, the time was ripe for African-Americans to defy the racial hierarchy. This challenge is often referred to as the *civil rights movement*.[4]

The following analysis concentrates on three distinct stages of activity during the civil rights movement: legalism, nonviolent direct action, and black power. Each stage is analytically distinguished by an emphasis on a particular *political* strategy and philosophy. The benefit of this approach is that it allows concentration on the *politics* of the movement. This means, however, less reliance on a strictly linear chronology. In other words, the analyses jump back in forth in time as the political stages of the movement overlap and accumulate.

LEGALISM: 1950–1958

Founded in 1911, the National Association of Colored People (NAACP) was created to educate the American public about the need for racial reform. In the early 1940s, the NAACP established its legal arm, the Legal Defense Fund (LDF) whose primary purpose was to fight segregation through litigation.[5] Led by future Supreme Court Justice Thurgood Marshall, the LDF pursued a strategy designed to push the laws of segregation (and the principles that supported them) directly up against the Constitution. In essence, the LDF intended to force the Court to choose between upholding the Constitution or upholding segregation.

The doctrine of "separate but equal" set in Plessy validated state-imposed racial discrimination for the first half of the 20th century. By the late 1940s, however, civil rights advocates had mounted a serious threat to the constitutionality of Plessy. In 1950, racial discrimination in graduate admissions was challenged in **Sweat v. Painter**.[6] *At issue was the admittance of an African-American student to the law school at the University of Texas. Consistent with Texas law, Homan Sweatt was denied admission to the University of Texas' law school because of the color of his skin. In a remarkable ruling, the state trial court allowed the University 6 months to provide Sweatt with comparable ("equal") educational facilities. When the Court did hear the case it was abundantly clear that the "new" law school did not measure up in any way to the law school at Austin (e.g., number and quality of faculty, library facilities, books, etc.). The Court ruled that it could not adjudicate in accordance with Plessy because ". . . legal education equivalent to that offered by the State . . ." was not available to Sweatt. Thus, the "Equal Protection Clause of the 14th Amendment requires that the petitioner be admitted to the University of Texas Law School."*

SWEATT V. PAINTER ET AL.

No. 44, SUPREME COURT OF THE UNITED STATES, 339 U.S. 629; 70 S. Ct. 848; 1950 U.S. LEXIS 1809; 94 L. Ed. 1114

April 4, 1950, Argued
June 5, 1950, Decided

OPINION: [*631] [**848] MR. CHIEF JUSTICE VINSON delivered the opinion of the Court.

[**849] [1]

This case and *McLaurin v. Oklahoma State Regents*, post, p. 637, present different aspects of this general question: To what extent does the Equal Protection
Clause of the 14th Amendment limit the power of a state to distinguish between students of different races in professional and graduate education in a
state university? Broader issues have been urged for our consideration, but
we adhere to the principle of deciding constitutional questions only in the
context of the particular case before the Court. We have frequently reiterated
that this Court will decide constitutional questions only when necessary to
the disposition of the case at hand, and that such decisions will be drawn as
narrowly as possible. *Rescue Army v. Municipal Court*, 331 U.S. 549 (1947),
[***5] and cases cited therein. Because of this traditional reluctance to extend
constitutional interpretations to situations or facts which are not before the
Court, much of the excellent research and detailed argument presented in
these cases is unnecessary to their disposition.

In the instant case, petitioner filed an application for admission to the University of Texas Law School for the February, 1946 term. His application was
rejected solely because he is a Negro.[n1] Petitioner thereupon brought this suit
for mandamus against the appropriate school officials, respondents here, to
compel his admission. At that time, there was no law school in Texas which
admitted Negroes.

The state trial court recognized that the action of the State in denying petitioner the opportunity to gain a legal education while granting it to others deprived him of the equal protection of the laws guaranteed by the 14th
Amendment. The court did not grant the relief requested, however, but continued the case for 6 months to allow the State to supply substantially equal
facilities. At the expiration of the 6 months, in December, 1946, the court denied the writ on the showing that the authorized university officials had
adopted an order calling for the opening of a law school for Negroes the following February. While petitioner's appeal was pending, such a school was
made available, but petitioner refused to register therein. The Texas Court of
Civil Appeals set aside the trial court's judgment and ordered the cause "remanded generally to the trial court for further proceedings without prejudice
to the rights of any party to this suit."

On remand, a hearing was held on the issue of the equality of the educational facilities at the newly established school as compared with the University of Texas Law School. Finding that the new school offered petitioner
"privileges, advantages, and opportunities for the study of law substantially
equivalent to those offered by the State to white students at the University of
Texas," the trial court denied mandamus. The Court of Civil Appeals affirmed. 210 S. W. 2d 442 (1948). Petitioner's application for a writ of error was
denied by the Texas Supreme Court. We granted certiorari, 338 U.S. 865 (1949),
because of the manifest importance of the constitutional issues involved.

The University of Texas Law School, from which petitioner was excluded,
was staffed by a faculty of 16 full-time and 3 part-time professors, some of
whom are nationally recognized authorities in their field. Its student body
numbered 850. The library contained over 65,000 volumes. Among the other

facilities available to the students were a law review, moot court facilities, scholarship funds, and Order of the Coif affiliation. The school's alumni occupy the most distinguished positions in the private practice of the law and in the public life of the [**850] State. It may properly be considered one of the nation's ranking law schools.

The law school for Negroes, which was to have opened in February, 1947, would have had no independent faculty or library. The teaching was to be carried on by four members of the University of Texas Law School faculty, who were to maintain their offices at the University of Texas while teaching at both institutions. Few of the 10,000 volumes ordered for the library had arrived; nor was there any full-time librarian. The school lacked accreditation.

Since the trial of this case, respondents report the opening of a law school at the Texas State University for Negroes. It is apparently on the road to full accreditation. It has a faculty of 5 full-time professors; a student body of 23; a library of some 16,500 volumes serviced by a full-time staff; a practice court and legal aid association; and one alumnus who has become a member of the Texas Bar.

Whether the University of Texas Law School is compared with the original or the new law school for Negroes, we cannot find substantial equality in the educational opportunities offered white and Negro law students by the State. In terms of number of the faculty, variety of courses and opportunity for specialization, size of the student body, scope of the library, availability of law review and similar activities, the University of Texas Law School is superior. What is more important, the University of Texas Law School possesses to a far greater degree those qualities which are incapable of objective measurement but which make for greatness in a law school. Such qualities, to name but a few, include reputation of the faculty, experience of the administration, position and influence of the alumni, standing in the community, traditions and prestige. It is difficult to believe that one who had a free choice between these law schools would consider the question close.

Moreover, although the law is a highly learned profession, we are well aware that it is an intensely practical one. The law school, the proving ground for legal learning and practice, cannot be effective in isolation from the individuals and institutions with which the law interacts. Few students and no one who has practiced law would choose to study in an academic vacuum, removed from the interplay of ideas and the exchange of views with which the law is concerned. The law school to which Texas is willing to admit petitioner excludes from its student body members of the racial groups which number 85% of the population of the State and include most of the lawyers, witnesses, jurors, judges and other officials with whom petitioner will inevitably be dealing when he becomes a member of the Texas Bar. With such a substantial and significant segment of society excluded, we cannot conclude that the education offered petitioner is substantially equal to that which he would receive if admitted to the University of Texas Law School. It may be argued that excluding petitioner from that school is no different from excluding white students from the new law school. This contention overlooks realities. It is unlikely that a member of a group so decisively in the majority, attending a school with rich traditions and prestige which only a history of consistently maintained excellence could command, would claim that the opportunities afforded him for legal education were unequal to those held open to petitioner.

That such a claim, if made, would be dishonored by the State, is no answer. "Equal protection of the laws is not achieved through indiscriminate imposition of inequalities." It is fundamental that these cases concern rights which are personal and present. This Court has stated unanimously that "The State must provide [legal education] for [petitioner] in conformity with the equal protection clause of the 14th Amendment and provide it as soon as it does for applicants of any other group."

That case "did not present the issue whether a state might not satisfy the equal protection clause of the 14th Amendment by establishing a separate law school for Negroes." In *Missouri ex rel. Gaines v. Canada*, 305 U.S. 337, 351 (1938), the Court, speaking through Chief Justice Hughes, declared that "petitioner's right was a personal one. It was as an individual that he was entitled to the equal protection of the laws, and the State was bound to furnish him within its borders facilities for legal education substantially equal to those which the State there afforded for persons of the white race, whether or not other Negroes sought the same opportunity." These are the only cases in this Court which present the issue of the constitutional validity of race distinctions in state-supported graduate and professional education.

In accordance with these cases, petitioner may claim his full constitutional right: legal education equivalent to that offered by the State to students of other races. Such education is not available to him in a separate law school as offered by the State. We cannot, therefore, agree with respondents that the doctrine of *Plessy v. Ferguson*, 163 U.S. 537 (1896), requires affirmance of the judgment below. Nor need we reach petitioner's contention that *Plessy v. Ferguson* should be reexamined in the light of contemporary knowledge respecting the purposes of the Fourteenth Amendment and the effects of racial segregation. We hold that the Equal Protection Clause of the 14th Amendment requires that petitioner be admitted to the University of Texas Law School. The judgment is reversed and the cause is remanded for proceedings not inconsistent with this opinion.

Reversed.

———————————————— ■ ————————————————

The significance of this case is that the Supreme Court demonstrated a willingness to notably depart from the precedence set in *Plessy*. In other words, while the Court still accepted the notion of racial segregation, the issue of equality was now under serious examination. The full doctrine, as set in *Plessy*, was ultimately overturned by a series of landmark school desegregation cases.

NOTE

n1 It appears that the University has been restricted to white students, in accordance with the State law. See Tex. Const., Art. VII, §§ 7, 14; Tex. Rev. Civ. Stat. (Vernon, 1925), Arts. 2643b (Supp. 1949), 2719, 2900.

Perhaps no other document altered the course of American race relations like the 1954 *Supreme Court decision in* **Brown v. Board of Education of Topeka**. *The action was actually comprised of four separate cases in Delaware, Virginia, South Carolina, and Kansas (Brown is the signature name simply because of alphabetical order). The legal issue turned on the constitutionality of excluding "Negro" schoolchildren from public schools simply because of the color of their skin. The LDF, representing the plaintiffs, argued that state-imposed segregation of educational facilities was in direct violation of the Equal Protection Clause of the 14th Amendment. In reference to the 14th Amendment, the LDF brief noted that ". . . it is indisputable that its primary purpose was to complete the emancipation provided by the 13th Amendment by ensuring to the Negro equality before the law."[7] Thurgood Marshall and the LDF legal team offered a compelling body of empirical evidence demonstrating that separate school facilities harmed black school children by stigmatizing them thus making it difficult to learn.[8] Moreover, the fact that separation was based on an arbitrary distinction such as skin color was an "irrational basis for governmental action."*

Writing for the majority, Chief Justice Warren noted the significance of public education as a central feature of democratic societies. Access to this public good, therefore, was important because, ". . . it is doubtful that any child may reasonably expected to succeed in life if he is denied the opportunity of an education." The Court ruled that ". . . in the field of public education the doctrine of "separate but equal has no place. Separate educational facilities are inherently unequal . . . we hold . . . that the plaintiffs are . . . deprived of the equal protection of the laws guaranteed by the 14th Amendment."

BROWN V. BOARD OF EDUCATION OF TOPEKA (1954)

■

Brown v. Board of Education, 503 U.S. 978

Mr. Chief Justice Warren delivered the opinion of the Court.

These cases come to us from the States of Kansas, South Carolina, Virginia, and Delaware. They are premised on different facts and different local conditions, but a common legal question justifies their consideration together in this consolidated opinion.

In each of the cases, minors of the Negro race, through their legal representatives, seek the aid of the courts in obtaining admission to the public schools of their community on a nonsegregated basis. In each instance, they had been denied admission to schools attended by white children under laws requiring or permitting segregation according to race. This segregation was alleged to deprive the plaintiffs of the equal protection of the laws under the Fourteenth Amendment. In each of the cases other than the Delaware case, a three-judge federal district court denied relief to the plaintiffs on the so-called "separate but equal" doctrine announced by this Court in *Plessy v. Ferguson*, 163 U. S. 537. Under that doctrine, equality of treatment is accorded when the races are provided substantially equal facilities, even though these facilities be separate. In the Delaware case, the Supreme Court of Delaware adhered to that doctrine, but ordered that the plaintiffs be admitted to the white schools because of their superiority to the Negro schools.

The plaintiffs contend that segregated public schools are not "equal" and cannot be made "equal," and that hence they are deprived of the equal protection of the laws. Because of the obvious importance of the question presented, the Court took jurisdiction. Argument was heard in the 1952 Term, and reargument was heard this Term on certain questions propounded by the Court.

Reargument was largely devoted to the circumstances surrounding the adoption of the 14th Amendment in 1868. It covered exhaustively consideration of the Amendment in Congress, ratification by the states, then existing practices in racial segregation, and the views of proponents and opponents of the Amendment. This discussion and our own investigation convince us that, although these sources cast some light, it is not enough to resolve the problem with which we are faced. At best, they are inconclusive. The most avid proponents of the post-War Amendments undoubtedly intended them to remove all legal distinctions among "all persons born or naturalized in the United States." Their opponents, just as certainly, were antagonistic to both the letter and the spirit of the Amendments and wished them to have the most limited effect. What others in Congress and the state legislatures had in mind cannot be determined with any degree of certainty.

An additional reason for the inconclusive nature of the Amendment's history, with respect to segregated schools, is the status of public education at that time. In the South, the movement toward free common schools, supported by general taxation, had not yet taken hold. Education of white children was largely in the hands of private groups. Education of Negroes was almost non-existent, and practically all of the race were illiterate. In fact, any education of Negroes was forbidden by law in some states. Today, in contrast, many Negroes have achieved outstanding success in the arts and sciences as well as in the business and professional world. It is true that public school education at the time of the Amendment had advanced further in the North, but the effect of the Amendment on Northern States was generally ignored in the congressional debates. Even in the North, the conditions of public education did not approximate those existing today. The curriculum was usually rudimentary; ungraded schools were common in rural areas; the school term was but three months a year in many states; and compulsory school attendance was virtually unknown. As a consequence, it is not surprising that there should be so little in the history of the 14th Amendment relating to its intended effect on public education.

In the first cases in this Court construing the 14th Amendment, decided shortly after its adoption, the Court interpreted it as proscribing all state imposed discriminations against the Negro race. The doctrine of "separate but equal" did not make its appearance in this Court until 1896 in the case of *Plessy* v. *Ferguson, supra*, involving not education but transportation. American courts have since labored with the doctrine for over half a century. In this Court, there have been six cases involving the "separate but equal" doctrine in the field of public education. In *Cumming* v. *County Board of Education*, 175 U. S. 528, and *Gong Lum* v. *Rice*, 275 U. S. 78, the validity of the doctrine itself was not challenged. In more recent cases, all on the graduate school level, inequality was found in that specific benefits enjoyed by white students were denied to Negro students of the same educational qualifications. *Missouri ex rel. Gaines* v. *Canada*, 305 U. S. 337; *Sipuel* v. *Oklahoma*, 332 U. S. 631; *Sweatt* v. *Painter*, 339 U. S. 629; *McLaurin* v. *Oklahoma State Regents*, 339 U. S. 637. In none of these cases was it necessary to re-examine the doctrine to grant relief to the Negro plaintiff. And in *Sweatt* v. *Painter, supra,* the Court expressly reserved decision on the question whether *Plessy v. Ferguson* should be held inapplicable to public education.

In the instant cases, that question is directly presented. Here, unlike *Sweatt v. Painter*, there are findings below that the Negro and white schools involved have been equalized, or are being equalized, with respect to buildings, curricula, qualifications and salaries of teachers, and other "tangible" factors. Our decision, therefore, cannot turn on merely a comparison of these tangible factors in the Negro and white schools involved in each of the cases. We must look instead to the effect of segregation itself on public education.

In approaching this problem, we cannot turn the clock back to 1868 when the Amendment was adopted, or even to 1896 when *Plessy v. Ferguson* was written. We must consider public education in the light of its full development and its present place in American life throughout the Nation. Only in this way can it be determined if segregation in public schools deprives these plaintiffs of the equal protection of the laws.

Today, education is perhaps the most important function of state and local governments. Compulsory school attendance laws and the great expenditures for education both demonstrate our recognition of the importance of education to our democratic society. It is required in the performance of our most basic public responsibilities, even service in the armed forces. It is the very foundation of good citizenship. Today it is a principal instrument in awakening the child to cultural values, in preparing him for later professional training, and in helping him to adjust normally to his environment. In these days, it is doubtful that any child may reasonably be expected to succeed in life if he is denied the opportunity of an education. Such an opportunity, where the state has undertaken to provide it, is a right which must be made available to all on equal terms.

We come then to the question presented: Does segregation of children in public schools solely on the basis of race, even though the physical facilities and other "tangible" factors may be equal, deprive the children of the minority group of equal educational opportunities? We believe that it does.

In *Sweatt* v. *Painter, supra,* in finding that a segregated law school for Negroes could not provide them equal educational opportunities, this Court relied in large part on "those qualities which are incapable of objective measurement but which make for greatness in a law school." In *McLaurin* v. *Oklahoma State Regents, supra,* the Court, in requiring that a Negro admitted to a white graduate school be treated like all other students, again resorted to intangible considerations: ". . . his ability to study, to engage in discussions and exchange views with other students, and, in general, to learn his profession." Such considerations apply with added force to children in grade and high schools. To separate them from others of similar age and qualifications solely because of their race generates a feeling of inferiority as to their status in the community that may affect their hearts and minds in a way unlikely ever to be undone. The effect of this separation on their educational opportunities was well stated by a finding in the Kansas case by a court which nevertheless felt compelled to rule against the Negro plaintiffs:

> "Segregation of white and colored children in public schools has a detrimental effect upon the colored children. The impact is greater when it has the sanction of the law; for the policy of separating the races is usually interpreted as denoting the inferiority of the Negro group. A sense of inferiority affects the motivation of a child to learn. Segregation with the sanction of law, therefore, has a tendency to [retard] the educational and mental development of Negro children and to deprive them of some of the benefits they would receive in a racial[ly] integrated school system."

Whatever may have been the extent of psychological knowledge at the time of *Plessy* v. *Ferguson*, this finding is amply supported by modern authority. Any language in *Plessy* v. *Ferguson* contrary to this finding is rejected.

We conclude that in the field of public education the doctrine of "separate but equal" has no place. Separate educational facilities are inherently unequal. Therefore, we hold that the plaintiffs and others similarly situated for whom the actions have been brought are, by reason of the segregation complained of, deprived of the equal protection of the laws guaranteed by the 14th Amendment. This disposition makes unnecessary any discussion whether such segregation also violates the Due Process Clause of the 14th Amendment.

Because these are class actions, because of the wide applicability of this decision, and because of the great variety of local conditions, the formulation of decrees in these cases presents problems of considerable complexity. On reargument, the consideration of appropriate relief was necessarily subordinated to the primary question—the constitutionality of segregation in public education. We have now announced that such segregation is a denial of the equal protection of the laws. In order that we may have the full assistance of the parties in formulating decrees, the cases will be restored to the docket, and the parties are requested to present further argument on Questions 4 and 5 previously propounded by the Court for the reargument this Term. The Attorney General of the United States is again invited to participate. The Attorneys General of the states requiring or permitting segregation in public education will also be permitted to appear as *amici curiae* upon request to do so by September 15, 1954, and submission of briefs by October 1, 1954.

It is so ordered.

The Court extended the Brown ruling in a related case having to do with school desegregation in the District of Columbia. In Bolling v. Sharpe *(1954) the LDF strategy employed in* Brown *was limited because the 14th Amendment is only applicable to the states. The LDF challenged the validity of racial segregation under the Due Process Clause of the 5th Amend-*

ment. Writing for the majority, Chief Justice Warren opined, ". . . Segregation in public education is not reasonably related to any proper governmental objective, and thus it imposes on Negro children of the District of Columbia a burden that constitutes an arbitrary deprivation of their liberty in violation of the Due Process Clause." The Court held that racial segregation of public schools in the District was a denial of blacks schoolchildren's due process of law.

BOLLING ET AL. V. SHARPE ET AL.

No. 8, Supreme Court of the United States, 347 U.S. 497; 74 S. Ct. 693; 1954 U.S.

OPINION: Mr. Chief Justice Warren delivered the opinion of the Court.

This case challenges the validity of segregation in the public schools of the District of Columbia. The petitioners, minors of the Negro race, allege that such segregation deprives them of due process of law under the Fifth Amendment. They were refused admission to a public school attended by white children solely because of their race. They sought the aid of the District Court for the District of Columbia in obtaining admission. That court dismissed their complaint. The Court granted a writ of certiorari before judgment in the Court of Appeals because of the importance of the constitutional question presented.

We have this day held that the Equal Protection Clause of the 14th Amendment prohibits the states from maintaining racially segregated public schools. The legal problem in the District of Columbia is somewhat different, however. The 5th Amendment, which is applicable in the District of Columbia, does not contain an equal protection clause as does the 14th Amendment which applies only to the states. But the concepts of equal protection and due process, both stemming from our American ideal of fairness, are not mutually exclusive. The "equal protection of the laws" is a more explicit safeguard of prohibited unfairness than "due process of law," and, therefore, we do not imply that the two are always interchangeable phrases. But, as this Court has recognized, discrimination may be so unjustifiable as to be violative of due process.

Classifications based solely upon race must be scrutinized with particular care, since they are contrary to our traditions and hence constitutionally suspect. As long ago as 1896, this Court declared the principle "that the Constitution of the United States, in its present form, forbids, so far as civil and political rights are concerned, discrimination by the General Government, or by the States, against any citizen because of his race." And in *Buchanan v. Warley*, 245 U.S. 60, the Court held that a statute which limited the right of a property owner to convey his property to a person of another race was, as an unreasonable discrimination, a denial of due process of law.

Although the Court has not assumed to define "liberty" with any great precision, that term is not confined to mere freedom from bodily restraint. Liberty under law extends to the full range of conduct which the individual is free to pursue, and it cannot be restricted except for a proper governmental objective.

Segregation in public education is not reasonably related to any proper governmental objective, and thus it imposes on Negro children of the District of Columbia a burden that constitutes an arbitrary deprivation of their liberty in violation of the Due Process Clause.

In view of our decision that the Constitution prohibits the states from maintaining racially segregated public schools, it would be unthinkable that the same Constitution would impose a lesser duty on the Federal Government. We hold that racial segregation in the public schools of the District of Columbia is a denial of the due process of law guaranteed by the 5th Amendment to the Constitution.

———————————————————————— ■ ————————————————————————

In the initial Brown *ruling (Brown I) Justice Warren stated the schools must desegregate with "all deliberate speed." The ambiguity of this order resulted in a second case that spelled out the details of implementing school desegregation. In* **Brown v. Board of Education of Topeka: An Enforcement Decree** *(Brown II), the Court recognized that "[F]ull implementation... may require solution of varied local school problems." As a result the Court mandated that implementing school integration fell most appropriately to the lower courts "[B]ecause of their proximity to local conditions." Leaving the implementation and enforcement authority in the hands of local southern officials quickly proved to be an obstacle for school integration.*

BROWN V. BOARD OF EDUCATION (1955)
———————————————————————— ■ ————————————————————————

Brown v. Board of Education, 349 U.S. 294, 75 S. Ct. 753, 99 L. Ed. 1083 (1955)

Chief Justice Warren delivered the opinion of the Court.

These cases were decided on May 17, 1954. [There] remains for consideration the manner in which relief is to be accorded.* * *

Full implementation of these constitutional principles may require solution of varied local school problems. School authorities have the primary responsibility for elucidating, assessing, and solving [them]; courts will have to consider whether the action of school authorities constitutes good faith implementation of the governing constitutional principles. Because of their proximity to local conditions and the possible need for further hearings, the courts which originally heard these cases can best perform this judicial appraisal. Accordingly, we believe it appropriate to remand the cases to those courts.

In fashioning and effectuating the decrees, the courts will be guided by equitable principles. Traditionally, equity has been characterized by a practical flexibility in shaping its remedies and by a facility for adjusting and reconciling public and private needs. [A]t stake is the personal interest of the plaintiffs in admission to public schools as soon as practicable on a nondiscriminatory basis. To effectuate this interest may call for elimination of a variety of obstacles in making the transition to school systems operated in accordance with the constitutional principles set forth in our May 17, 1954, decision. Courts of equity may properly take into account the public interest in the elimination of such obstacles in a systematic and effective manner. But it should go without saying that the vitality of these constitutional principles cannot be allowed to yield simply because of disagreement with them.

While giving weight to these public and private considerations, the courts will require that the defendants make a prompt and reasonable start toward full compliance with our May 17, 1954, ruling. Once such a start has been made, the courts may find that additional time is necessary to carry out the ruling in an effective manner. The burden rests upon the defendants to establish that such time is necessary in the public interest and is consistent with good faith compliance at the earliest practicable date. To that end, the courts may consider problems related to administration, arising from the physical condition of the school plant, the school transportation system, personnel, revision of school districts and attendance areas into compact units to achieve a system of determining admission to the public schools on a nonracial basis, and revision of local laws and regulations which may be necessary in solving the foregoing problems. They will also consider the adequacy of any plans the defendants may propose to meet these problems and to effectuate a transition to a racially nondiscriminatory school system. During this period of transition, the courts will retain jurisdiction of these cases.

The [cases are remanded] to take such proceedings and enter such orders and decrees consistent with this opinion as are necessary and proper to admit to public schools on a racially nondiscriminatory basis *with all deliberate speed* the parties to these cases.* * *

The school desegregation rulings symbolized the ascendancy of litigation as a strategy for African-American inclusion. For the first time in more than half a century, black rights were upheld and protected by the state. Integration in public education fundamentally altered the lives of millions of Americans—both black and white. As the African-American community once again tasted the spoils of political victory, southern whites quickly countermobilized to resist the ruling in *Brown*. In 1956, 101 United States Senators and Representatives issued the *Southern Manifesto* asserting that the *Brown* ruling was a clear-cut example of judicial abuse. As the members stated, "[W]e pledge ourselves to use all lawful means to bring about a reversal of this decision which is contrary to the Constitution and to prevent the use of force in its implementation." The significance of the Manifesto was that it sent a clear message to local officials and the southern public at large—state officials were in open defiance of the Supreme Court. The impact of this message on the implementation of school desegregation cannot be underestimated.

School boards in more than 21 states and the District of Columbia were demanded to take action as a result of the ruling in *Brown*. That school desegregation came to a head in Little Rock, Arkansas in 1957 was unexpected.[9] In response, the Little Rock School Board quickly and decisively moved to comply with *Brown*. By the fall of 1957, the plan was to enroll nine black students at Central High School. The night before the first day of classes Governor Orval Faubus came on television and announced that he couldn't maintain the peace if he was forced to integrate Central High. Faubus then ordered the National Guard to protect the school and deny admission to the black students. While white resistance was expected in Old Confederacy states like Alabama and Mississippi, the border South was perceived to be more moderate on racial matters. After a several weeks of white mob violence, a reluctant President Eisenhower sent federal troops to enforce the *Brown* ruling. In a public address about his actions in Little Rock President Eisenhower said, ". . . In that city, under the leadership of demagogic extremists, disorderly mobs have deliberately prevented the carrying out of proper orders from a federal court."[10]

In 1958, the Little Rock School Board sought from the district court a 2½ year postponement of the desegregation plan. Their reasoning was that public hostility was so intense that they could not adequately insure public safety nor could they provide public education. In **Cooper v. Aaron,** *the Supreme Court rejected the School Board's claim stating that ". . . the conditions they depict are directly traceable to the actions of legislators and executive officials of the State of Arkansas, taken in their official capacities, which reflect their own determination to resist this Court's decision in the Brown case." Thus, the violence and disruption surrounding the nine black school children attempting to attend Central High was seen as a direct result of state action. In the end, the Court rejected the plaintiff's claim to suspend the Little Rock desegregation plan.*

The significance of Cooper was at least two-fold. In the first instance, Cooper served as evidence that the strategy of legalism paid handsome dividends for civil rights advocates. The Supreme Court of the United States continued to uphold the civil rights of its black citizens. To the contrary, the case also pointed out some of the inherent weaknesses of legalism as a political strategy. For example, for all of its symbolic value, legalism produced small, incremental changes. In addition, it required tremendous resources. The LDF lawyers often worked pro bono or for little compensation. Further, litigation was expensive (e.g., expert witnesses, research, witnesses, etc.). Finally, the scope of legalism was narrow (i.e., a concentration on public education) and participation was exclusive—for the most part the central players were lawyers and elite activists. In essence, there was not a role for the burgeoning grassroots movement spreading across the South.

COOPER ET AL., MEMBERS OF THE BOARD OF DIRECTORS OF THE LITTLE ROCK, ARKANSAS, INDEPENDENT SCHOOL DISTRICT, ET AL. V. AARON ET AL.

No. 1, Supreme Court of the United States, 358 U.S. 1; 78 S. Ct. 1401; 1958 U.S.

September 11, 1958, Argued
September 12, 1958, Decided

OPINION By: Warren
OPINION: [*4] [**1402] Opinion of the Court by The Chief Justice, Mr. Justice Black, Mr. Justice Frankfurter, Mr. Justice Douglas, Mr. Justice Burton, Mr. Justice Clark, Mr. Justice Harlan, Mr. Justice Brennan, and Mr. Justice Whittaker.

[**1403] [1]

As this case reaches us it raises questions of the highest importance to the maintenance of our federal system of government. It necessarily involves a claim by the Governor and Legislature of a State that there is no duty on state officials to obey federal court orders resting on this Court's considered interpretation of the United States Constitution.

Specifically it involves actions by the Governor and Legislature of Arkansas upon the premise that they are not bound by our holding in *Brown* v. *Board of Education*, 347 U.S. 483. That holding was that the 14th Amendment forbids States to use their governmental powers to bar children on racial grounds from attending schools where there is state participation through any arrangement, management, funds or property. We are urged to uphold a suspension of the Little Rock School Board's plan to do away with segregated public schools in Little Rock until state laws and efforts to upset and nullify our holding in *Brown* v. *Board of Education* have been further challenged and tested in the courts. We reject these contentions.

The following are the facts and circumstances so far as necessary to show how the legal questions are presented.

On May 17, 1954, this Court decided that enforced racial segregation in the public schools of a State is a denial of the equal protection of the laws enjoined by the 14th Amendment. *Brown* v. *Board of Education*, 347 U.S. 483 [*6] The Court postponed, pending further argument, formulation of a decree to effectuate this decision. That decree was rendered May 31, 1955 *Brown* v. *Board of Education*, 349 U.S. 294. In the formulation of that decree the Court recognized that good faith compliance with the principles declared in Brown might in some situations "call for elimination of a variety of obstacles in making the transition to school systems operated in accordance with the constitutional principles set forth in our May 17, 1954, decision." *Id.*, at 300. The Court went on to state:

"Courts of equity may properly take into account the public interest in the elimination of such obstacles in a systematic and effective manner. But it should go without saying that [***9] the vitality of these constitutional principles cannot be allowed to yield simply because of disagreement with them.

While giving weight to these public and private considerations, the courts will require that the defendants make a prompt and reasonable start toward full compliance with our May 17, 1954, ruling. Once such a start has been made, the courts may find that additional time is necessary to carry out the ruling in an effective manner. The burden rests upon the defendants to establish that such time is necessary in the public interest and is consistent with good faith compliance at the earliest practicable date. To that end, the courts may consider problems related to administration, arising from the physical condition of the school plant, the school transportation system, personnel, revision of school districts and attendance areas into compact units to achieve a system of determining admission to the public schools on a nonracial basis, and revision of local laws and regulations which may be necessary in solving the foregoing problems." 349 U.S., at 300-301.

[*7] [2]

[3]

Under such circumstances, the District Courts were directed to require "a prompt and reasonable start toward full compliance," and to take such action as was necessary to bring about the end of racial segregation in the public schools "with all deliberate speed." *Ibid.* Of course, in many locations, obedience to the duty of desegregation would require the immediate general admission of Negro children, otherwise qualified as students for their appropriate classes, at particular schools. On the other hand, a District Court, after analysis of the relevant factors (which, of course, excludes hostility to racial desegregation), might conclude that justification existed for not requiring the present nonsegregated admission of all qualified Negro children. In such circumstances, however, the courts should scrutinize the program of the school authorities to make sure that they had developed arrangements pointed toward the earliest practicable completion of desegregation, and had taken appropriate steps to put their program into effective operation. It was made plain that delay in any guise in order to deny the constitutional rights of Negro children could not be countenaced, and that only a prompt start, diligently and earnestly pursued, to eliminate racial segregation from the public schools could constitute good faith compliance. State authorities were thus duty bound to devote every effort toward initiating desegregation and bringing about the elimination of racial discrimination in the public school system.

On May 20, 1954, three days after the first Brown opinion, the Little Rock District School Board adopted, and on May 23, 1954, made public, a statement of policy entitled "Supreme Court Decision*Segregation in Public Schools." In this statement the Board recognized that

"It is our responsibility to comply with Federal Constitutional Requirements and we intend to do so when the Supreme Court of the United States outlines the method to be followed."

[*8]

Thereafter the Board undertook studies of the administrative problems confronting the transition to a desegregated public school system at Little Rock. It instructed the Superintendent of Schools to prepare a plan for desegregation, and approved such a plan on May 24, 1955, seven days before the second *Brown* opinion. The plan provided for desegregation at the senior high school level (grades 10 through 12) as the first stage. Desegregation at the junior high and elementary levels was to follow. It was contemplated that desegregation at the high school level would commence in the fall of 1957, and the expectation was that complete desegregation of the school system would be accomplished by 1963. Following the adoption of this plan, the Superintendent of Schools discussed it with a large number of citizen groups in the city. As a result of these discussions, the Board reached the conclusion that "a large majority of the residents" of Little Rock were of "the belief . . . that the Plan, although objectionable in principle," from the point of view of those supporting segregated schools, "was still the best for the interests of all pupils in the District."

Upon challenge by a group of Negro plaintiffs desiring more rapid completion of the desegregation process, the District Court upheld the School Board's plan, *Aaron v. Cooper*, 143 F. Supp. 855.

While the School Board was thus going forward with its preparation for desegregating the Little Rock school system, other state authorities, in contrast, were actively pursuing a program designed to perpetuate in Arkansas the system of racial segregation which this Court had held violated the 14th Amendment. First came, in November 1956, an amendment to the State Constitution flatly commanding the Arkansas General Assembly to oppose "in every Constitutional manner the Un-constitutional desegregation decisions of May 17, 1954 and May 31, 1955 of the United States Supreme Court," Ark. Const., Amend. 44, and, through the initiative, a pupil assignment law, Ark. Stat. 80-1519 to 80-1524. Pursuant to this state constitutional command, a law relieving school children from compulsory attendance at racially mixed schools, Ark. Stat. 80-1525, and a law establishing a State Sovereignty Commission, Ark. Stat. 6-801 to 6-824, were enacted by the General Assembly in February 1957.

The School Board and the Superintendent of Schools nevertheless continued with preparations to carry out the first stage of the desegregation program. Nine Negro children were scheduled for admission in September 1957 to Central High School, which has more than two thousand students. Various administrative measures, designed to assure [***14] the smooth transition of this first stage of desegregation, were undertaken.

On September 2, 1957, the day before these Negro students were to enter Central High, the school authorities were met with drastic opposing action on the part of the Governor of Arkansas who dispatched units of the Arkansas National Guard to the Central High School grounds and placed the school "off limits" to colored students. As found by the District Court in subsequent proceedings, the Governor's action had not been requested by the school authorities, and was entirely unheralded. The findings were these:

"Up to this time [September 2], no crowds had gathered about Central High School and no acts of violence or threats of violence in connection with the carrying out of the plan had occurred. Nevertheless, out of an abundance of caution, the school authorities had frequently conferred with the Mayor and Chief of Police of Little Rock about taking appropriate [*10] steps by the Little Rock police to prevent any possible disturbances or acts of violence in connection with the attendance of the 9 colored students at Central High School. The Mayor considered that the Little Rock police force could [***15] adequately cope with any incidents [**1406] which might arise at the opening of school. The Mayor, the Chief of Police, and the school authorities made no request to the Governor or any representative of his for State assistance in maintaining peace and order at Central High School. Neither the Governor nor any other official of the State government consulted with the

Little Rock authorities about whether the Little Rock police were prepared to cope with any incidents which might arise at the school, about any need for State assistance in maintaining peace and order, or about stationing the Arkansas National Guard at Central High School." *Aaron v. Cooper*, 156 F. Supp. 220, 225.

The Board's petition for postponement in this proceeding states: "The effect of that action [of the Governor] was to harden the core of opposition to the Plan and cause many persons who theretofore had reluctantly accepted the Plan to believe there was some power in the State of Arkansas which, when exerted, could nullify the Federal law and permit disobedience of the decree of this [District] Court, and from that date hostility to the Plan was increased and criticism of the officials of the [School] District has become more bitter and unrestrained." The Governor's action caused the School Board to request the Negro students on September 2 not to attend the high school "until the legal dilemma was solved." The next day, September 3, 1957, the Board petitioned the District Court for instructions, and the court, after a hearing, found that the Board's [*11] request of the Negro students to stay away from the high school had been made because of the stationing of the military guards by the state authorities. The court determined that this was not a reason for departing from the approved plan, and ordered the School Board and Superintendent to proceed with it.

On the morning of the next day, September 4, 1957, the Negro children attempted to enter the high school but, as the District Court later found, units of the Arkansas National Guard "acting pursuant to the Governor's order, stood shoulder to shoulder at the school grounds and thereby forcibly prevented the 9 Negro students . . . from entering," as they continued to do every school day during the following three weeks. 156 F. Supp., at 225.

That same day, September 4, 1957, the United [***17] States Attorney for the Eastern District of Arkansas was requested by the District Court to begin an immediate investigation in order to fix responsibility for the interference with the orderly implementation of the District Court's direction to carry out the desegregation program. Three days later, September 7, the District Court denied a petition of the School Board and the Superintendent of Schools for an order temporarily suspending continuance of the program.

Upon completion of the United States Attorney's investigation, he and the Attorney General of the United States, at the District Court's request, entered the proceedings and filed a petition on behalf of the United States, as *amicus curiae*, to enjoin the Governor of Arkansas and officers of the Arkansas National Guard from further attempts to prevent obedience to the court's order. After hearings on the petition, the District Court found that the School Board's plan had been obstructed by the Governor through the use of National Guard troops, and granted a preliminary injunction on September [*12] 20, 1957, enjoining the Governor and the officers of the Guard from preventing the attendance of Negro children at [***18] Central High School, and from otherwise obstructing or interfering with the orders of the court in connection with the plan. 156 F. Supp. 220, affirmed, *Faubus v. United States*, 254 F. 2d 797. The National Guard was then withdrawn from the school.

[**1407] The next school day was Monday, September 23, 1957. The Negro children entered the high school that morning under the protection of the Little Rock Police Department and members of the Arkansas State Police. But the officers caused the children to be removed from the school during the morning because they had difficulty controlling a large and demonstrating crowd which had gathered at the high school. 163 F. Supp., at 16. On September 25, however, the President of the United States dispatched federal troops to Central High School and admission of the Negro students to the school was thereby effected. Regular army troops continued at the high school until November 27, 1957. They were then replaced by federalized National Guardsmen who remained throughout the balance of the school year. Eight of the Negro students remained in attendance at the school throughout the [***19] school year.

We come now to the aspect of the proceedings presently before us. On February 20, 1958, the School Board and the Superintendent of Schools filed a petition in the District Court seeking a postponement of their program for desegregation. Their position in essence was that because of extreme public hostility, which they stated had been engendered largely by the official attitudes and actions of the Governor and the Legislature, the maintenance of a sound educational program at Central High School, with the Negro students in attendance, would be impossible. The Board therefore proposed that the Negro students already admitted to the school be withdrawn [*13] and sent to segregated schools, and that all further steps to carry out the Board's desegregation program be postponed for a period later suggested by the Board to be two and one-half years.

After a hearing the District Court granted the relief requested by the Board. Among other things the court found that the past year at Central High School had been attended by conditions of "chaos, bedlam and turmoil"; that there were "repeated incidents of more or less serious violence directed against the Negro [***20] students and their property"; that there was "tension and unrest among the school administrators, the class-room teachers, the pupils, and the latters' parents, which inevitably had an adverse effect upon the educational program"; that a school official was threatened with violence; that a "serious financial burden" had been cast on the School District; that the education of the students had suffered "and under existing conditions will continue to suffer"; that the Board would continue to need "military assistance or its equivalent"; that the local police department would not be able "to detail enough men to afford the necessary protection"; and that the situation was "intolerable." 163 F. Supp., at 20–26.

In affirming the judgment of the Court of Appeals which reversed the District Court we have accepted without reservation the position of the School Board, the [*15] Superintendent of Schools, and their counsel that they displayed entire good faith in the conduct of these [***23] proceedings and in dealing with the unfortunate and distressing sequence of events which has been outlined. We likewise have accepted the findings of the District Court as to the conditions at Central High School during the 1957–1958 school year, and also the findings that the educational progress of all the students, white and colored, of that school has suffered and will continue to suffer if the conditions which prevailed last year are permitted to continue.

The significance of these findings, however, is to be considered in light of the fact, indisputably revealed by the record before us, that the conditions they depict are directly traceable to the actions of legislators and executive officials of the State of Arkansas, taken in their official capacities, which reflect their own determination to resist this Court's decision in the *Brown* case and which have brought about violent resistance to that decision in Arkansas. In its petition for certiorari filed in this Court, the School Board itself describes the situation in this language: "The legislative, executive, and judicial departments of the state government opposed the desegregation of Little Rock schools by enacting [***24] laws, calling out troops, making statements villifying federal law and federal courts, and failing to utilize state law enforcement agencies and judicial processes to maintain public peace." [5]

One may well sympathize with the position of the Board in the face of the frustrating conditions which have confronted it, but, regardless of the Board's good faith, the actions of the other stage agencies responsible for those conditions compel us to reject the Board's legal position. Had Central High School been under the direct management of the State itself, it could hardly be suggested [*16] that those immediately in charge of the school should be heard to assert their own good faith as a legal excuse for delay in implementing the constitutional rights of these respondents, when vindication of those rights was rendered difficult or impossible by the actions of other state officials. The situation here is in no different posture because the members of the School Board and the Superintendent of Schools are local officials; from the point of view of the 14th Amendment, they stand in this litigation as the agents of the State.

■

Study Questions

1. How did the decision in *Sweatt v. Painter* establish the foundation for the examination of the "separate but equal" clause established in the *Plessy v. Ferguson* case of 1896?

2. How did the Supreme Court decisions in school desegregation cases and the resulting Southern reaction show the limitations of the NAACP's Legal Defense Fund's approach to racial reform? What is the role of federalism and separation of powers in this analysis?

3. What is the significance of the *Bolling* decision? What are the implications for legalism as a strategy for civil rights advocacy?

4. What are the prospects for legalism as a keystone strategy for civil rights in the 21st century? What are the criteria for evaluation? Is it a more appropriate approach for some civil rights issues and not others? Why? Why not?

NOTES

1. *The Social and Economic Status of the Black Population in the United States: an Historical View, 1790–1978.* (Washington: U.S. Dept. of Commerce, Bureau of the Census).

2. Dianne M. Pinderhughes. *Race and ethnicity in Chicago politics: A reexamination of pluralist theory.* (Urbana, ILL: University of Illinois Press) 1987; Hanes Walton, Jr. *Black political parties* (New York: Free Press) 1972.

3. While there were certainly higher levels of integration in parts of the North, the fact remained that most people's socio-political networks were racially homogenous (Massey and Denton; and some other cites supporting the point of racial apartheid in the first half of the 20th century).

4. For other accounts of the civil rights movement, Sara Bullard, *A History of the Civil rights movement and Those Who Died in the Struggle.* (Cambridge: Oxford University Press) 1993; Clayborne Carson (ed.) *The Eyes on the prize: Civil Rights Reader: documents, speeches, and firsthand accounts from the Black freedom struggle, 1954–1990.* (Penguin Books: New York, New York) 1991; Glenn T. Eskew, But for Birmingham: *The Local and National Movement in the Civil Rights Struggle.* (Chapel Hill, North Carolina: University of North Carolina Press) 1997; Manning Marable, *Race, Reform, and Rebellion: The Second Reconstruction in Black America, 1945–1990* (Jackson: University of Mississippi Press) 1991.

5. Mark Tushnet. *The NAACP's legal strategy against segregated education, 1925–1950* (Chapel Hill: University of North Carolina Press) 1987.

6. The decision in *Sweatt* built upon earlier precedence set in *Missouri ex rel. Gaines v. Canada*. In this case Missouri state law stipulated that blacks could attend the University of Missouri's law school until a law school was built at predominantly black Lincoln University (or could provide for the payment of tuition fees in another state that admitted blacks). Gaines sought admission under this statute but was denied by the state Superintendent of Schools because ". . . it was contrary to the constitution, laws, and public policy of the state to admit a Negro as a student in the University of Missouri . . .". Adhering to *Plessy* (and pursuant to the 14th Amendment), the United States Supreme Court ruled that the existence of separate educational facilities rested upon ". . . the equality of the privileges which the laws give the separated groups within the State." Because Gaines was not provided the "enjoyment" of equal educational opportunities, the state had to admit him.

7. Deirde Mullane (ed.) *Crossing the danger water: Three hundred years of African-American writing.* (New York: Anchor Books) 1993.

8. Kenneth B. Clark. *Dark ghetto: dilemmas of social power.* (New York: Harper & Row) 1965.

9. Elizabeth Huckaby. *Crisis at Central High, Little Rock, 1957–58.* (Baton Rouge: Louisiana State University Press) 1980.

10. *NY Times,* September 25, 1957, cited in Blaustein and Zangrando.

Nonviolent Direct Action: 1955–1965

Whereas legalism was primarily concerned with desegregating public education, nonviolent direct action sought to integrate all elements of social life. Based on the concept of civil disobedience developed in India and Africa, this stage of the civil rights movement was much broader in scope and infinitely more inclusive. By the early 1950s the black community was positioned to take advantage of the rapid restructuring brought on by industrialization and the World Wars.[1] Throughout the South, black leaders met to devise a strategy to overthrow white domination. One common form of degradation was the requirement for blacks to sit at the back of public buses. In response, church-based leaders in Baton Rouge, Louisiana, broached the idea of a mass boycott to protest segregation in public transportation. Although less well known than other actions, the successful Baton Rouge Boycott of 1953 was the first significant event of the nonviolent direct action stage of the civil rights movement.

News of the gains in Baton Rouge quickly spread throughout the South via established communications networks of secular and religious leaders. For some time black leaders in Alabama had been thinking about staging a mass demonstration against discrimination in public transportation. Montgomery, like many Alabama cities, had an ordinance mandating blacks to ride at the back of the bus. Faculty at Alabama State College and members of Montgomery's black Women's Political Council begun to think about a boycott in earnest when, on two separate occasions, young black women had been thrown off the bus and arrested for refusing to give up their seats to white passengers. In each case, black leaders decided the conditions were not appropriate to stage a boycott.

On December 1, 1955, Ms. Rosa Parks was arrested for failing to comply with Montgomery's ordinance. Parks' stature as community leader made her the perfect rallying point for civil disobedience (e.g., her work with the NAACP, the Brotherhood of Sleeping Car Porters, and Highlander Folk School). Moreover, her pivotal involvement is emblematic of the under-emphasized role of women during the civil rights movement.[2] In the following selection from Taylor Branch's article "First Trombone," Martin Luther King, Jr. rises to local and national prominence with his lyrical analysis of the conditions in Montgomery and his powerful "call to arms." In his speech, King establishes the basic principles of nonviolent direct action—mass behavior, nonviolence, and legal and moral standing. King also expressed the sentiment of most black southerners when he said, "There comes a time, my friends, when people get tired of being thrown across the abyss of humiliation, where they experience the bleakness of nagging despair . . . There comes a time when people get tired of being pushed out of the glittering sunlight of life's July, and left standing amidst the piercing chill of an Alpine November." King made clear to a people and a nation that the black community intended to ". . . work with grim and bold determination—to gain justice on the buses in this city."

The Montgomery Bus Boycott had several key events.[3] Obviously the selection of King as spokesman was important. Although young and relatively new to Montgomery, King was able to articulate the black experience meaningfully to the nation and the world. Another critical component concerned sanctioning nonparticipating members of the community. This was typically accomplished through peer pressure, and in some cases, physical intimidation. Finally, the logistics of transporting large numbers of people each day for over one year was greatly aided by the blueprints developed in Baton Rouge and transmitted by an autonomous network of black clergy.

The boycott hit at the Achilles heel of white hegemony—the division between the old planter elite and a new commerce class. For example, Montgomery's merchants were placed under severe fiscal strain because the boycott disrupted downtown commerce.[4] After a year of bargaining and negotiation, the boycott finally came to an end, and the city ordinance was repealed. In quick fashion bus lines were desegregated all throughout the South as it became evident that the black community could and would engage in nonviolent mass behavior.

FIRST TROMBONE

Copyright 1999, Brookings Institution

L ate in the afternoon of Thursday, December 1, 1955, Rosa Parks was arrested in Montgomery, Alabama, for refusing to give up her seat on a public city bus to a white passenger. Over the weekend, leaders of the black community organized a bus boycott to begin on Monday morning. On Monday afternoon, December 5, Martin Luther King, Jr., the young pastor of Montgomery's Dexter Avenue Baptist Church, was chosen to lead the ongoing boycott and to speak at a mass meeting that evening at the Holt Street Baptist Church. King had less than half an hour to prepare his first political address.

King stood silently for a moment. When he greeted the enormous crowd of strangers, who were packed in the balconies and aisles, peering in through the windows and upward from seats on the floor, he spoke in a deep voice, stressing his diction in a slow introductory cadence. "We are here this evening—for serious business," he said, in even pulses, rising and then falling in pitch. When he paused, only one or two "yes" responses came up from the crowd, and they were quiet ones. It was a throng of shouters, he could see, but they were waiting to see where he would take them. "We are here in a general sense, because first and foremost—we are American citizens—and we are determined to apply our citizenship—to the fullness of its means" he said. "But we are here in a specific sense—because of the bus situation in Montgomery." A general murmur of assent came back to him, and the pitch of King's voice rose gradually through short, quickened sentences. "The situation is not at all new. The problem has existed over endless years. Just the other day—just last Thursday to be exact—one of the finest citizens in Montgomery—not one of the finest Negro citizens—but one of the finest citizens in Montgomery—was taken from a bus—and carried to jail and arrested—because she refused to give up—to give her seat to a white person."

The crowd punctuated each pause with scattered "Yeses" and "Amens." They were with him in rhythm, but lagged slightly behind in enthusiasm. Then King spoke of the law, saying that the arrest was doubtful even under the segregation ordinances, because reserved Negro and white bus sections were not specified in them. "The law has never been clarified at that point" he said, drawing an emphatic "Hell, no" from one man in his audience. "And I think I speak with—with legal authority—not that I have any legal authority—but I think I speak with legal authority behind me—that the law—the ordinance—the city ordinance has never been totally clarified." This sentence marked King as a speaker who took care with distinctions, but it took the crowd nowhere. King returned to the special nature of Rosa Parks. "And since it had to happen, I'm happy it happened to a person like Mrs. Parks," he said, "for nobody can doubt the boundless outreach of her integrity. Nobody can doubt the height of her character, nobody can doubt the depth of her Christian commitment." That's right, a soft chorus answered. "And just because she refused to get up, she was arrested," King repeated. The crowd was stirring now, following King at the speed of a medium walk.

He paused slightly longer. "And you know, my friends, there comes a time," he cried, "when people get tired of being trampled over by the iron feet of oppression." A flock of "Yeses" was coming back at him when suddenly the individual responses dissolved into a rising cheer and applause exploded beneath the cheer—all within the space of a second. The startling noise rolled on an on, like a wave that refused to break, and just when it seemed that the roar must finally weaken, a wall of sound came in from the enormous crowd outdoors to push the volume still higher. Thunder seemed to be added to the lower register—the sound of feet stomping on the wooden floor—until the loudness became something that was not so much heard as it was sensed by vibrations in the lungs. The giant cloud of noise shook the building and refused to go away. One sentence had set it loose somehow, pushing the call-and-response of the Negro church service past the din of a political rally and on to something else that King had never known before. There was a rabbit of awesome proportions in those bushes. As the noise finally fell back, King's voice rose above it to fire again. "There comes a time, my friends, when people get tired of being thrown across the abyss of humiliation, where they experience the bleakness of nagging despair," he declared. "There comes a time when people get tired of being pushed out of the glittering sunlight of life's July, and left standing amidst the piercing chill of an Alpine November. There. . . ." King was making a new run, but the crowd drowned him out. No one could tell whether the roar came in response to the nerve he had touched, or simply out of pride in

a speaker from whose tongue such rhetoric rolled so easily. "We are here because we are tired now," King repeated.

Perhaps daunted by the power that was bursting forth from the crowd,
King moved quickly to address the pitfalls of a boycott. "Now let us say that
we are not here advocating violence," he said. "We have overcome that." A
man in the crowd shouted, "Repeat that! Repeat that!" "I want it to be
known throughout Montgomery and throughout this nation that we are
Christian people," said King, putting three distinct syllables in "Christian."
"The only weapon that we have in our hands this evening is the weapon of
protest." There was a crisp shout of approval right on the beat of King's
pause. He and the audience moved into a slow trot. "If we were incarcerated
behind the iron curtains of a communistic nation—we couldn't do this. If we
were trapped in the dungeon of a totalitarian regime—we couldn't do this.
But the great glory of American democracy is the right to protest for right."
When the shouts of approval died down, King rose up with his final reason
to avoid violence, which was to distinguish themselves from their opponents in the Klan and the White Citizens Council. "There will be no crosses
burned at any bus stops in Montgomery," he said. "There will be no white
persons pulled out of their homes and taken out on some distant road and
murdered. There will be nobody among us who will stand up and defy the
Constitution of this nation."

King paused. The church was quiet but it was humming. "My friends,"
he said slowly, "I want it to be known—that we're going to work with grim
and bold determination—to gain justice on the buses in this city. And we are
not wrong. We are not wrong in what we are doing." There was a muffled
shout of anticipation, as the crowd sensed that King was moving closer to
the heart of his cause. "If we are wrong—the Supreme Court of this nation is
wrong," King sang out. He was rocking now, his voice seeming to be at once
deep and high pitched. "If we are wrong—God Almighty is wrong!" he
shouted, and the crowd seemed to explode a second time, as it had done
when he said they were tired. Wave after wave of noise broke over them,
cresting into the farthest reaches of the ceiling. They were far beyond Rosa
Parks or the bus laws. King's last cry had fused blasphemy to the edge of his
faith and the heart of theirs. The noise swelled until King cut through it to
move past a point of unbearable tension. "If we are wrong—Jesus of
Nazareth was merely a utopian dreamer and never came down to earth! If
we are wrong—justice is a lie." This was too much. He had to wait some
time before delivering his soaring conclusion, in a flight of anger mixed with
rapture: "And we are determined here in Montgomery—to work and fight
until justice runs down like water, and righteousness like a mighty stream!"
The audience all but smothered this passage from Amos, the lowly herds-
man prophet of Israel who, along with the priestly Isaiah, was King's favorite biblical authority on justice.

He backed off the emotion to speak of the need for unity, the dignity of
protest, the historical precedent of the labor movement. Comparatively speaking, his subject matter was mundane, but the crowd stayed with him even
through paraphrases of abstruse points from Niebuhr. "And I want to tell you

this evening that it is not enough for us to talk about love," he said. "Love is one of the pinnacle parts of the Christian faith. There is another side called justice. And justice is really love in calculation. Justice is love correcting that which would work against love." He said that God was not just the God of love: "He's also the God that standeth before the nations and says, 'Be still and know that I am God—and if you don't obey Me I'm gonna break the backbone of your power—and cast you out of the arms of your international and national relationships.'" Shouts and claps continued at a steady rhythm as King's audacity overflowed. "Standing beside love is always justice," he said. "Not only are we using the tools of persuasion—but we've got to use the tools of coercion." He called again for unity. For working together. He appealed to history, summoning his listeners to behave so that sages of the future would look back at the Negroes of Montgomery and say they were "a people who had the moral courage to stand up for their rights." He said they could do that. "God grant that we will do it before it's too late." Someone said, "Oh, yes." And King said, "As we proceed with our program—let us think on these things."

The crowd retreated into stunned silence as he stepped away from the pulpit. The ending was so abrupt, so anticlimactic. The crowd had been waiting for him to reach for the heights a third time at this conclusion, following the rules of oratory. A few seconds passed before memory and spirit overtook disappointment. The applause continued as King made his way out of the church, with people reaching out to touch him. Dexter members marveled, having never seen King let loose like that. [Ralph] Abernathy remained behind, reading negotiating demands from the pulpit. The boycott was on. King would work on his timing, but his oratory had just made him forever a public person. In the few short minutes of his first political address, a power of communion emerged from him that would speak inexorably to strangers who would both love and revile him, like all prophets. He was twenty-six, and had not quite twelve years and four months to live.

By the late 1950s, mass civil disobedience became the dominant political strategy. As Aldon Morris notes in the following selection from his book, **The Origins of the Civil Rights Movement***, student activists began to experiment with the "sit-in." This tactic was aimed at desegregating lunch counters at local "five and dime" stores like Woolworth's by taking up seats at the counter and quietly demanding to be served. Youth chapters from the main civil rights organizations—the NAACP, the Southern Christian Leadership Conference (a product of the Montgomery Bus Boycott), and the Congress on Racial Equality (a northern, interracial civil rights organization)—organized a number of sit-ins between 1957 and 1960. The Greensboro sit-in in 1960 catapulted the students into the national spotlight. Morris provides an empirical analysis of the role of black churches, colleges, and civil rights organizations to make the point that black gains were the result of developed infrasructure and rational action. Although Greensboro may have been the signature event, it was predated by a linear growth in the capacity of community-based organizations to engage in collective action. As Morris observes, "the early sit-ins were sponsored by indigenous resources of the black community; the leadership was black, the bulk of the demonstrators were black, the strategies and tactics were formulated by blacks, the finances came out of the pocket of blacks, and the psychological and spiritual support came from the black churches."*

ROOTS OF A TACTICAL INNOVATION: SIT-INS

Aldon Morris

Excerpt from The Origins of the Modern Civil Rights Movement

D uring the late 1950s activists associated with direct action organizations began experimenting with the sit-in tactic. The 1960 student sit-in movement followed naturally from the early efforts to mobilize for nonviolent direct action that took place in black communities across the South. Analysis of sit-ins of the late 1950s will reveal the basic components of the internal organization that was necessary for the emergence of the massive sit-ins of 1960.

EARLY SIT-INS: FORERUNNERS

On February 1, 1960, four black college students initiated a sit-in at the segregated lunch counter of the local Woolworth store in Greensboro, North Carolina. That day has come to be known as the opening of the sit-in movement. Civil rights activists, however, had conducted sit-ins between 1957 and 1960 in at least 16 cities: St. Louis, Missouri; Wichita and Kansas City, Kansas; Oklahoma City, Enid, Tulsa, and Stillwater, Oklahoma; Lexington and Louisville, Kentucky; Miami, Florida; Charleston, West Virginia; Sumter, South Carolina; East St. Louis, Illinois; Nashville, Tennessee; Atlanta, Georgia; and Durham, North Carolina. The Greensboro sit-ins are important as a unique link in a long chain of sit-ins. Although this book will concentrate on the uniqueness of the Greensboro link, there were important similarities in the entire chain. Previous studies have presented accounts of most of the earlier sit-ins, but without due appreciation of their scope, connections, and extensive organizational base.

The early sit-ins were initiated by direct action organizations. From interviews with participants in the early sit-ins and from published works, I found that civil rights organizations initiated sit-ins in 15 of the 16 cities I have identified. The NAACP, primarily its Youth Councils, either initiated or co-initiated sit-ins in nine of the 15 cities. CORE, usually working with the NAACP, played an important initiating role in seven. The SCLC initiated one case and was involved in another with CORE and FOR. Finally, the Durham Committee on Negro Affairs, working with the NAACP, initiated sit-ins in Durham. From these data we can conclude that the early sit-ins were a result of a multifaceted organizational effort.

Those sit-ins received substantial backing from their respective communities. The black church was the chief institutional force behind the sit-ins; nearly all of the direct action organizations that initiated them were closely associated with the church. The church supplied those organizations with not only an established communication network but also leaders and organized masses, finances, and a safe environment in which to hold political meetings. Direct action organizations clung to the church because their survival depended on it.

Not all black churches supported the sit-ins, and many tried to keep their support "invisible." Clara Luper, the organizer of the 1958 Oklahoma City sit-ins, wrote that the black church did not want to get involved, but church leaders told organizers "we could meet in their churches. They would take up a collection for us and make announcements concerning our worthwhile activities." Interviewed activists revealed that clusters of churches were usually directly involved with the sit-ins. In addition to community support generated through the churches, the activists also received support from parents of those participating in demonstrations.

The early sit-ins were organized by established leaders of the black community. The leaders did not spontaneously emerge in response to a crisis but were organizational actors in the fullest sense. Some sit-in leaders were also church leaders, taught school, and headed the local direct action organization; their extensive organizational linkages gave them access to a pool of individuals to serve as demonstrators. Clara Luper wrote, "The fact that I was teaching American History at Dungee High School in Spencer, Oklahoma, and was a member of the First Street Baptist Church furnished me with an ample number of young people who would become the nucleus of the Youth Council." Mrs. Luper's case is not isolated. Leaders of the early sit-ins were enmeshed in organizational networks and were integral members of the black community.

Rational planning was evident in this early wave of sit-ins. As we have seen, during the late 1950s the Reverends James Lawson and Kelly Miller Smith, both leaders of Nashville Christian Leadership Council, formed what they called a "nonviolent workshop." In them Lawson meticulously taught local college students the philosophy and tactics of nonviolent protest. In 1959 those students held "test" sit-ins in two department stores. Earlier, in 1957, members of the Oklahoma City NAACP Youth Council created what they called their "project," whose aim was to eliminate segregation in public accommodations. The project comprised various committees and groups that planned sit-in strategies. After a year of planning, the project group walked into the local Katz Drug Store and initiated a sit-in. In 1955 William Clay organized an NAACP Youth Council in St. Louis. Through careful planning and twelve months of demonstrations, its members were able to desegregate dining facilities at department stores. In Durham, North Carolina, in 1958 black activists of the Durham Committee on Negro Affairs conducted a survey of "five-and-dime" stores in Durham. It revealed that such stores were heavily dependent on black trade. Clearly, the sit-ins in Durham were based on rational planning.

Rational planning was evident in CORE's sit-ins during the late 1950s. CORE prepared for more direct action, including sit-ins, by conducting interracial workshops in Miami in September 1959 and January 1960. Dr. King assisted in the training of young people in one of the CORE workshops. In

April 1959 a newly formed Miami CORE group began conducting sit-ins at downtown variety store lunch counters. In July 1959 James Robinson, writing to affiliated CORE groups and others, stated: "You have probably read in the newspaper about the dramatic all-day sit-ins which Miami CORE has conducted at a number of lunch counters. Up to 50 people have participated at many of these sit-ins." In early September 1959 CORE conducted a 16-day workshop on direct action in Miami, called the September Action Institute. Robinson wrote of it: "The discussion of the theory and techniques of nonviolent direct action will become understandable to all Institute members precisely because their actual participation in action projects will illuminate what otherwise might remain intangible." While the institute was in session, sit-ins were conducted at the lunch counters of Jackson's-Byrons Department Store. According to Gordon Carey of CORE, "Six days of continuous sit-ins caused the owners of the lunch counter concession to close temporarily while considering a change of policy." Immediately following that store's closing, CORE activists began sitting in at Grant's Department Store. Carey wrote: "We sat at the lunch counter from three to six hours daily until the 2-week Institute ended on September 20." On September 19, 1959, officials of the Jackson's-Byrons Store informed CORE that Negroes would be served as of September 21. Four black CORE members went to the store on September 21 but were refused service. Carey's account continues:

> Miami CORE determined to return to Jackson's-Byrons every day. The lunch counter has about 40 seats: On September 23 we had 40 persons sitting-in. It is not easy to get 40 persons on a weekday to sitin from 10 A.M. till 3 P.M., but we maintained the demonstrations throughout the week. One woman who sat with us daily, works nights from 10 P.M. to 6 A.M. Cab drivers and off-duty Negro policemen joined us at the counter.

On September 25, 1959, city officials in Miami began arresting CORE members, and local whites physically attacked the protesters. Carey was told to be "out of Miami by Monday." Yet, Carey reports, "That day we had 80 persons sitting-in—half of them at Grant's." The Grant's store closed rather than serve blacks. On November 12, 1959, CORE made plans to sit in at the "white" waiting room of the Greenville, South Carolina, airport. The action was planned to protest the fact that the black baseball star Jackie Robinson had been ordered to leave the "white" waiting room a few days earlier. On January 23, just 10 days before the famous sit-in at Greensboro, North Carolina, the CORE organization in Sumter, South Carolina, reported that its teenage group was "testing counter service at dime store: manager says he plans to make a change." Again, the action in Sumter had long-range planning behind it: A year earlier, at CORE's National meeting of 1959, the Sumter group had reported that students were involved in its activities. The Sumter CORE organization also had expressed the opinion that "emphasis should be on students and children. In future projects [we] hope to attack employment in 10 stores, food stores and chain stores."

In the summer of 1959 the SCLC, CORE, and FOR jointly held a nonviolent workshop on the campus of Spelman College in Atlanta. When the conference ended, James Robinson, Executive Secretary of CORE, along with the Reverend Wyatt Walker, James McCain, Professor Guy Hershberger, and Elmer Newfield, headed for Dabbs, a segregated restaurant in Atlanta. This interracial group shocked everyone by sitting down and eating. In a CORE news release, James Robinson humorously wrote: "We all had agreed that it was the best coffee we had ever had—the extra tang of drinking your coffee interracially across the Georgia color bar is highly recommended!" Besides providing an example for the other workshop participants, these acts of defiance showed everyone how to protest. Marvin Rich of CORE explained: "They were being demonstrated in a public form, so people would just walk by and see it. And people who didn't think things were possible saw that they were possible, and six months later, in their own home town, they may try it out."

Finally, the early sit-ins were sponsored by indigenous resources of the black community; the leadership was black, the bulk of the demonstrators were black, the strategies and tactics were formulated by blacks, the finances came out of the pockets of blacks, and the psychological and spiritual support came from the black churches.

Most of the organizers of the early sit-ins knew each other and were well aware of each other's strategies of confrontation. Many of the activists belonged to the direct action wing of the NAACP. That group included such activists as Floyd McKissick, Daisy Bates, Ronald Walters, Hosea Williams, Barbara Posey, and Clara Luper, who thought of themselves as a distinct group because the national NAACP was usually disapproving or at best ambivalent about their direct action approach.

The NAACP activists built networks that bypassed the conservative channels and organizational positions of their superiors. At NAACP meetings and conferences they sought out situations where they could freely present their plans and desires to engage in confrontational politics and exchange information about strategies. Once acquainted, the activists remained in touch by phone and mail.

Thus it is no accident that sit-ins occurred between 1957 and 1960. Other instances of "direct action" also occurred during this period. Daisy Bates led black students affiliated with her NAACP Youth Council into the all-white Little Rock Central High School and forced President Eisenhower to send in federal troops. CORE, beginning to gain a foothold in the South, had the explicit goal of initiating direct action projects. We have already noted that CORE activists were in close contact with other activists of the period. Although the early sit-ins and related activities were not part of a grandiose scheme, they were tied together through organizational and personal networks.

THE SIT-IN CLUSTER OF THE LATE 1950S

Organizational and personal networks produced the first cluster of sit-ins in Oklahoma in 1958. In August 1958 the NAACP Youth Council of Wichita, Kansas, headed by Ronald Walters, initiated sit-ins at the lunch counters of a local drug store. At the same time Clara Luper and the young people in her NAACP Youth Council were training to conduct sit-ins in Oklahoma City. The adult leaders of the two groups knew each other: They worked for the same organization, so several members of the two groups traded numerous phone calls to exchange information and discuss mutual support. Direct contact was important, because the local press often refused to cover the sit-ins. Less than a week after Wichita, Clara Luper's group in Oklahoma City initiated its planned sit-ins.

Shortly thereafter sit-ins were conducted in Tulsa, Enid, and Stillwater, Oklahoma. Working through CORE and the local NAACP Youth Council, Clara Luper's friend Shirley Scaggins organized the sit-ins in Tulsa. Mrs. Scaggins had recently lived in Oklahoma City and knew the details of Mrs. Luper's sit-in project. The two leaders worked in concert. At the same time the NAACP Youth Council in Enid began to conduct sit-ins. Mr. Mitchell, who led that group, knew Mrs. Luper well. He had visited the Oklahoma Youth Council at the outset of its sit-in and had discussed sit-in tactics and mutual support. The Stillwater sit-ins appear to have been conducted independently by black college students.

The network that operated in Wichita and several Oklahoma communities reached as far as East St. Louis, Illinois. Homer Randolph, who in late 1958 organized the East St. Louis sit-ins, had previously lived in Oklahoma City, knew Mrs. Luper well, and had young relatives who participated in the Oklahoma City sit-ins.

In short, the first sit-in cluster occurred in Oklahoma in 1958 and spread to cities within a 100-mile radius through established organizational and personal networks. The majority of these early sit-ins were (1) connected rather than isolated, (2) initiated through organizations and personal ties, (3) rationally planned and led by established leaders and (4) supported by indigenous resources. Thus, the Greensboro sit-ins of February 1960 did not mark the movement's beginning but were a critical link in the chain, triggering sit-ins across the South at an incredible pace. What happened in the black community between the late 1950s and the early 1960s to produce such a movement?

In my view the early sit-ins did not give rise to a massive sit-in movement before 1960 because CORE and the NAACP Youth Council did not have a mass base. The SCLC, which did have a mass base, had not developed fully. Besides, direct action was just emerging as the dominant strategy during the late 1950s.

As the SCLC developed into a Southwide direct action organization between 1957 and 1960, it provided the mass base capable of sustaining a heavy volume of collective action. It augmented the activities of CORE and the NAACP Youth Councils, because they were closely tied to the church. Thus the SCLC, closely interlocked with NAACP Youth Councils and CORE chapters, had developed solid movement centers by late 1959. The centers usually had the following seven characteristics:

1. A cadre of social change-oriented ministers and their congregations. Often one minister would become the local leader of a given center, and his church would serve as the coordinating unit.

2. Direct action organizations of varied complexity. In many cities local churches served as quasi-direct action organizations, while in others ministers built complex church-related organizations (e.g., United Defense League of Baton Rouge, Montgomery Improvement Association, Alabama Christian Movement for Human Rights of Birmingham, Petersburg Improvement Association). NAACP Youth Councils and CORE affiliates also were components of the local centers.

3. Indigenous financing coordinated through the church.

4. Weekly mass meetings, which served as forums where local residents were informed of relevant information and strategies regarding the movement. These meetings also built solidarity among the participants.

5. Dissemination of nonviolent tactics and strategies. The leaders articulated to the black community the message that social change would occur only through nonviolent direct action carried out by masses.

6. Adaptation of a rich church culture to political purposes. The black spirituals, sermons, and prayers were used to deepen the participants' commitment to the struggle.

7. A mass-based orientation, rooted in the black community, through the church.

From the perspective of this study, the period between the 1950s bus boycotts and the 1960 sit-ins provided pivotal resources for the emerging civil rights movement. My analysis emphasizes that the organizational foundation of the civil rights movement was built during this period, and active local movement centers were created in numerous Southern black communities.

The sit-ins quickly spread throughout the South involving up to 70,000 students. By 1961 lunch counters in about 150 cities had been integrated. The sit-in technique was extended to include swimming pools, movie theaters, and pool halls. One of the more significant results was the creation of the Student Nonviolent Coordinating Committee (SNCC).[5] Formed at the urging of SCLC activist Ella Baker, SNCC played a central role in organizing and mobilizing college-aged students.[6] Developing from the youth chapters of the NAACP, SCLC, and fraternal organizations, SNCC trained cadres of student activists in the technique of passive resistance. These training sessions were especially important because student activists were commonly subjected to severe physical and psychological intimidation during attempts to integrate social accommodations.

Nonviolent direct action activities were primarily carried out in the South. The Supreme Court ruling in *Boynton v. Virginia*—prohibiting segregation in interstate travel accommodations—opened the door for the participation of northern organizations such as CORE. The "Freedom Rides" were designed to test the *Boynton* decision. Starting out from New York City, an interracial group of CORE activists "put the movement on wheels" by riding through the South on buses. While the "freedom riders" traveled without incident through Maryland and Virginia, they met stiff resistance in Rock Hill, South Carolina. Angry whites, armed with clubs and knifes, met the buses forcing a quick getaway. This pattern of resistance continued throughout the South and culminated in an ugly scene in Montgomery where 2,000 whites descended on the freedom riders. This incident attracted national media attention as several white CORE members were hospitalized. Nonetheless, nonviolent direct action was having its intended effect—social segregation was being toppled.

In 1963 Martin Luther King decided to stage another series of economic boycotts in Albany, Georgia. At issue was the failure of white merchants to desegregate the facilities and employ blacks. A central piece of nonviolent direct action strategy was built upon the concept of the "inelasticity" of the white power structure. That is, civil rights advocates counted on white elites to take reactionary positions. The "jail-in" was one of the more frequently used tactics to provoke white authorities. It involved a refusal to post bail for demonstrators who had been arrested for violating city ordinances (e.g., unlawful assembly, loitering, etc.). It was effective for at least two reasons. First, it placed a strain on cities' fiscal reserves (e.g., local officials did not budget for housing thousands of prisoners). Second, it was great theater. Media accounts and pictures of crowded prisons, to say nothing of the jailing of King, made news. The end result was growing sympathy for black protestors.

In Albany, Georgia King appeared to have met his match. The Albany police chief (Pritchett) refused to play into King's hands. Instead, he made arrangements with surrounding jurisdictions to handle the overflow of jailed protestors and instructed his force to handle the marchers with respect and dignity. In the end, Albany was seen as King's first major defeat. The event received little coverage and Albany's business elite resisted calls for desegregation. For the first time, King's leadership and tactics were questioned.

Malcolm X was the most articulate voice challenging the assumption that black integration into mainstream white society was the proper objective.[7] In **"Message to the Grass Roots"** *Malcolm described what he saw as the failure of black leadership–and the failure of King in Albany—to address the concerns of the black "nation." Malcolm criticized traditional civil rights leaders for being used by the "white man" against the "Negro revolution." In a stinging critique of passive resistance Malcolm argued that, "[J]ust as the slavemaster of that day used Tom, the house Negro, to keep the field Negroes in check, the same old slavemaster today has Negroes who are nothing but modern day Uncle Toms, 20th-century Uncle Toms, to keep you and me in check, to keep us under control, keep us passive and peaceful and nonviolent." Malcolm also mocked the tradition of singing "We Shall Overcome" saying, "You don't do that in a revolution. You don't do any singing, you're too busy swinging."*

MESSAGE TO THE GRASS ROOTS

Malcolm X

Excerpt from Malcolm X Speaks: Selected Speeches

In late 1963, the Detroit Council for Human Rights announced a Northern Negro Leadership Conference to be held in Detroit on November 9 and 10. When the council's chairman, Rev. C. L. Franklin, sought to exclude black nationalists and Freedom Now Party advocates from the conference, Rev. Albert B. Cleage, Jr., resigned from the council and, in collaboration with the Group On Advanced Leadership (GOAL), arranged for a Northern Negro Grass Roots Leadership Conference. This was held in Detroit at the same time as the more conservative gathering, which was addressed by Congressman Adam Clayton Powell among others. The two-day Grass Roots conference was climaxed by a large public rally at the King Solomon Baptist Church, with Rev. Cleage, journalist William Worthy and Malcolm X as the chief speakers. The audience, almost all black and with non-Muslims in the great majority, interrupted Malcolm with applause and laughter so often that he asked it to desist because of the lateness of the hour.

A few weeks after the conference, President Kennedy was assassinated and Elijah Muhammad silenced Malcolm X. This is, therefore, one of the last speeches Malcolm gave before leaving Muhammad's organization. It is the only specimen of his speeches as a Black Muslim included in this book. But it is not a typical Black Muslim speech. Even though Malcolm continued to preface certain statements with the phrase, "The Honorable Elijah Muhammad says," he was increasingly, in the period before the split, giving his own special stamp to the Black Muslims' ideas, including the idea of separation. The emphasis of this speech is considerably different from earlier ones of the type included in Louis E. Lomax's book, *When the Word Is Given. . . .*

The following selection consists of about one-half of the speech. The long-playing record, "Message to the Grass Roots by Malcolm X," published by the Afro-American Broadcasting and Recording Company, Detroit, is vastly superior to the written text in conveying the style and personality of Malcolm at his best—when he was speaking to a militant black audience.

We want to have just an off-the-cuff chat between you and me, us. We want to talk right down to earth in a language that everybody here can easily understand. We all agree tonight, all of the speakers have agreed, that America has a very serious problem. Not only does America have a very serious problem, but our people have a very serious problem. America's problem is us. We're her problem. The only reason she has a problem is she doesn't want us here. And every time you look at yourself, be you black, brown, red or yellow, a so-called Negro, you represent a person who poses such a serious problem for America because you're not wanted. Once you face this as a fact, then you can start plotting a course that will make you appear intelligent, instead of unintelligent.

What you and I need to do is learn to forget our differences. When we come together, we don't come together as Baptists or Methodists. You don't catch hell because you're a Baptist, and you don't catch hell because you're a

Methodist. You don't catch hell because you're a Methodist or Baptist, you don't catch hell because you're a Democrat or a Republican, you don't catch hell because you're a Mason or an Elk, and you sure don't catch hell because you're an American; because if you were an American, you wouldn't catch hell. You catch hell because you're a black man. You catch hell, all of us catch hell, for the same reason.

So we're all black people, so-called Negroes, second-class citizens, ex-slaves. You're nothing but an ex-slave. You don't like to be told that. But what else are you? You are ex-slaves. You didn't come here on the "Mayflower." You came here on a slave ship. In chains, like a horse, or a cow, or a chicken. And you were brought here by the people who came here on the "Mayflower," you were brought here by the so-called Pilgrims, or Founding Fathers. They were the ones who brought you here.

We have a common enemy. We have this in common: We have a common oppressor, a common exploiter, and a common discriminator. But once we all realize that we have a common enemy, then we unite—on the basis of what we have in common. And what we have foremost in common is that enemy—the white man. He's an enemy to all of us. I know some of you all think that some of them aren't enemies. Time will tell.

In Bandung back in, I think, 1954, was the first unity meeting in centuries of black people. And once you study what happened at the Bandung conference, and the results of the Bandung conference, it actually serves as a model for the same procedure you and I can use to get our problems solved. At Bandung all the nations came together, the dark nations from Africa and Asia. Some of them were Buddhists, some of them were Muslims, some of them were Christians, some were Confucianists, some were atheists. Despite their religious differences, they came together. Some were communists, some were socialists, some were capitalists—despite their economic and political differences, they came together. All of them were black, brown, red or yellow.

The number-one thing that was not allowed to attend the Bandung conference was the white man. He couldn't come. Once they excluded the white man, they found that they could get together. Once they kept him out, everybody else fell right in and fell in line. This is the thing that you and I have to understand. And these people who came together didn't have nuclear weapons, they didn't have jet planes, they didn't have all of the heavy armaments that the white man has. But they had unity.

They were able to submerge their little petty differences and agree on one thing: That there one African came from Kenya and was being colonized by the Englishman, and another African came from the Congo and was being colonized by the Belgian, and another African came from Guinea and was being colonized by the French, and another came from Angola and was being colonized by the Portuguese. When they came to the Bandung conference, they looked at the Portuguese, and at the Frenchman, and at the Englishman, and at the Dutchman, and learned or realized the one thing that all of them had in common—they were all from Europe, they were all Europeans, blond, blue-eyed and white skins. They began to recognize who their enemy was. The same man that was colonizing our people in Kenya was colonizing our people in the Congo. The same one in the Congo was colonizing our people in South Africa, and in Southern Rhodesia, and in Burma, and in India, and in Afghanistan, and in Pakistan. They realized all over the world where the dark man was being oppressed, he was being oppressed by the white man; where the dark man was being exploited, he was being exploited by the white man. So they got together on this basis—that they had a common enemy.

And when you and I here in Detroit and in Michigan and in America who have been awakened today look around us, we too realize here in America we all have a common enemy, whether he's in Georgia or Michigan, whether he's in California or New York. He's the same man—blue eyes and blond hair and pale skin—the same man. So what we have to do is what they did. They agreed to stop quarreling among themselves. Any little spat that they had, they'd settle it among themselves, go into a huddle—don't let the enemy know that you've got a disagreement.

Instead of airing our differences in public, we have to realize we're all the same family. And when you have a family squabble, you don't get out on the sidewalk. If you do, everybody calls you uncouth, unrefined, uncivilized, savage. If you don't make it at home, you settle it at home; you get in the closet, argue it out behind closed doors, and then when you come out on the street, you pose a common front, a united front. And this is what we need to do in the community, and in the city, and in the state. We need to stop airing our differences in front of the white man, put the white man out of our meetings, and then sit down and talk shop with each other. That's what we've got to do.

I would like to make a few comments concerning the difference between the black revolution and the Negro revolution. Are they both the same? And if they're not, what is the difference? What is the difference between a black revolution and a Negro revolution? First, what is a revolution? Sometimes I'm inclined to believe that many of our people are using this word "revolution" loosely, without taking careful consideration of what this word actually means, and what its historic characteristics are. When you study the historic nature of revolutions, the motive of a revolution, the objective of a revolution, the result of a revolution, and the methods used in a revolution, you may change words. You may devise another program, you may change your goal and you may change your mind.

Look at the American Revolution in 1776. That revolution was for what? For land. Why did they want land? Independence. How was it carried out? Bloodshed. Number one, it was based on land, the basis of independence. And the only way they could get it was bloodshed. The French Revolution— what was it based on? The landless against the landlord. What was it for? Land. How did they get it? Bloodshed. Was no love lost, was no compromise, was no negotiation. I'm telling you—you don't know what a revolution is. Because when you find out what it is, you'll get back in the alley, you'll get out of the way.

The Russian Revolution—what was it based on? Land; the landless against the landlord. How did they bring it about? Bloodshed. You haven't got a revolution that doesn't involve bloodshed. And you're afraid to bleed. I said, you're afraid to bleed.

As long as the white man sent you to Korea, you bled. He sent you to Germany, you bled. He sent you to the South Pacific to fight the Japanese, you bled. You bleed for white people, but when it comes to seeing your own churches being bombed and little black girls murdered, you haven't got any blood. You bleed when the white man says bleed; you bite when the white man says bite; and you bark when the white man says bark. I hate to say this about us, but it's true. How are you going to be nonviolent in Mississippi, as violent as you were in Korea? How can you justify being nonviolent in Mississippi and Alabama, when your churches are being bombed, and your little girls are being murdered, and at the same time you are going to get violent with Hitler, and Tojo, and somebody else you don't even know?

If violence is wrong in America, violence is wrong abroad. If it is wrong to be violent defending black women and black children and black babies and black men, then it is wrong for America to draft us and make us violent abroad in defense of her. And if it is right for America to draft us, and teach us how to be violent in defense of her, then it is right for you and me to do whatever is necessary to defend our own people right here in this country.

The Chinese Revolution—they wanted land. They threw the British out, along with the Uncle Tom Chinese. Yes, they did. They set a good example. When I was in prison, I read an article—don't be shocked when I say that I was in prison. You're still in prison. That's what America means: prison. When I was in prison, I read an article in *Life* magazine showing a little Chinese girl, nine years old; her father was on his hands and knees and she was pulling the trigger because he was an Uncle Tom Chinaman. When they had the revolution over there, they took a whole generation of Uncle Toms and just wiped them out. And within ten years that little girl became a full-grown woman. No more Toms in China. And today it's one of the toughest, roughest, most feared countries on this earth—by the white man. Because there are no Uncle Toms over there.

Of all our studies, history is best qualified to reward our research. And when you see that you've got problems, all you have to do is examine the historic method used all over the world by others who have problems similar to yours. Once you see how they got theirs straight, then you know how you can get yours straight. There's been a revolution, a black revolution, going on in Africa. In Kenya, the Mau Mau were revolutionary; they were the ones who brought the word "Uhuru" to the fore. The Mau Mau, they were revolutionary, they believed in scorched earth, they knocked everything aside that got in their way, and their revolution also was based on land, a desire for land. In Algeria, the northern part of Africa, a revolution took place. The Algerians were revolutionists, they wanted land. France offered to let them be integrated into France. They told France, to hell with France, they wanted some land, not some France. And they engaged in a bloody battle.

So I cite these various revolutions, brothers and sisters, to show you that you don't have a peaceful revolution. You don't have a turn-the-other-cheek revolution. There's no such thing as a nonviolent revolution. The only kind of revolution that is nonviolent is the Negro revolution. The only revolution in which the goal is loving your enemy is the Negro revolution. It's the only revolution in which the goal is a desegregated lunch counter, a desegregated theater, a desegregated park, and a desegregated public toilet; you can sit down next to white folks—on the toilet. That's no revolution. Revolution is based on land. Land is the basis of all independence. Land is the basis of freedom, Justice, and equality.

The white man knows what a revolution is. He knows that the black revolution is world-wide in scope and in nature. The black revolution is sweeping Asia, is sweeping Africa, is rearing its head in Latin America. The Cuban Revolution—that's a revolution. They overturned the system. Revolution is in Asia, revolution is in Africa, and the white man is screaming because he sees revolution in Latin America. How do you think he'll react to you when you learn what a real revolution is? You don't know what a revolution is. If you did, you wouldn't use that word.

Revolution is bloody, revolution is hostile, revolution knows no compromise, revolution overturns and destroys everything that gets in its way. And you, sitting around here like a knot on the wail, saying, "I'm going to love these folks no matter how much they hate me." No, you need a revolution. Whoever heard of a revolution where they lock arms, as Rev. Clenge was pointing out beautifully, singing "We Shall Overcome"? You don't do that in a revolution. You don't do any singing, you're too busy swinging. It's based on land. A revolutionary wants land so he can set up his own nation, an independent nation. These Negroes aren't asking for any nation—they're trying to crawl back on the plantation.

When you want a nation, that's called nationalism. When the white man became involved in a revolution in this country against England, what was it for? He wanted this land so he could set up another white nation. That's white nationalism. The American Revolution was white nationalism. The French Revolution was white nationalism. The Russian Revolution too—yes, it was—white nationalism. You don't think so? Why do you think Khrushchev and Mao can't get their heads together? White nationalism. All the revolutions that are going on in Asia and Africa today are based on what?—black nationalism. A revolutionary is a black nationalist. He wants a nation. I was reading some beautiful words by Rev. Cleage, pointing out why he couldn't get together with someone else in the city because all of them were afraid of being identified with black nationalism. If you're afraid of black nationalism, you're afraid of revolution. And if you love revolution, you love black nationalism.

To understand this, you have to go back to what the young brother here referred to as the house Negro and the field Negro back during slavery. There were two kinds of slaves, the house Negro and the field Negro. The house Negroes—they lived in the house with master, they dressed pretty good, they ate good because they ate his food—what he left. They lived in the attic or the basement, but still they lived near the master; and they loved the master more than the master loved himself. They would give their life to save the master's house—quicker than the master would. If the master said, "We got a good house here," the house Negro would say, "Yeah, we got a good house here." Whenever the master said "we," he said "we." That's how you can tell a house Negro.

If the master's house caught on fire, the house Negro would fight harder to put the blaze out than the master would. If the master got sick, the house Negro would say, "What's the matter, boss, *we* sick?" *We* sick! He identified himself with his master, more than his master identified with himself. And if you came to the house Negro and said, "Let's run away, let's escape, let's separate," the house Negro would look at you and say, "Man, you crazy. What you mean, separate? Where is there a better house than this? Where can I wear better clothes than this? Where can I eat better food than this?" That was that house Negro. In those days he was called a "house nigger." And that's what we call them today, because we've still got some house niggers running around here.

This modern house Negro loves his master. He wants to live near him. He'll pay three times as much as the house is worth just to live near his master, and then brag about "I'm the only Negro out here." "I'm the only one on my job." "I'm the only one in this school." You're nothing but a house Negro. And if someone comes to you right now and says, "Let's separate," you say the same thing that the house Negro said on the plantation. "What you mean, separate? From America, this good white man? Where you going to get a better job than you get here?" I mean, this is what you say. "I ain't left nothing in Africa," that's what you say. Why, you left your mind in Africa.

On that same plantation, there was the field Negro. The field Negroes— those were the masses. There were always more Negroes in the field than there were Negroes in the house. The Negro in the field caught hell. He ate leftovers. In the house they ate high up on the hog. The Negro in the field didn't get anything but what was left of the insides of the hog. They call it "chitt'lings" nowadays. In those days they called them what they were— guts. That's what you were—gut-eaters. And some of you are still gut-eaters.

The field Negro was beaten from morning to night; he lived in a shack, in a hut; he wore old, castoff clothes. He hated his master. I say he hated his master. He was intelligent. That house Negro loved his master, but that field Negro—remember, they were in the majority, and they hated the master. When the house caught on fire, he didn't try to put it out; that field Negro prayed for a wind, for a breeze. When the master got sick, the field Negro prayed that he'd die. If someone came to the field Negro and said, "Let's separate, let's run," he didn't say "Where we going?" He'd say, "Any place is better than here." You've got field Negroes in America today. I'm a field Negro. The masses are the field Negroes. When they see this man's house on fire, you don't hear the little Negroes talking about "*our* government is in trouble." They say, "*The* government is in trouble." Imagine a Negro: "*Our* government"! I even heard one say "*our* astronauts." They won't even let him near the plant—and "*our* astronauts"! "*Our* Navy"—that's a Negro that is out of his mind, a Negro that is out of his mind.

Just as the slavemaster of that day used Tom, the house Negro, to keep the field Negroes in check, the same old slavemaster today has Negroes who are nothing but modern Uncle Toms, 20th-century Uncle Toms, to keep you and me in check, to keep us under control, keep us passive and peaceful and nonviolent. That's Tom making you nonviolent. It's like when you go to the dentist, and the man's going to take your tooth. You're going to fight him when he starts pulling. So he squirts some stuff in your jaw called novocaine, to make you think they're not doing anything to you. So you sit there and because you've got all of that novocaine in your jaw, you suffer—peacefully. Blood running all down your jaw, and you don't know what's happening. Because someone has taught you to suffer—peacefully.

The white man does the same thing to you in the street, when he wants to put knots on your head and take advantage of you and not have to be afraid of your fighting back. To keep you from fighting back, he gets these old religious Uncle Toms to teach you and me, just like novocaine, to suffer peacefully. Don't stop suffering—just suffer peacefully. As Rev. Cleage pointed out, they say you should let your blood flow in the streets. This is a shame. You know he's a Christian preacher. If it's a shame to him, you know what it is to me.

There is nothing in our book, the Koran, that teaches us to suffer peacefully. Our religion teaches us to be intelligent. Be peaceful, be courteous, obey the law, respect everyone; but if someone puts his hand on you, send him to the cemetery. That's a good religion. In fact, that's that old-time religion. That's the one that Ma and Pa used to talk about: an eye for an eye, and a tooth for a tooth, and a head for a head, and a life for a life: That's a good religion. And nobody resents that kind of religion being taught but a wolf, who intends to make you his meal.

This is the way it is with the white man in America. He's a wolf—and you're sheep. Any time a shepherd, a pastor, teaches you and me not to run from the white man and, at the same time, teaches us not to flight the white man, he's a traitor to you and me. Don't lay down a life all by itself. No, preserve your life, it's the best thing you've got. And if you've got to give it up, let it be even-steven.

The slavemaster took Tom and dressed him well, fed him well and even gave him a little education—a *little* education; gave him a long coat and a top hat and made all the other slaves look up to him. Then he used Tom to control them. The same strategy that was used in those days is used today, by the same white man. He takes a Negro, a so-called Negro, and makes him prominent, builds him up, publicizes him, makes him a celebrity. And then he becomes a spokesman for Negroes—and a Negro leader.

I would like to mention just one other thing quickly, and that is the method that the white man uses, how the white man uses the "big guns," or Negro leaders, against the Negro revolution. They are not a part of the Negro revolution. They are used against the Negro revolution.

When Martin Luther King failed to desegregate Albany, Georgia, the civil-rights struggle in America reached its low point. King became bankrupt almost, as a leader. The Southern Christian Leadership Conference was in financial trouble; and it was in trouble, period, with the people when they failed to desegregate Albany, Georgia. Other Negro civil-rights leaders of so-called national stature became fallen idols. As they became fallen idols, began to lose their prestige and influence, local Negro leaders began to stir up the masses. In Cambridge, Maryland, Gloria Richardson; in Danville, Virginia, and other parts of the country, local leaders began to stir up our people at the grass-roots level. This was never done by these Negroes of national stature. They control you, but they have never incited you or excited you. They control you, they contain you, they have kept you on the plantation.

As soon as King failed in Birmingham, Negroes took to the streets. King went out to California to a big rally and raised I don't know how many thousands of dollars. He came to Detroit and had a march and raised some more thousands of dollars. And recall, right after that Roy Wilkins attacked King. He accused King and CORE [Congress Of Racial Equality] of starting trouble everywhere and then making the NAACP [National Association for the Advancement of Colored People] get them out of jail and spend a lot of money; they accused King and CORE of raising all the money and not paying it back. This happened; I've got it in documented evidence in the newspaper. Roy started attacking King, and King started attacking Roy, and Farmer started attacking both of them. And as these Negroes of national stature began to attack each other, they began to lose their control of the Negro masses.

The Negroes were out there in the streets. They were talking about how they were going to march on Washington. Right at that time Birmingham had exploded, and the Negroes in Birmingham—remember, they also exploded. They began to stab the crackers in the back and bust them up 'side their head—yes, they did. That's when Kennedy sent in the troops, down in Birmingham. After that, Kennedy got on the television and said "this is a moral issue." That's when he said he was going to put out a civil-rights bill. And when he mentioned civil-rights bill and the Southern crackers started talking about how they were going to boycott or filibuster it, then the Negroes started talking—about what? That they were going to march on Washington, march on the Senate, march on the White House, march on the Congress, and tie it up, bring it to a halt, not let the government proceed. They even said they were going out to the airport and lay down on the runway and not let any airplanes land. I'm telling you what they said. That was revolution. That was revolution. That was the black revolution.

It was the grass roots out there in the street. It scared the white man to death, scared the white power structure in Washington, D.C., to death; I was there. When they found out that this black steamroller was going to come down on the capital, they called in Wilkins, they called in Randolph, they called in these national Negro leaders that you respect and told them, "Call it off." Kennedy said, "Look, you all are letting this thing go too far." And Old Tom said, "Boss, I can't stop it, because I didn't start it." I'm telling you what they said. They said, "I'm not even in it, much less at the head of it." They said, "These Negroes are doing things on their own. They're running ahead of us." And that old shrewd fox, he said, "If you all aren't in it, I'll put you in it. I'll put you at the head of it. I'll endorse it. I'll welcome it. I'll help it. I'll join it."

A matter of hours went by. They had a meeting at the Carlyle Hotel in New York City. The Carlyle Hotel is owned by the Kennedy family; that's the hotel Kennedy spent the night at, two nights ago; it belongs to his family. A philanthropic society headed by a white man named Stephen Currier called all the top civil-rights leaders together at the Carlyle Hotel. And he told them, "By you all fighting each other, you are destroying the civil-rights movement. And since you're fighting over money from white liberals, let us set up what is known as the Council for United Civil Rights Leadership. Let's form this council, and all the civil-rights organizations will belong to it, and we'll use it for fund-raising purposes." Let me show you how tricky the white man is. As soon as they got it formed, they elected Whitney Young as its chairman, and who do you think became the co-chairman? Stephen Currier, the white man, a millionaire. Powell was talking about it down at Cobo Hall today. This is what he was talking about. Powell knows it happened. Randolph knows it happened. Wilkins knows it happened. King knows it happened. Every one of that Big Six—they know it happened.

Once they formed it, with the white man over it, he promised them and gave them $800,000 to split up among the Big Six; and told them that after the march was over they'd give them $700,000 more. A million and a half dollars—split up between leaders that you have been following, going to jail for, crying crocodile tears for. And they're nothing but Frank James and Jesse James and the what-do-you-call'em brothers.

As soon as they got the setup organized, the white man made available to them top public-relations experts; opened the news media across the country at their disposal, which then began to project these Big Six as the leaders of the march. Originally they weren't even in the march. You were talking this march talk on Hastings Street, you were talking march talk on Lenox Avenue, and on Fillmore Street, and on Central Avenue, and 32nd Street and 63rd Street. That's where the march talk was being talked. But the white man put the Big Six at the head of it; made them the march. They became the march. They took it over. And the first move they made after they took it over, they invited Walter Reuther, a white man; they invited a priest, a rabbi, and an old white preacher, yes, an old white preacher. The same white element that put Kennedy into power—labor, the Catholics, the Jews, and liberal Protestants; the same clique that put Kennedy in power, joined the march on Washington.

It's just like when you've got some coffee that's too black, which means it's too strong. What do you do? You integrate it with cream, you make it weak. But if you pour too much cream in it, you won't even know you ever had coffee. It used to be hot, it becomes cool. It used to be strong, it becomes weak. It used to wake you up, now it puts you to sleep. This is what they did with the march on Washington. They joined it. They didn't integrate it, they infiltrated it. They joined it, became a part of it, took it over. And as they took it over, it lost its militancy. It ceased to be angry, it ceased to be hot, it ceased to be uncompromising. Why, it even ceased to be a march. It became a picnic, a circus. Nothing but a circus, with clowns and all. You had one right here in Detroit—I saw it on television—with clowns leading it, white clowns and black clowns. I know you don't like what I'm saying, but I'm going to tell you anyway. Because I can prove what I'm saying. If you think I'm telling you wrong, you bring me Martin Luther King and A. Phillip Randolph and James Farmer and those other three, and see if they'll deny it over a microphone.

No, it was a sellout. It was a takeover. When James Baldwin came in from Paris, they wouldn't let him talk, because they couldn't make him go by the script. Burt Lancaster read the speech that Baldwin was supposed to make; they wouldn't let Baldwin get up there, because they know Baldwin is liable to say anything.

They controlled it so tight, they told those Negroes what time to hit town, how to come, where to stop, what signs to carry, what song to sing, what speech they could make, and what speech they couldn't make; and then told them to get out of town by sundown. And every one of those Toms was out of town by sundown. Now I know you don't like my saying this. But I can back it up. It was a circus, a performance that beat anything Hollywood could ever do, the performance of the year. Reuther and those other three devils should get an Academy Award for the best actors because they acted like they really loved Negroes and fooled a whole lot of Negroes. And the six Negro leaders should get an award too, for the best supporting cast.

Just as it seemed the blush was off the rose, King made a dramatic comeback in Birmingham, Alabama. The following selection from Harvard Sitkoff's **The Struggle for Black Equality**, *outlines King's strategy in Birmingham. Realizing that he needed a big victory to "rekindle the morale and momentum of the freedom struggle," King embarked on Project C (for confrontation). The Birmingham march called for an end to Jim Crow practices in employment and social accommodations. After several days of demonstrations, during which police chief Eugene "Bull" Connor routinely arrested the protestors, city officials issued an injunction "barring racial demonstrations." In open defiance, King violated the injunction and continued to march. Enraged, Connor publicly arrested King and his followers.*

WE SHALL OVERCOME

Harvard Sitkoff

Excerpt from The Struggle for Black Equality

Martin Luther King's determination to provoke a confrontation in Birmingham in 1963 resulted in a massive wave of nonviolent action—"the Negro Revolution." His action decisively changed both the nature of the struggle for racial justice and white attitudes toward civil rights. After more than twenty thousand blacks were jailed in hundreds of demonstrations, King's action eventuated the passage of the most comprehensive anti-discrimination legislation in American history.

The decision to launch a campaign to end segregation in Birmingham had been reached in a three-day strategy session conducted by the SCLC at its retreat near Savannah at the end of 1962. The motives were both personal and political, practical as well as philosophical. The Albany debacle weighted heavily on King and his aides. Malcolm X had said "the civil rights struggle in America reached its lowest point" in Albany, and many in the movement agreed. Albany brought into the open doubts about King's leadership and disillusionment with the established techniques of protest. The head of the SCLC wanted desperately to prove that nonviolence could still work, that "you can struggle without hating, you can fight without violence." King also believed it imperative to demonstrate his own courage and effectiveness. His reputation, and SCLC's influence, necessitated a daring, dramatic effort, especially since 1963 would be the year of the one hundredth anniversary of the Emancipation Proclamation.

King realized the need for some majestic achievement to rekindle the morale and momentum of the freedom struggle. Social movements require victories for sustenance, and civil rights gains had not kept pace with the rising expectations of blacks. Despair mounted in 1962, and King feared that if the movement faltered, blacks would turn to leaders like Malcolm X, who mocked nonviolence and had nothing but scorn for "integration"—a word, Malcolm said, "invented by a northern liberal." The SCLC leadership craved and needed a major triumph.

The time had come, moreover, to force Kennedy's hand. The President's policy of trying to show concern for blacks while at the same time avoiding action to inflame the white South, said King, had brought the movement nothing but delay and tokenism. By 1963, thirty-four African nations had freed themselves from colonial bondage, but more than two thousand school districts remained segregated in the South. Only 8 percent of the black children in the South attended class with whites. At this rate of progress, civil-rights leaders moaned, it would be the year 2054 before school desegregation became a reality, and it would be the year 2094 before blacks secured equality in job training and employment. Kennedy would have to be pushed, and pushed hard. "We've got to have a crisis to bargain with," Wyatt Tee Walker explained at the SCLC retreat. "To take a moderate approach hoping to get white help, doesn't help. They nail you to the cross, and it saps the enthusiasm of the followers. You've got to have a crisis."

Birmingham appeared to answer King's diverse needs. The Reverend Fred Lee Shuttlesworth, the head of the Alabama Christian Movement for Human Rights, a SCLC affiliate, had just invited King to conduct nonviolent demonstrations in Birmingham, the most segregated big city in America. No other undertaking would be more audacious. Absolute segregation was the rule— in schools, restaurants, rest rooms, drinking fountains, and department-store fitting rooms. Municipal officials closed down the city parks rather than comply with a federal court order to desegregate them. Birmingham abandoned its professional baseball team rather than allow it to play integrated clubs in the International League. Although over 40 percent of the population was black, fewer than ten thousand of the 80,000 registered voters were black. Despite the city's industrial prosperity, moreover, blacks remained restricted to menial and domestic jobs. Describing race relations in Birmingham, Harrison Salisbury wrote in the *New York Times*:

> Whites and blacks still walk the same streets. But the streets, the water supply and the sewer system are about the only public facilities they share. Ball parks and taxicabs are segregated. So are libraries. A book featuring black rabbits and

white rabbits was banned. A drive is on to forbid "Negro music" on "white" radio stations. Every channel of communication, every medium of mutual interest, every reasoned approach, every inch of middle ground has been fragmented by the emotional dynamite of racism, reinforced by the whip, the razor, the gun, the bomb, the torch, the club, the knife, the mob, the police and many branches of the state's apparatus.

To crack Birmingham's solid wall of segregation would be a mighty achievement.

Birmingham was more than unyielding on segregation. It had the reputation of a dangerous city. Blacks dubbed it "Bombing-ham" for the eighteen racial bombings and more than fifty cross-burning incidents that occurred between 1957 and 1963. Leading the vanguard of the brutal, last-ditch defenders of segregation was Eugene T. ("Bull") Connor. The jowly, thickset police commissioner prided himself on being as vigilant as he was cruel in "keeping the niggers in their place." The SCLC could count on Connor to respond viciously to any effort to alter the city's racial order, and that just might create the crisis that would force the President to act. King decided to aid Shuttlesworth, but to avoid having their nonviolent campaign used as a political football, they postponed the demonstrations until after the April 2 mayoralty runoff election. In the meantime, King and his associates prepared a top-secret plan which they called "Project C"—for *Confrontation*.

King and his task force arrived in Birmingham the day after the election. They promptly issued a manifesto spelling out the grievances of blacks in that city. It called for an immediate end to racist employment practices and Jim Crow public accommodations, and for the rapid formation of a biracial committee to plan for further desegregation. "The absence of justice and progress in Birmingham demands that we make a moral witness to give our community a chance to survive," the manifesto concluded; it reasoned that since Birmingham officials had resisted every attempt at mediation and compromise, the only recourse left to blacks was open protest. "We're tired of waiting," Shuttlesworth angrily reiterated to a packed church meeting that evening. "We've been waiting for 340 years for our rights. We want action. We want it now." As the congregation responded with feverish renditions of "Woke up This Mornin' with My Mind Stayed on Freedom" and "Ain't Gonna Let Nobody Turn Me 'Round," King rose to vow that he would lead an economic boycott and demonstrations against the downtown merchants until "Pharaoh lets God's people go."

The first stage of Project C began the next morning. Small groups of protesters staged sit-ins at the segregated downtown lunch counters. The anticipated arrests followed. King continued this tactic for several days, patiently piquing the concern of the Kennedy Administration and the interest of the national news media while arousing the black community. He carefully avoided provoking the racist fury of white Birmingham until these objectives were reasonably accomplished. To accelerate the process, King ordered Project C's second stage to start on April 6.

Some fifty blacks led by Shuttlesworth marched on City Hall that Saturday morning. Connor arrested them all. The next day, Palm Sunday, Connor similarly intercepted and jailed a column of blacks marching on City Hall headed by Martin Luther King's brother, the Reverend A. D. King. Day after day the public marches and arrests continued, all in the full glare of newspaper photographers and television cameras. King had counted on these incidents and the economic boycott accompanying them to activate larger numbers of Birmingham blacks, to focus national attention on the issue of civil rights, and to discomfort the city's economic elite. He had calculated right. On April 10, city officials secured an injunction barring racial demonstrations. They thought it would stop the SCLC campaign in its tracks, robbing King of his desired publicity and dampening the fervor of the black community. But King announced that he saw it as his duty to violate this immoral injunction and that he would do so on Good Friday, April 12. Accompanied by Abernathy and Al Hibbler, the popular blind blues singer, King led some fifty hymn-singing volunteers on yet another trek toward City Hall. Chanting "Freedom has come to Birmingham!" nearly a thousand blacks lined their route. An infuriated "Bull" Connor, now assisted by a squad of snarling, snapping police dogs, ordered their arrest. The national spotlight illuminated Birmingham's racial crisis as never before.

King used his time in jail to compose an eloquent essay justifying the strategy of the black freedom struggle. Ostensibly written to the eight Birmingham clergymen who had condemned the SCLC campaign as "unwise and untimely," King addressed his reply to the many whites and blacks who apparently shared his goals but questioned his tactics, especially those who urged the movement to be patient, moderate, and law-abiding. Begun in the margins of newspapers and continued on bits of scrap paper smuggled to him by a prison trusty, King worked for four days on his nineteen-page "Letter from the Birmingham Jail." Soon after, several national periodicals published it in its entirety and reprints were distributed across the nation. The news media frequently quoted it and, for the most part, cited it favorably. The letter proved to be a potent weapon in the propaganda battle to legitimate the direct-action movement. It quieted numerous critics of civil disobedience; it won significant new support for "Freedom Now."

Criticism of King for his "children's crusade" came from every quarter. Moderates anguished about the safety of the children. Conservatives denounced the tactic as cynical and exploitative. Radicals demeaned it as unmanly. "Real men," objected Malcolm X, "don't put their children on the firing line." King retorted that, by demonstrating, the children gained a "sense of their own stake in freedom and justice," as well as a heightened pride in their race and belief in their capacity to influence their future. He asked his white critics pointedly: Where had they been with their protective words when down through the years, Negro infants were born into ghettos, taking their first breath of life in a social atmosphere where the fresh air of freedom was crowded out by the stench of discrimination?

Words of reason no longer mattered, however. Action had taken precedence. The rules of the game had changed. Another thousand black children of Birmingham packed the Sixteenth Street Baptist Church that evening to shout their approval of King and his promise "Today was D Day. Tomorrow will be Double-D Day."

The *New York Times* account of the May 3 demonstrations began: "There was an ugly overtone to the events today that was not present yesterday." No one would accuse the reporter of overstatement. As an energed "Bull" Connor watched a thousand more students gather in the church to receive their demonstration assignments, he abandoned all restraint. He ordered his forces to bar the exits from the church, trapping inside about half the young protesters, and then had his men charge into those who escaped and had gathered in Kelly Ingram Park in front of the Sixteenth Street Baptist Church. The police, swinging nightsticks brutally and indiscriminately, beat demonstrators and onlookers. They sicced their dogs on the young, wounding several. When some adults in the park, horrified at the mistreatment of the children, hurled bricks and bottles at the policemen, Connor commanded the firemen with their high-pressure hoses: "Let 'em have it." With a sound like gunfire, streams of blistering water roared from the nozzles, blasting blacks against buildings and sweeping kids down slippery streets. The hundreds of pounds of pressure ripped the bark off trees; it also tore the clothes off young people's backs and cut through their skin. Those jailed that Friday brought the number of children arrested in two days to nearly thirteen hundred.

King had his confrontation, and more. On Saturday, an additional two hundred students were arrested, and several thousand adult blacks skirmished with the police, pelting them with rocks and stones. Again, scenes of clubbing, police dogs, and fire hoses appeared on the front pages of newspapers and on television sets throughout the country. The appalling pictures of snarling dogs lunging viciously at youthful marchers, of bands of policemen ganging up to beat children and women, of high-pressure hoses knocking the very young and the very old off their feet or into the air, brought a surge of anger and determination across black America and aroused the conscience, or guilt, of millions of whites. King suddenly had the support of much of the nation. Kennedy now had to act.

The pictures of violence in Birmingham made him "sick," the President admitted to a delegation from the Americans for Democratic Action that Saturday. Yet he doubted aloud that he had a constitutional mandate to act. He termed impossible the liberals' suggestion that he intervene immediately and forcefully in Birmingham, but acknowledged: "I am not asking for patience. I can well understand why the Negroes of Birmingham are tired of being asked to be patient." Privately, the President knew that the time had come to act. He had to resolve the conflict with the least possible political damage to himself. He shared the sense of national outrage at Southern white atrocities yet shrank from the prospect of using federal force to impose a new racial order. Kennedy simply wanted the quickest possible restoration of civil peace. Secretly he ordered Justice Department mediators to Birmingham to persuade the contending groups to negotiate a settlement. Concurrently, key Administration officials began an intensive campaign to pressure Birmingham's most influential businessmen, especially those connected with U.S. Steel, to accept a compromise agreement.

Until this moment in the crisis, the Senior Citizens' Committee, covertly organized by the Birmingham Chamber of Commerce to deal with desegregation problems, would not even talk with King and his associates. They were the so-called white moderates of the South—the gentlemen who said "nigra" rather than "nigger"—supposedly too busy making money to hate, yet for a month they had avoided even a hint of willingness to end the disorder and violence. Now, suddenly, they were ready to talk. They had felt the heat from Washington. They feared the city was on the verge of a major bloodletting. And they had reckoned the toll of the black boycott: sales in April had dropped more than a third in the downtown stores. So Birmingham's economic elite started to negotiate in earnest on May 4, even agreeing to hold all-night sessions. They talked and listened but would not accede. The SCLC would not back down. Deadlock. King ordered the demonstrations to continue.

The most massive black protest to date began early Monday, May 6, and police violence intensified accordingly. A flyer distributed near Negro schools urged all students: "Fight for freedom first, then go to school. Joint the thousands in jail who are making their witness for freedom. Come to the Sixteenth Street Baptist Church now . . . and we'll soon be free. It's up to you to free our teachers, our parents, yourself and our country." Once again, thousands of young blacks heeded the call. In some schools, attendance dropped nearly 90 percent. Preaching to a jammed church and to the thousands more in Ingram Park listening to loudspeakers, King reminded the students of their stake in this "righteous struggle for freedom and human dignity." He reiterated the necessity for nonviolence: "The world is watching you." Violence is impractical as well as immoral; the power of nonviolence is a greater weapon.

Dick Gregory, the well-known black comedian, led the first group of demonstrators out of the church. Police hurried them into the waiting paddy wagons as the students chanted: "Don't mind walking, 'cause I want my freedom now." Then another group left the church, shouting: "Freedom! Freedom! Freedom!" They, too, were quickly herded off to jail. Out came another group of young blacks, and then another, and another. For an hour, wave after wave of twenty to fifty black students, chanting and shouting for freedom, defiantly offered themselves up for arrest. The huge crowd in the park roared their approval for each contingent leaving the church. Many sang a new ditty: "It isn't nice to go to jail/There are nicer ways to do it/But the nice ways always fail."

The audacity of the students, the contempt of the blacks, stirred Connor's fear and loathing. After more than a thousand demonstrators had been seized, he turned his police on the crowd in the park. Shoving and kicking, the men in blue now vented their fury. As the television cameras rolled and the photographers focused their lenses, snapping police dogs once again leaped at the throats of taunting children, fire hoses bowled over rock-throwing blacks, and Connor's minions indiscriminately clubbed onlookers.

A shocked nation demanded federal action to end the conflict. Kennedy's mediators redoubled their efforts. They pressed King to yield on his demands for immediate desegregation and an end to discrimination in employment. They warned him of the folly of prolonging the crisis in the expectation of intervention by federal troops. Separately, the Justice Department officials urged the city's business establishment to make real concessions, not merely promises of future action. They threatened the white elite with the probable consequences of federal action and the economic effects of a bloodbath in Birmingham. Neither negotiating team would budge. The talks resumed, and so did the confrontation.

Tuesday, May 7, the conflict peaked. A larger number of students than ever before, and far less submissive, appeared on the streets. Rather than march from the church and orderly court arrest, some two thousand young blacks suddenly converged on the downtown area at noon. Most staged sit-ins. Others picketed the major stores. Some held pray-ins on the sidewalks. Several thousand adult spectators then spontaneously joined a raucous black parade through the business section. Over and over they sang "I ain't scared of your jail 'cause I want my freedom! . . . want my freedom!" "We're marching for freedom!" others chanted. "The police can't stop us now. Even 'Bull' Connor can't stop us now."

Connor certainly tried. Adding an armored police tank to his arsenal of hoses, dogs, clubs, and cattle prods, he ordered his men to drive the protesters back into the black ghetto. Brutally, they did so, eventually penning nearly four thousand in Ingram Park. Connor commanded that the high-pressure hoses be turned on the trapped blacks. The water shot from the nozzles whacked the bark off trees. It tore bricks loose from the walls. The crowd screamed, some for mercy, some in anger. Rocks flew. Bottles and bricks were hurled at the police. SCLC aides circulating in the crowd pleaded for nonviolence. Few could even hear them over the crashing of the huge hoses; and not many who could hear wanted to listen. Soon after Shuttlesworth entered the park to try to calm his followers, a blast of water slammed the minister against the side of a building. On hearing that an injured Shuttlesworth had just been placed in an ambulance, Connor laughed. "I waited a week to see Shuttlesworth get hit with a hose. I'm sorry I missed it. I wish they'd carried him away in a hearse." Not until the crowd had been thoroughly pacified and dispersed did the dogs cease biting, the clubs stop crashing bones, and the hoses end knocking blacks down and washing them along the sidewalks. A reporter who watched in despair mumbled "God bless America."

That noon, as the blacks demonstrated tumultuously downtown, a secret emergency meeting of the Senior Citizens' Committee resolved to end the disorder that had caused Birmingham to become an international byword for unrestrained police brutality. With the din of freedom chants in their ears, the business leaders directed their negotiators to come to terms with the SCLC. That evening a three-hour bargaining session brought the two sides close to agreement. Differences remained, but the premonition of unchecked violence affected both negotiating teams. Following three more days of talk, they reached agreement.

"I am very happy to be able to announce," King stated, "that we have come today to the climax of a long struggle for justice, freedom and human dignity in the city of Birmingham." The SCLC had won its demands for the "desegregation of lunch counters, rest rooms, fitting rooms and drinking fountains"; for the "upgrading and hiring of Negroes on a nondiscriminatory basis throughout the industrial community of Birmingham"; and for the formation of a biracial committee. It accepted, however, a timetable of planned stages, relenting on its insistence that these changes take effect immediately. The SCLC, moreover, acceded to the release of arrested demonstrators on bond, giving up its demand for the outright dismissal of all charges against them. Still and all, King could well claim with pride "the most magnificent victory for justice we've ever seen in the Deep South."

As Sitkoff points out, King was also under severe criticism by the clergy in Birmingham for engaging in what they perceived to be confrontational tactics. In response, King writes in **"A Letter from the Birmingham Jail"** *outlining the case for massive civil disobedience. The struggle for black rights entered the national consciousness as King's letter received national and international attention. Upon his release from jail King embarks on the final stage of his plan—the use of thousands of school children to continue the marches. The dissonance created by the images of carefree children being harassed by police in riot gear set off a wave of national sympathy for King's cause. The escalating violence surrounding the marches coupled with the predictably reactionary statements from Bull Connor were a national shame. A stunned and embarrassed President John Kennedy was finally moved to act. Justice Department officials were dispatched to broker a peace, and after several days of tense negotiation, King declared victory.*

LETTER FROM A BIRMINGHAM JAIL

Martin Luther King, Jr.

Author's Note: This response to a published statement by eight fellow clergymen from Alabama (Bishop C. C. J. Carpenter, Bishop Joseph A. Durick, Rabbi Hilton L. Grafman, Bishop Paul Hardim, Bishop Holan B. Harmon, i.e., Reverend George M. Murray, the Reverend Edward V. Ramage and the Reverend Earl Stallings) was composed under somewhat constricting circumstances. Begun on the margins of the newspaper in which the statement appeared while I was in jail, the letter was continued on scraps of writing paper supplied by a friendly Negro trusty, and concluded on a pad my attorneys were eventually permitted to leave me. Although the text remains in substance unaltered, I have indulged in the author's prerogative of polishing it for publication.

April 16, 1963

My Dear Fellow Clergymen

While confined here in the Birmingham city jail, I came across your recent statement calling my present activities "unwise and untimely." Seldom do I pause to answer criticism of my work and ideas. If I sought to answer all the criticisms that cross my desk, my secretaries would have little time for anything other than such correspondence in the course of the day, and I would have no time for constructive work. But since I feel that you are men of genuine good will and that your criticisms are sincerely set forth, I want to try to answer your statement in what I hope will be patient and reasonable terms.

I think I should indicate why I am here in Birmingham, since you have been influenced by the view which argues against "outsiders coming in." I have the honor of serving as president of the Southern Christian Leadership Conference, an organization operating in every southern state, with headquarters in Atlanta, Georgia. We have some 85 affiliated organizations across the South, and one of them is the Alabama Christian Movement for Human Rights. Frequently we share staff, educational and financial resources with our affiliates. Several months ago the affiliate here in Birmingham asked us to be on call to engage in a nonviolent direct-action program if such were deemed necessary. We readily consented, and when the hour came we lived up to our promise. So I, along with several members of my staff, am here because I was invited here. I am here because I have organizational ties here.

But more basically, I am in Birmingham because injustice is here. Just as the prophets of the 8th century B.C. left their villages and carried their "thus saith the Lord" far beyond the boundaries of their home towns, and just as the Apostle Paul left his village of Tarsus and carried the gospel of Jesus Christ to the far corners of the Greco-Roman world, so am I compelled to carry the gospel of freedom beyond my own home town. Like Paul, I must constantly respond to the Macedonian call for aid.

Moreover, I am cognizant of the interrelatedness of all communities and states. I cannot sit idly by in Atlanta and not be concerned about what happens in Birmingham. Injustice anywhere is a threat to justice everywhere. We are caught in an inescapable network of mutuality, tied in a single garment of destiny. Whatever affects one directly, affects all indirectly. Never again can we afford to live with the narrow, provincial "outside agitator" idea. Anyone who lives inside the United States can never be considered an outsider anywhere within its bounds.

You deplore the demonstrations taking place in Birmingham. But your statement, I am sorry to say, fails to express a similar concern for the conditions that brought about the demonstrations. I am sure that none of you would want to rest content with the superficial kind of social analysis that deals merely with effects and does not grapple with underlying causes. It is unfortunate that demonstrations are taking place in Birmingham, but it is even more unfortunate that the city's white power structure left the Negro community with no alternative.

In any nonviolent campaign there are four basic steps: collection of the facts to determine whether injustices exist; negotiation; self-purification; and direct action. We have gone through all these steps in Birmingham. There can be no gainsaying the fact that racial injustice engulfs this community. Birmingham is probably the most thoroughly segregated city in the United States. Its ugly record of brutality is widely known. Negroes have experienced grossly unjust treatment in the courts. There have been more unsolved bombings of Negro homes and churches in Birmingham than in any other city in the nation. These are the hard, brutal facts of the case. On the basis of these conditions, Negro leaders sought to negotiate with the city fathers. But the latter consistently refused to engage in good-faith negotiation.

Then, last September, came the opportunity to talk with leaders of Birmingham's economic community. In the course of the negotiations, certain promises were made by the merchants—for example, to remove the stores' humiliating racial signs. On the basis of these promises, the Reverend Fred Shuttlesworth and the leaders of the Alabama Christian Movement for Human Rights agreed to a moratorium on all demonstrations. As the weeks and months went by, we realized that we were the victims of a broken promise. A few signs, briefly removed, returned; the others remained.

As in so many past experiences, our hopes had been blasted, and the shadow of deep disappointment settled upon us. We had no alternative except to prepare for direct action, whereby we would present our very bodies as a means of laying our case before the conscience of the local and the national community. Mindful of the difficulties involved, we decided to undertake a process of self-purification. We began a series of workshops on nonviolence, and we repeatedly asked ourselves: "Are you able to accept blows without retaliating?" "Are you able to endure the ordeal of jail?" We decided to schedule our direct-action program for the Easter season, realizing that except for Christmas, this is the main shopping period of the year. Knowing that a strong economic-withdrawal program would be the by-product of direct action, we felt that this would be the best time to bring pressure to bear on the merchants for the needed change.

Then it occurred to us that Birmingham's mayoralty election was coming up in March, and we speedily decided to postpone action until after election day. When we discovered that the Commissioner of Public Safety, Eugene "Bull" Connor, had piled up enough votes to be in the run-off, we decided again to postpone action until the day after the run-off so that the demonstrations could not be used to cloud the issues. Like many others, we waited to see Mr. Connor defeated, and to this end we endured postponement after postponement. Having aided in this community need, we felt that our direct-action program could be delayed no longer.

You may well ask: "Why direct action? Why sit-ins, marches and so forth? Isn't negotiation a better path?" You are quite right in calling for negotiation. Indeed, this is the very purpose of direct action. Nonviolent direct action seeks to create such a crisis and foster such a tension that a community which has constantly refused to negotiate is forced to confront the issues. It seeks so to the issue that it can no longer be ignored. My citing the creation of tension as part of the work of the nonviolent-resister may sound rather shocking. But I must confess that I am not afraid of the word "tension." I have earnestly opposed violent tension, but there is a type of constructive, nonviolent tension which is necessary for growth. Just as Socrates felt that it was necessary to create a tension in the mind so that individuals could rise from the bondage of myths and half-truths to the unfettered realm of creative analysis and objective appraisal, so must we see the need for nonviolent gadflies to create the kind of tension in society that will help men rise from the dark depths of prejudice and racism to the majestic heights of understanding and brotherhood.

The purpose of our direct-action program is to create a situation so crisis-packed that it will inevitably open the door to negotiation. I therefore concur with you in your call for negotiation. Too long has our beloved Southland been bogged down in a tragic effort to live in monologue rather than dialogue.

One of the basic points in your statement is that the action that I and my associates have taken in Birmingham is untimely. Some have asked: "Why didn't you give the new city administration time to act?" The only answer that I can give to this query is that the new Birmingham administration must be prodded about as much as the outgoing one, before it will act. We are sadly mistaken if we feel that the election of Albert Boutwell as mayor will bring the millennium to Birmingham. While Mr. Boutwell is a much more gentle person than Mr. Connor, they are both segregationists, dedicated to maintenance of the status quo. I have hope that Mr. Boutwell will be reason-able enough to see the futility of massive resistance to desegregation. But he will not see this without pressure from devotees of civil rights. My friends, I must say to you that we have not made a single gain in civil rights without determined legal and nonviolent pressure. Lamentably, it is an historical fact that privileged groups seldom give up their privileges voluntarily. Individu-als may see the moral light and voluntarily give up their unjust posture; but, as Reinhold Niebuhr has reminded us, groups tend to be more immoral than individuals.

We know through painful experience that freedom is never voluntarily given by the oppressor; it must be demanded by the oppressed. Frankly, I have yet to engage in a direct-action campaign that was "well timed" in the view of those who have not suffered unduly from the disease of segregation. For years now I have heard the word "Wait!" It rings in the ear of every Negro with piercing familiarity. This "Wait" has almost always meant "Never." We must come to see, with one of our distinguished jurists, that "justice too long delayed is justice denied."

We have waited for more than 340 years for our constitutional and God-given rights. The nations of Asia and Africa are moving with jetlike speed to-ward gaining political independence, but we still creep at horse-and-buggy pace toward gaining a cup of coffee at a lunch counter. Perhaps it is easy for those who have never felt the stinging darts of segregation to say, "Wait." But when you have seen vicious mobs lynch your mothers and fathers at will and drown your sisters and brothers at whim; when you have seen hate-filled po-licemen curse, kick and even kill your black brothers and sisters; when you see the vast majority of your twenty million Negro brothers smothering in an airtight cage of poverty in the midst of an affluent society; when you sud-denly find your tongue twisted and your speech stammering as you seek to explain to your six-year-old daughter why she can't go to the public amuse-ment park that has just been advertised on television, and see tears welling up in her eyes when she is told that Funtown is closed to colored children, and see ominous clouds of inferiority beginning to form in her little mental sky, and see her beginning to distort her personality by developing an un-conscious bitterness toward white people; when you have to concoct an an-swer for a five-year-old son who is asking: "Daddy, why do white people treat colored people so mean?"; when you take a cross-country drive and find it necessary to sleep night after night in the uncomfortable corners of your automobile because no motel will accept you; when you are humiliated day in and day out by nagging signs reading "white" and "colored"; when you first name becomes "nigger," your middle name becomes "boy" (however old you are) and your last name becomes "John," and your wife and mother are never given the respected title "Mrs."; when you are harried by day and haunted by night by the fact that you are a Negro, living constantly at tiptoe distance, never quite knowing what to expect next, and are plagued with inner fears and outer resentments; when you are forever fighting a degenerating sense of "nobodiness"—then you will understand why we find it difficult to wait. There comes a time when the cup of endurance runs over, and men are no longer willing to be plunged into the abyss of despair I hope, sirs, you can understand our legitimate and an-avoidable impatience.

You express a great deal of anxiety over our willingness to break laws. This is certainly a legitimate concern. Since we so diligently urge people to obey the Supreme Court's decision of 1954 outlawing segregation in the public schools, at first glance it may seem rather paradoxical for us consciously to break laws. One may well ask: "How can you advocate breaking some laws and obeying others?" The answer lies in the fact that there are two types of laws: just and unjust. I would be the first to advocate obeying just laws. One has not only a legal but a moral responsibility to obey just laws. Conversely, one has a moral responsibility to disobey unjust laws. I would agree with St. Augustine that "an unjust law is no law at all."

Now, what is the difference between the two? How does one determine whether a law is just or unjust? A just law is a man-made code that squares with the moral law or the law of God. An unjust law is a code that is out of harmony with the moral law. To put it in the terms of St. Thomas Aquinas: An unjust law is a human law that is not rooted in eternal law and natural law. Any law that uplifts human personality is just. Any law that degrades human personality is unjust. All segregation statutes are unjust because segregation distorts the soul and damages the personality. It gives the segregator a false sense of superiority and the segregated a false sense of inferiority. Segregation, to use the terminology of the Jewish philosopher Martin Buber, substitutes an "I-it" relationship for an "I-thou" relationship and ends up relegating persons to the status of things. Hence segregation is not only politically, economically and sociologically unsound, it is morally wrong and sinful. Paul Tillich has said that sin is separation. Is not segregation an existential expression of man's tragic separation, his awful estrangement, his terrible sinfulness? Thus it is that I can urge men to obey the 1954 decision of the Supreme Court, for it is morally right; and I can urge them to disobey segregation ordinances, for they are morally wrong.

Let us consider a more concrete example of just and unjust laws. An unjust law is a code that a numerical or power majority group compels a minority group to obey but does not make binding on itself. This is *difference* made legal. By the same token, a just law is a code that a majority compels a minority to follow and that it is willing to follow itself. This is *sameness* made legal.

Let me give another explanation. A law is unjust if it is inflicted on a minority that, as a result of being denied the right to vote, had no part in enacting or devising the law. Who can say that the legislature of Alabama which set up that state's segregation laws was democratically elected? Throughout Alabama all sorts of devious methods are used to prevent Negroes from becoming registered voters, and there are some counties in which, even though Negroes constitute a majority of the population, not a single Negro is registered. Can any law enacted under such circumstances be considered democratically structured?

Sometimes a law is just on its face and unjust in its application. For instance, I have been arrested on a charge of *parading without a permit*. Now, there is nothing wrong in having an ordinance which requires a permit for a parade. But such an ordinance becomes unjust when it is used to maintain segregation and to deny citizens the First-Amendment privilege of peaceful assembly and protest.

I hope you are able to see the distinction I am trying to point out. In no sense do I advocate evading or defying the law, as would the rabid segregationist. That would lead to anarchy. One who breaks an unjust law must do so openly, lovingly, and with a willingness to accept the penalty. I submit that an individual who breaks a law that conscience tells him is unjust, and who willingly accepts the penalty of imprisonment in order to arouse the conscience of the community over its injustice, is in reality expressing the highest respect for law.

Of course, there is nothing new about this kind of civil disobedience. It was evidence sublimely in the refusal of Shadrach, Meshach and Abednego to obey the laws of Nebuchadnezzar, on the ground that a higher moral law was at stake. It was practiced superbly by the early Christians, who were willing to face hungry lions and the excruciating pain of chopping blocks rather than submit to certain unjust laws of the Roman Empire. To a degree, academic freedom is a reality today because Socrates practiced civil disobedience. In our own nation, the Boston Tea Party represented a massive act of civil disobedience.

We should never forget that everything Adolf Hitler did in Germany was "legal" and everything the Hungarian freedom fighters did in Hungary was "illegal." It was "illegal" to aid and comfort a Jew in Hitler's Germany. Even so, I am sure that, had I lived in Germany at the time, I would have aided and comforted my Jewish brothers. If today I lived in a Communist country where certain principles dear to the Christian faith are suppressed, I would openly advocate disobeying that country's antireligious laws.

I must make two honest confessions to you, my Christian and Jewish brothers. First, I must confess that over the past few years I have been gravely disappointed with the white moderate. I have almost reached the regrettable conclusion that the Negro's great stumbling block in his stride toward freedom is not the White Citizen's Counciler or the Ku Klux Klanner, but the white moderate, who is more devoted to "order" than to justice; who prefers a negative peace which is the absence of tension to a positive peace which is the presence of justice; who constantly says: "I agree with you in the goal you seek, but I cannot agree with your methods of direct action"; who paternalistically believes he can set the timetable for another man's freedom; who lives by a mythical concept of time and who constantly advises the Negro to wait for a "more convenient season." Shallow understanding from people of good will is more frustrating than absolute misunderstanding from people of ill will. Lukewarm acceptance is much more bewildering than outright rejection.

I had hoped that the white moderate would understand that law and order exist for the purpose of establishing justice and that when they fail in this purpose they become the dangerously structured dams that block the flow of social progress. I had hoped that the white moderate would understand that the present tension in the South is a necessary phase of the transition from an obnoxious negative peace, in which the Negro passively accepted his unjust plight, to a substantive and positive peace, in which all men will respect the dignity and worth of human personality. Actually, we who engage in nonviolent direct action are not the creators of tension. We merely bring to the surface the hidden tension that is already alive. We bring it out in the open, where it can be seen and dealt with. Like a boil that can never be cured so long as it is covered up but must be opened with all its ugliness to the natural medicines of air and light, injustice must be exposed, with all the tension its exposure creates, to the light of human conscience and the air of national opinion before it can be cured.

In your statement you assert that our actions, even though peaceful must be condemned because they precipitate violence. But is this a logical assertion? Isn't this like condemning a robbed man because his possession of money precipitated the evil act of robbery? Isn't this like condemning Socrates because his unswerving commitment to truth and his philosophical inquiries precipitated the act by the misguided populace in which they made him drink hemlock? Isn't this like condemning Jesus because his unique God-consciousness and never-ceasing devotion to God's will precipitated the evil act of crucifixion? We must come to see that, as the federal courts have consistently affirmed, it is wrong to urge an individual to cease his efforts to gain his basic constitutional rights because the quest may precipitate violence. Society must protect the robbed and punish the robber.

I had also hoped that the white moderate would reject the myth concerning time in relation to the struggle for freedom. I have just received a letter from a white brother in Texas. He writes: "All Christians know that the colored people will receive equal rights eventually, but it is possible that you are in too great a religious hurry. It has taken Christianity almost two thousand years to accomplish what it has. The teachings of Christ take time to come to earth." Such an attitude stems from a tragic misconception of time, from the strangely irrational notion that there is something in the very flow of time that will inevitably cure all ills. Actually, time itself is neutral; it can be used either destructively or constructively. More and more I feel that the people of ill will have used time much more effectively than have the people of good will. We will have to repent in this generation not merely for the hateful words and actions of the bad people but for the appalling silence of the good people. Human progress never rolls in on wheels of inevitability; it comes through the tireless efforts of men willing to be co-workers with God, and without this hard work, time itself becomes an ally of the forces of social stagnation. We must use time creatively, in the knowledge that the time is always ripe to do right. Now is the time to make real the promise of democracy and transform our pending national elegy into a creative psalm of brotherhood. Now is the time to lift our national policy from the quicksand of racial injustice to the solid rock of human dignity.

You speak of our activity in Birmingham as extreme. At first I was rather disappointed that fellow clergymen would see my nonviolent efforts as those of an extremist. I began thinking about the fact that I stand in the middle of two opposing forces in the Negro community. One is a force of complacency, made up in part of Negroes who, as a result of long years of oppression, are so drained of self-respect and a sense of "somebodiness" that they have adjusted to segregation; and in part of a few middleclass Negroes who, because of a degree of academic and economic security and because in some ways they profit by segregation, have become insensitive to the problems of the masses. The other force is one of bitterness and hatred, and it comes perilously close to advocating violence. It is expressed in the various black nationalist groups that are springing up across the nation, the largest and best-known being Elijah Muhammad's Muslim movement. Nourished by the Negro's frustration over the continued existence of racial discrimination, this movement is made up of people who have lost faith in America, who have absolutely repudiated Christianity, and who have concluded that the white man is an incorrigible "devil."

I have tried to stand between these two forces, saying that we need emulate neither the "do-nothingism" of the complacent nor the hatred and despair of the black nationalist. For there is the more excellent way of love and nonviolent protest. I am grateful to God that, through the influence of the Negro church, the way of nonviolence became an integral part of our struggle.

If this philosophy had not emerged, by now many streets of the South would, I am convinced, be flowing with blood. And I am further convinced that if our white brothers dismiss as "rabble-rousers" and "outside agitators" those of us who employ nonviolent direct action, and if they refuse to support our nonviolent efforts, millions of Negroes will, out of frustration and despair, seek solace and security in black-nationalist ideologies—a development that would inevitably lead to a frightening racial nightmare.

Oppressed people cannot remain oppressed forever. The yearning for freedom eventually manifests itself, and that is what has happened to the American Negro. Something within has reminded him of his birthright of freedom, and something without has reminded him that it can be gained. Consciously or unconsciously, he has been caught up by the *Zeitgeist*, and with his black brothers of Africa and his brown and yellow brothers of Asia, South America and the Caribbean, the United States Negro is moving with a sense of great urgency toward the promised land of racial justice. If one recognizes this vital urge that has engulfed the Negro community, one should readily understand why public demonstrations are taking place. The Negro has many peat-up resentments and latent frustrations, and he must release them. So let him march; let him make prayer pilgrimages to the city hall; let him go on free-dom rides—and try to understand why he must do so. If his repressed emotions are not released in nonviolent ways, they will seek expression through violence; this is not a threat but a fact of history. So I have not said to my people: "Get rid of your discontent." Rather, I have tried to say that this normal and healthy discontent can be channeled into the creative outlet of nonviolent direct action. And now this approach is being termed extremist.

But though I was initially disappointed at being categorized as an extremist, as I continued to think about the matter I gradually gained a measure of satisfaction from the label. Was not Jesus an extremist for love: "Love your enemies, bless them that curse you, do good to them that hate you, and pray for them which despitefully use you, and persecute you." Was not Amos an extremist for justice: "Let justice roll down like waters and righteousness like an ever-flowing stream." Was not Paul an extremist for the Christian gospel: "I bear in my body the marks of the Lord Jesus." Was not Martin Luther an extremist: "Here I stand; I cannot do otherwise, so help me God." And John Bunyan: "I will stay in jail to the end of my days before I make a butchery of my conscience." And Abraham Lincoln: "This nation cannot survive half slave and half free." And Thomas Jefferson: "We hold these truths to be self-evident, that all men are created equal . . ." So the question is not whether we will be extremists, but what kind of extremists we will be. Will we be extremists for hate or for love? Will we be extremists for the preservation of injustice or for the extension of justice? In that dramatic scene on Calvary's hill three men were crucified. We must never forget that all three were crucified for the same crime—the crime of extremism. Two were extremists for immorality, and thus fell below their environment. The other, Jesus Christ, was an extremist for love, truth and goodness, and there by rose above his environment. Perhaps the South, the nation and the world are in dire need of creative extremists.

I had hoped that the white moderate would see this need. Perhaps I was too optimistic; perhaps I expected too much. I suppose I should have realized that few members of the oppressor race can understand the deep groans and passionate yearnings of the oppressed race, and still fewer have the vision to see that injustice must be rooted out by strong, persistent and determined action. I am thankful, however, that some of our white brothers in the South have grasped the meaning of this social revolution and committed themselves to it. They are still all too few in quantity, but they are big in quality. Some—such as Ralph McGill, Lillian Smith, Harry Golden, James McBride Dabbs, Ann Braden and Sarah Patton Boyle—have written about our struggle in eloquent and prophetic terms. Others have marched with us down nameless streets of the South. They have languished in filthy, roach-infested jails, suffering the abuse and brutality of policemen who view them as "dirty nigger-lovers." Unlike so many of their moderate brothers and sisters, they have recognized the urgency of the moment and sensed the need for powerful "action" antidotes to combat the disease of segregation.

Let me take note of my other major disappointment I have been so greatly disappointed with the white church and its leadership. Of course, there are some notable exceptions. I am not unmindful of the fact that each of you has taken some significant stands on this issue. I commend you, Reverend Stallings, for your Christian stand on this past Sunday, in welcoming Negroes to your worship service on a nonsegregated basis. I commend the Catholic leaders of this state for integrating Spring Hill College several years ago.

But despite these notable exceptions, I must honestly reiterate that I have been disappointed with the church. I do not say this as one of those negative critics who can always find something wrong with the church. I say this as a minister of the gospel, who loves the church; who was nurtured in its bosom; who has been sustained by its spiritual blessings and who will remain true to it as long as the cord of life shall lengthen.

When I was suddenly catapulted into the leadership of the bus protest in Montgomery, Alabama, a few years ago, I felt we would be supported by the white church. I felt that the white ministers, priests and rabbis of the South would be among our strongest allies. Instead, some have been outright opponents, refusing to understand the freedom movement and misrepresenting its leaders; all too many others have been more cautious than courageous and have remained silent behind the anesthetizing security of stained-glass windows.

In spite of my shattered dreams, I came to Birmingham with the hope that the white religious leadership of this community would see the justice of our cause and, with deep moral concern, would serve as the channel through which our just grievances could reach the power structure. I had hoped that each of you would understand. But again I have been disappointed.

I have heard numerous southern religious leaders admonish their worshipers to comply with a desegregation decision because it is the law, but I have longed to hear white ministers declare: "Follow this decree because integration is morally right and because the Negro is your brother." In the midst of blatant injustices inflicted upon the Negro, I have watched white churchmen stand on the sideline and mouth pious irrelevancies and sanctimonious trivialities. In the midst of a mighty struggle to rid our nation of racial and economic injustice, I have heard many ministers say: "Those are social issues, with which the gospel has no real concern." And I have watched many churches commit themselves to a completely other-worldly religion which makes a strange, un-Biblical distinction between body and soul, between the sacred and the secular.

I have traveled the length and breadth of Alabama, Mississippi and all the other southern states. On sweltering summer days and crisp autumn mornings. I have looked at the South's beautiful churches with their lofty spires pointing heavenward. I have beheld the impressive outlines of her massive religious-education buildings. Over and over I have found myself asking: "What kind of people worship here? Who is their God? Where were their voices when the lips of Governor Barnett dripped with the words of interposition and nullification? Where were they when Governor Wallace gave a clarion call for defiance and hatred? Where were their voices of support to rise from the dark dungeons of complacency to the bright hills of creative protest?"

Yes, these questions are still in my mind. In deep disappointment I have wept over the laxity of the church. But be assured that my tears have been tears of love. There can be no deep disappointment where there is not deep love. Yes, I love the church. How could I do otherwise? I am in the rather unique position of being the son, the grandson and the great-grandson of preachers. Yes, I see the church as the body of Christ. But, oh! How we have blemished and scarred the body through social neglect and through fear of being nonconformists.

There was a time when the church was very powerful—in the time when the early Christians rejoiced at being deemed worthy to suffer for what they believed. In those days the church was not merely a thermometer that recorded the ideas and principles of popular opinions; it was a thermostat that transformed the mores of society. Whenever the early Christians entered a town, the people in power became disturbed and immediately sought to convict the Christians for being "disturbers of the peace" and "outside agitators." But the Christians pressed on, in the conviction that they were "a colony of heaven," called to obey God rather than man. Small in number, they were big in commitment. They were too God-intoxicated to be "astronomically intimidated." By their effort and example they brought an end to such ancient evils as infanticide and gladiatorial contests.

Things are different now. So often the contemporary church is a weak, ineffectual voice with an uncertain sound. So often it is an archdefender of the status quo. Far from being disturbed by the presence of the church, the power structure of the average community is consoled by the church's silent—and often even vocal—sanction of things as they are.

But the judgment of God is upon the church as never before. If today's church does not recapture the sacrificial spirit of the early church, it will lose its authenticity, forfeit the loyalty of millions, and be dismissed as an irrelevant social club with no meaning for the twentieth century. Every day I meet young people whose disappointment with the church has turned into outright disgust.

Perhaps I have once again been too optimistic. Is organized religion too inextricably bound to the status quo to save our nation and the world? Perhaps I must turn my faith to the inner spiritual church, the church within the church, as the true *ekklesia* and the hope of the world. But again I am thankful to God that some noble souls from the ranks of organized religion have broken loose from the paralyzing chains of conformity and joined us as active partners in the struggle for freedom. They have left their secure congregations and walked the streets of Albany, Georgia, with us. They have gone down the highways of the South on tortuous rides for freedom. Yes, they have gone to jail with us. Some have been dismissed from their churches, have lost the support of their bishops and fellow ministers. But they have acted in the faith that right defeated is stronger than evil triumphant. Their witness has been the spiritual salt that has preserved the true meaning of the gospel in these troubled times. They have carved a tunnel of hope through the dark mountain of disappointment.

I hope the church as a whole will meet the challenge of this decisive hour. But even if the church does not come to the aid of justice, I have no despair about the future. I have no fear about the outcome of our struggle in Birmingham, even if our motives are at present misunderstood. We will reach the goal of freedom in Birmingham and all over the nation, because the goal of America is freedom. Abused and scorned though we may be, our destiny is tied up with America's destiny. Before the pilgrims landed at Plymouth, we were here. Before the pen of Jefferson etched the majestic words of the Declaration on Independence across the pages of history, we were here. For more than two centuries our forebears labored in this country without wages; they made cotton king; they built the homes of their masters while suffering gross injustice and shameful humiliation—and yet out of a bottomless vitality they continued to thrive and develop. If the inexpressible cruelties of slavery could not stop us, the opposition we now face will surely fail. We will win our freedom because the scared heritage of our nation and the eternal will of God are embodied in our echoing demands.

Before closing I feel impelled to mention one other point in your statement that has troubled me profoundly. You warmly commended the Birmingham police force for keeping "order" and "preventing violence." I doubt that you would have so warmly commended the police force if you had seen its dogs sinking their teeth into unarmed, nonviolent Negroes. I doubt that you would so quickly comment the policemen if you were to observe their ugly and inhumane treatment of Negroes here in the city jail; if you were to watch them push and curse old Negro women and young Negro girls; if you were to see them slap and kick old Negro men and young boys; if you were to observe them, as they did on two occasions, refuse to give us food because we wanted to sing our grace together. I cannot join you in your praise of the Birmingham police department.

It is true that the police have exercised a degree of discipline in handling the demonstrators. In this sense they have conducted themselves rather "nonviolently" in public. But for what purpose? To preserve the evil system of segregation. Over the past few years I have consistently preached that nonviolence demands that the means we use must be as pure as the ends we seek. I have tried to make clear that it is wrong to use immoral means to attain moral ends. But now I must affirm that it is just as wrong, or perhaps even more so, to use moral means to preserve immoral ends. Perhaps Mr. Connor and his policemen have been rather nonviolent in public, as was Chief Pritchett in Albany, Georgia, but they have used the moral means of nonviolence to maintain the immoral end of racial injustice. As T. S. Eliot has said: "The last temptation is the greatest treason: To do the right deed for the wrong reason."

I wish you had commended the Negro sit-inners and demonstrators of Birmingham for their sublime courage, their willingness to suffer and their amazing discipline in the midst of great provocation. One day the South will recognize its real heroes. They will be the James Merediths, with the noble sense of purpose that enables them to face jeering and hostile mobs, and with the agonizing loneliness that characterizes the life of the pioneer. They will be old, oppressed, battered Negro women, symbolized in a 72-year-old woman in Montgomery, Alabama, who rose up with a sense of dignity and with her people decided not to ride segregated buses, and who responded with ungrammatical profundity to on who inquired about her weariness: "My feets is tired, but my soul is at rest." They will be the young high school and college students, the young ministers of the gospel and a host of their elders, courageously and nonviolently sitting in at lunch counters and willingly going to jail for conscience' sake. One day the South will know that when these disinherited children of God sat down at lunch counters, they were in reality standing up for what is best in the American dream and for the most sacred values in our Judeo-Christian heritage, thereby bringing our nation back to those great wells of democracy which were dug deep by the founding fathers in their formulation of the Constitution and the Declaration of Independence.

Never before have I written so long a letter. I'm afraid it is much too long to take your precious time. I can assure you that it would have been much shorter if I had been writing from a comfortable desk, but what else can one do when he is alone in a narrow jail cell, other than write long letters, think long thoughts and pray long prayers?

If I have said anything in this letter that overstates the truth and indicates an unreasonable impatience, I beg you to forgive me. If I have said anything that understates the truth and indicates my having a patience that allows me to settle for anything less than brotherhood, I beg God to forgive me.

I hope this letter find you strong in the faith. I also hope that circumstances will soon make it possible for me to meet each of you, not as an integrationist or a civil-rights leader but as a fellow clergyman and a Christian brother. Let us all hope that the dark clouds of racial prejudice will soon pass away and the deep fog of misunderstanding will be lifted from our fear-drenched communities, and in some not too distant tomorrow the radiant stars of love and brotherhood will shine over our great nation with all their scintillating beauty.

Yours for the cause of Peace and Brotherhood,

Martin Luther King, Jr.

In the year prior to the Birmingham incident, President Kennedy had submitted a new and broad civil rights bill to the Congress. The bill was intended to expand the provisions of two previous pieces of legislation: the 1957 Civil Rights Act and the 1960 Civil Rights Act. The 1957 Act established the Civil Rights Commission, while both pieces of legislation strengthened the Justice Department's authority to act on federal voting irregularities. Civil rights advocates believed that neither bill went far enough to protect minority rights.

As discussion of the pending civil rights bill took center stage, civil rights leaders began to make plans for another March on Washington. Support for the 1963 March came from many corners. Organized labor and religious groups provided monetary and administrative resources to augment the leadership of the main civil rights organizations. In many ways, the March on Washington was a watershed event in the civil rights movement. It represented the high point of the movement—a vast majority of civil rights organizations acted in a cooperative and concerted effort. Conversely, debates emerged between traditional organizations (e.g., SCLS and the NAACP) and the students of SNCC over the content of the speeches, the pace of change, and the proposed response to increasingly violent white resistance.[8] This behind-the-scene struggle foreshadowed the demise of large-scale collective action. For all outward appearances, however, the March was a shining triumph.

Contrary to the Kennedy administration's worst fears, the March was an exceedingly peaceful event. Crowd estimates ranged from 250,000 to more than 500,000 (with millions more watching on television). Whatever the correct number, the grounds of the Lincoln Memorial were filled with a multiracial sampling of Americans. The highlight of the event was Martin Luther King's majestic speech **"I Have a Dream."**

With his brilliant oratorical skills in full flight, King presented a vision of an integrated society in which ". . . little black boys and little black girls will be able to join hands with little white boys and white girls as sisters and brothers." A society that lived up to the "true meaning of its creed—we hold these truths to be self-evident, that all men are created equal." While at this exact point in time all things seemed possible, three months later America was once again tossed into racial discord.

I HAVE A DREAM
■

Martin Luther King Jr.

The year 1963 was the centennial of the signing of the Emancipation Proclamation. It was truly a momentous year in American History and in the life of Martin Luther King, Jr.

Despite opposition from the governors of Alabama and Mississippi, the president of the United States, John F. Kennedy, authorized federal marshals to escort a few black students to register at the University of Mississippi and the University of Alabama. "Bull" Connor, the head of Birmingham, Alabama's, police department ordered his officers to turn fire hoses and police dogs on young demonstrators; as television cameras captured this horrible scene, the nation gasped in disbelief and revulsion. Medgar Evers, a 37-year-old NAACP field secretary in Jackson, Mississippi, was murdered on his front porch on June 12. Riots occurred throughout the summer. The nation stood on the brink of racial civil war. It needed a prophet who could help see through the smoke left by gunpowder and bombs.

Martin Luther King, Jr., who published Why We Can't Wait *at this time, was the prophet of the hour. Although many of the phrases and themes that appear in "I Have a Dream" had often been repeated by Dr. King, this is his most well-known and most often quoted speech. He delivered it before the Lincoln Memorial on August 28, 1963, as the keynote address of the March on Washington, D.C., for Civil Rights. Television cameras allowed the entire nation to hear and see him plead for justice and freedom. Mrs. Coretta King once commented, "At that moment it seemed as if the Kingdom of God appeared. But it only lasted for a moment."*

I am happy to join with you today in what will go down in history as the greatest demonstration for freedom in the history of our nation.

Fivescore years ago, a great American, in whose symbolic shadow we stand today, signed the Emancipation Proclamation. This momentous decree came as a great beacon light of hope to millions of Negro slaves who had been seared in the flames of withering injustice. It came as a joyous daybreak to end the long night of their captivity.

But one hundred years later, the Negro still is not free; one hundred years later, the life of the Negro is still sadly crippled by the manacles of segregation and the chains of discrimination; one hundred years later, the Negro lives on a lonely island of poverty in the midst of a vast ocean of material prosperity; one hundred years later, the Negro is still languished in the corners of American society and finds himself in exile in his own land.

So we've come here today to dramatize a shameful condition. In a sense we've come to our nation's capital to cash a check. When the architects of our republic wrote the magnificent words of the Constitution and the Declaration of Independence, they were signing a promissory note to which every American was to fall heir. This note was the promise that all men, yes, black men as well as white men, would be guaranteed the unalienable rights of life, liberty, and the pursuit of happiness.

It is obvious today that America has defaulted on this promissory note in so far as her citizens of color are concerned. Instead of honoring this sacred obligation, America has given the Negro people a bad check; a check which has come back marked "insufficient funds." We refuse to believe that there are insufficient funds in the great vaults of opportunity of this nation. And so we've come to cash this check, a check that will give us upon demand the riches of freedom and the security of justice.

We have also come to this hallowed spot to remind America of the fierce urgency of now. This is not time to engage in the luxury of cooling off or to take the tranquilizing drug of gradualism. Now is the time to make real the promises of democracy; now is the time to rise from the dark and desolate valley of segregation to the sunlit path of racial justice; now is the time to lift our nation from the quicksands of racial injustice to the solid rock of brotherhood; now is the time to make justice a reality for all God's children. It would be fatal for the nation to overlook the urgency of the moment. This sweltering summer of the Negro's legitimate discontent will not pass until there is an invigorating autumn of freedom and equality.

Nineteen sixty-three is not an end, but a beginning. And those who hope that the Negro needed to blow off steam and will now be content, will have a rude awakening if the nation returns to business as usual.

There will be neither rest nor tranquility in America until the Negro is granted his citizenship rights. The whirlwinds of revolt will continue to shake the foundations of our nation until the bright day of justice emerges.

But there is something that I must say to my people who stand on the warm threshold which leads into the palace of justice. In the process of gaining our rightful place we must not be guilty of wrongful deeds.

Let us not seek to satisfy our thirst for freedom by drinking from the cup of bitterness and hatred. We must forever conduct our struggle on the high plane of dignity and discipline. We must not allow our creative protest to degenerate into physical violence. Again and again we must rise to the majestic heights of meeting physical force with soul force.

The marvelous new militancy which has engulfed the Negro community must not lead us to a distrust of all white people, for many of our white brothers, as evidenced by their presence here today, have come to realize that their destiny is tied up with our destiny and they have come to realize that their freedom is inextricably bound to our freedom. This offense we share mounted to storm the battlements of injustice must be carried forth by a biracial army. We cannot walk alone.

And as we walk, we must make the pledge that we shall always march ahead. We cannot turn back. There are those who are asking the devotees of civil rights, "When will you be satisfied?" We can never be satisfied as long as the Negro is the victim of the unspeakable horrors of police brutality.

We can never be satisfied as long as our bodies, heavy with fatigue of travel, cannot gain lodging in the motels of the highways and the hotels of the cities. We cannot be satisfied as long as the Negro's basic mobility is from a smaller ghetto to a larger one.

We can never be satisfied as long as our children are stripped of their selfhood and robbed of their dignity by signs stating "for whites only." We cannot be satisfied as long as a Negro in Mississippi cannot vote and a Negro in New York believes he has nothing for which to vote. No, we are not satisfied, and we will not be satisfied until justice rolls down like waters and righteousness like a mighty stream.

I am not unmindful that some of you come here out of excessive trials and tribulation. Some of you have come fresh from narrow jail cells. Some of you have come from areas where your quest for freedom left you battered by the storms of persecution and staggered by the winds of police brutality. You have been the veterans of creative suffering. Continue to work with the faith that unearned suffering is redemptive.

Go back to Mississippi; go back to Alabama; go back to South Carolina; go back to Georgia; go back to Louisiana; go back to the slums and ghettos of the northern cities, knowing that somehow this situation can, and will be changed. Let us not wallow in the valley of despair.

So I say to you, my friends that even though we must face the difficulties of today and tomorrow, I still have a dream. It is a dream deeply rooted in the American dream that one day this nation will rise up and live out the true meaning of its creed—we hold these truths to be self-evident, that all men are created equal.

I have a dream that one day on the red hills of Georgia, sons of former slaves and sons of former slave-owners will be able to sit down together at the table of brotherhood.

I have a dream that one day, even the state of Mississippi, a state sweltering with the heat of injustice, sweltering with the heat of oppression, will be transformed into an oasis of freedom and justice.

I have a dream my four little children will one day live in a nation where they will not be judged by the color of their skin but by the content of their character. I have a dream today!

I have a dream that one day, down in Alabama, with its vicious racists, with its governor having his lips dripping with the words of interposition and nullification, that one day, right there in Alabama, little black boys and black girls will be able to join hands with little white boys and white girls as sisters and brothers. I have a dream today!

I have a dream that one day every valley shall be exalted, every hill and mountain shall be made low, the rough places shall be made plain, and the crooked places shall be made straight and the glory of the Lord will be revealed and all flesh shall see it together.

This is our hope. This is the faith that I go back to the South with.

With this faith we will be able to hew out of the mountain of despair a stone of hope. With this faith we will be able to transform the jangling discords of our nation into a beautiful symphony of brotherhood.

With this faith we will be able to work together, to pray together, to struggle together, to go to jail together, to stand up for freedom together, knowing that we will be free one day. This will be the day when all of God's children will be able to sing with new meaning—"my country 'tis of thee; sweet land of liberty; of thee I sing; land where my fathers died, land of the pilgrim's pride; from every mountain side, let freedom ring"—and if America is to be a great nation, this must become true.

So let freedom ring from the prodigious hilltops of New Hampshire.

Let freedom ring from the mighty mountains of New York.

Let freedom ring from the heightening Alleghenies of Pennsylvania.

Let freedom ring from the snow-capped Rockies of Colorado.

Let freedom ring from the curvaceous slopes of California.

But not only that.

Let freedom ring from Stone Mountain of Georgia.

Let freedom ring from Lookout Mountain of Tennessee.

Let freedom ring from every hill and molehill of Mississippi, from every mountainside, let freedom ring.

And when we allow freedom to ring, when we let it ring from every village and hamlet, from every state and city, we will be able to speed up that day when all of God's children—black men and white men, Jews and Gentiles, Catholics and Protestants—will be able to join hands and to sing in the words of the old Negro spiritual, "Free at last, free at last; thank God Almighty, we are free at last."

The euphoria of the March on Washington quickly gave way to despair the following month as white supremacists bombed the 16th Street Baptist church in Birmingham killing four young girls attending Sunday school. The irony of the bombing was obvious—Birmingham had been the site of one of the Movement's greatest victories. The church bombing was a stark reminder of day-to-day racial "troubles" that continued to plague American society. The Kennedy assassination 2 months later compounded matters. When Texan Lyndon B. Johnson ascended to the presidency, civil rights activists were understandably concerned about the fate of the pending legislation.

As it turned out, Johnson's political acumen and legislative experience were critical to the final passage of the **Civil Rights Act of 1964**. *Overriding a southern filibuster, Congress enacted the most wide-sweeping civil rights bill of the 20th century. The Act was designed to protect African-American rights in almost every sphere of public life. Titles of the bill covered voting rights (Title I), public accommodations and education (Titles II, III, and IV), federally assisted programs (Title VI), and employment (Title VII). In addition, the bill extended the life of the Civil Rights Commission (Title V) created the Equal Employment Opportunity Commission (Title VII) and the Community Relations Service (Title X). The signature of the legislation was its provision of enforcement authority to the relevant government agencies. In essence, the Act gave "teeth" to the rights spelled out 100 years earlier in the Civil War Amendments. For example, to protect black rights in public accommodations, section 204(a) of Title II states that ". . . a civil action for preventive relief, including an application for a permanent or temporary injunction, restraining order, or other order, may be instituted by the person aggrieved and . . . the court may permit the Attorney General to intervene in such civil action." By providing federal support for judicial relief, the Civil Rights Act of 1964 paved the way for massive social change in America.*

CIVIL RIGHTS ACT(1964)

———————————————●———————————————

Civil Rights Act, P.L. 88–352 (1964)

TITLE I—VOTING RIGHTS

Sec.101. Section 2004 of the Revised Statutes (42 U.S.C. 1971), as amended by section 131 of the Civil Rights Act of 1957 (71 Stat. 637), and as further amended by section 601 of the Civil Rights Act of 1960 (74 Stat. 90), is further amended as follows:

(a) Insert "1" after "(a)" in subsection (a) and add at the end of subsection (a) the following new paragraphs:

"(2) No person acting under color of law shall—

"(A) in determining whether any individual is qualified under State law or laws to vote in any Federal election, apply any standard, practice, or procedure different from the standards, practices or procedures applied under such law or laws to other individuals within the same country, parish, or similar political subdivision who have been found by State officials to be qualified to vote;

"(B) deny the right of any individual to vote in any Federal election because of an error or omission on any record or paper relating to any application, registration, or other act requisite to voting, if such error or omission is not material in determining whether such individual is qualified under State law to vote in such election; or

"(C) employ any literacy test as a qualification for voting in any Federal election unless (i) such test is administered to each individual and is conducted wholly in writing, and (ii) a certified copy of the test and of the answers given by the individual is furnished to him within twenty-five days of the submission of his request made within the period of time during which records and papers are required to be retained and preserved pursuant to title III of the Civil Rights Act of 1960 (42 U.S.C. 1974-74e; 74 Stat. 88) : Provided, however, That the Attorney General may enter into agreements with appropriate State or local authorities that preparation, conduct, and maintenance of such tests in accordance with the provisions of applicable State or local law, including such special provisions as are necessary in the preparation, conduct, and maintenance of such tests for persons who are blind or otherwise physically handicapped, meet the purposes of this subparagraph and constitute compliance therewith.

TITLE II—INJUNCTIVE RELIEF AGAINST DISCRIMINATION IN PLACES OF PUBLIC ACCOMMODATION

Sec. 201. (a) All persons shall be entitled to the full and equal enjoyment of the goods, services, facilities, privileges, advantages, and accommodations of any place of public accommodation, as defined in this section, without discrimination or segregation on the ground of race, color, religion, or national origin.

TITLE III—DESEGREGATION OF PUBLIC FACILITIES

Sec. 301. (A) Whenever the Attorney General receives a complaint in writing signed by an individual to the effect that he is being deprived of or threatened with the loss of his right to the equal protection of the laws, on account of his race, color, religion, or national origin, by being denied equal utilization of any public facility which is owned, operated, or managed by or on behalf of any State or subdivision thereof, other than a public school or public college as defined in section 401 of title IV hereof, and the Attorney General believes the complaint is meritorious and certifies that the signer or signers of such complaint are unable, in his judgment, to initiate and maintain appropriate legal proceedings for relief and that the institution of an action will materially further the orderly progress of desegregation in public facilities, the Attorney General is authorized to institute for or in the name of the United States a civil action in any appropriate district court of the United States against such parties and for such relief as may be appropriate, and such court shall have and shall exercise jurisdiction of proceedings instituted pursuant to this section. The Attorney General may implead as defendants such additional parties as are or become necessary to the grant of effective relief hereunder.

TITLE IV—DESEGREGATION OF PUBLIC EDUCATION

Sec. 401. As used in this title—

    (a) "Commissioner" means the Commissioner of Education.

    (b) "Desegregation" means the assignment of students to public schools and within such schools without regard to their race, color, religion, or national origin, but "desegregation" shall not mean the assignment of students to public schools in order to overcome racial imbalance.

    (c) "Public school" means any elementary or secondary educational institution, and "public college" means any institution of higher education or any technical or vocational school above the secondary school level, provided that such public school or public college is operated by a State, subdivision of a State, or governmental agency within a State, or operated wholly or predominantly from or through the use of governmental funds or property, or funds or property derived from a governmental source.

    (d) "School board" means any agency or agencies which administer a system of one or more public schools and any other agency which is responsible for the assignment of students to or within such system.

Sec. 402. The commissioner shall conduct a survey and make a report to the President and the Congress, within two years of the enactment of this title, concerning the lack of availability of equal educational opportunities for individuals by reason of race, color, religion, or national origin in public educational institutions at all levels in the United States, its territories and possessions, and the District of Columbia.

TITLE V—COMMISSION ON CIVIL RIGHTS

Sec. 501. Section 102 of the Civil Rights Act of 1957 (42 U.S.C. 1975a; 71 Stat. 634) is amended to read as follows.

    "Sec. 104. (a) The Commission shall—

        "(1) investigate allegations in writing under oath or affirmation that certain citizens of the United States are being deprived of their right to vote and have that vote counted by reason of their color, race, religion, or national origin; which writing, under oath or affirmation, shall set forth the facts upon which such belief or beliefs are based;

"(2) study and collect information concerning legal developments constituting a denial of equal protection of the laws under the Constitution because of race, color, religion or national origin or in the administration of justice;

"(3) appraise the laws and policies of the Federal Government with respect to denials of equal protection of the laws under the Constitution because of race, color, religion or national origin or in the administration of justice;

"(4) serve as a national clearinghouse for information in respect to denials of equal protection of the laws because of race, color, religion or national origin, including but not limited to the fields of voting, education, housing, employment, the use of public facilities, and transportation, or in the administration of justice;

"(5) investigate allegations, made in writing and under oath or affirmation, that citizens of the United States are unlawfully being accorded or denied the right to vote, or to have their votes properly counted, in any election of presidential electors, Members of the United States Senate, or of the House of Representatives, as a result of any pattern or practice of fraud or discrimination in the conduct of such election; and . . ."

TITLE VI—NONDISCRIMINATION IN FEDERALLY ASSISTED PROGRAMS

Sec. 601. No person in the United States shall, on the ground of race, color, or national origin, be excluded from participation in, be denied the benefits of, or be subjected to discrimination under any program or activity receiving Federal financial assistance.

TITLE VII—EQUAL EMPLOYMENT OPPORTUNITY

Sec. 701. For the purposes of this title—

(a) The term "person" includes one or more individuals, labor unions, partnerships, associations, corporations, legal representatives,

DISCRIMINATION BECAUSE OF RACE, COLOR, RELIGION, SEX, OR NATIONAL ORIGIN

Sec. 703. (a) It shall be an unlawful employment practice for an employer—

(1) to fail or refuse to hire or to discharge any individual, or otherwise to discriminate against any individual with respect to his compensation, terms, conditions, or privileges of employment, because of such individual's race, color, religion, sex, or national origin; or

(2) to limit, segregate, or classify his employees in any way which would deprive or tend to deprive any individual of employment opportunities or otherwise adversely affect his status as an employee, because of such individual's race, color, religion, sex, or national origin.

(b) It shall be an unlawful employment practice for an employment agency to fail or refuse to refer for employment, or otherwise to discriminate against, any individual because of his race, color, religion, sex, or national origin, or to classify or refer for employment any individual on the basis of his race, color, religion, sex, or national origin.

EQUAL EMPLOYMENT OPPORTUNITY COMMISSION

Sec. 705. (a) There is hereby created a Commission to be known as the Equal Employment Opportunity Commission, which shall be composed of five members, not more than three of whom shall be members of the dame political party, who shall be appointed by the president by and with the advice and consent of the Senate.

(g) The Commission shall have power—

(1) to cooperate with and, with their consent, utilize regional, State, local, and other agencies, both public and private, and individuals;

(2) to pay to witnesses whose depositions are taken or who are summoned before the Commission or any of its agents the same witness and mileage fees as are paid to witnesses in the courts of the United States;

(3) to furnish to persons subject to this title such technical assistance as they may request to further their compliance with this title or an order issued thereunder;

(4) upon the request of (i) any employer, whose employees or some of them, or (ii) any labor organization, whose members or some of them, refuse or threaten to refuse to cooperate in effectuating the provisions of this title, to assist in such effectuation by conciliation or such other remedial action as is provided by this title;

(5) to make such technical studies as are appropriate to effectuate the purposes and policies of this title and to make the results of such studies available to the public;

(6) to refer matters to the Attorney General with recommendations for intervention in a civil action brought by an aggrieved party under section 706, or for the institution of a civil action by the Attorney General under section 707, and to advise, consult, and assist the Attorney General on such matters.

(h) Attorneys appointed under this section may, at the direction of the Commission, appear for and represent the Commission in any case in court.

(i) The Commission shall, in any of its educational or promotional activities, cooperate with other departments and agencies in the performance of such educational and promotional activities.

(j) All officers, agents, attorneys, and employees of the Commission shall be subject to the provisions of section 9 of the Act of August 2, 1939, as amended (the Hatch Act), not withstanding any exemption contained in such section.

TITLE X—ESTABLISHMENT OF COMMUNITY RELATIONS SERVICE

Sec. 1001. (a) There is hereby established in and as a part of the Department of Commerce a Community Relations Service (hereinafter referred to as the "Service"), which shall be headed by a Director who shall be appointed by the President with the advice and consent of the Senate for a term of four years. The Director is authorized to appoint, subject to the civil service laws and regulations, such other personnel as may be necessary to enable the Service to carry out its functions and duties, and to fix their compensation in accordance with the Classification Act of 1949, as amended The Director is further authorized to procure services as authorized by section 15 of the Act of August 2, 1946 (60 Sat. 810; 5 U.S.C. 55 (a)), but at rates for individuals no in excess of $75 per diem.

Sec. 1002. It shall be the function of the Service to provide assistance to communities and persons therein in resolving disputes, disagreements, or difficulties relating to discriminatory practices based on race, color, or national origin which impair the rights of persons in such communities under the Constitution or laws of the United States or which affect or may affect interstate commerce. The Service may offer its services in cases of such disputes, disagreements, or difficulties whenever, in its judgment, peaceful relations among the citizens of the community involved are threatened thereby, and it may offer its services either upon its own motion or upon the request of an appropriate State or local official or other interested person.

Although the Civil Rights Act of 1964 was a significant victory, widespread discrimination remained a fact of life for most southern blacks. In early 1965, King and the SCLC decided to up the ante by staging a protest march from Selma to Montgomery demanding black voting rights.[9] True to inelasticity assumption, Alabama Governor George Wallace ordered state troopers to attack the marchers with teargas and billyclubs. Tragically, two activists were killed during the height of the activities (the Reverend James Reeb and Viola Liuzzo—a white volunteer). Once again, federal troops were called in to restore order. In his famous "We Shall Overcome Speech" President Johnson informed a joint session of Congress of his intent to push forward on the issue of civil rights. Two days later, he submitted strict voting legislation for congressional approval.

Southern voting officials routinely engaged in obstructionist strategies designed to prevent blacks from exercising their right to vote. Massive civil disobedience nonetheless created a prevailing tide in public opinion that pushed Congress to shift the burden of proof from the victims to the perpetrators. In 1965, the Congress passed the **Voting Rights Act**. *The key provisions of the Act are presented in the following selection. The law was discretely applicable to the so-called "covered jurisdictions" in the states of Alabama, Alaska, Georgia, Louisiana, Mississippi, South Carolina, Virginia, and about 26 counties in North Carolina. These jurisdictions were identified as having maintained "tests or devices" as a prerequisite to voting and had less than 50% of the total voting-age population registered to vote in the 1964 presidential elections. The Act banned voting prequalifications (Section 2), suspended the use of literacy tests or other qualifying tests for voting (Section 4), required any changes in local election laws in covered jurisdictions to be precleared by the Department of Justice (Section 5), authorized the appointment of federal examiners empowered to order the registration of eligible voters in suspect jurisdictions (Section 6), and outlawed the poll tax as a precondition to voting (Section 10). The impact of the 1965 Voting Rights Act on black political participation cannot be overemphasized.*[10] *Federal voting rights protections such as the removal of voting "qualifications," "tests and devices," poll taxes, the appointment of federal examiners, and the threat of legal and financial sanctions against violators ensured the participation of a substantial number of new black voters.*

VOTING RIGHTS ACT (1965)

■

Excerpt from Voting Rights Act, P.L. 89–110 (1965)

Sec. 2. No voting qualification or prerequisite to voting, or standard, practice or procedure shall be imposed or applied by any State or political subdivision to deny or abridge the right of any citizen of the United States to vote on account of race or color.

Sec. 4. (a) To assure that the right of citizens of the United States to vote is not denied or abridged on account of race or color, no citizen shall be denied the right to vote in any Federal, State, or local election because of his failure to comply with any test or device in any State with respect to which the determinations have been made under subsection (b) or in any political subdivision with respect to which such determinations have been made as a separate unit, unless the United States District Court for the District of Columbia in an action for a declaratory judgment brought by such State or subdivision against the United States has determined that no such test or device has been used during the five years preceding the filing of the action for the purpose or with the effect of denying or abridging the right to vote on account of race or color: *Provided.* That no such declaratory judgment shall issue with respect to any plaintiff for a period of five years after the entry of a final judgment of any court of the United Staes, other than the denial of a declaratory judgment under this section, whether entered prior to or after the enactment of this Act, determining that denials or abridgments of the right to vote on account of race or color through the use of such tests or devices have occurred anywhere in the territory of such plaintiff.

Sec. 5. Whenever a State or political subdivision with respect to which the prohibitions set forth in section 4(a) are in effect shall enact or seek to administer any voting qualification or prerequisite to voting, or standard, practice, or procedure with respect to voting different from that in force or effect on November 1, 1964, such State or subdivision may institute an action in the United States District Court for the District of Columbia for a declaratory judgment that such qualification, prerequisite, standard, practice, or procedure does not have the purpose and will not have the effect of denying or abridging the right to vote on account of race or color, and unless and until the court enters such judgment no person shall be denied the right to vote for failure to comply with such qualification, prerequisite, standard, practice, or procedure.

Attorney General certifies with respect to any political subdivision named in, or included within the scope of, determinations made under section 4(b) that (1) he has received complaints in writing from twenty or more residents of such political subdivision alleging that they have been denied the right to vote under color of law on account of race or color, and that he believes such complaints to be meritorious, or (2) that in his judgment (considering, among other factors, whether the ratio of nonwhite persons to white persons registered to vote within such subdivision appears to him to be reasonably attributable to violations of the fifteenth amendment or whether substantial evidence exists that bona fide efforts are being made within such subdivision to comply with the 15th Amendment), the appointment of examiners is otherwise necessary to enforce the guarantees of the 15th Amendment, (the *Civil Service Commission* shall appoint as many examiners for such subdivision as it may deem appropriate to prepare and maintain lists of persons eligible to vote in Federal, State, and local elections.)

Sec. 10. (a) The Congress finds that the requirement of the payment of a poll tax as a precondition to voting (i) precludes persons of limited means from voting or imposes unreasonable financial hardship upon such persons as a precondition to their exercise of the franchise, (ii) does not bear a reasonable relationship to any legitimate State interest in the conduct of elections, and (iii) in some areas has the purpose or effect of denying persons the right to vote because of race or color. Upon the basis of these findings, Congress declares that the constitutional right of citizens to vote is denied or abridged in some areas by the requirement of the payment of a poll tax as a precondition to voting.

(b) In the exercise of the powers of Congress under section 5 of the fourteenth amendment and section 2 of the 15th Amendment, the Attorney General is authorized and directed to institute forthwith in the name of the

United States such actions, including actions against States or political sub-divisions, for declaratory judgment or injunctive relief against the enforcement of any requirement of the payment of a poll tax as a precondition to voting, or substitute therefore enacted after November 1, 1964, as will be necessary to implement the declaration of subsection (a) and the purposes of this section.

Although nonviolent direct action was basically a successful political tactic, it had limitations. In the first instance, it was logistically difficult to maintain—it required the mobilization and organization of thousands of volunteers. Second, it demanded a tremendous amount of emotional commitment—activists were asked to make great sacrifices in the face of economic, psychological, and physical intimidation. Third, the fact that activities were public meant that participants were visible targets for white reprisals—employers, bankers, and business associates. Finally, the presence of Malcolm X and the Nation of Islam, the increasing radicalization of SNCC, and the seeds of the Black Panthers presented serious challenges to the intellectual and organizational hegemony of the traditional civil rights organizations. Although nonviolent direct action changed the political and economic status of some African-Americans, the slow pace of change resulted in a splintering of the "traditional" coalition.

STUDY QUESTIONS

1. The Montgomery Bus Boycott was the first example of the nonviolent direct action approach to receive widespread public attention. The victory in Montgomery propelled people like Rosa Parks and Dr. Martin Luther King, Jr. to the forefront of the civil rights movement. What was the role of leadership during this phase of the movement? How did civil rights leaders establish legitimacy with the African-American community, on the one hand, and white leadership on the other? Which community assets were utilized by the civil rights leadership?

2. What role did television play in the nonviolent direct action stage of the civil rights movement? How was the issue "framed" in television accounts of the events in places like Montgomery and Birmingham? How did it effect the national dialogue on race? For instance, did television coverage of the March on Washington influence the public's perception of civil rights?

3. What are the central assumptions of the nonviolent direct action approach? What are the primary tactics? How were they employed by different groups of activists? Which tactics were most successful? Why?

4. In "*Message to the Grass Roots*" Malcolm X articulates his critique of King's platform for racial change. What is the basis for his criticism of nonviolent direct action? What are the key elements of Malcolm's

agenda for racial reform? How is it different from that presented by mainstream civil rights organizations? What role does the external white community have in his model?

5. How did the *Voting Rights Act* and the *Civil Rights Act* provide for racial equality? Were these two pieces of legislation a direct result of the nonviolent stage of the movement, or were there other factors that led to their passage? (e.g., the legislative skill of President Johnson). Have they, and their subsequent revisions, provided for equality today? If so, how? If not, what needs to be done to ensure the social and political rights of African-Americans?

Notes

1. See McAdam for a fuller discussion of this point.

2. Vicki L. Crawford et al. (eds) *Women in the civil rights movement: Trailblazers and torch-bearers, 1941–1965* (Brooklyn: Carlson Publishing); David J. Garrow. *The Montgomery bus boycott and the women who started it: The memoir of Jo Ann Gibson Robinson* (Knoxville: University of Tennessee Press) 1987.

3. Stewart Burns (ed.). *Daybreak of freedom: The Montgomery Bus Boycott.* (Chapel Hill, North Carolina: University of North Carolina Press) 1997.

4. Charles Bloom. *Class, Race, and the Civil rights movement* (Bloomington, Indiana: Indiana University Press) 1987.

5. Clayborne Carson. *In Struggle: SNCC and the Black awakening of the 1960s.* (Cambridge, Mass.: Harvard University Press) 1944.

6. Adult members of the black community claimed that these tactics were too confrontational. For example, jailing the students would give them a criminal record thus jeopardizing their futures. But as the strategy proved successful, adults supported SNCC activities.

7. Alex Haley (ed.) *The autobiography of Malcolm X.* (New York: Grove) 1965. Malcolm X. *Malcolm X speaks.* (New York: Grove Press) 1966; E. Victor Wolfenstein, *The victims of democracy: Malcolm X and the black revolution.* (Berkeley: University of California Press) 1981.

8. In perhaps the most well known rift, A. Phillip Randolph makes a personal plea to SNCC leadership to mute their criticism of Kennedy's record on civil rights. Also, refer back to Malcolm's **"Message to the Grassroots"** for a devastating critique of the march. Regarding white involvement Malcolm said, "It's just like when you've got some coffee that's too black, which means it's too strong. What do you do? You integrate it with cream, you make it weak. But if you pour too much cream in it, you won't even know you ever had coffee."

9. David J. Garrow. *Protest at Selma.* (New Haven: Yale University Press) 1978.

10. Chandler Davidson and Bernhard Grofman (eds.) *Quiet revolution in the South: The impact of the Voting Rights Act 1965—1990* (Princeton: Princeton University Press) 1994. Steven F. Lawson. *Black ballots: Voting rights in the South, 1944–1969.* (New York: Columbia University Press) 1976; Frank Parker. *Black votes count: Political empowerment in Mississippi after 1965* (Chapel Hill: University of North Carolina Press) 1990.

BLACK POWER: 1961–1972

As early as 1961, SNCC and CORE begun to question the premise that social change could bring on political and economic change. In essence, they wanted "more than a hamburger." Their initial goal was to wrest control of political authority in the South. Eating at lunch counters was relatively meaningless, they reasoned, if the black community had little control over public resources or was unable to hold local officials accountable.[1] Based on this logic, SNCC and CORE attempted to register five million black voters in the Deep South. The *Voter Education Project* was aimed not only at registering voters but also at raising political consciousness. The plan was to develop an indigenous political base with a leadership cadre and political institutions.

Early attempts at mobilization were not very successful. The black electorate lacked participatory values and there was severe white resistance (e.g., firebombings, lynchings, etc.). By 1963, it became clear that the Project needed better organization. To this end, the *Congress of Federated Organizations* (COFO) was established to serve as an administrative clearinghouse to transfer money and other resources from the headquarters in Atlanta to the various field operations. COFO's first public act was to stage a mock election in Mississippi to dramatize large-scale black disenfranchisement and to counter stereotypes about the failure of black voters to behave as "rational" voters. While over 800,000 ballots were cast (about 30% of the eligible black voters) in the "Freedom Vote," the event was unable to draw much national attention.

One of the political organizations that grew out of the Freedom Vote was the *Mississippi Freedom Democratic Party* (MFDP). Formed in 1964, MFDP's goal was to send a delegation to the Democratic Convention in Atlantic City. They claimed that they were the only true Democratic party representing Mississippi because the "regular" delegation was chosen by a "whites only" primary procedure. The MFDP made it to Atlantic City but was refused credentials although sympathetic journalists provided some delegates with press passes. The showdown came to a head when the Rules Committee offered the MFDP two seats and delegate Fannie Lou Hamer rejected them in a passionate televised speech. In the end, President Johnson intervened and threatened to withhold patronage from those who aided the MFDP.

COFO planned another massive voter registration drive in the summer of 1964. "Freedom Summer" was significant for several reasons. First, there was resistance from the traditional civil rights organizations who thought the strategy was too confrontational. Second, there was substantial white resistance as thousands of workers were arrested and churches and homes were firebombed. Third, for the first time in the Movement there was talk of limiting the role of white volunteers. Fourth, three white workers were killed quite naturally drawing the attention of the national press corps. Thus the failure of Freedom Summer to mobilize the black electorate and the heightened level of white violence caused COFO leaders to fundamentally rethink their base strategy.

In 1965 SNCC created the *Mississippi Freedom Labor Union* (MFLU) to organize black agricultural workers. The goal was to raise the pay of sharecroppers and cotton workers. The failure of these efforts led SNCC to try again in Lowndes County, Alabama. Exploiting a quirk in Alabama law, SNCC formed the Lowndes County Freedom Organization (LCFO) and took on the symbol of the Black Panther. They sent the cream of the organization (the so-called "Howard group")—Stokley Carmichael, Cleveland Sellers, Marion Barry, Ed Brown—who explicitly discussed excluding whites from leadership positions. LCFO attempts to mobilize voters ran into stiff resistance from both the white and black communities and was a symbolic victory at best. Nevertheless, the events in Mississippi and Alabama signaled the radicalization of the Movement. SNCC moved closer to identifying a nationalist ideology associated more with Malcolm X than with Martin Luther King.

Two events crystallized the ascendance of Black Power: the Los Angeles riots of 1965 and the draft for the Vietnam War. It was commonly understood at the time that the "race" problem was (predominantly) a "southern" problem.[2] Given massive upheavals in southern life surrounding race relations this view is understandable. In many respects the LA riots caught America off-guard. The **McCone Commission**—*empanelled by California Governor Edmund Brown to examine the causes and consequences of the "riots"—recognized this point in its report: "In Los Angeles, before the summer's explosion, there was a tendency to believe that the problems which caused the trouble elsewhere were not acute in this community." The Commission identified several key preconditions for the violence in Los Angeles. Part of the problem was endemic to northern and eastern cities that experienced significant black in-migration.[3] As the report states, "the fundamental causes were largely the same . . . : "[N]ot enough jobs to go around . . . not enough schooling . . . a resentment, even hatred of the police." The end result was a discrepancy between what people expected to receive and what they were, in fact, likely to receive. Put differently, the success of the Movement raised expectations—many blacks (and whites) believed they would soon witness a fundamental change in the social hierarchy. In reality, the gains were more symbolic than substantive. The Commission also cited two "aggravating events" that were specific to Los Angeles—empty promises regarding federal poverty program resources and the repeal of the* Rumford Fair Housing Act. *The Commission identified three recommendations as deserving priority:*

1. *improve "Negro" job opportunities in the skilled and semi-skilled in the service trades ". . . by cooperative programs for employment and training"*
2. *"a new and costly approach to educating the Negro child"*
3. *police reforms*

THE CRISIS—AN OVERVIEW

The McCone Commission Report on the Los Angeles Riots

The rioting in Los Angeles in the late, hot summer of 1965 took six days to run its full grievous course. In hindsight, the tinder-igniting incident is seen to have been the arrest of a drunken Negro youth about whose dangerous driving another Negro had complained to the Caucasian motorcycle officer who made the arrest. The arrest occurred under rather ordinary circumstances, near but not in the district known as Watts, at seven o'clock on the evening of 11 August, a Wednesday. The crisis ended in the afternoon of 17 August, a Tuesday, on Governor Brown's order to lift the curfew which had been imposed the Saturday before in an extensive area just south of the heart of the City.

In the ugliest interval, which lasted from Thursday through Saturday, perhaps as many as 10,000 Negroes took to the streets in marauding bands. They looted stores, set fires, beat up white passersby whom they hauled from stopped cars, many of which were turned upside down and burned, exchanged shots with law enforcement officers, and stoned and shot at firemen. The rioters seemed to have been caught up in an insensate rage of destruction. By Friday, the disorder spread to adjoining areas, and ultimately an area covering 46.5 square miles had to be controlled with the aid of military authority before public order was restored.

The entire Negro population of Los Angeles County, about two-thirds of whom live in this area, numbers more than 650,000. Observers estimate that only about 2% were involved in the disorder. Nevertheless, this violent fraction, however minor, has given the face of community relations in Los Angeles a sinister cast.

SOWING THE WIND

In the summer of 1964, Negro communities in seven eastern cities were stricken by riots (see Table 5-1). Although in each situation there were unique contributing circumstances not existing elsewhere, the fundamental causes were largely the same:

—Not enough jobs to go around, and within this scarcity not enough by a wide margin of a character which the untrained Negro could fill.

—Not enough schooling designed to meet the special needs of the disadvantaged Negro child, whose environment from infancy onward places him under a serious handicap.

—A resentment, even hatred, of the police, as the symbol of authority.

These riots were each a symptom of a sickness in the center of our cities. In almost every major city, Negroes pressing ever more densely into the central

■ TABLE 5-1

SUMMARY OF 1964 RIOTS

City	Date	Killed	Injured	Arrests	Stores Damaged
New York City	July 18–23	1	144	519	541
Rochester	July 24–25	4	350	976	204
Jersey City	August 2–4	0	46	52	71
Paterson	August 11–13	0	8	65	20
Elizabeth	August 11–13	0	6	18	17
Chicago (Dixmoor)	August 16–17	0	57	80	2
Philadelphia	August 28–30	0	341	774	225

city and occupying areas from which Caucasians have moved in their flight to the suburbs have developed an isolated existence with a feeling of separation from the community as a whole.

Many have moved to the city only in the last generation and are totally unprepared to meet the conditions of modern city life. At the core of the cities where they cluster, law and order have only tenuous hold; the conditions of life itself are often marginal; idleness leads to despair and finally, mass violence supplies a momentary relief from the malaise.

WHY LOS ANGELES?

In Los Angeles, before the summer's explosion, there was a tendency to believe, and with some reason, that the problems which caused the trouble elsewhere were not acute in this community. A "statistical portrait" drawn in 1964 by the Urban League which rated American cities in terms of ten basic aspects of Negro life—such as housing, employment, income—ranked Los Angeles first among the 68 cities that were examined. ("There is no question about it, this is the best city in the world," a young Negro leader told us with respect to housing for Negroes.) While the Negro districts of Los Angeles are not urban gems, neither are they slums. Watts, for example, is a community consisting mostly of one and two-story houses, a third of which are owned by the occupants. In the riot area, most streets are wide and usually quite clean; there are trees, parks, and playgrounds. A Negro in Los Angeles has long been able to sit where he wants in a bus or a movie house, to shop where he wishes, to vote, and to use public facilities without discrimination. The opportunity to succeed is probably unequaled in any other major American city.

Yet the riot did happen here, and there are special circumstances here which explain in part why it did. Perhaps the people of Los Angeles should have seen trouble gathering under the surface calm. In the last quarter century, the Negro population here has exploded. While the County's population has trebled, the

Negro population has increased almost tenfold from 75,000 in 1940 to 650,000 in 1965. Much of the increase came through *migration from Southern states* and many arrived with the anticipation that this dynamic city would somehow spell the end of life's endless problems. To those who have come with high hopes and great expectations and see the success of others so close at hand, failure brings a special measure of frustration and disillusionment. Moreover, the fundamental problems, which are the same here as in the cities which were racked by the 1964 riots, are intensified by what may well be the least adequate network of public transportation in any major city in America.

Looking back, we can also see that there was a series of aggravating events in the 12 months prior to the riots.

—Publicity given to the glowing promise of the Federal poverty program was paralleled by reports of controversy and bickering over the mechanism to handle the program here in Los Angeles, and when the projects did arrive, they did not live up to their press notices.

—Throughout the nation, unpunished violence and disobedience to law were widely reported, and almost daily there were exhortations, here and elsewhere, to take the most extreme and even illegal remedies to right a wide variety of wrongs, real and supposed.

—In addition, many Negroes here felt and were encouraged to feel that they had been affronted by the passage of Proposition 14—an initiative measure passed by two-thirds of the voters in November 1964 which *repealed the Rumford Fair Housing Act* and unless modified by the voters or invalidated by the courts will bar any attempt by state or local governments to enact similar laws.

When the rioting came to Los Angeles, it was not a race riot in the usual sense. What happened was *an explosion*—a formless, quite senseless, all but hopeless violent protest—engaged in by a few but bringing great distress to all.

Nor was the rioting exclusively a projection of the Negro problem It is part of an American problem which involves Negroes but which equally concerns other disadvantaged groups. In this report, our major conclusions and recommendations regarding the Negro problem in Los Angeles apply with equal force to the Mexican-Americans, a community which is almost equal in size to the Negro community and whose circumstances are similarly disadvantageous and demand equally urgent treatment. That the Mexican-American community did not riot is to it credit; it should not be to its disadvantage.

THE DULL DEVASTATING SPIRAL OF FAILURE

In examining the sickness in the center of our city, what has depressed and stunned us most is the dull, devastating spiral of failure that awaits the average disadvantaged child in the urban core. His home life all too often fails to give him the incentive and the elementary experience with words and ideas which prepares most children for school. Unprepared and unready, he may not learn to read or write at all; and because he shares his problem with 30 or more in the same classroom, even the efforts of the most dedicated teachers are unavailing. Age, not achievement, passes him on to higher grades, but in most cases he is unable to cope with courses in the upper grades because they demand basic skills which he does not possess. ("Try," a teacher said to us, "to teach history to a child who cannot read.")

Frustrated and disillusioned, the child becomes a discipline problem. Often he leaves school, sometimes before the end of junior high school. (About two-thirds of those who enter the three high schools in the center of the curfew area do not graduate.) He slips into the ranks of the permanent jobless, illiterate and untrained, unemployed and unemployable. All the talk about the millions which the government is spending to aid him raise his expectations but the benefits seldom reach him.

Reflecting this spiral of failure, unemployment in the disadvantaged areas runs two to three times the county average, and the employment available is too often intermittent. A family whose breadwinner is chronically out of work is almost invariably a disintegrating family. Crime rates soar and welfare rolls increase, even faster than the population.

This spiral of failure has a most damaging side effect. Because of the low standard of achievement in the schools in the urban core and adjacent areas, parents of the better students from advantaged backgrounds remove them from these schools, either by changing the location of the family home or by sending the children to private school. In turn, the average achievement level of the schools in the disadvantaged area sinks lower and lower. The evidence is that this chain reaction is one of the principal factors in maintaining de facto school segregation in the urban core and producing it in the adjacent areas where the Negro population is expanding. From our study, we are persuaded that there is a reasonable possibility that raising the achievement levels of the disadvantaged Negro child will materially lessen the tendency towards de facto segregation in education, and that this might possibly also make a substantial contribution to ending all de facto segregation.

ALL SEGMENTS OF SOCIETY

Perhaps for the first time our report will bring into clear focus, for all the citizens to see, the economic and sociological conditions in our city that underlay the gathering anger which impelled the rioters to escalate the routine arrest of a drunken driver into six days of violence. Yet, however powerful their grievances, the rioters had no legal or moral justification for the wounds they inflicted. Many crimes, a great many felonies, were committed. Even more dismaying, as we studied the record, was the large number of brutal exhortations to violence which were uttered by some Negroes. Rather than making proposals, they laid down ultimatums with the alternative being violence. All this nullified the admirable efforts of hundreds, if not thousands, both Negro and white, to quiet the situation and restore order.

What can be done to prevent a recurrence of the nightmare of August? It stands to reason that what we and other cities have been doing, costly as it all has been, is not enough. Improving the conditions of Negro life will demand adjustments on a scale unknown to any great society. The programs that we are recommending will be expensive and burdensome. And the burden, along with the expense, will fall on all segments of our society—on the public and private sectors, on industry and labor, on company presidents and hourly employees, and most indispensably, upon the members and leaders of the Negro community. For unless the disadvantaged are resolved to help themselves, whatever else is done by others is bound to fail.

The consequences of inaction, indifference, and inadequacy, we can all be sure now, would be far costlier in the long run than the cost of correction. If the city were to elect to stand aside, the walls of segregation would rise ever higher. The disadvantaged community would become more and more estranged and the risk of violence would rise. The cost of police protection would increase, and yet would never be adequate. Unemployment would climb; welfare costs would mount apace. And the preachers of division and demagoguery would have a matchless opportunity to tear our nation asunder.

OF FUNDAMENTAL AND DURABLE IMPORT

As a Commission, we are seriously concerned that the existing breach, if allowed to persist, could in time split our society irretrievably. So serious and so explosive is the situation that, unless it is checked, the August riots may seem by comparison to be only a curtain-raiser for what could blow up one day in the future.

Our recommendations will concern many areas where improvement can be made but three we consider to be of highest priority and greatest importance.

1. Because idleness brings a harvest of distressing problems, employment for those in the Negro community who are unemployed and able to work is a first priority. Our metropolitan area employs upwards of three millions of men and women in industry and in the service trades, and we face a shortage of skilled and semi-skilled workers as our economy expands. We recommend that our robust community take immediate steps to relieve the lack of *job opportunity* for Negroes by cooperative programs for employment and training, participated in by the Negro community, by governmental agencies, by employers and by organized labor.

2. In *education*, we recommend a new and costly approach to educating the Negro child who has been deprived of the early training that customarily starts at infancy and who because of early deficiencies advances through school on a basis of age rather than scholastic

attainment. What is clearly needed and what we recommend is an emergency program designed to raise the level of scholastic attainment of those who would otherwise fall behind. This requires pre-school education, intensive instruction in small classes, remedial courses and other special treatment. The cost will be great but until the level of scholastic achievement of the disadvantaged child is raised, we cannot expect to overcome the existing spiral of failure.

3. We recommend that *law enforcement* agencies place greater emphasis on their responsibilities for crime prevention as an essential element of the law enforcement task, and that they institute improved means for handling citizen complaints and community relationships.

The road to the improvement of the condition of the disadvantaged Negro which lies through education and employment is hard and long, but there is no shorter route. The avenue of violence and lawlessness leads to a dead end. To travel the long and difficult road will require courageous leadership and determined participation by all parts of our community, but no task in our times is more important. Of what shall it avail our nation if we can place a man on the moon but cannot cure the sickness in our cities?

———————————————————— ■ ————————————————————

The Los Angeles "riots" helped SNCC understand that racial inequalities in the South were connected to urban unrest in the North. That is, the same underlying dynamic was present in both contexts—black structural disadvantage. This point was amplified by the establishment of mandatory induction into military service for millions of American men and women. Well-connected whites were able to skirt military duty while blacks were inducted at higher rates and were more likely to be sent to the front lines. SNCC's inner circle began to connect what they saw as U.S imperialism abroad to a brand of domestic imperialism that sought to control racial minorities. Julian Bond, director of public relations (then recently elected to the Georgia House of Representatives but denied his seat) announced SNCC's formal opposition to the draft. In addition, SNCC picketed induction centers.

In this environment, SNCC decided to move their activities out of the South. Before they could relocate, however, they had to reformulate their ideology. During a series of meetings in late 1965 and early 1966 (known as the Atlanta Project) SNCC developed a position paper entitled **"The Basis of Black Power."** *The new ideology clearly sought independence from white control: "[I]f we are to proceed toward true liberation, we must cut ourselves off from white people. We must form our own institutions, credit unions, co-ops, political parties, write our own histories."4 It also had a cultural agenda that called for a "re-examination" of black identity, "[W]ho are black people, what are black people, and what is their relationship to American and the world?" Moreover, they challenged white hegemony over black culture. SNCC believed that the black community "allowed white people to interpret the importance and meaning of the cultural aspects of our society. We have allowed them to tell us what is good about our Afro-American music, art, and literature." In effect, SNCC was rejecting the notion that white cultural standards were the only standards. Finally, SNCC's position was explicitly comparative. Influenced by the writings of Franz Fanon and Mao Tse Tung, and en-*

couraged by the emergent liberation movement in Africa and Latin America, SNCC asserted that, "[T]he broad masses of black people react to American society in the same manner as colonial peoples react to the West in Africa and Latin America."

STUDENT NONVIOLENT COORDINATING COMMITTEE POSITION PAPER: THE BASIS OF BLACK POWER

This text is made available by the Sixties Project, sponsored by Viet Nam Generation Inc. and the Institute of Advanced Technology in the Humanities at the University of Virginia at Charlottesville. The Sixties Project is a collective of humanities scholars working together on the Internet to use electronic resources to provide routes of collaboration and make available primary and secondary sources for researchers, students, teachers, writers and librarians interested in the 1960s.

The myth that the Negro is somehow incapable of liberating himself, is lazy, etc., came out of the American experience. In the books that children read, whites are always "good" (good symbols are white), blacks are "evil" or seen as savages in movies, their language is referred to as a "dialect," and black people in this country are supposedly descended from savages.

Any white person who comes into the movement has the concepts in his mind about black people, if only subconsciously. He cannot escape them because the whole society has geared his subconscious in that direction.

Miss America coming from Mississippi has a chance to represent all of America, but a black person from either Mississippi or New York will never represent America. Thus the white people coming into the movement cannot relate to the black experience, cannot relate to the word "black," cannot relate to the "nitty gritty," cannot relate to the experience that brought such a word into existence, cannot relate to chitterlings, hog's head cheese, pig feet, ham hocks, and cannot relate to slavery, because these things are not a part of their experience. They also cannot relate to the black religious experience, nor to the black church, unless, of course, this church has taken on white manifestations.

WHITE POWER

Negroes in this country have never been allowed to organize themselves because of white interference. As a result of this, the stereotype has been reinforced that blacks cannot organize themselves. The white psychology that blacks have to be watched, also reinforces this stereotype. Blacks, in fact, feel intimidated by the presence of whites, because of their knowledge of the power that whites have over their lives. One white person can come into a meeting of black people and change the complexion of that meeting, where a meeting unless he was an obvious Uncle Tom. People would immediately start talking about "brotherhood," "love," etc.; race would not be discussed.

If people must express themselves freely, there has to be a climate in which they can do this. If blacks feel intimidated by whites, then they are not liable to vent the rage that they feel about whites in the presence of whites—especially not the black people whom we are trying to organize, i.e., the broad masses of black people. A climate has to be created whereby blacks can express themselves. The reasons that whites must be excluded is not that one is anti-white, but because the effects that one is trying to achieve cannot succeed because whites have an intimidating effect. Ofttimes, the intimidating effect is in direct proportion to the amount of degradation that black people have suffered at the hands of white people.

ROLES OF WHITES AND BLACKS

It must be offered that white people who desire change in this country should go where that problem (racism) is most manifest. The problem is not in the black community. The white people should go into white communities where the whites have created power for the express purpose of denying blacks human dignity and self-determination. Whites who come into the black community with ideas of change seem to want to absolve the power structure of its responsibility for what it is doing, and saying that change can only come through black unity, which is the worst kind of paternalism. This is not to say that whites have not had an important role in the movement. In the case of Mississippi, their role was very key in that they helped give blacks the right to organize, but that role is now over, and it should be.

People now have the right to picket, the right to give out leaflets, the right to vote, the right to demonstrate, the right to print.

These things which revolve around the right to organize have been accomplished mainly because of the entrance of white people into Mississippi, in the summer of 1964. Since these goals have now been accomplished, whites' role in the movement has now ended. What does it mean if black people, once having the right to organize, are not allowed to organize themselves? It means that blacks' ideas about inferiority are being reinforced. Shouldn't people be able to organize themselves? Blacks should be given this right. Further, white participation means in the eyes of the black community that whites are the "brains" behind the movement, and that blacks cannot function without whites. This only serves to perpetuate existing attitudes within the existing society, i.e., blacks are "dumb," "unable to take care of business," etc. Whites are "smart," the "brains" behind the whole thing.

How do blacks relate to other blacks as such? How do we react to Willie Mays as against Mickey Mantle? What is our response to Mays hitting a home run against Mantel performing the same deed? One has to come to the conclusion that it is because of black participation in baseball. Negroes still identify with the Dodgers because of Jackie Robinson's efforts with the Dodgers. Negroes would instinctively champion all-black teams if they opposed all white or predominantly white teams. The same principle operates for the movement as it does for baseball: a mystique must be created whereby Negroes can identify with the movement.

Thus an all-black project is needed in order for the people to free themselves. This has to exist from the beginning. This relates to what can be called "coalition politics." There is no doubt in our minds that some whites are just as disgusted with this system as we are. But it is meaningless to talk about coalition if there is no one to align ourselves with, because of the lack of organization in the white communities. There can be no talk of "hooking up" unless black people organize blacks and white people organize whites. If these conditions are met, then perhaps at some later date—and if we are going in the same direction—talks about exchange of personnel, coalition, and other meaningful alliances can be discussed.

In the beginning of the movement, we had fallen into a trap whereby we thought that our problems revolved around the right to eat at certain lunch counters or the right to vote, or to organize our communities. We have seen, however, that the problem is much deeper. The problem of this country, as we had seen it, concerned all blacks and all whites and therefore if decisions were left to the young people, then solutions would be arrived at. But this negates the history of black people and whites. We have dealt stringently with the problem of "Uncle Tom," but we have not yet gotten around to Simon Legree. We must ask ourselves, who is the real villain—Uncle Tom or Simon Legree? Everybody knows Uncle Tom, but who knows Simon Legree? So what we have now in SNCC is a closed society, a clique. Black people cannot relate to SNCC because of its unrealistic, nonracial atmosphere; denying their experience of America as a racist society. In contrast, the Southern Christian Leadership Conference of Martin Luther King, Jr., has a staff that at least maintains a black facade. The front office is virtually all black, but nobody accuses SCLC of being racist.

If we are to proceed toward true liberation, we must cut ourselves off from white people. We must form our own institutions, credit unions, co-ops, political parties, write our own histories.

To proceed further, let us make some comparisons between the Black Movement of the early 1900s and the movement of the 1960s—i.e., compare the National Association for the advancement of Colored People with SNCC. Whites subverted the Niagara movement (the forerunner of the NAACP) which, at the outset, was an all-black movement. The name of the new organization was also very revealing, in that it presupposed blacks have to advanced to the level of whites. We are now aware that the NAACP has grown reactionary, is controlled by the black power structure itself, and stands as one of the main roadblocks to black freedom. SNCC, by allowing the whites to remain in the organization, can have its efforts subverted in much the same manner, i.e., through having them play important roles such as community organizers, etc. Indigenous leadership cannot be built with whites in the positions they now hold.

These facts do not mean that whites cannot help. They can participate on a voluntary basis. We can contract work out to them, but in no way can they participate on a policy-making level.

BLACK SELF-DETERMINATION

The charge may be made that we are "racists," but whites who are sensitive to our problems will realize that we must determine our own destiny.

In an attempt to find a solution to our dilemma, we propose that our organization (SNCC) should be black-staffed, black-controlled, and black-financed. We do not want to fall into a similar dilemma that other civil rights organizations have fallen into. If we continue to rely upon white financial support we will find ourselves entwined in the tentacles of the white power complex that controls this country. It is also important that a black organization (devoid of cultism) be projected to our people so that it can be demonstrated that such organizations are viable.

More and more we see black people in this country being used as a tool of the white liberal establishment. Liberal whites have not begun to address themselves to the real problem of black people in this country—witness their bewilderment, fear, and anxiety when nationalism is mentioned concerning black people. An analysis of the white liberal's reaction to the word "nationalism" alone reveals a very meaningful attitude of whites of an ideological persuasion toward blacks in this country. It means previous solutions to black problems in this country have been made in the interests of those whites dealing with these problems and not in the best interests of black people in the country. Whites can only subvert our true search and struggles for self-determination, self-identification, and liberation in this country. Reevaluation of the white and black roles must *now* take place so that white no longer designate roles that black people play but rather black people define white people's roles.

Too long have we allowed white people to interpret the importance and meaning of the cultural aspects of our society. We have allowed them to tell us what was good about our Afro-American music, art, and literature. How many black critics do we have on the "jazz" scene? How can a white person who is not part of the black psyche (except in the oppressor's role) interpret the meaning of the blues to us who are manifestations of the song themselves?

It must be pointed out that on whatever level of contact blacks and whites come together, that meeting or confrontation is not on the level of the blacks but always on the level of the whites. This only means that our everyday contact with whites is a reinforcement of the myth of white supremacy. Whites are the ones who must try to raise themselves to our humanistic level. We are not, after all, the ones who are responsible for a genocidal war in Vietnam; we are not the ones who are responsible for neocolonialism in Africa and Latin America; we are not the ones who held a people in animalistic bondage over 400 years. We reject the American dream as defined by white people and must work to construct an American reality defined by Afro-Americans.

WHITE RADICALS

One of the criticisms of white militants and radicals is that when we view the masses of white people we view the overall reality of America, we view the racism, the bigotry, and the distortion of personality, we view man's inhumanity to man; we view in reality 180 million racists. The sensitive white intellectual and radical who is fighting to bring about change is conscious of this fact, but does not have the courage to admit this. When he admits this reality, then he must also admit his involvement because he is a part of the collective white America. It is only to the extent that he recognizes this that he will be able to change this reality.

Another common concern is, how does the white radical view the black community, and how does he view the poor white community, in terms of organizing? So far, we have found that most white radicals have sought to escape the horrible reality of America by going into the black community and attempting to organize black people while neglecting the organization of their own people's racist communities. How can one clean up someone else's yard when one's own yard is untidy? Again we feel that SNCC and the civil rights movement in general is in many aspects similar to the anticolonial situations in the African and Asian countries. We have the whites in the movement corresponding to the white civil servants and missionaries in the colonial countries who have worked with the colonial people for a long period of time and have developed a paternalistic attitude toward them. The reality of the colonial people taking over their own lives and controlling their own destiny must be faced. Having to move aside and letting the natural process of growth and development take place must be faced.

These views should not be equated with outside influence or outside agitation but should be viewed as the natural process of growth and development within a movement; so that the move by the black militants and SNCC in this direction should be viewed as a turn toward self-determination.

It is very ironic and curious that aware whites in the country can champion anticolonialism in other countries in Africa, Asia, and Latin America, but when black people move toward similar goals of self-determination in this country they are viewed as racists and anti-white by these same progressive whites. In proceeding further, it can be said that this attitude derives from the overall point of view of the white psyche as it concerns the black people. This attitude stems from the era of the slave revolts when every white man was a potential deputy or sheriff or guardian of the state. Because when black people get together among themselves to workout their problems, it becomes a threat to white people, because such meetings were potential slave revolts.

It can be maintained that this attitude or way of thinking has perpetuated itself to this current period and that it is part of the psyche of white people in this country whatever their political persuasion might be. It is part of the white fear-guilt complex resulting from the slave revolts. There have been examples of whites who stated that they can deal with black fellows on an individual basis but become threatened or menaced by the presence of groups of blacks. It can be maintained that this attitude is held by the majority of progressive whites in this country.

BLACK IDENTITY

A thorough re-examination must be made by black people concerning the contributions that we have made in shaping this country. If this re-examination and re-evaluation is not made, and black people are not given their proper due and respect, then the antagonisms and contradictions are going to become more and more glaring, more and more intense, until a national explosion may result.

When people attempt to move from these conclusions it would be faulty reasoning to say they are ordered by racism, because, in this country and in the West, racism has functioned as a type of white nationalism when dealing with black people. We all know the habit that this has created throughout the world and particularly among nonwhite people in this country.

Therefore any re-evaluation that we must make will, for the most part, deal with identification. Who are black people, what are black people, what is their relationship to America and the world?

It must be repeated that the whole myth of "Negro citizenship," perpetuated by the white elite, has confused the thinking of radical and progressive blacks and whites in this country. The broad masses of black people react to American society in the same manner as colonial peoples react to the West in Africa and Latin America, and had the same relationship—that of the colonized toward the colonizer.

———————————————— ■ ————————————————

SNCC's new ideology was quickly tested. In 1966, James Meredith, the first black to attend the University of Mississippi, attempted to stage a one-man march from Memphis to Jackson to dramatize the fear most blacks lived under in the South. Meredith was shot on the second day of the march. Civil rights leaders—including King and SNCC's new chair Stokley Carmichael—rushed to Memphis vowing to continue the march, and the national media followed. Controversy quickly ensued between the key civil rights organizations resulting in the withdrawal of the NAACP and the Urban League. SNCC and the SCLC individually pressed ahead with the march. SNCC's message, however, was fundamentally different from King's vision. In a public statement they said, "I'm not going to beg the white man for anything I deserve, I'm going to take it." SNCC encapsulated their new ideology with the term "Black Power" during "call and response" segments of SNCC rallies. The speaker would ask the crowd, "what do we want" and the crowd would respond "Black Power." The visual and linguistic force jumped out of the television. King even urged them to use a different phrase (Black Equality). SNCC now turned their attention to moving north.

SNCC operatives shortly discovered that many northern and eastern cities were politically crowded. In one way or another The NAACP, the Urban League, the Democratic party, organized labor, and white leftist organizations were all competing for public resources. In addition, the Nation of Islam (even in the wake of Malcolm's murder) had established itself as a contender for black interests. On the other hand, SNCC could not remain in the South. White violence was escalating and northern philanthropic money was drying up. In a sense, SNCC was pushed into a holding pattern.

During essentially the same time period, the underlying dynamic of oppression, isolation, and marginalization lead a group of young African-Americans in Oakland, California to create a new political organization—the Black Panther Party for Self-Defense. In 1966, they published the **Black Panther Party Platform and Program** *or the "Ten Point Program." The Panthers, like SNCC, sought political, economic, and cultural self-determination. Unlike SNCC, the Panthers also had explicitly political goals. They demanded immediate release of ". . . all black men held in federal, state, county and city prisons and jails." They sought exemption from military service. They wanted ". . . black people when brought to trial to be tried by a jury of their peer group or people from their black communities." More ambitiously, they wanted the United Nations to supervise a ". . . plebiscite . . . for the purpose of determining the will of black people as to their national destiny."*

OCTOBER 1966 BLACK PANTHER PARTY PLATFORM AND PROGRAM

Collected from the Black Panther Party in Oakland, California on November 14, 1966

WHAT WE WANT

The program is usually divided into one section of ten points entitled "What We Want" and then ten paragraphs explaining these points in a section entitled "What We Believe."

WHAT WE BELIEVE

For the sake of clarity, we have put each one of the ten points in "What We Want" immediately above its corresponding paragraph in "What We Believe."

1. *We want freedom. We want power to determine the destiny of our Black Community.*

   We believe that black people will not be free until we are able to determine our destiny.

2. *We want full employment for our people.*

We believe that the federal government is responsible and obligated to give every man employment or a guaranteed income. We believe that if the white American businessmen will not give full employment, then the means of production should be taken from the businessmen and placed in the community so that the people of the community can organize and employ all of its people and give a high standard of living.

3. *We want an end to the robbery by the white man of our Black Community.*

We believe that this racist government has robbed us and now we are demanding the overdue debt of forty acres and two mules. Forty acres and two mules was promised 100 years ago as restitution for slave labor and mass murder of black people. We will accept the payment in currency which will be distributed to our many communities. The Germans are now aiding the Jews in Israel for the genocide of the Jewish people. The Germans murdered six million Jews. The American racist has taken part in the slaughter of over fifty million black people: therefore, we feel that this is a modest demand that we make.

4. *We want decent housing, fit for shelter of human beings.*

We believe that if the white landlords will not give decent housing to our black community, then the housing and the land should be made into cooperatives so that our community, with government aid, can build and make decent housing for its people.

5. *We want education for our people that exposes the true nature of this decadent American society. We want education that teaches us our true history and our role in the present-day society.*

We believe in an educational system that will give to our people a knowledge of self. If a man does not have knowledge of himself and his position in society and the world, then he has little chance to relate to anything else.

6. *We want all black men to be exempt from military service.*

We believe that Black people should not be forced to fight in the military service to defend a racist government that does not protect us. We will not fight and kill other people of color in the world who, like black people, are being victimized by the white racist government of America. We will protect ourselves from the force and violence of the racist police and the racist military, by whatever means necessary.

7. *We want an immediate end to POLICE BRUTALITY and MURDER of black people.*

We believe we can end police brutality in our black community by organizing black self-defense groups that are dedicated to defending our black community from racist police oppression and brutality. The 2nd Amendment to the Constitution of the United States gives a right to bear arms. We therefore believe that all black people should arm themselves for self defense.

8. *We want freedom for all black men held in federal, state, county and city prisons and jails.*

   We believe that all black people should be released from the many jails and prisons because they have not received a fair and impartial trial.

9. *We want all black people when brought to trial to be tried in court by a jury of their peer group or people from their black communities, as defined by the Constitution of the United States.*

   We believe that the courts should follow the United States Constitution so that black people will receive fair trials. The 14th Amendment of the U.S. Constitution gives a man a right to be tried by his peer group. A peer is a person from a similar economic, social, religious, geographical, environmental, historical and racial background. To do this the court will be forced to select a jury from the black community from which the black defendant came. We have been, and are being tried by all-white juries that have no understanding of the "average reasoning man" of the black community.

10. *We want land, bread, housing, education, clothing, justice and peace. And as our major political objective, a United Nations-supervised plebiscite to be held throughout the black colony in which only black colonial subjects will be allowed to participate, for the purpose of determining the will of black people as to their national destiny.*

    When, in the course of human events, it becomes necessary for one people to dissolve the political bonds which have connected them with another, and to assume, among the powers of the earth, the separate and equal station to which the laws of nature and nature's God entitle them, a decent respect to the opinions of mankind requires that they should declare the causes which impel them to the separation.

    We hold these truths to be self-evident, that all men are created equal; that they are endowed by their Creator with certain unalienable rights; that among these are life, liberty, and the pursuit of happiness. *That, to secure these rights, governments are instituted among men, deriving their just powers from the consent of the governed; that, whenever any form of government becomes destructive of these ends. It is the right of the people to alter or to abolish it, and to institute a new government, laying its foundation on such principles, and organizing its powers in such form, as to them shall seem most likely to effect their safety and happiness.* Prudence, indeed, will dictate that governments long established should not be changed for light and transient causes; and, accordingly, all experience hath shown, that mankind are more disposed to suffer, while evils are sufferable, than to right themselves by abolishing the forms to which they are accustomed. *But, when a long train of abuses and usurpations, pursuing invariably the same object, evinces a design to reduce*

them under absolute despotism, it is their right. It is their duty, to throw off
such government, and to provide new guards for their future security.

FREE HUEY NOW

GUNS BABY GUNS

The rise of the Panthers is chronicled in David Hilliard's autobiography **This Side of**
Glory*. Like many young blacks, the words of Malcolm X and the events in Los Angeles and*
other northern cities had a significant impact on Hilliard.[5] He sensed the urgency of black in-
surrection but lacked a viable outlet of expression. The Nation of Islam was a living contradic-
tion for him, and he flatly rejected the passive approach of King ("there's no glory in getting
your brains beat out"). Hilliard's long time friend Huey Newton told him about a new black po-
litical organization formed by students at Merritt College in Oakland. Taking advantage of a
California law allowing citizens to carry loaded weapons as long as they are not concealed, the
Panthers organized patrols to monitor police activity in the community. As the buzz surround-
ing the Panthers grew, Hilliard was drawn to the organization. Additionally, Newton expanded
his world-view by exposing him to Fanon and Mao. Hilliard now had ". . . a different existence,
a calling, something that removes me from my aimlessness, gives my days reason and purpose."
Hilliard's experience was not unique as the Panther membership grew appreciably.[6]

THIS SIDE OF GLORY:
THE AUTOBIOGRAPHY OF DAVID HILLIARD
AND THE STORY OF THE BLACK PANTHER PARTY

David Hilliard and Lewis Cole

Excerpt from This Side of Glory

I agree with Malcolm and the Muslims about America: a white man's
heaven is a black man's hell. And Malcolm—with his razor-sharp mind
and wit—speaks my language. He's no *saditi*; he could easily hang on the corner
with us. But I don't return to the mosque after my one visit, and stay away even
after Malcolm's television appearance. For one thing, my street buddies won't
go, and I like running with my partners. Plus, the Nation of Islam is a living con-
tradiction for me. I respect their personal discipline, but like to drink, dress up,
and party; I champion their militancy, but relish American culture. I don't want
to opt out of America. I like America. I think and feel American. I don't have a
problem if I want out of the society. My problem comes from wanting in.

I have equally divided feelings about the people who are fighting to be
included.

I'm impressed by the oratorical ability of Martin Luther King—Martin
Luther Cool, Chico calls him—and his precise, clever imagery: "We have
come to cash a check and the system has returned it to us saying insufficient
funds." I admire that. I envy his power to move and influence people. Listening to him, I recall the minister in the Mobile True Vine Baptist Church
and experience the same excitement that overwhelmed me as a boy, loving

the give-and-take of the sermon, answering him back, swept up in the crowd and the euphoria he manages to create.

But I completely disagree with him. First of all, he *is* a preacher and I've never overcome my contempt for our local ministers who would accept tithes from their poor, hard-working, spellbound congregations: they preached false glory, and King's no better. In fact, he's worse. There's not false glory, there's *no* glory in getting your brains beat out.

"Why don't these people fight back?" I ask Pat angrily as the Alabama police pursue the crowd stumbling off the Selma bridge. The passivity of the civil rights demonstrators contradicts my family's most fundamental belief: you don't stand idly by and be kicked, you fight for yourself.

"What is wrong with them to allow this to happen?" I ask. I am so incensed I want to cry.

At the same time, the idea of taking political action into my own hands is completely foreign to me. Local organizations made up of people working out of the unions and community organizers like Mark Comfort, who's been trying to mobilize West Oakland for some time, are trying to meld the militancy of the Muslims with the broader vision of the civil rights movement. But I have no experience with organizations, no faith in my own power.

Then, one afternoon—we're in the summer of 1965—we hear there's a riot in Watts, the center of the black community in Los Angeles. For the next few days I stay glued to the television, recognizing the street corners, liquor stores, beauty shops, and bars that have become a war zone. The images of troops marching down the avenues remind me of Don Winslow; but now it's guys like Bo, my little nephew, who are Devil Dogs tossing Molotov cocktails. I cheer them on, envying Bojack, a wild thrill rising in me. Burn! I think, glued to the chaos on the screen. Burn! This is what should happen! We should never accept our situation! Hate and fury flow through me. Before, such powerful feelings have always pulled me inward, making me clenched inside. Now my rage and contempt pour out, as though they're a song or a kind of exuberant, defiant love.

On the corner we talk about the riots, everybody saying the brothers are right to defend themselves. Fired by the example, I apply the lesson to an immediate problem, intimidating a store owner who threatens to repossess some furniture Pat and I have stopped making payments on.

"Listen," I say to him, liquored up and furious, "and you'd better listen carefully because I'm only gonna say this once: You bother me again about this furniture and we're gonna burn your store. So stay away from me."

Then the excitement of Watts fades. I realize my life still hasn't changed. And that's what I want, a different existence, a calling, something that removes me from my aimlessness, gives my days reason and purpose. Even working a good, new job on the docks that earns me weekly expenses in two or three days and provides me with the finest whiskeys and brandies money can buy, I remain deeply discontent. The next summer the Cleveland black community goes to war, guys my age seizing the Hough for two days. I start in awe at pictures of them on television and in *Life* magazine. Their courage and defiance is monumental. What do you want? the radio interviewer asks them. More ammunition, they say. I start to read again, first the books Russ the Finn, suggested, then others. Malcolm's *Autobiography* has recently come out. I buy the book and, for the next days, don't leave the house, don't drink, just lie on the bed, putting the words together, feeling I am not reading Malcolm's life but my own.

In the midst of this period, Huey starts coming over—he's recently served a short term in the Alameda County Jail, including a month in solitary, the notorious "hole"—drifting by at night, partying with me, June, and old high school friends, talking and drinking the cognac that the Japanese sailors sell cheap for American dollars.

One afternoon he announces he's putting together a new political organization and mentions Malcolm's name. I'm instantly excited.

"I got to be part of this stuff," I say. "You don't understand, Huey. I mean this is what I'm reading. What are you gonna do?"

"We're gonna defend ourselves," he answers. He refers to Malcolm again "Malcolm talked about the right to defend ourselves by any means necessary—"

I interrupt him because the night before I read Malcolm on self-defense. "Huey," I say, "this is amazing. I was just reading the man."

Huey smiles. "We're gonna be the personification of Malcolm X's dreams. "I gotta be part of this," I say.

Huey tells me he's creating the organization with a brother named Bobb Seale, an aspiring stand-up coming whom Huey has done political organizing with at Merritt College. We drive over to Seale's mother's house, a ramblin, ranch house with a spotless living room, the couch and chairs sheltered in side clear plastic slipcovers.

In the back Huey introduces me to his new friends. He tells them about the old days, says I was one of the bravest fighter he's ever known. Then he shows me the guns: shotgun, revolver, a .45, one or two smaller pistols, an M1.

"But what are you going to do?" I ask. My head swims. I feel proud to be connected to Huey and his plan—things will definitely happen in Oakland now. But the guns scare as much as thrill me, and the whys, hows, and whats of the organization baffle me. I only know he's talking about an organization that will right some wrongs against black people.

"We're gonna organize the brothers," Huey says. "All these other organizations deal with students or the churches. We're gonna get the brothers and sisters off the block like you and me. Like Malcolm would have done."

I nod my head—what Huey says makes sense—and ask, "To do what?"

"Get power," Huey says. "True power is the ability to define a phenomenon and make it act in a desired manner. That's what none of the brothers have. None of us have it. And we have to band together to create it."

Bobby shows me the Ten Point Program. The document has two parts: What We Want and What We Believe.

What We Want: We want freedom. We want power to determine the destiny of our black community.

What We Believe: We believe that black people will not be free until we are able to determine our destiny.

What We Want: jobs, housing, education, an end to white businessmen ripping off the black community, an end to police brutality, trials by juries of our peers, freedom for all the brothers and sisters in jail, and finally a UN-sponsored plebiscite to determine whether we want to be part of America. (The final section in the What We Believe part is a quote from the opening of the American Declaration of Independence.)

"We call ourselves the Black Panther Party for Self-Defense," Huey says. He explains that the name originates from Lowndes County, Alabama, where Student Noviolent Coordinating Committee (SNCC) organizers formed the first all-black party. "The nature of the panther is that he never attacks," explains Huey. "But if anyone attacks him or backs him into a corner, the panther comes up to wipe that aggressor or that attacker out, absolutely, resolutely, wholly, thoroughly, and completely." He tells me about the police patrols. Under California law a citizen can carry a loaded gun as long as the weapon is not concealed. Taking advantage of the law, the Panthers have been driving around armed with their guns and a law book. When they see an incident occurring between a cop and a brother they stop and make sure the officer follows the law. The cops have been totally furious and scared at the sight of blacks with guns, but so far the police have always backed down and there have been no shots fired.

Bobby straps on his over-the-shoulder holster, sets his beret at a perfect angle; Huey slings the bandolier over his chest and picks up his shotgun. Until this moment I've imagined Huey was talking abstractly—as though all this would happen someday in the future. Not now. Certainly not today.

"Where you going?" I ask them.

"On patrol," Huey says, getting into the car.

"To patrol the police?" I ask. Bobby lives on a quiet block lined with the usual stucco homes. I ask myself, Is this really happening? Here? Now?

"That's right," he says and closes the car door. And it becomes clear to me why he's not asking me to join them: Huey wants me to make up my own mind. He's giving me the choice.

"Power to the people, David," he says, and raises his clenched fist.

"Power to the people, Huey," I answer.

The next few days I am totally preoccupied. What am I going to do? Go with Huey or not?

Aware of what I'm thinking, Pat worries about my next move.

"Huey came by," she remembers.

I wouldn't even open the door for him. I knew he was into the civil rights movement and I knew what the problems were here in Oakland. But I had known Huey from before, in high school, and he was crazy. He was always very pretty, neat as a pin, and from his appearance you wouldn't think he would do what he did. But he was crazy. One time he got into a fight with some boys about his light skin. They got the better of him because they jumped him. But then he came back two weeks later with a hatchet and he got his revenge and had them jumping out of windows and stuff. So when he came around now I still had in the back of my head how he had protected himself then, and I was afraid he'd take you away—that you wouldn't be around me and the kids and would get involved in the movement.

June is also ambivalent about my working with the Party. "Man, you don't need to get into that," he says. "Just stick with your job."

I do, but I also make up my mind, telling Huey I want to go on patrol.

The next night we drive over to Bobby's. There, inside the car, Huey gives me the handgun. I'm really wired, not knowing what to expect. I've never backed down from a fight, but I don't relish confronting armed police at night in West Oakland.

"Let me carry the shotgun," I say. I want to overcome my fear and embarrassment that these other guys are more courageous than I.

"Actually," Huey answers, "I think I should carry the shotgun."

"You can trust me," I argue. "Like when we were young."

Enjoying the situation, his eyes shine, but he speaks with great authority. "I carry the shotgun. You carry this. Now let's go."

As I drive the car down the street I ask my next question—I have questions all the time now. "Now what should we do if the police stop us."

"If they stop us we have to defend ourselves," he explains.

"Oh," I say, looking down at the gun in my lap. In the back of my mind I still think that somehow Huey doesn't really mean his statement, that he's fronting—a lot of guys threaten to shoot cops and then let themselves be arrested. I don't blame them. I'm a realist. I don't expect them—and I don't expect Huey—actually to shoot it out with the police. He'll still command my respect. So I imagine his actual plan is for some talk, some compromises, a tit for tat in which they lower their guns and we lower ours.

The evening is an anticlimax, no confrontation with the police. But when I come home finally, the M1 in hand—Huey has given me the rifle to keep—I am utterly exhausted, completely wound up. I store the gun in the closet and Pat asks what I'm doing. I haven't even thought about asking her permission. Not out of disrespect; her opinion simply doesn't matter. My mind and heart have been captured. The Party—not another woman—has taken me away from her. For the first time since I can remember I no longer feel adrift.

During the next several weeks Huey and Bobby become local heroes from their standoffs with police. After the tense scenes, Huey comes by, sipping cognac and telling me incredible tales, talking a mile a minute, no different from the 12-year-old kid with whom I used to walk to school, his head full of brilliant, mischievous, fascinating ideas.

But he's also a different Huey. I've been wrong. The Panther confrontations the last weeks have proved these guys are *not* like everybody else. They're not fronting. They're for real. They put on guns, load their ammunition, and don't back down when they find trouble.

And I ask myself, How do they do it?

Because I've never known anybody like that before.

But Huey I have known.

And yet, Huey is one of them.

And not just one of them—but their *leader*, the one they look up to.

And I know Huey and I've always been equal to Huey. In fact, when we were growing up Huey would come down to run with *us*.

So the past tells me I can join him. Huey's no superman; Huey's only Huey, the same person as ever, my friend, running partner, brother. And it's not Huey testing me, but a part of Huey inside myself, urging me, You can do this, David, meaning not just shoot at police, but—what scares me much more—take the intellectual and moral leap from the street corner into this world of action, ideas, and revolution.

"Why should I read it?" I challenge Huey. We're riding in the Volkswagen that belongs to LaVerne, his girlfriend. Huey's been going on about Castro, China, Aleister Crowley's *The Greatest Beast* all in the same breath, and now tells me I must study a book by an Algerian psychiatrist. "What's an Algerian psychiatrist gonna know about America?"

"Because he's talking about us. The wretched of the earth. That's what we are, David. The lumpen, the field niggers, the oppressed, the implacables. In Algeria the wretched of the earth threw out the French and created a revolutionary socialist society. Which is what we have to do here. So he has a lot to say to us. Revolutionary nationalists like us are not narrowly parochial, David."

We're driving down San Pablo, going to the Bos'un Locker, the bar where we hang out. The same sense of unreality and disbelief I've experienced before overcomes me, a kind of light-headed wooziness as I look at the familiar streets and people and see them in a new light: battlegrounds and revolutionaries.

"Huey," I say. "How do you know all these things? How'd you get so smart?"

"Reading," he says. "You can do it. I'll teach you. I'll tell you what to read. You can do it."

Maybe I can. One night Betty Shabazz, the widow of Malcolm X, comes to speak in San Francisco and the Party joins with another Bay Area group who also call themselves Panthers to serve as her bodyguard. I'm at work when the groups meet Betty Shabazz's plane, but when I attend her speech I hear there was a showdown at *Ramparts* magazine: Huey stood down the police, but the other group was fronting, with no ammunition in their guns, and would have been useless if a real shoot-out had occurred.

"They're not Panthers," I say and remember a phrase I've come across in Mao's Little Red Book. "They're paper panthers."

"That's right," Huey says. "That's good, David. Paper panthers."

I enjoy the moment. I've applied an idea to a situation—analyzed something. Maybe I have a gift for revolution after all.

I get Huey's book, *The Wretched of the Earth* by Frantz Fanon. I lie down, unconscious of my family's presence, my mind totally absorbed with the Party and politics, eager to absorb the lessons of what Huey calls "the black bible."

I open the yellow and black cover, struggle through the preface written by a Frenchman named Jean-Paul Sartre, and start reading the first chapter, "Concerning Violence."

"National liberation, national renaissance, the restoration of nationhood to the people, commonwealth: whatever may be the headings used or the new formula introduced, decolonization is always a violent phenomenon."

What?

I reread the paragraph.

I'm lost. I have the dictionary in one hand, the book in the other, and I can't get past the first page, can't get past the first paragraph, barely the first sentence. I might as well be reading a foreign language. Practically every word is unknown to me. I shuttle from the book to the dictionary, looking up these abstract, abstruse concepts—colonialism, decolonization, spontaneity, self-consciousness, tabula rasa, mutatis mutandis—figuring out the dictionary definition, then trying to apply the meaning to the sentence. By the time I've put one together, I've forgotten the previous two.

I close the book.

I feel as frustrated as when I'm on the job. Only this time ideas are falling down, not boxes of baby food, and I can't give up because Huey has told me this book will help enlighten me, and I trust Huey's opinions.

I skip ahead:

"You do not turn any society, however primitive it may be, upside down with such a program if you are not decided from the very beginning, that is to say from the actual formulation of that program, to overcome all the obstacles that you will come across in so doing."

Try another page:

"The natives' challenge to the colonial world is not a rational confrontation of points of view."

And one more:

"At times, this Manichaeism goes to its logical conclusion and dehumanizes the native, or to speak plainly it turns him into an animal."

That's it.

I drive over to Huey's house, furious at him for recommending this bedeviling book and at myself for not understanding it.

"Look, man," I say to Huey as he lies in bed—Huey always does a lot of his most important thinking in bed. "How the hell are we ever gonna educate people? *I* don't even know what's going on. I mean I read Malcolm X and I understood him, but I don't understand this at all! So how can I get other black people to understand it. They don't even understand *me* when I'm talking about Malcolm!"

"Let me tell you a story," Huey answers. He doesn't speak like a guru but in a fast, light voice, his words practically tripping over one another, his eyes darting, Geiger counters measuring his articulation and my comprehension; he's brilliant, spellbinding chatterbox.

"Imagine people living in a cave. They've been there all their lives. At the end of the cave shines a light. Now one person among them knows the light is the sun. The rest are afraid of the light. They've lived in darkness and think the light is some kind of evil. Now let's say the person who knows about the light tells them it's not evil and tries to lead them out of the cave. They'll fight and probably overpower and maybe even kill him. Because all they know is darkness, and so quite logically they would be fearful of the light. So instead he has to gradually lead them toward the light. Well, it's the same with knowledge. Gradually you have to lead people toward an understanding of

what's happening. So don't take this stuff all together. Just bit by bit understand it, and as you understand it you can give it to other people. Remember:
One never drops a flowerpot on the head of the masses."

His words don't help me to understand Fanon, not one bit.

But the story does give me hope. Huey's right. I myself have been in the
dark. But if I read and study the book, apply myself, struggle to understand
the concepts, rather than just become frustrated by them, I will begin to understand what Fanon is saying. *The wretched of the earth*—that's not only the
peasants Fanon talks about, but us, myself, J.J., Ernest, Chico.

Soon after, I attend one of the Party's political education classes. Bobby
leads the session. He's talking about national culture, discussing dashikis,
using the terms of colonizer and mother country, but speaking plainly so we
can understand.

"We're nationalists," Bobby says, "because we see ourselves as a nation
within a nation. But we're revolutionary nationalists. We don't see ourselves
as a national unit for racist reasons but as a necessity for us to progress as
human beings and live on the face of this earth. We don't fight racism with
racism. We fight racism with solidarity. We don't fight exploitative capitalism with black capitalism. We fight capitalism with revolutionary socialism.
All of us are laboring people—employed or unemployed, and our unity has
got to be based on the practical necessities of life, liberty, and the pursuit of
happiness. It's got to be based on the practical things like the survival of
people and people's right to self-determination, to iron out their problems
by themselves without the interference of the police or CIA or armed forces
of the USA. We don't care about changing what we wear; we want power—
later for what we wear. Dashikis don't free nobody and pork chops don't oppress nobody."

With their guns, the Panthers demonstrate in North Richmond against
the police killing of a young brother named Denzil Dowell. Shortly afterward, I drive with Huey and Bobby to San Francisco; there we meet Eldridge Cleaver and other Panthers and put out a four-page mimeographed
sheet with the headline "Why Was Denzil Dowell Killed?" That April a bill
is introduced in the California legislature to ban people from carrying guns
in public. Huey sees the possibility of a "colossal event." He decides to send
Bobby and a delegation of thirty Panthers—twenty-four men and six
women—right to the statehouse in Sacramento, loaded with guns and with
a message to the people:

America has historically reserved its most barbaric treatment for non-
white people. . . . The enslavement of Black people at the very founding of
this country, the genocide practiced on the America Indians and the confine-
ment of the survivors on reservations, the savage lynching of thousands of
Black men and women, the dropping of atomic bombs on Hiroshima and Na-
gasaki, and now the cowardly massacre of Vietnam all testify to the fact that
toward people of color the racist power structure of America has but one policy: repression, genocide, terror, and the big stick.

Black people have begged, prayed, petitioned and demonstrated, among
other things, to get the racist power structure of America to right the wrongs

which have historically been perpetrated against Black people. All of these efforts have been answered by more repression, deceit, and hypocrisy. As the aggression of the racist American government escalates in Vietnam, the police agencies of America escalate the repression of Black people through the ghettos of America.

The Black Panther Party for Self-Defense believes that the time has come for Black people to arm themselves against this terror before it is too late. . . . A people who have suffered so much for so long at the hands of a racist society must draw the line somewhere. We believe that the Black communities of America must rise up as one man to halt the progression of a trend that leads inevitably to their total destruction.

After carrying their guns into the State Assembly and reading Huey's message to reporters, the Panthers are arrested on a variety of trumped-up charges and put up on bail. To free them, Huey and I invest part of five hundred dollars he gets for speaking at San Francisco State—his first paid speaking engagement—in a pound of marijuana, breaking it down into "nickels" that we'll sell on the street.

As we're transporting the dope in the Volkswagen, a cop car drives by. I understand this could be a very, very bad situation because not only do we have the dope but we also have the guns in the car as usual.

"Hey, Huey," I say, "what are we supposed to do if the police stop us?"

Huey laughs. "We *shoot* them. You know, we fight."

Even with the preparation of the last several weeks, I am unprepared for the answer.

He goes on. "We don't give up our guns. We don't give up our dope. I mean, that's what I don't understand about these brothers. They get busted and they have guns with them, which is all the police have, but they give up their guns *and* their property. No. If the police come and mess around here, they've stopped the wrong car."

I look at him. Huey's completely serene, not scared or macho, just real clearheaded about the situation, certain of one thing: if the cops stop us, they are going to be the ones in trouble, not us.

The silence grows. I have to answer him. In my mind history has always happened differently, almost as though the events I read about were according to plan. What Huey and the rest of us are doing all seems much less organized, erratic. And I still doubt myself: Can we really be something of value? And yet Huey's knowledge and supreme self-confidence and my own excitement make the idea of turning back absolutely unacceptable.

"Okay," I say, watching the police car draw away in the rearview mirror. "Okay."

That fall of 1967, the students in the Bay Area organize a demonstration called Stop the Draft Week. For five days they try to shut down the Oakland recruiting station using nonviolent tactics. Neither Oakland nor the rest of the country has seen anything like these white kids—mother country radicals, Huey calls them, adopting one of Fanon's terms—defying the laws and police, "shutting the mother down," as they say, making chaos be the cost of the war.

Throughout the week, Huey and I sell papers at the demonstration. I listen to people's speeches over loudspeakers and mikes and then refer to the subject I've just heard as I hawk the paper: "Buy *The Black Panther*! Our paper speaks to this issue and our program—"

And people respond. "Yeah? What's this?"

"We're the Panthers! Want to see? Buy the paper!"

I sell a hundred papers in thirty minutes. Huey—who has first sold Red Books with Bobby on the Berkeley campus to get money for the Party—says, "God, you can really sell papers!"

My days become fractured. Some mornings I work longshore. I wake at five, Bobby driving me to the San Francisco dispatch hall and back to Oakland once my number is assigned a job. Then he takes the car, going off on Party business while I work in the hold. We load rawhides onto pallets, crisscrossing the leathers to secure them on the platforms. I hate the work; flies teem around the still-bloody, rancid-smelling skins. Overhead the walking boss looks down into the hold, shouting orders at me. The smell, dark, and insects nauseate me; I'm back in the outhouse in my mother's backyard at Mobile, and I curse the man every time his shadow passes.

Some mornings I don't report at all. I let a member of my crew sign for me and meet them at the dock or have someone else altogether use my number. They show up for work and I collect the paycheck, splitting the money.

"You gotta get to work," June tells me, getting on my case one morning after I say I'm too tired for the shape-up. "You're gonna lose your job. You got a family to support."

I get angry with him, curse him out, saying he has a slave mentality and that he should free himself from the white man's world. But Huey has the same attitude.

"Keep the job, man," he says. "Besides, it's a good job. I gotta get me a job myself. My girlfriend is getting on me."

"I hate the job," I tell Huey.

We talk at his girlfriend's house. It's the afternoon. Huey's hung over from our drunk at the Bos'un Locker the night before. He's lying in bed, reading Fanon.

"We gotta figure out what to do, David," he says, planted on the bed. "Things are really not going well. What are we gonna do?"

Together we review the past and formulate plans for the future. We've got a tubful of weed we can sell to raise some money, plus June's buddies like to play poker and we can hold a poker party at my house, serving and charging for spaghetti and fried chicken and taking a percentage of the pot.

By now it's four or five and we're ready to roll; there's a Congress of Racial Equality (CORE) rally this afternoon that Huey thinks we should attend.

"We need to revive the spirit of the Party," Huey says as we cruise through West Oakland. "We need a colossal event."

"Well what are we gonna do?" I ask.

He doesn't know. We stop on Seventh Street and Huey notices a good looking hooker holding a clipboard.

"What are you doing," Huey asks her.

"Studying sociology," she says.

Huey cracks up. "Well interview me," he jokes.

At the CORE rally Huey stands by the door debating with people. When it's over we drift down to the Bos'un Locker.

"This is how you organize," Huey tells me in the car. "This is what Castro did. You talk to people. You organize the peasants. And the people here are the bars."

Gene McKinney and some other guys from the old days are already there Huey asks for three zombies, stiff drinks, and bets he can down all three, one after the other. Now June and his buddies join us. June is skeptical and stand-offish toward Huey, but he buys him a drink too because—even as critical as he is—he loves to loosen Huey's tongue and make him talk on revolution.

"Go on, Huey!" they encourage him. "Talk!"

By now Huey is well into it, discussing Marxism and the Russian Revolution. I listen to his fervid oratory, fascinated by his knowledge and brilliance. Huey raps on Soviets and communes, the Bolsheviks and Me*** sheviks. The foreign names and distant countries no longer intimidate me Instead I'm excited by them. Once all these people and organizations were the same as Huey and Bobby and me.

"Huey," I say that night as we drive home, "I gotta learn about the Russian Revolution and Marxism."

"Go see *Doctor Zhivago*," he says.

"What?"

"It's a movie. Go see it. Then we can talk about it."

I have other questions, but it's late; besides, there are always others questions; every answer raises another question. I want to continue—I feel an urgent need to know everything because I also believe I have never learned anything before this; the entire world is opening up to my understanding things always dark and impossible to fathom are now perfectly clear, perfectly comprehensible—but I've got to get to work the next morning.

The next morning I'm tired and the stench from the cowhides is nauseating. From the first moment, the walking boss is on me:

"Get a move on, Hilliard! Move your ass!"

I explode at his irritating barks. "I'm moving as fast as I want!" I shout back. The other workers check me out.

"Don't you be yelling at me! You got something to say you come down here and say it to my face! I'm sick and tired of you standing up there yelling down at me! What the hell do you think this is? A slave ship? I'm gonna move as fast as I please. I'm not a slave anymore. And if you think differently you'd best not be up there when I come up!"

That night June gets after me. Pat remembers the scene.

"We were in the car," Pat says.

June was saying, "Man, you don't need to get into that. Just stick with your job."

But with me it was like, whatever you did was all right. I didn't want you to join because I was scared of death. But you wanted to join. You felt a need for yourself. That this was your chance to do something.

I said, "You do whatever you want. I'll work and take care of the kids. Just make sure the kids are okay."

———————————————— ■ ————————————————

The Panthers catapulted to national prominence as a result of four separate events. The first was the addition of Eldridge Cleaver as Minister of Education. Cleaver had gained celebrity as a result of essays he had written while a prisoner at Folsom Prison.[7] The second was their protest of the Mulford Anti-Gun bill that ended up with the Panthers on the floor of the California State Assembly armed and dressed in black. The third was their participation in Stop the Draft Week in 1967. The Panthers, like SNCC, formally opposed the war and collaborated with other anti-war groups to stage rallies across the country. The fourth incident was an offshoot of the Panthers involvement in the anti-war movement. Law enforcement officials targeted Newton as one of the key players and while driving home from a party, he was stopped by the Oakland police. Things escalated and shots were fired. One officer died and another was wounded. Newton was also shot and ended up being jailed without bail. The Panthers started a "Free Huey" movement and regularly held rallies outside of the jail that received extensive media coverage.

Black power advocates convened a meeting in Newark, New Jersey to debate the "black nation" question. The Panthers and SNCC demanded United Nations status and initiated discussions about partitioning a portion in the continental United States. On the basis of this initial collaboration, the two groups began to think about a more formal alliance. SNCC was looking to leave the South but needed a place to "land" in the North. SNCCs had two desirable assets: an experienced cadre of leaders who had earned their marks in the toughest places in the Deep South; and, a more a solid intellectual grasp of Black Nationalism. On the other hand, the Panthers offered a well-developed program of activities (e.g., school breakfasts, sickle cell research, economic cooperatives, nationalist schools, and neighborhood watch patrols). In addition the Party was expanding to other cities in the North.

On its face, the alliance seemed quite plausible. Behind the scenes, though, strong personalities fought for dominance and the alliance quickly fell apart. The disintegration was aided by intense pressure from outside sources. The FBI, CIA, and other law enforcement agencies stepped up their repression of "black radicals." Authorities killed Bobby Hutton in an attack on the Oakland headquarters, Fred Hampton was gunned down in Chicago, and Newton was convicted on murder charges. Although Bobby Seale ran a respectable campaign for mayor of Oakland in 1973, the Party began to disintegrate. Similarly, SNCC never found a foothold in the North after the failed alliance with the Panthers in the late 1960s.

With murder charges hanging over his head, Newton jumped bail in 1974 and left for Cuba. In her autobiography, A Taste of Power, Elaine Brown describes how she assumed leadership of the party. As she notes, "[A] woman in the Black power movement was considered, at best, irrelevant . . . [I]f a black woman assumed a role of leadership, she was said to be eroding black manhood, to be hindering the progress of the black race. She was an enemy of black people." Brown exposes a sore point of the entire movement—a failure to reconcile issues of race and gender. In other words, although black men were fighting for the freedom of their people, they did so under the cloak of sexism. For Brown, the phrase Black Power ". . . symbolized . . . . the denial of black women in favor of the freedom of the black man." Although Brown was able to temporarily hold the party together, the Black Power phase of the civil rights movement was essentially over.

A WOMAN'S REVOLUTION

Elaine Brown

Excerpt from A Taste of Power: A Black Woman's Story

A woman in the Black Power movement was considered, at best, irrelevant. A woman asserting herself was a pariah. A woman attempting the role of leadership was, to my proud black Brothers, making an alliance with the "counter-revolutionary, man-hating, lesbian, feminist white bitches." It was a violation of some Black Power principle that was left undefined. If a black woman assumed a role of leadership, she was said to be eroding black manhood, to be hindering the progress of the black race. She was an enemy of black people.

I knew I would have to muster something mighty to manage the Black Panther Party. My quick decision to get Huey to ordain Larry Henson as the new chief of staff had been the most important step in that direction. Larry's own male chauvinism would, I concluded, be held in check by his serious commitment to the dictates of the party. Whatever problems it presented would be outweighed by his fearlessness, and by the relentlessness and even savagery with which he always carried out orders. He was capable of hoisting me above the battlefield of men who might resist or challenge my leadership.

During the critical two weeks after Huey's departure, before I announced my new role to the membership, Larry proved he would tolerate no disrespect of me or the orders that flowed from the Central Committee that I was quickly reconstituting. He proved he could and would put down usurpers, that he could manage the military arm of the party and would unquestioningly support all party decisions with the force of that arm. With Larry behind me, I was unfaltering when I announced to the entire party that Huey Newton was in exile and that I was taking his place.

Like most new arrivals from other chapters, Larry had been assigned menial work. He worked in the party's day-care facilities, where he had as carefully and conscientiously washed babies and cooked their food as he had taken his turn on the overnight security watch. He cleaned the child-care facilities during the day as diligently as he cleaned the guns June Hilliard gave him at night. He was reliable, loyal to the point of killing or dying. His record earned him a place in the special security ranks. Now he was chief of staff of a party that could survive only, I believed, under his sure hand.

Within a month of Huey's exile, Larry had shaped our straggling army. He had ordered the guns and asserted authority over the hardest of the men, aboveground and underground. He was carefully reorganizing the next link in his chain of command, elevating the toughest and truest men, like Perkins and Ricardo and Big Bob. He also had put down a series of disruptions on the Oakland streets that came as news of Huey's exile spread.

By the time Tony moved to Sacramento, he had been elevated to the Cabinet post of legal affairs secretary to the governor, and I had announced my candidacy for a seat on the City Council of Oakland. My candidacy had been on our agenda since the last campaign. Huey had talked with me about it a great deal. It was more important now than ever to pursue this goal, he advised me over the telephone from Cuba, where he had settled into exile.

There was very little time left before the election in April 1975. I had no idea how I could at once run for office and steer the Black Panther Party, but there was too little time to waste worrying.

I installed Beth Meador, a black law student, as my campaign manager. Impressively, I was able to get black businessman Otho Green to be finance manager of the campaign. Green had been Bobby Seale's only black opponent for the mayor's seat. Inside the party, I placed Phyllis Jackson, who had been one of the mainstays of the previous campaign, as coordinator of party campaign workers. I positioned Ericka Huggins to fill the vacancy of administrator of our school and its affiliate programs and projects. I had already appointed Joan Kelley administrator of our nonmilitary apparatus, such as the Survival Programs and legal matters, and Norma Armour, coordinator of the ministry of finance. I made Michael Fultz, from the Boston branch, coeditor of the newspaper with David Du Bois. The pieces were in place.

There was one result of all this I had failed to think through: I had introduced a number of women in the party's administration. There were too many women in command of the affairs of the Black Panther Party, numerous men were grumbling.

"I hear we can't call them bitches no more," one Brother actually stated to me in the middle of an extraordinarily hectic day.

"No, motherfucker," I responded unendearingly, "you may not call *them* bitches 'no more.'" I turned brusquely to Bill, my bodyguard, and told him to make a note for Larry to deal with "my Brother here."

It was a given that the entire Black Power movement was handicapped by the limited roles the Brothers allowed the Sisters and by the outright oppressive behavior of men toward women. This had meant little to me personally, however. The party was so far to the left of the civil rights and black nationalist men, nothing in their philosophies was dreamt of in ours. And because of Huey—and now Larry—I had been able to deflect most of the chauvinism of Black Panther men. My leadership was secure. Thus, in installing Sisters in key positions, I had not considered this business. I had only considered the issue of merit, which had no gender.

The grumbling over the elevation of women grew louder. I had to call upon Larry to shut all mouths.

. . . I mustered all the energy I had to struggle through the last two months of the campaign. Aggravating the situation like a gnat was one of my lesser opponents, an unknown young Negro.

He was suggesting to little gatherings of prospective supporters that I had an unsalutary lifestyle, as exhibited by my cocaine case and by what he labeled as my secret sexual life. "Those in the know," he stated, were sure I was a "man-hating lesbian." He pointed to the number of women who had suddenly "taken over" the party, especially now that the great Huey P. Newton was out of sight.

Oddly, I had never thought of myself as a feminist. I had even been denounced by certain radical feminist collectives as a "lackey" for men. That charge was based on my having written and sung two albums of songs that my female accusers claimed elevated and praised men. Resenting that label, I had joined the majority of black women in America in denouncing feminism. It was an idea reserved for white women, I said, assailing the women's movement, wholesale, as either racist or inconsequential to black people.

Sexism was a secondary problem. Capitalism and racism were primary. I had maintained that position even in the face of my exasperation with the chauvinism of Black Power men in general and Black Panther men in particular.

Now hearing the ugly intent of my opponent's words, I trembled with a fury long buried. I recognized the true meaning of his words. He was not talking about making love with women—he was attacking me for *valuing* women.

The feminists were right. The value of my life had been obliterated as much by being female as by being black and poor. Racism and sexism in America were equal partners in my oppression.

Even men who were themselves oppressed wanted power over women. Whatever social stigma had been intended by the label "lesbian"—always invoked when men felt threatened, I observed with the benefit of hindsight—did not concern me. It was simply the rattle of a man terrorized by a social order dominated by other men. It was a social order I was bent on destroying. But his accusations did wake me.

There would be no further impositions on me by men, including black men, including Black Panther men. I would support every assertion of human rights by women—from the right to abortion to the right of equality with men as laborers and leaders. I would declare that the agenda of the Black Panther Party and our revolution to free black people from oppression specifically included black women.

I would denounce loudly the philosophies of the Karengas, who raised the name of Africa to justify the suppression of black women. I would lambaste the civil-rights men who had dismissed the importance of women like Fannie Lou Hamer and Ella Baker and Daisy Bates and even Kathleen Cleaver. I would not tolerate any raised fists in my face or any Black Power handshakes, or even the phrase "Black Power," for all of it now symbolized to me the denial of black women in favor of the freedom of "the black man."

I would claim my womanhood and my place. If that gave rise to my being labeled a "man-hating lesbian, feminist bitch," I would be the most radical of them.

I made it clear that no more discussion would be had regarding my personnel decisions. The women I had positioned would be accepted for what they were: the most capable. I would be very hard on those who questioned me on the basis of my genitalia.

It was with this attitude that I insisted on attending the disciplinary session I ordered for a Brother who had blackened the eye of the Sister with whom he was "relating," because she had not properly cooked his greens. It was with this attitude that I had Larry and Perkins accompany me to a meeting with my accusatory campaign opponent, in which we threatened him with bodily harm if he ever so much as spoke my name again in public.

The Black Power phase ended by the mid-1970s and marks the closing of the civil rights movement.[8] A number of factors made this strategy difficult to sustain. First, its confrontational nature evoked a punitive response from white governmental officials. "Black militants" were typically blamed for mass rioting in a number of American cities between 1967 and 1970. For example, Richard Nixon won the presidency in 1968 on the strength of a "law and order" platform promising to control urban unrest. The police routinely harassed Black Power activists and many of them, including Carmichael, Newton, and Seale, left the country. Second, a portion of the leadership was co-opted into mainstream structures. Poverty and urban redevelopment funds pouring into black ghettos were attractive to many leaders and were directed to those willing to "play the game." Third, while the Panthers and SNCC received national attention, their memberships were never large. It appears that a majority of the black community accepted elements of "cultural nationalism" (e.g., wearing dashikis, growing Afros, rejecting "slave names") but few people endorsed such nationalist goals as partitioning the U.S, returning to Africa, or remaining in segregated communities.

None of this is to say that the movement has ended. To be sure, black people and communities continue to litigate, mobilize, and protest racial inequality. The Million Man March notwithstanding, contemporary efforts are neither as coordinated nor sustained as the activities of the 1950s and 1960s. As we will discover in the next section, the legacy of the movement continues to bob and weave through the difficult terrain of current racial politics in America.

STUDY QUESTIONS

1. SNCC's position paper "*The Basis of Black Power*" and the "*Black Panther Party Platform and Program*" articulate a more aggressive approach to achieving a black voice in America. What is the black power platform? What is the role of white people (and others) in this new approach? How ought one to evaluate the success of this part of the movement? What was the governmental response to black power? Can a black power model be successful in today's world?

2. What were the underlying causes of the Watts riot of 1965? How much different are they than the causes of urban unrest in the last decade of the 20th century? What was (and has been) the governmental response? What should a new approach look like?

3. What were the gender politics of the black power movement? More generally, what are the tensions between feminism and a black nationalist agenda? How might these tensions be resolved? What are the implications for modern day gender politics within the African-American community?

4. Why did young people like David Hilliard join the Black Panther Party in the 1960s? Were his motivations different than those of young blacks who join gangs in today's society?

NOTES

1. Charles V. Hamilton and Stokley Carmichael. *Black power: the politics of liberation in America*. (London: Cape) 1968.

2. Vincent Harding. *There is a river: the Black struggle for freedom in America* (New York: Harcourt Brace Jovanovich) 1981.

3. Nicholas Lemann, *The Promised Land: The Great Black Migration and How it Changed America*. (New York: Knopf) 1991.

4. Even "conscious" whites were considered a liability because "[W]hites who come into the black community with ideas of change may want to absolve the power structure of its responsibility for what it is doing."

5. *National Advisory Committee on Civil Disorders*, 1967 (The Kerner Report).

6. For a fuller discussion of the Panthers, Charles E. Jones (ed.). *The Black Panther Party reconsidered*. (Baltimore: Black Classic Press) 1998.

7. *Soul on Ice*. Ramparts: New York 1968.

8. William L. Van Deburg. *New day in Babylon: The Black Power Movement and American culture*. (Chicago: University of Chicago Press) 1992.

The Contemporary Consequences of the Struggle for African-American Liberation

In their book *Issue Evolution* James Carmines and Edward Stimson introduce the notion of *easy* and *hard* issues to explain why some issues are resolved with relative dispatch and others persist with acrimony on the public agenda.[1] Easy issues are characterized by clearly definitions of the problem, readily identifiable advocates and opponents with distinct views, and clear and attainable solutions. The imperative for equal rights made race an "easy" issue in the middle portion of the century. The government could take reasonably distinct and demonstrable "action steps" (e.g., school integration, voting protections, fair housing, etc.) and, for the most part, the public was able to identify the interests of heroes (e.g., King, Malcolm, Johnson) and villains (e.g., Conner, Wallace, Nixon). Thus between 1964 and 1978 a flurry of government action—often referred to as the "Great Society"—was designed to, among others things, promote the concerns of African-Americans. The basic premise was that government intervention would be the engine for black uplift.

There is little doubt that many things have changed as a result of the civil rights movement. Economically, African-Americans own banks, newspapers, sports franchises, insurance companies, radio stations, and television networks. Socially, open displays of racism are no longer tolerated and most white Americans subscribe to the principle of racial equality. For the most part, black Americans can go to the restaurants, movie theaters, hotels, and golf courses of their choice. In addition, African-Americans are among the country's most popular icons (e.g., Colin Powell, Oprah Winfrey, Michael Jordon) and are active contributors to the cultural life of the society (e.g., Toni Morrison, Walter Moseley, August Wilson, Wynton Marsalis). Finally, blacks have held mayoral seats in almost every large American city, have served in the Senate, the House, and the Cabinet, and have even run for president. In short, the life chances of black Americans have improved substantially over the last twenty-five years or so.

Still, there is farther to go. While some blacks have enjoyed the material fruits of American society, a significant portion remains mired in poverty, isolation, and hopelessness, and even middle-class blacks have a tenuous hold on the American dream. Racism, although more subtle (and more difficult to detect), still exists, and from time to time racial incidents resemble events from the first third of the century (e.g., the Byrd killing in Texas). Moreover, for all the talk about integration, the society remains deeply segregated when it comes to education, housing, and religion. Thus, for most white Americans the media becomes an important source of information about blacks. Given the tendency of American media to distort the realities of day-to-day black life, it is not surprising that many white Americans perceive blacks to be culturally deficient. Lastly, black political empowerment has generally been limited to aging cities, racially homogenous congressional districts, and bureaucratic posts subject to the pleasure of a (white) chief executive. From this view, gains that have been made are largely superficial—whites are still the superordinate group and blacks remain the subordinate group.

Thus in the post-civil rights era race has become a "hard" issue. Racial goals are unclear and significant disagreement exists about appropriate public remedies. Unlike the 1950s and 1960s it is much more difficult to distinguish between the "good guys" and the "bad guys." Is Ward Connerly good or bad? Louis Farakhan? Bill Clinton? Moreover, whites and blacks clearly perceive different realities. Thus race remains a divisive issue in American social and political life.

WHITHER RACISM?

A central underlying goal of the civil rights movement was to eradicate racist attitudes among the white public. Integration, it was believed, would reduce racial fears and promote equality. On the surface, white support for racial equality has risen dramatically over the last 40 years. In their book, *Racial Attitudes in America*, Howard Schuman and his colleagues show that support for the formal principles of racial equality increased substantially between the early 1940s and the early 1980s. For example, less than 50% of white Americans supported integrated transportation in 1942 but almost 90% supported it by 1970. Likewise, support for school integration rose from about one-third in 1942 to more than 85% in 1982, and support for integrated public accommodations increased from 73% in 1963 to 88% by 1970. Thus, there appears to be widespread acceptance of the principle of racial equality.[2] In contrast, this prima facie progress did not translate into support for implementation of the principles. Data from the Schuman study indicate that support for busing actually decreased by 15 percentage points between 1964 and 1978. Schuman et al., refer to this as the "principle-implementation gap." That is, the discrepancy between what people will support in theory and what they will support in practice.

Nonetheless, there has been progress. The American public does not generally tolerate overt displays of racist attitudes. Moreover, there are whole communities where the dominant ethos is racial tolerance (e.g., Walnut, California). Yet, anti-black sentiments persist among a nontrivial segment of the white population. For instance, a 1992 study of Los Angeles residents found that 40% of the white sample rated blacks negatively—60% said that blacks were dependent on welfare, 40% believed blacks to be less intelligent and hard to get along with, and around 30% opposed living in black neighborhoods or marrying blacks.[3] Thus, it is not surprising that whites and blacks perceive fundamentally different realities. The Joint Center for Political and Economic Studies' 1997 national poll on race relations reports that African-Americans (compared to whites) were significantly more likely to believe that: race relations were poor in their communities, discrimination against blacks "remains common," the situation for African-Americans has either stayed the same or gotten worse in the last 5 years, and the police harass and discriminate against blacks.[4] As the Center concludes, ". . . the state of race relations remains troubled."[5]

Researchers have provided several explanations for enduring racism in American society. In their book, **Divided by Color: Racial Politics and Democratic Ideals**, *Don Kinder and Lynn Sanders review three basic models of contemporary racial attitudes. The first position argues that a new form of racism has emerged to replace the "open bigotry" of old-fashioned (or "red-neck") racism. According to this view, whites interpreted urban violence associated with Black Power ideology in the late 1960s and early 1970s as a violation of cherished American values. In addition, the campaigns of Wallace, Nixon, and Reagan ". . . gave public expression to simmering racial resentments." The core belief was that formal racism had been outlawed, opportunities existed, and blacks should stop complaining and making demands. Instead, they should pull themselves up by the "bootstraps" like other minority groups in American society. As Kinder and Sanders observe, "[A]t the core of this question was not whether blacks possessed the inborn ability to succeed, but rather whether they would try."[6]*

There appears to be little doubt that racial resentment exists or that it has an impact on how whites think on racial policy matters. For example, the Kinder and Sanders data shows that a majority of whites subscribe to the view that black demands are illegitimate. Further, racial resentment is shown to have a measurable impact on white attitudes toward a wide range of pro-black public policies (e.g., school desegregation, preferential hiring, fair employment).

A rival theory maintains that white Americans' attitudes toward blacks are affected by a commitment to a bundle of traditional American values (i.e., equality, economic individualism, and limited government). Opposition to black interests, according to this view, is not a function of simple anti-black sentiment but rather an assessment based on evaluations of fairness, individual responsibility, and government action. For example, white opposition to increased federal spending is thought to be a judgement about the appropriate role of the government, not a judgement against blacks per se. Kinder and Sanders conclude that the evidence for this model is mixed. On the one hand, there is widespread support for the "American Creed." In addition, ". . . equality loomed the largest in public opinion on matters of race." On the other hand, economic individualism and limited government failed to produce consistent effects on racial policy preferences.[7]

The third viewpoint contends that "[W]hites resist policies promoting racial equality . . . out of a sense that such policies threaten their collective interests." The basis for this model is "realistic group conflict" theory. The argument is that because groups are in a state of competition over finite public resources, anything that advances one group will be opposed by the other (i.e., a "zero sum" game). Over time, members make an assessment of their group's relative position in the society. Black gains in the 1960s and 1970s, on this line of logic, slowed white advancement thus representing a threat to historic white hegemony. As Kinder and Sanders show, the perception of threat is driven more by white world views than by "social circumstances" or economic threat. The perception of threat, however, does appear to influence support for race-specific policies. For example, whites that perceived racial group threat were less likely to support policies such as school desegregation, preferential hiring, and college quotas.[8]

DIVIDED BY COLOR:
RACIAL POLITICS AND DEMOCRATIC IDEALS

Donald R. Kinder and Lynn M. Sanders

Excerpt from Divided by Color: Racial Politics and Democratic Ideals

If the civil rights movement and the flagrantly racist reaction it incited compelled many white Americans to express their support for racial equality as a matter of principle, the riots and the new belligerent rhetoric pushed them in quite a different direction. As we saw earlier, civil rights was widely regarded as the nation's most important problem in 1964 and 1965, but began to fade soon thereafter and disappeared entirely by the mid-1970s. Whites seemed to believe that the national government had successfully swept away all the barriers and obstacles that had stood in the way of black participation in American society. Segregation was being dismantled. Discrimination was illegal. Voting rights were being enforced. In the view of many white Americans, the problem of race was solved.

Or rather *that* problem of race was solved. Public discussion of the "race problem" in America no longer referred to ensuring equal rights and opportunities for blacks—that, apparently, had already been accomplished. Instead, discussion centered on the threat that inner-city blacks posed to social order and public safety. As Americans lost interest in civil rights, they became preoccupied with violence and disorder in the cities.

This change reflects a transformation in the characterization of race relations dominating news reports and public discourse. Before Watts, the typical picture looked something like this: neatly dressed blacks, petitioning peacefully for their basic rights, crouched on the ground, being pummeled with nightsticks and set upon by police dogs. After Watts, Americans were instead witness to pictures of mobs of young city blacks, hurling bricks at police cars, torching their own neighborhoods, and looting stores of all that they could carry. Such pictures invited the conclusion from whites that after all that had been done for blacks, after all that had been given to them, it was not enough. Blacks wanted more, they demanded more—and they took it.

The riots opened up a huge racial rift. Fear and revulsion against the violence were widespread among both white and black Americans, but whites were much more likely to condemn those who participated in the riots and more eager for the police and National Guard to retaliate against them. Where blacks saw the riots as expressions of legitimate grievances, whites were inclined to explain them as eruptions of black hatred and senseless criminality incited by outside agitators. To many white Americans, then, the civil disorders of the 1960s amounted to an appalling collective mugging.

Understood in this way, the riots created a crisis for liberalism. President Johnson attempted to distinguish between the movement for civil rights—the "orderly struggle for civil rights that has ennobled the last decade"—and the violence and destruction that were sweeping through American cities. This was a difficult distinction to sell, and the political advantage moved decisively to the conservatives:

> Liberals faced the burden of explaining why the riots occurred after so many of the things which they had promised would solve the problems had already been done. They faced accusations that they were unwilling to uphold public order and were proposing to reward rather than punish communities that had spawned mass violence. Politically, liberals suddenly found themselves on the defensive, no longer occupying the high moral ground. Intellectually, they were far from certain about what was required or what would work.

After the riots, conservative arguments took on new appeal, now in tune with white apprehensions. There was less talk about equality and more about law and order. Onto the national stage strutted George Wallace, followed in short order by the "new" Richard Nixon and by Ronald Reagan. Each, in his own way, gave public expression to simmering racial resentments. By interpreting inner-city violence and poverty as glaring manifestations of the failure of blacks to live up to American values, and by placing these problems at the center of their campaigns, Wallace, Nixon, and Reagan, among others, helped to create and legitimize a new form of prejudice. They did not promote biological racism: they were not white supremacists; they did not allege genetic impairments; they did not promise a return to segregation; they did not imply that blacks were second-class citizens or that they should be treated differently than anyone else. Their message was subtle, rather than blatant: it was that blacks should behave themselves. They should take quiet advantage of the ample opportunities now provided them. Government had been too generous, had given blacks too much, and blacks, for their part, had accepted these gifts all too readily. Discrimination was illegal, opportunities were plentiful. Blacks should work their way up without handouts or special favors in a society that was now color-blind.

At the core of this new resentment was not whether blacks possessed the inborn ability to succeed, but rather whether they would try. Now that all major obstacles to their improvement had supposedly been removed, would blacks apply themselves, as others had before them? One might say that black Americans would now be judged as Martin Luther King had wished, that is, by the "content of their character." The riots specifically and inner-city life generally were interpreted by many whites as repudiations of individualism, sacred American commitments to hard work, discipline, and self-sacrifice.

And more was to come. The riots that had handed the political advantage to conservatives were followed by a series of contentious public issues entangled in race, which, to many whites, exposed both the misguided benevolence of major American institutions and the moral deficiency of blacks unwilling to make it honestly on their own. These included allegations of fraud and abuse in the welfare system, explosions of crime, the dissolution of the traditional family, the plague of drugs, and dependence on government handouts. Most recently, public debate on matters of race has focused on affirmative action. Opponents of affirmative action see government requiring employers to give jobs and promotions to underqualified blacks, schools filling up with ill-prepared and undeserving black students, judges redrawing district lines to guarantee black candidates safe election, and colleges caving in to black students with codes that restrict speech and multicultural curricula that ridicule traditional learning.

Each of these episodes has provided a public stage for the creation and expression of racial animosity. A new form of prejudice has come to prominence, one that is preoccupied with matters of moral character, informed by the virtues associated with the traditions of individualism. At its center are the contentions that blacks do not try hard enough to overcome the difficulties they face and that they take what they have not earned. Today, we say, prejudice is expressed in the language of American individualism.

THE MEANING AND
MEASUREMENT OF RACIAL RESENTMENT

With these developments in mind, we attempted to measure racial resentment with a battery of six questions included in the 1986 NES. Each question was presented as an assertion; whites were asked to indicate whether they agreed or disagreed with each, and how strongly they did so:

> Irish, Italian, Jewish and many other minorities overcame prejudice and worked their way up. Blacks should do the same without any special favors.
> Generations of slavery and discrimination have created conditions that make it difficult for blacks to work their way out of the lower class.
> It's really a matter of some people not trying hard enough; if blacks would only try harder they could be just as well off as whites.
> Over the past few years, blacks have gotten less than they deserve.
> Most blacks who receive money from welfare programs could get along without it if they tried.
> Government officials usually pay less attention to a request or complaint from a black person than from a white person.

Compared with most efforts to measure racial animosity, these questions should appear rather subtle. They do not require whites to declare in straight-forward fashion that blacks are dim-witted or lazy or promiscuous. Their approach is more roundabout. The questions distinguish between those whites who are generally sympathetic toward blacks and those who are generally unsympathetic. It could be said that our questions do for race what Adorno's *Authoritarian Personality* did for anti-Semitism. The famous "F-scale" that Adorno and his research team employed to measure authoritarianism was composed of questions that resemble ours, in that they were carefully formulated, as Roger Brown put it, "to express a subtle hostility without seeming to offend the democratic values that most subjects would feel bound to support. Each question has a kind of fair-minded and reasonable veneer. It is sometimes rather difficult to find the sting."

As Table 6-1 reveals, many white Americans are quite prepared to express such a "subtle hostility" toward blacks. Substantial majorities agreed that if blacks would only try harder they could be just as well off as whites; that most blacks who receive money from welfare programs could get along without it if they tried; and that blacks should overcome prejudice on their own

RACIAL RESENTMENT AMONG WHITE AMERICANS

1. Most blacks who receive money from welfare programs could get along without it if they tried.

Agree strongly	25.4%
Agree somewhat	35.3
Neither agree nor disagree	14.2
Disagree somewhat	18.7
Disagree strongly	6.5

2. Over the past few years, blacks have gotten less than they deserve.

Agree strongly	3.3
Agree somewhat	15.4
Neither agree nor disagree	22.8
Disagree somewhat	38.0
Disagree strongly	20.5

3. Government officials usually pay less attention to a request or complaint from a black person than from a white person.

Agree strongly	3.9
Agree somewhat	17.8
Neither agree nor disagree	28.3
Disagree somewhat	30.5
Disagree strongly	19.4

4. Irish, Italian, Jewish and many other minorities overcame prejudice and worked their way up. Blacks should do the same without any special favors.

Agree strongly	32.9
Agree somewhat	33.7
Neither agree nor disagree	12.4
Disagree somewhat	16.2
Disagree strongly	4.7

[In past studies, we have asked people why they think white people seem to get more of the good things in life in America—such as better jobs and more money—than black people do. These are some of the reasons given by both blacks and whites.]

5. It's really a matter of some people not trying hard enough; if blacks would only try harder they could be just as well off as whites.

Agree strongly	22.4
Agree somewhat	36.9
Neither agree nor disagree	13.3
Disagree somewhat	19.1
Disagree strongly	8.2

6. Generations of slavery and discrimination have created conditions that make it difficult for blacks to work their way out of the lower class.

Agree strongly	17.0
Agree somewhat	41.1
Neither agree nor disagree	9.8
Disagree somewhat	19.2
Disagree strongly	12.9

SOURCE: 1986 National Election Study.

without any special favors. Likewise, many rejected the assertion that blacks have gotten less than they deserve in recent years; that blacks receive less attention from government officials than whites do; or that generations of slavery and discrimination have created conditions that make it difficult for blacks to work their way into the middle class.

RACIAL RESENTMENT AND RACE POLICY

Our immediate purpose is to estimate the impact of racial resentment where it is likely to be most pronounced: on policies that deal explicitly and unambiguously with race. On matters of school desegregation and affirmative action, black Americans are the intended primary beneficiaries, and all our questions name them as such. If racial resentment is to come into play in public opinion at all, it should show up most plainly here.

In this first analysis, we also take into account, in addition to racial resentment, the effects due to material threats to self-interest, opposition to the intrusions of government in private affairs, a wide array of social background characteristics (age, region, gender, Hispanic ethnicity, family income, education, occupational status), as well as race of interviewer.

Column 1 of Table 6-2 presents the results. The rows of the table correspond to each of the six race policies included in the 1986 NES. The estimated effect of racial resentment is provided in each case by ordinary least squares regression. Keeping in mind that the policy questions, like the racial resentment scale, are coded on the 0–1 interval, the coefficients on display in column 1 of Table 6-2 indicate a very substantial effect of racial resentment on white opinion.

Consider, as a typical example, the question of whether the federal government should provide special assistance to black Americans. According to Table 6-2, the regression estimate of the effect of racial resentment on this question of policy is .44. This means that two white Americans, identical in social background and political outlook, who differ only in that one is racially sympathetic (scoring 0 on the racial resentment scale) while the other is racially resentful (a score of 1.0), will differ from each other on the question of federal assistance by a value of .44. When we consider that the effects due to other considerations are taken into account, and that the policy scale itself ranges from 0, meaning that the government has a special obligation to blacks, to 1, meaning that blacks should get ahead on their own without the help of government, a difference of .44 is large.

Indeed, column 1 of Table 6-2 presents nothing but sizable coefficients. The effect of racial resentment is greatest on the question of quotas in college admissions and smallest—though still appreciable—on the question of school desegregation. These results imply that white Americans' objections to policies intended to diminish racial inequalities are expressions, in large part, of racial resentment.

■ **TABLE 6-2**

IMPACT OF RACIAL RESENTMENT ON WHITE AMERICANS' OPINIONS ON RACE POLICY

Policy	1986		1988		1992	
	(1)	(2)	(3)	(4)	(5)	(6)
Fair employment	.57	.57	.51	.63	.63	.51
School desegregation	.30	.28	.18	–	.40	.17
Federal spending	.45	.44	.36	.41	.59	.73
Government effort	.44	.44	.37	.53	.51	.59
Preferential hiring	.40	.40	.38	.42	.47	.41
College quotas	.60	.61	.59	.63	.71	.60

SOURCE: 1986, 1988, 1992 National Election Studies.

NOTE: Table entry is B, the unstandardized regression coefficient representing the effect of racial resentment (coded 0–1) on whites' views on race policy (also coded 0–1). All coefficients are statistically significant.

MATTERS OF PRINCIPLE

One strong current in the history of Western political thought, closely associated with Aristotle, insists that politics and morality never be divorced. Aristotle argued in the *Ethics* that moral judgments must be integrated into political life. In the *Politics*, he suggested that a necessary criterion for judging the worthiness of a governmental regime or constitution was whether it allowed a good man to be a good citizen. Our purpose here is to investigate the proposition that public opinion on matters of race is based in part on principles, much as Aristotle would have wished.

Our analysis takes for granted that people are neither detached nor indifferent to their world; that they "do not stop with a sheerly factual view of their experience. Explicitly or implicitly, they are continually regarding things as good or bad, pleasant or unpleasant, beautiful or ugly, appropriate or inappropriate, true or false, virtues or vices." Americans, like people everywhere, engage in these kinds of normative assessments in politics as in other realms of human experience. Indeed, Americans may do this more than others; principles may play a more prominent role in American political life than elsewhere. For America, it is said, originated in a conscious political act, in the proclamation of certain basic political principles. And Americans, it is argued, are unified by a commitment to a "creed"—a set of governing principles that guides their views on politics and society. We are skeptical of such sweeping claims, but we shall see. Here we consider the possibility that public opinion on matters of race is influenced by core American principles, by the ideas of *equality, economic individualism,* and *limited government*, in particular.

We take up these three and not others because each has received detailed attention in studies of the American political tradition. Each has played a prominent role in national debates on issues of race. Each is neither so general as to be vacuous nor so specific as to be of little use in guiding the variety of views that make up an outlook on politics. And finally, each of the three provokes genuine disagreement. Not all Americans are swept away by the call of equality; not everyone takes hard work and individual initiative to be virtues; not all Americans think of the national government as encroaching on their rights. Differences on these general matters of principle may therefore translate into corresponding differences on specific matters of policy. That, at least, is the hypothesis that we bring to our analysis here.

It may seem odd that we consider this a working hypothesis rather than a settled conclusion. Starting with Alexis de Tocqueville, many perceptive observers, liberal and conservative, white and black alike, have confidently placed these three themes at the center of the American political experience. And yet we have just begun to accumulate systematic evidence on what ordinary Americans think about such principles—whether they think about them at all—and the extent to which they might take such principles into account as they reach their political views.

We believe that principles are important to opinion, but we want to begin our analysis cautiously, grounded in realistic expectations. Too often, it seems to us, principles are imbued with a kind of wondrous and awesome power. Sometimes it seems as if American principles did work on their own, that people had nothing to do with ideas, or at least that once ideas appeared on the scene, people could do little to stop them. By some accounts, the American Creed virtually defines the nation. More so than a common religion, ethnic heritage, or linguistic background, a commitment to principles is supposedly what unifies the American people. And if principles can define and build a nation, then why shouldn't they also provide the means for the country to overcome its most vexing problem, that of slavery and its lingering aftermath of racial conflict?

This is the position taken by Gunnar Myrdal, in his justly celebrated and massive study of American race relations, now fifty years old. Myrdal was shocked at the place of blacks in American society and impressed with how deeply entrenched were patterns of racial segregation and discrimination. Nevertheless, Myrdal emerged from his investigation optimistic about America's future, and his optimism derived from the power he invested in the American Creed: "Americans of all national origins, classes, regions, creeds, and colors, have something in common: a social *ethos*, a political creed. It is hard to avoid the judgment that this 'American Creed' is the cement in the structure of this great and disparate nation."

For Myrdal, the creed was the ideological inheritance that drove American political development. As discrimination and prejudice were supported by "mere" tradition and interest, surely they would retreat in the face of the inexorably advancing creed, where "the American thinks, talks, and acts under the influence of high national and Christian precepts." Myrdal's faith in the power of American principles to set things right is striking, given the object of his study, and also, we think, naive, but it is by no means unusual.

A common companion to the claim that principles exercise an extraordinary power is the contention that they transcend their times. If not quite eternal, principles are often portrayed as if they were essentially unchanging. Thus Myrdal's reference to the American Creed, an ideological inheritance traced back in a straight line to Enlightenment ideals. Thus Lipset's influential argument that the entire length of American political history can be read as a perpetual struggle between two essentially fixed ideas, equality and achievement. Thus Tocqueville's observation that "two things are surprising in the United States: the mutability of the greater part of human actions, and the singular stability of certain principles. Men are in constant motion; the mind of man appears almost unmoved."

We don't think so. America is no longer a dependent colony but free and independent, the world's only superpower. Where once the country was largely rural and sparsely populated, it is now predominantly urban, industrial, and heavily populated. At special moments and again now, the nation has faced the challenge of absorbing huge numbers of "alien elements." Is it reasonable to assume that in the face of all these dramatic transformations, the founding principles have somehow been perfectly preserved?

We believe to the contrary, that the core principles of equality, economic individualism, and limited government are not fixed but evolving. Principles are used in political argument, they help to shape political reality, and are themselves altered as certain constructions become obsolete and new political conditions arise. Like Rodgers, we believe that the history of political principles in America is not a story of "a slowly unfolding tradition" but rather an account of "contention, argument, and power." Like Rodgers, we are interested in how principles are "put to use, and in this way fashioned and re-fashioned: not what the American political tradition *means*, but how various aspects of the Creed have been *used*: how they were employed and for what ends, how they rose in power, withered, and collapsed, how they were invented, stolen for other ends, remade, abandoned."

Finally, we presume that opinions typically reflect conflict and compromise among *multiple* principles. We do not wish to repeat the search for the Holy Grail of ideology, the largely fruitless pursuit for the one sweeping ideological idea that would unlock the mysteries of American public opinion that has so preoccupied research over the last thirty years. Rather, we assume here multiple principles at play simultaneously. Opinions on race policy are likely to reflect a person's thinking about the importance and desirability of equality, the claim of individualism, the propriety of government intervention, and perhaps more. People ordinarily take into account more than a single principle when confronting public policy.

Not only is this the way things likely are, it's the way things should be, according to Robert Lane:

> Just as the person who is bound entirely by his ideology, so that experience does not have the power to change its elements, is an ideologue and unfree, so the person who governs all his policy recommendations by a single value is close to "obsession" or borders on "fixation" and is similarly unfree. The healthy person has

multiple values, and he finds them often in conflict; his health is revealed in his toleration of the conflict and the means he chooses to reconcile the conflict, not in the way he makes all policy recommendations serve a single value, however economical that might be for him.

Our framework takes Lane's point a few steps further. We also think that Americans take into account several principles, not just one. But we also insist that Americans are juggling other considerations as well: they are pursuing their own diverse interests, they are concerned about the interests of their group, and they are using policy questions as an opportunity to express their various social sympathies and resentments. All of these elements shape opinions on race policy. Principles play a role, but probably not the overriding one often attributed to them. Our analysis must be sensitive to the malleability and complexity of values and to the particular ways they may be constructed and activated in political debate.

CONCLUSIONS AND IMPLICATIONS

In scores of commentaries over more than a century, principles have been given a prominent place in the analysis of American politics, and none more than the three we have just examined: equality, economic individualism, and limited government. Bold claims are not the same as systematic evidence, of course, and it is systematic evidence (of a particular kind) that we have done our best to supply here.

In some respects, what we found supports the widespread and apparently growing enthusiasm for principles as a way to understand American public opinion. Principles do matter; they are, by our evidence at least, an important part of the story of public opinion. This is particularly true for equality, but it also applies, if less forcefully, for limited government. Our results stand up well to replication, and they hold for black Americans as for whites.

Principles matter, then, but the imprint they leave on opinion is not uniformly strong. Indeed, in the case of economic individualism, the imprint is faint almost to the vanishing point. But even more generally, the effects that we manage to turn up here have a contingency and specificity about them that are out of keeping with the common portrayal of principles as unstoppable forces that level all opposition. Equality may be, as Douglas Rae and his colleagues maintain, "the most distinctive and compelling element of our national ideology," but not all Americans find equality compelling. And it may even be that, as Huntington would have it, "Opposition to power, and suspicion of government as the most dangerous embodiment of power, are the central themes of American political thought," but not all Americans seem to regard government as dangerous, and even when they do, they do not necessarily take such sentiments into account as they form opinions on policy. In their modesty and specificity, our results do not measure up all that well to the grand declarations often made on behalf of American political principles.

Modesty and specificity do not trouble us, of course. We would have been surprised had things turned out the other way. We don't mean to imply that we were clear-eyed about exactly what form such contingency and specificity would take. There were more than a few surprises, and two seem worth noting here.

The first concerns equality. Of the three principles we examined, equality loomed the largest in public opinion on matters of race. What we find most impressive is not so much that equality made a large difference as that the magnitude of equality's effect depended so acutely on exactly which issues were under consideration. In Chapter 2 we suggested that the six race policy questions examined in greatest detail here reflect three distinct, but closely related, facets of current debate. But what we took to be rather fine distinctions among the three related domains the American public obviously takes very seriously: we see this in the highly variable role played by equality across the domains. Equality is extremely important when it comes to school desegregation and fair employment, the two issues that best represent the struggle for equal rights and opportunities carried forward by the civil rights movement. It is perhaps not surprising that the principle of equality would enter most forcefully into public opinion on precisely these questions. But the extent to which this is true, for whites and blacks alike, in 1992 and in 1986, is surprising.

At the same time, equality simply disappears from public opinion on issues of affirmative action. This disappearance is instructive: it tells us something both about affirmative action and about equality; it suggests that opponents and supporters of affirmative action can enlist equality as justification for their views. Opponents can reject affirmative action in the name of equality by arguing that affirmative action violates equal treatment; supporters can embrace affirmative action in the name of equality by arguing that affirmative action brings the formal idea of equal opportunity to life. Equality is complicated and elastic; it can be stretched to more than one use, "furnishing rival interests," as Pole once wrote, "with equally satisfying terms of moral reference."

Yet another surprise was the quite spectacular failure of economic individualism. Faith that hard work brings success has very little to do with opinions on matters of race. This holds generally for whites as for blacks, and in the 1985 NES data as in the major study of opinion on issues of race undertaken by NES in 1986. These results challenge the contention that contemporary debate over affirmative action and welfare reform is first and foremost a discussion about the virtues of hard work and individual responsibility.

Finally, that principles matter at all in public opinion implies a particular conception of politics, one that puts justification and discussion at the center of political life. Stoker puts this point well:

> Politics is not simply an arena where citizen preferences are articulated and aggregated but one where public goals and policies are debated and political goals

must be publicly justified. When citizen assess public policies, events, and leaders or consider their own political choices, they are not merely trying to figure out what or who they like or what it is they want. They are also trying to figure out what or who is *good* and what is *right*.

The development of the idea of group interest owes much to realistic group conflict theory, introduced in rudimentary form at the turn of the century by William Graham Sumner in his famous *Folkways*. The theory begins with the assertion that antagonism between groups is rooted in actual conflict: groups have incompatible goals, and they compete for scarce resources. In this analysis, racial groups are neither vestiges of premodern society nor convenient outlets for psychological distress but rather, as Giles and Evans put it, "vehicles for the pursuit of interest in modern pluralist societies," "participants in ongoing competition for control of economic, political, and social structures." Conflicts of interest cause intergroup conflict, and conflict between groups is most intense where the real conflicts of interest are greatest, where the groups have the most at stake.

The relevance of realistic group conflict theory to American race relations is supported by a line of empirical work that extends back to V.O. Key's *Southern Politics*. Key showed in fine detail that politics in the American South through the middle of the twentieth century was most reactionary in the so-called black belt: an arc that extended from the Chesapeake Bay in the northeast, through the eastern shore of the Carolinas, down through the midlands of Georgia and Alabama, along the rivers of Mississippi, Arkansas, and Louisiana, and into east Texas. It was in the black belt where the plantation system and slavery had flourished and where, as Key put it, whites possessed "the deepest and most immediate concern with the maintenance of white supremacy." Racism prevailed throughout the South, of course, but it was whites in the black belt, because they had the most to lose, who acted on their racism. Inside the black belt, the threat was real and serious; outside it, "blacks were neither so central to the local economy nor so sizable a bloc of prospective voters in local elections." Accordingly, it was within the black belt where support for secession and war was most adamant, where the subsequent drive for black disfranchisement came with greatest force, where the Populist revolt was crushed, and where, in the 1950s and 1960s, defense of segregation was most ferocious.

Key's observations in Southern Politics have been corroborated by scores of more modest investigations. This work demonstrates the lingering significance of the black belt in Southern politics and establishes the more general point of the political importance of sheer numbers. As the great migration carried blacks out of the rural South into the cities, South and North, miniature black belts were created everywhere. And time and again, as the black share of the population increased, whites became more reactionary in their views on race.

This evidence is certainly consistent with realistic group-conflict theory, and we have no particular quarrel with this interpretation. It is worth pointing out, however, that no study actually attempts to measure the perception of threat, the theory's pivotal concept. Threat is inferred, not directly measured. This means that we cannot know for certain whether, say, whites in the black belt in fact felt threatened by large black populations. Nor can we know, if they did feel threatened, whether the threat was experienced as a danger to themselves personally, or to their group collectively.

Granted that the level of analysis for realistic group conflict theory is primarily the group, not the individual, the theory nevertheless carries "inevitable implications for psychological processes." Our analysis takes such implications seriously by directly measuring the individual's perception of group threat. Again, the threat singled out here is not personal but collective, involving the welfare of whites in general. Whites resist policies promoting racial equality, in this view, out of a sense that such policies threaten their collective interests.

Another limitation of the empirical literature motivated by realistic group-conflict theory is that it has been preoccupied entirely with the political response of whites. The vocabulary of realistic group-conflict theory, which we have simply appropriated here, is oriented to threat, not to advantage, takes the perspective of whites threatened by blacks.

Our purpose here, then, is to test realistic group-conflict theory with evidence hand-tailored to the individual level, taking into account both that whites might be motivated by a sense of group threat and that blacks might be motivated by a sense of group advantage.

GROUP THREAT AND WHITE RESISTANCE TO RACIAL EQUALITY

We do so by capitalizing on questions appearing on the 1986 NES that inquire into citizens' views of the consequences of affirmative action policies for blacks and whites considered as social groups. These questions, shown in Table 6-3, parallel the self-interest questions we analyzed earlier in the chapter, except that references to families are replaced by references to racial groups. As Table 6-3 indicates, many white Americans believe that affirmative action policies harm the interests of whites. A majority (57.4%) agreed that affirmative action programs for blacks have reduced whites' chances for jobs, promotions, and admissions to schools and training programs. Three-quarters of whites (74.9%) said that it was very or somewhat likely that a white person wouldn't get a job or promotion while an equally or less qualified black person got one instead. And almost as many (69.0%) believed that it was very or somewhat likely that a white person would not get admitted to a school while an equally or less qualified black person got in instead.

Among white Americans, these perceptions of racial group threat are very consistent: those who believe that affirmative action programs for blacks have reduced whites' opportunities also are inclined to think that whites often get turned down for jobs or promotions that go instead to blacks, and they also

▪ TABLE 6-3

PERCEPTION OF RACIAL GROUP THREAT AMONG WHITE AMERICANS

Affirmative action programs for blacks have reduced whites' chances for jobs, promotions, and admission to schools and training programs.

Strongly agree	29.8%
Agree	27.6
Disagree	27.5
Strongly disagree	15.1

What do you think the chances are these days that a white person won't get admitted to a school while an equally or less qualified black person gets admitted instead?

Very likely	27.6
Somewhat likely	41.4
Not very likely	31.1

What do you think the chances are these days that a white person won't get a job or promotion while an equally or less qualified black person gets one instead?

Very likely	26.6
Somewhat likely	48.3
Not very likely	25.1

SOURCE: 1986 National Election Study.

tend to believe that white applicants are regularly turned away from schools while blacks are invited in. Indeed, the pattern here is perhaps too consistent. The correlations are so high that the perception of group threat resembles more a tidy ideology than a realistic assessment of a messy social reality.

Equally worrisome is that perceptions of group threat are highly correlated with perceptions of threat to family. The correlation between responses to the two kinds of threat, one centered on the family, the other on the group, is little different, on average, from the typical correlation among the group threat questions (average Pearson $r = .46$ and $.52$, respectively). As a purely empirical matter, then, personal and group racial threats among white Americans are not as distinct as we had hoped.

These simple and preliminary results lead us immediately to question the extent to which whites' perceptions of racial group threat can be regarded as realistic. Earlier we found that the perception of personal racial threat is largely unconnected to actual circumstance but is tightly bound to feelings of racial resentment. Exactly the same suspicion arises here, since personal and collective racial threats seem so intertwined in the minds of white Americans.

Indeed, we find essentially the same pattern of results for racial group threat as we did in our previous analysis of personal racial threat. In both instances, the perception of racial threat among white Americans is connected, but weakly, to personal economic insecurities and to living and working in close proximity to blacks. And in both instances, the perception of racial threat is predicted best, far and away, by the resentments whites feel toward blacks. In theory, the sources of perceived threat are found in real conflicts of interest. Threat is supposed to be, in a word, realistic. Here again we see that

■ TABLE 6-4

IMPACT OF GROUP INTEREST ON WHITE SUPPORT FOR RACIAL POLICY

	School Desegregation	Fair Employment	Government Help	Federal Programs	Preferential Hiring	College Quotes
Perception of racial Group threat	– .17 (.06)	– .10 (.06)	– .11 (.03)	– .11 (.04)	– .20 (.04)	– .25 (.05)

SOURCE: 1986 National Elections Study.

NOTE: Entry is B, the unstandardized regression coefficient, with standard errors presented in parentheses underneath. All variables coded 0–1. Each regression equation also included measures of age, region, sex, marital status, union membership, religion, race of interviewer, and racial resentment.

it is not. Our results suggest that the perception of threat is a product not so much of the social circumstances white Americans find themselves in, but of how they look at the social world, and especially whether or not they regard blacks with suspicion and resentment.

This brings us finally to the central business of determining the effects of racial group threat on public opinion. We expect these effects to be most pronounced on opinions toward affirmative action, since the group-interest questions themselves refer to the consequences of affirmative action policies. Because racial resentment is so strongly implicated in whites' perceptions of the threats that blacks appear to pose to their collective interests, our analysis of white opinion must take into account its impact as well.

The regression results, summarized in Table 6-4, indicate that white Americans who believe that blacks threaten their collective interests are less supportive of policies designed to reduce racial inequalities, consistent with theoretical expectations. The effect is statistically significant in each of the six policies we examine; it ranges in size from modest, in the case of federal programs, to sizable, in the case of affirmative action. Thus the effect is most visible just where it should be. Moreover, when we repeated this analysis, making use of the 1985 NES that carried many of the same questions, we uncovered virtually the identical pattern of results. We take these findings to mean that interests matter to whites' views on matters of race. Group interests matter. Insofar as interests figure prominently in white opinion on race, it is through the threats blacks appear to pose to whites' collective well-being, not their personal welfare.

Jody David Armour offers another explanation for white antagonism toward blacks in his book, **Negrophobia**. *Here he presents the case (and critique) of the "Intelligent Bayesian." The central argument is that blacks' perceived proclivity for anti-social behavior justifies racial bias. In other words, racism is a function of simple probabilistic estimates, or, the "objectivity of the numbers." Armour writes, "[T]he Bayesian's argument is simple: As much as I regret it, I must act differently toward blacks because it is logical to do so." Thus, if blacks commit more violent crime, it is rational for shopkeepers and cabdrivers, for instance, to discriminate.*

Likewise, if black motorists are more likely to have warrants, violate traffic laws, and be in possession of narcotics, it is also rational for the police to indiscriminately stop black drivers.

Armour offers several criticisms of this approach. He begins by noting that the core assumptions of the model are flawed. For example, people simply do not have enough information to make accurate calculations about the actions and attitudes of racial group members. Moreover, the information they do have is often distorted. The high levels of residential segregation discussed in Chapter 6 imply that most whites do not have an experiential basis with which to judge African-Americans. As a result, they merely on second-hand information provided by the mass media. Given the routine distortions of black life depicted on the main source of public information—television—it is not surprising that whites are unable to make accurate assessments about black life.

THE "INTELLIGENT BAYESIAN": RECKONING WITH RATIONAL DISCRIMINATION

Jody David Armour

Excerpt from Negrophobia and Reasonable Racism: The Hidden Costs of Being Black in America

There is nothing more painful to me at this stage in my life than to walk down the street and hear footsteps and start thinking about robbery—then look around and see somebody White and feel relieved.

—THE REVEREND JESSE JACKSON, IN A SPEECH TO A BLACK CONGREGATION

IN CHICAGO DECRYING BLACK-ON-BLACK CRIME

White America craves absolution. At least according to *U.S. News & World Report* it does. By admitting he sometimes fears young Black men, the Reverend Jackson "seemed to be offering sympathetic Whites something for which they hungered: absolution," declared *U.S. News.* For other journalists, Jackson's comments were as much about vindication as absolution—in their view, his comments put an acceptable face on their own discriminatory beliefs and practices. Richard Cohen of the *Washington Post,* for example, announced in his column that Jackson's remarks "pithily paraphrase what I wrote" in 1986. He was referring to a 1986 column in which he asserted that if he were a shopkeeper, he would lock his doors "to keep young Black men out." For Cohen, Jackson's remarks proved that "it is not racism to recognize a potential threat posed by someone with certain characteristics."

Cohen's advocacy of discrimination against young Black men raises a second argument advanced to justify acting on race-based assumptions, namely, that, given statistics demonstrating Blacks' disproportionate engagement in crime, it is reasonable to perceive a greater threat from someone Black than someone White. Walter Williams, a conservative Black economist, refers to someone like Cohen as an "Intelligent Bayesian," named for Sir Thomas

Bayes, the father of statistics. For Williams, stereotypes are merely statistical generalizations, probabilistic rules of thumb that, when accurate, help people make speedy and often difficult decisions in a world of imperfect information. Whether "intelligent" is an apt adjective for a person who discriminates on the basis of stereotypes remains to be seen. For now we shall simply refer to such a person as a "Bayesian."

On its surface, the contention of the Bayesian appears relatively free of the troubling implications of the Reasonable Racist's defense. While the Reasonable Racist explicitly admits his prejudice and bases his claim for exoneration on the prevalence of irrational racial bias, the Bayesian invokes the "objectivity" of numbers. The Bayesian's argument is simple: "As much as I regret it, I must act differently toward Blacks because it is logical to do so." The Bayesian relies on numbers that reflect not the prevalence of racist attitudes among Whites, but the statistical disproportionality with which Blacks commit crimes.

A threshold problem with the Bayesian's profession of pristine rationality concerns the "scrambled eggs" problem described earlier—that is, the practical impossibility of unscrambling the rational and irrational sources of racial fears. For countless Americans, fears of Black violence stem from, among other things, the complex interaction of cultural stereotypes, racial antagonisms, and unremitting overrepresentations of Black violence in the mass media. As for the mass media, especially television news, recall the letter in the Introduction from the would-be Bayesian who remarked, "If I saw Blacks in my neighborhood I would be on the lookout, and for a good reason." The "good reason" he cites for his hypervigilance about Blacks is television. Few Americans keep copies of FBI Uniform Crime Reports by their bedsides: when asked in a *Los Angeles Times* survey (February 13, 1994) from where they got their information about crime, 65% of respondents said they learned about it from the mass media. But television journalism on crime and violence has been proven to reveal, and project, a consistent racial bias.

Even if media reporting on crime and violence were not biased, our minds simply do not process information about Blacks and other stereotyped groups the way the Bayesian assumes. The Bayesian assumes that our minds can passively mirror the world around us, that they can operate like calculators, and that social stereotypes can be represented in our minds as mere bits of statistical information, as malleable and subject to ongoing revision as the batting averages of active major-league baseball players. Each of these assumptions flies in the face of what modern psychology reveals about the workings of the human mind.

Further, the Bayesian's contention that she can delicately balance the racial factor in her calculations is refuted by recent discoveries about the psychological impact of stereotypes. A stereotype, unlike ordinary statistical information, radically alters our mindset, unconsciously bringing about a sea change in our perceptual readiness. Under the influence of a stereotype, we tend to see *what the stereotype primes us to see*. If violence is part of the stereotype, we are primed to construe ambiguous behavior as evincing violence, not on a retail but on a wholesale level. Thus, even if race marginally increases the probability that an "ambiguous" person is an assailant, decision makers inevitably exaggerate the *weight* properly accorded to this fact. Whatever merit there is to the contention that it is appropriate to consider a person's race as one—just one—of the factors defining the "kind" of person who poses a danger, the racial factor assumes overriding psychological significance when the supposed assailant is Black.

To the extent that Blacks do commit disproportionate numbers of violent street crimes, socioeconomic status largely explains such overrepresentation. Crime rates are inextricably linked to poverty and unemployment. Genetic explanations of crime statistics founder on the fact that crime and delinquency rates of the African American middle class are virtually identical to those of Whites similarly situated.

Recognizing the socioeconomic factors that drive violent street crime, the Bayesian may insist that he views race merely as a proxy for information with admittedly greater predictive value—such as income, education, and prospects for the future—but that costs more to obtain. "Thus," says the Bayesian, "I consider a wealthy Black graduate of the Harvard Law School who is making six figures at a major Wall Street law firm to pose a lower risk of armed robbery than a poor and illiterate White high school dropout with little hope of gainful employment."

"However," he continues, "ascertaining an individual's schooling and income may require a personal interview and reference checks. The costs of obtaining such particularized information may be prohibitive in many situations. Surely you can't expect shopkeepers, cabdrivers, or people in the position of our hypothetical bank patron to incur such costs, to get a person's life story before he fingers his buzzer, stops his taxi, or uses deadly defensive force against a 'suspicious' person. When obtaining such information is prohibitively costly, we must economize by using stereotypes and playing the odds."

Viewed in this light, the Bayesian's claim that race can serve merely as a proxy for socioeconomic status might seem persuasive. But if race is a proxy for socioeconomic factors, then race loses its predictive value when one controls for those factors. Thus, if an individual is walking through an impoverished, "crime-prone neighborhood," as the Reverend Jackson may have had in mind, and if he has already weighed the character of the neighborhood in judging the dangerousness of his situation, then it is illogical for him to consider the racial identity of the person whose suspicious footsteps he hears. For he has already taken into account the socioeconomic factors for which race is a proxy, and considering the racial identity of the ambiguous person under such circumstances constitutes "double counting."

Since our hypothetical scenario takes place in a predominantly White upper-middle-class neighborhood, it does not seem to implicate the double-counting problem. Further, the discussion shall proceed on the basis of two assumptions: first, that the rate of robberies is "significantly" higher for Blacks than for non-Blacks; second, and most unrealistic, that the defendant's greater fear of Blacks results entirely from his analysis of crime statistics. Given these assumptions, what objections to the argument of the Bayesian remain? Surely admitting statistics, carrying logic and objectivity on the rising and plunging curves of their graphs like Vulcans on dolphin-back, better promotes the accuracy, rationality, and fairness of the fact-finding process than not admitting them.

WHY RATIONAL DISCRIMINATION IS NOT REASONABLE

The most readily apparent objection to the reasonableness claim of the Bayesian challenges the statistical *method* he employs to assess the victim's dangerousness. Neither private nor judicial judgments about a particular member of a class, the argument goes, should rest on evidence about the class to which he or she belongs. Despite the attractiveness of this principle, and occasional court admonitions to avoid statistical inferences about individuals, private and judicial decision makers routinely rely on statistical evidence to judge past facts and predict future behavior. Lenders use statistics concerning age, marital status, location or residence, income, and assets to predict whether a borrower will repay a loan. Parole commissions may also use statistical techniques to predict parole success, considering factors such as number of prior convictions, type of crime, employment history, and family ties. And courts consider nonindividualized statistical probabilities when deciding whether to allow injured litigants to use epidemiological proof of causation in their lawsuits.

Consider one example of the injustices that lurk in the Bayesian's lopsided attention to rationality. Ira Glasser of the American Civil Liberties Union tells the story of a Black couple who, some years ago, took in a movie in Times Square. It was raining when they came out of the theater about 11 P.M., so the husband went by himself for the car, which was parked in a garage several blocks away. When he returned to pick up his wife, she had disappeared. The man eventually discovered that his wife, who was five months pregnant, had been arrested by the police, put in jail, strip-searched and booked on charges of loitering for the purpose of prostitution.

The arresting officer in this shocking incident may well have viewed himself as an Intelligent Bayesian. Perhaps wrongly, let's assume that at the time he made the arrest, there was a high incidence of prostitution in Times Square, most of the prostitutes were unescorted women, a disproportionate number of them were Black, and most transactions occurred between 10 P.M. and 2 A.M.. The officer might assert that, from his stand-point, there was significant evidence to support his factual judgment that the woman was a prostitute—she was a woman, Black, unescorted, and in Times Square at 11 o'clock at night. Even if we assume that his belief was rational in the sense that there was factual support for it, his *decision* to act on this belief in the way he did was patently *unreasonable*, not to mention outrageous and reprehensible. The reason his actions were unreasonable is because the costs of potential mistakes were so grievous. Given the enormous costs of potential mistakes, we rightly condemn him for not doing more to reduce the risk of being mistaken before subjecting this woman to such treatment. Many of us may express our concerns about the terrible costs of being wrong in this situation as doubt about whether the officer's factual judgments were rational. But, upon careful reflection, we see that we are really saying that given the potential for mistakes and the terrible consequences of his mistake, the actions of the officer were unreasonable, even if his factual judgment was rational in the sense that there were circumstances to support it.

The Bayesian tries to avoid discussion of the consequences of error by focusing solely on his subjective factual judgments, specifically, on whether his hastier conclusion that the "ambiguous" Black man was about to attack him was rational given that Blacks pose a marginally greater risk of assault than Whites. It is true that judging that one knows something may be a subjective thought process, a "state of mind." For example, when the officer, upon seeing the unescorted Black woman in Times Square in the late evening, concluded that she is a prostitute, something purely subjective occurred in his thought processes. What the Bayesian overlooks, however, is that the hastier conclusion that he is under attack leads him to make a decision to *more hastily shoot* a Black man. The reasonableness of that *decision* and *act* (hastier use of deadly force against Blacks) is just as much at issue in these situations as the rationality of hastier factual judgment that he was about to be attacked.

As these readings demonstrate, racial politics in the post-civil rights era is nothing if not complex.[11] In a time of "political correctness," "superficial tolerance," and "reverse racism," it is difficult to find one's way on racial matters. No longer are there clear-cut solutions such as integrating lunch counters or protecting voting rights. In addition, even middle class blacks are challenging the base assumptions of integrationism instead preferring to live in black middle-class housing enclaves (e.g., Prince George's County, Maryland and Ladera Heights, California) and send their children to historically black colleges and universities. Likewise many white Americans have retreated to "walled" communities in an attempt to isolate themselves from the vagaries of urban life. Given these patterns there has been a great deal of hand wringing over the appropriate steps toward racial equality in America. The following selections offer two contrasting visions of future race relations in the United States.

*In his book, **Color Blind**, Ellis Cose offers "twelve steps toward a race-neutral nation." He takes up the daunting question of what it would take for America to become a "color-blind society." His assumption, of course, is that "conscious" whites and blacks actually have a desire to create a bias-free society. "His goal is to move the dialogue about race '. . . beyond the realm of reassuring yet empty platitudes.'" Several of his suggestions are temporal in nature. Thus, for the society to move toward race neutrality, people must quit waiting for time to heal things, recognize that progress on some fronts is only part of the journey, and that however difficult, the conversation about race is an on-going process. Society must be vigilant in breaking down residential segregation and, in turn, vigorously enforce anti-discrimination laws. Progress toward a race-neutral society should also recognize that "race relations is not a zero-sum game." To Cose, the lives of all Americans are interconnected. It therefore makes* *sense to seek interracial collaborations whenever possible. Finally, we should quit looking for a single bromide to America's racial problems. There is no simple solution, no "silver bullet."*

TWELVE STEPS TOWARD
A RACE-NEUTRAL NATION

■

Ellis Cose

Excerpt from Color Blind: Seeing Beyond Race in a Race-Obsessed World

In *The Fire Next Time*, James Baldwin offered an eloquent and urgent plea: "If we—and now I mean the relatively conscious whites and the relatively conscious blacks, who must, like lovers, insist on, or create, the consciousness of the others—do not falter in our duty now, we may be able, handful that we are, to end the racial nightmare, and achieve our country, and change the history of the world."

For people who cling to the dream of a bias-free society and believe in the power of words, in people's endless capacity for enlightenment, Baldwin's prayer resounds like an anthem, defining the challenge that still lies before us. Indeed, in some quarters, the message (albeit in a more multiethnic version) seems even more urgent now than it did some three decades ago when Baldwin first set down those words.

Forecasting the future of a society is inevitably a risky proposition, and I would not be so foolish or so pessimistic as to proclaim that the race-related problems the United States faces today will always be with us. Indeed, one thing that is virtually certain is that many of the particulars will change.

America is in the midst of a seismic shift in racial composition, and our racial definitions are not likely to survive it intact. Whether or not the government sanctions a multiracial category or declares Latino to be a race, Americans have no choice but to acknowledge that the racial mix is becoming more complex—and individuals less subject to pigeonholing—than ever before in the country's history. That demographic transformation, at the least, provides an opportunity to ask whether as we change the meaning of race, we can also render it less important.

A number of analysts, as I noted earlier, claim that we have already done so—that if it was not for those noisy group-rights people, we could pretty much put the issue of race behind us. I don't happen to be convinced, but I find the prospect a tantalizing possibility—enough so that it should be put to the test. I, for one, would find it fascinating, for instance, if the foes of the Voting Rights Act really put their theories into practice and took it upon themselves to recruit scores of accomplished people of color from around the country to run in what are now considered "white" districts and monitor the presumably color-blind results. I would find it even more exciting if those who are so adamantly opposed to affirmative action in college admissions would organize efforts to upgrade the schools and the level of instruction in every slum in America, so those who are black and brown and poor would be better prepared to complete on an equal footing with the middle-class, white children who find it so easy to belittle their achievements.

But whether or not the prophets of the color-blind state are willing to put their speculations to the test, I believe that Americans of goodwill, and certainly those who count themselves among the "relatively conscious," have a responsibility in this increasingly racially ambiguous age to ask what kind of future we want to make. Are we at all serious when we talk about a society in which people are no longer judged by the color of their skin? After conducting some sixty-five interviews for *Black, White, Other*, Lise Funderburg apparently felt we are not. She became convinced, she wrote, "that the pressures in our country to separate black and white—and to make biracial people choose one over the other—are epidemic." Yet—and one must inject a *yet* because the other side of the coin is impossible to ignore—more than ever before, people are crossing racial lines to find friends, colleagues, and spouses. Many are trying, as best they can, to tune out the racial craziness all around as they search for a way out of the continuing American nightmare. Given that, I think we have to ask the question—if only as an experiment in thought: What would it take to create a society that is truly race neutral? Do we have the vaguest idea how we would go about trying to create such a place?

The short answer, I suspect, is no, otherwise we would probably be much further along the way than we are. Still, I believe we can at least sketch some ideas of what needs to happen to get us there, of what sort of things we should be thinking about beyond such platitudes as "let's just love one another," which is the verbal equivalent of throwing up our hands in noble resignation. Why not instead conjure up a vision of a possible future—rooted not in dreams of some benevolent deity ushering in an era of universal brotherhood, but in recognition of the fact that our racial problem can only be solved by attacking its myriad components. Enumerating steps our society could take toward racial sanity is obviously not the same as putting America's racial goblins to rest. It is, however, a necessary prelude to moving the dialogue beyond the realm of reassuring yet empty platitudes.

So what would some of those steps be?

1. **We must stop expecting time to solve the problem for us.**

   In the 1967 film *Guess Who's Coming to Dinner*, there is a scene in which Sidney Poitier (who plays a physician in his 30s who is in love with a young white woman) turns, in a fit of rage, to the actor playing his father. Only when the older generation is dead and gone, Poitier declares, will prejudice wither away. The sobering realization is that Poitier is now older than his movie-land father was then, and the problem, obviously, is still with us.

   Nonetheless, many people assume that there is magic in the passage of years. "Eventually white Americans will be ready for a black in this position," they may say at one point. "Yes, inner-city conditions are bad, but eventually they will be better," they will say at another.

   In his 1965 interview in *Playboy*, Martin Luther King, Jr., pointed out the absurdity in such an attitude. "Where progress for the Negro in America is concerned, there is a tragic misconception of time among whites," he said. "They seem to cherish a strange, irrational notion that something in the very flow of time will cure all ills. In truth, time itself is only neutral. Increasingly, I feel that time has been used destructively by people of ill will much more than it has been constructively by those of good will."

Time doesn't heal all wounds; it certainly doesn't solve all problems. It is often merely an excuse for allowing them to fester. Our problems, including our racial problems, belong to us—not to our descendants.

2. **We must recognize that ending hate is the beginning, not the end, of our mission.**

Occasionally, I turn on my television and am greeted by some celebrity exhorting me to stop "the hate," or words to that effect. I always wonder about the target audience for that particular broadside. I suspect that it is aimed mostly at people who don't hate anyone— perhaps as a reminder of our virtue. I certainly can't imagine a card-carrying member of the local Nazi group or the Ku Klux Klan getting so fired up by the message that he turns to the television and exclaims, "Yes, you're right. I must immediately stop the hate."

The fact is that stopping the hate does little to bring people of different races or ethnic groups together. Certainly, it's better than stoking hate, but discrimination and stereotyping are not primarily the result of hatred. They never have been. Slave owners, for the most part, did not hate their slaves. They simply didn't see them as full human beings, and they certainly did not consider them equals. Tolerance and even affection often come in the same package as prejudice. Thus, if we tell ourselves that the only problem is hate, we avoid facing the reality—as has much of Latin America—that it is mostly nice, nonhating people (such as those who boasted to Eneid Routté-Gómez, in Chapter 7, about the not-quite-equal housekeeper who was "*de la familia*") who perpetuate racial inequality.

3. **We must accept the fact that equality is not a halfway proposition.**

For as long as the idea of equal treatment has been around, Americans have been trying to figure out a way to accomplish it short of *really* accomplishing it. Booker T. Washington's most famous speech, delivered at the Atlanta Exposition in 1895, was calculated to reassure the nervous and non-integration-minded on that point: "In all things that are purely social we can be as separate as the fingers, yet one as the hand in all things essential to mutual progress."

Several months later, John Marshall Harlan's famous dissent in *Plessy v. Ferguson* pointed out that equal treatment did not necessarily mean equality: "The white race deems itself to be the dominant race in this country. And . . . will continue to be for all time, if it remains true to its great heritage, and holds fast to the principles of constitutional liberty."

This century has seen huge changes in the status of black Americans. It has also seen the growth of largely segregated school systems, the development and maintenance of segregated neighborhoods, and the congealing of the assumption that blacks and whites belong to fundamentally different communities. The mistake was in the notion that social, economic, and political equality are not interrelated, that it was possible to go on living in largely segregated neighborhoods, socialize in largely segregated circles, and even attend segregated places of worship and yet somehow have a workplace and a polity where race ceased to be a factor. As long as we cling to the notion that equality is fine in some spheres and not in others, we will be clinging to a lie.

4. **We must end American apartheid.**

Martin Luther King, Jr., recognized from the beginning that America's racial problem cannot be divorced from the conditions in which so many blacks live. In an interview in 1967, he observed, "Some ninety-two percent of the Negroes of the United States find themselves living in cities, and they find themselves in a triple ghetto in these cities on the whole: a ghetto of race, a ghetto of poverty, and a ghetto of human misery." Such circumstances, he noted, breed lack of opportunity and despair.

Hundreds of scholars and activists since then have confirmed King's observation. In *American Apartheid*, for instance, sociologists Douglas Massey and Nancy Denton concluded: "For America, the failure to end segregation will perpetuate a bitter dilemma that has long divided the nation. If segregation is permitted to continue, poverty will inevitably deepen and become more persistent within a large share of the black community, crime and drugs will become more fully rooted, and social institutions will fragment further under the weight of deteriorating conditions. As racial inequality sharpens, white fears will grow, racial prejudices will be reinforced, and hostility toward blacks will increase, making the problems of racial justice and equal opportunity even more insoluble."

In investigating why residents of Brooklyn's Red Hook neighborhood had such a hard time getting jobs even though several employers were located in the area, social scientists Philip Kasinitz and Jan Rosenberg concluded that racial discrimination against blacks and Puerto Ricans was only part of the problem. The very neighborhood itself, an isolated urban slum, was seen as so undesirable that anyone who lived there had a rough time getting work. "In Red Hook, being a member of a stigmatized race, living in a stigmatized place, and not having sufficient diversity of social connections all come together to block residents' access to jobs, even—perhaps particularly—to those located virtually on their door steps," Kasinitz and Rosenberg concluded.

Much the same could be said about countless ghettos across America in which blacks and some Latinos are housed. And America seems less than eager to change that circumstance. As I write this chapter, the Chicago newspapers are running stories of a conflict in the Northwest Side community of Hiawatha Park. Many residents in that white working-class area are up in arms about a proposal by the Habitat Company to place a small building for low-income residents in their neighborhood. A *Chicago Tribune* article by Flynn McRoberts reported:

> In the spring of 1966, Martin Luther King Jr. waged his campaign for civil rights and open housing from a three-flat building on Chicago's West Side. He and the marchers he led were met with taunts and bottles.
>
> Three decades later, another Chicago three–flat is at the center of a fight over fair housing for minorities. This time, those opposed to the idea have set the bottles aside, but the message is the same: We don't want you here. . . .
>
> Walking among the more than 200 people who turned out Tuesday night in a gym at Hiawatha Park, one could sense the venom and the desperation.
>
> "They don't work, they don't pay taxes!" one woman yelled. . . .
>
> "Where are you going to go?" [a] city worker asked. "Wherever you go, they're going to follow you."
>
> The evening was filled with talk of imperiled property values, of how a poor family "getting something for nothing" had no right to live in the same neighborhood as someone working three jobs to pay a mortgage.
>
> It absolutely is not, the residents insisted, an issue of racism.
>
> But all the talk of property values and other concerns usually comes with the words "these people." After some prodding, one life-long Hiawatha Park resident offered his translation. "When they say 'they,' they mean blacks.

In analyzing 1990 census data, University of Chicago sociologist Martha Van Haitsma discovered that roughly 60% of black Chicagoans lived in census tracts that were 95% or more black. In contrast, only .5% of Chicago's Mexicans and Mexican Americans lived in areas 95% or more Mexican—and none lived in census tracts in which 99% of the population was of Mexican descent. The extreme isolation of the black population made it easy for non-blacks to feel both psychological and political estrangement. Cross-racial political coalitions would be difficult, surmised Van Haitsma, "as long as poor blacks remain so incredibly segregated that any policies that affect a black neighborhood are confined to blacks."

Chicago is not, in all respects, typical. A 1996 study by University of Michigan demographers William Frey and Reynolds Farley found that in certain areas with fast-growing Latino and Asian populations, black segregation seemed to be declining a bit—even as segregation of Asians and Latinos was growing. Nonetheless, blacks remain, by far, the most segregated minority group in America.

Americans have paid much homage of late to King's dream of a society where people would be judged only by the content of their character—even as they have yanked children out of schools when a delicate racial balance "tipped," or planted themselves in neighbor-hoods determinedly monochromatic, or fought programs that would provide housing for poor blacks outside of the slums. There is some-thing fundamentally incongruous in the idea of judging people by the content of their character and yet consigning so many Americans at birth to communities in which they are written off even before their character has been shaped.

5. **We must recognize that race relations is not a zero-sum game.**

The stubborn survival of segregation is both a reflection and a re-sult of the tendency of many Americans to assume that the problems of one race have little impact on another. Whites can look upon a dis-tant black community and conclude, as Van Haitsma puts it, that if blacks suffer "they are the only ones who suffer." John Marshall Har-lan was right, however, when he argued a century ago that the "des-tinies of the . . . races, in this country, are indissolubly linked." The notion that "mainstream" America can completely shut itself off from the problems wreaking havoc in its ghettos is a dangerous myth. As NAACP head Kweisi Mfume told journalist Michel Mar-riott, "You can't create within a subculture a people that you have written off and expect that you will never encounter them."

The presumption that America is a zero-sum society, that if one race advances another must regress, is every bit as wrongheaded. Yet it accounts, in large measure, for the shrill and often illogical re-action to programs that aim to improve life for minorities—and most especially to affirmative action. Zero-sum thinking even explains some of the hostility that periodically surfaces within and between members of so-called minority groups. *Can only one person of color rise within a given organization?* One hopes not. *Does an increase in Latino clout portend a decline in blacks' well-being?* It shouldn't, though people often act as if it does. Undoubtedly, in some circumstances, the zero-sum model makes sense. There are times when one individ-ual's success only comes at the price of another's. But the larger truth of any society is that the fates of its members are intercon-nected. Ideally, we can all progress together. Unfortunately, we have too often revealed in political rhetoric that puts across the opposite message; and we have too often rewarded politicians who, through their demagoguery, exploit our anxiety and insecurities—as opposed to those politicians who demonstrate the willingness and ability to harness our faith in each other and in ourselves.

6. **We must replace a presumption that minorities will fail with an expectation of their success.**

When doing research with young drug dealers in California, an-thropologist John Ogbu found himself both impressed and im-mensely saddened. "Those guys have a sense of the economy. They have talents that could be used on Wall Street," he remarked. "They have intelligence—but not the belief that they can succeed in the mainstream." Somewhere along the line, probably long before they became drug dealers, that belief had been wrenched out of them.

Creating an atmosphere in which people learn they cannot achieve is tantamount to creating failure. "There is no defense or security for any of us except in the development of the highest intelligence of all," declared Booker T. Washington in the famous speech that made his reputation. America has been much too efficient at creating factories for failure. There is no reason why we can't do better at creating laboratories for success.

The various academic programs that do wonders with "at-risk" youths share a rock-hard belief in the ability of the young people in their care. These programs manage to create an atmosphere in which the "success syndrome" can thrive. Much like the general managers in John Kotter's study, *The General Managers* (discussed in Chapter 6), the more fortunate young scholars are challenged and supported at crucial junctures in their development.

One reason why theories about the heritability of intelligence are so appealing is that many people like to consider merit a fixed quality: Either you have it or you don't; either you are born talented or you are not. The real world is not so simple. How well you do in life and how good you are at a job depend greatly on what opportunities you were offered and what challenges were provided. Instead of focusing so much attention on whether people with less merit are getting various slots, we should be focusing (through the sorts of enrichment programs noted previously and, more broadly, by making achievement a priority in communities where it is generally discouraged) on how to widen—and reward—the pool of meritorious people.

7. **We must stop playing the blame game.**

Too often America's racial debate is sidetracked by a search for racial scapegoats. And more often than not, those scapegoats end up being the people on the other side of the debate. "It's your fault because you're a racist." "No, it's your fault because you expect something for nothing." "It's white skin privilege." "It's reverse racism." "If white people weren't so self-centered . . ." "If black people weren't so crime-prone . . ." And on and on it goes.

American culture, with its bellicose talk-show hosts and pugnacious politicians, rewards those who cast aspersions at the top of their lungs. And American law, with its concept of damages and reparations, encourages the practice of allocating blame. Although denying the past is dishonest and even sometimes maddening, obsessing about past wrongs is ultimately futile.

Certainly, loudmouths will always be among us and will continue to say obnoxious and foolish things, but it would be wonderful if more opinion leaders who engage in what passes for public discourse would recognize an obvious reality: It hardly matters who is responsible for things being screwed up; the only relevant question is, "How do we make them better?"

8. **We must do a better job at leveling the playing field.**

As long as roughly a third of black Americans sit on the bottom of the nation's economic pyramid and have little chance of moving up, the United States will have a serious racial problem on its hands. There is simply no way around that cold reality. As Latin Americans are realizing, it is rather pointless to say that the problem is class, not race, if race and class are tightly linked.

During the past several decades, Americans have witnessed an esoteric debate over whether society must provide equality of opportunity to minorities or somehow ensure equality of result. It is, however, something of a phony debate, for the two concepts are not altogether separate things. If America was, in fact, providing equality of opportunity, then we would certainly have something closer to equality of racial result than we do at present. The problem is that equality of opportunity has generally been defined quite narrowly—such as simply letting blacks and whites take the same test, or apply for the same job. Yet as Oliver and Shapiro made clear, equality of opportunity is meaningless when inherited wealth is such a large determinant of what schools one attends (and even whether one goes to school), what neighborhoods one can live in, and what influences and contacts one is exposed to.

Most blacks, Oliver and Shapiro pointed out, have virtually no wealth—even if they do earn a decent income. A mere two thousand dollars in financial assets, according to their calculations, is sufficient to put one among the wealthiest one-fifth of black house-holds. Whites with equal educational levels to blacks typically have five to ten times as much wealth, they estimated, largely because whites are much more likely than blacks to inherit or receive gifts of substantial unearned assets. This disparity is a direct result of Jim Crow practices and discriminatory laws and policies that prevented most blacks, until recently, from amassing much of anything that could be passed on to their children.

Clearly, at this juncture, America is not about to adopt any scheme (justifiable though it may be) to redistribute resources materially. What Americans must do, however, if we are at all serious about equality of opportunity, is to make it easier for those without substantial resources to have secure housing outside urban ghettos, to receive a high-quality education, and to have access to decent jobs.

In *When Work Disappears*, William Julius Wilson made the startling point: that for the first time in this century most adults in America's inner ghettos are without work. Joblessness, in and of itself, is bad enough; but as Wilson made clear, it also fuels a host of other ills—including crime, family dissolution, and despair. To talk about economic equality without also talking about jobs for those in America's most distressed communities is to talk nonsense. Similarly, a theoretical commitment to equal educational opportunity is meaningless without a genuine commitment to ensuring that all Americans can receive a good education.

Foes of academic affirmative action inevitably point to how poorly prepared some students of color are for a college education. They tend to be silent when it comes to offering support for programs that could boost those students' achievement long before they knock at the university door. Their silence is not only socially irresponsible, it is unconscionable.

9. **We must become serious about fighting discrimination.**

It's impossible to ensure access to better jobs and better housing without actively taking on the residual discrimination in our society. Shelby Steele was right when he suggested (see Chapter 6) that discrimination is evil and that morality requires resisting it, although that is a message a lot of people would prefer not to hear.

In their rush to declare this society color blind, some Americans have leaped to the conclusion that discrimination has largely disappeared. They explain away what little discrimination they believe exists as the fault of a few isolated individuals or the result of the oversensitivity of minorities or by observing that most Americans, being decent people, would not dare to break the law by practicing discrimination. A white talk-show host on the West Coast once told me—seriously, I think—that the treatment he received when he walked around the city in blue jeans was probably no different from what a similarly dressed black man would encounter. On any given day, that may or may not be true. The point is that assuming it is true is not the same as ensuring that it is.

As Rice observed, we would not do away with the Internal Revenue Service out of an assumption that Americans, left to their own devices, generally obey the law. Instead, we empower the IRS to audit their returns, confiscate their property, and put them in jail if they don't pay the proper amount. We certainly don't leave it up to individuals who feel cheated out of their fellow citizens' tax dollars to take the delinquents to court.

Making discrimination a felony is probably not a solution, but more aggressive monitoring and prosecution—especially in housing and employment situations—would not be a bad start. Instead, many Americans seem determined to make discrimination easier to ignore. The Equal Employment Opportunity Commission is perennially underfunded and backlogged. (EEOC chairman Gilbert Casellas was so frustrated after sixteen months on his job that he bitterly complained to a *Washington Post* reporter, "Nobody gives a crap about us.") And politicians are calling for cutbacks in the use of interracial "testers" who investigate discrimination in housing markets. Just as one cannot get beyond race by treating different races differently, one cannot get beyond discrimination by refusing to acknowledge it. One can get beyond discrimination only by fighting it vigorously wherever it is found.

10. **We must keep the conversation going.**

   Dialogue clearly is no cure-all for racial estrangement. Conversations, as opposed to confrontations, about race are inevitably aimed at a select few—those who are "relatively conscious," those who make up the empathic elite. Many (probably most) Americans have virtually no interest in race until a racial situation explodes in their backyard. Yet, limited as the audience may be, the ongoing discourse is crucial. It gives those who are sincerely interested in examining their attitudes and behavior an opportunity to do so, and, in some instances, can even lead to change, assuming that individuals are willing to do so.

   During the 1996 Democratic Convention, Bill Bradley presided over an "UnConvention" that focused on interracial communication. The meeting, sponsored by the Human Relations Foundation of Chicago, featured several big-name authors, including Toni Morrison, Cornel West, Bharati Mukherjee, and David Henry Hwang. Bradley reasoned that writers, particularly those who cross racial lines in their fiction, might be able to help people to see the world through the eyes of another race. He also hoped the event would attract enough attention to serve as an inspiration to President Clinton, and to persuade him of the importance of speaking more regularly on racial issues. The president of the United States has a mighty microphone, said Bradley. "Why not take this microphone and take people on a journey toward racial healing."

   Although the UnConvention drew a crowd of enthusiastic Chicagoans, it did not attract much attention from the media or from delegates to the DNC. Yet when I spoke with Bradley the following day, he refused to believe the news media's indifference was indicative of the feelings of ordinary people. Many Americans, he argued, were eager for an in-depth conversation exploring racial issues. One can only hope that he is right; for dialogue at its best, as Lester suggested, can provide the wisdom and grace that enable us to focus on useful strategies and to discard those that are not. It clarifies issues that, sooner or later, will become important to everyone; it defines the goals that the nation must strive to reach—even those goals that seem impossible or currently unachievable.

   As Baldwin observed: "[In] our time, as in every time, the impossible is the least that one can demand—and one is, after all, emboldened by the spectacle of human history in general, and American Negro history in particular, for it testifies to nothing less than the perpetual achievement of the impossible."

11. **We must seize opportunities for interracial collaboration.**

   Dovidio has an irrefutable point: Even those who have no interest in talking about the so-called *racial situation*, can, through the process of working with (and having to depend on) people of other races, begin to see beyond skin color. Conversation, in short, has its limits. Only through doing things together—things that typically have nothing specifically to do with race—will people succeed in breaking down racial barriers.

The Changing Relations Project, a Ford Foundation-funded effort to promote cooperation among immigrants and established residents, examined relations among various groups in six U.S. communities and concluded that successful efforts rarely had an explicitly racial agenda. "When groups come together to participate in a shared task, the inspiration is usually a desire to improve specific community conditions—to secure better social services or housing, or to battle neighborhood crime and deterioration. The groups are not searching consciously for cross-cultural means to improve an abstract sense of 'quality of life.' Rather . . . they are struggling together over a loss of control in the face of dramatic changes in their standard of living. Shared activities reduce tension and competition and build bonds of trust among groups," the board's report concluded.

"If you can establish a sense of groupness, of being on the same team even artificially and temporarily, that begins to create a foundation on which people can have more personal, deeper discussions and understanding," observed Dovidio.

Those who are truly concerned about bridging the racial ravine cannot afford to ignore that insight. Facing common problems as community groups, as work colleagues, or as classmates can provide a focus and reduce self-conscious awkwardness in a way that simple conversation cannot.

12. We must stop looking for one solution to all our racial problems.

Meetings on racial justice often resemble nothing so much as a bazaar filled with peddlers offering the all-purpose answer. "What we need is a national dialogue," says one person. "No, we need more entrepreneurship," says another. "No, we need to talk about integration." "What we really need is self-help." "Well, what about education?" "If we could just get rid of affirmative action . . ." "No, it's values. What we need to do is restore spirituality and high moral values to our communities." "You're wrong, we need to focus on stopping the hate." "No, we need to save the children."

The reality is that the problem has no single or simple solution. If there is one answer, it lies in recognizing how complex the issue has become and in not using that complexity as an excuse for inaction. In short, if we are to achieve our country, we must attack the enemy on many fronts.

It is too much to dream that all the points just discussed will have relevance to every reader. I hope, however, that they will provide a useful framework for those who are searching for a sense of the possible and grappling with the difficult question, "Where do we go from here?" I hope as well that these points, and the rest of this book, will help to spark a more honest racial debate—one that acknowledges real problems for what they are but that also illuminates the fact that, intractable as those problems may seem, they are not unsolvable.

———————————————■———————————————

*In his fable, **"The Racial Preference Licensing Act"** (from Faces at the Bottom of the Well), Derek Bell offers a fundamentally different prescription for America's racial ills. Bell tells the story of a new statute that ". . . represented a realistic advance in race relations." The law is based on the assumption that racism is endemic to the society and it is impossible to change behavior by "policing morality." The marketplace, in contrast, is better at balancing the rights of white and black citizens. The law required a license to engage in discriminatory behavior. Businesses had to pay a hefty fee to obtain it, prominently display it in their place of business and ". . . operate their business in accordance with racially selective policies set out in their license." Discrimination charges against business not holding a license required the plaintiff to carry the burden of proof, and if the charges were found to have merit the plaintiff would be awarded ". . . ten thousand dollars per instance of unlicensed discrimination." Additionally, all fees would be held in an "equality fund" used to provide benefits to blacks.*

In this fable, Bell is visited by his "guardian angel," Geneva Crenshaw. Geneva routinely challenges Bell's thinking and it is she who came up with the idea for the Act. In the final part of the fable, Geneva justifies the new law on three grounds: one, it counters the claim that integration is "forced association"; two, ". . . the law may dilute the financial and psychological benefits of racism"; and three, black people will not have to guess whether white actions are based on discriminatory intent. In short, this proposal forces civil rights advocates to ". . . see the racial world as it is."

THE RACIAL PREFERENCE LICENSING ACT

———————————————■———————————————

Derek Bell

Excerpt from Faces at the Bottom of the Well

Racial nepotism rather than racial animus is the major motivation for much of the discrimination blacks experience.

—MATTHEW S. GOLDBERG

It was enacted as the Racial Preference Licensing Act. At an elaborate, nationally televised signing ceremony, the President—elected as a "racial moderate"—assured the nation that the new statute represented a realistic advance in race relations. "It is," he insisted, "certainly not a return to the segregation policies granted constitutional protection under the stigma-inflicting 'separate but equal' standard of *Plessy* v. *Ferguson* established roughly a century ago.

"Far from being a retreat into our unhappy racial past," he explained, "the new law embodies a daring attempt to create a brighter racial future for all our citizens. Racial realism is the key to understanding this new law. *It does not assume a* nonexistent racial tolerance, but holdly proclaims its commitment to racial justice through the working of a marketplace that recognizes and seeks to balance the rights of our black citizens to fair treatment and the no less important right of some whites to an unfettered choice of customers, employees, and contractees."

Under the new act, all employers, proprietors of public facilities, and owners and managers of dwelling places, homes, and apartments could, on application to the federal government, obtain a license authorizing the holders, their managers, agents, and employees to exclude or separate persons on the basis of race and color. The license itself was expensive, though not prohibitively so. Once obtained, it required payment to a government commission of a tax of 3% of the income derived from whites employed, whites served, or products sold to whites during each quarter in which a policy of "racial preference" was in effect. Congress based its authority for the act on the commerce clause, the taxing power, and the general welfare clause of the Constitution.

License holders were required both to display their licenses prominently in a public place and to operate their businesses in accordance with the racially selective policies set out on their license. Specifically, discrimination had to be practiced in accordance with the license on a nonselective basis. Licenses were not available to those who, for example, might hire or rent to one token black and then discriminate against other applicants, using the license as a shield against discrimination suits. Persons of color wishing to charge discrimination against a facility not holding a license would carry the burden of proof, but such burden might be met with statistical and circumstantial as well as with direct evidence provided by white "testers."* Under the act, successful complainants would be entitled to damages set at ten thousand dollars per instance of unlicensed discrimination, including attorneys' fees.

License fees and commissions paid by license holders would be placed in an "equality fund" used to underwrite black businesses, to offer no-interest mortgage loans for black home buyers, and to provide scholarships for black students seeking college and vocational education. To counter charges that black people, as under *Plessy*, would be both segregated and never gain any significant benefit from the quality fund, the act provided that five major civil rights organizations (each named in the statute) would submit the name of a representative who would serve on the commission for one, nonrenewable three-year term.

---

* Testing is an effective, but too little utilized, technique to ferret out bias in the sale and rental of housing or in employment practices. Generally, in testing, people who are alike in virtually every way except race or ethnicity are sent to apply for jobs, housing, or mortgages. The results are then analyzed for how differently whites are treated compared with black or Hispanic people. In 1982, the Supreme Court found that testers in a housing discrimination suit, and the housing association to which they were attached, had standing to sue in their own right as injured parties.

The President committed himself and his administration to the effective enforcement of the Racial Preference Licensing Act. "It is time," he declared, "to bring hard-headed realism rather than well-intentioned idealism to bear on our long-standing racial problems. Policies adopted because they seemed right have usually failed. Actions taken to promote justice for blacks have brought injustice to whites without appreciably improving the status or standards of living for blacks, particularly for those who most need the protection those actions were intended to provide.

"Within the memories of many of our citizens, this nation has both affirmed policies of racial segregation and advocated polices of racial integration. Neither approach has been either satisfactory or effective in furthering harmony and domestic tranquillity." Recalling the Civil Rights Act of 1964 and its 1991 amendments, the President pointed out that while the once-controversial public-accommodation provisions in the original 1964 act received unanimous judicial approval in the year of its adoption, even three decades later the act's protective function, particularly in the employment area, had been undermined by both unenthusiastic enforcement and judicial decisions construing its provisions ever more narrowly.

"As we all know," the President continued "the Supreme Court has now raised grave questions about the continued validity of the 1964 Act and the Fair Housing Act of 1968—along with their various predecessors and supplemental amendments as applied to racial discrimination. The Court stopped just short of declaring unconstitutional all laws prohibiting racial discrimination, and found that the existing civil rights acts were inconsistent with what it viewed as the essential 'racial forgiveness' principle in the landmark decision of *Brown* v. *Board of Education* of 1954. The Court announced further that nothing in its decision was intended to affect the validity of the statutes' protection against discrimination based on sex, national origin, or religion.

"This is, of course, not an occasion for a legal seminar, but it is important that all citizens understand the background of the new racial preference statute we sign this evening. The Supreme Court expressed its concern that existing civil rights statues created racial categories that failed to meet the heavy burden of justification placed on any governmental policy that seeks to classify persons on the basis of race. In 1989, the Court held that this heavy burden, called the 'strict scrutiny' standard, applied to remedial as well as to invidious racial classifications. Our highest court reasoned that its 1954 decision in the landmark case of *Brown* v. *Board of Education* did not seek to identify and punish wrongdoers, and the implementation order in *Brown II* a year later did not require immediate enforcement. Rather, *Brown II* asserted that delay was required, not only to permit time for the major changes required in Southern school policies, but also—and this is important—to enable accommodation to school integration which ran counter to the views and strong emotions of most Southern whites.

"In line with this reasoning," the President continued, "the Court referred with approval to the views of the late Yale law professor Alexander Bickel, who contended that any effort to enforce *Brown* as a criminal law would have failed, as have alcohol prohibition, antigambling, most sex laws, and other laws policing morals. Bickel said, 'It follows that in achieving integration, the task of the law . . . was not to punish law breakers but to diminish their number.'

"Now the Court has found Professor Bickel's argument compelling. Viewed from the perspective provided by four decades, the Court says now that *Brown* was basically a call for a higher morality rather than a judicial decree authorizing Congress to coerce behavior allegedly unjust to blacks because that behavior recognized generally acknowledged differences in racial groups. This characterization of *Brown* explains why *Brown* was no more effective as an enforcement tool than were other 'morals-policing' laws such as alcohol prohibition, antigambling, and sex laws, all of which are hard to enforce precisely because they seek to protect our citizens' health and welfare against what a legislature deems self-abuse.

"Relying on this reasoning, the Court determined that laws requiring cessation of white conduct deemed harmful to blacks are hard to enforce because they seek to 'police morality.' While conceding both the states' and the federal government's broad powers to protect the health, safety, and welfare of its citizens, the Court found nothing in the Constitution authorizing regulation of what government at any particular time might deem appropriate 'moral' behavior. The exercise of such authority, the Court feared, could lead Congress to control the perceptions of what some whites believe about the humanity of some blacks. On this point," the President said, "I want to quote the opinion the Supreme Court has just handed down: 'Whatever the good intentions of such an undertaking, it clearly aimed for a spiritual result that might be urged by a religion but is beyond the reach of government coercion.'

"Many of us, of both political persuasions," the President went on, "were emboldened by the Court to seek racial harmony and justice along the route of mutual respect as suggested in its decision. This bill I now sign into law is the result of long debate and good-faith compromise. It is, as its opponents charge and its proponents concede, a radical new approach to the nation's continuing tensions over racial status. It maximizes freedom of racial choice for all our citizens while guaranteeing that people of color will benefit either directly from equal access or indirectly from the fruits of the license taxes paid by those who choose policies of racial exclusion.

"A few, final words. I respect the views of those who vigorously opposed this new law. And yet the course we take today was determined by many forces too powerful to ignore, too popular to resist, and too pregnant with potential to deny. We have vacillated long enough. We must move on toward what I predict will be a new and more candid and collaborative relationship among all our citizens. May God help us all as we seek with His help to pioneer a new path in our continuing crusade to bring justice and harmony to all races in America."

Well, Geneva, you've done it again, I thought to myself as I finished this second story well after midnight. After all our battles, I thought I'd finally pulled myself up to your advanced level of racial thinking—but the Racial Preference Licensing Act is too much.

"You still don't get it, do you?"

I looked up. There she was—the ultimate African queen—sitting on the small couch in my study. The mass of gray dreadlocks framing Geneva's strong features made a beautiful contrast with her smooth blue-black skin. She greeted me with her old smile, warm yet authoritative.

"Welcome," I said, trying to mask my shock with a bit of savoir-faire. "Do you always visit folks at two o'clock in the morning?"

She smiled, "I decided I could not leave it to you to figure out the real significance of my story."

"Well," I said, "I'm delighted to see you!" As indeed I was. It had been almost five years since Geneva disappeared at the close of the climactic civil rights conference that ended my book *And We Are Not Saved*. Seeing her now made me realize how much I had missed her, and I slipped back easily into our old relationship.

"Tell me, Geneva, how can you justify this law? After all, if the Fourteenth Amendment's equal protection clause retains any viability, it is to bar government-sponsored racial segregation. Even if—as is likely—you convince me of your law's potential, what are civil rights advocates going to say when I present it to them? As you know, it has taken me years to regain some acceptance within the civil rights community—since I suggested in print that civil rights lawyers who urge racial-balance remedies in all school desegregation cases were giving priority to their integration ideals over their clients' educational needs. Much as I respect your insight on racial issues, Geneva, I think your story's going to turn the civil rights community against us at a time when our goal is to persuade them to broaden their thinking beyond traditional, integration-oriented goals."

"Oh ye of little faith!" she responded. "Even after all these years, you remain as suspicious of my truths as you are faithful to the civil rights ideals that events long ago rendered obsolete. Whatever its cost to relationships with your civil rights friends, accept the inevitability of my Racial Preference Licensing Act. And believe—if not me—yourself.

"Although you maintain your faith in the viability of the Fourteenth Amendment, in your writings you have acknowledged, albeit reluctantly, that whatever the civil rights law or constitutional provision, blacks gain little protection against one or another form of racial discrimination unless granting blacks a measure of relief will serve some interest of importance to whites. Virtually every piece of civil rights legislation beginning with the Emancipation Proclamation supports your position. Your beloved 14th Amendment is a key illustration of this white self-interest principle. Enacted in 1868 to provide citizenship to the former slaves and their offspring, support for the Amendment reflected Republicans' concern after the Civil War that the Southern Democrats, having lost the war, might win the peace. This was not a groundless fear. If the Southern states could rejoin the union, bar blacks from voting, and regain control of state government, they might soon become the dominant power in the federal government as well.

"Of course, within a decade, when Republican interests changed and the society grew weary of racial remedies and was ready to sacrifice black rights to political expediency, both the Supreme Court and the nation simply ignored the original stated purpose of the Fourteenth Amendment's equal protection guarantee. In 1896, the *Plessy v. Ferguson* precedent gave legal validity to this distortion and then to a torrent of Jim Crow statutes. Separate but equal' was the judicial promise. Racial subordination became the legally enforceable fact."

"Well, sure," I mustered a response, "the 14th Amendment's history is a definitive example of white self-interest lawmaking, but what is its relevance to your Racial Preference Licensing Act? It seems to me—and certainly will seem to most civil rights advocates—like a new, more subtle, but hardly less pernicious 'separate but equal' law. Is there something I'm missing?"

"You are—which is precisely why I am here."

"I could certainly," I said, "use more of an explanation for a law that entrusts our rights to free-market forces. The law and economics experts might welcome civil rights protections in this form,* but virtually all civil rights professionals will view legalizing racist practices as nothing less than a particularly vicious means of setting the struggle for racial justice back a century. I doubt I could communicate them effectively to most black people."

"Of course you can't! Neither they nor you really want to come to grips with the real role of racism in this country."

"And that is?"

"My friend, know it! Racism is more than a group of bad white folks whose discriminatory predilections can be controlled by well-formed laws, vigorously enforced. Traditional civil rights laws tend to be ineffective because they are built on a law enforcement model. They assume that most citizens will obey the law; and when law breakers are held liable, a strong warning goes out that will discourage violators and encourage compliance. But the law enforcement model for civil rights breaks down when a great number of whites are willing—because of convenience, habit, distaste, fear, or simple preference—to violate the law. It then becomes almost impossible to enforce, because so many whites, though not discriminating themselves, identify more easily with those who do than with their victims."

"That much I understand," I replied. "Managers of hotels, restaurants, and other places of public accommodation have complied with antidiscrimination laws because they have discovered that, for the most part, it is far more profitable to serve blacks than to exclude or segregate them. On the other hand, these same establishments regularly discriminate against blacks seeking jobs."

"Precisely right, friend. A single establishment, often a single individual, can be inconsistent for any number of reasons, including the desire not to upset or inconvenience white customers or white employees. More often, management would prefer to hire the white than the black applicant. As one

---

* A similar economically based principle underlay the action of the Connecticut Legislature when in 1973 it enacted a statute mandating penalties equal to the capital and operating costs saved by not installing and operating equipment to meet applicable regulatory limits. In 1977, Congress added "noncompliance penalties" patterned after the Connecticut compliance program to section 120 of the Clean Air Act. As of 1988, section 173(I)(A) of the Clean Air Act in effect permits the introduction of new pollution sources if "total allowable emissions" from existing and new sources are "sufficiently less than total emissions from existing sources allowed under the applicable implementation plan."

economist has argued, 'racial nepotism' rather than 'racial animus' is the major motivation for much of the discrimination blacks experience."

"But nepotism," I objected, "is a preference for family members or relatives. What does it have to do with racial discrimination?"

Geneva gave me her "you are not serious" smile.

Then it hit me. "Of course! You're right, Geneva, it is hard to get out of the law enforcement model. You're suggesting that whites tend to treat one another like family, at least when there's a choice between them and us. So that terms like 'merit' and 'best qualified' are infinitely manipulable if and when whites must explain why they reject blacks to hire 'relatives'—even when the only relationship is that of race. So, unless there's some pressing reason for hiring, renting to, or otherwise dealing with a black, many whites will prefer to hire, rent to, sell to, or otherwise deal with a white—including one less qualified by objective measures and certainly one who is by any measure better qualified."

"Lord, I knew the man could figure it out! He just needed my presence."

"Well, since a little sarcasm is the usual price of gaining face-to-face access to your insight, Geneva, I am willing to pay. Actually, as I think about it, racial licensing is like that approach adopted some years ago by environmentalists who felt that licensing undesirable conduct was the best means of dealing with industry's arguments that it could not immediately comply with laws to protect the environment. The idea is, as I recall, that a sufficiently high licensing fee would make it profitable for industry to take steps to control the emissions (or whatever), and that thereby it would be possible to reduce damage to health and property much more cheaply than an attempt to control the entire polluting activity.

"Come to think of it, Geneva, there's even a precedent, of sorts, for the Equality Fund. College football's Fiesta Bowl authorities no doubt had a similar principle in mind when they announced in 1990 that they would create a minority scholarship fund of one hundred thousand dollars or endow an academic chair for minority students at each competing university; the aim was to induce colleges to participate in the Fiesta Bowl in Arizona, a state whose populace has refused to recognize the Martin Luther King, Jr., holiday. Sunkist Growers, Inc., the event's sponsor, agreed to match the amount. Further 'sweetening the pot,' one university president promised to donate all net proceeds to university programs benefiting minority students."

These law and economics experts, especially Richard Posner and John J. Donohue, accept Gary Becker's theory that markets drive out discriminatory employers because discrimination tends to minimize profits. The essence of Posner and Donohue's debate on Title VII (the Equal Employment Opportunity Act) is whether "[l]egislation that prohibits employment discrimination . . . actually enhance[s] rather than impair[s] economic efficiency." Donohue argues that the effects of the Title VII statutory scheme are to increase the rate at which discriminators are driven out of the market from the base rate, which many economists steeped in the neoclassical tradition would argue is the optimal rate. Posner questions whether this effect (the increased rate) occurs; and, significantly, also raises questions about whether the regulatory scheme, designed to decrease discrimination against blacks in employment decisions and thereby increase the net welfare of blacks, actually succeeds in doing so. If neither assumption is accurate, he states that the costs of enforcement and all other costs associated with administering Title VII "are a dead weight social loss that cannot be justified on grounds [not only of efficiency but] of social equity."

Posner and David A. Strauss both make statements that would seem to indicate openness to such measures as the Racial Preference Licensing Act. Posner writes that "it might be that a tax on those whites [who discriminate because of an aversion to blacks and therefore would seek a license] for the benefit of blacks would be justifiable on the grounds of social equity [although this is not an *efficiency* justification in the wealth maximization sense]." And Strauss asks, "Why would the objectives of compensatory justice and avoiding racial stratification not be better served, at less cost, if the legal system permitted statistical discrimination; captured the efficiency gains (and the gains for reduced administrative costs) through taxation, and transferred the proceeds to African Americans?"

"Both examples," remarked Geneva, "illustrate how pocketbook issues are always near the top of the list of motives for racial behavior. That's why compliance with traditional civil rights laws is particularly tough during a period of great economic uncertainty, white nepotism becoming most prevalent when jobs and reasonably priced housing are in short supply. During such times, racial tolerance dissolves into hostility."

"Just as during the 1890s," I interjected, "when economic conditions for the working classes were at another low point, and there was intense labor and racial strife. Today, whites have concluded, as they did a century ago, that the country has done enough for black people despite the flood of evidence to the contrary. The Supreme Court's civil rights decisions reflect the public's lack of interest. In the meantime, enforcement of civil rights laws, never vigorous, has dawdled into the doldrums, and this inertia encourages open violation and discourages victims from filing complaints they fear will only add futility and possible retaliation to their misery."

"All true," Geneva agreed.

"But given the already strong anti–civil rights trends," I argued, "wouldn't the Racial Preference Licensing Act simply encourage them?"

"You are resistant," Geneva replied. "Don't you see? For the very reasons you offer, urging stronger civil rights laws barring discrimination in this period is not simply foolhardy; it's the waste of a valuable opportunity."

"Well," I acknowledged, "I have no doubt that a great many white people would prefer the Racial Preference Licensing Act to traditional civil rights laws. The licensing feature provides legal protection for their racially discriminatory policies—particularly in employment and housing—which whites have practiced covertly, despite the presence on the books of civil rights laws and Court decisions declaring those practices unlawful."

"It is even more attractive," Geneva said, "in that thoughtful whites will view the new law as a means of giving moral legitimacy to their discriminatory preferences by adopting the theory that whites have a right of non-association (with blacks), and that this right should be recognized in law."

"On those grounds," I put in, "the act could expect support from white civil libertarins who think racial discrimination abhorrent but are troubled by the need to coerce correct behavior. Whites will not be happy about the Equality Fund, though these provisions might attract the support of black separatists who would see the fund as a fair trade for the integration they always distrusted. But, believe me, Geneva, no such benefits will assuage the absolute opposition of most civil rights professionals—black and white. They remain committed—to the point of obsession—with integration notions that, however widely held in the 1960s, are woefully beyond reach today."

"Don't start again!" Geneva threw up her hands. "I understand and sympathize with your civil rights friends' unwillingness to accept the legalized reincarnation of Jim Crow. They remember all too well how many of our people suffered and sacrificed to bury those obnoxious signs 'Colored' and 'White.' I think that even if I could prove that the Racial Preference Licensing Act would usher in the racial millennium, civil rights professionals would be unwilling to—as they might put it—'squander our high principles in return for a mess of segregation-tainted pottage.' Victory on such grounds is, they would conclude, no victory at all."

"You mock them, Geneva, but integration advocates would see themselves as standing by their principles."

"Principles, hell! What I do not understand—and this is what I really want to get clear—is what principle is so compelling as to justify continued allegiance to obsolete civil rights strategies that have done little to prevent—and may have contributed to—the contemporary statistics regarding black crime, broken families, devastated neighborhoods, alcohol and drug abuse, out-of-wedlock births, illiteracy, unemployment, and welfare dependency?"

She stopped to take a deep breath, then went on. "Racial segregation was surely hateful, but let me tell you, friend, that if I knew that its return would restore our black communities to what they were before desegregation, I would think such a trade entitled to serious thought. I would not dismiss it self-righteously, as you tell me many black leaders would do. Black people simply cannot afford the luxury of rigidity on racial issues. This story is not intended to urge actual adoption of a racial preference licensing law, but to provoke blacks and their white allies to look beyond traditional civil rights views. We must learn to examine every racial policy, including those that seem most hostile to blacks, and determine whether there is unintended potential African Americans can exploit.

"Think about it! Given the way things have gone historically, if all existing civil rights laws were invalidated, legislation like the Racial Preference Licensing Act might be all African Americans could expect. And it could prove no less—and perhaps more—effective than those laws that now provide us the promise of protection without either the will or the resources to honor that promise."

"Most civil rights advocates," I replied, "would, on hearing that argument, likely respond by linking arms and singing three choruses of 'We Shall Overcome.'"

"You're probably right, friend—but it is your job, is it not, to make them see that racist opposition has polluted the dream that phrase once inspired? However comforting, the dream distracts us from the harsh racial reality closing in around you and ours."

As I did not respond, Geneva continued. "You have to make people *see*. Just as parents used to tell children stories about the stork to avoid telling them about sex, so for similarly evasive reasons many black people hold to dreams about a truly integrated society that is brought into being by the enforcement of laws barring discriminatory conduct. History and—one would hope—common sense tells us that dream is never coming true."

"Dreams and ideals are not evil, Geneva."

"Of course, they aren't, but we need to be realistic about our present and future civil rights activities. The question is whether the activity reflects and is intended to challenge the actual barriers we face rather than those that seem a threat to the integration ideology."

"That's all very high-sounding, Geneva, and I agree that we need a more realistic perspective, but how can I bring others to recognize that need?"

"We might begin by considering the advantages of such a radical measure as the Racial Preference Licensing Act. First, by authorizing racial discrimination, such a law would, as I suggested earlier, remove the long-argued concern that civil rights laws deny anyone the right of non-association.* With the compulsive element removed, people who discriminate against blacks without getting the license authorized by law, may not retain the unspoken but real public sympathy they now enjoy. They may be viewed as what they are: law breakers who deserve punishment.

"Second, by requiring the discriminator both to publicize and to pay all blacks a price for that 'right,' the law may dilute both the financial and the psychological benefits of racism. Today even the worst racist denies being a racist. Most whites pay a tremendous price for their reflexive and often unconscious racism, but few are ready to post their racial preferences on a public license and even less ready to make direct payments for the privilege of practicing discrimination. Paradoxically, gaining the right to practice openly what people now enthusiastically practice covertly, will take a lot of the joy out of discrimination and replace that joy with some costly pain.

"Third, black people will no longer have to divine—as we have regularly to do in this antidiscrimination era—whether an employer, a realtor, or a proprietor wants to exclude them. The license will give them—and the world—ample notice. Those who seek to discriminate without a license will place their businesses at risk of serious, even ruinous, penalties."

"It seems crazy," I began.

"Racism is hardly based on logic. We need to fight racism the way a forest ranger fights fire with fire."

---

* Herbert Wechser, for example, has suggested the decision in *Brown v. Board of Education* might be criticized as requiring "integration [that] forces an association upon those for whom it is unpleasant or repugnant."

"Sounds to me," I said, "like trying to fight for civil rights the way Brer Rabbit got himself out of Brer Fox's clutches in the old Uncle Remus story."

"Something like that." Geneva smiled, sensing that she was penetrating my skepticism. "In a bad situation he lacks the power to get out of, Brer Rabbit uses his wits. He doesn't waste any energy asking Brer Fox to set him free. He doesn't rely on his constitutional rights. Rather, he sets about pleading with Brer Fox that throwing him in the briar patch would be a fate worse than death. Convinced that the worst thing he could do to Brer Rabbit was the very thing Brer Rabbit didn't want him to do, Brer Fox threw Brer Rabbit right into the middle of the briar patch. And, of course, once in the brambles, Brer Rabbit easily slips through them and escapes."

"So," I pursued, "even if civil rights advocates strenuously resisted seeing any benefits in the Racial Preference Licensing Act, they may have their consciousness raised so as to seek out other sorts of briar patch?"

"Exactly. Civil rights advocates must first see the racial world as it is, determined by the need to maintain economic stability. And then, in the light of that reality, they must try to structure both initiatives and responses. We need, for example, to push for more money and more effective plans for curriculum in all-black schools rather than exhaust ourselves and our resources on ethereal integration in mainly white suburbs."

Drawing a deep breath, she asked, "Do you understand?"

"Understanding is not my problem," I replied. "It's conviction that comes hard. And selling your position will require real conviction on my part. Even so, before committing it to my book, I'll try it out in my next law review article."

"I rather think law review editors and many of their readers will see my point more easily than you. They, unlike many of you who have worked for integration for decades, may not harbor fond hopes of America as having reached a racially integrated millennium. And they may be willing to look for potential gain even in the face of racial disaster. Perhaps if *they* accept your article, you will come to see the merits of my approach."

"Geneva!" I protested. "I don't need a law review editor to give legitimacy to your far-out notions about race."

She smiled. "Let's just say that the editor's approval will give my approach acceptability."

"In other words, you're saying I'll see its merits if white folks think it is a good idea. I don't think that's fair."

"Don't worry, friend. We black women are amazingly tolerant of our men's frailties in that area. Speaking of which," she added, "I assume you will be sending me that new story of yours that tests black women's tolerance in the ever-sensitive area of interracial romance."

I told her I would transmit it quite soon. Geneva rose to her full six feet. Still smiling, she bent and kissed me before heading toward the door. "Though you are impossible as ever, I have missed you."

The usually squeaky door to my study opened and closed, still not rousing my two large Weimaraner hounds which, usually alert to the slightest sound, had slept soundly through Geneva's visit.

Could I myself have been sleeping and imagined she'd been there? No, there on my monitor was every word of our conversation, miraculously transcribed.

———————————————————— ■ ————————————————————

The upshot of these readings raises serious questions about the goals of the society *vis-a-vis* race. What does it mean to be black in American society? Can people of African descent ever really be Americans? What is the relationship between African-American culture and the culture of the broader society? Put differently, how does the modern discourse on race understand and characterize the African-American condition? These questions motivate the next chapter.

STUDY QUESTIONS

1. Taxi drivers in cities like Washington, D.C. and New York routinely refuse to pick up black fares. Their common justification is not based on skin color; rather it is based on the belief (and experience?) that blacks are much more likely to leave the cab without paying and/or are more likely to have high crime areas as their destination. Is the behavior of the taxi drivers justified?

2. What are the differences between the group interest and racial resentment models of racial attitudes? How do they conceive the notion of material interest? How do these models situate attitudes associated with old-fashioned or "redneck" racism?

3. Is Derrick Bell right? That is, aren't we much better off as a society if we acknowledge that racism exists and that it is unlikely to abate in the future? Or, should we intensify our efforts to produce a color-blind society? What are the political and policy implications of these contrasting views?

4. Can people oppose policies designed to advance racial equality without being racist? In other words, is white resistance to contemporary racial policy more a function of ideology than race? What is the relationship between conservative ideology and racism?

NOTES

1. Edward G. Carmines, and James A. Stimson. *Issue evolution: Race and the transformation of American politics.* (Princeton: Princeton University Press) 1989.

2. Howard Schuman, Charlotte Steeh, and Lawrence D. Bobo. *Racial attitudes in America: trends and interpretations.* (Cambridge: Harvard University Press) 1985.

3. Lawrence D. Bobo et al., *Public opinion before and after a spring of discontent: A preliminary report on the 1992 Los Angeles Social Survey* (UCLA: Center for the Study of Urban Poverty) 1992.

4. *National Opinion Poll — Race Relations* (Washington, D.C: The Joint Center for Political and Economic Studies) 1997.

5. Thomas B. Edsall and Mary D. Edsall. Chain reaction: *The impact of race, rights, and taxes on American politics.* (New York: W.W. Norton) 1992; Jennifer Hochschild. *Facing up to the American Dream: Race, class, and the soul of a nation* (Princeton: Princeton University Press) 1995. Andrew Hacker. *Two nations: Black and White, separate, hostile, unequal.* (New York: Scribner's) 1992.

6. David O. Sears, "Symbolic Racism" in P.A. Katz and D.A. Taylor (eds.) *Eliminating racism: Profiles in controversy.* (New York: Plenum Press) 1988.

7. Paul M. Sniderman and Thomas Piazza. *The scar of race.* (Cambridge: Belknap, Harvard) 1993.

8. Lawrence D. Bobo "Whites opposition to busing: Symbolic racism or realistic group conflict?" *Journal of Personality and Social Psychology,* 45 (1988):1196–1210.

9. But see, American Civil Liberties Union. *Driving while black: Racial profiling on our nation's highways.* An American Civil Liberties Union Special Report, June 1999.

10. See, C. Campbell, *Race, myth and the news.* (Thousand Oaks, C.A.: Russell Sage) 1995. Mark Crispin-Miller. *Crime news in Baltimore: The economic cost of local TV's bodybag journalism* (New York: Project on Media Ownership) 1998; Robert M. Entman, "Blacks in the News: Television, modern racism, and cultural change." *Journalism Quarterly* 69 (1992): 341 1; Robert M. Entman, "Modern Racism and the Images of Blacks in Local Television News." *Critical Studies in Mass Communication.* 7: (1990): 332; Herman Gray, *Watching race: Television and the struggle for blackness.* (Minneapolis: University of Minnesota Press) 1995; E. Guerrere, *Framing Blackness: The African-American image in film.* (Philadelphia: Temple University Press) 1993. Franklin D. Gilliam, Jr. and Shanto Iyengar, 2000. "Prime suspects: the impact of local television news on attitudes about crime & race" *American Journal of Political Science* 44, 3:560–573.

11. Jon Hurwitz and Mark Peffley (eds.) 1998. *Perception and prejudice: Race and politics in the United States* (New Haven: Yale University Press).

Ideology, Identity, and Black Political Thought

Cultural values and symbols have a profound impact on the way people interact with the political process. This system of beliefs, or *ideology*, mediates political meaning and determines political action. Put differently, to what extent do African-Americans share a common set of attitudes and opinions. Does this distinctively "black" worldview influence politics and policy in a patterned fashion? For instance, on what terms does the community evaluate itself and the broader society? What is the proper relationship to other racial and ethnic groups? The purpose of black political thought is to provide answers to these questions. In short, ideology serves to theoretically capture black identity and structure the public's discourse on racial politics.[1]

Historically, black identity was shaped by a quest for authenticity and emancipation.[2] The initial goal was to articulate a conception of African-Americans as fully developed human beings capable of intellectual sovereignty. Thus, 19th century black thought sought to demonstrate that blacks were neither child-like creatures in need of protection nor beast-like heathens requiring strict social control.[3] This vision of black life, for example, animated the abolitionist movement before the Civil War.[4] Moreover, it resurfaced in the latter part of the century in response to Jim Crow era policies. By the turn of the century, however, African-American thinkers began to articulate new visions of the African-American experience.

This chapter examines three ideologies that have dominated black political thought in 20th century.[5] The first belief system is associated with the notion of a "black nation." The core assumption is that inter-group competition necessarily leads one group to seek dominance over others in the society.[6] In turn, this imperative requires the hegemonic group to erase or modify the cultures of competing subgroups. In response, oppressed people, or, a "nation within a nation," must do all they can to preserve cultural autonomy. In essence, nationalist ideology rejects the values and mores of dominant culture in favor of self-determination. In contrast, integrationist ideologies accept the basic values and institutions of the majority society. The problem, from this view, is that racial subgroups are not accorded full citizenship rights and privileges. Collective action, therefore, is necessary to express the group's grievances but it should be done within the confines of broadly accepted forms of behavior. The end game is to have full access to and participation in the benefits of "mainstream" society. The third ideology starts from the belief that there is no singular black worldview. Rather, there are several different identity subtypes that crosscut and sit orthogonal to the standard integration/separation dichotomy. Identity, according to the pluralist model, is malleable. For example, individual group members may switch identities over the course of a lifetime as personal circumstances vary and contexts change. In sum, the following selections represent all three ideologies.

BLACK NATIONALISM

Marcus Garvey established the United Negro Improvement Association (UNIA) in 1917 to "... improve the general conditions of Negroes everywhere."[7] In the **"Declaration of Rights of the Negro Peoples of the World,"** *the UNIA laid out their plans for black liberation. The first section of the document is a list of grievances or complaints about the treatment of people of African descent. Although it clearly called attention to racial discrimination in America, it also connected the oppression of American blacks to Western imperialism worldwide. The second section of the Declaration outlined 54 "demands" including the claim that "... all men, women, and children of our blood" were "... free citizens of Africa the Motherland of all Negroes." The demands also asserted political, cultural, religious, and economic autonomy for "the Negro."*

The most well-known activity of the UNIA was the creation of the Black Star Steamship Corporation designed to transport blacks "back to Africa." The "Black Star Line," however, was never fully operational and its vessels ran aground in the Caribbean. By the mid-1920s the UNIA was in deep financial trouble. Additionally, the federal government—believing Garvey was a legitimate threat to the social order—applied severe legal pressure. Ultimately, Garvey was incarcerated for mail fraud in 1925, and the UNIA never regained prominence in the black community.

DECLARATION OF RIGHTS OF THE NEGRO PEOPLES OF THE WORLD (1920)

Marcus Garvey

UNIVERSAL NEGRO IMPROVEMENT ASSOCIATION

Be it Resolved, That the Negro people of the world, through their chosen representatives in convention assembled in Liberty Hall, in the City of New York and United States of America, from August 1 to August 31, in the year of our Lord, one thousand nine hundred and twenty, protest against the wrongs injustices they are suffering at the hands of their white brethren, and state what they deem their fair and just rights, as well as the treatment they propose to demand of all men in the future.

We complain:

I. That nowhere in the world, with few exceptions, are black men accorded equal treatment with white men, although in the same situation and circumstances, but, on the contrary, are discriminated
against and denied the common rights due to human beings for no
other reason than their race and color.

    We are not willingly accepted as guests in the public hotels and
inns of the world for no other reason than our race and color.

II. In certain parts of the United States of America our race is denied
the right of public trial accorded to other races when accused of
crime, but are lynched and burned by mobs, and such brutal and
inhuman treatment is even practised upon our women.

III. That European nations have parcelled out among themselves and
taken possession of nearly all of the continent of Africa, and the natives are compelled to surrender their lands to aliens and are
treated in most instances like slaves.

IV. In the southern portion of the United States of America, although
citizens under the Federal Constitution, and in some states almost
equal to the whites in population and are qualified land owners and
taxpayers, we are, nevertheless, denied all voice in the making and
administration of the laws and are taxed without representation by
the state governments, and at the same time compelled to do military service in defense of the country.

V. On the public conveyances and common carriers in the Southern
portion of the United States we are jim-crowed and compelled to
accept separate and inferior accommodations and made to pay the
same fare charged for first-class accommodations, and our families
are often humiliated and insulted by drunken white men who ha-
bitually pass through the jim-crow cars going to the smoking car.

VI. The physicians of our race are denied the right to attend their patients while in the public hospitals of the cities and states where
they reside in certain parts of the United States.

    Our children are forced to attend inferior separate schools for
shorter terms than white children, and the public school funds are
unequally divided between the white and colored schools.

VII. We are discriminated against and denied an equal chance to earn
wages for the support of our families, and in many instances are refused admission into labor unions, and nearly everywhere are paid
smaller wages than white men.

VIII. In Civil Service and departmental offices we are everywhere discriminated against and made to feel that to be a black man in Europe, America and the West Indies is equivalent to being an outcast
and a leper among the races of men, no matter what the character
and attainments of the black man may be.

IX. In the British and other West Indian Islands and colonies, Negroes
are secretly and cunningly discriminated against, and denied those

fuller rights in government to which white citizens are appointed, nominated and elected.

X. That our people in those parts are forced to work for lower wages than the average standard of white men and are kept in conditions repugnant to good civilized tastes and customs.

XI. That the many acts of injustice against members of our race before the courts of law in the respective islands and colonies are of such nature as to create disgust and disrespect for the white man's sense of justice.

XII. Against all such inhuman, unchristian and uncivilized treatment we here and now emphatically protest, and invoke the condemnation of all mankind.

In order to encourage our race all over the world and to stimulate it to a higher and grander destiny, we demand and insist on the following Declaration of Rights:

1. Be it known to all men that whereas, all men are created equal and entitled to the rights of life, liberty and the pursuit of happiness, and because of this we, the duly elected representatives of the Negro peoples of the world, invoking the aid of the just and Almighty God do declare all men women and children of our blood throughout the world free citizens, and do claim them as free citizens of Africa, the Motherland of all Negroes.

2. That we believe in the supreme authority of our race in all things racial; that all things are created and given to man as a common possession; that there should be an equitable distribution and apportionment of all such things, and in consideration of the fact that as a race we are now deprived of those things that are morally and legally ours, we believe it right that all such things should be acquired and held by whatsoever means possible.

3. That we believe the Negro, like any other race, should be governed by the ethics of civilization, and, therefore, should not be deprived of any of those rights or privileges common to other human beings.

4. We declare that Negroes, wheresoever they form a community among themselves, should be given the right to elect their own representatives to represent them in legislatures, courts of law, or such institutions as may exercise control over that particular community.

5. We assert that the Negro is entitled to even-handed justice before all courts of law and equity in whatever country he may be found, and when this is denied him on account of his race or color such denial is an insult to the race as a whole and should be resented by the entire body of Negroes.

6. We declare it unfair and prejudicial to the rights of Negroes in communities where they exist in considerable numbers to be tried by a

judge and jury composed entirely of an alien race, but in all such cases members of our race are entitled to representation on the jury.

7. We believe that any law or practice that tends to deprive any African of his land or the privileges of free citizenship within his country is unjust and immoral, and no native should respect any such law or practice.

8. We declare taxation without representation unjust and tyrannous, and there should be no obligation on the part of the Negro to obey the levy of a tax by any law-making body from which he is excluded and denied representation on account of his race and color.

9. We believe that any law especially directed against the Negro to his detriment and singling him out because of his race or color is unfair and immoral, and should not be respected.

10. We believe all men entitled to common human respect, and that our race should in no way tolerate any insults that may be interpreted to mean disrespect to our color.

11. We deprecate the use of the term "nigger" as applied to Negroes, and demand that the word 'Negro' be written with a capital "N".

12. We believe that the Negro should adopt every means to protect himself against barbarous practices inflicted upon him because of color.

13. We believe in the freedom of Africa for the Negro people of the world, and by the principle of Europe for the Europeans and Asia for the Asiatics; we also demand Africa for the Africans at home and abroad.

14. We believe in the inherent right of the Negro to possess himself of Africa, and that his possession of same shall not be regarded as an infringement on any claim or purchase made by any race or nation.

15. We strongly condemn the cupidity of those nations of the world who, by open aggression or secret schemes, have seized the territories and inexhaustible natural wealth of Africa, and we place on record our most solemn determination to reclaim the treasures and possession of the vast continent of our forefathers.

16. We believe all men should live in peace one with the other, but when races and nations provoke the ire of other races and nations by attempting to infringe upon their rights, war becomes inevitable, and the attempt in any way to free one's self or protect one's rights or heritage becomes justifiable.

17. Whereas, the lynching, by burning, hanging or any other means, of human beings is a barbarous practice, and a shame and disgrace to civilization, we therefore declare any country guilty of such atrocities outside the pale of civilization.

18. We protest against the atrocious crime of whipping, flogging and overworking of the native tribes of Africa and Negroes everywhere. These are methods that should be abolished, and all means should be taken to prevent a continuance of such brutal practices.

19. We protest against the atrocious practice of shaving the heads of Africans, especially of African women or individuals of Negro blood, when placed in prison as a punishment for crime by an alien race.

20. We protest against segregated districts, separate public conveyances, industrial discrimination, lynchings and limitations of political privileges of any Negro citizen in any part of the world on account of race, color or creed, and will exert our full influence and power against all such.

21. We protest against any punishment inflicted upon a Negro with severity, as against lighter punishment inflicted upon another of an alien race for like offense, as an act of prejudice and injustice, and should be resented by the entire race.

22. We protest against the system of education in any country where Negroes are denied the same privileges and advantages as other races.

23. We declare it inhuman and unfair to boycott Negroes from industries and labor in any part of the world.

24. We believe in the doctrine of the freedom of the press, and we therefore emphatically protest against the suppression of Negro newspapers and periodicals in various parts of the world, and call upon Negroes everywhere to employ all available means to prevent such suppression.

25. We further demand free speech universally for all men.

26. We hereby protest against the publication of scandalous and inflammatory articles by an alien press tending to create racial strife and the exhibition of picture films showing the Negro as a cannibal.

27. We believe in the self-determination of all peoples.

28. We declare for the freedom of religious worship.

29. With the help of Almighty God, we declare ourselves the sworn protectors of the honor and virtue of our women and children, and pledge our lives for their protection and defense everywhere, and under all circumstances from wrongs and outrages.

30. We demand the right of unlimited and unprejudiced education for ourselves and our posterity forever.

31. We declare that the teaching in any school by alien teachers to our boys and girls, that the alien race is superior to the Negro race, is an insult to the Negro people of the world.

32. Where Negroes form a part of the citizenry of any country, and pass the civil service examination of such country, we declare them entitled to the same consideration as other citizens as to appointments in such civil service.

33. We vigorously protest against the increasingly unfair and unjust treatment accorded Negro travelers on land and sea by the agents

and employees of railroad and steamship companies and insist that for equal fare we receive equal privileges with travelers of other races.

34. We declare it unjust for any country, State or nation to enact laws tending to hinder and obstruct the free immigration of Negroes on account of their race and color.

35. That the right of the Negro to travel unmolested throughout the world be not abridged by any person or persons, and all Negroes are called upon to give aid to a fellow Negro when thus molested.

36. We declare that all Negroes are entitled to the same right to travel over the world as other men.

37. We hereby demand that the governments of the world recognize our leader and his representatives chosen by the race to look after the welfare of our people under such governments.

38. We demand complete control of our social institutions without interference by any alien race or races.

39. That the colors, Red, Black and Green, be the colors of the Negro race.

40. Resolved, That the anthem 'Ethiopia, Thou Land of Our Fathers,' etc., shall be the anthem of the Negro race.

41. We believe that any limited liberty which deprives one of the complete rights and prerogatives of full citizenship is but a modified form of slavery.

42. We declare it an injustice to our people and a serious impediment to the health of the race to deny to competent licensed Negro physicians the right to practise in the public hospitals of the communities in which they reside, for no other reason than their race and color.

43. We call upon the various governments of the world to accept and acknowledge Negro representatives who shall be sent to the said governments to represent the general welfare of the Negro peoples of the world.

44. We deplore and protest against the practice of confining juvenile prisoners in prisons with adults, and we recommend that such youthful prisoners be taught gainful trades under humane supervision.

45. Be it further resolved, that we as a race of people declare the League of Nations null and void as far as the Negro is concerned, in that it seeks to deprive Negroes of their liberty.

46. We demand of all men to do unto us as we would do unto them, in the name of justice; and we cheerfully accord to all men all the rights we claim herein for ourselves.

47. We declare that no Negro shall engage himself in battle for an alien race without first obtaining the consent of the leader of the Negro people of the world, except in a matter of national self-defense.

48. We protest against the practice of drafting Negroes and sending them to war with alien forces without proper training, and demand in all cases that Negro soldiers be given the same training as the aliens.

49. We demand that instructions given Negro children in schools include the subject of "Negro History," to their benefit.

50. We demand a free and unfettered commercial intercourse with all the Negro people of the world.

51. We declare for the absolute freedom of the seas for all peoples.

52. We demand that our duly accredited representatives be given proper recognition in all leagues, conferences, conventions or courts of international arbitration wherever human rights are discussed.

53. We proclaim the 31st day of August of each year to be an international holiday to be observed by all Negroes.

54. We want all men to know we shall maintain and contend for the freedom and equality of every man, woman and child of our race, with our lives, our fortunes and our sacred honor.

These rights we believe to be justly ours and proper for the protection of the Negro race at large, and because of this belief we, on behalf of the four hundred million Negroes of the world, do pledge herein the sacred blood of the race in defense, and we hereby subscribe our names as a guarantee of the truthfulness and faithfulness hereof in the presence of Almighty God on the 13th day of August, in the year of our Lord one thousand nine hundred and twenty.

Black Nationalism was revived as a dominant ideology during the Black Power phase of the civil rights movement. While differing in specifics, Elijah Muhammad, Malcolm X, Maulana Karenga, the Black Panther Party, and SNCC, among others, shared a vision of black life that was insular and self-determined.[8] By the mid-1970s (as noted in Chapter 6), most Black Power advocates had either changed philosophies, left the country, or been killed. Even the Nation of Islam, under the guidance of Elijah Muhammad's son Wallace, pursued a reformed philosophy. Into this breach stepped Minister Louis Farrakhan, leader of Harlem's Temple No. 7. In 1975, Farrakhan broke with Wallace Muhammad and reclaimed the name of the Nation. In keeping with the core tenets of Black Nationalism, Farrakhan preached a brand of self-sufficiency and self-determination that catapulted him to national prominence. In 1995, Farrakhan organized the "Million Man March" and became the undisputed leader of the Black Nationalist movement.[9]

The intellectual framework for contemporary Black Nationalism is commonly associated with the work of Molefi Asante. In his book, *The Afrocentric Idea*, Asante introduced the concept of "Afrocentricity." The primary assumption is that African ideals must be at the center of any analysis that involves the culture and behavior of people of African descent.[10] The rationale is that different cultural and historical experiences result in different perceptions about the relevant social codes, customs, and mores that constitute public life. The Afrocentric tradition places a premium on more "circular" forms of reasoning utilizing the spoken word—or oral tradition—to interpret and understand the human condition. For example, black preachers, political leaders, and even rappers commonly use the technique of indirection to articulate the black experience. In contrast, the Eurocentric value system favors linear lines of discourse that seek prediction and control. Political debates are a prime example of the "linearity" of European thinking. A problem is identified, each side of the issue is presented, and a panel of "objective" judges evaluate the arguments and determine the appropriate solution. Thus, the vast discrepancy between worldviews explains the "failure" of large segments of the black population to accept and adhere to Eurocentric values. In essence, they cannot assimilate because they do not have the proper frame of reference.[11]

*In the following selection, **"The Afrocentric Idea in Education,"** Asante applies Afrocentricity to the field of education. He maintains that, in most U.S. classrooms, whites are ". . . located in the center perspective position." Especially invasive is the idea that ". . . Eurocentricity presents the particular historical reality of Europeans as the sum total of the human experience." As a result, black school children are marginalized and stigmatized. Afrocentricity, on the other hand, does not seek to invalidate the experiences of other groups, rather ". . . the person of African descent should be centered in his or her experiences as an African . . . ." Interestingly, Asante sees the Afrocentric perspective as a "stepping stone" for multiculturalism in education because it starts from the assumption that ". . . all humans have contributed to world development." At the end of the essay, Asante points out the dangers of an educational system steeped in "distorted information" and argues that Afrocentric education is the best means to improve the educational achievement of black school children.*

THE AFROCENTRIC IDEA IN EDUCATION

Molefi Asante

INTRODUCTION

Many of the principles that govern the development of the Afrocentric idea in education were first established by Carter G. Woodson in *The Mis-education of the Negro* (1933). Indeed, Woodson's classic reveals the fundamental problems pertaining to the education of the African person in America. As Woodson contends, African Americans have been educated away from their own culture and traditions and attached to the fringes of European culture; thus dislocated from themselves, Woodson asserts that African Americans often valorize European culture to the detriment of their own heritage. Although Woodson does not advocate rejection of American citizenship or nationality, he believed that assuming African Americans hold the same position as European Americans vis-á-vis the realities of American would lead to the psychological and cultural death of the African American population. Furthermore, if education is ever to be substantive and meaningful within the context of American society, Woodson argues, it must first address the African's historical experiences, both in Africa and America. That is why he places on education, and particularly on the traditionally African American colleges, the burden of teaching the African American to be responsive to the long traditions and history of Africa as well as America. Woodson's alert recognition, more than 50 years ago, that something is severely wrong with the way African Americans are educated provides the principal impetus for the Afrocentric approach to American education. . . .

DEFINITIONS

. . . In education, *centricity* refers to a perspective that involves locating students within the context of their own cultural references so that they can relate socially and psychologically to other cultural perspectives. Centricity is a concept that can be applied to any culture. The centrist paradigm is supported by research showing that the most productive method of teaching any student is to place his or her group within the center of the context of knowledge. For White students in America this is easy because almost all the experiences discussed in American classrooms are approached from the standpoint of White perspectives and history. American education, however, is not centric; it is Eurocentric.

Consequently, non-White students are also made to see themselves and their groups as the "acted upon." Only rarely do they read or hear of non-White people as active participants in history. This is as true for a discussion of the American Revolution as it is for a discussion of Dante's *Inferno*; for instance, most classroom discussions of the European slave trade concentrate on the activities of Whites rather than on the resistance efforts of Africans. A person educated in a truly centric fashion comes to view all groups' contributions as significant and useful. Even a White person educated in such a system does not assume superiority based upon racist notions. Thus, a truly centric education is different from a Eurocentric, racist (that is, White supremacist) education.

Afrocentricity is a frame of reference wherein phenomena are viewed from the perspective of the African person. The Afrocentric approach seeks in every situation the appropriate centrality of the African person. In education this means that teachers provide students the opportunity to study the world and its people, concepts, and history from an African world view. In most classrooms, whatever the subject, Whites are located in the center perspective position. How alien the African American child must feel, how like an outsider! The little African American child who sits in a classroom and is taught to accept as heroes and heroines individuals who defamed African people is being actively de-centered, dislocated, and made into a nonperson, one whose aim in life might be to one day shed that "badge of inferiority": his or her Blackness. In Afrocentric educational settings, however, teachers do not marginalize African American children by causing them to question their own self-worth because their people's story is seldom told. By seeing themselves as the subjects rather than the objects of education—be the discipline biology, medicine, literature, or social studies—African American students come to see themselves not merely as seekers of knowledge but as integral participants in it. Because all content areas are adaptable to an Afrocentric approach, African American students can be made to see themselves as centered in the reality of any discipline.

It must be emphasized that Afrocentricity is *not* a Black version of Eurocentricity. Eurocentricity is based on White supremacist notions whose purposes are to protect White privilege and advantage in education, economics, politics, and so forth. Unlike Eurocentricity, Afrocentricity does not condone ethnocentric valorization at the expense of degrading other groups' perspectives.

Moreover, Eurocentricity presents the particular historical reality of Europeans as the sum total of the human experience. It imposes Eurocentric realities as "universal"; i.e., that which is White is presented as applying to the human condition in general, while that which is non-White is viewed as group-specific and therefore not "human." This explains why some scholars and artists of African descent rush to deny their Blackness; they believe that to exist as a Black person is not to exist as a universal human being. They are the individuals Woodson identified as preferring European art, language, and culture over African art, language, and culture; they believe that anything of European origin is inherently better than anything produced by or issuing from their own people. Naturally, the person of African descent should be centered in his or her historical experiences as an African, but Eurocentric curricula produce such aberrations of perspective among persons of color.

Multiculturalism in education is a nonhierarchical approach that respects and celebrates a variety of cultural perspectives on world phenomena. The multicultural approach holds that although European culture is the majority culture in the United States, that is not sufficient reason for it to be imposed on diverse student populations as "universal." Multiculturalists assert that education, to have integrity, must begin with the proposition that all humans have contributed to world development and the flow of knowledge and information, and that most human achievements are the result of mutually interactive, international effort. Without a multicultural education, students remain essentially ignorant of the contributions of a major portion of the world's people. A multicultural education is thus a fundamental necessity for anyone who wishes to achieve competency in almost any subject.

The Afrocentric idea must be the stepping-stone from which the multicultural idea is launched. A truly authentic multicultural education, therefore, must be based upon the Afrocentric initiative. If this step is skipped, multicultural curricula, as they are increasingly being defined by White "resisters" ... will evolve without any substantive infusion of African American content, and the African American child will continue to be lost in the Eurocentric framework of education. In other words, the African American child will neither be confirmed nor affirmed in his or her own cultural information. For the mutual benefit of all Americans, this tragedy, which leads to the psychological and cultural dislocation of African American children, can and should be avoided. . . .

THE CONDITION OF EUROCENTRIC EDUCATION

Institutions such as schools are conditioned by the character of the nation in which they are developed. Just as crime and politics are different in different nations, so, too, is education. In the United States a "Whites-only" orientation has predominated in education. This has had a profound impact on the quality of education for children of all races and ethnic groups. The African American child has suffered disproportionately, but White children are also the victims of monoculturally diseased curricula.

THE TRAGEDY OF IGNORANCE

During the past five years many White students and parents have approached me after presentations with tears in their eyes or expressing their anger about the absence of information about African Americans in the schools. A recent comment from a young White man at a major university in the Northeast was especially striking. As he said to me: "My teacher told us that Martin Luther King was a commie and went on with the class." Because this student's teacher made no effort to discuss King's ideas, the student maliciously had been kept ignorant. The vast majority of White Americans are likewise ignorant about the bountiful reservoirs of African and African American history, culture, and contributions. For example, few Americans of any color have heard the names of Cheikh Anta Diop, Anna Julia Cooper, C. L. R. James, or J. A. Rogers. All were historians who contributed greatly to our understanding of the African world. Indeed, very few teachers have ever taken a course in African American Studies; therefore, most are unable to provide systematic information about African Americans. . . .

CORRECTING DISTORTED INFORMATION

Hegemonic education can exist only so long as true and accurate information is withheld. Hegemonic Eurocentric education can exist only so long as Whites maintain that Africans and other non-Whites have never contributed to world civilization. It is largely upon such false ideas that invidious distinctions are made. The truth, however, gives one insight into the real reasons behind human actions, whether one chooses to follow the paths of others or not. For example, one cannot remain comfortable teaching that art and philosophy originated in Greece if one learns that the Greeks themselves taught that the study of these subjects originated in Africa, specifically ancient Kemet.

The first philosophers were the Egyptians Kagemni, Khun-anup, Ptahhotep, Kete, and Seti; but Eurocentric education is so disjointed that students have no way of discovering this and other knowledge of the organic relationship of Africa to the rest of human history. Not only did Africa contribute to human history, African civilizations predate all other civilizations. Indeed, the human species originated on the continent of Africa—this is true whether one looks at either archaeological or biological evidence.

Two other notions must be refuted. There are those who say that African American history should begin with the arrival of Africans as slaves in 1619, but it has been shown that Africans visited and inhabited North and South America long before European settlers "discovered" the "New World." Secondly, although America became something of a home for those Africans who survived the horrors of the Middle Passage, their experiences on the slave ships and during slavery resulted in their having an entirely different (and often tainted) perspective about America from that of the Europeans and others who came, for the most part, of their own free will seeking opportunities not available to them in their native lands. Afrocentricity therefore seeks to recognize this divergence in perspective and create centeredness for African American students.

CONCLUSION

The reigning initiative for total curricular change is the movement that is being proposed and led by Africans, namely, the Afrocentric idea. When I wrote the first book on Afrocentricity, now in its fifth printing, I had no idea that in 10 years the idea would both shake up and shape discussions in education, art, fashion, and politics. Since the publication of my subsequent works, *The Afrocentric Idea* and *Kemet, Afrocentricity, and Knowledge,* the debate has been joined in earnest. Still, for many White Americans (and some African Americans) the most unsettling aspect of the discussion about Afrocentricity is that its intellectual source lies in the research and writings of African American scholars. Whites are accustomed to being in charge of the major ideas circulating in the American academy. . . .

Afrocentricity provides all Americans an opportunity to examine the perspective of the African person in this society and the world. The resisters claim that Afrocentricity is anti-White; yet, if Afrocentricity as a theory is against anything it is against racism, ignorance, and monoethnic hegemony in the curriculum.

Afrocentricity is not anti-White; it is, however, pro-human. Further, the aim of the Afrocentric curriculum is not to divide America, it is to make America flourish as it ought to flourish. This nation has long been divided with regard to the educational opportunities afforded to children. By virtue of the protection provided by society and reinforced by the Eurocentric curriculum, the White child is already ahead of the African American child by first grade. Our efforts thus must concentrate on giving the African American child greater opportunities for learning at the kindergarten level. However, the kind of assistance the African American child needs is as much cultural as it is academic. If the proper cultural information is provided, the academic performance will surely follow suit.

When it comes to educating African American children, the American educational system does not need a tune-up, it needs an overhaul. Black children have been maligned by this system. Black teachers have been maligned. Black history has been maligned. Africa has been maligned. Nonetheless, two truisms can be stated about education in America. First, some teachers *can and do* effectively teach African American children; secondly, if some teachers can do it, others can, too. We must learn all we can about what makes these teachers' attitudes and approaches successful, and then work diligently to see that their successes are replicated on a broad scale. By raising the same questions that Woodson posed more than 50 years ago, Afrocentric education, along with a significant reorientation of the American educational enterprise, seeks to respond to the African person's psychological and cultural dislocation. By providing philosophical and theoretical guidelines and criteria that are centered in an African perception of reality and by placing the African American child in his or her proper historical context and setting, Afrocentricity may be just the "escape hatch" African Americans so desperately need to facilitate academic success and "steal away" from the cycle of miseducation and dislocation.

———————————————————— ■ ————————————————————

INTEGRATIONISM

The primary debate among integrationists has historically been over the appropriate strategy for black inclusion in mainstream society. In **"The Talented Tenth"** *W.E.B. Dubois argued that "[T]he Negro race, like all races, is going to be saved by its exceptional men." He staked this claim on three empirical observations. First, he showed that it was ". . . the educated and intelligent of the Negro people that have led and elevated the masses . . ." In the second instance, Dubois described a training plan based on the assumption that "[T]he best and most capable . . . must be schooled in the colleges and universities of the land." Dubois summarized his findings (not presented here) on the "function" of college-educated blacks in the following way: "[H]e is, as he ought to be, the group leader, the man who sets the ideals of the community where he lives, directs its thoughts and heads its social movements." Dubois also noted the tremendous side-benefit to investing in black higher education—many college-educated blacks went on to become teachers themselves. Dubois ends the essay by discussing how investment in the "talented tenth" contributes to addressing the broader "negro problem." Although he supported technical training, Dubois argued for the added value of investing in the elite—". . . the culture of the surrounding world trickles through and is handed on by the graduates of higher schools." In sum, integration must start by raising the "talented tenth."*

THE TALENTED TENTH

W.E.B. Du Bois, Burghardt

The Negro race, like all races, is going to be saved by its exceptional men. The problem of education, then, among Negroes must first of all deal with the Talented Tenth; it is the problem of developing the Best of this race that they may guide the Mass away from the contamination and death of the Worst, in their own and other races. Now the training of men is a difficult and intricate task. Its technique is a matter for educational experts, but its object is for the vision of seers. If we make money the object of man-training, we shall develop money-makers but not necessarily men; if we make technical skill the object of education, we may possess artisans but not, in nature, men. Men we shall have only as we make manhood the object of the work of the schools—intelligence, broad sympathy, knowledge of the world that was and is, and of the relation of men to it—this is the curriculum of that Higher Education which must underlie true life. On this foundation we may build bread winning, skill of hand and quickness of brain, with never a fear lest the child and man mistake the means of living for the object of life.

If this be true—and who can deny it—three tasks lay before me; first to show from the past that the Talented Tenth as they have risen among American Negroes have been worthy of leadership; secondly, to show how these men may be educated and developed; and thirdly, to show their relation to the Negro problem.

You misjudge us because you do not know us. From the very first it has been the educated and intelligent of the Negro people that have led and elevated the mass, and the sole obstacles that nullified and retarded their efforts were slavery and race prejudice; for what is slavery but the legalized survival of the unfit and the nullification of the work of natural internal leadership? Negro leadership, therefore, sought from the first to rid the race of this awful incubus that it might make way for natural selection and the survival of the fittest. In colonial days came Phillis Wheatley and Paul Cuffe striving against the bars of prejudice.

Then came Dr. James Derham, who could tell even the learned Dr. Rush something of medicine, and Lemuel Haynes, to whom Middlebury College gave an honorary A. M. in 1804. These and others we may call the Revolutionary group of distinguished Negroes they were persons of marked ability, leaders of a Talented Tenth, standing conspicuously among the best of their time. They strove by word and deed to save the color line from becoming the line between the bond and free, but all they could do was nullified by Eli Whitney and the Curse of Gold. So they passed into forgetfulness.

But their spirit did not wholly die; here and there in the early part of the century came other exceptional men. Some were natural sons of unnatural fathers and were given often a liberal training and thus a race of educated mulattoes sprang up to plead for black men's rights.

There was Purvis and Remond, Pennington and Highland Garnett, Sojourner Truth and Alexander Crummel, and above all, Frederick Douglass—What would the abolition movement have been without them? They stood as living examples of the possibilities of the Negro race, their own hard experiences and well wrought culture said silently more than all the drawn periods of orators—they were the men who made American slavery impossible.

Where were these black abolitionists trained? Some, like Frederick Douglass, were self-trained, but yet trained liberally; others, like Alexander Crummell and McCune Smith, graduated from famous foreign universities. Most of them rose up through the colored schools of New York and Philadelphia and Boston, taught by college-bred men like Russworm, of Dartmouth, and college-bred white men like Neau and Benezet.

After emancipation came a new group of educated and gifted leaders: Langston, Bruce and Elliot, Greener, Williams and Payne. Through political organization, historical and polemic writing and moral regeneration, these men strove to uplift their people.

How then shall the leaders of a struggling people be trained and the hands of the risen few strengthened? There can be but one answer: The best and most capable of their youth must be schooled in the colleges and universities of the land. We will not quarrel as to just what the university of the Negro should teach or how it should teach it—I willingly admit that each soul and each race-soul needs its own peculiar curriculum. But this is true: A university is a human invention for the transmission of knowledge and culture from generation to generation, through the training of quick minds and pure hearts, and for this work no other human invention will suffice, not even trade and industrial schools.

All men cannot go to college but some men must; every isolated group or nation must have its yeast, must have for the talented few centers of training where men are not so mystified and befuddled by the hard and necessary toil of earning a living, as to have no aims higher than their bellies, and no God greater than Gold. This is true training, and thus in the beginning were the favored sons of the freedmen trained.

These figures illustrate vividly the function of the college-bred Negro. He is, as he ought to be, the group leader, the man who sets the ideals of the community where he lives, directs its thoughts and heads its social movements.

It has, however, been in the furnishing of teachers that the Negro college has found its peculiar function. Few persons realize how vast a work, how mighty a revolution has been thus accomplished. To furnish five millions and more of ignorant people with teachers of their own race and blood, in one generation, was not only a very difficult undertaking, but a very important one, in that, it placed before the eyes of almost every Negro child an attainable ideal. It brought the masses of the blacks in contact with modern civilization, made black men the leaders of their communities and trainers of the new generation. In this work college-bred Negroes were first teachers, and then teachers of teachers. And here it is that the broad culture of college work has been of peculiar value. Knowledge of life and its wider meaning, has been the point of the Negro's deepest ignorance, and the sending out of teachers whose training has not been simply for bread winning, but also for human culture, has been of inestimable value in the training of these men.

The problem of training the Negro is to-day immensely complicated by the fact that the whole question of the efficiency and appropriateness of our present systems of education, for any kind of child, is a matter of active debate, in which final settlement seems still afar off. Consequently it often happens that persons arguing for or against certain systems of education for Negroes, have these controversies in mind and miss the real question at issue. The main question, so far as the Southern Negro is concerned, is: What under the present circumstance, must a system of education do in order to raise the Negro as quickly as possible in the scale of civilization? The answer to this question seems to me clear: It must strengthen the Negro's character, increase his knowledge and teach him to earn a living. Now it goes without saying, that it is hard to do all these things simultaneously or suddenly, and that at the same time it will not do to give all the attention to one and neglect the others; we could give black boys trades, but that alone will not civilize a race of ex-slaves; we might simply increase their knowledge of the world, but this would not necessarily make them wish to use this knowledge honestly; we might seek to strengthen character and purpose, but to what end if this people have nothing to eat or to wear? A system of education is not one thing, nor does it have a single definite object, nor is it a mere matter of schools. Education is that whole system of human training within and without the school house walls, which molds and develops men.

I would not deny, or for a moment seem to deny, the paramount necessity of teaching the Negro to work, and to work steadily and skillfully; or seem to depreciate in the slightest degree the important part industrial schools must play in the accomplishment of these ends, but I do say, and insist upon it, that it is industrialism drunk with its vision of success, to imagine that its own work can be accomplished without providing for the training of broadly cultured men and women to teach its own teachers, and to teach the teachers of the public schools.

But I have already said that human education is not simply a matter of schools; it is much more a matter of family and group life—the training of one's home, of one's daily companions, of one's social class. Now the black boy of the South moves in a black world—a world with its own leaders, its own thoughts, its own ideals. In this world he gets by far the larger part of his life training, and through the eyes of this dark world he peers into the veiled world beyond. Who guides and determines the education which he receives in his world? His teachers here are the group-leaders of the Negro physicians and clergymen, the trained fathers and mothers, the influential and forceful men about him of all kinds; here it is, if at all, that the culture of the surrounding world trickles through and is handed on by the graduates

of the higher schools. Can such culture training of group leaders be neglected? Can we afford to ignore it? Do you think that if the leaders of
thought among Negroes are not trained and educated thinkers, that they
will have no leaders? On the contrary a hundred half-trained demagogues
will still hold the places they so largely occupy now, and hundreds of vocif-
erous busy-bodies will multiply. You have no choice; either you must help
furnish this race from within its own ranks with thoughtful men of trained
leadership, or you must suffer the evil consequences of a headless misguided rabble.

I am an earnest advocate of manual training and trade teaching for black
boys, and for white boys, too. I believe that next to the founding of Negro colleges the most valuable addition to Negro education since the war, has been
industrial training for black boys. Nevertheless, I insist that the object of all
true education is not to make men carpenters, it is to make carpenters men;
there are two means of making the carpenter a man, each equally important:
the first is to give the group and community in which he works, liberally
trained teachers and leaders to teach him and his family what life means; the
second is to give him sufficient intelligence and technical skill to make him an
efficient workman; the first object demands the Negro college and college-
bred men—not a quantity of such colleges, but a few of excellent quality; not
too many college-bred men, but enough to leaven the lump, to inspire the
masses, to raise the Talented Tenth to leadership; the second object demands
a good system of common schools, well-taught, conveniently located and
properly equipped.

Men of America, the problem is plain before you. Here is a race trans-
planted through the criminal foolishness of your fathers. Whether you like it
or not the millions are here, and here they will remain. If you do not lift them
up, they will pull you down. Education and work are the levers to uplift a
people. Work alone will not do it unless inspired by the right ideals and
guided by intelligence. Education must not simply teach work—it must teach
Life. The Talented Tenth of the Negro race must be made leaders of thought
and missionaries of culture among their people. No others can do this work
and Negro colleges must train men for it. The Negro race, like all other races,
is going to be saved by its exceptional men.

————————————————————■————————————————————

*Booker T. Washington, in the "**Atlanta Exposition Address**," told African-Americans to
"cast down your buckets where you are." This metaphor was the basis for a vision of integration in which black Americans, particularly in the South, were to develop applied skills in agriculture, commerce, mechanics, the professions, and domestic service. Washington's belief was
that blacks would only succeed when they understood that ". . . there is a much dignity in tilling a field as writing a poem." Moreover, he reached out to white Southerners by suggesting
that blacks had no desire for social equality and had every intention of being ". . . patient, faithful, law-abiding, and unresentful people. . . ." In short, Washington roundly refuted the vision
of integration set forth by Dubois when he said: "[I]t is at the bottom of life we must begin, and
not at the top." Black progress, from this perspective, rested on enhanced labor marketability:
"[N]o race that has anything to contribute to the markets of the world is long in any degree
ostracized."*

THE ATLANTA EXPOSITION ADDRESS, 1919

Booker T. Washington

The Atlanta Exposition, at which I had been asked to make an address as a representative of the Negro race, as stated in the last chapter, was opened with a short address from Governor Bullock. After other interesting exercises, including an invocation from Bishop Nelson, of Georgia, a dedicatory ode by Albert Howell, Jr., and addresses by the President of the Exposition and Mrs. Joseph Thompson, the President of the Woman's Board, Governor Bullock introduced me with the words, "We have with us to-day a representative of Negro enterprise and Negro civilization."

When I arose to speak, there was considerable cheering, especially from the coloured people. As I remember it now, the thing that was uppermost in my mind was the desire to say something that would cement the friendship of the races and bring about hearty cooperation between them. So far as my outward surroundings were concerned, the only thing that I recall distinctly now is that when I got up, I saw thousands of eyes looking intently into my face. The following is the address which I delivered:—

MR. PRESIDENT AND GENTLEMEN OF THE BOARD OF DIRECTORS AND CITIZENS.

One-third of the population of the South is of the Negro race. No enterprise seeking the material, civil, or moral welfare of this section can disregard this element of our population and reach the highest success. I but convey to you, Mr. President and Directors, the sentiment of the masses of my race when I say that in no way have the values and manhood of the American Negro been more fittingly and generously recognized than by the managers of this magnificent Exposition at every stage of its progress. It is a recognition that will do more to cement the friendship of the two races than any occurrence since the dawn of our freedom.

Not only this, but the opportunity here afforded will awaken among us a new era of industrial progress. Ignorant and inexperienced, it is not strange that in the first years of our new life we began at the top instead of at the bottom; that a seat in Congress or the state legislature was more sought than real estate or industrial skill; that the political convention of stump speaking had more attractions than starting a dairy farm or truck garden.

A ship lost at sea for many days suddenly sighted friendly vessel. From the mast of the unfortunate vessel was seen a signal, "Water, water; we die of thirst!" The answer from the friendly vessel at once came back, "Cast down your bucket where you are." A second time the signal, "Water, water; send us water!" ran up from the distressed vessel, and was answered, "Cast down your bucket where you are." And a third and fourth signal for water was answered, "Cast down your bucket where you are." The captain of the distressed vessel, at last heeding the injunction, cast down his bucket, and it came up full of fresh, sparkling water from the mouth of the Amazon River. To those of my race who depend on bettering their condition in a foreign land or who underestimate the importance of cultivating friendly relations with the Southern white man, who is their next-door neighbour, I would say: "Cast down your bucket where you are"—cast it down in making friends in every manly way of the people of all races by whom we are surrounded.

Cast it down in agriculture, mechanics, in commerce, in domestic service, and in the professions. And in this connection it is well to bear in mind that whatever other sins the South may be called to bear, when it comes to business, pure and simple, it is in the South that the Negro is given a man's chance in the commercial world, and in nothing is this Exposition more eloquent than in emphasizing this chance. Our greatest danger is that in the great leap from slavery to freedom we may overlook the fact that the masses of us are to live by the productions of our hands, and fail to keep in mind that we shall prosper in proportion as we learn to dignify and glorify common labour and put brains and skill into the common occupations of life; shall prosper in proportion as we learn to draw the line between the superficial and the substantial, the ornamental gewgaws of life and the useful. No race can prosper till it learns that there is as much dignity in tilling a field as in writing a poem. It is at the bottom of life we must begin, and not at the top. Nor should we permit our grievances to overshadow our opportunities.

To those of the white race who look to the incoming of those of foreign birth and strange tongue and habits for the prosperity of the South, were I permitted I would repeat what I say to my own race, "Cast down your bucket where you are." Cast it down among the eight millions of Negroes whose habits you know, whose fidelity and love you have tested in days when to have proved treacherous meant the ruin of your firesides. Cast down your bucket among these people who have, without strikes and labour wars, tilled your fields, cleared your forests, builded your railroads and cities, and brought forth treasures from the bowels of the earth, and helped make possible this magnificent representation of the progress of the South. Casting down your bucket among my people, helping and encouraging them as you are doing on these grounds, and to education of head, hand, and heart, you will find that they will buy your surplus land, make blossom the waste places in your fields, and run your factories. While doing this, you can be sure in the future, as in the past, that you and your families will be surrounded by the most patient, faithful, law-abiding, and unresentful people that the world has seen. As we have proved our loyalty to you in the past, in nursing your children, watching by the sickbed of your mothers and fathers, and often following them with tear-dimmed eyes to their graves, so in the future, in our humble way, we shall stand by you with a devotion that no foreigner can approach, ready to lay down our lives, if need be, in defence of yours, interlacing our industrial, commercial, civil, and religious life with yours in a way that shall make the interests of both races one. In all things that are purely social we can be as separate as the fingers, yet one as the hand in all things essential to mutual progress.

There is no defence or security for any of us except in the highest intelligence and development of all. If anywhere there are efforts tending to curtail the fullest growth of the Negro, let these efforts be turned into stimulating, encouraging, and making him the most useful and intelligent citizen. Effort or means so invested will pay a thousand per cent interest. These efforts will be twice blessed—"blessing him that gives and him that takes."

Nearly sixteen millions of hands will aid you in pulling the load upward, or they will pull against you the load downward. We shall constitute one-third and more of the ignorance and crime of the South, or one-third its intelligence and progress; we shall contribute one-third to the business and industrial prosperity of the South, or we shall prove a veritable body of death, stagnating, depressing, retarding every effort to advance the body politic.

Gentlemen of the Exposition, as we present to you our humble effort at an exhibition of our progress, you must not expect overmuch. Starting thirty years ago with ownership here and there in a few quilts and pumpkins and chickens (gathered from miscellaneous sources), remember the path that has led from these to the inventions and production of agricultural implements, buggies, steam-engines, newspapers, books, statuary, carving, paintings, the management of drug-stores and banks, has not been trodden without contact with thorns and thistles. While we take pride in what we exhibit as a result of our independent efforts, we do not for a moment forget that our part in this exhibition would fall far short of your expectations but for the constant help that has come to our educational life, not only from the Southern states, but especially from Northern philanthropists, who have made their gifts a constant stream of blessing and encouragement.

The wisest among my race understand that the agitation of questions of social equality is the extremest folly, and that progress in the enjoyment of all the privileges that will come to us must be the result of severe and constant struggle rather than of artificial forcing. No race that has anything to contribute to the markets of the world is long in any degree ostracized. It is important and right that all privileges of the law be ours, but it is vastly more important that we be prepared for the exercises of these privileges. The opportunity to earn a dollar in a factory just now is worth infinitely more than the opportunity to spend a dollar in an opera-house.

In conclusion, may I repeat that nothing in thirty years has given us more hope and encouragement, and drawn us so near to you of the white race, as this opportunity offered by the Exposition; and here bending, as it were, over the altar that represents the results of the struggles of your race and mine, both starting practically empty-handed three decades ago. I pledged that in your effort to work out the great and intricate problem which God has laid at the doors of the South, you shall have at all times the patient, sympathetic help of my race; only let this be constantly in mind, that, while from representations in these buildings of the product of field, of forest, of mine, of factory, letters, and art, much good will come, yet far above and beyond material benefits will be that higher good, that, let us pray God, will come, in a blotting out of sectional differences and racial animosities and suspicions, in a determination to administer absolute justice, in a willing obedience among all classes to the mandates of law. This, then, coupled with our material prosperity, will bring into our beloved South a new heaven and a new earth.

The first thing that I remember, after I had finished speaking, was that Governor Bullock rushed across the platform and took me by the hand, and that others did the same. I received so many and such hearty congratulations that I found it difficult to get out of the building. I did not appreciate to any degree, however, the impression which my address seemed to have made, until the next morning, when I went into the business part of the city.

As soon as I was recognized, I was surprised to find myself pointed out and surrounded by a crowd of men who wished to shake hands with me. This was kept up on every street on to which I went, to an extent which embarrassed me so much that I went back to my boarding-place. The next morning I returned to Tuskegee. At the station in Atlanta, and at almost all of the stations at which the train stopped between that city and Tuskegee, I found a crowd of people anxious to shake hands with me.

The papers in all parts of the United States published the address in full, and for months afterward there were complimentary editorial references to it. Mr. Clark Howell, the editor of the Atlanta *Constitution*, telegraphed to a New York paper, among other words, the following, "I do not exaggerate when I say that Professor Booker T. Washington's address yesterday was one of the most notable speeches, both as to character and as to the warmth of its reception, ever delivered to a Southern audience. The address was a revelation. The whole speech is a platform upon which blacks and whites can stand with full justice to each other."

The postmodern extension of Washington's ideology is found in neo-conservative political thought.[12] *In a chapter entitled* **"Race-Holding,"** *Shelby Steele identifies several elements of post-civil rights era black conservative philosophy.*[13] *The core belief is that black Americans should be (and should want to be) judged solely on the basis of their achievements. Government programs such as affirmative action are "handouts" that produce white backlash and black insecurity. Steele is particularly critical of blacks that he identifies as "race holders," or people who use perceived racism as a crutch to hide fear and protect self-doubt. This view rejects the notion that racial discrimination is the best predictor of black life chances. As Steele contests, "[I]nstead of admitting that racism has declined, we argue all the harder that it is still alive and more insidious than ever. We hold race up to shield us from what we do not want to see in ourselves."*

Neo-conservative ideology trades on the assumption that ". . . a margin of choice is open to blacks . . ." In other words, because individuals possess free will (agency), they have the opportunity to engage in morally right or morally wrong decisions. Black anti-social behavior is more a product of individual choice than structural impediments. Thus, "[C]hoice lives in even the most blighted of circumstances." In the final analysis, black progress is dependent on the willingness of the community to accept individual responsibility and fully avail themselves of opportunities presented by an increasingly tolerant society.

THE CONTENT OF OUR CHARACTER
·

Shelby Steele

Excerpt from Chapter 2

RACE-HOLDING

I am a fortyish, middle-class, black American male with a teaching position at a large state university in California. I have owned my own home for more than ten years, as well as the two cars that are the minimal requirement for life in California. And I will confess to a moderate strain of yuppie hedonism. Year after year my two children are the sole representatives of their race in their classrooms, a fact they sometimes have difficulty remembering. We are the only black family in our suburban neighborhood, and even this claim to specialness is diminished by the fact that my wife is white. I think we are called an "integrated" family, though no one has ever used the term with me. For me to be among large numbers of blacks requires conscientiousness and a long car ride, and in truth, I have not been very conscientious lately. Though I was raised in an all-black community just south of Chicago, I only occasionally feel nostalgia for such places. Trips to the barbershop now and then usually satisfy this need, though recently, in the interest of convenience, I've taken to letting my wife cut my hair.

I see in people's eyes from time to time, and hear often in the media, what amounts to a judgment of people like myself: You have moved into the great amorphous middle class and lost your connection to your people and your cultural roots. You have become a genuine invisible man. This is a judgment with many obvious dimensions, many arrows of guilt. But, in essence, it charges me with selfishness and inauthenticity.

At one point I romanticized my situation, thought of myself as a marginal man. The seductive imagery of alienation supported me in this. But in America today racial marginality is hard to sell as the stuff of tragedy. The position brings with it an ugly note of self-insistence that annoys people in a society that is, at least officially, desegregated.

For better or worse, I'm not very marginal. In my middle-American world I see people like myself everywhere. We nod coolly at stoplights, our eyes connect for an awkward instant in shopping malls, we hear about one another from our white friends. "Have you met the new doctor at the hospital . . . the engineer at IBM . . . the new professor in history?" The black middle class is growing. We are often said to be sneaking or slipping or creeping unnoticed into the middle class, as though images of stealth best characterized our movement. I picture a kind of underground railroad, delivering us in the dead of night from the inner city to the suburbs.

But even if we aren't very marginal, we are very shy with one another, at least until we've had a chance to meet privately and take our readings. When we first meet, we experience a trapped feeling, as if we had walked into a cage of racial expectations that would rob us of our individuality by reducing us to an exclusively racial dimension. We are a threat, at first, to one another's uniqueness. I have seen the same well-dressed black woman in the supermarket for more than a year now. We do not speak, and we usually pretend not to see each other. But, when we turn a corner suddenly and find ourselves staring squarely into each other's eyes, her face freezes and she moves on. I believe she is insisting that both of us be more than black—that we interact only when we have a reason other than the mere fact of our race. Her chilliness enforces a priority I agree with—individuality over group identity.

But I believe I see something else in this woman that I also see in myself and in many other middle-class blacks. It is a kind of race fatigue, a deep weariness with things racial, which comes from the fact that our lives are more integrated than they have ever been before. Race does not determine our fates as powerfully as it once did, which means it is not the vital personal concern it once was. Before the sixties, race set the boundaries of black life. Now, especially for middle-class blacks, it is far less a factor, though we don't always like to admit it. Blacks still suffer from racism, so we must be concerned, but this need to be concerned with what is not so personally urgent makes for race fatigue.

I have a friend who did poorly in the insurance business for years. "People won't buy insurance from a black man," he always said. Two years ago another black man and a black woman joined his office. Almost immediately both did twice the business my friend was doing, with the same largely white client base.

Integration shock is essentially the shock of being suddenly accountable on strictly personal terms. It occurs in situations that disallow race as an excuse for personal shortcomings and it therefore exposes vulnerabilities that previously were hidden. One response to such shock is to face up to the self-confrontation it brings and then to act on the basis of what we learn about ourselves. After some struggle, my friend was able to do this. He completely revised his sales technique, asked himself some hard questions about his motivation, and resolved to work harder.

But when one lacks the courage to face oneself fully, a fear of hidden vulnerabilities triggers a fright-flight response to integration shock. Instead of admitting that racism has declined, we argue all the harder that it is still alive and more insidious than ever. We hold race up to shield us from what we do not want to see in ourselves. My friend did this at first, saying that the two blacks in this office were doing better than he was because they knew how to "kiss white ass." Here he was *race-holding*, using race to keep from looking at himself.

Recently I read an article in the local paper that explored the question of whether blacks could feel comfortable living in the largely white Silicon Valley. The article focused on a black family that had been living for more than a decade in Saratoga, a very well-to-do white community. Their neighborhood, their children's schools, their places of employment, their shopping areas and parks—their entire physical environment—were populated by affluent whites. Yet during the interview the wife said they had made two firm rules for their children: that they go to all-black colleges back east and that they do "no dating outside the race, period."

I have pushed enough black history and culture on my own children to be able to identify with the impulse behind the first of these rules. Black children in largely white situations must understand and appreciate their cultural background. But the rigidity of these rules, not to mention the rules themselves, points to more than a concern with transmitting heritage or gaining experience with other blacks. Rigidity arises from fear and self-doubt. These people, I believe, were afraid of something.

What was striking to me about their rules, especially the one prohibiting interracial dating, was their tone of rejection. The black parents seemed as determined to reject the white world as to embrace the black one. Why? I would say because of integration shock. Their integrated lives have opened up vulnerabilities they do not wish to face. But what vulnerabilities? In this case, I think a particularly embarrassing one. On some level, I suspect, they doubt whether they are as good as the white people who live around them. You cannot be raised in a culture that was for centuries committed to the notion of your inferiority and not have some doubt in this regard—doubt that is likely to be aggravated most in integrated situations. So the rejecting tone of their rules is self-protective: *I will reject you before you have a chance to reject me.* But all of this is covered over by race. The high value of racial pride is invoked to shield them from a doubt that they are afraid to acknowledge. Unacknowledged, this doubt gains a negative power inside the personality that expresses itself in the rigidity and absolutism of their rules. Repressed fears tend always to escalate their campaign for our attention by pushing us further and further into irrationality and rigidity.

The refusal to see something unflattering in ourselves always triggers the snap from race fatigue to race-holding. And once that happens, we are caught, like this family, in a jumble of racial ironies. The parents in Saratoga, who have chosen to live integrated lives, impose a kind of segregation on their children. Rules that would be racist in the mouth of any white person are created and enforced with pride. Their unexamined self-doubt also leaves them unable to exploit fully the freedom they have attained. Race fatigue makes them run to a place like Saratoga, but integration shock makes them hold race protectively. They end up clinging to what they've run from.

Once race-holding is triggered by fear, it ensnares us in a web of self-defeating attitudes that end up circumventing the new freedoms we've won over the past several decades. I have seen its corrosive effects in my own life and in the lives of virtually every black person I've known. Some are only mildly touched by it, while others seem incapacitated by it. But race-holding is as unavoidable as defensiveness itself, and I am convinced that it is one of the most debilitating, yet unrecognized, forces in black life today.

I define a *holding* as any self-description that serves to justify or camouflage a person's fears, weaknesses, and inadequacies. Holdings are the little and big exaggerations, distortions, and lies about ourselves that prop us up and let us move along the compromised paths we follow. They develop to defend against threats to our self-esteem, threats that make us feel vulnerable and that plant a seed of fear. This fear can work like wind on a brushfire, spreading self-doubt far beyond what the initial threat would warrant, so that we become even more weakened and more needy of holdings. Since holdings justify our reticence and cowardice, they are usually expressed in the form of high belief or earthy wisdom. A man whose business fails from his own indifference holds an image of himself as a man too honest to be a good businessman—a self-description that draws a veil over his weakness.

For some years I have noticed that I can walk into any of my classes on the first day of the semester, identify the black students, and be sadly confident that on the last day of the semester a disproportionate number of them will be at the bottom of the class, far behind any number of white students of equal or even lesser native ability. More to the point, they will have performed far beneath their own native ability. Self-fulfilling prophesy theory says that their schools have always expected them to do poorly, and that they have internalized this message and *done* poorly. But this deterministic theory sees blacks only as victims, without any margin of choice. It cannot fully explain the poor performances of these black students because it identifies only the forces that *pressure* them to do poorly. By overlooking the margin of choice open to them, this theory fails to recognize the degree to which they are responsible for their own poor showing. (The irony of this oversight is that it takes the power for positive change away from the students and puts it in the hands of the very institutions that failed them in the first place.)

The theory of race-holding is based on the assumption that a margin of choice is always open to blacks (even slaves had some choice). And it tries to make clear the mechanisms by which we relinquish that choice in the name of race. With the decline in racism the margin of black choice has greatly expanded, which is probably why race-holding is so much more visible today than ever before. But anything that prevents us from exploiting our new freedom to the fullest is now as serious a barrier to us as racism once was.

The self-fulfilling prophesy theory is no doubt correct that black students, like the ones I regularly see, internalize a message of inferiority that they receive from school and the larger society around them. But the relevant question in the 1990s is why they *choose* to internalize this view of themselves. Why do they voluntarily perceive themselves as inferior? We can talk about the weakened black family and countless other scars of oppression and poverty. And certainly these things have much to do with the image these students have of themselves. But they do not fully explain this self-image because none of them entirely eliminates the margin of choice that remains open. Choice lives in even the most blighted circumstances, and it certainly lives in the lives of these black college students.

I think they *choose* to believe in their inferiority, not to fulfill society's prophesy about them, but for the comforts and rationalizations their racial "inferiority" affords them. They hold their race to evade individual responsibility. Their margin of choice scares them, as it does all people. They are naturally intimidated by that eternal tussle between the freedom to act and the responsibility we must take for our actions. To some extent all of us balk in the face of this. The difference is that these students use their race to conceal the fact that they are balking. Their "inferiority" shields them from having to see that they are afraid of all-out competition with white students. And it isn't even an honest inferiority. I don't think they really believe it. It is a false inferiority, *chosen* over an honest and productive confrontation with white students and with their real fears—a strategy that allows them to stay comfortably on the sidelines in a university environment that all but showers them with opportunity.

"I'm doing okay for a black student," a student once told me. "I'm doing well considering where I came from," I have told myself. Race allows us both to hide from the real question, which is, "Am I doing what I can, considering my talents and energies?"

I see all of this as pretty much a subconscious process, fear working on a subterranean level to let us reduce our margin of choice in the name of race. Consciously, we tell ourselves that we are only identifying with our race, but fear bloats our racial identity to an unnatural size and then uses it as cover for its subversive work. The more severe the integration shock, the more fear cover is needed.

Doesn't race enhance individuality? I think it does, but only when individuality is nurtured and developed apart from race. The race-holder, inside the bubble of his separate self, feels inadequate or insecure and then seeks reassurance through race. When, instead, a sense of self arises from individual achievement and self-realization. When self-esteem is established apart from race, then racial identity can only enhance because it is no longer needed for any other purpose.

The word *individualism* began to connote selfishness and even betrayal for many blacks during the sixties. Individualism was seen as a threat to the solidarity blacks needed during those years of social confrontation. Despite the decline in racism, these connotations have lingered. Race-holding keeps them alive because they serve the race-holder's need to exaggerate the importance of race as well as to justify a fear of individual responsibility. Race-holding makes fluid the boundary between race and self, group and individual identity, so that race can swing over at a moment's notice and fill in where fears leave a vacuum.

This is a worse problem than is at first apparent because the individual is the seat of all energy, creativity, motivation, and power. We are most strongly motivated when we want something for ourselves. When our personal wants are best achieved through group action, as in the civil rights movement, we lend our energy to the group, and it becomes as strong as the sum of our energies. When the need for group action recedes, more energy is available to us as individuals. But race-holding intercedes here by affixing the race-holder too tightly to this racial identity and by causing him to see the locus of power in race rather than in himself. In this way race-holding corrupts the greatest source of power and strength available to blacks—the energy latent in our personal desires.

One of my favorite passages in Ralph Ellison's *Invisible Man* is his description of the problem of blacks as

> not actually one of creating the uncreated conscience of [our] race, but of creating the *uncreated features of* [our] *face*. Our task is that of making ourselves individuals. . . . We create the race by creating ourselves and then to our great astonishment we will have created something far more important: we will have created a culture.

These lines hold up well, more than thirty years after they were written. They seem to suggest a kind of Adam Smith vision of culture: When the individual makes himself, he makes culture. An "invisible hand" uses individual effort to define and broaden culture. In the 1990s we blacks are more than ever in a position where our common good will best be served by the determined pursuit of our most personal aspirations.

I think the means to this, and the answer to race-holding generally, is personal responsibility, a source of great power that race-holding does its best to conceal.

Some years ago I made a mistake at a neighbor's cocktail party that taught me something about personal responsibility. I went to the party for the thinnest of reasons—mere politeness—though the afternoon was hot and I was already in a peevish mood. The event would have been problematic even if I weren't the only black at the party. But I was, and on this afternoon I *chose* to make note of the fact, though it was hardly a new experience for me. As I strolled around the sun-baked patio, avoiding people more than engaging them, I held this fact more and more tightly until I came to believe it had a profound meaning I needed to understand. After a while I decided that others needed to understand it, too.

In the sixties, blacks and white liberals often engaged in something that might be called the harangue-flagellation ritual. Blacks felt anger, white liberals felt guilt, and when they came together, blacks would vent their anger by haranguing the whites, who often allowed themselves to be scourged as a kind of penance. The "official" black purpose of this rite was to "educate" whites on the issue of race, and in the sixties this purpose may sometimes have been served. But in the eighties, after a marked decline in racism and two decades of consciousness-raising, the rite had become both anachronistic and, I think, irresponsible. Nevertheless, it suited my mood on this hot afternoon, so I retrieved it from its dusty bin and tried to make it fashionable again.

A woman at the party said how much she liked Jesse Jackson's rhetorical style. Was "style" the only thing she liked? I asked, with an edge to my voice. The woman gave me a curious and exasperated look, but I pushed on anyway. Soon I was lecturing the six or seven people around me: I told them that racism had been driven underground in the sixties and seventies, where more insidious strategies for foiling the possibilities of black people had evolved. I pointed to the black unemployment rate, the continued segregation of many schools, housing discrimination, and so on. Soon I saw that the old harangue-flagellation ritual was firmly back in place. I was shaming these people, and they nodded at what I said in a way that gratified me.

But at home that night I felt a stinging shame, and even weeks later the thought of that afternoon made me cringe. Eventually I saw why. For one thing, I was trading on my race with those people, using the very thing I claimed to be so concerned with to buy my way out of certain anxieties. Like the Saratoga family, I was race-holding in response to the integration shock I felt in this integrated situation. I had begun to feel vulnerable, and I hit those people with race before they could hit me with it. My vulnerabilities, of course, were essentially the same as the Saratoga family's. On some level I doubted myself in relation to these whites, and my insecurities drove me into an offense that was really a defense. The shame I began to feel, though I could not identify it at the time, was essentially the shame of cowardice. I felt as though I'd run away from something and used race to cover my tracks.

This shame had another dimension that was even more humiliating than the cowardice I had felt. On that patio I was complaining to white people, beseeching them to see how badly blacks were still treated, and I was gratified to see their heads nod as though they understood. My voice contained no audible whine, but at least some of what I said amounted to a whine. And this is what put the sting in my shame. Cowardice was a common enough fault, but whining was quite another thing.

The race-holder whines, or complains indiscriminately, not because he seeks redress but because he seeks the status of victim, a status that excuses him from what he fears. A victim is not responsible for his condition, and by claiming a victim's status the race-holder gives up the sense of personal responsibility he needs to better his condition. His unseen purpose is to hide rather than fight, so the anger and, more importantly, the energy that real racism breeds in him is squandered in self-serving complaint. The price he pays for the false comfort of his victim's status is a kind of impotence.

The difference between the race-holder who merely complains and the honest protester is that the latter keeps the responsibility for his condition in his own hands. The honest protester may be victimized, but he is not solely a victim. He thinks of himself as fully human and asks only that the rules of the game be made fair. Through fairness, rather than entitlement, he retains his personal responsibility and the power that grows out of it. But he also understands that he must keep this responsibility whether or not society is fair. His purpose is to realize himself, to live the fullest possible life, and he is responsible for this, like all men, regardless of how society treats him.

Personal responsibility is the brick and mortar of power. The responsible person knows that the quality of his life is something that he will have to make inside the limits of his fate. Some of these limits he can push back, some he cannot, but in any case the quality of his life will pretty much reflect the quality of his efforts. When this link between well-being and action is truly accepted, the result is power. With this understanding and the knowledge that he is responsible, a person can see his margin of choice. He can choose and act, and choose and act again, without illusion. He can create himself and make himself felt in the world. Such a person has power.

I was neither responsible nor powerful as I stood on my neighbor's patio complaining about racism to these polite people. In effect I was asking them to be fully responsible for something that blacks and whites *share* responsibility for. Whites must guarantee a free and fair society. But blacks must be responsible for actualizing their own lives. If I had said this to the people at the party, maybe they would have gone away with a clearer sense of their own responsibilities. But I never considered it because the real goal of my complaining was to disguise a fear I didn't want to acknowledge.

The barriers to black progress in America today are clearly as much psychological as they are social or economic. We have suffered as much as any group in human history, and if this suffering has ennobled us, it has also wounded us and pushed us into defensive strategies that are often self-defeating. But we haven't fully admitted this to ourselves. The psychological realm is murky, frightening, and just plain embarrassing. And a risk is involved in exploring it: the risk of discovering the ways in which we contribute to, if not create, the reality in which we live. Denial, avoidance, and repression intervene to save us from this risk. But, of course, they only energize what is repressed with more and more negative power, so that we are victimized as much by our own buried fears as by racism.

In the deepest sense, the long struggle of blacks in America has always been a struggle to retrieve our full humanity. But now the reactive stance we adopted to defend ourselves against oppression binds us to the same racial views that oppressed us in the first place. Snakelike, our defense has turned on us. I think it is now the last barrier to the kind of self-possession that will give us our full humanity, and we must overcome it ourselves.

■

PLURALISM

In **"The Pitfalls of Racial Reasoning,"** *Cornel West puts forward "... a new framework for black thought and practice" based on a prophetic model of moral reasoning.[14] This paradigm rejects appeals to black authenticity and replaces them with a viewpoint based on the "... moral quality of black responses to undeniable racist denigration ..." Moreover, the prophetic model does not assume that there is "... a black essence that all black people share nor one black perspective to which all black people should adhere." West analyzes the Anita Hill–Clarence Thomas hearings to demonstrate how "racial reasoning" paralyzes black leadership.[15] The failure of black leaders to reject Thomas' claims to racial authenticity (e.g., a sharecropper's son, a "hi-tech" lynching), for example, is seen as emblematic of a "closed-ranks mentality." The attendant consequence is that "racial reasoning" encourages a cultural conservatism that is patriarchal (and homophobic).[16] In other words, by presenting opposition to his appointment as an attack on the "black social order," Thomas was able to reinforce male power and neutralize black support for Hill. The resulting irony, as West points out, was that Hill's support came from her ideological opponents—"... progressive feminists, liberals, and some black folk." In sum, a prophetic framework promotes a "black* *cultural democracy" that seeks coalition with nonblacks who are ". . . deeply committed to the antiracist struggle." It trumpets a mature black identity that is capable of a ". . . moral assessment of the variety of perspectives held by black people and selects those views based on black dignity and decency that eschew putting any group of people or culture on a pedestal or in the gutter."*

RACE MATTERS

Cornell West

Excerpt from Chapter 2: The Pitfalls of Racial Reasoning

Insistence on patriarchal values, on equating black liberation with black men gaining access to male privilege that would enable them to assert power over black women, was one of the most significant forces undermining radical struggle. Thorough critiques of gender would have compelled leaders of black liberation struggles to envision new strategies and to talk about black subjectivity in a visionary manner.

—BELL HOOKS, *YEARNING: RACE, GENDER, AND CULTURAL POLITICS* (1990)

The most depressing feature of the Clarence Thomas/Anita Hill hearings was neither the mean-spirited attacks of the Republicans nor the spineless silences of the Democrats—both reveal the predictable inability of most white politicians to talk candidly about race and gender. Rather what was most disturbing was the low level of political discussion in black America about these hearings—a crude discourse about race and gender that bespeaks a failure of nerve of black leadership.

This failure of nerve already was manifest in the selection and confirmation process of Clarence Thomas. Bush's choice of Thomas caught most black leaders off guard. Few had the courage to say publicly that this was an act of cynical tokenism concealed by outright lies about Thomas being the most qualified candidate regardless of race. Thomas had an undistinguished record as a student (mere graduation from Yale Law School does not qualify one for the Supreme Court); he left thirteen thousand age discrimination cases dying on the vine for lack of investigation in his turbulent eight years at the EEOC; and his performance during his short fifteen months as an appellate court judge was mediocre. The very fact that no black leader could utter publicly that a black appointee for the Supreme Court was *unqualified* shows how captive they are to white racist stereotypes about black intellectual talent. The point here is not simply that if Thomas were white they would have no trouble shouting this fact from the rooftops. The point is also that their silence reveals that black leaders may entertain the possibility that the racist stereotype may be true. Hence their attempt to cover Thomas's mediocrity with silence. Of course, some privately admit his mediocrity while pointing out the mediocrity of Justice Souter and other members of the Court—as if white mediocrity were a justification of black mediocrity. No double standards here, the argument goes, if a black man is unqualified one can defend and excuse him by appealing to other unqualified white judges. This chimes well with a cynical tokenism of the lowest common denominator—with little concern for the goal of shattering the racist stereotype or for furthering the public interest of the nation. It also renders invisible highly qualified black judges who deserve serious consideration for selection to the Court.

How did much of black leadership get in this bind? Why did so many of them capitulate to Bush's cynical strategy? First, Thomas's claim to racial authenticity—his birth in Jim Crow Georgia, his childhood as the grandson of a black sharecropper, his undeniably black phenotype degraded by racist ideals of beauty, and his gallant black struggle for achievement in racist America. Second, the complex relation of this claim to racial authenticity to the increasing closing-ranks mentality in black America. Escalating black nationalist sentiments—the notion that America's will to racial justice is weak and therefore black people must close ranks for survival in a hostile country—rests principally upon claims to racial authenticity. Third, the way in which black nationalist sentiments promote and encourage black cultural conservatism, especially black patriarchal (and homophobic) power. The idea of black people closing ranks against hostile white Americans reinforces black male power exercised over black women (e.g., to protect, regulate, subordinate, and hence usually, though not always, to use and abuse women) in order to preserve black social order under circumstances of white literal attack and symbolic assault. (This process is discussed in more detail in chapter 7.)

Most black leaders got lost in this thicket of reasoning and hence got caught in a vulgar form of racial reasoning: black authenticity → black closing-ranks mentality → black male subordination of black women in the interests of the black community in a hostile white racist country. Such a line of racial reasoning leads to such questions as: "Is Thomas really black?" "Is he black enough to be defended?" "Is he just black on the outside?" In fact, these kinds of questions were asked, debated, and answered throughout black America in barber shops, beauty salons, living rooms, churches, mosques, and schoolrooms.

Unfortunately, the very framework of racial reasoning was not called into question. Yet as long as racial reasoning regulates black thought and action, Clarence Thomases will continue to haunt black America—as Bush and other conservatives sit back, watch, and prosper. How does one undermine the framework of racial reasoning? By dismantling each pillar slowly and systematically. The fundamental aim of this undermining and dismantling is to replace racial reasoning with moral reasoning, to understand the black freedom struggle not as an affair of skin pigmentation and racial phenotype but rather as a matter of ethical principles and wise politics, and to combat the black nationalist attempt to subordinate the issues and interests of black women by linking mature black self-love and self-respect to egalitarian relations within and outside black communities. The failure of nerve of black leadership is its refusal to undermine and dismantle the framework of racial reasoning.

Let us begin with the claim to racial authenticity—a claim Bush made about Thomas, Thomas made about himself in the hearings, and black nationalists make about themselves. What is black authenticity? Who is really black? First, blackness has no meaning outside of a system of race-conscious people and practices. After centuries of racist degradation, exploitation, and oppression in America, being black means being minimally subject to white supremacist abuse and being part of a rich culture and community that has struggled against such abuse. All people with black skin and African phenotype are subject to potential white supremacist abuse. Hence, all black Americans have some interest in resisting racism—even if their interest is confined solely to themselves as individuals rather than to larger black communities. Yet how this "interest" is defined and how individuals and communities are understood vary. Hence any claim to black authenticity—beyond that of being a potential object of racist abuse and an heir to a grand tradition of black struggle—is contingent on one's political definition of black interest and one's ethical understanding of how this interest relates to individuals and communities in and outside black America. In short, blackness is a political and ethical construct. Appeals to black authenticity ignore this fact; such appeals hide and conceal the political and ethical dimension of blackness. This is why claims to racial authenticity trump political and ethical argument—and why racial reasoning discourages moral reasoning. Every claim to racial authenticity presupposes elaborate conceptions of political and ethical relations of interests, individuals, and communities. Racial reasoning conceals these presuppositions behind a deceptive cloak of racial consensus—yet racial reasoning is seductive because it invokes an undeniable history of racial abuse and racial struggle. This is why Bush's claims to Thomas's black authenticity, Thomas's claims about his own black authenticity, and black nationalist claims about black authenticity all highlight histories of black abuse and black struggle.

But if claims to black authenticity are political and ethical conceptions of the relation of black interests, individuals, and communities, then any attempt to confine black authenticity to black nationalist politics or black male interests warrants suspicion. For example, black leaders failed to highlight the problematic statements Clarence Thomas made about his sister, Emma Mae, regarding her experience with the welfare system. In front of a conservative audience in San Francisco, Thomas implied she was a welfare cheat dependent on state support. Yet, like most black women in American history, Emma Mae is a hard-working person. She was sensitive enough to take care of her sick aunt even though she was unable to work for a short period of time. After she left welfare, she worked two jobs—until 3:00 in the morning! Thomas's statements reveal his own lack of integrity and character. But the failure of black leaders to highlight his statements discloses a conception of black authenticity confined to black male interests, individuals, and communities. In short, the refusal by most black leaders to give weight to the interests of black women was already apparent before Anita Hill appeared on the scene.

The claims to black authenticity that feed on the closing-ranks mentality of black people are dangerous precisely because this closing of ranks is usually done at the expense of black women. It also tends to ignore the divisions of class and sexual orientation in black America—divisions that require attention if *all* black interests, individuals, and communities are to be taken into consideration. Thomas's conservative Republican politics do not promote a closing-ranks mentality; instead Thomas claims black authenticity for self-promotion, to gain power and prestige. All his professional life he has championed individual achievement and race-free standards. Yet when it looked as though the Senate would not confirm his appointment to the Supreme Court, he played the racial card of black victimization and black solidarity at the expense of Anita Hill. Like his sister, Emma Mae, Anita Hill could be used and abused for his own self-interested conception of black authenticity and racial solidarity.

Thomas played this racial card with success—first with appeals to his victimization in Jim Crow Georgia and later to his victimization by a "hi-tech lynching"—primarily because of the deep cultural conservatism in white and black America. In white America, cultural conservatism takes the form of a chronic racism, sexism, and homophobia. Hence, only certain kinds of black people deserve high positions, that is, those who accept the rules of the game played by white America. In black America, cultural conservatism takes the form of a inchoate xenophobia (e.g., against whites, Jews, and Asians), systemic sexism, and homophobia. Like all conservatisms rooted in a quest for order, the pervasive disorder in white and, especially, black American fans and fuels the channeling of rage toward the most vulnerable and degraded members of the community. For white America, this means primarily scapegoating black people, women, gay men, and lesbians. For black America, this means principally attacking black women and black gay men and lesbians. In this way, black nationalist and black male-centered claims to black authenticity reinforce black cultural conservatism. The support of Louis Farrakhan's Nation of Islam for Clarence Thomas—despite Farrakhan's critique of Republican Party racist and conservative policies—highlights this fact. It also shows how racial reasoning leads different and disparate viewpoints in black America to the same dead end—with substantive ethical principles and savvy wise politics left out.

The undermining and dismantling of the framework of racial reasoning—especially the basic notions of black authenticity, closed-ranks mentality, and black cultural conservatism—lead toward a new framework for black thought and practice. This new framework should be a *prophetic* one of moral reasoning with its fundamental ideas of a mature black identity, coalition strategy, and black cultural democracy. Instead of cathartic appeals to black authenticity, a prophetic viewpoint bases mature black self-love and self-respect on the moral quality of black responses to undeniable racist degradation in the American past and present. These responses assume neither a black essence that all black people share nor one black perspective to which all black people should adhere. Rather, a prophetic framework encourages *moral* assessment of the variety of perspectives held by black people and selects those views based on black dignity and decency that eschew putting any group of people or culture on a pedestal or in the gutter. Instead, blackness is understood to be either the perennial possibility of white supremacist abuse or the distinct styles and dominant modes of expression found in black cultures and communities. These styles and modes are diverse—yet they do stand apart from those of other groups (even as they are shaped by and shape those of other groups). And all such styles and modes stand in need of ethical evaluation. Mature black identity results from an acknowledgment of the specific black responses to white supremacist abuses and a moral assessment of these responses such that the humanity of black people does not rest on deifying or demonizing others.

Instead of a closing-ranks mentality, a prophetic framework encourages a coalition strategy that solicits genuine solidarity with those deeply committed to antiracist struggle. This strategy is neither naive nor opportunistic; black suspicion of whites, Latinos, Jews, and Asians runs deep for historical reasons. Yet there are slight thought significant antiracist traditions among whites, Asians, and especially Latinos, Jews, and indigenous people that must not be cast aside. Such coalitions are important precisely because they not only enhance the plight of black people but also because they enrich the quality of life in America.

Last, a prophetic framework replaces black cultural conservatism with black cultural democracy. Instead of authoritarian sensibilities that subordinate women or degrade gay men and lesbians, black cultural democracy promotes the equality of black women and men and the humanity of black gay men and lesbians. In short, black cultural democracy rejects the pervasive patriarchy and homophobia in black American life.

If most black leaders had adopted a prophetic framework of moral reasoning rather than a narrow framework of racial reasoning, the debate over the Clarence Thomas/Anita Hill hearings would have proceeded in a quite different manner in black America. For example, both Thomas and Hill would be viewed as two black Republican conservative supporters of some of the most vicious policies to besiege black working and poor communities since Jim and Jane Crow segregation. Both Thomas and Hill supported an unprecedented redistribution of wealth from working people to well-to-do people in the form of regressive taxation, deregulation policies, cutbacks and slowdowns in public service programs, take-backs at the negotiation table between workers and management, and military buildups at the Pentagon. Both Thomas and Hill supported the unleashing of unbridled capitalist market forces on a level never witnessed in the United States before that have devastated black working and poor communities. These market forces took the principal form of unregulated corporative and financial expansion and intense entrepreneurial activity. This tremendous ferment in big and small businesses—including enormous bonanzas in speculation, leverage buyouts and mergers, as well as high levels of corruption and graft—contributed to a new kind of culture of consumption in white and black America. Never before has the seductive market way of life held such sway in nearly every sphere of American life. This market way of life promotes addictions to stimulation and obsessions with comfort and convenience. Addictions and obsessions—centered primarily around bodily pleasures and status rankings—constitute market moralities of various sorts. The common denominator is a rugged and ragged individualism and rapacious hedonism in quest of a perennial "high" in body and mind.

In the hearings, the image of Clarence Thomas that emerged was one of an exemplary hedonist, a consumer of pornography, captive to a stereotypical self-image of the powerful black man who revels in sexual prowess in a racist society. Anita Hill appeared as the exemplary careerist addicted to job promotion and captive to the stereotypical self-image of the sacrificial black woman who suffers silently and alone. There was reason to suspect that Thomas was not telling the whole truth. He was silent about *Roe v. Wade*, his intentions in the antiabortion essay on Lewis Lehrmann, and the contours of his conservative political philosophy. Furthermore, his obdurate stonewalling in regard to his private life was disturbing. There also should be little doubt that Anita Hill's decision to testify was a break from her careerist ambitions. On the one hand, she strikes me as a person of integrity and honesty. On the other hand, she indeed put a premium on job advancement—even at painful personal cost. Yet her speaking out disrupted this pattern of behavior and she found herself supported only by people who opposed the very conservative Republican policies she otherwise championed, namely, progressive feminists, liberals, and some black folk. How strange she must feel being a hero to her former foes. One wonders whether Judge Bork supported her as fervently as she did him a few years ago.

A prophetic framework of moral reasoning would have liberated black leaders from the racial guilt of opposing a black man for the highest court in the land and of the feeling that one had to choose between a black woman and a black man. Like the Black Congressional Caucus (minus one?), black people could have simply opposed Thomas based on qualifications and principle. And one could have chosen between two black right-wing figures based on their sworn testimonies in light of the patterns of their behavior in the recent past. Similarly, black leaders could have avoided being duped by Thomas's desperate and vulgar appeals to racial victimization by a white male Senate committee who handled him gently (no questions about his private life). Like Senator Hollings, who knows racial intimidation when he sees it (given his past experiences with it), black leaders could have seen through the rhetorical charade and called a moral spade a moral spade.

Unfortunately, most black leaders remained caught in a framework of racial reasoning—even when they opposed Thomas and/or supported Hill. Rarely did we have a black leader highlight the moral content of a mature black identity, accent the crucial role of coalition strategy in the struggle for justice, or promote the ideal of black cultural democracy. Instead, the debate evolved around glib formulations of a black "role model" based on mere pigmentation, an atavistic defense of blackness that mirrors the increasing xenophobia in American life, and circled around a silence about the ugly authoritarian practices in black America that range from sexual harassment to indescribable violence against women. Hence a grand opportunity for substantive discussion and struggle over race and gender was missed in black America and the larger society. And black leadership must share some of the blame. As long as black leaders remain caught in a frame-work of racial reasoning, they will not rise above the manipulative lan-guage of Bush and Thomas—just as the state of siege (the death, disease, and destruction) raging in much of black America creates more urban wastelands and combat zones. Where there is no vision, the people perish; where there is no framework of moral reasoning, the people close ranks in a war of all against all. The growing gangsterization of America results in part from a market-driven racial reasoning that links the White House to the ghetto projects. In this sense, George Bush, David Duke, and many gangster rap artists speak the same language from different social loca-tions—only racial reasoning can save us. Yet I hear a cloud of witnesses from afar—Sojourner Truth, Wendell Phillips, Emma Goldman, A. Phillip Randolph, Ella Baker, Myles Horton, Fannie Lou Hamer, Michael Harring-ton, Abraham Joshua Heschel, Tom Hayden, Harvey Milk, Robert Moses, Barbara Ehrenreich, Martin Luther King, Jr., and many anonymous others who championed the struggle for freedom and justice in a prophetic frame-work of moral reasoning. They understood that the pitfalls of racial reason-ing are too costly in mind, body, and soul—especially for a downtrodden and despised people like black Americans. The best of our leadership rec-ognized this valuable truth—and more must do so in the future if America is to survive with any moral sense.

———————————————————■———————————————————

The Hill–Thomas hearings point to another construction of black identity; namely, black feminist thought. In **"Defining Black Feminist Thought"** *Patricia Hill-Collins discusses two central tensions in black feminist identity: (i) who can be a black feminist? (ii) what con-stitutes black feminism? To the first question, Hill-Collins identifies three possibilities in the literature. Black feminists are either characterized as all African-American women, as selected African-Americans (primarily women) who have a feminist consciousness, or as selected African-American women with a feminist consciousness. The problem with these views, ac-cording to Hill-Collins, is that they treat race as "immutable," thus ignoring the significance of the social construction of race. Moreover, although the interjection of feminism provides more flexibility, most analyses fail to successfully integrate biology and ideology into a coher-ent account of who can be a black feminist.*

Hill-Collins also critiques standard thinking on the constituent parts of black feminist thought. If black feminism is "the exclusive province of African-American women," then being black and/or female ". . . automatically determine the variants of Black and/or feminist con-sciousness." This, of course, discounts the notion that people often change their ideas over time. It also fails to recognize substantive differences among black feminists.

Hill-Collins proposes an alternative paradigm that requires a ". . . reassessing the central-ity Black women intellectuals assume in producing Black feminist thought." This view also calls attention to the possibility of coalitions with other people with "distinctive standpoints" (e.g., black men, people of color, white women). On this line of reasoning, the life experiences of black women play an important role in the development of black feminist thought. Further, black women intellectuals occupy an especially significant vantage point from which to artic-ulate a black women's standpoint, provide leadership, and create group autonomy. Finally, the core constituent parts of black feminist thought should be imbued with a "humanist vision" that places the struggle of African-American women in the context of a wider global struggle for "human dignity and empowerment."

BLACK FEMINIST THOUGHT: KNOWLEDGE, CONSCIOUSNESS, AND THE POLITICS OF EMPOWERMENT

Patricia Hill-Collins

Excerpt from Chapter 2, Defining Black Feminist Thought

Widely used yet rarely defined, Black feminist thought encompasses diverse and contradictory meanings. Two interrelated tensions highlight issues in defining Black feminist thought. The first concerns the thorny question of who can be a Black feminist. One current response, explicit in Patricia Bell Scott's (1982b) "Selected Bibliography on Black Feminism," classifies all African-American women, regardless of the content of our ideas, as Black feminists. From this perspective, living as Black women provides experiences to stimulate a Black feminist consciousness. Yet indiscriminately labeling all Black women in this way simultaneously conflates the terms *woman* and *feminist* and identifies being of African descent—a questionable biological category—as being the sole determinant of a Black feminist consciousness. As Cheryl Clarke points out, "I criticized Scott. Some of the women she cited as 'black feminists' were clearly not feminist at the time they wrote their books and still are not to this day" (1983, 94).

The term *Black feminist* has also been used to apply to selected African-Americans—primarily women—who possess some version of a feminist consciousness. Beverly Guy-Sheftall (1986) contends that both men and women can be "Black feminists" and names Frederick Douglass and William E. B. DuBois as prominent examples of Black male feminists. Guy-Sheftall also identifies some distinguishing features of Black feminist ideas: namely, that Black women's experiences with both racial and gender oppression that result in needs and problems distinct from white women and Black men, and that Black women must struggle for equality both as women and as African-Americans. Guy-Sheftall's definition is helpful in that its use of ideological criteria fosters a definition of Black feminist thought that encompasses both experiences and ideas. In other words, she suggests that experiences gained from living as African-American women stimulate a Black feminist sensibility. But her definition is simultaneously troublesome because it makes the biological category of Blackness the prerequisite for possessing such thought. Furthermore, it does not explain why these particular ideological criteria and not others are the distinguishing ones.

The term Black feminist has also been used to describe selected African-American women who possess some version of a feminist consciousness (Beale 1970; Hooks 1981; Barbara Smith 1983; White 1984). This usage of the term yields the most restrictive notion of who can be a Black feminist. The ground-breaking Combahee River Collective (1982) document, "A Black Feminist Statement," implicitly relies on this definition. The Collective claims that "as Black women we find any type of biological determinism a particularly dangerous and reactionary basis upon which to build a politic" (p. 17). But in spite of this statement, by implying that only African-American women can be Black feminists, they require a biological prerequisite for race and gender consciousness. The Collective also offers its own ideological criteria for identifying Black feminist ideas. In contrast to Beverly Guy-Sheftall, the Collective places a stronger emphasis on capitalism as a source of Black women's oppression and on political activism as a distinguishing feature of Black feminism.

Biologically deterministic criteria for the term *black* and the accompanying assumption that being of African descent somehow produces a certain consciousness or perspective are inherent in these definitions. By presenting race as being fixed and immutable—something rooted in nature—these approaches mask the historical construction of racial categories, the shifting meaning of race, and the crucial role of politics and ideology in shaping conceptions of race (Gould 11981; Omi and Winant 1986). In contrast, much greater variation is afforded the term feminist. Feminists are seen as ranging from biologically determined—as is the case in radical feminist thought, which argues that only women can be feminists—to notions of feminists as individuals who have undergone some type of political transformation theoretically achievable by anyone.

Though the term Black feminist could also be used to describe any individual who embraces Black feminist ideas, the separation of biology from ideology required for this usage is rarely seen in the works of Black women intellectuals. Sometimes the contradictions among these competing definitions can be so great that Black women writers use all simultaneously. Consider the following passage from Deborah McDowell's essay "New Directions for Black Feminist Criticism":

> I use the term here simply to refer to Black female critics who analyze the works of Black female writers from a feminist political perspective. But the term can also apply to any criticism written by a Black woman regardless of her subject or perspective—a book written by a male from a feminist or political perspective, a book written by a Black woman or about Black women authors in general, or any writings by women. (1985, 191)

While McDowell implies that elite white men could be "black feminists," she is clearly unwilling to state so categorically. From McDowell's perspective, whites and Black men who embrace a specific political perspective, and Black women regardless of political perspective, could all potentially be deemed Black feminist critics.

The ambiguity surrounding current perspectives on who can be a Black feminist is directly tied to a second definitional tension in Black feminist thought: the question of what constitutes Black feminism. The range of assumptions concerning the relationship between ideas and their advocates as illustrated in the works of Patricia Bell Scott, Beverly Guy-Sheftall, the Combahee River Collective, and Deborah McDowell leads to problems in defining

Black feminist theory itself. Once a person is labeled a "Black feminist," then ideas forwarded by that individual often become defined as Black feminist thought. This practice accounts for neither changes in the thinking of an individual nor differences among Black feminist theorists.

A definition of Black feminist thought is needed that avoids the materialist position that being Black and/or female generates certain experiences that automatically determine variants of a Black and/or feminist consciousness. Claims that Black feminist thought is the exclusive province of African-American women, regardless of the experiences and worldview of such women, typify this position. But a definition of Black feminist thought must also avoid the idealist position that ideas can be evaluated in isolation from the groups that create them. Definitions claiming that anyone can produce and develop Black feminist thought risk obscuring the special angle of vision that Black women bring to the knowledge production process.

THE DIMENSIONS OF
A BLACK WOMEN'S STANDPOINT

Developing adequate definitions of Black feminist thought involves facing this complex nexus of relationships among biological classification, the social construction of race and gender as categories of analysis, the material conditions accompanying these changing social constructions, and Black women's consciousness about these themes. One way of addressing the definitional tensions in Black feminist thought is to specify the relationship between a Black women's standpoint—those experiences and ideas shared by African-American women that provide a unique angle of vision on self, community, and society—and theories that interpret these experiences.[1] I suggest that Black feminist thought consists of specialized knowledge created by African-American women which clarifies a standpoint of and for Black women. In other words, Black feminist thought encompasses theoretical interpretations of Black women's reality by those who live it.

This definition does not mean that all African-American women generate such thought or that other groups do not play a critical role in its production.

WHO CAN BE A BLACK FEMINIST?:
THE CENTRALITY OF BLACK WOMEN
INTELLECTUALS TO THE PRODUCTION
OF BLACK FEMINIST THOUGHT

I aim to develop a definition of Black feminist thought that relies exclusively neither on a materialist analysis—one whereby all African-American women by virtue of biology become automatically registered as "authentic Black feminists"—nor on an idealist analysis whereby the background, worldview, and interests of the thinker are deemed irrelevant in assessing his or her ideas. Resolving the tension between these two extremes involves reassessing the centrality Black women intellectuals assume in producing Black feminist thought. It also requires examining the importance of coalitions with Black men, white women, people of color, and other groups with distinctive standpoints. Such coalitions are essential in order to foster other groups' contributions as critics, teachers, advocates, and disseminators of a self-defined Afrocentric feminist standpoint.

Black women's concrete experiences as members of specific race, class, and gender groups as well as our concrete historical situations necessarily play significant roles in our perspective on the world. No standpoint is neutral because no individual or group exists unembedded in the world. Knowledge is gained not by solitary individuals but by Black women as socially constituted members of a group (Narayan 1989). These factors all frame the definitional tensions in Black feminist thought.

Black women intellectuals are central to Black feminist thought for several reasons. First, our experiences as African-American women provide us with a unique standpoint on Black womanhood unavailable to other groups. It is more likely for Black women as members of an oppressed group to have critical insights into the condition of our own oppression than it is for those who live outside those structures. One of the characters in Frances Ellen Watkins Harper's 1892 novel, *Iola Leroy*, expresses this belief in the special vision of those who have experienced oppression:

> Miss Leroy, out of the race must come its own thinkers and writers. Authors belonging to the white race have written good books, for which I am deeply grateful, but it seems to be almost impossible for a white man to put himself completely in our place. No man can feel the iron which enters another man's soul. (Carby 1987, 62)

Only African-American women occupy this center and can "feel the iron" that enters Black women's souls, because we are the only group that has experienced race, gender, and class oppression as Black women experience them. The importance of Black women's leadership in producing Black feminist thought does not mean that others cannot participate. It does mean that the primary responsibility for defining one's own reality lies with the people who live that reality, who actually have those experiences.

Second, Black women intellectuals provide unique leadership for Black women's empowerment and resistance. In discussing Black women's involvement in the feminist movement, Sheila Radford-Hill points out the connections among self-definition, empowerment, and taking actions in one's own behalf:

> Black women now realize that part of the problem within the movement was our insistence that white women do for/with us what we must do for/with ourselves:

namely, frame our own social action around our own agenda for change. . . . Critical to this discussion is the right to organize on one's own behalf. . . . Criticism by black feminists must reaffirm this principle. (1986, 162)

Black feminist thought cannot challenge race, gender, and class oppression without empowering African-American women. "Oppressed people resist by identifying themselves as subjects, by defining their reality, shaping their new identity, naming their history, telling their story," notes Bell Hooks (1989, 43). Because self-definition is key to individual and group empowerment, using an epistemology that cedes the power of self-definition to other groups, no matter how well-meaning, in essence perpetuates Black women's subordination. As Black feminist sociologist Deborah K. King succinctly states, "Black feminism asserts self-determination as essential" (1988, 72).

Stressing the importance of Black women's centrality to Black feminist thought does not mean that all African-American women exert this leadership. While being an African-American woman generally provides the experiential base for an Afrocentric feminist consciousness, these same conditions suppress its articulation. It is not acquired as a finished product but must continually develop in relation to changing conditions.

Bonnie Johnson emphasizes the importance of self-definition. In her critique of Patricia Bell Scott's bibliography on Black feminism, she challenges both Scott's categorization of all works by Black women as being Black feminist and Scott's identification of a wide range of African-American women as Black feminists: "Whether I think they're feminists is irrelevant. *They* would not call themselves feminist" (Clarke et al. 1983, 94). As Patrice L. Dickerson contends, "a person comes into being and knows herself by her achievements, and through her efforts to become and know herself, she achieves" (personal correspondence 1988). Here is the heart of the matter. An Afrocentric feminist consciousness constantly emerges and is part of a self-conscious struggle to merge thought and action.

Third, Black women intellectuals are central in the production of Black feminist thought because we alone can create the group autonomy that must precede effective coalitions with other groups. This autonomy is quite distinct from separatist positions whereby Black women withdraw from other groups and engage in exclusionary politics. In her introduction to *Home Girls, A Black Feminist Anthology*, Barbara Smith describes this difference: "Autonomy and separatism are fundamentally different. Whereas autonomy comes from a position of strength, separatism comes from a position of fear. When we're truly autonomous we can deal with other kinds of people, a multiplicity of issues, and with difference, because we have formed a solid base of strength" (1983, xl). Black women intellectuals who articulate an autonomous, self-defined standpoint are in a position to examine the usefulness of coalitions with other groups, both scholarly and activist, in order to develop new models for social change. However, autonomy to develop a self-defined, independent analysis does not mean that Black feminist thought has relevance only for African-American women or that we must confine ourselves to analyzing our own experiences. As Sonia Sanchez points out, "I've always known that if you write from a black experience, you're writing from a universal experience as well. . . . I know you don't have to whitewash yourself to be universal" (in Tate 1983, 142).

While Black feminist thought may originate with Black feminist intellectuals, it cannot flourish isolated from the experiences and ideas of other groups. The dilemma is that Black women intellectuals must place our own experiences and consciousness at the center of any serious efforts to develop Black feminist thought yet not have that thought become separatist and exclusionary. Bell Hooks offers a solution to this problem by suggesting that we shift from statements such as "I am a feminist" to those such as "I advocate feminism." Such an approach could "serve as a way women who are concerned about feminism as well as other political movements could express their support while avoiding linguistic structures that give primacy to one particular group" (1984, 30).

By advocating, refining, and disseminating Black feminist thought, other groups—such as Black men, white women, white men, and other people of color—further its development. Black women can produce an attenuated version of Black feminist thought separated from other groups. Other groups cannot produce Black feminist thought without African-American women. Such groups can, however, develop self-defined knowledge reflecting their own standpoints. But the full actualization of Black feminist thought requires a collaborative enterprise with Black women at the center of a community based on coalitions among autonomous groups.

Coalitions such as these require dialogues among Black women intellectuals and within the larger African-American women's community. Exploring the common themes of a Black women's standpoint is an important first step. Moreover, finding ways of handling internal dissent is especially important for the Black women's intellectual community. Evelynn Hammond describes how maintaining a united front for whites stifles her thinking: "What I need to do is challenge my thinking, to grow. On white publications sometimes I feel like I'm holding up the banner of black womanhood. And that doesn't allow me to be as critical as I would like to be" (in Clarke et al. 1983, 104). Cheryl Clarke observes that she has two dialogues: one with the public and the private ones in which she feels free to criticize the work of other Black women. Clarke states that the private dialogues are the ones that "have changed my life, have shaped the way I feel . . . have mattered to me" (p. 103).

Coalitions also require dialogues with other groups. Rather than rejecting our marginality, Black women intellectuals can use our outsider-within stance as a position of strength in building effective coalitions and stimulating dialogue. Barbara Smith suggests that Black women develop dialogues based on a "commitment to principled coalitions, based not upon expediency, but upon our actual need for each other" (1983, xxxiii). Dialogues among and coalitions with a range of groups, each with its own distinctive set of experiences and specialized thought embedded in those experiences, form the larger, more general terrain of intellectual and political discourse necessary for furthering Black feminism. Through dialogues exploring how relations of domination and subordination are maintained and changed, parallels between Black women's experiences and those of other groups become the focus of investigation.

Dialogue and principled coalition create possibilities for new versions of truth. Alice Walker's answer to the question of what she felt were the major differences between the literature of African-Americans and whites offers a provocative glimpse of the types of truths that might emerge through an epistemology based on dialogue and coalition. Walker did not spend much time considering this question, since it was not the difference between them that interested her, but, rather, the way Black writers and white writers seemed to be writing one immense story, with different parts of the story coming from a multitude of different perspectives. In a conversation with her mother, Walker refines this epistemological vision: "I believe that the truth about any subject only comes when all sides of the story are put together, and all their different meanings make one new one. Each writer writes the missing parts to the other writer's story. And the whole story is what I'm after" (1983, 49). Her mother's response to Walker's vision of the possibilities of dialogues and coalitions hints at the difficulty of sustaining such dialogues under oppressive conditions: "Well, I doubt if you can ever get the *true* missing parts of anything away from the white folks,' my mother says softly, so as not to offend the waitress who is mopping up a nearby table; 'they've sat on the truth so long by now they've mashed the life out of it'" (1983, 49).

WHAT CONSTITUTES BLACK FEMINISM? THE RECURRING HUMANIST VISION

A wide range of African-American women intellectuals have advanced the view that Black women's struggles are part of a wider struggle for human dignity and empowerment. In an 1893 speech to women, Anna Julia Cooper cogently expressed this alternative worldview:

> We take our stand on the solidarity of humanity, the oneness of life, and the unnaturalness and injustice of all special favoritisms, whether of sex, race, country, or condition. . . . The colored woman feels that woman's cause is one and universal; and that . . . not till race, color, sex, and condition are seen as accidents, and not the substance of life; not till the universal title of humanity to life, liberty, and the pursuit of happiness is conceded to be inalienable to all; not till then is woman's lesson taught and woman's cause won—not the white woman's nor the black woman's, not the red woman's but the cause of every man and of every woman who has writhed silently under a mighty wrong. (Loewenberg and Bogin 1976, 330–31)

Like Cooper, many African-American women intellectuals embrace this perspective regardless of particular political solutions we propose, our fields of study, or our historical periods. Whether we advocate working through separate Black women's organizations, becoming part of women's organizations, working within existing political structures, or supporting Black community institutions, African-American women intellectuals repeatedly identify political actions such as these as a *means* for human empowerment rather than ends in and of themselves. Thus the primary guiding principle of Black feminism is a recurring humanist vision (Steady 1981, 1987).

Alice Walker's preference for the term *womanist*, a term she describes as "womanist is to feminist as purple is to lavender," addresses this notion of the solidarity of humanity. To Walker, one is "womanist" when one is "committed to the survival and wholeness of entire people, male and female." A womanist is "not a separatist, except periodically for health" and is "traditionally universalist, as is 'Mama, why are we brown, pink, and yellow, and our cousins are white, beige, and black?' Ans.: 'Well, you know the colored race is just like a flower garden, with every color flower represented'" (1983, xi). By redefining all people as "people of color," Walker universalizes what are typically seen as individual struggles while simultaneously allowing space for autonomous movements of self-determination.

In assessing the sexism of the Black nationalist movement of the 1960s, Black feminist lawyer Pauli Murray identifies the dangers inherent in separatism as opposed to autonomy, and also echoes Cooper's concern with the solidarity of humanity:

> The lesson of history that all human rights are indivisible and that the failure to adhere to this principle jeopardizes the rights of all is particularly applicable here. A built-in hazard of an aggressive ethnocentric movement which disregards the interests of other disadvantaged groups is that it will become parochial and ultimately self-defeating in the face of hostile reactions, dwindling allies, and mounting frustrations. . . . Only a broad movement for human rights can prevent the Black Revolution from becoming isolated and can insure ultimate success. (Murray 1970, 102)

Without a commitment to human solidarity, suggests Murray, any political movement—whether nationalist, feminist or antielitist—may be doomed to ultimate failure.

As we move into a new century, Dubois' conception of African-American identity—"two souls, two thoughts, two unreconciled strivings, two warring ideals in one dark body"—is as relevant as ever. On the one hand, integrationist ideology has successfully moved blacks into the mainstream of the society. Fifty years ago, for example, it would have been unthinkable for distinctively black cultural elements (e.g., language, letters, and music) to be central to the nation's overall identity. Indeed, Maya Angelou, Michael Jordan, and Colin Powell are national icons. Blacks run Fortune 500 companies (e.g., American Express), major cities (e.g., San Francisco), and television networks (e.g., BET). Blacks have even been credited with spawning the rebirth of public intellectualism.[17]

The critique of "mainstreaming," however, is that it comes with a price tag—the loss of substantive cultural heritage. From this view, the fact that Malcolm X hats can be purchased at Nordstrom's signals the commodification and trivialization of black culture.[18] Put differently, appropriation is not integration. Further, even mainstream success cannot protect achieving African-Americans from common racial indignities such as police harassment, inferior service, and mistaken identity.[19] In this context, racial solidarity becomes a welcome relief from the anxieties of the black experience in America. Is it possible that the more blacks succeed, the more attractive nationalist ideologies become?

Finally, changing demographics suggest that the fundamental conception of race is likely to undergo significant transformation in the 21st century. The emergence of black immigrants from the Caribbean and South America call into question standard interpretations of black identity. Similarly, the rise in out-marriage rates means that claims to racial authenticity will grow weaker over time.[20] In sum, the struggle for identity and validation remains uncertain.

STUDY QUESTIONS

1. What is the role of identity in the construction of a black worldview? How does identity structure the discourse on racial politics? Is identity a matter of phenotype or cultural consciousness?

2. What are the central points of disagreement between DuBois and Washington? Which model of black inclusion do you find most compelling? Why? How applicable are these views to the contemporary politics of race?

3. How does nationalist ideology capture and explain the black condition in America? How popular is nationalist thought in the black community? Are non-blacks more threatened by black nationalism than other models of the black experience? If so, why?

4. Conservatives argue that too many blacks use racism as an excuse to rationalize black failings. How much credence do you place in this view? If this view is accurate, what are the implications for public policy initiatives in the African-American community? What is the proper role of black intellectual and political leadership from the conservative perspective? What are the obligations of individual blacks?

5. How should one think about the interaction between race and gender? Put differently, where does black feminist thought fit in the construction of an African-American worldview? Who can be a black feminist? Are there conflicts between feminist thought and other models of the black condition?

NOTES

1. Harold Cruse. *The crisis of the Negro intellectual: A historical analysis of the failure of black leadership.* (New York: Quill) 1984.

2. William Van Deburg. *Modern Black Nationalism: From Marcus Garvey to Louis Farrakhan.* (New York: New York University Press) 1997.

3. Bennett, pp. 86–140.

4. James M. McPherson. *The struggle for equality: Abolitionists and the Negro in the Civil War and Reconstruction* (Princeton: Princeton University Press) 1964.

5. Charles P. Henry. *Culture and African-American politics.* (Bloomington: Indiana University Press) 1990; Robert C. Smith and Richard Seltzer. *Race, class, and culture: A study in Afro-American mass opinion.* (Albany: State University of New York Press) 1992.

6. Jim Sidanius and Felicia Pratto. *Social dominance: an intergroup theory of social hierarchy and oppression* (Cambridge, UK: Cambridge University Press) 1999.

7. Amy Jacques Garvey, *Garvey and Garveyism* (New York: Collier) 1972. As cited in Van Deburg.

8. Robert I. Allen, *Dialectics of black power* (Boston, Mass.: New England Free Press)1968; Stokely Carmichael and Charles Hamilton *Black power; the politics of liberation in America* (New York: Random House) 1967; E.U. Essien-Udom. *Black Nationalism.* (New York: Dell) 1962; Wilson Jeremiah Moses (ed.) *Classical Black Nationalism: from the American Revolution to Marcus Garvey.* (New York: New York University Press) 1996; Alphonso Pinkney, *Red, black, and green: Black Nationalism in the United States.* (Cambridge: Cambridge University Press) 1976.

9. Van Deburg, pp. 315–327.

10. Molefi K. Asante. *The Afrocentric idea* (Philadelphia: Temple University Press) 1987. But, Mary R. Lefkowitz and Guy MacLean Rogers (eds.) *Black Athena Revisited.* (Chapel Hill: U of North Carolina Press) 1996.

11. See also, Gerald Early, "Understanding Afrocentrism: Why blacks dream of a world without whites". *Civilization* July/August 1995: 31–39.

12. While conservatism reached its zenith in the black community (and the nation) during the Reagan administration, the promulgation of conservative ideas is not new in black life. Early black conservatives such as George S. Schuyler and Zora Neale Hurston were frequent critics of liberal black leadership.

13. Shelby Steele. *The content of our character: a new vision of race in America* (New York: St. Martin's Press) 1990. also, Stephen Carter. *Reflections of an affirmative action baby.* (New York: Basic Books) 1991; Glenn C. Loury, *One by one from the inside out: essays and reviews on race and responsibility in America* (New York: Free Press) 1995; Thomas Sowell. *Race and economics.* (New York: D. McKay Co) 1975, *Markets and minorities* (New York: Basic Books) 1981; Walter E. Williams. *The state against Blacks* (New York: New Press) 1982.

14. Cornel West. *Race matters* (Boston: Beacon Press) 1993.

15. Toni Morrison (ed.) *Race-ing, Justice, En-gendering power: Essays on Anita Hill, Clarence Thomas, and the construction of social reality.* (New York: Pantheon) 1992.

16. For a fuller discussion of race and gender Margaret L. Andersen and Patricia Hill Collins. *Race, class, and gender.* (Belmot, CA: Wadsworth) 1992; Patricia Hill Collins. *Knowledge, consciousness, and the politics of empowerment.* (New York: Routledge) 1989; Kimberle Williams Crenshaw, "Mapping the margins: intersectionality, identity politics, and violence against women of color," *Stanford Law Review* 43:6 1991 pp.1241–1299; Paula Giddings *Where I enter: The impact of black women on race and sex in America.* (New York: William Morrow) 1984.

17. Robert S. Boynton, "The new intellectuals," *Atlantic Monthly* 275:3 March 1995:53–66.

18. See, Robin D.G. Kelley. *Race rebels: Culture, politics, and the black working class.* (New York: Basic Books) 1990.

19. Ellis Cose. *The rage of a privileged class: Why are middle class blacks angry? Why should America care?* (New York: Harper, Collins) 1993.

20. See, M. Belinda Tucker and Claudia Mitchell-Kernan (eds.). *The decline in marriage among African-Americans: Causes, consequences, and policy implications.* (New York: Russell Sage Foundation) 1995.

RACIAL POLITICS IN URBAN AMERICA

The politics of race in contemporary America most commonly plays out in urban centers. The intense interracial struggles for political power in cities such as Los Angeles, New York, Chicago, Atlanta, and a host of other cities bear testimony to this claim.[1] In the post-civil rights era, there has been a significant increase in the number of black elected officials. In 1970, there were less than 1500 black elected officials nationwide. By 1996, there were more than 8000.[2] The majority of these officials were elected in local jurisdictions, such as counties and municipalities.[3]

There are at least three basic reasons for these trends. First, drawn by the lure of stable employment, large-scale in-migration to the cities between 1940 and 1970 provided black leadership with the necessary numbers and infrastructure to mobilize the black electorate. Churches, fraternal organizations, and civil rights groups were the engines of black political empowerment. Second, organizational capabilities developed during the civil rights movement were directly transferable to the electoral arena. Thus, by the 1970s, mobilizing large numbers of people had become "old hat." Third, "white-flight" magnified the political impact of black voters. In other words, African-Americans became numerical majorities in several of the country's largest cities. In short, the rapidly growing black population was willing and able to capitalize on access to political structures.[4]

There are two basic reasons why African-Americans have devoted tremendous energy toward securing local political power. The first is that ascension to public office provides a basis for the exercise of political power. That is, it allows for greater control over the measure and direction of public resources. For example, local black elected officials have provided their core constituents with benefits in employment, housing, education, and business development.[5] Second, the presence of minority elected officials has significant symbolic effects for populations that have historically been denied access to the organs of government. Group identity and pride is no doubt bolstered by the presence of group members who hold high public office. Put differently, minority citizens are more psychologically engaged in politics when they are visibly included into public structures.[6]

In 1967 Richard Hatcher became the first black mayor (of a major city) in the 20th century. He outlined the central agenda of black political empowerment in his **"Inaugural Address."** *Early in the speech he identified the cause of black poverty as blocked opportunities and pledged* *to give black citizens a ". . . share of the good life" by "tearing down the slums" and creating job opportunities. Hatcher called for black equality and indicated that the city would not tolerate people who ". . . peddle the poison of racism." Throughout the speech, the new mayor argued the city could not advance politically or economically unless the citizenry was willing to accept the value of diversity. Even political reform could be aided by a black-led administration: "[G]ood government comes in assorted colors and nationalities." Hatcher ends the address by emphasizing that there must be a break with the past and a step into a new beginning that "shatters the walls of the ghetto for all time."*

INAUGURAL ADDRESS (1967)

Richard Hatcher

My fellow Americans. Today we are witnessing a rebirth of Gary's determination to take its rightful place among the great cities of our nation. With a resolute mind we embark upon a four-year journey, to change the face of our city and unite the hearts of our citizens; to tear down slums and build healthy bodies; to destroy crime and create beauty; to expand industry and restrict pollution.

Gary, Indiana is a warm city—it has welcomed in large numbers into its midst emigrants from southern Europe, black people from the deep South and those who come from South of the border. In diversity, we have found strength; however, today is a new day. Let it be known that as of this moment, there are some who are no longer welcome in Gary, Indiana. Those who have made a profession of violating our laws—are no longer welcome. He who would stick up our businessmen and rape our women—is no longer welcome. Those who would bribe our policemen and other public officials and those public officials who accept bribes are no longer welcome and those who would sow the seeds of discord and peddle the poison of racism, let it be clearly understood, are no longer welcome in Gary, Indiana.

A special word to my brothers and sisters who because of circumstances beyond your control, find yourselves locked into miserable slums, without enough food to eat, inadequate clothing for your children and no hope for tomorrow. It is a primary goal of this administration to make your life better. To give you a decent place to live. To help create job opportunities for you and to assist you in every way in breaking the vicious chain of poverty. To give you your rightful share of the good life.

To our business community, including United States Steel Corporation and other large corporations, I say that Gary has been good to you, but it can be better. We assure you that this administration stands ready to support you in your efforts to rejuvenate our downtown, that it will work closely with you in attempting to attract new industry and enterprise in developing a healthy economic climate. In return, we shall ask you to roll up your sleeves and stand with us as we attempt to rebuild this city. Share with us your technical expertise, and your know-how and your money. Help us save our city. Each of you has a moral commitment to this community, and to your fellow man.

And if you think so, now's the time to say so. There is nothing sacred in silence, nothing Christian in cowardice, nothing temperate in timidity.

To organized labor, we make a special plea that in the great tradition of your movement and out of your deep concern for the little man, the average man, you join us in this effort. Join us as we attempt to put into practice the great principles espoused by Samuel Gompers long ago and Joseph Germano more recently . . . "To every man his due."

To those who will be employees of this city, I say that the highest standards of integrity will be expected of you and anyone who fails to meet that requirement will be summarily discharged. Graft and corruption shall end and efficiency shall begin.

Today we have sworn in a new City Council. Represented there are men and women of integrity and great ability. I look forward to working closely with them for I am honored to call them all friend. Their responsibility is clear cut—to give to you the citizens of Gary four years of the finest, most progressive government in this city's history. To engage in constructive criticism and opposition to this administration when conscience so dictates, but never to oppose simply for opposition's sake. Our city is suffering. And unless the right medicine is administered, it may die. We have long since passed the point where either this administration or this Council can afford the luxury of playing politics with the lives of our people.

To the press, we ask your understanding, patience and help—all of our judgments shall not be correct, but they shall be honestly made. You have a responsibility not only to report the news accurately, but to interpret it with restraint.

Let me for a moment speak to our young people. Your city needs you. We shall seek ways to capture your spirit, imagination and creativity in order that they may be true assets in our city's fight to improve itself. Our future depends upon the dedication of our young people today.

And finally, to all of our citizens, whether you live in Glen Park, in Midtown or in Miller, I make a special appeal. We cannot solve our problems, we cannot save our city if we all are divided. The great promise of our city will not be realized until we treat each other as equals without respect to race or religion. To quote our president, "Until justice is blind to color, until education is unaware of race, until opportunity is unconcerned with the color of men's skins, emancipation will be a proclamation and not a fact. The Negro today asks justice. We do not answer him when we reply by asking patience." We have talked long enough in this city about equality. The time is here to live it. If we really want good government, peace and unity, now's the time to practice what we preach. Good government comes in assorted colors and nationalities.

Together, we shall walk through our valleys of hope; together we shall climb the steep mountains of opportunity, for we seek a high and beautiful new plateau—a new plateau of economy and efficiency in government, a new plateau of progress in government: a new plateau where every man, democrat and republican, rich and poor, Jew and Gentile, black and white, shall live in peace and dignity.

And so my fellow Americans, as we go from this place, let us understand clearly our role and responsibility. This is a God-given opportunity to become builders of the future instead of guardians of a barren past, and we must not waste it. Let us pray for this wisdom and guidance. Let us dare to make a new beginning. Let us shatter the walls of the ghetto for all time. Let us build a new city and a new man to inhabit it. Let each and everyone of us have the courage to do what we all know must be done. For we here in Gary, Indiana have much to say about what will happen in urban America.

Our problems are many. But our determination is great and we feel as Tennyson must have felt when he said:

> Oh yet we trust that somehow good will be the final goal of ill. . . .
> That nothing walks with aimless feet
> That not one life shall be destroyed
> or cast as rubbish to the void
>
> When God hath made the pile complete
> Behold, we know not anything
> I can but trust that good shall fall
> At last—far off—at last to all
> And every winter change to Spring.

And every Winter change to Spring. In Gary, together, we seek to change all winters to Spring. We know the way is difficult, but that does not discourage us. One of America's outstanding black poets, a scholar and a wise man, Professor Arna Bontemps, once wrote the following:

> We are not come to make a strife
> With words upon this hill;
> It is not wise to waste the life
> Against a stubborn will
> Yet we would die as some have done,
> Beating a way for the rising sun.

Gary is a rising sun. Together, we shall beat a way; together, we shall turn darkness into light, despair into hope and promise into progress. For God's sake, for Gary's sake—Let's get ourselves together.

———————————————————————— ■ ————————————————————————

In their article, **"Race, socio-political participation, and black empowerment,"** *Lawrence Bobo and Frank Gilliam offer a theoretical (and empirical) framework for understanding the impact of black political empowerment on mass attitudes and behavior. They define empowerment as, ". . . the extent to which a group has achieved significant influence in political decision making." Operationalizing empowerment as holding the mayor's office is taken as a reflection of black office-holding across a wide range of political offices (e.g., city council, school board, county boards, etc.). Their basic hypothesis is that holding "positions of authority" and wielding political power increases blacks' political involvement by raising levels of trust, efficacy, and knowledge. In other words, ". . . black empowerment is a contextual cue of likely policy responsiveness that encourages blacks to feel that participation has intrinsic value." Although not reported here, Bobo and Gilliam present national survey data to demonstrate that empowerment increases participation and ". . . leads to a more engaged . . .*

orientation to politics." In fact, they found that blacks in empowered areas actually had higher rates of participation compared to whites in high empowerment areas. Although the authors conclude that black empowerment has a significant effect on black attitudes and behavior, they are cautious about the ability of post-civil rights black elected officials to alter the structure of power fundamentally in most large cities.

RACE, SOCIO-POLITICAL PARTICIPATION, AND BLACK EMPOWERMENT

Lawrence D. Bobo and Franklin D. Gilliam, Jr.

BLACK POLITICAL EMPOWERMENT

Understanding black participation in the contemporary period, we believe, requires taking into account the likely effects of black political empowerment. By political empowerment—or political incorporation, as some have called it (Browning, Marshall, and Tabb 1984)—we mean the extent to which a group has achieved significant representation and influence in political decision making.

The business of U.S. politics is transacted on several levels. Black gains in public office-holding, however, have primarily been at the state and local levels (Joint Center for Political Studies 1988, 8). Blacks have made tremendous strides in obtaining seats in state legislatures and on city councils and school boards (p. 13). The most notable black gains, we believe, have been at the mayoral level (see Persons 1987). In major cities such as Atlanta, Detroit, Gary, Los Angeles, and others, black mayors have controlled city hall for more than a decade. Conceptually, we focus on whether blacks have captured the mayor's office because it involves the highest degree of local empowerment, usually signaling both a high level of organization among elites in the African-American community and a relatively high degree of control over local decision making (Browning, Marshal, and Tabb 1984; Nelson and Meranto 1977).

There are two interrelated reasons why such empowerment should influence mass sociopolitical participation. First, empowerment should influence participation because sociopolitical behavior has a heavily instrumental basis. Like Wolfinger and Rosenstone (1980), we believe that people participate because the perceived benefits of doing so outweigh the perceived costs. Second, empowerment should influence participation because macro level aspects of a person's sociopolitical environment affect cost-benefit calculations. There is a large literature on the effects of political contexts on cost-benefit calculations relevant to participation. Studies have emphasized legal factors (Ashenfelter and Kelley 1975; Wolfinger and Rosenstone 1980), electoral factors (Gilliam 1985; Patterson and Caldeira 1983), organizational factors such as mobilization efforts by political parties (Flanigan and Zingale

1979; Key 1949), and cues from political figures indicating likely policy re-sponsiveness (Bullock 1981; Whitby 1987). Our primary interest is in this lat-ter type of contextual influence. We hypothesize that where blacks hold more positions of authority, wield political power, and have done so for longer pe-riods of time, greater numbers of blacks should see value in sociopolitical involvement.

We expect, then, that the greater the level of empowerment, the more likely it is that blacks will become politically involved (Hamilton 1986). Em-powerment should increase participation because of its effects on several social psychological factors, in particular, its impact on levels of political trust, efficacy, and knowledge about politics. Blacks in high empowerment areas should feel more trusting of government, express higher levels of effi-cacy, and become more knowledgeable about politics than blacks in low-empowerment areas. All of which should, in turn, contribute to higher levels of participation.

The impact of empowerment on levels of trust and efficacy among blacks should also change the nature of *black-white differences* in the extent and cor-relates of participation. In areas of high black empowerment, blacks should participate at rates equal to, or greater than, whites (all other things being equal). In areas of relatively low black empowerment, blacks should partici-pate at rates lower than whites. Furthermore, black empowerment should bring greater similarity between blacks and whites in the relationship of po-litical orientations to sociopolitical participation. Earlier research found that the most active blacks were politically discontented; that is, they exhibited a combination of low levels of trust in government and high levels of personal political efficacy. In contrast, the most active whites were found among those aptly labeled "politically engaged"—those individuals with high levels of trust and high levels of efficacy. Growing black empowerment suggests a shift of the most active blacks to the same type of "engaged" orientation of the most active whites.

DISCUSSION AND CONCLUSIONS

Our results show, first, that where blacks hold positions of political power, they are more active and participate at higher rates than whites of compara-ble socioeconomic status. Second, black empowerment is a contextual cue of likely policy responsiveness that encourages blacks to feel that participation has intrinsic value. This conclusion is based on the finding that empower-ment leads to higher levels of political knowledge and that it leads to a more engaged (i.e., trusting and efficacious) orientation to politics.

An alternative interpretation of these results holds that black empower-ment is the outcome of higher participation brought about by registration and turnout drives when a viable black candidate emerges. This explanation of our results is unconvincing on logical and empirical grounds even though we agree that the mobilization of black voters is a necessary component of the accomplishment of empowerment (Browning, Marshall, and Tabb 1984). First, blacks are not newcomers to elective office in most of the "empowered" areas in our sample, and our dependent variables are general patterns of individual behavior. Hence, it is unlikely that we have found merely the short-term effects of black voter mobilization efforts. What is more, the effects of empowerment are not restricted to electoral turnout. Second, if the association between empowerment and participation were merely the result of voter mobilization drives by black candidates, we should have found strong direct effects of empowerment on participation among blacks. Instead, the data show that empowerment works through the psychological factors of political orientation and (especially) level of actual political knowledge. We suggest that black empowerment, whatever heightened mobilization this feat initially requires, has broad and lasting consequences on how often, and why, blacks become active participants in the political process. One sign of the potential for such effects is that whites, too, are affected. Recall the finding that whites in high-black-empowerment areas are less politically knowledgeable than whites in low-black-empowerment areas.

These results call for changes in our empirical and theoretical ideas about black sociopolitical behavior. Studies of sociopolitical participation based on data from the late 1950s and into the 1960s found that blacks participated less than whites, that blacks were more active than whites at any given level of socioeconomic status, and that greater black involvement was rooted in group consciousness and a sense of political discontent. Substantively, these patterns were correctly read as showing that (1) blacks were fighting for basic civic inclusion and to obtain the larger goal of improving the material status of the group and (2) that full understanding of patterns of sociopolitical participation in the United States required one to take race into account.

The significance of race for sociopolitical behavior has evidently changed. On the one hand, we find that blacks generally participate at the same rate as whites of comparable socioeconomic status and that the politically engaged are the most active segment of both groups. It is tempting to conclude, therefore, that the importance of race for patterns of sociopolitical participation has greatly declined. On the other hand, blacks are more active than comparable whites in areas of high black political empowerment. In addition, level of empowerment shapes both blacks' likelihood of adopting an "engaged" orientation to politics and their basic levels of knowledge about political affairs. These psychological orientations to politics, in turn, powerfully affect a person's level of sociopolitical involvement. It is more accurate, then, to conclude that race now shapes sociopolitical behavior in different ways and for somewhat different reasons than held in the past.

In our judgment, these differences reflect broad legal-political-economic changes that improved the general social standing of many blacks and, most directly, brought a tremendous increase in the number and influence of black elected officials. To be sure, the core political goals of blacks have steadily been full and fair inclusion in all domains of U.S. society (Hamilton 1984; Jones 1972; Walton 1985). When the pathways to these objectives were fundamentally blocked, different strategies and orientations were necessary than now seem appropriate in a context of significant wielding of institutional power by blacks. With the goal of basic civic inclusion largely accomplished, the black political agenda has shifted to the goal of maintaining, exploiting, and expanding the political and economic resources available to the black community (Hamilton 1986).

Nonetheless, the degree of black political empowerment and general social progress must be kept in perspective. Blacks gained control of mayoral offices at a time when the power of urban political machines continued to decline, when population and commerce were shifting to suburban areas (Wilson 1980), and when federal programs became less generous (Moore 1988). Hindrances to black empowerment in the form of cumbersome voter registration procedures, district boundaries that dilute the black vote, gerrymandering, hostility to black candidates among a significant number of whites (Williams and Morris 1987), and the cooptation of some black leaders (Browning, Marshall, and Tabb 1984; Jennings 1984) are still problematic. In addition, the persisting social segregation and economic disadvantages of blacks (Farley and Allen 1987; Wilson 1987) constitute structural bases for black racial identity formation (Allen, Dawson, and Brown 1989) as well as for sharp black-white political polarization over race relations issues (Bobo 1988), social welfare policy attitudes (Bobo n.d.; Gilliam and Whitby 1989), and basic life satisfaction (Thomas and Hughes 1986). Black progress and political empowerment are still partial and incomplete even though they have advanced far enough to affect how often, and why, blacks become politically active.

Further investigations of changing black sociopolitical behavior and the influence of black empowerment will require studies with larger samples of blacks. Future research should develop direct indicators of whether black respondents think black officials are more responsive to their needs than white officials (Jackson and Oliver 1988). Full exploration of these ideas will require data on whether black officials have the inclination and resources to produce desired outcomes for their constituents (Eisinger 1982). Tapping the reactions of whites to black elected officials is a necessary component of this research. In addition, the empowerment model may be extended to other U.S. minority groups. The growing electoral power of Latinos, for example, might be fruitfully studied within the empowerment framework we developed here.

———————————————— ■ ————————————————

Aldon Morris, in **"The Future of Black Politics: Substance versus Process and Formality,"** *critiques the empowerment thesis on the grounds that it confuses office-holding with "real empowerment." He raises the possibility that ". . . this strategy of political office seeking . . . could push the black community even lower than its present subordinate position." Morris' core claim is that black elected officials do not have sufficient power to influence the allocation of important economic resources. Black politicians, according to Morris, do not have an interest in promoting this agenda because they do not possess the authority to make the changes necessary for black economic advancement. To the extent that black leaders have exercised power, it has been to mainly promote the political interests of the black middle class. He goes on to say that black politicians are essentially the caretakers of white concerns because the structures they preside over were designed to ". . . protect and promote the economic interests of America's white upper classes."*

Morris challenges black thinkers and leaders to debate a political-economy approach to black empowerment based on implementing ". . . fundamental economic change within the black community." He raises three points to frame the debate. First, such a discussion should seek to bridge the gap between the black "haves" and "have nots." Second, the lesson from the civil rights movement is that black protest politics has the ability to strike at the heart of white economic power (i.e., Birmingham Bus Boycott). Third, black empowerment must be more inclusive and use the intellect of African-American women—there are 2.5 times more male elected officials than females.[7] In short, black office-holding is more style than substance.

THE FUTURE OF BLACK POLITICS: SUBSTANCE VERSUS PROCESS AND FORMALITY

Aldon Morris

A s the decade of the 1990s opens, the material conditions of the black masses have deteriorated drastically. Yet, at the same time the number of black elected officials has skyrocketed to an all-time high. This is a paradox that was not supposed to happen. During the heyday of the civil rights and black power movements, it was widely believed that attaining the ballot, and the political power it would generate, were the keys that would unlock the doors of black empowerment. Black leaders, activists, and ordinary people marched, went to jail, and endured physical violence to obtain the ballot. Some even paid the supreme price by sacrificing their life so that African Americans could achieve the ballot. But twenty-five years later a bitter revelation stares the scholar and lay person in the face: the election of black politicians does not automatically empower the African-American community, and it is even possible for that community to become less empowered as the number of black elected officials increases.

The civil rights movement was successful in its effort to seize the franchise for millions of southern blacks and create favorable political conditions for the exercise of the franchise by blacks outside the South. Indeed, "the number of black elected officials has risen from a few dozens in 1940 to over 6,800 in 1988" (Jayne and Williams, 1989:15). As Bobo and Gilliam point out, black elected officials are to be found in state legislatures, city councils, and school boards, and as mayors of major cities. Currently there is a black governor of Virginia, and Andrew Young conducted an impressive but unsuccessful campaign to become the first black governor of Georgia. Reflecting this trend of black political progress, a black man—Ron Brown—is the current National Chairman of the Democratic party, and Jesse Jackson waged significant campaigns to become president of the United States in 1984 and 1988. In short, the civil rights movement ushered in a small-scale revolution in electoral politics, making it possible for significant numbers of blacks to hold office for the first time since Reconstruction.

Nevertheless, office-holding and real empowerment can be two different realities altogether, as the data already cited suggest with respect to the black community. Moreover, in many cases black mayors, for example, have had sufficient time to empower the black community, for in "major cities such as Atlanta, Detroit, Gary, Los Angeles, and others, black mayors have controlled city hall for more than a decade" (Bobo and Gilliam, 1990:379). In my view, it is time to seriously consider the argument that black elected officials, no matter how well intended, cannot empower the black community. If true, this is a harsh conclusion, given the heroic struggles in the past by African-Americans to obtain the franchise, and the current obsession with electoral politics by black leaders. But these are precisely the reasons why this strategy of political office seeking must be questioned, for such a myopic quest could push the black community even lower than its present subordinate position.

The ability to exercise power is the essence of politics. Empowerment means having the leverage to allocate to one's constituency valuable resources that are unequally distributed within a society. In America valuable resources—money, wealth, good jobs, access to medical and legal services, ability to engage in consequential decision making, and the like—are unequally distributed along class, race, and gender lines. Thus, the black community is in a subordinate position because historically and currently it has been the victim of an interlocking system of class, race, and gender oppression. This oppression has left the black community relatively powerless, because it lacks the leverage to allocate valuable resources to its members. From this vantage point, black empowerment refers to a state in which political and economic representatives of the black community have real power to allocate valuable resources—especially economic resources—to their community, enabling it to effectively compete and bargain with other communities from a position of strength, rather than of dependency.

The analytical value of this political-economy approach to black empowerment seems obvious. Yet black empowerment is often defined as mere representation and influence, rather than as the actual exercise of power (Bobo and Gilliam, 1990). Employing these narrow criteria of empowerment, analysts often conclude that significant black empowerment has already occurred. This restricted view of empowerment probably stems from the tremendous political struggles African-Americans had to wage to break into electoral politics on a significant level. It is important to remember, however, that black people had to generate real power outside conventional channels in order to gain widespread access to the electoral arena. It was protest politics in the context of a grass-roots social movement that made electoral politics accessible to the black community.

A major reason why politicians and political apparatus emerge within a group is to solidify, manage, and protect group interest, especially economic interests. In this respect the paramount responsibility of the American state and its associated political parties is to protect and promote the economic interests of America's white upper classes. In the black community this process has worked in the reverse. Black politicians and black political machinery are proliferating, while the black community remains economically oppressed and locked out of the economic mainstream of the larger society. In many cases blacks are seeking and winning political offices already permeated with an institutional logic that protects and promotes white interest. In any case, black politicians usually find themselves seeking and presiding over political structures only marginally attached to their own group's interests. The essence of such politics is to substitute procedures and formality for substantive group interest. Under such conditions black politics have become the art of warring over empty shells, while the masses bear the cross of hunger and pain.

The analysis here is that real black empowerment flows from economic resources rather than from the mere acquisition of political office. Yet contemporary black politicians proceed as if their election to office is tantamount to black empowerment. The black masses are urged to register, vote, and mobilize the community for the purpose of electing blacks. What becomes paramount is winning city hall, seats in Congress, the governor's mansion, an aldermanic post, and the White House. In this logic the silent promise of the politician is "vote for me and I will set you free." The masses are convinced on a subtle level that once elected, black politicians will provide them with good jobs, economic parity, and social justice.

The question of whether black politicians have the wherewithal to empower the black community is sidestepped. Yet it is the real question that must be addressed head on by black politicians, leaders, and community activists if black politics are to be pursued intelligently. If this fails to happen, the black community may very well be rushing toward a political train disguised as a black liberator, but whose real destination is deeper black subordination. From all indications, office seeking appears to be the black politics of the future. The major strategy discussions in the community and leadership circles center around how to run the best campaign, how to appeal to white voters, how to select the best candidate, and how to appeal to a fragile black electorate riddled with class differences.

It is curious that debates addressing black economic empowerment and the development of strategies to accomplish such empowerment are virtually nonexistent among black political leaders. Yet it was precisely this agenda that emerged logically from the political struggles of the 1950s and 1960s. This quest for black economic empowerment led to the assassinations of black protest leaders and the heavy repression of the civil rights and black power movements. Indeed, white economic and political elites realized that money and other valuable resources would have to be distributed more equally in order for blacks and the poor to become economically empowered.

There are good reasons why black political leaders avoid generating or sharpening a debate focusing on black economic empowerment. Such a debate would reveal their lack of capacity to actually implement fundamental economic change within the black community. The masses would come to see that the winning of political offices is not synonymous with empowerment, and that such political behavior is susceptible to becoming largely a ritual of process and formal office-holding. Therefore black political leaders engage in the far-easier task of debating formal political procedures and how to win office. Electoral politics are probably the black politics of the future because black political leaders have developed a vested interest in steering the community down this barren route.

Nonetheless, an ongoing national debate on black economic empowerment would be fruitful for black political leaders and for the larger African-American community. To be useful, this debate would have to be pursued vigorously and honestly and include serious input from black political leaders, activists, scholars, business leaders, and clearly, as well as members of the African-American community. Such a debate should be deeply rooted in hard economic and political data, as well as in philosophy, and speculative thinking. It should be conducted within the institutions of the African-American community, and it should be democratic so as to prevent any particular segment of the community form directing it into narrow channels.

I believe that from this debate would emerge a number of important conclusions that could be utilized in building a politics of substance for the future. First, a dynamic relationship between black political leaders and the black masses must develop and be promoted if black politics are to become empowering and politically significant. Such a relationship is essential, because the inherent dynamics of electoral politics separate politicians from the masses and encourage only those superficial ties geared toward mobilizing the vote for the next election. This separation is catastrophic for the African-American community, because, unlike the white politician, whose role is to manage and protect an already-empowered constituency, the black politician must work for empowerment itself, which can only be accomplished in concert with the masses. In the absence of a dynamic relationship that unites leaders and masses, black politics will remain trapped in procedures and formalities and be characterized by internecine warfare among politicians, similar to that that erupted in Chicago following the death of Harold Washington.

Second, black electoral politics must embrace black protest politics; otherwise the former will remain impotent in terms of black empowerment. It is now commonplace for politicians and the black masses to view protest politics as weapons of the 1960s that have become obsolete for the modern period, where "real politics" are conducted in legislative halls and the offices of politicians. However, for a potent black politics to emerge capable of generating real empowerment, black politicians themselves must become empowered. Mass black protest is a critical ingredient capable of empowering black politicians. With the election of black politicians, the black masses have tended to become politically quiescent, believing either that their elected officials would realize their interests, or that protest would embarrass black office-holders or be perceived by hostile white forces as public attacks against black office-holders. This is unfortunate, because black protest could create the social conditions under which black politicians could more effectively wrestle economic and social goods from a recalcitrant society and could utilize those resources in an overall effort to empower the African-American community. In short, a mobilized protesting constituency is one that cannot be ignored and that in fact, becomes an important factor in the equation of power politics.

Black protest would also serve to counter the conservative tendencies inherent in electoral politics. Black politicians, like all politicians, must be kept honest and focused on the goal of black empowerment, and it is black protest that can keep them in check. Moreover, black protest is a central force that pulls the black community into the political process making them knowledgeable and politically efficacious. Without mass involvement and protest, it is unlikely that large economic corporations, the government, and other powerful white interests will share societal resources more equitably with the African-American community. Thus, the election of black officials ought to generate black protest rather than repel it, and black leaders, especially activists, must function as the vanguard in the generation and management of black protest. Black protest politics and electoral politics are the twin cornerstones necessary in the empowerment of the African-American community.

Third, black electoral politics are not likely to be dynamic and creative if they continue to be dominated by black males. What the African-American political community needs now are new, fresh, ideas concerning the strategies that should be explored and implemented in the search for black empowerment. Black women have unique insights rooted in their experience of class, race, and gender oppression and their familiarity with black family dynamics. These insights need to be incorporated into the political dialogue by the African-American community. For example, knowledge of how women support families on few resources is important, because it would help inform us about how to economically empower black families. Black women political leaders could also help empower the black community by revealing how sexism operates in this context. Sexism is a real liability in the black community, because it works against the mobilization and productivity of women and men.

In conclusion, I have argued that the current obsession with black electoral process, at the expense of actually empowering the African-American community, is a disturbing development. The current brand of black electoral politics stresses political procedures and office holding rather than actual activities and ideas capable of producing black empowerment. It was also stressed that economic empowerment is the crucial step that must be undertaken if black politics are to remain meaningful and useful. If black politicians fail to grapple with real economic empowerment, they will have rejected the historic mission hammered out by the heroic struggles of the civil rights and black power movements. Finally, we need a critical political science and sociology that will be able to conceptualize exactly what constitutes black empowerment and the tools that can measure the degree to which black empowerment has occurred as well as the degree to which the goal continues to elude us. It is time to open debate on how to achieve complete black liberation.

———————————————————◼———————————————————

*A second critique of empowerment theory is that it clings to a style of politics that is passe. In **"End of the Rainbow"** Jim Sleeper argues that the model of "Rainbow" politics forwarded by most black mayors in the 1970s and 1980s has led to "identity politics" that exacerbate, rather than subdue racial tensions. "Rainbow I" mayors are a protest elite centered in the traditional civil rights organizations. They are typically committed to an agenda of "racial group rights" based on their "victim" status. In contrast, the changing demographics of most large cities has spawned a new style of urban leadership that Sleeper dubs "Rainbow II." These mayors are typically white businessmen or black technocrats who ". . . practice fiscal conservatism* *and reject race-based politics." Richard Riordan (LA), Rudolph Giuliani (NY), Michael White (Cleveland), William Campbell (Atlanta), and Dennis Archer (Detroit) are all examples of Rainbow II mayors. Their strategy has been to develop a coalition among white voters disenchanted with civil rights era politics, other racial minorities who feel excluded (e.g., Asians and Latinos), and broker an alliance with some portions of the black political establishment. Rainbow I politics, from this perspective, polarize racial groups and lead to balkanization. Sleeper concluded that, "[O]nly if Rainbow II succeeds will cities regain their promise . . ."[8]*

THE END OF THE RAINBOW

Jim Sleeper

Copyright The New Republic, *Inc. (1993)*

On a trip to Israel in July, New York Mayor David Dinkins's eyes welled with tears as he recalled a close friendship with his accountant of many years, the late Abe Nowick, a Jew, in which racial differences had mattered so little that "one didn't know what the other was." It was a moment emblematic of the healer New Yorkers hoped Dinkins would be when they elected him over U.S. Attorney Rudolph Giuliani in 1989, shortly after young whites in Brooklyn's Bensonhurst section murdered Yusef Hawkins, a black youth who had wandered onto their turf to look at a used car. It was emblematic, too, of the promise of black "Rainbow" mayoralties in multiracial cities in the 1970s and 1980s—Tom Bradley in Los Angeles, Harold Washington in Chicago, and Wilson Goode in Philadelphia, to name a few.

Yet, just as those other rainbows have faded, the ecumenical side of Dinkins on display in Jerusalem has been eclipsed in the years since his "Vote your hopes, not your fears" victory four years ago. Challenged by Giuliani again this year, Dinkins has been reduced in part to running a "Vote your fears" campaign. A string of recent public claims by Dinkins supporters that Giuliani is backed by the Ku Klux Klan, fascists and Reaganites (although conservatives such as William Bennett and Pat Buchanan denounce Giuliani as a liberal) may coax some voters back into Dinkins' corner. But a victory at this price would hardly repeat the harmonic convergence that was once the rationale for a Dinkins candidacy.

What went wrong? There are two reasons for the decay of Dinkins's rainbow politics, neither peculiar to New York. First, a deep recession and economic upheaval demand a "reinventing" of local government that seems utterly beyond the reach of a mayor whose political style is more common in Europe than in America: that of a social-democratic wheelhorse. Dinkins's failure to articulate a rationale for municipal restructuring, much less attempt it against union and black clubhouse opposition, is one reason his government is torn by racial and other subgroup squabbling over jobs, entitlements and preferments.

Second, Dinkins's failures of leadership during a long, black boycott of Korean stores and amid black rioting against Hasidic Jews in Crown Heights are only the best-known of many abdications to the politics of victimization (among them his year-long delay of a contract for street toilets in deference to activists' demands that each one be wheelchair accessible). Such muddlings highlight the rainbow ideology's tendency to deepen racial and other differences in the name of respecting them; in the zero-sum game of urban governance, identity politics implodes.

Meanwhile Giuliani, the erstwhile altar boy with a Savonarola streak and a mostly-white inner circle, has created a Republican-liberal "fusion" slate, with Herman Badillo, the city's most distinguished Hispanic politician, running for comptroller. They claim they want to subordinate parochial grievances to a single, uniform civic standard. Alluding to the Korean boycott, Giuliani says he wants to convince blacks that "If I were mayor and some Italian-Americans were intimidating a black shopkeeper, I'd come down on them hard and fast. People have to be able to feel confident that they'll be protected, whatever the mayor's color."

It's a familiar pattern. Beyond New York, the Rainbow habit of crying racism has found itself discounted by voters of all colors who want better governance and less rhetoric. Politically centrist mayoral candidates, many of them, ironically, white men, have drawn substantial numbers of nonwhite voters into new coalitions—call them Rainbow II—by touting a can-do pragmatism and a common civic identity that is more than the sum of skin tones, genders, sexual orientations, and resentments. The truth they've grasped remains obscure only to some in liberal Democratic circles and the academy: The more genuinely multicultural and racially diverse a city becomes, the less "liberal" it is in the Rainbow I sense of the term.

The pattern emerges from half a dozen donnybrooks of the past three years, including Houston and Philadelphia in 1991 and Los Angeles and Jersey City in 1992. In each, the liberal candidate, usually a person of color, had the mantle of the civil rights movement, the support of a multiracial, multicultural coalition, and the endorsement of Jesse Jackson. He was militantly pro-choice, anti-death penalty and in favor of the most expansive gay rights and immigrant rights agendas around. He was applauded in black churches and endorsed by liberal newspapers. He may not have had much of an economic program, but he branded his white male opponent a closet Reaganite and sounded the trumpet for "progressive" unity.

The white male opponent, who typically had never held elective office, posed as a businesslike reformer, promising to clean house and create new jobs through commercial deregulation, better public safety, less onerous taxation, and tougher union contracts. Preaching tolerance rather than correctness and touting endorsements from prominent Latinos and other minority leaders who had broken with the civil rights establishment, he vowed to unite the city across racial and partisan lines.

Closer examination turns up telling ironies. In Chicago's 1989 special election to fill out the late Harold Washington's term, Richard M. Daley, a son of—but also a reformer of—his father's infamous machine, trounced alderman Timothy Evans, who claimed the mantle of Washington's paradigmatic Rainbow I coalition and was backed enthusiastically by Jackson. Two years later, against a black former judge running on the Harold Washington party line, Daley carried 80 percent of the city's small but critical Latino vote and 26 percent of the black vote (up from just 7 percent in 1989).

Similarly, in Houston in 1991, Robert Lanier, a wealthy white real estate developer and native New Yorker, took 70 percent of the Latino vote to defeat Sylvester Turner, a black, Harvard-educated state legislator backed solidly by blacks and white Rainbow I liberals tied to former Mayor Kathy Whitmire. The popular Lanier—the first candidate in 20 years to be elected mayor with virtually no support from the 25 percent of the city's electorate that is black— is a shoo-in this fall for another two-year term.

That same year in Philadelphia, Edward Rendell, a Jewish New York native and, like Giuliani, a tough-talking ex-prosecutor, won the mayoralty by preaching fiscal austerity and municipal restructuring in a city facing bankruptcy. Campaigning energetically in the black community, he took 20 percent of the black vote against three black Democratic primary opponents before trouncing a Republican to succeed Philadelphia's first black mayor, Wilson Goode.

In July of this year, Los Angeles's Richard Riordan, another native New Yorker and a Wall Street investor, succeeded five-termer Bradley in the 58 percent non-white city by carrying 43 percent of the Latino vote, 31 percent of the Asian American vote, 14 percent of the black vote and 67 percent of the white vote against Rainbow I Democrat Michael Woo, a councilman who had led the opposition against Police Chief Daryl Gates. Riordan's Rainbow II is embryonic, at best, however: 72 percent of those who voted in the election were white. He has responded with high-level appointments of blacks, Latinos, Asians, and gays.

Across the continent in Jersey City, both mayoral finalists this spring were white, yet the Rainbow II scenario was otherwise unchanged. Republican Wall Street investor Bret Schundler, yet another ex-New Yorker, beat a Jackson-backed Democrat by winning 40 percent of the black vote and 60 percent of the Latino vote in that majority nonwhite city. This, even after Jackson warned in radio spots that his candidate represented "the values of the usa— the United States of America," while a vote for Schundler was a vote for "the values of the usa—the Union of South Africa."

It was, of course, nothing of the kind. Neither was Daley's victory in Chicago—which Jackson tried to prevent by linking Daley to his father's infamous "shoot to kill" order against arsonists in 1968—simply a white racist restoration. The new mayors have won by tapping a growing disillusionment with old-style "civil rights" politics among voters whom the movement has betrayed, and by including new racial minorities who feel excluded by black-led Rainbow I administrations.

The new mayors depart, respectfully but firmly, from the politics of such trailblazing black mayors as Gary, Indiana's Richard Hatcher, Cleveland's Carl Stokes, Atlanta's Maynard Jackson, Detroit's Coleman Young, New Orleans's Ernest "Dutch" Morial, Chicago's Harold Washington, and the District of Columbia's Marion Barry. Most of these men were broad-shouldered veterans of elemental, often brutal struggles for racial justice that had honed their leadership qualities and introduced them to class—as well as race-consciousness. Most won narrowly against unyielding white hostility.

In office, they had to outmaneuver scheming white politicians, censorious editorial boards and rebellious subordinates in heavily white municipal work forces. With rhetoric, if not redress, they had to relieve the pent-up frustrations of blacks long exiled from city politics and jobs. Civic elites demanded that they end black crime. Businessmen, taking advantage of the mayors' desperation about economic decay, co-opted them into "big bang" development schemes that siphoned city resources from poor neighborhoods. Detroit's Young became defensive and bitter, Marion Barry dissolute and corrupt. Harold Washington seemed to thrive on frustration, towering over his more parochial black supporters and white adversaries alike, but he died in office. Literally and figuratively, the hearts of black mayors were broken by their divided cities.

At the same time, though, some black trailblazers and their Rainbow I successors have shifted from protecting basic individual rights and mobilizing economic coalitions to touting racial group rights and policies that are gratuitously destructive of traditional families. It's almost as if Rainbow I administrations simply presume, and so accelerate, civic and social balkanization. They often pit blacks against almost everyone else, not just against declining white electorates.

It is here, in the interaction of shifting civil rights strategies and changing urban demographics, that Rainbow I meets its end. In the years after 1970, 10 million immigrants, the vast majority of them nonwhite, entered American cities. Today, 40 percent of Angelenos and 30 percent of New Yorkers are foreign-born. These Mexican and Filipino laborers, Chinese and Puerto Rican seamstresses, Pakistani and Haitian cabbies and Korean and Dominican merchants often bring with them notions of race that are more fluid and ecumenical than those of American blacks or whites. They don't necessarily embrace a Rainbow I agenda of affirmative action and group rights-oriented litigation that presumes victimization by white racism. They rely more heavily on family and communal ties in order to achieve success.

For example, the immigrants of color in New York City's poorest census tracts are three times more likely than their American black and Puerto Rican neighbors to live in two-parent households. They're more likely to work within ethnic niches of the economy and to favor public spending on police and schools rather than on welfare, foster care, homeless shelters, and drug treatment. The median incomes of Caribbean blacks and Asian Indians exceed those of American blacks, blunting charges of institutional racism. Chinese and Mexican immigrants' incomes are lower, but their family structures and values point upward. Even the high level of welfare dependency among Soviet refugees only underscores that culture, not racism, is the key variable in urban success.

Polls and voting patterns suggest that most newcomers are wary of the stigma and polarization that often accompany race-based politics and programs such as all-black schools, racial districting, municipal affirmative action quotas and multicultural curricula. In recent New York City school board elections, ten of thirteen Asian candidates, and half of the Hispanic candidates, ran against a liberal "Children of the Rainbow" curriculum, backed by Dinkins, and Giuliani has sometimes led Dinkins in polls of Asians and Latinos.

The future is visible in an editorial in San Diego's Mexican-American newspaper *La Prensa*, cited recently by Jack Miles in *The Atlantic*, that heralds Latinos as the new "bridge between blacks, whites, Asians and Latinos. They [Latinos] will have to bring an end to class, color and ethnic warfare. To succeed, they will have to do what the blacks failed to do: incorporate all into the human race and exclude no one."

Demographic change is also accelerating Rainbow I's passing by diminishing black clout. Latinos, vital to Rainbow II victories, now outnumber blacks in Los Angeles and will do so in New York, Houston and Jersey City by the next census. Latinos have long outnumbered blacks in such Sunbelt and Western cities as Miami, San Antonio and Denver; the last two elected Henry Cisneros and Federico Pena, both now in Clinton's Cabinet, an honor shared by no former black mayor. The risk is that the new, multiracial coalitions will be openly anti-black.

Yet Rainbow II politics are by no means off-limits to black mayors, who do well among whites when they abandon a Rainbow I agenda. In 1989 Cleveland's Michael White became Rainbow II's first prominent black mayoral standard-bearer after defeating a "blacker-than-thou" opponent; he is a shoo-in for re-election next month. Denver and Seattle, both about 70 percent white, elected Wellington Webb and Norman Rice, black mayors who defy Rainbow I stereotypes. Both practice fiscal conservatism and reject race-based politics. Similarly, Chester Jenkins, the black mayor of mostly white Durham, North Carolina, credits Jesse Jackson with energizing black voters, but, describing his own campaign, says, "I didn't speak of a rainbow coalition. I'm sure that turns a lot of white people off. People think that when a black person is running, he is going to be a big taxer and spender. I'm not that way." Even in heavily black cities, where the first black mayors have left the field to black candidates hawking everything from nationalist paranoia to race-neutral economic realism, debate is less often foreclosed by charges that any candidate's views are racist.

But it's one thing for Rainbow II mayors to win by arguing that the poor, who want to live decently, and the middle class, which wants to live safely, have a common interest in restructuring government. Actually shifting government's emphasis from bureaucratic compassion to urban reconstruction is harder. A disabled federal government—the legacy of Reaganomics—forces mayors to choose between aiding today's casualties and making investments that might prevent more casualties tomorrow.

There's a flawed Democratic legacy at work here, too: In the 1960s, Great Society funding drove cities to increase the social welfare portions of their budgets from around 15 percent to as much as 30 percent. Today, most cities can't meet their needs merely through tough bargaining, more productivity and privatization. The choices mayors face do follow racial fault lines, imperiling efforts to put civic-consciousness above race-consciousness.

One who seems undaunted by these risks is Edward Rendell, the new mayor of Philadelphia. A city of 1.6 million people, it is about half white, 40 percent black and 6 percent Latino. A son of Manhattan's West Side with a voice like Mel Brooks, he moved to Philadelphia to attend the University of

Pennsylvania and served as district attorney before winning the mayoralty in 1991.

The city had become insolvent in the late 1980s under its first black mayor, Wilson Goode. Its bonds had been downgraded, it was borrowing at credit card rates and it was running a structural deficit amounting to 10 percent of its $2.3 billion budget, owing to the collapse of its manufacturing base, federal cutbacks, and generous union contracts. Goode, a stiff Wharton manager and a passive subscriber to Rainbow I nostrums, had alienated blacks as well as whites while deferring necessary reforms. His infamous bombing of move headquarters in 1985, which destroyed a block of residential homes, was only a symptom of his lack of command.

With Goode retiring, Rendell decided to run against three black Democratic candidates by presenting himself as a "New Democrat," an apostle of David Osborne's and Ted Gaebler's Reinventing Government. When the candidates were asked whether they would accept a strike of city workers if it was necessary to turn the city around, "the other three hemmed and hawed," Rendell recalled in an interview with *Newsday*. "I looked in the camera and said, 'I hope it doesn't become necessary, but there's a decent chance it will. The answer to your question is yes. I don't want a strike, but if a strike's necessary to bring about the type of changes we need, then I'm ready.'" Rendell's strong personality and the city's desperate straits made the election a referendum on whether Philadelphia could look beyond color for candor about its condition.

Rendell could promise not to roll back blacks' political gains relative to whites' because, thanks to enlightened civil service reforms in the '50s, Philadelphia had long had a municipal work force as black as its population. As early as 1964, its police department had been 22 percent black, while nearby Newark and Detroit were at 5 percent. Equally important, Philadelphia has a 20-year-old black political establishment that predated Goode and doesn't countenance the super-heated racial rhetoric common in New York or Detroit. Rendell won an absolute majority in a four-way primary, carrying 20 percent of the black vote against his black opponents. "It's not that the era of the black mayor is over," he reflected, "The era of blacks voting lockstep for black candidates is over."

In office, Rendell forged an alliance with newly elected City Council President John Street. "He handled the transition very smoothly, made deals with the black political leadership," comments Philadelphia Inquirer columnist Acel Moore. The city's mayors often have been at loggerheads with its council for institutional, not racial, reasons. Rendell courted Street, giving him an implicit veto on some initiatives.

That meant giving ground on privatization—keeping the new convention center under city management, for example, lest black jobs be lost. Yet Rendell privatized custodial services, prison health services, and other functions, and says that similar initiatives will soon save $40 million. He insists that all whose jobs are privatized can be hired by other agencies or private contractors. But the contractors impose steep pay and benefit cuts, the point of privatization being to save money at workers' expense. And, as recent New

York City scandals involving asbestos removal and parking ticket collections show, privatization can bring corruption and incompetence. Rendell counters that most city unions can avoid such troubles by changing their own work rules to improve productivity.

Rendell and Street also scaled back, by roughly $100 million, a fat trash collection contract negotiated by Goode. That meant weathering the feared strike. When union leaders cried that "an administration of white guys in suits" was beating up on black employees, the new mayor challenged black voters: "Do you get twenty paid sick days on your job? Do you get fourteen paid holidays?" The strike lasted less than a day after Rendell gave union leaders face-saving exits.

Philadelphia is still a city in decline. Its large public housing authority, which shelters 10 percent of the populace, is mired in patronage and corruption. Its industrial areas are in ruins. Its tax structure is a mess. But Rendell is at least candid about his city's options. Rainbow I mayors like Goode (and, notably, Dinkins) tend to live in denial, railing at Washington without seriously rethinking their own emphasis on rights and re-distributive services. Rendell argues that mayors who want a new federal urban policy will have credibility "only if we come to Washington with clean hands."

Rendell is not the only Rainbow II trailblazer. In Cleveland, Michael White, a self-described street fighter from the city's tough East Side, combines an "attitude" toward powerful elites with a fierce determination to reinforce conservative social values in a distinctively black idiom. He ran for mayor in 1989 as a maverick state senator and won partly on a fluke: the two white candidates in the primary were so equally matched that they canceled out each other, and White squeaked past them into a runoff with the most powerful black politician in town, City Council President George Forbes. For the first time, Cleveland's electorate, half black, half white, faced a choice between two blacks.

White had made the runoff partly on his own steam, too, with a forceful campaign against black crime, school busing and Forbes's penchant for playing the race card, which had enraged many whites. "White articulated a vision and said the same thing on both sides of town," says *Plain Dealer* columnist Brent Larkin. He argued that blacks who opposed busing didn't have to fear saying so just because whites opposed it, too. In an ugly runoff with Forbes, White won with 30 percent of the black vote and 90 percent of the white vote—an inauspicious beginning for a black mayor by Rainbow I standards, but one he soon turned to his advantage among blacks.

Since the rocky reign of its first black mayor, Carl Stokes, in the late 1960s, Cleveland's population has dropped roughly 30 percent, to 505,000. Under a succession of white mayors, including ethnic populist Dennis Kucinich and corporate darling George Voinovich, Cleveland touted itself as a comeback city with a sleek new skyline and, not far off, a $365 million stadium for the Indians that will rival Baltimore's Camden Yards. But more than a third of Cleveland's population lives below the poverty line, and much of its East Side is an inner-city moonscape.

White has tackled some problems that his white predecessors avoided. Although he doesn't run the city's elected school board, he backed a winning, insurgent, biracial slate opposed to busing. He won give-backs, reduced overtime and one-cop patrol cars from city unions. He backed cops in crack-house evictions and a controversial case involving the death in police custody of a drug-abusing black suspected of car theft.

White has been criticized by blacks and white liberals for these positions and for scolding Jesse Jackson at the 1992 Democratic National Convention in New York, when Jackson criticized Bill Clinton after his nomination was inevitable. White's obvious pride in being black has helped him on the East Side, but "he has consciously attempted not to be a 'black' mayor," Larkin says. "If anything, he makes a conscious effort to be a mayor who happens to be black." Civil rights leaders may not like that, but Cleveland's voters do.

As White's and Rendell's accomplishments mirror one another, Rainbow II moves to the center of urban politics from both sides of the racial divide. This is nowhere more clear than in New York, where a Dinkins defeat would mark the first time that a big city's first black mayor has ever lost a re-election bid. Such a defeat, especially amid the liberal fear-mongering about racism and fascism now underway in New York, would be a telling repudiation of 20 years of misguided racial politics.

But a Giuliani victory would not settle the question of whether Rainbow II administrations can regenerate American cities as places where new products, ideas and people circulate freely across the lines of color and class. Full black participation in that exchange is what the early civil rights movement sought, and what more recent black attacks on the liberal civic culture have repelled. Can new mayors outflank or creatively redirect such assaults?

The challenge ought to be irresistible to Democrats, who bring to cities a sophistication at governing and a love of urbanity. But those who cling to Rainbow I social-welfare spending and identity politics will continue to default to Republican neophytes such as Los Angeles's Riordan, Jersey City's Schundler or, indeed, Giuliani. Only if Democrats follow the example of candidate Clinton, who spoke for those "who work hard and play by the rules," and who rebuffed that consummate Rainbow I phony, Sister Souljah, can they expect to win like Rendell and White. Only if Rainbow II succeeds will cities regain their promise and, not incidentally, nourish the occasional friendship where "one didn't know what the other was."

Raphael Sonenshein, in his article **"The Battle Over Liquor Stores in South Central Los Angeles,"** *shows the inherent difficulties for advocates of coalition politics in large multiethnic cities. As he points out, ethnic and racial conflict in American cities is increasingly played out as relations between various nonwhite communities. Using the debate between African-Americans and Koreans over liquor stores in the wake of the Los Angeles urban unrest of 1992 as a case study, Sonenshein identifies three critical variables in assessing the potential for interminority coalitions: group interest, shared racial ideology, and the role of leadership. It was clear from the outset that blacks and Koreans had fundamentally different material interests. On the one hand, Korean merchants had a vested financial stake in the liquor stores. Any attempt to impose regulations represented a threat to their livelihood. On the other, leaders in the African-American community viewed the liquor stores as damaging to the social fabric of their environment. Moreover, the two communities had very little common ideological ground.*

Thus, the critical factor to a compromise was the vision and willingness of leaders on both sides to reject framing the issue as a racial and ethnic conflict. Instead, they were able to focus attention on questions of community development; questions that both sides agreed were essential to the economic and social viability of South Central Los Angeles. The broader implications of the case study speak to the idea that the resolution of interminority conflict—even in the presence of competing group interests and weak ideological ties—depends on the willingness of community leaders to resist the short-term gains of identity politics in favor of identifying shared goals.

THE BATTLE OVER LIQUOR STORES IN SOUTH CENTRAL LOS ANGELES: THE MANAGEMENT OF AN INTERMINORITY CONFLICT

Raphael J. Sonenshein

Urban Affairs Review, *Vol. 31, No. 6, July 1996 710–737, 1996 Sage Publications, Inc.*

Most of the literature on interracial conflict and coalition is drawn from the relationship between blacks and whites. These explorations have helped illuminate the possibilities for interracial coalitions and the likelihood of broad interracial polarization.

The civil unrest that struck Los Angeles in 1992 and the earlier violence that hit Miami in 1981 have forcefully shown the need to study conflicts and coalitions among nonwhite communities. Conflict between blacks and Hispanics in Miami is at the core of the city's racial polarization (Portes and Stepick 1993), and in the Los Angeles violence of 1992, most of the commercial establishments that were destroyed were owned by Korean Americans (Tierney 1994; Ong and Hee 1993).

For those who live in inner cities, relationships with other minorities are clear and present, more immediate, and closer to home than the building of broad political coalitions. The population of U.S. cities is changing dramatically as new groups enter and existing groups decline. Inner-city residents are increasingly interacting with other minorities on a daily basis (Oliver and Johnson 1984). Life in the inner city has much to do with negotiations over resources and territory among minority groups. The outcome of these negotiations could greatly affect the ability of people in the inner city to obtain and exercise power over their own environment.

What are the prospects for interminority coalitions in the intense cauldron of the inner city? Those who favor rainbow coalitions might be encouraged that such interminority contacts could create communities of color able to pursue common objectives in a political coalition (Henry 1980). However, in much of the literature, scholars have focused on interminority conflict as the most likely outcome (Johnson and Oliver 1989; Miles 1992).

Theoretical notions advanced in the study of coalitions between blacks and whites might be helpful in understanding interminority dynamics. There have long been lively debates about interracial coalitions and the basis on which they might be built.

In their classic book *Black Power*, Carmichael and Hamilton (1967) high-lighted the role of self-interest in coalitions, arguing that only groups with an independent power base and their own interests in mind can form productive coalitions. They made a crucial contribution by moving the discussion of coalition beyond sentimental notions of goodwill alone as the basis for coalitions.

In *Protest Is Not Enough*, Browning, Marshall, and Tabb (1984) argued that racial ideology played a central role in the development of interracial coalitions. Shared racial liberalism fostered the ability of blacks and Hispanics to win a share of power in city politics in the 10 northern California cities they studied. Successful biracial and multiracial coalitions between minorities and liberal whites marked those cities in which there was the greatest degree of minority political success.

Ideology and interest, however, are insufficient to explain the dynamics of interracial politics and of coalitions in general. Even in the same community, interracial coalitions rise and fall. In her critique of traditional coalition theory, Hinckley (1981) noted that trust among leaders is an essential factor in coalition success. Leadership plays a highly underrated role in the resolution of ethnic and racial conflicts.

In an earlier study (Sonenshein 1993), I presented an alternative theory of interracial coalitions. Shared ideology—in this case, racial liberalism—is indeed an essential feature of interracial coalition politics. However, once shared ideology is in place, self-interest plays an important role in the extent of coalition success. Leadership plays a crucial and very human role in whether shared ideology can build on interest alliances or transcend interest conflict. Thus interracial political coalitions can be analyzed as the interplay among interest, ideology, and leadership.

BACKGROUND

Los Angeles, the second-largest city in the United States, has become the frontier outpost of ethnic and racial diversity. With its large and varied population, Los Angeles may be on the verge of developing a new multiethnic politics. Whites now constitute less than 40% of the population, and Hispanics and Asian-Americans represent half the city. The proportion of blacks has declined to about 14%.

In pure numbers, racial minorities constitute a majority of the city. But there are many obstacles in the way of such a new majority. As Erie, Brackman, and Ingram (1993, 67) have noted. "The rainbow model is an ideological gloss that obscures as much as it illuminates the realities of ethnic power in Los Angeles."

Electoral politics in Los Angeles is still largely a matter involving blacks and whites and, to a lesser degree, Hispanics, although the inner-city community itself is more and more a rainbow. Of the eligible votes, three-fourths are either white or black (Pactech Data and Research, Inc. 1992). In the April 1993 mayoral primary, fully 86% of those who voted were either white (68%) or black (18%). Only 8% were Hispanic and 4% were Asian-American (*Los*

Angeles Times, 22 April 1993). Of those who voted in the general election, 72% were white, 12% were black, 10% were Hispanic, and 4% were Asian-American (*Los Angeles Times,* 10 June 1993).

South Central Los Angeles (which will later be referred to as South Central), once the heart of the black community, is now a poor and working-class community in which space is uneasily shared among three groups: blacks, who have a great deal of political representation but a depressed economic situation; a young immigrant Hispanic community, working at low wages and having virtually no political representation; and Korean Americans, who constitute a merchant class, not residing in South Central and coexisting uneasily in the neighborhoods.

Along the three dimensions of interest, ideology, and leadership (Sonenshein 1993), the South Central community faces major obstacles to coalition. Of the three groups, only blacks are fully active in the political arena and are recognizably liberal and Democratic. The represent the vast share of the registered voters of South Central. Rather than needing coalition politics, blacks hold a virtual monopoly of political power in the area at the same time that they have lost substantial power citywide.

In South Central, blacks retain virtually all the official political power, holding city council, state assembly, state senate, and county supervisorial posts. The public institutions of South Central, such as public hospitals, are largely run by blacks, although the clientele is overwhelmingly Hispanic.

There are few ideological linkages between blacks and Korean Americans (Jackson 1988). In addition to the hostilities that have grown up between the two communities, there is little evidence of shared political values or commitments. Indeed, there is substantial evidence of ill will (Thornton and Taylor 1988; Jo 1992).

At the same time, economic investment is most visibly dominated by the mom-and-pop stores that dot the community, which are principally owned by Korean Americans. The relationship between blacks and Korean Americans, particularly in the liquor store controversy, reveals a clear conflict of interest. The most obvious conflict is that the movement to limit liquor stores directly affects the store owners' livelihoods.

In inner-city neighborhoods from New York City to Chicago to Los Angeles, the role of liquor stores has become an important political issue (*New York Times,* 29 November 1992). As other businesses leave the inner city, the sign that reads "liquor" remains a troubling symbol of remaining economic activity—as well as a constant reminder of the social problems of poverty.

The prominence of liquor stores has set off community protests in a number of cities. Community groups have pressured liquor companies to stop encouraging young people in the inner city to drink alcohol, especially the most fortified brands. They have demanded that liquor stores already in operation take some responsibility for the effects of their presence in the community. Some groups have sought to limit new liquor stores or to close existing stores.

The conflict over liquor stores has developed overtones of interethnic conflict in recent years. At times, these controversies have pitted blacks against store owners of different ethnic and racial backgrounds—particularly Korean Americans. These battles have overlapped with the even more complex question of ethnic control of small businesses in minority neighborhoods in an era of rising immigration to U.S. cities (Light and Bonacich 1988).

New York City has witnessed major conflict between black activists and Korean-American store owners, leading to an extremely bitter boycott of a Korean-American grocery store in Brooklyn in 1990 (*New York Times*, 25 September 1990). In Indianapolis, a militant black organization pressured the Korean-American owner of a beauty supply store to respond to its demands (Indianapolis *Star*, 16 May 1993).

The Los Angeles violence of 1992 highlighted the growing importance of the uncomfortable relationship between inner-city residents and Korean-American merchants. A number of Korean Americans lost their lives to armed robbers, and in a dramatic case, a young black woman, LaTasha Harlins, was shot and killed by a Korean-American grocer, Soon Ja Du, after an altercation in the store. Activists in the black community organized a 1991 boycott of several Korean-owned stores (Freer 1994).

In the context of interest conflict and lack of ideological common ground, the burden of leadership has been acute in the management of the conflict over liquor stores. In particular, in the midst of interethnic conflict, leaders could potentially influence whether the liquor store controversy would be seen exclusively within the volatile framework of the conflict between blacks and Korean Americans.

RESEARCH

This research, largely conducted in late 1992 and throughout 1993, was based on interviews with key participants in the liquor store controversy, examination of newspaper and magazine articles in the black and Korean-American communities, attendance at city hall hearings, examination of city council files, and examination of legal documents in a lawsuit on liquor stores. The controversy has been explored from the perspectives of the community activists in South Central, the liquor store owners (many of whom are Korean Americans), and governmental decision makers.

LIQUOR AND SOUTH CENTRAL LOS ANGELES

The exodus of bank branches, large grocery stores, and movie theaters from South Central has created a major gap that has been increasingly filled by stores in which the most profitable commodity is liquor. Stores that cash checks, sell groceries, and offer convenience items fill a major functional role in the community. They also provide a vehicle for the liquor industry to sell its products in areas in which there is much money to be made.

The sale and location of liquor licenses are regulated by the state of California through the Department of Alcoholic Beverage Control. Although a state formula limits the concentration of liquor stores, it operates only by county. There are no state restrictions on liquor license location *within* counties. There is nothing to prevent most or even all liquor licenses in one county from being concentrated in a single area. In addition, some liquor stores gained approval by providing *public conveniences and necessities,* such as selling groceries or providing check-cashing services, that are not widely available in a neighborhood. These gaps in state law have combined with the short supply of normal commercial institutions to create the conditions for the overconcentration of liquor stores in South Central.

There are an astonishing number of liquor stores in South Central. A mayoral task force reported that "in a 40 square mile area, there are 682 licenses. This equates to 17 licenses per square mile, compared to 1.6 per square mile in the remainder of Los Angeles County" (Mayor Bradley's South Central Community/Merchant Liquor Task Force 1992, 1). Liquor stores have been located on virtually every corner. In South Central, the two main institutions still present in great numbers are liquor stores and churches (*Los Angeles Times*, 24 October 1983).

Beginning in the early 1980s, and accelerating by 1986, there was a major change of ownership of liquor stores in South Central. The transfer of liquor licenses from one owner to another did not constitute a new mode of operation and did not trigger the conditional-use process. From then on, the liquor store issue developed a new interracial and interethnic focus.

The ownership of liquor stores in South Central was not the main form of business for the thousands of Korean Americans who were flocking to Los Angeles. Indeed, by one estimate, only 9% of Korean-American businesses were even located in South Central (Kwong 1992, 29). A *Los Angeles Times* survey of Korean Americans within Los Angeles County conducted just before the civil unrest found that only 4% were involved in the liquor store business (*Los Angeles Times* Poll 1992). Those Korean Americans who came to South Central were the least affluent Korean-American merchants, attracted by low prices of entry in the face of many dangers of doing business (Fruto and Wibecan 1992).

Conflicts developed quickly and were often attributed to cultural misunderstandings. Violent incidents occurred with alarming frequency, and a number of Korean-American shopkeepers were killed in their stores. As mentioned earlier, in 1991, a Korean-American storekeeper shot and killed a young black woman. The Black-Korean Alliance, which was originally formed in 1986, tried to bridge the troubled waters (*Los Angeles Times*, 9 November 1992), but tensions continued at a high level.

Cultural misunderstandings were only part of the story. On top of the inherent tensions between owners of small shops and inner-city residents, the pace of Korean-American entry into the community was somewhat unlike that of earlier groups. Many Korean Americans were very recent immigrants. Heer and Herman (1990, 5) estimated that between 1980 and 1986, the overall Korean-American population of Los Angeles County increased by 98.7%.

Some came to South Central after several years of building capital, and others brought capital with them from the sale of real estate in Korea (Fruto and Wibecan 1992). Many had no idea what they were getting into and were unprepared for doing business in a tense and polarized inner city. Language was itself a major obstacle. The *Los Angeles Times Poll* (1992) reported that 61% of those Korean Americans who were in the United States five years or less indicated that they did not speak English well. Nearly 50% of all Korean Americans in the survey indicated that language was far and away the major obstacle holding their group back in Southern California. The situation was ripe for conflict.

The merchants also pursued a strategy of legal threat, an area about which the city government was extremely sensitive. When the city passed the emergency ordinance that required public hearings for rebuilding liquor stores, the store owners filed a lawsuit in superior court. The city attorney's very cautious approach may have reflected concern about leaving the city vulnerable to legal action.

In sum, as the city deliberated over what to do about liquor stores in South Central in the aftermath of the violence, two major constituencies had made an appearance. One was the long-standing South Central community. The other was a newly emergent Korean-American community, alert to the need to protect its damaged interests. Both sides sought to influence leaders and public opinion and to mount effective legal campaigns. How did government officials deal with these intense cross pressures?

Walters' original amendment, which had not passed the council, had called for a wholly new procedure for evaluating liquor stores. In the view of Dale Goldsmith (private attorney and the coalition's legal advisor, interview with the author, 24 February 1993),

> the city ended up compromising between the one extreme, which was the community wanting a full new conditional-use permit review, treating these uses as essentially new uses which could be approved, and then the other would be the owners and KAGRO who wanted nothing at all. So the city, in its Solomon-like wisdom, set up the plan approval process.

The plan approval process led both sides into a long-lasting, case-by-case review of each request for rebuilding.

The city attorney, James K. Hahn, was particularly careful to protect the city from legal liability. Despite his electoral base in the black community, Hahn drew a narrow interpretation of the planning commission's power to limit liquor stores. When the owners took the city to court anyway, the coalition filed a motion to intervene on the city's side, fearing that the city would protect only its own interests (*Korean American Legal Advocacy Foundation, Inc. v. City of Los Angeles* [28 Cal. 2d 530, 1994], ex parte application for leave to intervene, 18 June 1993, 10–11).

The coalition pursued its case both in the planning commission and in the zoning commission. The zoning commission has the power to prevent the sale of liquor on the grounds that the store represents a nuisance. The procedure

requires the imposition of conditions and a six-month evaluation period before the zoning commission can act, subject to override by the city council.
Bass (interview, 5 March 1993) noted, "It's always been our tactic to file revo-
cations and to go after the rebuilds, to hit it from all sides, as well as to block.
It was a three-pronged strategy."

Over the next few months, city hall officials floated a number of ideas to
settle the controversy. The first was the method often used to preserve Mayor
Bradley's coalition—the outside task force. On 29 June 1992, Bradley and
Ridley-Thomas (eighth district), chairperson of the council's Ad Hoc Committee on Recovery and Revitalization, appointed a South Central Commu-
nity/Merchant Liquor Task Force. Cochaired by one black and one Korean
American and assisted by various city officials, the task force was to issue a
report to Ridley-Thomas's ad hoc council committee. For a time, the task
force played the role of diffusing and defusing controversy; questions about
how the city would respond could be referred to the task force. Many assumed that the task force would find a way to compensate store owners for
not reopening liquor stores.

However, the final report of the task force (Mayor Bradley's South Central
Community/Merchant Liquor Task Force 1992), issued on 18 November
1992, was marked by an agreement to disagree. Revealingly, each side submitted a separate attachment to the report. The issue could not be resolved
without outside money to buy out the store owners. The various funding
sources, from the city's Community Redevelopment Agency to the federal
government to private foundations, were unable to meet the need. The attempt to build a coalition of opposed groups had failed, and the controversy
went back to city hall. Further evidence that matters had reached an impasse
came with the formal breakup of the Black-Korean Alliance after six years of
effort (*Korea Times*, 9 December 1992).

The action continued in planning commission hearings on rebuild applications by liquor store owners. The coalition fought these applications on a
case-by-case basis. The conditional-use process, backed by city attorney opinions, seemed to limit what the planning commission could do. So the coalition took what it could get, documenting community impact from the stores
and demanding the hiring of security guards, restrictions on graffiti, and limits on the sale of cups and individual bottles. Ridley-Thomas helped establish
offices to receive community complaints about liquor stores (*Sentinel*, 23 July
1992). Ridley-Thomas and Walters appeared at a number of the hearings to
testify against the store owners. Police officers often backed up the coalition's
arguments.

On the other side, Song and other Korean-American leaders spoke in defense of the liquor store owners, arguing that there was no clear evidence that
the stores caused crime. They emphasized that Korean-American store owners were law-abiding merchants who were in danger of being victimized
twice—once in the civil unrest and again in these legal proceedings (Corecia
J. Davis, research assistant, participant-observation, 16, 18 February 1993).

Without an overall city policy, the planning commission was confused and
uncomfortable. Members had been told by the city attorney that they could

not legally stop a liquor store from being rebuilt. One member of the commission, Lydia Kennard, felt strongly that this interpretation was incorrect and often voted to prevent liquor stores from rebuilding (*Sentinel*, 17 June 1993). Although rebuilding conditions were often expensive and uncomfortable, the merchants generally won permission to rebuild in the planning commission.

Goldsmith (interview, 24 February 1993) then found a different way to pursue the coalition's goals. Goldsmith had generally represented developers against challenges by slow-growth groups on the city's affluent west side. He devised a legal strategy that borrowed from the tactics of the groups that had been making life miserable for his own corporate clients: appeals to the California Environmental Quality Act of 1970.

In addition to questioning the city attorney's interpretation of the powers of the planning commission, Goldsmith argued that the city had an obligation to enforce environmental standards throughout the city. If liquor stores could be shown to present an environmental hazard to public safety, then the rebuilding of liquor stores would require "negative declarations" or the more bulky Environmental Impact Report. This view received some support from the city attorney and within the planning commission and seemed certain to further slow down the rebuilding process—an explicit goal of the strategy.

Goldsmith (interview, 24 February 1993) recalled an ironic moment "at the commission before the Fox hearing" (a major controversy over the expansion of the 20th Century Fox studio on the west side): "there were quite a few anti-Fox people in the council chambers waiting for their item to come up, and when they heard the testimony of the community, were cheering for it." The environmental strategy had crucial political implications. Under this argument, the South Central community was neither seeking special treatment in opposition to vested property interests nor contesting ethnic ownership of stores. Rather, the coalition sought to extend to a poor community the power to regulate its environment, a power long championed in middle-class communities. Thus, in a remarkable irony, the very zoning power that had often been used to exclude minorities and the poor from middle-class areas could be used to protect the environment in the inner city. This approach also allowed the coalition to pursue links with environmental groups and with anti-liquor-store forces in other parts of the city.

The environmental approach reinforced a nonracial discourse in the liquor store controversy. If the issue were framed as blacks against Korean Americans, the community activists would likely lose. It was only by pulling back from the anti-Korean sentiment that was undoubtedly present in the community that the coalition was able to challenge effectively the presence of the liquor stores, no matter who owned them.

From the standpoint of the merchants, there were advantages and disadvantages to a discourse of ethnicity. Korean-American store owners had become targets of community hostility, and to frame the issue in ethnic terms could only increase the danger within which they operated. At the same time, the portrait of the merchants as an embattled minority provided greater potential for political support than an undifferentiated mass of liquor store owners.

The merchants were best able to convert this portrait into political support among Republican legislators in the state capitol. The state of California still plays the central role in the ultimate legal decisions on liquor stores, and there, the liquor store owners were in a stronger position.

Representatives of the beverage industry concentrate their efforts on the state capitol in Sacramento. Rather than intervening at each city hall, they seek to use state power to preempt local decisions. Thus, in 1993, when Archie-Hudson introduced another piece of legislation to limit liquor stores in South Central, her proposal was again defeated.

Archie-Hudson's bill would have enabled authorities to revoke licenses at problem liquor stores and would have limited liquor stores in cities to one for every 2,500 residents. The Los Angeles City Council backed the measure, and Walters traveled to Sacramento to testify on its behalf. It failed to clear the Assembly Governmental Organization Committee on a 6–6 vote because of strong opposition from the beer and wine lobby (*Los Angeles Times*, 12 May 1993).

In May 1993, the matter made its way into superior court when the merchants filed suit against the city, with the coalition entering as an interested party. The merchants' suit charged that the state had ultimate authority over liquor stores and that the city had overstepped its legal powers by requiring the planning commission hearings after the civil unrest. Further, they charged that they had suffered severe financial losses as a result. The city argued that it was well within its powers to regulate liquor stores as a land use. The coalition's supporting brief presented the social impact of the liquor stores and referred to the serious losses incurred by community residents from the presence of the stores.

On 12 June 1993, Judge Robert O'Brien of the superior court, ruled in favor of the city and against the merchants. He concluded that the city could regulate land use even though it could not control licenses to sell liquor (*Sentinel*, 24–30 June 1993). Thus the limited powers the city had claimed were upheld by the court, and the merchants' request for a preliminary injunction was denied. The merchants appealed the decision to the state court of appeals but lost there as well in 1994.

Meanwhile, a bill was wending its way through the state legislature that would invalidate the entire city process. Sponsored by Assemblyman Paul Horcher (R-Whittier), it became the vehicle for Korean-American groups seeking to overturn the city's policy.

The coalition actively lobbied against the Horcher bill, trying to dissuade Horcher and other legislators from preempting the city legislative process. Bass and her allies sought to bring Richard Riordan, mayor of Los Angeles, into the debate. With his ties to state Republicans and to the business community, his support of the city's position could provide crucial political support (Bass, interview, 5 March 1993).

With strong opposition from Los Angeles's black elected officials, the measure failed to pass the senate. By July, it had become inactive, following Mayor Riordan's request that the legislators let Los Angeles work out the matter. Horcher removed the bill at the request of Riordan, and when it was introduced again in August 1994, a coalition of Democrats killed it in committee over the objections of a Republican minority. This had clearly become a more partisan issue at the state level than in the city of Los Angeles. In the face of defeat, Horcher charged that blacks in Los Angeles simply wanted to drive Korean Americans out of South Central (*Los Angeles Times*, 30 August 1994). However, Bass's ability to frame the issue as environmental, rather than racial, undermined Horcher's argument.

A TENTATIVE COMPROMISE

In the midst of this stalemate, a modest opening emerged with an agreement at city hall to help liquor store owners convert their operations to laundromats. The concept of conversion had gained momentum when it became obvious that there were insufficient funds in public coffers or in the private sector to compensate liquor store owners for abandoning their businesses.

The conversion idea was pursued by a group of progressive Asian-Americans known as the Asian Pacific Planning Council. In March 1993, they submitted a proposal to the city council calling for a $260,650 program to help convert a number of liquor stores to other businesses.

In June, the city council adopted the general concept and applied it to laundromats, allocating $260,000 to a pilot conversion program. In addition, the council removed a crucial barrier to conversion by waiving the sewer hookup fee for new laundromats. Without that waiver, the conversion would have been far too costly—as much as $2,200 per machine (*Los Angeles Times*, 3 June 1993).

Although it did not resolve the basic controversy, the laundromat plan was a breakthrough. Opinions of its value varied. The coalition was extremely supportive of the project and was included as part of an advisory committee. The program reinforced their position that they did not oppose Korean Americans doing business in South Central as long as their main product was not liquor. Some Korean Americans were pleased with this first step. Kim (telephone interview with Ji-Young Lee, 15 July 1993) said,

> It's one of the few alternatives offered to merchants right now. We're just beginning this program. Converting businesses into laundromats is the first attempt. The possibility is virtually limitless. We hope to help merchants convert their businesses in other areas like fast-food franchises, auto care, etc.

Song (telephone interview with Ji-Young Lee, 15 July 1993) was much less optimistic, saying,

> As long as it's a workable program, I'm all for it. The response that I get from the victims, however, is that they don't like it. Many victims claim that the profit margins are not satisfactory. If laundromats were a profitable business, it would

> have already existed in the area. Even if incentives like the hookup fees are waived, they've lost everything. There are no quick fixes.

Despite the mixed feelings, the laundromat conversion program represented the first successful effort to bridge the gap between the two opposed camps. Even with the beginnings of compromise, however, the liquor store controversy was not going to go away easily, neatly, or quickly. Both sides were deeply committed. To the coalition, the drive to limit liquor stores was a statement that an inner-city community can take control of its own environment as effectively as an affluent neighborhood. To the merchants and to the Korean-American community, a major investment of money and even lives had gone into the small businesses of Koreatown and South Central. The viability of immigrant families was now poised against the viability of a community.

LEADERSHIP AND THE MANAGEMENT OF INTERMINORITY CONFLICT

It is hard to imagine a clearer conflict of interest between two groups. On one hand, Korean Americans have invested their lives' savings in stores that they operate under difficult conditions, working long hours for unpredictable rewards. On the other hand, blacks in the inner city fear that their already-threatened environment is being further devastated by the social impact of liquor stores. Without a foundation of ideological agreement and with a recent history of intergroup dislike, alliance building is extremely difficult.

As people seek to bridge the differences in interest and ideology between blacks and Korean Americans (Freer 1994), these dynamics may change for the better. But in a situation like the liquor store controversy, interests are in conflict and ideology is a weak link. In that setting, leadership can be expected to play a crucial role. Not only can leaders design and implement strategies but they can also shape the issue itself. This flexibility is particularly important in issues involving interethnic conflict.

Some key leaders of both groups were adamant that the conflict was economic and social, not racial and ethnic, and they actively lobbied the media to avoid cultural explanations for the issue. Although it was an uphill battle to alter media coverage, some leaders in both communities at least tried to reframe the debate.

Song offered on example of how difficult it can be to influence the media perception. He and Bass were invited to appear on a television program to discuss the liquor store issue. Song (interview, 2 February 1993) recalled that

> We were talking about the issue before we got on the air, and we pretty much agreed that it is not a black-Korean issue anyway. There is a common goal to have a better community, but their focus is on getting rid of the liquor store. Our foremost interest is to protect the investment. Other than that, if it can be

resolved, then we have a common goal, actually. It's good business sense to have a good relation with the community anyway. As we were talking, somebody from the news department came in and said, "Would you mind not talking too much before we get it out on the air?" So I realized they wanted us to fight.

The failure of the Black-Korean Alliance or the mayor's task force to find a solution to this conflict was hardly surprising. Leaders had limited leeway to reach balanced resolutions in these forums. For example, when Kim was perceived as too quick to sympathize with the black community's position, he came under intense political attack within the Korean-American community (Kim, interview, 30 March 1993).

It is particularly unrealistic to expect the relationship between blacks and Korean Americans to match the long history of coalition between blacks and Jews in Los Angeles. Blacks and Jews in Los Angeles met as political equals—outsiders in a political system dominated by hostile conservatives (Sonenshein 1989, 1993). Today, imbalances abound between blacks and Korean Americans. As Korean-American activist T. S. Chung (attorney and cochair of Mayor Bradley's South Central Community/Merchant Liquor Task Force, interview with Ji-Young Lee, 23 April 1993) noted, blacks perceive Korean Americans to be dominating them economically, whereas Korean Americans perceive blacks to be controlling them politically.

Middleman minorities are trapped between their dependence on outside economic forces and the perception within the community that they are exploiters. As Chung (interview, 23 April 1993) noted, "you shouldn't generalize the black-Korean relationship based upon the relationship between Korean merchants and black customers in South Central—a very poor set of circumstances that are bound to create a bad relationship."

The liquor store controversy provides some important insights into the dynamics of interracial coalitions. In the evolving world of interminority relations, the concepts of coalition and conflict are too limiting. When groups are in conflict, these interactions can be managed in different ways. When leaders pursue pragmatic approaches even though polarization might bring immediate political rewards, the possibility of devising successful agreements will obviously be enhanced. By focusing on liquor rather than on ethnic rivalries, the coalition chose not to make the issue "Who owns the stores?" but, rather, "What are the stores selling, and how are they selling it?" That focus provides some grounds for hope.

Theoretical notions about who should make good coalition partners do not always hold up in the real world. The bonds among nonwhite communities depend heavily on the circumstances under which the groups encounter one another. Indeed, if that encounter is as fraught with conflict as the presence of liquor stores in South Central, the potential bond may deteriorate into a state of perceived enmity. Only the most thoughtful and creative leaders, able to find alternative ways to build a relationship without being devastated by the conflict, can find a path to sharing power and resources.

STUDY QUESTIONS

1. Why has the largest increase in African-American office-holding occurred at the local level of government? What does this say about politics as an avenue for development in the African-American community? What is the relationship between political and economic power?

2. What are the central tenets of the empowerment model? In what ways does black political empowerment influence mass attitudes and behaviors? How does political empowerment operate at the community level? What is the significance of symbolic politics?

3. What are the major criticisms of the empowerment approach? What is the difference between descriptive and substantive representation? What are the class dimensions of empowerment politics? What is the role of traditional African-American political leadership in the new urban environment?

4. Changing demographics have fundamentally altered the political landscape of most large American cities. The arrival of new entrants into the political process poses a number of challenges to black political empowerment. What are these challenges and how should the black political community respond?

NOTES

1. Like other American minority groups, blacks have pursued local politics as a stepping stone to mainstream acceptance. For example, Steven P. Erie. *Rainbow's end: Irish-Americans and the dilemmas of urban machine politics, 1840–1985.* (Berkeley: University of California Press) 1988.

2. *Black elected officials: A national roster.* (Washington: Joint Center for Political and Economic Studies) 1992.

3. In 1998 there were 12 African-Americans elected to statewide offices in the continental United States, David A. Bostis, "The black vote in '98," *The Joint Center for Political and Economic Studies,* November 1998.

4. Patricia Gurin, Shirley Hatchett and James S. Jackson. *Hope and independence: Blacks' response to electoral and party politics.* (New York: Sage) 1989; K.C. Minion Morrison. *Black political mobilization.* (Albany: State University of New York Press) 1987; Michael B. Preston et al., (eds.) *The new black politics.* (New York: Longman) 1982.

5. Rufus Browning, Dale Rogers Marshall and David H. Tabb. *Protest is not enough: The struggle of blacks and hispanics for equality in urban politics.* (Berkeley: University of California Press); Peter K. Eisinger, "Black employment in municipal jobs: The impact of black political power," *American Political Science Review* 4:76; 1982:330–52; Albert Karnig and Susan Welch. *Black representation and urban policy.* (Chicago: University of Chicago Press) 1980; Gary Orfield and Carol Ashkinaze. *The closing door: Conservative policy and black opportunity.* (Chicago: University of Chicago Press) 1991; Huey L. Perry, "Black politics and mayoral leadership in Birmingham and New Orleans," *National Political Science Review* 2 1990:154–160; Raphael J. Sonenshein. *Politics in black and white: Race and power in Los Angeles.* (Princeton: Princeton University Press).

6. Franklin D. Gilliam, Jr., "Exploring minority empowerment: Symbolic politics, governing coalitions, and traces of political style in Los Angeles," *American Journal of Political*

Science, 40:1, 1996:56–81; Franklin D. Gilliam, Jr. and Karen M. Kaufmann, "Is there an empowerment life-cycle? Long-term black empowerment and its influence on voter participation," *Urban Affairs Review*, 33:6, 1999:741–766.

7. David Bositis. *Black Elected Officials: A Statistical Summary, 1993–1997* (Washington, D.C.: Joint Center for Political and Economic Studies) 1998.

8. For more on the deracialization thesis see, Jack Miles, "Blacks vs. Browns: The struggle for the bottom rung," *Atlantic Monthly* (October) 1992; Michael B. Preston and Bruce Cain (eds.) *Racial and ethnic politics in California.* (Berkeley: IGS Press) 1998; Carol A. Pierannunzi and John D. Hutcheson, Jr, "Deracialization in the Deep South: Mayoral politics in Atlanta," *Urban Affairs Quarterly* 27,2 December 1991: 192–201; Robert Starks, "A commentary and response to "Exploring the meaning and implication of deracialization in African-American urban politics." *Urban Affairs Quarterly* 27 (1991): 222; Stephan Thernstrom and Abigail Thernstrom. *America in black and white: One nation indivisible* (New York: Simon and Schuster) 1997.

RACIAL POLITICS AT THE NATIONAL LEVEL: THE PRESIDENCY, THE CONGRESS, AND THE SUPREME COURT

African-American political influence at the national level is best characterized as indirect. For instance, there has not been a black president or vice-president in the history of the United States. Likewise, there have only been two black Supreme Court justices (Thurgood Marshall and Clarence Thomas). And while there has been substantial black office-holding in Congress—there has not been a black Speaker of the House nor Senate Majority Leader and there have only been two black Senators in the post-civil rights era: Edward Brooke (R., Mass.) and Carol Mosley-Braun (D., Ill.). The paucity of black elected officials does not mean that black interests have not been represented at the national level. Nor does it mean that only black politicians can represent black interests. Rather, it suggests that black political power is wielded through a filter. Put differently, the political interests of the black community are primarily dependent on the actions of non-black political actors. The upshot, of course, is that a hostile presidential administration (e.g., Reagan/Bush), Supreme Court (e.g., the Rehnquist court), or Congress (e.g., 1994 Republican Congress) can easily threaten black interests.

THE PRESIDENCY

In **"Blacks and Presidential Policy Making"** *Robert Smith examines black influence in the post-civil rights executive branch. As Smith notes, blacks were excluded from cabinet positions and rarely called upon to offer advice prior to the Nixon administration. In other words, blacks had little formal impact on executive decision-making in the first two-thirds of the 20th century. Smith focuses on the effectiveness of high-level black executive branch appointees in three post-1960s administrations—Nixon, Carter and Reagan. His conclusion about the impact of black appointees is that, ". . . the evidence reviewed here . . . suggests that they brought into the government the perspectives of the black community." Nevertheless, there was significant variation across administrations in response to ideological and structural concerns. Black appointees, like the representatives of any specific constituency, were affected by the tension between speaking for the administration and speaking for their "community." In some cases, black appointees broke with the administration's position. For example, appointees in the Nixon administration were instrumental in developing the*

"Philadelphia Plan" which ultimately became the cornerstone of affirmative action policy. Likewise, Samuel Pierce, Secretary of Housing and Urban Development in the Reagan Administration ". . . persuaded Reagan to support strengthening the enforcement provisions of the Fair Housing Act of 1968." In other cases, black appointees sided with the administration in opposition to community consensus (e.g., Clarence Thomas, chair of the Equal Employment Opportunity Commission and Clarence Pendleton, chair of the Civil Rights Commission during Reagan). In short, the evidence on the impact of black appointees is mixed at best.

WE HAVE NO LEADERS: AFRICAN-AMERICANS IN THE POST-CIVIL RIGHTS ERA

Robert C. Smith

Excerpt from Chapter 5: Blacks and Presidential Policy Making: Neglect, Policy, Symbols, and Cooptation

What differences has it made that in the last 20 years blacks have become routine participants in the presidential and congressional decision-making processes? An important assumption by proponents of black incorporation is that blacks will become advocates of black interests in the policy-making process; that where they have the capacity to make or influence decisions they will reflect the values of the group. The theoretical discussion in Chapter 1 suggests an alternative hypothesis about the consequences of incorporation, namely that rather than advancing the interests or values of the race, the consequence of institutionalization will instead be the adoption by individuals of the interests and values of the institutions; and the more powerful a person becomes within an institution the more likely he or she is to hold its values. It is essentially these alternative assumptions that we examine empirically in this and later chapters dealing with black participation during the last 20 years in presidential, congressional and Democratic Party institutional processes.

In this chapter the focus is on the presidency and executive branch decision making. What can be said of the institutional legacy left behind by those blacks who have held high-level appointments in the executive branch? Did they work toward solving the problems of race? Did they have the president's ear? Were they effective? These are the questions examined in this chapter. The focus is on the post-civil rights era administrations—Nixon-Ford, Carter, Reagan and to an extent Bush—first because this period is the focus of the book as a whole but also because the phenomenon itself is largely a post-civil rights era one. Prior to the 1960s blacks simply were not a part of the executive branch of government. Black participation in executive policy making was generally limited to the occasional advice a president might seek informally from one or more blacks in whom he had personal confidence (Frederick Douglas's counsel to President Lincoln and Booker Washington's to Theodore Roosevelt are perhaps the best known instances of this practice), or to advice on racial matters from the so-called black cabinets that emerged in the administrations of William Taft and Franklin Roosevelt. In the Kennedy and Johnson administrations the handful of black appointees would occasionally gather informally to discuss civil rights and related issues but overall blacks in the executive branch were by and large uninvolved in the formulation of the civil rights and Great Society initiatives of the 1960s. Essentially, then, black participation in decisions of the executive on more than an occasional or ad hoc basis is a post-civil rights era phenomenon beginning with the Nixon administration.

THE NIXON ADMINISTRATIONS

As the first post–civil rights era president, Nixon appointed about 30 blacks to subcabinet positions in his administration. This represented at that time the largest number of African-Americans ever to serve in the government, nearly three times the number appointed by President Johnson. Nixon had campaigned for office on a vaguely antiblack or anti–civil rights platform, with antibusing and law-and-order rhetoric designed to appeal to the unreconstructed white south and the Wallace vote. Consequently, unlike in 1960 when he received roughly a quarter of the black vote, in 1968 he received less than 10%. Nevertheless, consistent with the logic of incorporation or systemic integration ongoing when he took office, Nixon did not, indeed by 1969 could not, revert to the practice of the Eisenhower administration of excluding blacks from the government. Although probably in deference to his white southern constituency Nixon did not appoint a black to a highly visible cabinet post, he did make subcabinet appointments as well as appointments at the independent agencies and regulatory commissions. The process of black incorporation by the late 1960s had become irreversible, party and ideology notwithstanding.

The Nixon administration came to power at about the same time that the black power principles of race solidarity and organization were being adopted by the black leadership establishment. This had an important effect on this new group of government officials, leading them early in the administration to form a separatist race group caucus called the Council of Black Appointees. The significance of the group's formation was not in terms of its impact on policy but rather that in the late 1960s and early 1970s blacks in the administration felt they had a responsibility to try to advance the interests of the race in the councils of government. They did not see themselves as simply officials who merely happened to be black; rather, their sense of race consciousness and solidarity was such that they felt compelled to try to organize collectively to advance what they understood to be the interests of the race, even when these ran counter to the publicly stated position of the President. In all likelihood their sensitivity to their roles as race advocates was influenced by the salience of the ethos of black power during this period. This interpretation is supported to some extent by the fact that the kind of race solidarity and organization exhibited by blacks in the Nixon administration is not observed in subsequent administrations. In the Reagan administration in fact, the contrary is observed; black appointees, rather than challenging policies generally thought to be adverse to black interests, became instead their enthusiastic advocates. The Council of Black Appointees *as a group* sought to influence administration decision making on only one issue, school busing. This, however, was the most controversial race-specific issue during Nixon's tenure. This issue not only was a source of black-white tensions but it also divided the black community at both the elite and mass levels. Yet the black leadership establishment (from whence the leading blacks in the administration were drawn) was, publicly at least, united in support of court-ordered busing as one option to desegregate the schools, while the president was just as firmly committed to an antibusing policy as a strategic calculus to shore up his support among southern whites and among those northern blue-collar white voters who had supported George Wallace in the 1968 election. Thus, the issue throughout the late 1960s and early 1970s pitted the black establishment against the policy and political interests of the president. Black appointees in this conflict sided with the leadership of black America rather than their president.

During its first year the Nixon administration in an unprecedented act asked the federal courts to delay the desegregation of certain southern school systems. Although a unanimous Supreme Court rejected the request, this was the first time the federal government had intervened in court in opposition to school desegregation. This action sparked a revolt in the government's civil rights bureaucracy; attorneys in the Justice Department's Civil Rights Division filed a written protest, and several resigned. Leon Panetta, director of HEW's Office of Civil Rights, resigned in protest, and James Allen, the Commissioner of Education, was fired, in part for his strong opposition to administration policy. Later, in a nationwide television address the president proposed declaring a "moratorium" on all school busing for purposes of school desegregation until passage of his Equal Educational Opportunity Act, a bill which in effect nullified the right of the courts to order busing for purposes of school desegregation. Finally, Vice President Agnew suggested that the administration, if all else failed, would consider a constitutional amendment to ban all busing for purposes of school desegregation. In response to these developments the Council of Black Appointees prepared and sent to the president a detailed, formal position paper setting forth its objections to the administration's proposals, particularly the idea raised by the vice president of a constitutional amendment. The president ignored the council's missive. A second paper was sent and again no acknowledgment by the president or his senior staff. Finally, feeling that the president (or his staff) was seeking to ignore the group's statement, the council sent a third copy, and this time issued a press release indicating that the group had sent a position paper to the president relative to his school desegregation policy. The group emphasized that it was not its intention to publicly oppose the president, that it remained loyal to the administration but felt the press attention was the only way "to get around Nixon's palace guard and make sure he got

the statement and also to some extent to let the public know our position."
Asked what was the impact on the president's school desegregation policy of
the council's efforts, Constance Newman, then chairperson, replied, "Well, he
did not support the constitutional amendment and we would like to think we
played some role in that, yet we were of course disappointed by his support
of antibusing legislation." Yet the president had never publicly supported a
constitutional amendment, and many Washington observers felt the Agnew
statement was only a "trial balloon" floated to make the president's legislative proposals seem more responsible. Thus, on an issue perceived as of signal importance to blacks, black appointees found it difficult to gain even an
audience with the president to present their position and on the record had
no impact on the eventual policy.

Feeling increasingly frustrated about their inability to have an effect on the
president's decision, and with black leaders attacking the administration in
increasingly harsh language (the NAACP's board chairman called the administration the first openly antiblack administration since Woodrow Wilson's), black appointees decided to make public their internal policy
disagreements with the president. This was done through a series of not-for-
attribution interviews by several black appointees with Paul Delaney, a black
correspondent for the *New York Times*. In the published story, the appointees
urged the president to, among other things, issue a "major policy statement"
committing his administration to equality of rights and an improvement in
the enforcement of civil rights law. Otherwise, they implied, they might re-
sign in protest, raising the possibility that all senior-level blacks might leave
the government. In spite of these efforts the administration continued to pursue its antibusing rhetoric and policy proposals, and the black appointees
were powerless despite a year-long effort to affect the decision-making
process. At least, however, the record shows that they tried, and on an issue
of paramount political importance to the president.

If busing was the most controversial race issue during the late 1960s and
early 1970s, by the end of the decade it had been replaced by affirmative action, the series of policies and programs designed to take race into account as
means to overcome past patterns and practices of racism, to diversify educational institutions and the workplace and to enforce relevant provisions of
the Civil Rights Act of 1964. Like busing, affirmative action is an issue that divides the nation on race lines, divides the black community but nevertheless
is overwhelmingly supported by the black leadership establishment. Black
appointees have been intimately involved in the shaping of national policy
on affirmative action, going back to the Kennedy and Johnson administrations. The roles they have played during this thirty-year period provide interesting contrasts on the part played by black appointees in advancing the
interests of the race. In the conservative Republican Nixon administration
black appointees played an important role in developing affirmative action policy as we know it today, while in the Democratic Carter administration other black appointees sought to effectively destroy it.

The government developed and began to implement affirmative action in
the Kennedy and Johnson administrations, but the process reached its full

doctrinal and practical application in the Nixon administration in the form of its Philadelphia Plan. The Philadelphia Plan began to take shape originally in the Johnson administration. Although the logic and procedures of the Philadelphia Plan have become the model for affirmative action programs in government, the academy and business, in areas such as university admissions, private and public employment and government contracting, it was originally designed to deal with the peculiar problems of discrimination in the construction industry.

In 1966 Labor Secretary Willard Wirtz created the Office of Federal Contract Compliance as the administrative unit to enforce Executive Order 11246. As its first director he appointed Edward Sylvester, who was then a relatively low-level staff person in the department's international bureau. Graham writes that Sylvester had a reputation as a "tough, competent and dedicated administrator" and that "By 1967 the OFCC, like the EEOC but on a smaller scale, was accumulating a staff of activist blacks and white liberal reformers, whose zeal for enforcement mirrored that of their young, attractive and aggressive leaders—Edward Sylvester at OFCC and Clifford Alexander at the EEOC." Sylvester shortly after taking office began to develop a plan to deal with discrimination in the construction trades. What he proposed was the "Cleveland Plan." Under its provisions local compliance committees were established. These committees, while not setting firm target numbers for black contractors, would require that before a final contract could be signed the winning bidder would be required to submit detailed reports that listed by trade or craft in all phases of the work the specific number of black workers to be hired. This plan resulted in protests from the AFL-CIO, business groups, the construction companies, conservative Republicans and liberal (labor-connected) Democrats in the Congress, who all charged that the Cleveland and later Philadelphia Plans in effect established de facto racial hiring quotas in violation of the 1964 Civil Rights Act. Because of this opposition in the Congress and elsewhere, the comptroller general (head of the Congress's independent General Accounting Office) was asked by members of Congress to review the plans in order to determine if they were consistent with government bidding and contracting procedures. The comptroller general ruled that Sylvester's plan was illegal not because of its alleged racial quotas but because it violated standard government bidding and contracting procedures which require that contracts be awarded "only on the basis of the lowest bid, with all specifications or requirements spelled out before the bidding." In other words, if a contractor were to be required to employ a targeted number of blacks this would have to be spelled out in advance in the invitation to bid. As Graham notes, this created for Sylvester a dilemma; if the plan required explicit numbers prior to the award of the contract then it would be called an illegal quota; but if the numbers remained vague then they would violate the comptroller general's ruling that bidders be specifically informed in advance of all requirements. Given the comptroller general's ruling and the widespread opposition, Sylvester was forced to rescind the plan.

In spite of his skillful and dedicated work, Sylvester left office in 1969 without having put into effect an effective plan to enforce nondiscrimination in employment by government contractors. This was in part because time ran out in the last year of Johnson's lame duck presidency and because of the opposition not only from business and congressional conservatives but liberals and labor, key constituent groups along with blacks in the Democratic party coalition." One would have thought that any hope for the Sylvester Plan would have died with the election of the conservative, Republican business-oriented Nixon administration, especially given Nixon's election year anti–civil rights rhetoric. However, Sylvester's plan was revived, strengthened and implemented, and again this was in part a result of the skillful and dedicated work of two Nixon administration black appointees.

Nixon selected as his Labor Secretary George Schultz, an economist at the University of Chicago with a reputation as a moderate on civil rights and race issues. Shultz, for reasons that are not entirely clear from the records reviewed by Graham and Hood, apparently decided to revive the Sylvester Plan and was able to persuade the president to go along. Whatever the reasons, the Nixon administration, in spite of the opposition of business and congressional conservatives, embraced the Johnson administration's affirmative action strategy. Shultz reorganized the Department and created a new assistant secretary for Wage and Labor Standards, with the head of OFCC reporting to him rather than directly to the secretary. For this new position he choose Arthur Fletcher, a black Republican who had run for Lieutenant Governor in Washington. Fletcher said when asked to take the job, he insisted on two things: one, that he be allowed to make equal employment a "labor standard" and two, that he be allowed to pick his own deputy who would head OFCC. In fact, Fletcher in a personal interview told me, "The Philadelphia Plan was my baby. When I came in there was no specific standard for equal opportunity. It was viewed as social engineering and not as labor standard enforceable at law. So, one of my conditions for accepting the job was that I could make equal opportunity a labor standard. When Shultz asked me to take the job this is what I told him." Fletcher overstates his role, overlooking, for example, the origins of the Philadelphia Plan in the Johnson administration and Shultz's leadership. It is probably more accurate to say as Graham writes that "Fletcher presided with Shultz's blessings over the redesign of the Philadelphia Plan."

With his deputy John Wilks (also black) at OFCC, Fletcher set about immediately to revise the Sylvester Plan in a way that would overcome the objections of GAO. The revised plan issued six months after the took office avoided the quota issue by establishing target goals for minority employment which bidders would agree to try to meet. The GAO objection was met by the plan's prohibition on any negotiations after contracts were awarded. In announcing the plan Fletcher indicated that it would eventually apply not only to Philadelphia but to all cities across the country "as soon as possible" and he forthrightly defended goals or targets for black employment as "necessary because of historic segregation and discrimination." The comptroller general ruled that Fletcher's revised plan was still illegal, this time because it used race or national origin as a determinative factor in employment decisions which, he held, was a violation of Title VII of the Civil Rights Act.

Opponents said then, as they do now, that the notion of targets or goals were simply euphemisms for racial quotas. After a series of congressional hearings, opponents of the plan in the Senate passed an amendment to an appropriations bill that prohibited the expenditure of any federal funds on any contract which the comptroller general holds to be in contravention of any federal stature. After intense lobbying by Shultz and the president, the House rejected this amendment by a vote of 208 to 156. A majority of House Democrats (including many northern liberals) voted for the amendment while Republicans opposed it by a margin of 124 to 41. The irony here of course is that affirmative action received its initial legislative ratification over the objections of the Democratic majority in Congress and only with the support of the conservative Republican president and legislative majorities. Twenty years later this ideological and partisan alignment on affirmative action is completely reversed, as indicated by the debate and vote on the Civil Rights Act of 1991 (see Chapter 6).

Given the amendment's defeat, Fletcher and Wilks shortly thereafter issued a revised order applying principles and procedures of the Philadelphia Plan to all government contractors. This was a radical change in policy, since Sylvester's original affirmative action plan was ostensibly narrowly designed to address the unique problems of racism in the craft unions, where there were ample empirical findings to establish employment discrimination. This new order simply assumed historical racism or discrimination and applied the Philadelphia Plan nationwide, covering by Fletcher's estimate from one third to one half of the national workforce. This new order led to renewed attacks from congressional opponents, but to no avail, and the order in its final form was issued in February 1970. It required government contractors (with contracts of at least $50,000 and fifty or more employees) to file an acceptable affirmative action plan that would include (1) an analysis of all job categories to determine the underutilization of minorities (underutilization was defined as having fewer minorities in a particular job category than would reasonably be expected by their availability in the relevant labor force) and (2) a specific plan with goals and timetables to correct any identified underutilization.

This revised and extended Philadelphia Plan subsequently became the model for voluntary affirmative action programs throughout American society. It is today the source of bitter partisan, ideological and race conflict. The key point for purposes of this analysis is that the policy is substantially the result of the work of black appointees—Sylvester in Johnson's administration and Fletcher and Wilks in Nixon's—who used their positions in government to advance a policy that they perceived to be in the interests of blacks. This case shows that black appointees did make a difference. As Graham writes, "what was new by 1970 was the growing insider role of the civil rights lobby within the executive establishment. . . ." This insider role of blacks in the executive branch has grown substantially in numbers since 1970. However, the policy impact or consequence has not been commensurate. Indeed, the early years of the Nixon administration in many ways represents the high point of black attempts to shape executive branch decision making.

THE CARTER ADMINISTRATION

President Carter appointed three times more blacks to high-level office than did President Nixon. Yet, a review of the record of the Carter presidency on issues of concern to blacks shows this relatively large number of persons had only a marginal effect on decision making. Although blacks in the Carter administration did not form a separatist caucus or council, black appointees did meet on an ad hoc, informal basis on several occasions in order to discuss race-related issues.

Thus, whatever the record shows in terms of the actual effect of these individuals on race-related policy decisions, it is clear that most were inclined to try to use their positions to advance the interests of the race.

Andrew Young, President Carter's fellow Georgian and his principal supporter among black leaders during the campaign, was the most prominent black appointee in the administration. In the scores of books and memoirs reviewed, he is by far the most frequently mentioned black official in the administration. Most of the references, however, are to the role he played in Carter's 1976 campaign, the significance of a black as the first United Nations ambassador, his often controversial remarks and to his firing as a result of an unauthorized meeting with representatives of the Palestine Liberation Organization. Gaddis Smith's observations are typical: "President Carter's appointment of Andrew Young as United States Ambassador to the United Nations, the first black to hold such a high diplomatic position, was a signal to both Africans and to a domestic constituency. He immediately became an uninhibited spokesman who won acclaim among black African leaders and caused consternation among South African whites and some conservative Americans because he belittled the Soviet threat." Young clearly thought he had a special mandate to participate in shaping U.S. foreign policy toward Africa, especially southern Africa. And, as Smith points out, he had a view (consistent with that of most black leaders) that U.S. policy in the region reflected too much concern with the Soviet threat and not enough with African issues on their merits. In this view, Young in Carter policy deliberations was allied with his nominal superior, Cyrus Vance, the secretary of state, while Zbigniew Brzezinski, the national security advisor, took the traditional cold war view that the major threat to American interests in the region was the Soviet-Cuban presence. Abernathy writes that the administration eventually established as its goal in the region to "set in motion a peaceful and progressive transformation of South Africa toward a biracial democracy . . . while forging elsewhere a coalition of moderate black leaders in order to stem continual radicalization and eliminate the Soviet-Cuban presence from the continent." And he writes, "Andrew Young played a key role." Other sources, however, are less clear on the goals of U.S. policy in the region or Young's role in shaping it. Mollenhoff writes that it is unclear what Young's influence on the president was in terms of African policy; and Smith concluded that it was inconsequential. In fact he argues that "Young was fired because of his unauthorized conversations with a Palestinian leader, but more generally because his philosophy was contrary to the administration's new direction. African policy now reflected more concern with meeting Soviet influence and less with African issues per se." Overall, then, the evidence of Ambassador Young's influence on administration decision making in his area of special interests and concern is ambiguous. He certainly made an effort to turn U.S. policy away from its cold war mentality in southern Africa; what is ambiguous is how effective he was in his efforts.

Aside from Young, HUD Secretary Harris is the most frequently mentioned appointee. Shull writes that she had good rapport with Carter and frequently sent him memos with recommendations on housing and welfare policy. Several sources indicate that she played a major role in shaping Carter's welfare reform and urban policy proposals. The urban policy proposal was the first attempt by a president to develop a comprehensive approach to the nation's urban problems. It therefore resulted in a range of jurisdictional disputes between HUD, HEW and the Departments of Commerce, Labor and Agriculture. Early in 1977 Carter appointed Harris to chair an interagency task force—the Urban and Regional Policy Group—to manage these jurisdictional disputes and to develop the administration's urban policy.

Harris's task force proceeded slowly until the Urban League's Vernon Jordan in a July 1977 speech attacked the administration for its inattention to urban and minority problems. Jordan's attack angered the president but resulted in instructions to his staff and to Harris's task force to speed up development of the urban policy proposals. With the active involvement of Stuart Eizenstat, the president's principal domestic policy advisor, Harris's task force in late October prepared a draft report recommending to the president that the administration's urban policy focus exclusively on the nation's largest, most distressed central cities and that all existing federal programs be targeted toward these cities in a comprehensive strategy. The task force also proposed additional targeted programs at a cost of ten to twenty billion dollars. After this document was leaked to the press, conservatives and rural and suburban members of congress criticized the proposed policy because of its central city focus and its cost. President Carter then directed Harris to revise the proposal to remove its exclusive focus on central cities and drastically scale back its costs. At this point, Eizenstadt and the White House staff increased their role in the policy formulation process and Harris's role in the development of the final policy apparently diminished. The final Carter urban policy submitted to the Congress was a scaled-down version of Harris's original recommendations, focusing less on the largely black central cities and with no additional money for targeted programs.

If the Young and Harris records reveal some attempts on their parts to advance race interests in administration decision making on issues within their scopes of responsibility, the records of the next two persons—Drew Days and Wade McCree at the Department of Justice—show the opposite. During the Johnson and Nixon administrations, black appointees played important roles in the development and implementation of affirmative action as national policy. Ironically, in the Carter administration Days and McCree sought to destroy their work by taking the now familiar right-wing view that it is impermissible under the Constitution for the government to take race into account in order to remedy historical or institutional racism or to diversify the nation's workplace or institutions of higher education. McCree, the solicitor general, and Days, the assistant attorney general for civil rights, were both men with distinguished legal credentials, both card-carrying members of the liberal black establishment. They were also appointed largely because they were black. Carter's nomination for attorney genderal of his friend, Georgia appeals court judge Griffin Bell, resulted in criticism from blacks, who alleged that Bell had a record of insensitivity if not hostility to civil rights. In part to appease his critics, Bell selected McCree and Days to run the department's two divisions most responsible for civil rights decision making.

THE REAGAN ADMINISTRATION

Forty-nine books or memories on the Reagan administration were reviewed and the indices were searched for information about twelve senior-level black appointees and on eleven race-related issues including the renewal of the Voting Rights Act, the Bob Jones case, Executive Order 11246, South Africa and welfare reform. In these sources, entries were found on only four senior level officials—HUD Secretary Samuel Pierce, National Security Advisor Colin Powell, EEOC Chair Clarence Thomas and Clarence Pendleton, Chair of the Civil Rights Commission. In addition, two low-level black White House staff aides were mentioned in connection with the Bob Jones tuition tax exemption controversy.

Of the four senior level black officials, most of the material is on Pierce (except for Powell; there is considerable material on his role in national security decision making, which I do not include here given my focus on issues of race). References to Thomas and Pendleton are limited largely to discussion of the circumstances of their appointments. For example, in an essay by Robert Thompson in Tinsley Yarbourgh's edited volume *The Reagan Administration and Human Rights*, Pendleton's appointment is described in terms of his long-time association with Reagan aide Edwin Meese. Thompson writes, "Pendleton's principal [qualification] . . . seems to have been his association with Ed Meese whose views on civil rights were consistent with those of the administration." Thompson also quotes Pendleton as telling a reporter that his views on affirmative action were consistent with Reagan's because "whatever the administration's policy is in this respect, I have no choice but to support that policy." And several sources refer to Pendleton's dissent in a 1982 Civil Rights Commission report endorsing busing for purposes of school desegregation. In one case the sources differ as to Pendleton's role. Early in the administration the Civil Rights Commission requested that executive departments and agencies submit information on their civil rights enforcement activities and affirmative action. The Departments of Labor and Education refused. The commission then threatened to issue a subpoena. Thompson indicates that Pendleton voted against the subpoena, while Dugger reports that he joined with his fellow commissioners in the threat to issue the subpoena if needed to obtain the information (the subpoena was not issued as the two departments voluntarily supplied the material). Most of the sources, how-ever, deal with Pierce's role in administration decision making on issues rel-evant to his department and on race issues generally.

Samuel Pierce as the only black cabinet member dealt not only with issues relevant to his department but with the full range of race-related or civil rights issues. Unlike Pendleton, Thomas and most other senior black appointees, Pierce was not a new right conservative or "Reaganut," rather he was a prod-uct of the eastern, liberal Republican tradition. Evans and Novak describe Pierce as the "only bona fide liberal" in the cabinet. Liberal is an exaggeration here, since except for civil rights Pierce described himself as a "true believer" in the Reagan revolution, arguing, "I really believe his programs are grounded on solid economic principles. . . . The one area where I might differ—and this ap-plies more to several top aides than to the president—is in the area of civil rights. I've spoken to the president about civil rights on several occasions. He has assured me that he's committed to racial justice. And I believe that."

Evans and Novak describe Pierce as a liberal because, they write, he was Reagan's "only constant adversary" who "constantly defended HUD pro-grams that had been growing since the days of LBJ's Great Society." Other ac-counts differ on Pierce's role in defending his department's programs. Dugger describes the massive cuts in the HUD budget and concludes that Pierce was not much different from the rest of the administration except for being black. Similarly, Brownstein refers to Pierce's "steady dismantling of Johnson's Great Society programs." What seems to distinguish evaluation of Pierce's tenure at HUD is effort versus results. Stockman, Evans and Novak and even Brown-stein seem to agree that in internal administration discussions Pierce made an effort to defend some of HUD's programs from the massive budget cuts pro-posed by the White House budget office but that he generally failed. One ex-ception, noted by several sources, is Pierce's successful defense of HUD's Urban Development Action Grants (UDAG), which provided for local eco-nomic development projects. Stockman writes that he wanted to eliminate the program. "But Secretary of Housing and Urban Development Sam Pierce launched a noisy campaign to spare this turkey, and soon the White House switch board was flooded with HUD orchestrated distress calls from local Re-publican mayors and businessmen who happened to be in the redevelopment and construction business." With this exception, the sources indicate that Stockman won every budget battle with Pierce, with the results that in his tenure Pierce presided over the near total decimation of government support for low and moderate income housing, seeing budget authority drop from $35 billion in 1980 to $10 billion by 1988, representing the largest decline in budget authority and appropriations than in any other domestic program category. His private misgivings notwithstanding, Pierce before Congress and in the press ardently defended these massive cuts. Thus, the record here is one of ef-fort, perhaps, but little effectiveness in defending programs that dispropor-tionately benefitted low income Americans, particularly blacks. Therefore Pierce's effectiveness as an advocate of black interests cannot be established on the basis of his record at HUD. And to some extent even his dedication to the preservation of HUD programs might be questioned, given his "true believer" commitment to Reaganomics. Pierce, for example, said that while the cuts hurt blacks they were necessary to turn the economy around.

On civil rights issues the available studies indicate that Pierce was both more active and effective. Pierce departed from the administration's civil rights stance, and he argued that he felt "a special responsibility to tell the administration what's on the minds of black Americans." Pierce was involved in administration decision making on all the major civil rights issues. In his own area of responsibility—the implementation of antidiscrimination in the sale and rental of housing—Pierce is credited with persuading Reagan to support strengthening the enforcement provisions of the Fair Housing Act of 1968. The Fair Housing Amendments of 1988 were introduced during the Carter administration and by the 1980s enjoyed widespread congressional support; however, the law as Lamb writes "was plainly inconsistent" with Reagan's previous record on civil rights. Enforcement of antidiscrimination in housing under the 1968 act was limited to expensive and time-consuming pattern or practice litigation by the Justice Department or through "conference, conciliation and persuasion" by HUD. Given the well-documented continuation of pervasive housing discrimination since passage of the 1968 act, most authorities were agreed that the enforcement provisions were inadequate. Under the 1988 amendments, when HUD conciliation fails, the department may issue a "discrimination charge" and the Justice Department is then obligated to pursue the matter as a civil suit, if the parties agree to choose federal court resolution of the charges. If the parties do not choose to go to court, the HUD Secretary may refer the case to an administrative law judge within the department. If the law judge finds that the discrimination charge is valid he may provide relief in the form of damages, attorney's fees and civil penalties of up to $50,000. These provisions in the minds of most observers added "teeth to fair housing policy for the first time."

Outside of his responsibilities at HUD, Pierce was also involved in administration decision making on renewal of the Voting Rights Act in 1982, on maintenance of the affirmative action Executive Order 11246 and on the Bob Jones tax exemption controversy. On each of these issues he appears to have had some moderating effect on the anti-civil rights posture of Reagan and his more conservative cabinet secretaries and White House aides. Although Pierce was attacked in the press for supporting a provision that would have allowed states to "bail out" from the Voting Rights Act's preclearance provision (which requires covered jurisdictions to clear any proposed changes in their election processes with the Justice Department on a showing that they had ended discrimination), he argues that in cabinet deliberations he only did this as a means of laying before the president all of his options but that he from the outset strongly urged the president to support a straight-forward extension of the Act for 25 years, including the controversial effects rather intent standard of proof. Reagan initially rejected the effects test and supported the bail-out provisions, positions which Pierce says "disappointed" him. In the end, however, under pressure from moderate congressional Republicans, Reagan reluctantly signed the 1982 Voting Rights Act which included the effects test as supported by Pierce and the civil rights lobby.

CONCLUSION

Until the advent of the Reagan administration it may be generally said that black appointees did try to represent the interests of the race as these are conventionally understood. On the range of race-related issues of the last 25 years—school desegregation, affirmative action, voting rights, housing discrimination and South Africa policy—the evidence reviewed here, while not definitive, suggests that they brought into the government the perspectives of the black community. Yet, as Holden writes:

> No executive appointee, no senior bureaucrat, automatically represents the "interest" with which he has in the past been most identified merely because of past identification. The bureaucratic enterprise contains its own incentives which impose directions and constraints upon the functionary. Thus, it is fatuous to expect that a Black functionary will automatically "represent Black interests" or that if he attempts to do this he will automatically be effective, without some external relationships. The bureaucracy, like Congress, depends on constituency relationship.

The evidence reviewed here shows how the incentives or imperatives of the "bureaucratic enterprise" or the logic of institutionalization shaped the behavior of black appointees in several administrations. This is particularly the case for blacks serving in Republican administrations, since blacks are an insignificant part of the party's electoral coalition. This raises the question of whether in right-wing administrations the interests of the black community would be better served if there were no black appointees at all, a position some critics took with respect to the Thomas Supreme Court appointment, arguing that it would be better to have an all-white Supreme Court than one with a black right-wing conservative ideologue. In any event, this study of 25 years of black involvement in presidential policy making suggests that more than mere statistical incorporation is required if the causes advanced by blacks are to become public policy. What is needed is a powerful constituency outside of government so that any president and his appointees, black or white, will feel the pressure to act on the needs of the race. Without such a powerful constituency, the incorporation of blacks into the executive branch will remain largely symbolic.

───────────────────────── ■ ─────────────────────────

President Bill Clinton has appointed more high-ranking African-Americans than any other American president.[1] Not only did he appoint more cabinet officers than his predecessors, he appointed them to positions not typically associated with black interest—Ron Brown (Commerce), Hazel O'Leary (Energy), Mike Espy (Agriculture), Alexis Herman (Energy), and Rodney Slater (Transportation). Additionally, blacks held several other visible high-ranking positions in the administration (e.g., Franklin Raines, Office of Management and Budget; David Kennard, Federal Communications Commission; Deval Patrick, Department of Justice; Jocelyn Elders and David Satcher, Surgeons General). Although it is too early to evaluate the impact of these appointees definitively, it is clear that many of them have been strong advocates for black interests. Ron Brown, for example, provided access to capital and markets for black businesses before his untimely death in a plane crash. Secretary Kennard has been a strong voice for greater equity in the ownership of radio and television stations. Nonetheless, these appointees, like black appointees before them, must reconcile the tension between supporting the administration's interests and the interests of the broader black community.

Ultimate power in the executive branch, of course, lies with the office of the presidency. To date, there has not been an African-American president. Nonetheless, several black candidates have run for office (e.g., Shirley Chisholm, Lenora Fulani, Alan Keyes). Perhaps the most significant was Jesse Jackson's campaign in 1984. In this election, Jackson ran competitively in the early primaries before eventually losing the nomination to former Vice President Walter Mondale. The following selection is Jackson's 1984 **"Address before the Democratic National Convention."** *In the speech, Jackson outlined his "rainbow coalition" vision for the Democratic Party. He began the speech by connecting with his core constituency, ". . . the desperate, the damned, the disinherited, the disrespected, and the despised." He utilized the metaphor of a "quilt" to convey that ". . . many patches, many pieces, many colors, many sizes, all woven and held together by a common thread." He went on to claim the legacy of civil rights icons like Hamer, Malcolm, King, and the Kennedys in an attempt to reach out to a Jewish community skeptical of his intentions. He made it clear that the rainbow was to be inclusive and called for the Party to be tolerant and understanding of divergent views and cultures. In the latter part of the speech, Jackson emphasized the importance of voting rights protections, gender equity, and Pan-Africanism. In brief, Jackson argued that the "time had come" for a redefinition of American politics and society.[2]*

ADDRESS BEFORE
THE DEMOCRATIC NATIONAL CONVENTION

Jesse Jackson

July 18, 1984, Wednesday

Tonight we come together bound by our faith in a mighty God, with genuine respect and love for our country, and inheriting the legacy of a great party, the Democratic Party, which is the best hope for redirecting our nation on a more humane, just and peaceful course.

This is not a perfect party. We are not a perfect people. Yet, we are called to a perfect mission to feed the hungry; to clothe the naked; to house the homeless; to teach the illiterate; to provide jobs for the jobless; and to choose the human race over the nuclear race. (Applause)

We are gathered here this week to nominate a candidate and adopt a platform which will expand, unify, direct and inspire our Party and the Nation to fulfill this mission.

My constituency is the desperate, the damned, the disinherited, the disrespected, and the despised. They are restless and seek relief. They've voted in record numbers. They have invested faith, hope and trust that they have in us. The Democratic Party must send them a signal that we care. I pledge my best to not let them down.

Our flag is red, white and blue, but our nations is a rainbow—red, yellow, brown, black and white—and we're all precious in God's sight.

America is not like a blanket—one piece of unbroken cloth, the same color, the same texture, the same size. America is more like a quilt—many patches, many pieces, many colors, many sizes, all woven and held together by a common thread. The white, the Hispanic, the black, the Arab, the Jew, the woman, the native American, the small farmer, the businessperson, the environmentalist, the peace activist, the young, the old, the lesbian, the gay and the disabled make up the American quilt. (Applause)

Even in our fractured state, all of us count and all of us fit somewhere. We have proven that we can survive without each other. But we have not proven that we can win and progress without each other. We must come together. (Applause)

From Fannie Lou Hamer in Atlantic City in 1964 to the Rainbow Coalition in San Francisco today; from the Atlantic to the Pacific, we have experienced pain but progress as we ended American apartheid laws, we got public accommodation, we secured voting right, we obtained open housing, as young people got the right to vote. We lost Malcolm, Martin, Medgar, Bobby, John and Viola. The team that got us here must be expanded, not abandoned. (Applause)

Twenty years ago, tears welled up in our eyes as the bodies of Schwerner, Goodman and Chaney were dredged from the depths of a river in Mississippi. Twenty years later, our communities, black and Jewish, are in anguish, anger and pain. Feelings have been hurt on both sides.

There is a crisis in communications. Confusion is in the air. But we cannot afford to lose our way. We may agree to agree; or agree to disagree on issues; we must bring back civility to these tensions.

We are co-partners in a long and rich religious history—the Judeo-Christian traditions. Many blacks and Jews have a shared passion for social justice at home and peace abroad. We must seek a revival of the spirit, inspired by anew vision and new possibilities. We must return to higher ground. (Applause)

We are bound by Moses and Jesus, but also connected with Islam and Mohammed. These three great religions, Judaism, Christianity and Islam, were all born in the revered and holy city of Jerusalem.

We are bound by Dr. Martin Luther King Jr. and Rabbi Abraham Heschel, crying out from their graves for us to reach common ground. We are bound by shared blood and shared sacrifices. We are much too intelligent; much too bound by our Judeo-Christian heritage; much too victimized by racism, sexism, militarism and anti-Semitism; much too threatened as historical scapegoats to go on divided one from another. We must turn from finger pointing to clasped hands. We must share our burdens and our joys with each other once again. We must turn to each other and not on each other and choose higher ground. (Applause)

Twenty years later, we cannot be satisfied by just restoring the old coalition. Old wine skins must make room for new wine. We must heal and expand. The Rainbow Coalition is making room for Arab Americans. They, too, know the pain and hurt of racial and religious rejection. They must not continue to be made pariahs. The Rainbow Coalition is making room for Hispanic Americans who this very night are living under the threat of the Simpson-Mazzoli bill. (Applause) And farm workers from Ohio who are fighting the Campbell Soup Company with a boycott to achieve legitimate workers' rights. (Applause)

The Rainbow is making room for the Native American, the most exploited people of all, a people with the greatest moral claim amongst us. We support them as they seek the restoration of their ancient land and claim amongst us. We support them as they seek the restoration of land and water rights, as they seek to preserve their ancestral homelands and the beauty of a land that was once all theirs. They can never receive a fair share for all they have given us. They must finally have a fair chance to develop their great resources and to preserve their people and their culture.

The Rainbow Coalition includes Asian Americans, now being killed in our streets, scapegoats for the failures of corporate, industrial and economic policies.

The Rainbow is making room for the young Americans. Twenty years ago, our young people were dying in a war for which they could not even vote. Twenty years later, young America has the power to stop a war in Central America and the responsibility to vote in great numbers. (Applause) Young America must be politically active in 1984. The choice is war or peace. We must make room for young America.

The Rainbow includes disabled veterans. The color scheme fits in the Rainbow. The disabled have their handicap revealed and their genius concealed; while the able-bodied have their genius revealed and their disability concealed. But ultimately, we must judge people by their values and their contribution. Don't leave anybody out. I would rather have Roosevelt in a wheelchair than Reagan on a horse. (Applause)

The Rainbow includes for small farmers. They have suffered tremendously under the Reagan regime. They will either receive 90% parity or 100% charity. We must address their concerns and make room for them.

The Rainbow includes lesbians and gays. No American citizen ought to be denied equal protection from the law.

We must be unusually committed and caring as we expand our family to include new members. All of us must be tolerant and understanding as the fears and anxieties of the rejected and of the party leadership express themselves in so many different ways. Too often what we call hate—as if it were some deeply rooted in philosophy or strategy—it is simply ignorance, anxiety, paranoia, fear and insecurity. (Applause)

When we think, on this journey from slaveship to championship, that we have gone from the planks of the Boardwalk in Atlantic City in 1964 to fighting to help write the planks in the platform in San Francisco in 1984 there is a deep and abiding sense of joy in our souls in spite of the tears in our eyes. Though there are missing plans, there is a solid foundation upon which to build. Our party can win, but we must provide hope, which will inspire people to struggle and achieve; provide a plan that shows a way out of our dilemma and then lead the way.

In 1984, my heart is made to feel glad because I know there is a way out—justice. The requirement for rebuilding America is justice. The linchpin of progressive politics in our nation will not come from the North, they in fact will come from the South.

That is why I argue over and over again. We look from Virginia around to Texas, there's only one black Congressperson out of 115. Nineteen years later, we're locked out the Congress, the Senate and the Governor's mansion.

What does this large black vote mean? Why do I fight to win second primaries and fight gerrymandering and annexation and at-large elections? Why do we fight over that? Because I tell you, you cannot hold someone in the ditch unless you linger there with them. (Applause) Unless you linger there. (Applause)

If you want a change in this nation, you enforce that voting rights act. We'll get 12 to 20 Black, Hispanics, female and progressive congresspersons from the South. We can save the cotton, but we have got to fight the boll weevils. We have to make a judgment. We have got to make a judgment.

It is not enough to hope that ERA will pass. How can we pass ERA? If Blacks vote in great numbers, progressive Whites win. It is the only way progressive Whites win. If Blacks vote in great numbers, Hispanics win. When Blacks, Hispanics and progressive Whites vote, women win. When women win, children win. When women and children win, workers win. We must all come together. We must come together. (Spontaneous demonstration) Thank you.

I tell you, in all our joy and excitement, we must not save the world and lose our souls. We should never short-circuit enforcing the Voting Rights Act at every level. When one of us rises, all of us will rise. Justice is the way out. Peace is the way out. We should not act as if nuclear weaponry is negotiable and debatable.

We look at Africa. We cannot just focus on Apartheid in Southern Africa. We must fight for trade with Africa, and not just aid to Africa. We cannot stand idly by and say we will not relate to Nicaragua unless they have elections there, and then embrace military regimes in Africa overthrowing democratic governments in Nigeria and Liberia and Ghana. We must fight for democracy all around the world, and play the game by one set of rules.

Peace in this world. Our present formula for peace in the Middle East is inadequate. It will not work. There are 22 nations in the Middle East. Our nation must be able to talk and act and influence all of them. We must build upon Camp David, and measure human rights by one yard stick, In that region we have too many interests and too few friends.

We leave this place looking for the sunny side because there's a brighter side somewhere. I am more convinced than ever that we can win. We will vault up the rough side of the mountain. We can win. I just want young America to do me one favor, just one favor.

Exercise the right to dream. You must face reality, that which is. But then dream of a reality that ought to be, that must be. Live beyond the pain of reality with the dream of a bright tomorrow. Use hope and imagination as weapons of survival and progress. Use love to motivate you and obligate you to serve the human family.

Young America, dream. Choose the human race over the nuclear race. Bury the weapons and don't burn the people. Dream—dream of a new value system. Teachers who teach for life and not just for living; teach because they can't help it. Dream of lawyers more concerned about justice than a judgeship. Dream of doctors more concerned about public health than personal wealth. (Applause) Dream of preachers and priests who will prophesy and not just profiteer. Preach and dream! Our time has come. Our time has come.

Suffering breeds character. Character breeds faith, and in the end faith will not disappoint. Or time has come. Our faith, hope and dreams have prevailed. Our time has come. Weeping has endured for nights but that joy cometh in the morning.

Our time has come. No grave can hold our body down. Our time has come. No lie can live forever. Our time has come. We must leave the racial battle ground and come to the economic common ground and moral higher ground. America, our time has come.

We come from disgrace to amazing grace. Our time has come. Give me your tired, give me our poor, your huddled masses who yearn to breathe free and come November, their will be a change because our time has come.

Thank you and God bless you.

———————————————•———————————————

Jackson's two failed presidential bids were part and parcel of a larger transformation of American presidential politics in the 1980s of which race was a primary factor.[3] In the following selection, "White Suburbs and a Divided Black Community," Thomas and Mary Edsall describe how the Bush campaign used white racial fears to mobilize voters in support of Bush's presidential candidacy. Trailing Massachusetts Governor Michael Dukakis in the midsummer polls, the Bush team sought to reenergize disaffected white suburban voters, particularly in the South, who had voted for Ronald Reagan in 1980 and 1984. As Edsall and Edsall write, "Few events could be better suited . . . than the crimes of William (Willie) Horton, Jr." Horton had been convicted of first-degree murder and was sentenced to life in prison. Released under a weekend work furlough, Horton pistol-whipped an Oxon Hill, Maryland man and raped his fiancée. The political rub was that Governor Dukakis had earlier vetoed a bill that would have "prohibited furloughs of first-degree murderers." The Edsalls show how the Bush campaign used the Horton case as an example of a liberal agenda gone awry.

CHAIN REACTION: THE IMPACT OF RACE, RIGHTS, AND TAXES ON AMERICAN POLITICS

———————————————•———————————————

Thomas Byrne Edsall with Mary D. Edsall

Excerpt from Chapter 11: White Suburbs and a Divided Black Community

In preparing for the 1988 election, Republican strategists planning the campaign of George Bush faced a new set of problems: the fires that had fueled the conservative revolution had been banked; the combustibility of the issues of race, rights, and taxes had been reduced—in large part because the

Reagan administration had fulfilled many of its implicit promises to key white constituents. The anger and resentment in the white working and lower-middle class, which had helped the GOP in the elections of 1980 and 1984, had been blunted by the successes of the Reagan revolution. It was not difficult, however, to reignite those fires.

By 1988, the perception of a link between the Democratic party and controversial government policies on race, rights, and taxes had become imbedded in the conscious and unconscious memory of American politics—a perception still close enough to the surface to be accessible to political manipulation. This perception often exerted influence on an unarticulated level, a level at which the national Democratic party was still tied, in the minds of many voters, to the problems of crime, welfare, school failure, family dissolution, spreading urban squalor, an eroding work ethic, and global retreat.

In 1988, the Bush campaign assembled and deployed a range of symbols and images designed to tap into these submerged concerns—concerns often clustering around the nexus of racial, ethnic, cultural, and "values" anxieties that had helped to fuel the conservative politics of the post-civil rights era. The symbols of the Bush campaign—Willie Horton, the ACLU, the death penalty, the Pledge of Allegiance, the American flag, "no new taxes," the "L-word," and "Harvard boutique liberal"—conjured up the criminal defendants' and prisoners' rights movements, black crime, permissive liberal elites, a revenue-hungry state, eroding traditional values, tattered patriotism, and declining American prestige. Themes and symbols tapping these issues became for the Republican party the means of restoring the salience of associations damaging to Democrats, and the means of maintaining the vitality of the majority conservative coalition.

The 1988 Bush campaign strategy essentially looked backwards, organized around the conflicts and schisms of the previous 25 years. The campaign was fought on the battleground of the civil rights and the broader rights movements, focusing on the liabilities that had accumulated around the liberal wing of the national Democratic party.

The 1988 Bush campaign masked, in many respects, what were, in fact, far more complex social developments. Some of these developments suggest the potential for a *lessening* of racial isolation in the next decades, and include not only the sustained growth of the black middle class, but include also the continued ascension of increasing numbers of blacks to positions of power and authority in the public and private sectors; the increased willingness of whites to vote for a black candidate; and the possibility that partisan competition for black support will break the logjam now impeding black economic and social advancement. Developments springing from the increasing upward mobility of large numbers of black Americans have the potential to release each party from calcified positions in a fixed ideological debate, and from rigid policy alternatives lacking in innovation and vigor.

Conversely, however, there is another set of forces at work in America *intensifying* racial separation, particularly the separation, if not segregation, of poor blacks—and these forces have the potential to institutionalize racially separate structures in the political and economic spheres. Such forces could well make superfluous the divisive tactics of Republican political strategists. There may prove to be enough internal logic and cohesion to a right-of-center, top-down coalition that explicit polarizations over issues of race, rights, and taxes—such as those characterizing the 1988 Bush campaign—will no longer be necessary.

If this set of trends continues, racial and other, parallel divisions may become so ingrained in the composition and organization of American society that explicit political strategies to bring them to the surface will be unneeded.

The most important of these segregating forces is the ascendance of the suburban electorate to virtual majority status, empowering an overwhelmingly white segment of the voting population to address basic social service needs (schooling, recreation, libraries, roads, police and fire protection) through local suburban government and through locally generated revenues, and to further sever already weak ties to increasingly black urban constituencies.

In mid-summer 1988, long-range historical developments were far from the thinking of campaign operatives staffing the battle between Vice-President Bush and Massachusetts Governor Dukakis. With Dukakis far ahead in the polls, the central goal of the Bush campaign was to reignite social issue conservatism, and to counteract the successes of the Reagan revolution—success in quieting the most insistent demands of those seeking insulation from liberal government and success in deflating the pressures on working and lower-middle class whites—the very pressures that had led such voters to join in a top-down coalition with the conservative right.

Diminished white discontent over race and taxes combined with administration corruption, the Iran-Contra scandal, and growing income disparities to set the stage for an election in which the Democratic party had a chance at presidential victory. The size of the 17-percentage point lead in the polls held by Dukakis in July 1988 was unsustainable through the general election, but it reflected a restoration of Democratic loyalty that strategists for the presidential campaign of George Bush recognized as a substantial threat.

Lee Atwater, manager and central strategist of the 1988 Bush campaign, was acutely aware of the danger of economic discontent to the GOP and to his candidate:

> You see a new group who are not quite of age, they are 32–37. They grew up same time I grew up. My parents taught me that if I got a college degree, I've got it made. I was taught that the whole world was an oyster. These people believe all that and grow up. . . . All of a sudden these people who grew up thinking they'd get the white collar college jobs, all of a sudden they really are getting [what amount to] blue collar jobs. They say, 'I can see where I end up. Here I am the number two guy in my hometown Rexall Drugs, I'm making 28 grand, and I know if I stay here another 20 years, I can be the number one guy making 36 grand. For the first time in my life, I realize, Boy, it ain't going to happen.'

Atwater, who cut his political teeth in ex-Democrat, ex-segregationist Strom Thurmond's 1970 South Carolina Republican senatorial campaign, derived his strategies from the race-driven politics of the South, a region of hardball race-coded campaigning where Atwater—and other native politicians, including top Republican strategist Charles Black of North Carolina—learned to use racial and social issues to break the partisan loyalties of white Democrats and to fracture their decisive majority. "Republicans in the South could not win elections simply by showing various issues and talking about various issues. You had to make the case that the other guy, the other candidate is a bad guy and I'm a good guy. You simply could not get out in a universe where 60% of the people were Democrats and 28% Republican, and win by talking about your issues. The more you can make a Democrat a 'national Democrat' and a symbol of the national Democratic Party, the better off you are," said Atwater in 1984, looking back on his South Carolina experience.

In developing a strategy to break the 17-point advantage held by Dukakis in mid-summer, 1988, Atwater drew on his understanding of the dynamics of Southern voting, an understanding that had become increasing applicable to national contests. In a 1984 analysis of domestic politics Atwater wrote:

> "We have as the main voting groups in Southern politics 1) country clubbers ['reliably Republican'], 2) populists, 3) blacks ['reliably Democratic']. . . . The class struggle in the South continues, with the populists serving as the trump card. . . . Populists have always been liberal on economics. So long as the crucial issues were generally confined to economics—as during the New Deal—the liberal candidate would expect to get most of the populist vote. But populists are conservatives on most social issues. . . . As for race, it was hardly an issue—it went without saying that the populists' chosen leaders were hardcore segregationists. . . . After Carter's defeat [in 1980], the Democrats backed away from their Great Society rhetoric and diverted public attention from busing, affirmative action, etc., and toward clear economic issues. In 1982, we discovered we could not hold the populist vote on economic issues alone. When social and cultural issues died down, the populists were left with no compelling reason to vote Republican. . . . When Republicans are successful in getting certain social issues to the forefront, the populist vote is ours. The trick we must master is choosing those social issues that do not alienate the country clubbers since, again, we need their votes and the populists' to win in the South.

Few events could be better suited to focus public attention on the liabilities of Democratic liberalism than the crimes of William R. (Willie) Horton, Jr.,—a black felon featured in a barrage of Republican television commercials, speeches, and leaflets throughout the 1988 campaign. Convicted of the first-degree murder of a 17-year-old gas station attendant and sentenced to life in Massachusetts prison without possibility of parole, Horton was granted ten weekend furloughs under a program first initiated in 1972 in the early stages of the prisoners' rights movement.

That was the year the national Democratic party platform committed the party to "Recognition of the constitutional and human rights of prisoners; realistic therapeutic, vocational, wage-earning, education, alcoholism, and drug treatment programs. . . . Emergency, educational and work-release furlough programs as an available technique."

In 1976, Dukakis, two years into his first term as Massachusetts governor, vetoed a bill that would have prohibited furloughs of first-degree murderers, contending that such a bill would "cut the heart out of efforts at inmate rehabilitation." Ten years later, on June 6, 1986, Horton, on his tenth weekend furlough, disappeared.

In eight months, Horton resurfaced in Maryland. On April 3, 1987, Horton forced his way into the Oxon Hill, Maryland, home of Clifford Barnes and his financee, Angela Miller, who was out that evening. Horton beat Barnes with a pistol, cut him 22 times on his stomach and chest, tied and gagged him in the cellar. When Angela Miller returned home, Horton tied her up and raped her twice over a four-hour period. Barnes, in the cellar, broke free and called the police from a neighbor's house. After a car chase, Horton was captured and tried in Maryland where he was sentenced to two consecutive life terms plus 85 years. The judge refused to send him back to Massachusetts, saying, "I'm not prepared to take the chance that Mr. Horton might again be furloughed or otherwise released. This man should never draw a breath of free air again."

The Dukakis administration dealt with the furor that developed after Horton's 1987 arrest in Maryland with evasion. Dukakis did not apologize to Miller or to Barnes, rejected the requests of the press, particularly of the Lawrence *Eagle-Tribune*, for information on the records of Horton and other furloughed prisoners, and continued to defend the furlough program. "Don't forget that Mr. Horton had nine previous successful furloughs," Philip Johnston, Dukakis's secretary of Human Services, told reporters.

Atwater, who had assigned a campaign staffer to unearth weaknesses in the Dukakis record, could not contain himself on learning the details of the Horton case. At a meeting with southern Republicans in Atlanta on July 9, two weeks before the Democratic convention, Atwater held forth in a gleeful stream of consciousness:

> I can't wait until this Dukakis fellow gets down here [the South]. There are quite a few questions he ought to have to answer every day he's down here, and every time he gives the answer, there's going to be votes coming up just like in a cash register. Can you imagine him trying to answer how in the world as governor, a responsible position like governor, he was in favor of this furlough program that allowed first-degree murderers and drug pushers to go on weekend vacations where they could murder, sell drugs and do all the rest of this stuff? There is a story about a fellow named Willie Horton who for all I know may end up to be Dukakis' running mate. Dukakis is making Hamlet look like the rock of Gibraltar in the way he's acted on this [Atwater was referring to Dukakis' procedure for selecting a running mate.] The guy [Dukakis] was on TV about a month ago and he said you'll never see me standing in the driveway of my house talking to these candidates [referring to Mondale's protracted search in 1984 for a running mate, interviewing prospects at his Minnesota home]. And guess what, on Monday, I saw in the driveway of his [Dukakis's] house? Jesse Jackson. So anyway, maybe he'll put this Willie Horton guy on the ticket after all is said and done. And Willie

Horton is the fellow who was a convicted murderer and rapist who got let out on eight [Atwater got the figure wrong] of these weekend furloughs, and on the ninth one, he brutally and wantonly raped this woman. . . . And do you know what the response was from the Dukakis crowd: 'Well he didn't do anything on the other eight.

With Horton creating a case study, at the extreme, of the costs of Democratic liberalism, the more abstract issues of Dukakis's membership in the ACLU, his veto of legislation requiring teachers to lead the Pledge of Allegiance, his opposition to the death penalty, his wife's confession to a history of amphetamine abuse, and his generally rights-oriented, liberal stance provided the means for the Bush campaign to wrap the collective agenda of race, rights, and values around the neck of the Democratic presidential nominee.

Willie Horton represented for key sectors of the electorate the consequences of an aggressively expansive liberalism, a liberalism running up against public opinion, against "traditional" values, and, to a certain degree, against common sense. In the mind of many voters, the Willie Horton case came to stand for the blurring by liberalism of legitimate goals, such as modest help for prisoners judged suitable for rehabilitation (prisoners, for example, without long records of violence), with the *il*legitimate goal, in the majority view, of "coddling" violent and dangerous criminals whom much of society judged irredeemable.

Republican strategists correctly perceived that the furlough of Willie Horton epitomized an evolution of the far-reaching rights movement and of post-war liberalism, an evolution that was resented and disapproved of by significant numbers of voters who saw crime as existing on a *continuum* with other social and moral problems aggravated by liberalism. For these voters, the evolving rights movement was seen as extending the same public access to hard-core pornography as to *Lady Chatterley's Lover*; as allowing welfare recipients to avoid the responsibility for supporting their own children; as fostering drug use, illegitimacy, homosexual promiscuity, and an AIDS epidemic—all leading to demands on taxpayers to foot skyrocketing health-care and social service bills—bills traceable, in this view, to behavior commonly judged "immoral," and incurred disproportionately by blacks and Hispanics.

Crime became a shorthand *signal*, to crucial numbers of white voters, of broader issues of social disorder, tapping powerful ideas about authority, status, morality, self-control, and race. If criminal defendants in the years preceding the rights revolution had been, like many other beneficiaries of that movement, in fact subject to arbitrary authority and to random cruelty, by the 1980s they had completely lost their public status as victims. Populist legitimacy and sympathy had shifted decisively from victims of law enforcement to the victims of criminal violence, and in general to those who felt themselves to be victimized by the rights revolution and by social change—"average" citizens whose own rights seemed to them to be unprotected by the liberal state.

"On no other issue is the dividing line so clear, on no other issue is my opponent's philosophy so completely at odds with mine, and I would say with the common sense attitudes of the American people, than on the issue of crime," Bush declared in a October 7, 1988, campaign speech to police officers in Xenia, Ohio. "There are some—and I would list my opponent among them—who have wandered off the clear-cut path of common sense and have become lost in the thickets of liberal sociology. Just as when it comes to foreign policy, they always `Blame America First,' when it comes to crime and criminals, they always seem to 'Blame Society First'. . . . [Criminal justice under Dukakis is] a 'Twilight Zone' world where prisoners' 'right to privacy' has more weight than the citizen's right to safety."

The rise of Republican suburbs in a "white noose" around declining cities with majority, or near-majority, black and Hispanic populations is becoming the central characteristic of politics in such key states as New York, Michigan, Illinois, and Ohio. From 1968 to 1988, the total vote cast by the heavily Democratic New York City counties of Queens, the Bronx, Kings (Brooklyn), and New York (Manhattan) has fallen from 2.4 million to 1.9 million, while the surrounding Republican-leaning counties (Westchester, Nassau, Suffolk, and Richmond) have risen from 1.5 million to 1.6 million, for a net gain of just under 600,000 votes in favor of the Republican counties. In Illinois during the same 20-year period, the 1.9 million-vote advantage in 1968 of Democratic Cook County (Chicago and environs) over the surrounding GOP counties of DuPage, Will, and Lake, dropped by 1988 to a 1.4 million vote advantage. In Michigan, Wayne County (Detroit and surrounding communities) in 1968 cast 1.03 million votes, 470,000 *more* than the 560,000 cast in neighboring Oakland and McComb counties; by 1988, Wayne county (62% white, 38% black and Hispanic) cast 748,156 votes, 5,448 less than the 753,604 voters who went to the polls in McComb (97% white) and Oakland counties (93% white). In terms of actual vote outcomes, Humphrey in 1968 came out 433,096 votes ahead in these three counties; Dukakis in 1988 lost the three counties by 13,164 votes.

What all this suggests is that a politics of suburban hegemony will come to characterize presidential elections. With a majority of the electorate equipped to address its own needs through local government, not only will urban blacks become increasingly isolated by city-county boundaries, but support for the federal government, a primary driving force behind black advancement, is likely to diminish.

For those seeking to maintain and nurture a right-of-center coalition, suburban hegemony provides the ideal setting for the repeated mobilization of an election-day majority without depending upon divisive 'wedge' issues to prevent the restoration of the more economically-based Democratic coalition.

———————————————————————■———————————————————————

In **"The Public Presidency Hits the Wall: Clinton's Presidential Initiative on Race,"** *Renee Smith analyzes the impact of President Clinton's efforts to lead a dialogue on race relations in the United States. Her central concern is whether the president can use the "bully pulpit" to influence public discourse and policy on complex social issues. Smith contends that* *the initiative failed to generate much public discussion about racial issues. Citing public opinion data, Smith shows that the president's pronouncement did little to change the importance of racism as a major public concern. Further, the president's approval ratings moved very little as a result of the town hall meetings he convened. Smith identifies five reasons for the president's failure to energize the public discourse about race. First, it was less than clear that the public believed such an initiative was needed. This is not surprising given the large numbers of whites who believe that the rate of racial progress is "about right." Second, the initiative stumbled badly out of the gate. The advisory board meetings took some time to get underway, its composition was a matter of concern, and staffing was a problem. Third, the advisory board met publicly. This obviously constrained free and open discussions. Further, critics asserted that the board spent too much time listening to researchers and not enough time listening to citizens. Fourth, the town-hall meeting approach insured that media coverage would be episodic, thus deemphasizing the contextual framework of American race relations. Finally, the Monica Lewinsky scandal meant that the president had little energy to devote to the initiative. While the jury is still out, Smith concludes, ". . . the public presidency, as practiced by Clinton, hit the wall." Put differently, given the complexities of racial politics in the United States, it is very difficult for any president to move the public discourse on race from the "bully pulpit."[4]*

THE PUBLIC PRESIDENCY HITS THE WALL: CLINTON'S PRESIDENTIAL INITIATIVE ON RACE

Renee M. Smith

President Clinton, June 14, 1997

When President Bill Clinton made a public appeal for all Americans to begin "a candid conversation on the state of race relations today," he promised both to lead the dialogue and to encourage public officials and citizens to take action based on the conclusions reached in these conversations.(1) In the days following Clinton's announcement of the President's Initiative on Race, administration officials asserted three goals—study, dialogue, and action—for the initiative. To help him meet these goals, President Clinton appointed a seven-member advisory board whose tasks he initially specified as educating Americans about racial issues, promoting community dialogue about race relations, supporting and recruiting leaders to bridge racial divides, and recommending concrete solutions for racial problems. He also pledged to meet with and listen to citizens' views in a series of "town-hall" meetings—a format he used successfully in his presidential campaigns.

But can the "bully pulpit" be used successfully to encourage dialogue and to obtain policy change on the basis of that conversation? In the age of the "public" or "rhetorical" presidency,(2) can a president elicit a national conversation and legislative action on topics as complicated as racism or racial inequality without a coinciding crisis or important event to call citizens' attention to the issues and to coalesce opinion around specific policy alterna-tives? Existing scholarship on the presidency suggests that Clinton's race ini-tiative was doomed from the moment he decided to use his favored town-hall meetings as a tactic to promote discussions of race relations. Rather than generating dialogue about racial issues, these town meetings produced discussions about Clinton's performance during them and about his willing-ness to listen to all points of view. In addition, his use of forums allowing public feedback created expectations among citizens that the meetings of his advisory board, required by law to be open to the public, would necessarily allow for extensive citizen participation.

EXISTING SCHOLARSHIP

Existing scholarship on the public presidency suggests that Clinton's race initiative, based in large part on obtaining a response from the public, was likely to fail. For instance, Woodrow Wilson's arguments that presidents should engage in the leadership of public opinion by "interpreting" citi-zens' preferences seems to imply a top-down type of leadership in which a president first discerns and then molds public opinion to use it as leverage in policy battles with Congress. While Wilson implied that a president could mold existing and partially formed preferences by making public ad-dresses, he did not suggest that a president could spur the formation of pol-icy preferences in the absence of public concern over an issue, nor did he suggest that public opinion should be discerned by direct feedback from a small group of citizens.(3)

Similarly, Neustadt argued that presidents must often serve as teachers, educating the public on important issues of the day. Unfortunately, this task will be difficult, Neustadt said, because the public is generally inat-tentive unless an event occurs to stimulate concern. And while presidents can sometimes manufacture such events, "No matter how cooperative the press, a President needs quiet from competitive events if what he does is to be noticed as a happening."(4) In addition, recent experimental research shows that whether citizens think political leaders should take responsi-bility for solutions to problems of racial inequality and poverty depends on whether media coverage of these events is episodic (focusing on dis-crete events) or thematic (focusing on events within their societal and his-torical contexts).(5)

Finally, many presidential scholars have noted the debilitating paradox that can arise for presidents in the age of the public presidency. To the extent that presidents more frequently use public opinion as the basis for their pol-icy decisions, they may weaken their long-run leadership capacities because each public appeal raises citizens' expectations about the president's power to solve problems. Like a marathon runner with only a few miles to finish, the public presidency will sometimes "hit the wall."

THE EMPIRICAL EVIDENCE

The empirical evidence related to Clinton's Presidential Initiative on Race also shows that his strategy to promote dialogue about racial issues by using public speeches and nationally televised town-hall meetings has failed.(6) For instance, Clinton's national approval rating, which stood at 57% in May 1997, remained at that level even as news of his upcoming plans to address racial issues surfaced. And ten days after the June 14, 1997, speech in which he announced his initiative, Clinton's approval rating was recorded as 55% (a percentage that is not statistically different from his rating prior to the speech).(7) Clinton's approval ratings before and after each of his town-hall meetings were 59 and 61% bracketing the December 3, 1997, meeting in Akron, Ohio (televised on C-SPAN); 67 and 66% before and after his meeting featuring black athletes on April 1, 1998, in Houston (televised on ESPN); and 60 and 61% bracketing his July 8, 1998, roundtable discussion with eight authors, educators, and journalists (televised on PBS). In each case, there was no statistically discernible difference in Clinton's approval rating before and after he met with citizens and others.(8)

Examining a more direct measure of public concern with racial issues also shows that Clinton's call for dialogue had no discernible effect on citizen's opinions. In January 1997, racism was not a major public concern—only 4% of all responses to a survey question about the nation's most important problem dealt with racism. That age remained constant in the ensuing year and a half, despite Clinton's highly publicized speech announcing the initiative and two town-hall and seven advisory board meetings.(9)

EXPLAINING THE CLINTON FAILURE

Why have Clinton's efforts to influence the national agenda failed? First, while Clinton hoped to establish a historical legacy for himself by taking on the issues of race relations and racial inequality, the public was divided over whether such an initiative was needed. Second, the initiative initially lacked focus, which resulted in early miscues. Third, the advisory board was forced to meet publicly, which dampened the panelists' ability to engage in open dialogue and raised citizens expectations that obtaining public feedback would be the primary focus of each meeting. Fourth, Clinton's town-hall meetings encouraged episodic media coverage of his initiative, which hindered Clinton's ability to focus the public on policy alternatives. Fifth, just when the advisory board and the initiative began to pick up steam, Clinton was hit with the allegations that he had sexual relations with Monica Lewinsky. Clinton's improprieties dominated and continue to hold the attention of the mass media, crowding out news of other presidential actions. They also forced Clinton and his staff to pour considerable energy into responding to the political consequences, thereby using time and resources that might have been devoted to other issues.

PUBLIC OPINION ON RACE RELATIONS

Despite Clinton's desire to focus on race relations in the United States, the public was divided over whether such an effort was necessary. In June 1997, 76% of whites and 49% of blacks said they thought blacks were treated equally in local communities.(10) Despite the large gap in the perceptions of blacks and whites, it is difficult to argue that there is a crisis in race relations when almost half of all blacks say they think they are treated equally and when three-fourths of whites do not acknowledge a problem. That Clinton's efforts had little effect also can be seen in the results of an April 1998 poll in which only small majorities of whites (54%) and nonwhites (59%) agreed that the initiative was needed.

LACK OF FOCUS

Despite its immediate formation, the advisory board did not meet publicly until September 30, 1997. In fact, the board had no staff until Judith Winston became its executive director at the beginning of August. It took her another month to hire and train additional staff. Throughout that period, board members struggled to determine the panel's charge. Should it deal only with black-white race relations? To what degree was the advisory board, appointed by Clinton, able to act independently? In addition, Clinton and the board were criticized because the board was not representative of all minorities and did not contain members representing conservative views on U.S. race relations. The lack of focus by Clinton and the advisory board even extended into Clinton's third and final town-hall meeting in July 1998 at which Clinton and the participants spent most of their time "talking about talking bluntly about race."(11)

PUBLIC ADVISORY BOARD MEETINGS

By law, the advisory board was required to meet in public. Given the divisive nature of racial issues, public meetings hindered the ability of board members to speak freely, especially since some of them held positions in business or education that could be jeopardized by public statements on such a sensitive issue. More important, because Clinton pledged to hold town-hall meetings and solicit direct feedback from the audience, the advisory board was often criticized for spending too much time listening to the reports of researchers on the effects of race in the areas of housing, education, and criminal justice and not enough time allowing citizens to address the board and state their views.(12) When they did hear from citizens, there was little dialogue but instead "serial monologue, an airing of grievances and personal perspectives."(13) John Hope Franklin, head of the president's advisory board, in his one-year evaluation of the race initiative, commented, "We have learned how difficult it is to hold productive discussions about race under the glare of television lights and cameras, in large meetings among relative strangers, and among people who expect more than an advisory board can reasonably deliver.(14)

EPISODIC MEDIA COVERAGE

By using a town-hall meeting approach, Clinton all but guaranteed that media coverage of his race initiative would be episodic, focusing on each meeting as a discrete event rather than focusing on the issue of race within its societal and historical contexts. This became true of the advisory board's meetings as well because of media and public expectations that citizens' feedback would play an important role. My review of media coverage by the Wall Street Journal, the New York Times, the Washington Post, and the Christian Science Monitor shows that news reports on Clinton's race initiative were dominated by discussions of the spectacle provided by each town-hall or advisory board meeting rather than by the issues of discrimination, injustice, or affirmative action within a broader context. One prominent feature of news reports and analyses of the race initiative was the emphasis on Clinton as a media performer. For instance, commentators called Clinton the "first conversationalist"(15) and "chief talker"(16) and referred to his initiative as "a national gabfest,"(17) "the jaw, jaw approach,"(18) and governing by therapy.(19) To the extent that media coverage was episodic, the complex causes of and solutions to racial conflict were ignored by the media and, hence, by citizens.

Although Clinton thought his town-hall meetings would benefit his cause (as they did during his presidential campaigns), he later realized that for the case of race relations, such "events" could not galvanize public opinion. "It's very hard to pierce through the public consciousness and to do a sustained public education campaign in the absence of some great conflict," Clinton was quoted as saying.(20) In this case, it seems that, just as Neustadt predicted, the president as teacher needed real, rather than manufactured, events to raise citizens' awareness.

CHARGES OF MISCONDUCT

Clinton held his first town-hall meeting on December 3, 1997. Two weeks later, the advisory board met for the third time, and shortly thereafter, Clinton hosted nine national leaders who held conservative views on U.S. race relations at the White House. At this point, the initiative began to pick up steam. To ensure his staff maintained its focus on the initiative, Clinton began requiring weekly reports from executive departments that discussed realized or contemplated events or policies aimed at solving race-related problems.

The advisory board, Clinton staff, and Clinton himself were finally working together, or at least working, and seemed poised to make headway after the December holidays.

Once the allegations surfaced that Clinton had sexual relations with a White House intern and may have perjured himself, neither Clinton nor administration officials had time to push the race initiative. By March 1998, a news report on Clinton's upcoming town-hall meeting with sports officials and athletes noted, "The meeting will be Mr. Clinton's second town hall session on race since he started his initiative last June. The national dialogue has been eclipsed in recent months by the possibility of war with Iraq and the accusations of sexual impropriety against Mr. Clinton, who has devoted little public time promoting the initiative."(21)

CONCLUSION

Technically, the President's Initiative on Race is not over. What remains is to see whether Congress approves any of the additional funds that Clinton has requested for race-related programs. Clinton has also promised to issue a report summarizing the findings of the advisory board and others who participated in the race initiative. The president's report, which reportedly "will include a 'significant public policy component' as well as 'bully pulpit' leadership,"(22) is expected no later than January 1999.

For all intents and purposes, the President's Initiative on Race was over almost as soon as it began. The public presidency, however well suited it may be for stirring up short-term support for a president or a one-shot dose of support for a specific public policy, is not well suited for eliciting general public debate on complex and sensitive issues such as race relations. Nor is it well suited for coalescing diverse opinions on policy alternatives. As one commentator wrote, "Sure, a televised meeting or march can help promote a cause once it is defined, but it is not much good at formulating or working out any sort of plan for the tangle of matters that have come to define the problem of race."(23) In that sense, the public presidency, as practiced by Clinton, hit the wall. Whether he or any other similarly situated president can, before a national audience, run through the pain to reach a finish line is an open question.

NOTES

(1.) President William Clinton, "Remarks by the President at University of California at San Diego Commencement," June 14, 1997. On-line. Available at http://www. whitehouse.gov/Initiative/OneAmerica/speech.html. July 7 1998.

(2.) George C. Edwards, The Public Presidency (New York: St. Martin's, 1983); Jeffrey Tulis, The Rhetorical Presidency (Princeton, NJ: Princeton University Press, 1987).

(3.) Woodrow Wilson, Constitutional Government in the United States (New York: Columbia University Press, 1908).

(4.) Richard Neustadt, Presidential Power, 2d ed. (New York: John Wiley, 1980), pp. 74–79.

(5.) Shanto Iyengar, Is Anyone Responsible? How Television Frames Political Issues (Chicago: University of Chicago Press, 1991), pp. 63–68.

(6.) My article deals with Clinton's effort to encourage national dialogue. The Clinton administration cites numerous requests for budget increases in the fiscal year 1999 budget as evidence of its policy actions. These requests are in the areas of civil rights enforcement, education, aid to minority businesses, job access, housing, crime, health, and child care. In addition, by the one-year mark, there had been eight advisory meetings, nine hundred campus discussions, and more than one hundred community meetings. For a summary, see http://www.whitehouse.gov/Initiative/OneAmerica/accompreport.html.

(7.) The Gallup Poll. On-line. Available at http://www.gallup.com/Gallup_Poll_Data/ratepres/jobapp.htm, August 10, 1998.

(8.) Ibid.

(9.) Only 2% of responses were related to concerns with racism, according to an April 1998 Gallup poll. See The Gallup Poll. On-line. Available at http://www.gallup.com/Gallup_Poll_Data/mood/problem.htm, August 10, 1998.

(10.) The Gallup Poll. "Special Reports: Black/White Relations in the U.S." June 10, 1997. On-line. Available at http:/www.gallup.com/Gallup_Poll_Data/Special_Reports/race.htm, August 10, 1998.

(11.) Jim Lehrer, quoted in "Clinton at Race Forum, Is Confronted on Affirmative Action," New York Times, July 9, 1998, p. 23.

(12.) Steven A. Holmes, "President Nudges His Race Panel to Take Action," New York Times, October 1, 1997, p. 23.

(13.) Felicia R. Lee, "The Honest Dialogue That is Neither," New York Times (late edition), December 7, 1997, p. 5.

(14.) John Hope Franklin, "Talking, Not Shouting, about Race," New York Times, June 13, 1998, p. 15.

(15.) Lee, "The Honest Dialogue."

(16.) Walter Goodman, "Where Image Prevails, Talk about Race Turns Bland," New York Times, December 9, 1997, sec. E, p. 2.

(17.) Russell Baker, "We've Got to Talk," New York Times, June 17, 1997, p. 21.

(18.) Skip Thurman, "Next Clinton Focus: Healing Racial Rifts," Christian Science Monitor, June 3, 1997.

(19.) Glenn C. Loury, "Why Talk about Race? Welfare and Crime Demand More Than Feel Good Chat," Washington Post, December 7, 1997.

(20.) President William Clinton, quoted in Stephen A. Holmes and James Bennett, "A Renewed Sense of Purpose for Clinton's Panel on Race," New York Times, January 14, 1998, p. 1.

(21.) Steven ah. Holmes, "Race Forum Will Seek New Focus," New York Times, March 20, 1998, p. 21.

(22.) Peter Baker and Michael Fletcher, "'Conversations about Race': Just Talk? White House Searching For a Way to Turn Rhetoric into Change," Washington Post, June 14, 1998, sec. A.

(23.) Goodman, "Where Image Prevails.

Between 1869 and 1901, 22 blacks served in the United States Congress (all were Republicans). This period of initial black institutional empowerment was relatively short-lived, however, as no blacks served between 1901 and 1928. The second surge of black congressional empowerment followed the election of Oscar DePriest of Illinois in 1928 and, by 1973, 52 blacks had held Congressional seats. Black representation in Congress grew most dramatically in the post-civil rights era. [5] For example, between 1975 and 1998, the black congressional delegation averaged approximately 23 members. Further, in the 1990s, the average was around 35 members.[6]

The Congressional Black Caucus has been the primary instrument for advancing black interests in the legislative branch. [7] The caucus was established in 1971 and grew out of the "Democratic Select Steering Committee." Rep. Charles Diggs formed the committee to ". . . promote communication between himself and other Black House members."[8] The purpose of the CBC is to ". . . promote the public welfare through legislation designed to meet the needs of millions of neglected citizens." Members' duties encompass both particularized efforts for their electoral constituencies and promoting the interests of the national black community.[9] The increase in the size of the modern Caucus quite naturally means that there is greater variation in opinion among the delegation. Republican members like Watts and Franks have openly feuded with the Caucus and even Democratic stalwarts Bill Gray and Mike Espy bolted the "party line" on particular issues.[10]

The increasing variation of views among members of the CBC coupled with the racially liberal voting records of several white members has challenged conceptions of how and by whom black interests are represented in Congress. Perhaps the most controversial question surrounding black representation in the modern Congress is "racial redistricting," or the practice of redrawing congressional district lines for racial reasons.[11] The historical context of racial redistricting is found in the response of southern state and local officials to Voting Rights Act of 1965.[12] The primary tool of white resistance was to alter jurisdictional boundaries in such a way as to dilute black voting strength. In this way, black voters were often denied the opportunity to elect the candidate of their choice. During the 1980s, Congress and the Supreme Court cleared the path to the creation of majority-minority congressional districts following the 1990 Census. By the mid-1990s, however, racial redistricting came under political and judicial scrutiny.

In *Miller v. Johnson (1995)*, the Court sought to clarify its new position on racial redistricting. Striking down a race-based districting plan in Georgia, the Court made plain its view that race may not be the predominant factor in drawing districts lines. In **"The Future of Black Representation,"** Carol Swain contends that far from diminishing black legislative influence, the Miller ruling ". . . may well enhance minority influence in Congress." Swain constructs her argument on three points. First, fewer majority-minority districts heightens the probability that black votes can be spread out in support of liberal, non-black *candidates. Second, Miller will not hurt the re-election chances of black incumbents from black majority districts. Likewise, black incumbents from white majority districts, who do not have to rely on black numerical majorities, will also be unaffected by the Miller ruling. Third, the creation of majority-minority districts costs the Democrats seats in the 1994-midterm elections.[13] The upshot, of course, is that the presence of more Republicans means less substantive representation for black interests. Swain ends the article with a critique of the role of the Congressional Black Caucus in furthering the interests of the African-American community.*

THE FUTURE OF BLACK REPRESENTATION

Carol M. Swain

T The Supreme Court has "eviscerated" the Voting Rights Act, a *New York Times* editorial declared on June 30, the day after the Court ruled five to four that it is unconstitutional to use the race of voters as the "predominant" factor in drawing the lines of congressional districts. A dejected Cynthia Mc-Kinney, whose Georgia district was the focus of the Court's scrutiny, warned that the decision in *Miller v. Johnson* might lead to the "ultimate bleaching of the U.S. Congress." Some melodramatic critics even likened the *Miller* decision to *Dred Scott*, the 1857 Court ruling that blacks were not citizens of the U.S. and "had no rights which the white man was bound to respect."

If the critics of *Miller* are right, the future of black political representation in Congress is grim, and blacks ought to mobilize to salvage what they can of racial districting. But another interpretation suggests a different response. The Court's decision may not diminish black influence in congressional elections, and it may not doom black candidates for Congress. And rather than diminishing the legislative strength of minorities, the decision may well enhance minority influence in Congress by enabling liberal candidates with agendas more friendly to African Americans to get elected in districts adjacent to some of the current black-majority districts. The Supreme Court handed down a decision; it didn't hand down the future. Much of what happens now depends on how the Congressional Black Caucus and other black leaders respond to new judicial and political realities.

WHY MILLER ISN'T FATAL

Critics of the *Miller* decision have greatly overstated its likely impact on minority representatives. The redrawing of the offending district lines does not mean that current black and Latino incumbents will automatically lose their re-election bids.

Most current black incumbents will not be fatally affected by the *Miller* ruling. Racial gerrymandering is not an issue for the numerous black representatives of geographical areas with large compact minority populations. The growing number of black politicians elected from districts without black majorities will also have little cause for concern over the Court's ruling. Black Democrats Ronald Dellums, Alan Wheat, and Bill Clay and black Republicans Gary Franks and J.C. Watts have shown that white voters in congressional elections will support black candidates. Similarly, the elections of Illinois Senator Carol Moseley Braun, former Virginia Governor L. Douglas Wilder. Ohio Treasurer J. Kenneth Blackwell, and New York Comptroller Carl McCall show that race is no longer an insurmountable barrier to black electoral success at the state level as well. Carl McCall's victory was especially significant as he was the only New York Democrat to win statewide in 1994.

Many black incumbents, moreover, have been anticipating that the Supreme Court would rule against race-conscious districting since last year's decisions in two earlier cases, *Johnson v. DeGrandy* and *Holder v. Hall*, and have been gathering resources in anticipation of more competitive campaigns. Georgia's McKinney and North Carolina's Mel Watts, for example, have reached out to white voters and eagerly sought to build biracial coalitions. They will now be in a stronger position to gain white votes than in previous elections.

Critics of *Miller* are also missing two other important facts. First, the Court did not authorize white officials to return to the old practice of breaking up compact minority populations into separate districts to dilute their voting power. *Miller* does not overturn *Beer v. United States* (1976), which led to a no-retrogression policy interpreted by the courts to mean that a redistricting plan or an electoral change cannot leave minority voters worse off. Thus, while partisan gerrymanders are certainly possible, black incumbents in compact minority districts have some protection against regressive redistricting plans.

Second, even if the Court had approved race-conscious districting, the strategy of grouping together black voters in the same district to elect blacks to Congress has nearly been exhausted. Today there are few places where African Americans are concentrated enough to create more black-majority districts. Philadelphia's 1st district, New York's 16th and 17th, and Mississippi's 4th are among the last remaining areas where such a strategy has any hope for increasing black representation. If black interests are to be better represented in Congress, racial gerrymandering is not the way.

PUTTING COLOR BEFORE SUBSTANCE

Most people would agree that African-Americans lost substantive representation in 1994: The new Republican Congress represents their interests less than the previous Democratic one even though the new Congress has more black members. What went wrong? One answer is that the strategy to enhance minority representation through racial gerrymandering had the unintended consequence—unintended, that is, by most voting-rights advocates—of increasing Republican strength.

It was clearly the intention of the architects of the minority districts to give greater voting power to both African-Americans and Latinos, two predominantly Democratic groups. Indeed, 13 blacks and 5 Hispanics were elected in the 18 newly created minority districts in 1992. The newly elected blacks, all Democrats, were reelected in 1994, but other members of their party did not fare as well. The Democrats' loss of 52 House seats in 1994 gave the Republicans 12 more than they needed for control. Race-conscious redistricting, the evidence suggests, cost the Democrats enough seats to shift the balance of power in the House. By concentrating liberal voting strength in a few minority districts with supermajorities of Democratic voters, Democratic candidates in nearby districts were deprived of allies in their contests with more conservative Republicans.

Moreover, some white Democrats at the state and local level lost because minority voters failed to turn out for the general elections in districts where congressional black incumbents had no serious competition. In several congressional districts, Republicans declined even to run candidates against black incumbents. Since the elections in these districts were not actively contested, some black voters stayed home and failed to cast votes for white Democratic candidates running for other offices.

Some critics have disputed this analysis. Soon after the election, the Legal Defense Fund (LDF) of the NAACP issued a detailed analysis of what was then thought to be a Democratic loss of 54 seats (later narrowed to 52 after a couple of cliff-hangers were resolved). That analysis showed that Republicans captured 24 seats in states where there were no nonwhite-majority districts and 15 seats in white-majority districts surrounded by other white-majority districts. Of the remaining 15 districts, 8 gained minority voters and 6 remained the same. According to the LDF report, far from impeding the re-election rate of white Democrats in the South, race-conscious districting helped save Democrats in such states as Mississippi and Georgia. The report concludes that Democrats lost seats for the simplest of reasons: A majority of white voters shifted to the Republican Party.

But the LDF report fails to provide a satisfactory account of such states as Georgia, where two black-majority districts were added to the one that previously existed. The Georgia plan was largely designed to unseat Newt Gingrich by obliterating his old district and forcing him to move his residence. As it turned out, race-conscious redistricting gave him a safer Republican constituency, cutting black voters from 14% of his district in 1990 (when he won by only 974 votes) to 6% in 1992 and after.

The dismemberment of Gingrich's former district contributed directly to the defeat of 12-term Democrat Richard Ray, and redistricting led three other white Democrats to retire. Since redistricting, a nine-to-one seat Democratic advantage has turned into a seven-to-three Republican advantage (with Republicans picking up one seat when white Democrat Nathan

Deal switched parties). Now Georgia's only Democrats in the House are blacks representing districts where the voting-age population is over 57% black.

North Carolina, which created two black majority congressional districts, is another case that illustrates how redistricting backfired. Although its six Democratic incumbents survived the 1992 elections, they were decimated in 1994 when Democrats lost two incumbents and three open seats. Before redistricting, North-Carolina Democrats held an eight-to-four advantage; after 1994 the Republicans had a seven-to-four advantage. Two of the state's four Democrats are black, and one of the white Democrats, Charlie Rose, was barely reelected. The time may come when southern officeholders primarily consist of black Democrats and white Republicans.

North Carolina's second district was the one most directly affected by the concentration of black voters in nearby districts. Before redistricting, blacks made up 37% of the voting-age population; after redistricting, they constituted only 20%. Tim Valentine, the six-term Democratic incumbent, retired after his re-election margin dropped from 75% in 1990 to 54% in 1992. His Republican successor David Funderburk, a former U.S. ambassador to Romania, won the district with 56% of the vote. Commenting on Funderburk's qualifications, Valentine said, "He was an attractive candidate, a smart, articulate man who had written several books. He's also probably to the right of Jesse Helms."

Other Democrats whose losses were related to redistricting include Joan Kelley Horn of Missouri, who was barely elected in 1990 and then defeated in 1992 after losing more than 8,000 black voters to the district of a 13-term black Democrat, Bill Clay, Alabama's five-term Ben Erdreich, Maryland's three-term Tom McMillen, and Louisiana's ten-term Jerry Huckaby are among the other casualties of redistricting.

These results should scarcely be surprising. After all, the coalition to racialize voting districts included not only blacks and Hispanics, but also Republicans. Why should a party otherwise opposed to affirmative action have advocated quotas in the electoral system by supporting specially drawn racial districts that would surely elect Democrats? Could it be that the Republicans knew something about the effect of concentrating their opponents' strength in a few nonwhite-majority districts that escaped less discerning analysts?

Defending the strategy of race-conscious redistricting, the Reverend Jesse Jackson declared, "These new districts are beneficial because they've made the U.S. Congress look more like America. It's white, it's black, it's Hispanic, it's Asian, it's Native American, it's male, and it's female." And "it's also Republican," as Steven Holmes of the *New York Times* pointed out after the election.

Racial districting has had an impact not only on the makeup of Congress, but on the disposition of white representatives after black voters were stripped from their districts. In a study of the voting patterns of the white Democrats in the last Congress who had lost black voters through redistricting, political scientists L. Marvin Overby and Kenneth Cosgrove found that they became more conservative and less supportive of policies preferred by African-Americans.

Although a number of analysts had predicted that the black and Hispanic empowerment strategy would backfire, voting-rights activists and minority-group leaders, almost all Democrats, forged ahead with their unholy alliance with the Republicans. The upshot was that black voters lost power and influence. Black politicians gained safer seats in a hostile Congress where many now consider themselves under siege. With the Republican capture of the House of Representatives, all but two of the African-American representatives in Congress have become minority members of the minority party. African-Americans lost 3 chairmanships of full committees and 17 chairmanships of subcommittees as well as other important leadership posts.

THE REPUBLICAN AGENDA AND THE BLACK CAUCUS

Blacks in America are bound to suffer in the new political milieu of the mid-1990s, as Republicans advance their ambitious agenda to eliminate affirmative action, curtail social programs such as free school lunches, and reduce taxes. The Democratic Party has traditionally represented the policy preferences of African-Americans much more effectively than have the Republicans, and the power of the Congressional Black Caucus depends on Democratic control.

During the last Congress, the Black Caucus became a major player in shaping the budget, the crime bill, the space program (which passed by a single vote), and other legislation. Caucus members were prominent in debates on health care. NAFTA, the ban on assault weapons, welfare reform, and environmental policy. The caucus provided the margin of victory on 16 of 87 key votes during the first session of the last Congress.

The Republican decision to reduce the size of all standing committees meant that under seniority rules, the most junior Democrats lost their assignments on the more prestigious committees. Blacks and Hispanics who had been in Congress for less than two terms were disproportionately affected. Carrie Meeks of Florida, with the lowest seniority, lost her place on the Appropriations Committee. Mel Reynolds and Cleo Fields lost their seats on Ways and Means. Bobby Rush of Illinois lost his seats on Banking and Financial Services and on the Science Committee. Before the 1994 elections, blacks were represented on all standing committees except Natural Resources. Ron Dellums of California chaired the Armed Services Committee, John Conyers of Michigan chaired Government Operations, and Bill Clay of Missouri chaired the Post Office and Civil Service Committee. (Clay had also been in line to chair the important Education and Labor Committee.) After the 1994 election, blacks lost all these positions and many others as well.

The resurgent Republicans also eliminated more than 600 committee staff jobs, many of which were held by blacks. Hundreds of personal staffers of defeated Democrats lost their jobs; many of these too were black, since Democrats in recent years have often reached out to hire more blacks.

The Congressional Black Caucus must bear some responsibility for what has happened. Bolstered by its increased size during the 103rd Congress, the caucus under Chairman Kweisi Mfume of Maryland took highly publicized aggressive stances against President Clinton and the Democratic congressional leadership. Caucus members publicly chastised the president over such issues as the withdrawal of Lani Guinier's nomination as head of the Civil Rights Division of the Justice Department, the racial justice provisions of the crime bill, and U.S. policy toward Haiti. Perhaps because caucus members often represent poorer-than-average congressional districts, they fought vigorously against provisions to ban contributions from political action committees, a key element of campaign reform.

A combination of factors, including the group's larger size, its aggressiveness, and the increased media attention paid to race-conscious districting, worked in concert to ensure that the caucus received more press coverage than ever before. On more than one occasion President Clinton was portrayed as kowtowing to the caucus's demands. The CBS show *60 Minutes*, for instance, portrayed the caucus as goading President Clinton to intervene militarily in Haiti to restore power to exiled president Jean-Bertrand Aristide. Although some caucus members opposed the invasion, the segment suggested the group was a monolithic far-left power bloc with substantial influence over the president. Conservative talk-show host John McLaughlin, after criticizing Mfume for trying to direct the military efforts in Haiti, referred to him as "General Mfume."

But the most costly public mistake made by the group was probably its apparent embrace of Louis Farrakhan at its annual legislative weekend, which was aired on C-SPAN and coincidentally occurred during the historic week when Israel signed its peace agreement with the Palestine Liberation Organization. After a number of groups denounced the caucus's action, individual members placed the blame on Mfume, who they said acted without their authority. Two months later Khalid Muhammad, a disciple of Farrakhan, delivered a venomous speech at Kean College attacking Jews, Catholics, and other groups. The ensuing public outrage was so great that it led the Congress, for the first time in history, to pass a resolution condemning the speech of a private citizen. Twenty caucus members voted for the resolution, eleven voted against, four voted present, and three failed to vote as the measure passed the House 361 to 34. Mfume later reported that during 1994 the caucus had received thousands of racist threats and "buckets of hate mail." A more reflective and circumspect Congressional Black Caucus could have avoided that response.

"Black people have no permanent friends, no permanent enemies . . . just permanent interests," runs the Black Caucus motto. To pursue those interests, blacks in Congress need more friends and fewer enemies. In response to *Miller*, black Democrats need to reach out across partisan and racial lines to form coalitions with those who share their values. In some cases, they may have to work with sympathetic Republicans to craft new policies that depart from traditional approaches to the problems that perennially affect African-Americans.

Rather than constitute a disaster, the *Miller* ruling is good for the Democratic Party, good for the Congressional Black Caucus, and good for the vast majority of African-Americans who need more representation of their liberal views of policy than they need people who look like them. Minority-group leaders have encouraged voters to confuse increased black and brown faces in legislative assemblies with greater power and influence, but the two are obviously not the same. African-Americans can succeed politically only when they build broader coalitions. As a result of *Miller*, a more dispersed black population may enable enough Democrats to defeat Republicans to recapture the House of Representatives. More blacks in white-dominated districts will have a moderating influence on many Democrats and Republicans. So rather than decrease African-American representation, the Miller decision may actually serve to increase it and to get Congress to become more solicitous of black interests, whatever the count of black faces.

Another critique of majority-minority districting calls attention to bias of winner-take-all electoral arrangements. In **"The Representation of Minority Interests,"** *Lani Guinier offers three limits of racial districting. An often overlooked goal of creating race-based districts is to encourage higher levels of minority voter turnout. On this point, Guinier contends that single-member districts insulate black incumbents from electoral threat, thus reducing competition. In turn, turnout is low and minority incumbents are often less accountable to their core constituents. A second, and related, criticism is that single-member districts inhibit accountable debate and encourage the "politics of individualism." That is, meaningful discussion of significant public issues is stymied by the fact that candidates are frequently unwilling to take on hot-button issues that make it difficult to attract the large number of voters in the political center. Finally, Guinier questions the "token inclusion" of minority representatives who are politically isolated once inside the governing body.*

Guinier proposes two alternatives to racial redistricting. The first is based on the notion of minority influence districts. The goal of this plan is to create "pockets of electoral influence" where minority voters are in a position to influence the outcome of elections between majority group candidates. This strategy has the side-benefit of strengthening minority influence in the legislative process because vote-seeking politicians pay attention to concentrated and motivated sources of political power. The second alternative is the creation of multimember electoral districts where candidates are elected through a cumulative voting system.[14] This configuration would allow voters to "cast multiple votes up to the number of open seats." Thus, the "strategic use of multiple voting possibilities" allows minority voters a better expression of their preferences. In either case, Guinier calls for nothing short of a fundamental restructuring of the electoral rules of the game.

THE REPRESENTATION OF MINORITY INTERESTS

Lani Guinier

Majority black electoral districts are the remedy of choice in most voting rights cases brought by black plaintiffs. This preference is consistent with the particular bias toward winner-take-all single-member electoral districts common in the United States. This article focuses on the limits of districting as a method for representing minority interests.

Elections based on multimember districts and proportional or semipro-portional representation may work better than districting as a remedy for vote dilution. These alternatives would assure fair minority representation and would better reflect all voters' true preferences. Semiproportional, mul-timember electoral systems do not rely on territorial or residential location as a fixed proxy for interests. Instead, these alternative electoral systems allow voters to establish their own communities of interest at each election. Unlike race-conscious districting, which predetermines voting options based on a concept of group representation, these alternative electoral systems allow contenders to win representation based on their proportion of the votes actu-ally cast.

For example, in an at-large system with cumulative voting, voters can cast multiple votes for one candidate. Although each voter possesses the same total number of votes, a voter has the option of plumping or cumulating her votes to express the intensity of her preferences. Instead of creating one ma-jority black single-member district in a jurisdiction with a black electoral mi-nority of 30% and three county commissioners, each voter would create her own election district by the way she distributed her votes. If voting for a black candidate was important to her, she could give the black candidate all three of her votes. If the 30% black voting minority all felt this way and was therefore politically cohesive, it could not be denied at least one representa-tive of its choice.

By juggling the number of legislative positions within each multimember district, a jurisdiction can set a community-specific threshold of exclusion— something less than 50% but more than 5%—to approximate the actual pop-ulation percentage of minority voters in the locality. The threshold of exclusion can be set high enough to eliminate real fringe groups or marginal claims, yet low enough to empower many other politically cohesive minori-ties, including white liberals who live in Republican-dominated suburbs, white women who are not geographically concentrated, and Latinos who live in small, dispersed concentrations.

By contrast, winner-take-all districting gives those who get the most votes all the power. Thus, votes cast for "losers" are wasted. This submerges the voting strength of all voters who do not support the winning candidate. Given the preference of incumbents for safe districts, even some for the votes cast for winners may be wasted. Moreover, the decennial process of district-ing, in which incumbents enjoy inordinate control, often produces voter dis-interest in noncompetitive election contents.

Because they remove the power of districting from self-interested incum-bents, multimember districts with cumulative voting may generate greater voter interest in competitive election contests. In addition, negative cam-paigning less effective in elections with multiple winners than in elections with only one opponent. As a result, candidates may have to offer more than name recognition, thereby reducing the incentive for contests based solely on television advertising and negative campaigning.

Candidates may turn to political parties to assist them in identifying inter-est constituencies. The lowered exclusion threshold gives third political parties a real chance to win representation. This might revive community-based, local political organizations, which could play an important role in educating and mobilizing grass-roots support for ideas rather than just for career politicians. If so, these alternatives would accomplish many of the objectives of term limitations.

Even if they are not actually implemented as remedies in vote dilution cases, semiproportional election systems also serve as a baseline for measuring the political fairness of existing systems. As such, they focus our attention on the value of direct rather than virtual representation of interests. They also redirect the responsibility for establishing interest constituencies away from incumbent politicians and back to the voters themselves. They introduce, without the immutable and separatist nature of its contemporary stigma, the concept of proportionality. By at least raising some of these ideas, a discussion of alternative election systems may inject new meaning into the debate about political fairness.

REMEDIAL ALTERNATIVES TO MAJORITY BLACK DISTRICTS

MINORITY INFLUENCE DISTRICTS

One alternative to creating majority black districts is to disperse the black voting population, creating pockets of electoral influence. A few courts, commentators, and litigators have urged the adoption of districting plans in which blacks are in electoral minority in several districts rather than an electoral majority in just a few. These critics of majority black districts claim that minority influence districts would better integrate minorities into the political process.

In its strongest version, an influence district is a district in which minority voters enjoy electoral influence and legislative clout despite the fact they are a numerical minority and voting is racially polarized. For example, an electoral minority may have influence where it can determine the outcome of an election contest between competing majority preferred candidates. Although the minority voters cannot sponsor their own representative, they may influence which majority candidate gets elected.

At the legislative decision-making stage, the strong minority influence claim would be that the power of minority voters is superior because minority voters enjoy influence over multiple representatives rather than concentrated control over one or two. Because minority voters must work with other groups in order to enjoy either electoral or legislative power, influence districts arguably mobilize cross-racial alliances in particular and political participation throughout the extended political process in general.

There is also a weak influence claim in which influence occurs only *under the right combination of circumstances.* The weak influence claim is based on three alternative assumptions. First, the majority may be influential despite its numerical scarcity *where voting is not racially polarized.* Second, even where the electorate is racially polarized, the racial minority may be influential if there are multiple racial groups that coalesce around a single minority sponsored candidate. Third, even where voting is racially polarized, the racial minority might be influential where there is unusual fragmentation within the white community and the aggregating decisional rule is a plurality, not a majority, vote threshold.

MULTIMEMBER DISTRICTS THAT ARE NOT WINNER-TAKE-ALL

Alternative election systems, which lower the threshold of inclusion to less than 50%, may be preferable to minority influence districts. For example, cumulative voting systems enable a minority of less than 50% to exercise electoral control *and* legislative influence.

Under cumulative voting, voters cast multiple votes up to the number of open seats. Voters may choose to express the intensity of their performances by aggregating all of their votes for a single candidate. If voting is polarized along racial lines, as voting rights litigation cases hypothesize, semiproportional systems of representation, such as cumulative voting, generally operate to provide at least a minimal level of minority representation. Unlike districting, however, they allow minority group members to self-identify their allegiance and their preferences based on their strategic use of multiple voting possibilities. In this sense, they allow voluntary interest constituencies to form at each election. Voters "district" themselves every election.

Because of concerns with procedural fairness, a cumulative voting system that relies on voluntary districting by each voter is a reasonable, and in many cases, preferable alternative to geographic districting. Cumulative voting would abandon districting altogether to represent fairly minority voters who do not enjoy either the numerical strength to become an electoral majority within a district or who are geographically dispersed within a large area such that their strength cannot be maximized within one or more single-member districts.

Political boundaries traditionally define a community of interest. However, structures for fairly representing divergent interests within a large, heterogeneous body are necessary, especially to the extent local government structures become more regionally based. To meet the increasing suburbanization of America, demands are growing for metropolitan government and interdistrict planning. Unless voting rights advocates are preoccupied by the importance of black control of increasingly poor, isolated urban areas, they too may begin to seek representational strategies within a metropolitan, not simply a citywide, area.

Alternatives such as cumulative voting are one such strategy. Cumulative voting lowers the threshold of representation to encourage local political organizations to form. Minority political organizations or third political parties might then reclaim, at a newly invigorated grass-roots level, the traditional party role of mobilizing voter participation. Additionally, locally based political parties might then organize around issues or issue-based coalitions. Since the potential support for the minority political party is not confined to a geographic or racial base, cross-racial and pan-geographic coalitions are possible.

The interjection of an issue-oriented dimension might potentially transform what has essentially become the celebrity politics of candidate-centered campaigns. As a spokesperson for the Ross Perot petition campaign put it: "Back in the 70s, the parties lost to television advertising their role as the main source of the nation's political information. Reaching voters through emotion-based image-making became far more efficient than trying to enlist them as party members."

I propose these alternative election systems as a substitute for term limits because they allow for greater turnover among incumbents who no longer enjoy exclusive control over the districting process. Incumbent politicians, who fear that term limits will prematurely shorten their careers, may be persuaded to support alternative election systems, which also promote accountable citizen legislators as preferable and less arbitrary election reform.

───────────────────────────── ■ ─────────────────────────────

In **"Representation in Congress: Line Drawing and Minorities,"** *Kenny J. Whitby and Franklin D. Gilliam, Jr. evaluate the "case against racial redistricting." They evaluate several claims made by opponents of "majority-minority" districts. One criticism is that such districts violate the principle of individualism. After a brief review of the history of black suffrage, Whitby and Gilliam conclude that, "[T]he fact that blacks were excluded as a group and that the system is group based surely undermines the notion that remedies such as racial redistricting violate a principled commitment to individualism." A second critique maintains that racial redistricting violates the principles of color-blindness. On this point the authors argue that a historical reading of voting rights policy indicates that vote dilution schemes and the unwillingness of many whites to vote for black candidates presents a ". . . severe challenge to notions of color-blindness." A third reason to oppose racial redistricting is that increasing the number of "safe" black seats actually harms the overall policy concerns of the community. In other words, creating majority-minority districts increases the likelihood that more Republicans will be elected thus working against the interests of the broader black community.[15] Whitby and Gilliam also urge caution when interpreting election results from the early 1990s. Racial redistricting wasn't the only factor at work. For instance, the country was in a general anti-Democrat mood that clearly cost the party seats.[16]*

Opponents of race-based districting also contend that liberal white legislators represent black interests in ways comparable to black members. To this, Whitby and Gilliam contend that critics have a narrow conception of substantive representation. Put differently, substantive representation is more than final roll-call votes in a particular Congress.[17] As the authors note, ". . . the impact of race is a function of the particular bills voted on by representatives in any given Congress." In other words, race is most important when the legislation under consideration has overt racial implications. Finally, opponents underestimate the institutional and psychological benefits of racial redistricting. Typically elected from "black" districts, long-term black incumbents ". . . are included in the queue for leadership positions in Congress." Visible incorporation into the political structures of the society provides the community with a voice in the public discourse. In the final analysis, Whitby and Gilliam argue that while majority-minority districts play a significant role in the representation of black interests, they must not be adhered to at any cost.

REPRESENTATION IN CONGRESS:
LINE DRAWING AND MINORITIES

■

Kenny J. Whitby and Franklin D. Gilliam, Jr.

T he process of drawing congressional district boundary lines is crucial to representation in Congress. To a very large extent, districting defines who the actors can be in congressional politics. The ideal of "one person, one vote" was defined initially in the famous U.S. Supreme Court case of *Baker v. Carr* (1962), and thereby "the reapportionment revolution was born" (Dixon 1968: 3). Three decades after the *Baker* decision, important issues of congressional representation remain alive, above all, the issue of the representation of African Americans.

The current maelstrom over racial redistricting revisits an old theme in American politics: the inclusionary rules for racial minorities in representative government. These rules define important features of the stage on which the drama of congressional elections unfolds. Ralph J. Bunche once observed that "minority populations, and particularly racial minorities, striving to exist in any theoretically democratic modern society, are compelled to struggle strenuously for even a moderate participation in the democratic game" (quoted in Meier, Rudwick, & Broderick 1965: 184). Bunche knew that representation is intrinsically valuable but not equally attainable by all people in American society. From the debate over slavery at the Constitutional Convention (1787) to recent court decisions such as the 1995 decision in *Miller v. Johnson* (a case involving racial redistricting in Georgia) and the 1996 *Bush v. Vera* ruling (a racial-redistricting case in Texas), the United States has struggled to find the appropriate remedy for proven exclusion of racial minorities from the representational process.

Race-conscious districting is the latest remedy for the diminution of minority-vote influence, but it is not without its critics. The case against creating "majority–minority" districts is largely based on three points. First, people such as Justices Antonin Scalia and Clarence Thomas argue that representation should be defined solely in formal terms, that is, as the right of individuals to vote for the candidate of their choice. Put differently, they argue that a democratic society's obligation is to provide only for universal suffrage, not to promote the political rights of particular groups.

A second criticism is that race-conscious districting violates the principles of "color-blindness." Proponents of this view highlight the divisiveness of race in American society. Conservatives and liberals converge on the point that all race-based policy making is suspicious on its face because it recognizes skin color as the defining factor. In *Shaw v. Reno* (1993), Justice Sandra Day O'Connor echoes this sentiment when she notes that:

A reapportionment plan that includes in one district individuals who belong to the same race, but who are otherwise widely separated by geographical and political boundaries, and who may have little in common with one another but the color of their skin, bears an uncomfortable resemblance to political apartheid. (p. 2827)

The third attack on racial redistricting concerns substantive policy out-comes reflected by the roll call votes of members of Congress. This position is based on two related arguments. Some observers challenge the notion that racial minorities are better served by legislators from their group. Carol Swain (1993) is often cited as proof that there are few differences in the voting records of liberal white and African-American legislators. Similarly, many be-lieve that the increase in African-Americans in Congress after the 1990 round of redistricting was largely responsible for dramatic gains by Republicans in the South (Hill 1995; Lublin 1995). Thus, if Republicans *generally* do not share black political interests, then it is optimal to prefer an increase in liberal white legislators at the expense of a decrease in the number of majority–minority districts.

In this chapter we examine the case against racial redistricting. The first section studies the historical case to determine if individual rights are the sole basis for inclusion. Here we briefly remind readers of the group nature of African-American exclusion prior to the 1965 Voting Rights Act.

Next, we consider the notion that contemporary American society can, and does, proceed on the basis of color-blindness. Our analysis elevates two important mechanisms of color consciousness—minority-vote dilu-tion schemes devised by public officials and racially polarized voting behavior among the electorate. The long-term consequences of these vari-ables seriously call into question the principle of color-blindness. The irony is that the very failure to adhere to the principle of color-blindness produced the impetus toward districting to promote minority representa-tion. In this discussion, we highlight the exogenous impact of the U.S. Supreme Court.

The last section of the chapter concerns substantive representation. Our ar-gument on this issue unpacks two interconnected points. First, we present evidence that constrains the argument about the ability of nonblacks to rep-resent black policy interests. There are differences—black legislators do more often vote the common policy interests of African-Americans than do non-blacks. We make the case that most analysts conceive of substantive repre-sentation far too narrowly. We advocate a broader view of the concept that takes into account the context of the times (i.e., the nature of the legislative proposal lawmakers are asked to vote on in any given Congress), a more nu-anced understanding of the legislative process (i.e., indicators other than floor votes), the power of symbolic politics, and the value of long-term insti-tutional representation. Second, we study the question of whether increasing minority representation actually harms black policy interests by increasing the number of Republicans. Our review of the evidence suggests a more tem-pered version of that claim. It is still debatable whether racial redistricting was the sole, or most important, determinant of Republican seat gain. We conclude the chapter by considering the prospects of racial redistricting and the likely consequences for electoral politics, congressional behavior, and rep-resentative democracy. We end by calling for refined racial-redistricting strategies.

HISTORICAL CONTEXT:
GROUP BASIS OF RACIAL POLITICS

The modern mechanisms for racial representation in American political life are historically rooted in a complex weave of economic, social, and political factors. It is widely known that the issue of black inclusion posed a dilemma for America's Founding Fathers at the Constitutional Convention of 1787. Whether best understood as compromising politicians or self-interested elites, the Framers forged an uneasy consensus regarding the status of blacks. The Three-Fifths Compromise, the slavery commerce clause, and, later, the fugitive slave law triggered a pattern of political exclusion that extended from the national level down to the states and localities. These constitutional provisions provided a basis for a pattern of exclusion best characterized as the "slave codes." The codes were a method of social control to maintain the advantages of cheap, black labor (Franklin 1964; Jarvis 1992; Quarles 1964). Although conditions varied across the colonies, the imposition of the codes meant that enslaved blacks could not own property, vote, make contracts, have standing in court, or control the lives of their children. As James McGregor Burns (1982: 143) notes, "In general, the life of the enslaved Afro-American was nasty, poor, brutish, and often short." The effect was to deny blacks, en masse, basic citizenship rights and institutionalize their marginal status in the society.

It is beyond the scope of this chapter to devote the necessary space to the significance of the Civil War, Radical Reconstruction, and Jim Crow. It is enough to say that before passage of the Voting Rights Act of 1965, blacks were routinely prevented from voting by such practices as physical intimidation, literacy tests, and poll taxes (Foner 1988; Jarvis 1992; Lawson 1976; Matthews and Prothro 1967). To illustrate the effectiveness of disenfranchising practices in 1947, only 20% of eligible blacks were registered to vote, and only 25% were registered in 1956 and 1958 (Matthews and Prothro 1967: 184). While there were a few nonsouthern states where blacks could fully participate in electoral politics, the fact remained that as a group, blacks were unable to impact governmental decisions through the electoral system.

The Voting Rights Act (VRA) of 1965 is generally regarded as the most effective federal voting-rights law enacted since Reconstruction. The VRA targeted those states (Alabama, Georgia, Louisiana, Mississippi, South Carolina, Virginia, and parts of North Carolina and Arizona) where white conservative politicians had succeeded in systematically disenfranchising a large segment of the black voting-age population through voter registration barriers, intimidation, and outright violence.

There are three key provisions in the VRA. The first (Section 2) bars the adoption of any electoral devices that would result in the denial of the vote to any person because of race and color. Second, the Section 4 "triggering formula" suspends the use of literacy tests in any political subdivision or state where less than 50% of the voting-age population was registered to vote in 1964, and so authorizes federal registrars to register voters and monitor elections in these areas. The third major provision (Section 5) is designed to prevent the dilution of minority-voter strength. This provision states that political units in areas covered by the act may make no change in their voting practices without preclearance by the U.S. attorney general or the Federal District Court for the District of Columbia.

To date, the VRA has been extended and strengthened on three occasions, in 1970, 1975, and most recently, in 1982. The extension of the act in 1970, along with passage of the Twenty-sixth Amendment, lowered the minimum age for voting from twenty-one to eighteen in all elections. It also banned the use of literacy tests. The 1975 extension boosted the number of Hispanic and Asian voters by requiring bilingual ballots. The 1982 amendments to the Voting Rights Act were especially noteworthy because they were designed to encourage a more benign form of racial gerrymandering to promote minority representation. Section 2 of the law has been revised to stipulate that a violation could be proven by the existence of an election procedure that "results in the denial or abridgement" of the right to vote. The revision is significant because it replaces the "intent" standard of proof applied in the *Mobile* case (discussed in the next section). In short, the 1982 extension is a significant attempt to more clearly define the rules of inclusion for American racial and ethnic minorities.

In this section we have argued for a rejection of the idea that representative government only recognizes individual rights. In an ideal world, this might be the case. But the history of America is such that race is much more than a biological category. It is a political category born of a system that systematically excluded certain groups. Moreover, it is a form of government more plural than democratic in nature. That is, it has, and does, recognize the political interests of groups. The fact that blacks were excluded as a group and that the system is group based surely undermines the notion that remedies such as racial redistricting violate a principled commitment to individualism.

COLOR-BLINDNESS VERSUS COLOR-CONSCIOUSNESS

Shortly after the passage of the VRA, state and local officials attempted to continue the pattern of representational exclusion by configuring district boundaries to frustrate the electoral opportunities of minority-supported candidates. *Negative gerrymandering* was the most common vote dilution practice. Officials typically employed two strategies: packing—the overconcentration of minorities in one district to prevent them from having much influence in another—and cracking—the dispersion of concentrated minorities across districts to prevent them from having much influence in any one district. The Court's response to these tactics ultimately created pressures for group-based remedies such as majority-minority districts.

In *White v. Regester* (1973), a Texas legislative reapportionment case involving the claim by minority plaintiffs of vote dilution, the Supreme Court held that although the Texas plan was not invidiously discriminatory, and thus was not automatically unconstitutional, it could be rejected on the grounds that it appeared to decrease minority-voting strength. In *Beer v. United States* (1976), the Supreme Court continued to refine its views on what the VRA required. In this case, the issue was whether a New Orleans redistricting plan providing for two black majority districts was acceptable even though a different redistricting plan could have provided the chance for the election of black city council members in addition to more black representatives. Although the Court ruled in favor of the New Orleans plan, it noted that an electoral plan was only acceptable as long as there was no electoral scheme devised to dilute minority voting power.

In *United Jewish Organizations v. Carrey* (1977), the Supreme Court took another step in the direction of redistricting to achieve a specific electoral outcome. The case involved a redistricting plan that divided the Hasidic Jewish community in Brooklyn, New York, to create an additional black-majority district. The Supreme Court rejected the claim by the affected Hasidic community that the redistricting plan was unconstitutional. In effect, the Court ruled that the VRA could be used as a device for improving the lot of protected groups, most notably, black voters.

The movement toward redistricting to improve minority electoral prospects was soon curtailed as a result of the Supreme Court's decision in *City of Mobile v. Bolden* (1980). The case focused on whether the at-large election system in Mobile, Alabama, provided black voters with a realistic chance of electing black commissioners to the three-person governing body. The Supreme Court ruled that the Voting Rights Act required that voting rights plaintiffs show "intent" to discriminate before there could be a violation under Section 2 of the act. In effect, the Court rejected the ruling in *White v. Regester*, which stated that plaintiffs could provide circumstantial evidence (e.g., past history of discrimination) as proof of discriminatory intent. In sum, by the early 1980s there was considerable judicial tension between a focus on "expected outcome" and a focus on "discriminatory intent" as the central interpretative tool for the VRA.

In 1982, Congress overturned the *Mobile* decision by revising Section 2 of the VRA. The 1982 amendments replace the intent test with the results test. The revised law opened the way for another important Supreme Court ruling that would soon bring the issue of minority-controlled districts to center stage in the decennial battles over fair representation. In essence, the 1982 amendments sought to rectify the continuing problem of racial-bloc voting and vote dilution practices in America. It was an effort to tie the voting practices of the white electorate to the vote dilution schemes of public officials. In *Thornburg v. Gingles* (1986), a case involving whether or not redistricting of North Carolina's multimember legislative districts violated the VRA by diluting black-voter strength, the high court accepted the new results test in the revised Section 2 provision of the VRA.

In the *Thornburg* case, the Court set out three criteria for determining what constitutes a violation of Section 2 of the VRA: polarization, compactness, and cohesiveness. Polarization refers to the relationship between votes for minority candidates and the racial composition of voting precincts. Polarization is said to exist when the majority votes as a bloc to defeat the minority's preferred candidate.[1] Compactness considers whether or not minority voters can constitute a majority in a compact enough geographic area. Given America's peculiar racial differences in residential patterns (Massey and Denton 1993), the Court was concerned about the ability of proposed plans to draw reasonable district lines to create black majorities. Finally, the issue of cohesiveness asks for evidence that the minority group solidly votes for its preferred candidate. Creating black-majority districts would obviously be irrelevant if the community did not vote as a bloc for a single candidate of choice.

The combination of the 1982 amendments and the *Thornburg* decision paved the way of the "color-conscious" creation of majority–minority districts. Following the 1990 census, a record number of congressional districts were consciously created to give minority voters numerical majorities. A total of thirty-two African-American districts (up from seventeen in 1990), and twenty Hispanic districts (compared to nine in 1990) were created for the 1992 elections. These districts were initially supported by Democrats, who assumed that minority-controlled districts would enhance the electoral fortunes of Democratic representatives. Republicans, however, have become increasingly supportive of redistricting plans that would produce more minority-controlled districts, reasoning that concentrating minority voters in a few districts would make adjoining districts whiter, more conservative, and more likely to elect Republican representatives.

The post-1990 redistricting to promote minority electoral prospects has been controversial. White voters have filed federal court lawsuits in several states claiming a violation of their rights to equal protection under the 14th Amendment. One of the first lawsuits to reach the Supreme Court was *Shaw v. Reno* (1993). In this case, white voters claimed that North Carolina's redrawn Twelfth District (majority-black) violated their constitutional rights (see Figure 9-1). The *Shaw* case turned on the compactness test. Because of asymmetrical residential patterns, blacks do not always live in a compact configuration (particularly in the South). To get around this problem of geographical dispersion, some state legislatures abandoned traditional redistricting standards of compactness and contiguity and drew oddly shaped district boundaries. Justice Sandra Day O'Connor, writing for the Court majority in this 5–4 decision, asserted that if district boundaries were so "bizarre" as to be indefensible on any grounds other than an effort to elect minorities to political office, white voters would have legal justification for claiming that they had been the victims of unconstitutional racial gerrymandering. Although the Supreme Court had never previously held that compactness was an independent federal constitutional requirement, the Court gave legal standing to challenges to any congressional redistricting plans with an oddly shaped majority-minority district.

In *Shaw*, the Court sidestepped the general question of what actually constitutes racial gerrymandering. The vagueness of the ruling has opened the way for challenges by white voters to the drawing of these districts. A number of states, mostly in the South, have challenged the constitutionality of

■ FIGURE 9-1

GERRYMANDERING IN NORTH CAROLINA (1993)

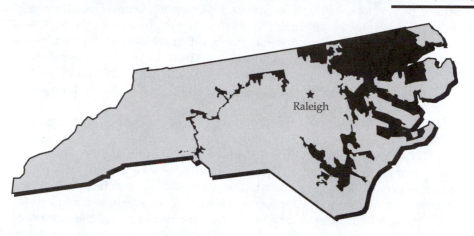

★
Raleigh

majority-minority districts. In *Miller v. Johnson* (1995), the Court began to address the extent to which race could be used as a factor in drawing district boundaries. In its ruling, the Court declared that Georgia's 1992 congressional map was unconstitutional because race played a dominant role in the configuration of the Eleventh District. Writing for the majority in the 5–4 opinion, Justice Anthony M. Kennedy attempted to clarify the compactness ruling rendered in *Shaw*. He also attempted to define more clearly the Court's position on racial gerrymandering. According to Kennedy, a constitutional violation may exist in any case in which race was the "predominant" factor in determining the configuration of district lines. While the Court struck down the "race-based" redistricting plan in Georgia, it provided little direction on how redistricting authorities in Georgia or other states should draw new maps.

In *Bush v. Vera* (1996), which was decided by another 5–4 vote, the Court once again left many questions unanswered about the proper role of race in the districting process. In this Texas ruling involving one majority-Hispanic district (Twenty-ninth District) and two majority-black districts (Eighteenth and Thirtieth Districts), the high court decided that the state had relied too heavily on race and thus moved too far from traditional districting principles. Despite the Court's intentions, neither *Miller* nor *Bush* spell out when race is the "predominant" factor in district line drawing. Consequently, it is still unclear which race-based redistricting plans will be acceptable to the federal courts in the future.

In sum, we contend that vote dilution schemes and racially polarized voting present a severe challenge to notions of color-blindness. Seemingly, the majority of justices on the Supreme Court are willing to concede that the color-blind argument is not totally defensible on constitutional grounds. In effect, the high court has stopped short of saying that there is no room for color-consciousness in configuring district boundaries.

SUBSTANTIVE REPRESENTATION

From a policy perspective, does it matter if Congress is not a racially or ethnically representative assembly? To a large degree, the use of the VRA as a tool to elect more racial minorities to public office is based on the putative assumption that the race of the member does affect the quality of substantive representation for minorities. Put somewhat differently, racial minorities will, on average, receive better policy representation from minority lawmakers than they will from white legislators.

Theoretical tradition in the literature on congressional representation holds that the need to face the electorate forces lawmakers to be responsive to all significant groups in their constituencies. So, for instance, a representative from a blue-collar district will be responsive to blue-collar constituents even if he or she is not a blue-collar worker. From this perspective, legislators should be judged in terms of how well they perform their legislative duties and not in terms of whether they mirror the social characteristics of their constituents (Eulau and Karps 1977; Pitkin 1967). However, many who feel that they are not well represented in Congress (e.g., women, African Americans, Native Americans) believe that the quality of representation is directly related to the number of congressional representatives from their group.

One simple way of testing for racial differences in congressional voting is to examine the mean scores of representatives. Relying on roll call votes in the post-redistricting Congresses (103rd Congress, 1993–4; 104th Congress, 1995–6) for which complete data were available, we use this testing procedure to learn more about who in Congress best represents the policy interests of racial minorities. First, it should be established that racial minorities generally favor liberal policies. That is, they prefer greater governmental intervention on behalf of the federal government in eliminating racial discrimination and assisting the economically disadvantaged. Public opinion research reveals that the black community as a whole holds markedly more liberal views than whites (Gilliam and Whitby 1989; Jaynes and Williams 1989; Schuman, Steeh, and Bobo 1985; Wood 1990). Previous studies also reveal that Hispanic citizens on average tend to be more liberal than whites (de la Garza et al. 1992; Hero and Tolbert 1995; Welch and Hibbing, 1984).

Taking party into account produces some interesting distinctions (Table 9-1). While the discrepancy between white Democrats and white Republicans is expected, there is also about a 17 point average difference between white Democrats and black Democrats in the 103rd Congress, and the mean difference is about 14-percentage points in the 104th. The findings also reveal that both white and Hispanic Democratic legislators vote considerably more liberally than their aggregate group averages. Finally, because of the very small number of black and Hispanic Republicans in both Congresses, we do not generalize too much about their roll call voting scores.

Table 9-2 breaks down the data more discretely by including region. The analysis is restricted to House Democrats so that we can present a clearer pic-

▪ TABLE 9-1

MEAN LIBERAL ROLL-CALL VOTING SCORES OF
U.S. REPRESENTATIVES BY RACE AND PARTY

	ADA	COPE	LCCRa
103rd Congress (1993–94)			
Democrats			
Black (37)[a]	92	94	95
Hispanic (14)	79	86	90
White (204)	70	79	80
Republicans			
Black (1)[b]	15	22	21
Hispanic (3)	20	51	45
White (171)	14	20	22
104th Congress[c]			
Democrats			
Black (36)	90	99	94
Hispanic (14)	83	95	90
White (146)	75	88	78
Republicans			
Black (2)[d]	13	4	18
Hispanic (3)	12	14	55
White (229)	7	6	19

[a]Total number of representatives (in parentheses).

[b]Scores of Gary Franks, Connecticut.

[c]First session (1995) mean ADA and COPE scores.

[d]Average scores of Gary Franks and J. C. Watts of Oklahoma.

ture of the role of race in legislative voting behavior. Not surprisingly, non-southern Democrats, on average, are more liberal than southern Democrats. While it is true that the voting behavior of southern Democrats is less conservative than it was two decades ago, it is some distance away from the more liberal voting of nonsouthern Democrats.

Table 9-1 conveys three additional findings of note. First, there is significant regional variation in voting scores for white members, but not for black members. Across our three measures (103rd Congress), white Democrats not from the South score an average of 24 points higher than their southern partisan colleagues. The magnitude of difference is 20 points across the three measures in the 104th Congress. Conversely, the mean scores of black Democrats in both regions are 90% or better on each interest-group scale.

This finding is noteworthy because redistricting after the 1990 census was a major factor in the election of twelve first-term black representatives in the South (it is significant that this new cohort had mean voting scores on a par

■ **TABLE 9-2**

MEAN LIBERAL SCORES OF DEMOCRATIC U.S. REPRESENTATIVES
BY RACE AND REGION

	ADA	COPE	LCCR
103rd Congress (1993–94)			
Nonsouthern Democrats			
Black (20)[a]	95	96	97
Hispanic (10)	89	88	96
White (149)	77	84	87
Southern Democrats			
Black (17)	90	92	92
Hispanic (4)	53	79	73
White (55)	49	65	63
104th Congress[b]			
Nonsouthern Democrats			
Black (19)	89	100	95
Hispanic (10)	92	99	95
White (111)	80	93	83
Southern Democrats			
Black (17)	92	95	94
Hispanic (4)	60	85	50
White (35)	61	73	62

[a]Total number of representatives in parentheses.

[b]First session (1995) mean ADA and COPE scores.

with the other members of the Congressional Black Caucus). Second, while interracial differences (103rd Congress) in voting scores between black and white Democrats average about 13 points outside the South, the average difference in the South is 32 points across the three voting scales. Similarity, in the 104th Congress, interracial differences constitute, on average, 9-percentage points in the North and approximately 28 points in the South. Third, the small number of Hispanic legislators (particularly in the South) makes it difficult to interpret their voting scores. It is intriguing, however, that the scores of nonsouthern Hispanic legislators are more similar to those of blacks than whites.

There are two additional ways that the conception of substantive representation might be expanded. Although early researchers (Eulau and Karps 1977; Pitkin 1967) recognized the importance of symbolic representation, very little attention has been paid to this component of majority–minority districts. Race is a powerful cognitive cue, which goes beyond the notion of, "My representative looks like me." One cannot underestimate the power of symbolic representation to groups long excluded from the political system. The fact that members of the group noticeably participate in public decisions produces a wide array of psychic benefits such as higher political efficacy (see Bobo and Gilliam 1990). Visible and numerous African-American members of Congress represent a "black voice" in the public decision-making process. Members such as Charles Rangel and Kweisi Mfume (before his resignation to become head of the National Association for the Advancement of Colored People) became "regulars" on the most important public forums—television news programs. In the broadest sense, then, the high visibility of African-American legislators evokes group pride and symbolizes the fact that the community's interests are being conveyed (Edelman 1964; Gilliam 1996; Sears 1993).

Another, more tangible way that majority-minority districts serve black interests is by providing the opportunity for long-term black empowerment. The tenure that incumbency affords, we believe, means that black representatives are included in the queue for leadership positions in Congress. Provided the Democrats can manage to win back a majority of the seats in the House, several black members are poised to ascend to important committee positions.[2] In sum, these are positive results for pluralist and democratic theorists because the involvement of previously disenfranchised groups supports the legitimacy, and hence stability, of the political system.

Does racial redistricting affect the partisan composition of Congress? Republican gains in the House have led to widespread speculation that the creation of majority-minority districts mightily contributed to the demise of Democratic candidates. Kevin Hill (1995), in his analysis of the partisan consequences of racial redistricting for the 1992 elections, reports that the Democrats lost at least four seats in the South as a result. David Lublin (1995), responding to the Legal Defense Fund's analysis of the role of redistricting in the 1994 elections (which argues that Democratic losses were the result of white voter defection), presents evidence indicating that racial redistricting cost the Democrats thirteen seats. Swain (1995) echoes Lublin's sentiments when she argues that racial redistricting was largely responsible for the Republican takeover of the House after the 1994 elections.

This line of research, however, generally suffers from a rather limited view of the 1992 and 1994 House elections. John Petrocik and Scott Desposato (1995) argue for a more complex effect on electoral outcomes. They content that neither the loss of African-American constituents in southern districts nor the shifts in the white population to accommodate majority-minority districts can, alone, account for the Democratic demise. Rather, Democratic losses are best understood as a combination of the twin forces of racial redistricting (the loss of black voters and the addition of white voters unfamiliar with the Democratic incumbent) plus a dramatic anti-Democratic national tide in 1994.

In conclusion, researchers must be careful not to overinterpret election results. While the creation of majority-minority districts hurt the Democrats in some areas, this was not the sole story of the 1992 or 1994 House elections. A more complex understanding of majority-minority districts is needed, suggesting that the issue merits further, systematic investigation.[3]

CONCLUSION AND IMPLICATIONS

The creation of a record number of majority-minority districts after the 1990 census reopened an old wound in American politics: what constitutes fair and equal treatment for minorities under the current system of electing members to legislative assemblies? Our review leads us to the conclusion that the critics of racial redistricting have failed to make their case on three grounds. First, American politics is fundamentally about groups. While the notion of individual rights is a lofty ideal, the reality of daily political life is that groups matter. The history of African-American exclusion is testimony to the fact that race is not simply a biological construct, but rather a social and racial category. Second, vote dilution techniques employed by public officials and racially polarized voting indicate that we are far from the ideal of a color-blind society. Race matters, and does so in a big way. While we do not believe this outcome is inevitable, and we surely wish the reality were different, we must acknowledge this fact if we are to have productive dialogue and constructive remedies. Third, there is great psychic and institutional value to increasing black office holding. A "seat at the table" is important. Furthermore, having an opportunity to occasionally sit at the head of the table is immeasurably significant at this point in history.

We recognize that our view comes with consequences. It is a mathematical fact that only a finite number of these districts can be drawn. This is hardly troubling to us because nowhere in our position is the argument that African-Americans could not seek coalition partners. We also do not denigrate the notion that nonblacks cannot represent black interests. We must, however, point out the fact that there are still significant racial differences in legislative behavior when the issues of the day are racially charged (i.e., affirmative action) and at other stages of the legislative process (e.g., bill sponsorship, committee work, amendment votes). Additionally, the viability of the Congressional Black Caucus is an issue of concern. The caucus played a major role early in the Clinton administration on such issues as the North American Free Trade Agreement, the ban on assault weapons, and the crime bill. Setbacks on welfare reform and the treatment of Haitian refugees and the reduction of committee sizes by the new Republican majority have pointed out that the number of members is not the only issue. African-American politicians and their constituencies must recognize the subtleties of power politics. We are optimistic that this will come about with time.

A final comment concerns the linkage of recent Republican gains to the increase in majority-minority districts. From our view, this calls for a "fine-tuning" of line drawing rather than a rejection of principle. Providing underrepresented groups with a fair chance to elect candidates of their choice should not fall hostage to a mechanistic application of the 65% rule, which holds that the black population should not fall below this threshold level. Advocates should carefully study given jurisdictions for voting patterns, political climate, partisan balance, and geography. In some instances, given a particular weave of cultural, social, and economic factors, extraordinary districts may have to be drawn. On the other hand, some districts may need fewer than a 50% African-American threshold to effectively run and elect candidates of their choosing.

The 1996 elections for membership in the 105th Congress are interesting from this point of view.[4] On the one hand, four black congressional candidates (Georgia's Sanford Bishop and Cynthia McKinney, Oklahoma's J. C. Watts, and Indian's Julia Carson) won in districts with white majorities. On the other hand, Gary Franks (R-CT) lost in a majority-white district. The rub is that four of the candidates (Bishop, McKinney, Franks, and Watts) were incumbents, making it difficult to disentangle the effects of incumbency from race. The election results are an optimistic sign that large numbers of white voters voted for black candidates who won. But because race and incumbency are conflated, it is premature to conclude that there has been a significant decline in racially polarized voting.

The mechanistic application of any strategy, we believe, decreases the possibility of a successful remedy. The best recommendation is for malleability, because this debate will surely continue in the future. Only with a more sophisticated understanding of race and representation should hard policy decisions be made in the future.

Notes

1. Evidence for racially polarized voting is well documented in the social science literature. For some research on the topic, see Grofman, Migalski, and Noviello (1985); Wildgen (1988); Engstrom and McDonald (1988); Loewen (1990); Ards and Lewis (1992); Grofman, Handley, and Niemi (1992); Firebaugh (1993).

2. Two African Americans served as chairs of important committees in the 103rd Congress. They were Ron Dellums of California (chair of the Armed Services Committee) and John Conyers of Michigan (chair of the Government and Operations Committee). Several other African-American members served as chairs of subcommittees.

3. Another potential harmful effect of racial redistricting is that representatives might become less responsive to minority constituents as a result of losing significant numbers of minority voters in their districts. Charles Bullock's analysis of the voting behavior of southern representatives in 1993 reveals that white representatives did not modify their voting behavior as a result of constituency changes. More research is needed in this area because the behavioral consequences of racial redistricting may be a long-term phenomenon (see Bullock 1995). For the impact of racial redistricting on House incumbents' behavior, see Overby and Cosgrove (1996).

4. The number of African-American and Hispanic members of the 105th Congress will closely resemble those in the 103rd and 104th Congresses. A total of forty African Americans (including Senator Carol Moseley-Braun of Illinois and nonvoting delegates Eleanor Holmes Norton from the District of Columbia and Donna Christian Green from the Virgin Islands, both of whom are Democrats) will serve. Also, nineteen Hispanics were elected to serve in the 105th Congress (including nonvoting Democratic representative Carlos Romero-Barcelo from Puerto-Rico) (*Congressional Quarterly Weekly Report*, January 4, 1997, p. 28).

THE SUPREME COURT

Constitutional and statutory interpretations are two important functions of the Supreme Court that have a direct impact on the political interests of African-Americans. The ruling in *Plessy* and *Brown*, for example, involved interpretations of the constitutional protections afforded black Americans. Similarly, such cases as *Gingles* and *Miller* focused on the application of the 1982 amendments to the Voting Rights Act. However, whether or not the Court rules in favor black interests is often a political matter.[18] In other words, the political leanings of the justices, the political climate of the nation, and the partisanship of the party in power play a significant role in determining judicial policy. In particular, the power of presidential appointment has had a profound effect on the relationship between the Court and the African-American community. For instance, it is widely agreed that the appointments of presidents Reagan and Bush have resulted in a clear conservative majority that has generally peeled back gains from the civil rights movement.[19] In education, employment, voting rights, and economic development the Rehnquist Court has consistently ruled against the agenda of many in the black community.

In their article **"Blacks and United States Supreme Court,"** *James Gibson and Greg Caldeira examine African-American attitudes toward the Supreme Court. They, too, begin with the observation that the Supreme Court of the 1950s and 1960s held the black community in "high esteem," however the Court of the last 20 or so years has been decidedly less friendly. They hypothesize two plausible explanations of contemporary black attitudes toward the Court. The first notion is that black evaluations of the Court are dependent on the nature of judicial policy. When the Court rules against black interests, blacks should have harsher perceptions of the Court. Thus blacks in the recent period should harbor more negative attitudes. On the other hand, when the Court is seen as supporting black interest, blacks are more favorably disposed to the Court. The second proposition is that black attitudes toward the Court exhibit cohort effects. That is, because older African-Americans were socialized during the period in which the Warren Court frequently upheld black claims they are likely to have more positive views of the Court. Utilizing a national opinion survey of African-Americans, the authors find that blacks do show less support for the Court than do whites. On the other hand, this lack of support is not as large as one might expect as a function of blacks' evaluations of discrete judicial policies. Rather, the residual positive evaluation of older blacks socialized during the Warren Court mutes dissatisfaction with current judicial policies. As the authors point out, however, if future appointments to the Court result in more favorable rulings, black attitudes toward the Court can quickly change.*

BLACKS AND THE SUPREME COURT: MODELS OF DIFFUSE SUPPORT

■

James L. Gibson and Gregory A. Caldeira

THE SUPREME COURT AND BLACK RIGHTS AND OPPORTUNITIES

Perhaps more than any other national political institution in recent decades, the Supreme Court has protected the interests of black Americans. From the early days of the Warren Court onward through the beginning of the 1960s, the Court stood as a beacon of hope and light for black Americans amidst an otherwise hostile political system. Senior southern chairmen in both houses of Congress, buttressed by the institution of the "filibuster" in the Senate and the Rules Committee in the House, bottled up attempts to legislate against lynching, intimidation at the polls, and all manner of racial discrimination. To be sure, chief executives from Franklin Roosevelt through John Kennedy proved more receptive to the political cause of blacks than did Congress, but not until Lyndon Johnson did the executive branch invest the full force of its authority in favor of black civil rights.

Even prior to the 1930s, the Court from time to time struck blows for racial equality. The Court's decisions on the issue of race prior to the 1940s hardly seem revolutionary in the light of history and the justices showed considerable inconsistency, but the black community saw sufficient promise to place heavy weight on the judiciary in the struggle for freedom and equality. Thus, for example, the NAACP mobilized in an impressive way to help to defeat Judge John J. Parker's nomination to the Supreme Court in 1930. The leader in this battle, Walter White, saw Parker as a threat to the gains blacks had made in the past and hoped to see in the future in the Supreme Court (see, e.g., Hine 1977; Watson 1963). Older black Americans have witnessed great changes in the degree to which the Supreme Court has shown sympathy to their interests.

The NAACP Legal Defense Fund's well-documented, systematic, and relatively successful use of the federal courts to achieve greater racial equality in a number of areas of the law is a classic example of how the Court was drawn in and assumed an instrumental role in the lives of blacks (see Vose 1959 and Tushnet 1987). During the 1950s and 1960s, the apogee of "Warren Court liberalism," the Supreme Court with the help of a number of interest groups steadfastly vindicated and expanded the rights of blacks. Shapiro (1979) has put the matter well in describing blacks—along with organized labor, government workers, and poor people—as the chief constituencies of the Warren Court. From the 1920s through the late 1960s, the Supreme Court became increasingly supportive of the rights and liberties of blacks, and in the 1950s and 1960s this movement accelerated. Especially following World War II through the close of the 1960s, then, black Americans had good reason to hold the Supreme Court in high esteem.

Black Americans in the last two decades have not found the Supreme Court the loyal and constant ally of the past. Indeed, as an empirical matter, the claims of blacks have met with much less success and received less sympathy from the Burger Court (see, for examples, Ulmer and Thompson 1981; Baum 1987, 1988; Blasi 1983). From the early 1970s through the present, blacks and other constituents of the Warren Court have increasingly turned— often in desperation—for vindication of rights and liberties to the Congress and, in some areas, to the state courts. In the late Burger Court and during the first years of the Rehnquist Court, the justices have shown less and less sympathy for the policy agenda of the black community, instead cultivating constituencies among state, local, and federal governments, businesses of varying sizes, and social conservatives. Accordingly, litigators for African Americans can point to few victories in the Supreme Court in recent years. To be sure, we can identify some expansions of the rights of blacks during the Burger Court era in a few selected policy areas, but, whatever view one might take of the whole picture, it is clear that the black community could no longer take the Court for granted as a friend (for a brief review of shifts in policy see Shapiro 1990, 62–64). Thus, if blacks saw the Court in a particularly positive light during the Warren Era as a result of its aid and comfort in the struggle for civil rights, today they surely have little or no reasons to hold the Court in the high esteem of yesteryear.

What, if any, implications do these basic changes in policy have for black attitudes toward the Supreme Court? To assess this question, we must initially turn to prior research on black support for the Court.

BLACKS' VIEWS OF THE SUPREME COURT

Early research on black-white differences in support for the Supreme Court pictured blacks as substantially more supportive of the institution than whites. For instance, Hirsch and Donohew (1968)—based on data collected in 1964, the heyday of the Court's activism on racial issues—reported that not only were black attitudes toward the Court extremely favorable, but that twice as many blacks were favorable than were whites. This research assumed a connection between policy and support; support for the Court in this view flowed from favorable judicial decisions.

We can use earlier research to trace in a rough-and-ready fashion changes in black attitudes toward the Court.[1] According to the measures employed at the time, blacks were considerably more supportive of the Court (or at lest its policy outputs) than were whites during the 1960s (Hirsch and Donohew 1968; see also Murphy, Tanenhaus, and Kastner 1973). By the 1970s, however, racial differences in attitudes had shrunken considerably (Handberg and Maddox 1982; Sigelman 1979; Glenn 1974–1975). This change in views in the black community most likely reflected changing evaluations of the Court's decisions, rather than change in fundamental commitments to the institution. By the end of the 1970s, black-white differences had largely disappeared. On at least one dimension of support—confidence in the Court—blacks manifested an orientation toward that institution just as *unfavorable* as whites (Sigelman 1979). Sigelman interpreted this finding as an indication of a "bottoming out" of the attitudes of both blacks and whites in the wake of the so-called Watergate crisis. Unfortunately, problems in both the measurement of diffuse support and the small numbers of blacks included in the samples make us wary of placing too much confidence in these findings.

In general, there is some evidence that black political attitudes are more reality-based than are white attitudes. For instance, black trust in government seems to be closely connected to satisfaction with incumbents and particularly with the election of black political leaders (Howell and Fagan 1988; Abney and Hutcheson 1981; Bobo and Gilliam 1990). The evidence is fragmentary, but it seems that the reservoir of good will toward the political system is shallower among blacks than among whites.

Thus, two major hypotheses emerge from this earlier, largely descriptive literature.[2] The first envisions diffuse support among blacks as a reflection of levels of specific support. That is, to the extent that unfavorable policy decisions are forthcoming, blacks will not extend support for the Supreme Court. Consequently, we may find a diminished utility in distinguishing between diffuse and specific support among blacks.

To the extent that black attitudes toward the Court reflect the degree of favorable judicial policies, we would predict a less positive orientation toward the Court among blacks than whites, than they were in the past. Indeed, it would not be too much of a caricature to argue that most of the Court's decisions of the 1960s on balance favored blacks, that they were more mixed in the 1970s, and that in the 1980s blacks have been decidedly disadvantaged by the course of judicial policy, at least in relative terms. If diffuse support among blacks is a function of the nature of policy outputs, then we would expect to find blacks today less favorably oriented toward the Court than are whites. Of course, we have in our possession only cross-sectional evidence, so we have to remain guarded in what we say about these dynamic propositions.

Second, black attitudes toward the Court may be closely related to the degree to which individuals have experienced a Supreme Court favorably disposed to the interests of their community. Young black Americans have never lived in a period during which the Supreme Court has acted in a uniformly sympathetic fashion toward black political and social interests. Accordingly, if this interpretation based on cohorts holds water, we expect to find considerable generational differences in diffuse support associated with these changes in the Court's policy over the last several decades.

Two aspects stand out sharply. First, blacks, like whites, are in the main favorably oriented toward the Supreme Court as an institution. For instance, a majority of both blacks and whites would *not* support the abolition of judicial review of congressional action. Of those willing to express a view (i.e., of those who are not uncertain), substantial majorities indicate support of the Court. There is obviously a fair amount of variability in the views of both whites and blacks. Yet we should understand this variability within the general context of positive orientations toward the high bench.

Second, on every single item blacks show less support for the Court than do whites, and in every instance the difference is highly statistically significant. This pattern results in part because blacks are more likely than whites to profess uncertainty toward the Court.[3] Nonetheless, even discounting that, we find blacks less supportive of the institution.

This result stands in stark contrast to the findings reported in earlier work—in those studies, blacks showed either greater support for the Court than did whites, or at the very least, in recent years, no difference. Even if we take into account differences in measurement in earlier studies, we think it likely that our results represent an important shift downward in the level of support for the Court among blacks relative to whites.

THE RELATIONSHIP OF DIFFUSE AND SPECIFIC SUPPORT

Extant literature suggests that black attitudes toward the Court are strongly driven by the favorability of the policy outputs of the Court toward black political and social interests. When the Court finds in favor of blacks' claims, it receives support; when its decisions go against the interests of blacks, support declines. Earlier research thus leads us to expect a close connection between specific and diffuse support among black Americans.

Specific support is the evaluations citizens hold of the current policy outputs of the institution. We measured specific support by asking the respondents whether the Supreme Court is "too liberal or too conservative or about right in its decisions?" Roughly 54% of our black respondents judge the Supreme Court as "about right." Among those dissatisfied with Court outputs, there is more than a two to one balance in favor of the view that the Court has been too conservative. Thus, a bare majority of blacks gives specific support to the Court.

This question as asked is *not* a measure of specific support. Instead, we must transform it into a dichotomous variable indicating satisfaction or dissatisfaction with the Court. Specific support refers to whether the subject is satisfied or dissatisfied with the outputs of the institution, not whether the respondent views the policy as too liberal or too conservative.[4]

From this perspective, we find little relationship between diffuse and specific support. Among blacks, the relationship between diffuse and specific support is not strong, and if anything, there is a slight tendency for those who express dissatisfaction with the Court's current outputs to show *higher* levels of diffuse support. For instance, among those who think the Court has been too conservative, 35% express high levels of diffuse support; among those who view the institution as too liberal only 9% express high support (16% of those satisfied with the Court are high in diffuse support). This no doubt reflects the submerged impact of ideology in our measure of specific support. Dissatisfaction does not in and of itself predict levels of diffuse support. This is comforting from the point of view of measurement.

BLACK COHORTS AND SUPPORT FOR THE SUPREME COURT

It is quite possible that some portion of the remaining reservoir of diffuse support among blacks represents a "hangover" from the earlier strong institutional regard generated during the heyday of the liberal Warren Court.[5] After a sustained period during which the high bench stood in the forefront of the civil rights movement, and after *white* Americans themselves had made the Supreme Court such a vivid symbol of the movement toward greater racial integration, we might find only a gradual erosion of fundamental support among blacks as the Court changed its policy orientations and adopted a more conservative stance. This scenario would explain the decoupling of ideology, policy attitudes, specific support, and diffuse support within the minds of contemporary black Americans.

We can conduct a weak test of this hypothesis through an analysis of black cohorts. We have divided our subjects into three categories.[6] The first consists of those who largely came of political age after the Warren Court revolution. We identify this group as those who were born after 1953. By the time these people had reached their fifteenth birthday, the Supreme Court had begun its rightward move. For nearly all of the adult lives of these subjects, the Supreme Court has not found in favor of blacks' interests as consistently as had the Warren Court.[7] Although we recognize that affective orientations toward political institutions are instilled at a quite early age (see Easton 1965, for example), we also believe that these beliefs can be extinguished relatively early in life if they are not reinforced.[8]

The second category of citizens includes those who most strongly and directly experienced the Warren Court's rulings. This group we define as those who were born between 1933 and 1953. These are the individuals most likely to have directly experienced the desegregation brought about by the Court. Moreover, their political views hardened during the period in which the U.S. Supreme Court was the most, if not only, responsive institution to black political and social interests. It is this group that we most strongly suspect developed stalwart and nearly immutable attitudes toward the Court. Even after a fairly lengthy period of conservative rulings by the Court, we expect that this group will exhibit the highest levels of diffuse support for the institution.

The final category encompasses those who have experienced supreme courts of greatly varying hues. These old black Americans were born prior to 1933 and lived through periods in which the Supreme Court was sometimes—but more often not—responsive to black interests. Indeed, during the period of the bulk of this cohort's greatest receptivity to political learning, the Court's policy on race was relatively conservative, and for this reason we hypothesize that these subjects are the least likely of our three cohorts to express diffuse support for the Court.

The hypothesis is fairly strongly supported by the data. The "Warren Court" cohort exhibits an unusually high level of support for the Supreme Court. Slightly more than a quarter of the middle cohort exhibited a high level of diffuse support; a significantly smaller proportion of the other cohorts show up in the category of highest esteem for the Court. The top row of the table makes the difference even clearer. For instance, only one third of this group is low in diffuse support, compared to 59% for the older cohort and 48% for the younger cohort. This is a substantial difference. Those who were most clearly and directly influenced by the Supreme Court during their early adult years are the most supportive of the institution. The disjunction between this generation and our youngest cohort of blacks is particularly striking.

SUMMARY AND CONCLUSIONS

Here we have discovered or reaffirmed several important attributes of black opinions toward the U.S. Supreme Court. First, blacks are on balance fairly positive toward the Court, but they are decidedly less positive than whites. Second, at the same time, black attitudes toward the institution are not as negative as one might predict if attitudes were formed primarily by whether one is pleased or displeased with current judicial policies. Third, we can explain a portion of the reason why blacks "over-support" the Court as a residue of positive affect created largely during the era of the Warren Court. Among both younger and older blacks, attitudes toward the institution reflect levels of policy satisfaction. Only this "Warren Court" cohort shows a willingness to defined the Court as an institution even in the face of disagreement with the outputs of the current incumbents. These results strongly suggest the extraordinary resiliency of orientations learned early in the life cycle.

For the Supreme Court, the blacks of the Warren Era remain a relatively solid and faithful constituency in comparison to those from other eras. The Supreme Court, in creating controversial policies, naturally makes many enemies, and this problem draws much attention from journalists, politicians, and scholars. But we seem to forget the other side of controversial choices. The Court often makes firm friends as it hands down a series of tough decisions. The Court, like other political institutions, has a set of constituencies, and, like other institutions, it relies on the support of those constituents against its political opposition. We should not think of constituencies as equally important, loyal, or coherent. Fissures will develop even within the most clearly identifiable and unified constituencies, of which black Americans constitute perhaps the best example. Nor should we consider the political landscape as fixed in stone; the Court's constituencies will change substantially over time as the Court itself and its policy agenda change. Indeed, as diffuse support among blacks erodes over the long haul in response to unfavorable policy outputs, we would anticipate a concomitant increase in support among those constituencies now favored in the Supreme Court's decisions. Here we have investigated some sources of support for the Court among one of its most important constituencies, black Americans, and found that one generation in particular has shown extraordinary loyalty to the institution.

NOTES

1. It is always difficult to evaluate research on black and white differences for several methodological reasons. First, the number of black respondents is typically small, and the pooling of surveys using the same sampling frame is only a partial palliative. Second, we have an abiding suspicion that considerable segments of the black community are systematically underrepresented in opinion surveys. Third, it is never clear that statistical controls for black-white differences in socioeconomic status in fact capture and remove all (e.g., linear and nonlinear) of the interracial differences. Thus, we must take care in interpreting this literature.

2. We might also suggest a third hypothesis: the findings in the research might differ because they used quite different measures of support for the Supreme Court. Because the measurement approaches differed so considerably, our extraction of hypotheses from this literature must be treated as highly tentative.

3. It is certainly true that some of the difference between blacks and whites is a function of a greater tendency for blacks to be uncertain or not to have an opinion on these issues. Nevertheless, when we exclude these respondents from the analysis, the racial difference on three of the five items is still significant beyond .001, the difference on one item is significant at .01, and one difference is not significant. For instance, of those with opinions, 24% of the black sample would like to reduce the powers of the Supreme Court; only 12% of the white sample is so inclined.

4. Scholars have operationalized specific support in a number of different manners. Thus, for example, Murphy, Tanenhaus, and Kastner (1973) create a summated scale derived from open-ended responses to queries about what the individual liked and disliked about the Supreme Court's decisions—modeled on the Survey Research Center's batteries on evaluations of the parties and candidates in presidential contests. Others have asked a series of closed-ended items about specific decisions and used them to generate an overall score. We can see some value in both approaches. We opted for ours on grounds of parsimony.

   Relatively few members of the public think along ideological lines and connect particular issues to the left-right continuum. Does our measure of specific support miss the mark for those who do not connect this ideological continuum to specific decisions of the Court? That is, what if an individual likes or dislikes the content of the Court's decisions but does not see them as liberal or conservative? Our impression is that respondents pass over ideological terms and tell the interviewers essentially whether they like or dislike the Court's decisions. Few of the respondents refused to answer the item—in stark contrast to the substantial number who cannot or will not identify themselves on the ideological continuum.

5. Scholars differ on the persistence throughout the life-cycle of political orientations learned in adolescence or early adulthood. Some make claims for substantial continuity, for the primacy of attitudes learned early in life; others argue for minimal persistence except for the most fundamental orientations. The truth seems to lie somewhere between the two extremes. Kinder and Sears' authoritative review of the literature puts it well:

   Adults steadily resist any systematic pressure to change their longstanding predispositions. . . . Any major resocialization, even in early adulthood, apparently demands an exacting and unusually powerful social situation. . . . In its simplest form, then, the persistence view overstates the case. More plausible is a view that takes into account continuing socialization and occasional resocialization through adolescence and diminishing but still noticeable levels of change thereafter (1985, 724).

6. No doubt others will think of other points at which to divide the three cohorts, and some might prefer different numbers of cohorts. We think the divisions we have specified make good substantive sense, and on practical grounds we could not afford to break the sample into more subsets. The results reported in succeeding tables seem solid. Our experiments with alternative cohorts did not indicate any particular sensitivity to the break points.

7. The Court's rightward shift did not occur in one fell swoop after the retirement of Earl Warren and installation of Warren Burger in 1969, Harry Blackmun in 1970, and Lewis Powell and William Rehnquist in 1971. It happened gradually. Nevertheless, the various media, political elites, and the black community spoke of these changes in personnel as though they marked sharp, significant shifts in judicial policy. For our purposes, perceptions among black leaders and the black community are more important than subtle interpretations of doctrinal change.

8. Evidence on the onset of affective attachments to the Supreme Court among young Americans is in scant supply and of problematic quality. Still, the two main studies (Easton and Dennis 1969; Caldeira 1977) seem united on one point: young people develop knowledge of and feelings toward the Court at a much later age than for the president.

In the conclusion to his book **Race Against the Supreme Court**, *Girardeau Spann summarizes his critique of the ability of the Supreme Court to protect the interests of racial minorities. His core claim is that inherent majoritarian biases in the structure and functioning of the Court preclude it from protecting the interests of blacks (and other racial minorities) from the tyranny of the majority. Spann's argument rests on two broad points. In the first instance, Spann argues that the structure of the Court is designed to serve the interests of majority rather than nonmajority interests, thus the Court cannot fully satisfy its traditional role of protecting minority rights (i.e., judicial review). For example, "... the Court consists of socialized justices who possess the values and dispositions of the same political majority that controls the representative branches." Moreover, the insulating effects of lifetime tenure cannot counter this tendency because judges have tremendous discretionary authority to give operative meaning to legal principles. The second leg of the argument is that the Supreme Court develops legal doctrines that govern race relations from a position of majoritarian bias. He offers three examples in support of this view. One, minorities are given a false sense of security by the principle of judicial review which creates "judicial dependency" that deters from using black political power to blunt "self-determined political action." Two, by centralizing affirmative action law, the Court has muted the influence of black political empowerment at the local level. Three, the Court has institutionalized a set of assumptions based on the notion that there are "fundamental rights that the government cannot abridge" (and those rights are set forth by the Court). Thus blacks cannot demand rights outside of this legal paradigm. In sum, Spann contends that the pro-majority biases of the Supreme Court hinder its ability to be a champion of minority rights.*[20]

RACE AGAINST THE COURT: THE SUPREME COURT AND MINORITIES IN CONTEMPORARY AMERICA

Girardeau A. Spann

Excerpt from Chapter 10: Summary and Conclusion

For racial minorities, judicial review has proven to be more of a curse than a blessing. Rather than protecting racial minority interests from the tyranny of the majority, the Supreme Court has done just the opposite. It has protected the majority from claims of equality by racial minorities. During the early history of the Supreme Court, the Court was fairly explicit in its sacrifice of minority interests for majoritarian gain. Whether the Court was abandoning the Cherokee Tribe in the face of majoritarian hostility as it did in *Cherokee Nation v. State of Georgia*, denying citizenship to blacks in gratuitously demeaning terms as it did in *Dred Scott*, invalidating Reconstruction civil rights legislation as it did in *The Civil Rights Cases*, or proclaiming the virtues of *de jure* segregation as it did in *Plessy*, the 19th-century Supreme Court was fairly transparent in the implementation of its mission to protect white majority interests. In the post-*Brown* 20th century, the Court has been more opaque in the implementation of its mission, but the mission has remained the same. Racial minority interests have still been sacrificed to majoritarian desires, but the doctrinal mechanisms on which the Court has relied to effect the sacrifice have been more sophisticated, lurking in the interstices of complex and esoteric constitutional rules. The Court has even mastered the extremely sophisticated strategy of dressing minority losses in the attire of minority gains when it serves majoritarian ends to grant such apparent concessions, as the Court did in *Brown v. Board of Education*. The structural reasons for which the Court is destined to serve majoritarian rather than countermajoritarian ends have been discussed in Part I, and they are summarized below. The ways in which the Court's veiled majoritarianism have contributed to the perpetuation of minority subordination in contemporary culture have been discussed in Part II, and they too are summarized below. Despite the sense of hopelessness that continued Supreme Court "protection" portends, all of this suggests a rather intriguing conclusion for racial minorities who are seemingly trapped in the predicament of judicial review. The efficacy of this conclusion, however, depends upon a subtle appreciation of the precise locus of the contest that presently exists between the Supreme Court and racial minorities in America.

SUMMARY OF PART I

Part I of this book has described how Supreme Court adjudication fails to serve the countermajoritarian judicial function that is traditionally ascribed to it. The framers initially designed a system of government in which individual liberty and property rights were to be protected by the political safeguards of federalism and separation of powers. During the New Deal, however, those safeguards were largely eviscerated, in accordance with majoritarian political preferences. As a result, the task of protecting individual rights has fallen to the Supreme Court. Under the *Marbury*-based traditional model of judicial review, the Court is an appropriate guardian of individual rights because it possesses institutional advantages over the representative branches that promote sensitivity to politically impotent interests. Because of this sensitivity, the Court is able to honor rights that an unconstrained political branch of government would prefer to exploit for majoritarian purposes. The rights of racial minorities, like the rights of individuals, are subject to similar majoritarian exploitation because of the relative political powerlessness that racial minorities have historically been forced to endure. Accordingly, the traditional model of judicial review requires the Court to protect the interests of racial minorities from majoritarian abrogation, just as it requires the Court to protect the rights of individuals. Under the traditional model, the ability of the Supreme Court to operate in a countermajoritarian manner is essential. Although the Court is commonly perceived to be performing its prophylactic function in an acceptable manner, the Court in fact does not possess the countermajoritarian capacity that the traditional model attributes to it. Moreover, the Court not only lacks the ability to serve as a guardian against majority preferences, it actually advances those preferences through its adjudications.

The Supreme Court as currently conceived cannot possess the countermajoritarian capacity required for traditional judicial review because the membership of the Court consists of socialized justices who possess the values and predispositions of the same elite political majority that controls the representative branches. As a statistical matter, therefore, those majoritarian-influenced jurists will exercise judicial discretion in the same way that the members of the representative branches exercise political discretion, unless unique features of the judicial process successfully constrain the exercise of judicial discretion. Although both formal and operational safeguards have been built into the judicial process in order to guarantee its countermajoritarian capabilities, those safeguards are ineffective.

The formal safeguards of life tenure and salary protection are designed to protect the judiciary from overt political pressures that might be exerted by the representative branches in order to affect the outcome of particular cases. It is unlikely that these safeguards are effective in attaining this limited objective, but more important, they are not even addressed to the majoritarian influences that the process of socialization has exerted over judicial attitudes and values. The operational safeguard of principled adjudication, which arguably *is* addressed to the problem of socialized judicial preferences, cannot ultimately serve the desired insulating function, because the legal principles on which the adjudicatory process relies themselves depend upon unconstrained discretionary input in order to derive their operative meanings.

Many legal principles expressly incorporate majoritarian preferences into their meanings, because the governing legal standard is defined to coincide with whatever meaning a majoritarian branch has given it. More subtly, the same result is often accomplished through deferential standards of review, which permit majoritarian preferences to govern the content of a principle because the Court will not intervene to alter its majoritarian meaning. Although not all legal principles incorporate majoritarian preferences into their meanings, it is the Supreme Court that must decide which principles do and which do not. This decision requires an act of judicial discretion, and it poses all of the dangers associated with the exercise of such discretion.

If the present thesis concerning the necessary correspondence between majoritarian and countermajoritarian dispositions of minority interests is correct, one would expect the Supreme Court to preserve for itself opportunities to submit to majoritarian desires. Whether done intentionally or unconsciously, the formulation of doctrinal rules whose applications require significant amounts of judicial discretion has ensured the continued presence of enough doctrinal latitude for majoritarian influences to operate effectively within the judicial process. Without imputing improper motives to the Court, it is sufficient to note that if one were to design a sophisticated judicial system that would optimize the protection of majority interests in the face of minority demands for better treatment, it would look very much like our present judicial system. Accordingly, it is unrealistic to conceive of the Supreme Court as anything other than a veiled majoritarian institution. And because it is a majoritarian institution, one of the primary tasks that has tacitly been assigned to the Supreme Court is to effectuate the majoritarian preference for the continued subordination of racial minorities.

Part II of this book has described how the Supreme Court developed the legal doctrines that govern race relations in a way that permits the subtle perpetuation of minority subordination. Because the Supreme Court operates in a veiled majoritarian manner, racial minorities could rationally prefer the overt political process to the Supreme Court adjudicatory process as the most promising means for advancing racial minority interests. The process of positive politics is pure in the sense that it purports to be nothing more than what it is—a process for generating outcomes in a pluralist political environment. Unlike the process of Supreme Court adjudication, which purports to have normative content that places it above the realm of mere crass political exchange, the positive political process has no doctrinal pretensions behind which the majority can hide as it extracts resources from racial minorities.

Contemporary racial minorities possess a degree of political power that enables them to operate effectively in the pluralist political process. By pooling their political resources, individual minority groups can increase their inherent political strength. Minorities can further enhance their political strength by forming political coalitions with sympathetic majority interest groups on both short and long term bases. The fact that racial minority interests have historically fared better before the representative branches of government than before the Supreme Court not only illustrates the viability of such a political strategy, but suggests that the simplicity of the overt political process is more advantageous to minorities than the complexities of Supreme Court politics.

The fact that the Supreme Court will inevitably be involved in the formulation of social policies that affect racial minority interests means that minority interests will be subject to surreptitious sacrifice for the benefit of the white majority. There are three ways in which the Supreme Court places minorities at a systemic disadvantage in their quest to secure racial justice. The first is by promoting continued belief in the countermajoritarian model of judicial review, which has lulled racial minorities into a dependency relationship with the Supreme Court under which minorities have come to rely on judicial review rather than on minority political strength for the protection of minority interests. The second is by centralizing the law of affirmative action in a way that makes it difficult for minorities to capitalize on the local political power that they do possess. The third is by legitimating a set of counterproductive assumptions about the operation of the legal system, and the worth of racial minorities, that can reduce the will of even minorities themselves to achieve equal status with whites.

The first way in which the Supreme Court has systemically disadvantaged racial minorities is by successfully consigning minorities to the status of Supreme Court dependents. The Court accomplished this through issuance of its decision in *Brown v. Board of Education*. Although *Brown* promised to desegregate the schools and to eliminate race-based governmental classifications, it did neither. *Brown* merely replaced *de jure* segregation with *de facto* segregation in a way that simply prompted governmental policymakers to rely on racial correlates rather than race itself when they wished to utilize a race-based classification. *Brown* is better understood as a majoritarian decision that inflicted national foreign policy preferences on the regional south than as a countermajoritarian decision that imposed the rule of law on a massively resistant majority.

Notwithstanding its true majoritarian nature, *Brown* has come to be viewed as proof of the Supreme Court's countermajoritarian capabilities. Because racial minorities have come to share this view of *Brown* they have permitted the Court to dictate *minority* political policy to them. Racial minorities have disregarded their own progressive political and intellectual leaders and have manifested their dependence upon the Supreme Court in electing to pursue the elusive goal of integrated education, rather than the goal of high quality education in minority-controlled schools. Moreover, they continue to do so even though this strategy has resulted in nearly 40 post-*Brown* years of inferior education for minority school children.

This submissiveness on the part of racial minorities reflects a deeper minority dependence on the Supreme Court as the institution that prescribes the ways in which minorities conceptualize the problems associated with race. Most notably, this dependence has prompted minority acceptance of the Court's prescription for assimilation rather than self-determination as the aspirational goal for right-thinking racial minority groups to pursue. On an even deeper level, it is dependence upon Supreme Court paternalism that has led minorities to eschew aggressive, self-determined political action in favor of the safety inherent in continued minority status as wards of the Supreme Court.

The second way in which the Supreme Court has systemically disadvantaged racial minorities is by centralizing the law of affirmative action. With the demise of *de jure* segregation, the law of affirmative action has become the most significant area of the law affecting racial minority interests. The statistical nature of contemporary racial discrimination means that only statistical allocations of societal resources offer any hope of promoting racial equality. However, it is in the interest of members of the white majority as rational wealth maximizers to allocate to themselves as large a share of societal resources as possible without either provoking minorities to adopt extra-legal strategies of resistance or causing the majority to view itself in unflatteringly selfish terms. The Supreme Court has served the function of advancing this majoritarian interest by upholding the constitutionality of only those affirmative action programs that are adopted at the national rather than the local level.

By centralizing the law of affirmative action to permit national but not local affirmative action programs, the Court has permitted the majority to retain its goodwill and positive self-image by allowing it to adopt *some* affirmative action programs. However, racial minorities possess more political power at the local level, where there can be heavy concentrations of minority voting strength, than at the national level, where minorities will comprise only a small percentage of the total electorate. As a result, Supreme Court validation of only centralized affirmative action programs turns out to be a political bargain for the white majority, because it will not result in *many* affirmative action programs actually taking effect.

More subtly, the Supreme Court's centralization of the law of affirmative action reflects our prevailing cultural preferences for universalism, rational objectivity, and race neutrality over the parochialism, irrational subjectivity, and racial bias that have come to be associated with decentralization. In a culture that is as inescapably race-conscious as contemporary American culture, allocations of societal resources are significantly dependent upon race. It is implausible to suggest that some race-neutral concept such as merit could override the racial factors that go into making resource allocation determinations. However, the Supreme Court's centralization of the law of affirmative action ultimately permits the white majority to view the race-conscious allocation of resources to racial minorities as a suspect racial preference while viewing the equally race-conscious allocation of resources to itself as the commendable exercise of race neutrality. This not only helps the majority to feel comfortable with its disproportionate allocation of societal resources, but it deters minorities from embracing nationalist strategies for the advancement of racial interests that offer the greatest hope for promoting racial equality and self-determination.

The third way in which the Supreme Court has systemically disadvantaged racial minorities is by legitimating a set of counterproductive assumptions about the nature of the legal process, and ultimately about racial minorities themselves. The process of legitimation operates by causing an unstated assumption to be accepted without scrutiny while analytical attention has been diverted to a more salient consequence of the legitimated assumption. Using this technique, the Supreme Court has legitimated three unstated assumptions that are relevant to the minority struggle for racial equality. It has legitimated the liberal assumption that there exists a category of fundamental rights that the government cannot abridge. It has also legitimated the assumption that the Supreme Court is the final expositor of the content of those rights. Finally, it has legitimated the assumption that minorities cannot properly make demands upon the majority that exceed the scope of the fundamental rights as expounded by the Court.

All of these assumptions serve the interests of the white majority, but they do not serve the interests of racial minorities. The liberal rights assumption is counterproductive because it tends to backfire on racial minorities. Its most frequent historic use has been in the protection of white property interests. Similarly, its contemporary majoritarian value lies in its use to invalidate affirmative action programs on the grounds that they interfere with majoritarian interests. The assumption that the Supreme Court is the final expositor of the content of rights is counterproductive because it authorizes the mostly white, mostly male Supreme Court to referee disputes between the majority and racial minorities over the proper allocation of resources in a way that is largely immune from political modification. Historically, this has been an arbitration system that favors the majority over racial minorities, and there is no reason to believe that this built-in bias is about to change. The assumption that minorities are not entitled to anything more than what the Supreme Court grants them not only solidifies the dependency relationship that racial minorities have with the Supreme Court, but it conveys negative connotations about the indolent ingratitude of racial minorities that perpetuate perceptions of racial minorities as inferior. To the extent that these perceptions are shared by racial minorities themselves, legitimation of this assumption frustrates minority perceptions of self-worth and inhibits the aggressiveness with which minorities will pursue their claims for racial justice.

CONCLUSION

The traditional model of judicial review is hopelessly disingenuous. Not only is the Supreme Court precluded from protecting minority interests by its veiled majoritarian nature, but it seems that the Court's true institutional function is to perpetuate the subordination of racial minorities for majority gain. As a matter of constitutional theory, this leads to a rather paradoxical conclusion. Although contemporary constitutional debate centers around the continued viability of the *Marbury* model, in the final analysis, it simply does not much matter whether the traditional model of judicial review is valid or not. The Supreme Court has cast far too strong a spell of necessity over the constituents of judicial review to be thwarted by mere insights into its operational deficiencies. The legal academics, operating in the name of constraining scrutiny, have also provided their share of aid and comfort to the endeavor. The more transparent the Court's deficiencies have become, the more abundant has become the flow of theory to obfuscate the transparency. And racial minorities themselves, wanting desperately to become a part of the whole, have chosen to root for the success of the undertaking. They have viewed the recurrence of judicial betrayal as an unsightly blemish upon an otherwise noble aspiration. Like the white majority, racial minorities have resisted the inference that persistent perfidy reveals a flaw at the inception of the enterprise. Everyone seems to want the system to work, no matter how unworkable the system seems to become.

In this environment, racial minorities armed with insights about the inescapable majoritarianism of the Supreme Court could do no more than treat the Court as an antagonistic political institution rather than as a hospitable benefactor. But to be effective in their political treatment, minorities would still have to file the same briefs before the Court, offer the same oral arguments, and pronounce the words "Your Honor" with the same degree of deference. No matter how enlightened it were to become, political use of the Court would still legitimate the countermajoritarian assumptions on which the traditional model is based, thereby perversely implicating racial minorities in the perpetuation of their own subordination. Sadly, the assumption that racial minorities are Supreme Court dependents who are incapable of political self-determination seems to be self-fulfilling. This poses an inescapable dilemma for minorities in search of racial justice.

Thankfully, the dilemma is only syllogistic. It is an artifact of the same sorts of rational discourse and logical analysis that could permit a social institution as regressive as the Supreme Court to become recognized as the champion of oppressed minorities. Once freed from the epistemological constraints of syllogistic analysis, racial minorities could also free themselves from the constraints of Supreme Court protection. Consider that the vision of an omnipotent God exerts enormous influence over the attitudes and behavior of the adherents to that vision. But it is of no consequence whatsoever to those for whom the vision holds no attraction. Similarly, Freud's conception of unconscious determinism is of paramount importance to those who have chosen to pursue psychoanalytic strategies for self-realization. But it is little more than a source of amusement to those for whom hard-edged conceptions of freewill offer a more comfortable account of human behavior. Even assuming that an external reality remains constant across epistemological perspectives, it is the perspectives themselves—not the underlying reality—that give life and meaning to experience. It follows that the way for racial minorities to escape the reality of Supreme Court subordination is to think about that reality differently. . . .

Thought about differently, it is not at all surprising that a Supreme Court nominally committed to the protection of minority interests would resist the escape of racial minorities from its protective custody. While it is true that under the *Marbury* model of judicial review, minorities are consigned to a role of perpetual Supreme Court dependency, minority dependence is the lesser of the two dependencies that are created by the traditional model. Under the *Marbury* model, if there were no politically impotent minorities for the Supreme Court to protect, there could be no judicial review. And without judicial review, the Supreme Court would be deprived of its distinctive significance in the American political system. Ironically, it is the Supreme Court that is actually dependent upon the continued vulnerability of minorities in order to sustain its own constitutional legitimacy. This, of course, gives racial minorities an enormous source of power over the Court. By choosing to relinquish their vulnerability, racial minorities would also terminate the traditional utility of the Supreme Court.

To date, racial minorities have charitably served as sacrificial recipients of Supreme Court largess in a way that has protected the fragile esteem of this governmental institution—an institution whose only real power lies in the continued obeisance of its minority charges. But that has proven to be a counterproductive endeavor. The society has remained unjust despite its invocation of judicial review as the symbol for its commitment to inchoate equal justice. Racial minorities have demonstrated remarkable tolerance with the shortcomings of the Court. They have treated its decisions with the patience and restraint that one would accord the misdeeds of a wayward child whose deficient parenting was properly to blame for the child's poor conduct.

Nevertheless, even racial minority tolerance must eventually come to an end. The adjudicatory path to racial justice has proven unworkable, and it is now time for minorities to cease their protection of the Supreme Court. It is time to leave the Court to its fate. The continued self-sacrifice of minority interests solely to shore up the institutional importance of the Supreme Court, and the unworkable approach to justice that it represents, would serve no useful purpose. The era of the Court has come, and it has gone. And minorities must now show concern for themselves rather than continuing to protect this obsolete institution and the social order for which it stands.

Although minorities may not ultimately possess the power to control the manner in which the legal process deals with their welfare, they do possess the power to control their conception of that process. Which may be every bit as good.

As noted previously, there have been two African-American Supreme Court justices— Thurgood Marshall and Clarence Thomas. Whereas Marshall is lionized for his support of black interests, Thomas has been bitterly attacked as being antithetical to the political agenda supported by the majority of the black community.[21] In the following selection entitled, "On Justice Clarence Thomas," Stephen Smith argues that the scathing attacks on Justice Thomas are a function of the tenuous hold black liberal leadership has on the majority of the community. Smith starts his defense by observing that there has always been disagreement among black thinkers about the appropriate model for racial equality. From this view, Justice Thomas is part of a long tradition of black dissent. Smith goes on to note the Thomas' views are "well within the black mainstream" and cites public opinion data that reveals significant support for conservatism among African-Americans.[22] Finally, Smith maintains that Thomas' stated support of color-blind reasoning in his positions on the Court show that he has "remained true to both the Constitution and to the traditional civil rights objective that the government must treat all of its citizens as individuals, without regard to their race." In short, Smith believes that black liberals who are clinging on to the threads of a worn ideology have unfairly attacked Justice Thomas. Thus, by implication, the Supreme Court is a body capable of protecting the rights of minority citizens.

ON JUSTICE CLARENCE THOMAS

Stephen F. Smith

Copyright National Affairs Inc. 1996

It has been almost five years since Associate Justice Clarence Thomas was confirmed as the 106th Justice of the Supreme Court of the United States. During that time, he has come under sharp and unrelenting criticism from the liberal media. He has also been criticized by those who one would have expected to welcome the ascent of a black American to the pinnacle of his profession: the civil-rights community. To give but one example, at the 1995 convention of the National Association for the Advancement of Colored People (NAACP), Thomas was repeatedly called a "pimp" and a "traitor."

Is all this part of some personal vendetta against Justice Thomas? Maybe in part, but far more is at work here. Simply put, the incessant assaults on

Thomas are part of a larger political struggle for the hearts and minds of black America. The traditional liberal black leadership is fighting to maintain its increasingly tenuous hold on power within the black community, and the liberal Democrats to maintain their control over one of their last remaining core constituencies.

Thomas has triggered this struggle because he, more than any other individual, personifies the rise of black conservatism in America. The symbolism is inevitable, for Justice Thomas's seat on the nation's high Court makes him not only one of the most powerful people in America but also the highest ranking black legal officer in the country. It is thus not surprising that civil-rights leaders and other Thomas critics single him out for denunciation. The continued spread of conservative ideas in the black community poses a direct threat to the status quo in that community and could someday fill the leadership vacuum that currently exists there.

The accusations have been many, but the most scandalous is that Thomas holds views that no "true" black person could. It is important to understand at the outset just how absurd the claim is. According to this view, the color of one's skin dictates one's views; if one is black, one simply must support, for instance, affirmative action or federal welfare programs. The view has a rather paradoxical corollary, namely that one's views dictate one's skin color; thus Thomas is said to be not really black, which is what it mean to call him an "Uncle Tom" or a "traitor" to his race.

The view that all blacks must think alike is racist on its face, as well as untrue: Black people are not, and never have been, monolithic in their views. To the contrary, there has always been a healthy diversity of opinion within the black community, as in the white community. This is true even in regard to civil-rights issues. Most famously perhaps, in the decades that followed enactment of the constitutional amendments abolishing slavery and guaranteeing blacks and all other persons the equal protection of the laws, W. E. B. Du Bois argued for an immediate end to all forms of political and social discrimination.

Others, however, favored the more gradual approach of Booker T. Washington. Although it has become fashionable of late to say that Washington was an apologist for segregation the reality is otherwise. Washington advocated temporarily deferring explosive social issues to focus, instead, on achieving economic self-sufficiency and equality for blacks. This debate raged on well after the turn of the century. Indeed, the NAACP got its start in 1910 as a dissenting voice in that debate; the fledgling group began as a challenge to the tyranny of the so-called "Washington machine" and urged, in agreement with Du Bois, that blacks should first fight to win full political and civil equality.

This tradition of dissent within the black community has continued up to the present day. In the early part of the twentieth century, some blacks, including Marcus Garvey, argued against integration and in favor of American blacks moving to Africa or elsewhere. Others, including then-attorney Thurgood Marshall, believed that integration into every aspect of American life was the key to black progress. Similarly, during the 1960s, the mainstream civil-rights movement, led by Martin Luther King, Jr., favored peaceful, nonviolent means of protest, whereas more radical forces, such as Malcolm X and the Black Panther Party, were willing to resort to violence. Today, of course, many in the black community agitate for race-conscious remedies, such as affirmative action, in the belief that white racism constitutes an insuperable barrier to black progress. Others, including Thomas, Glenn Loury, and Shelby Steele, oppose affirmative action and argue that, having achieved equality before the law and basic civil rights, blacks should now work to improve schools, to rebuild neighborhoods, and to maintain strong family structures. It is clear, therefore, that Thomas's critics are simply wrong in arguing that all blacks do, and must, think alike; there have always been divergent voices in the black community.

Thomas and the other black thinkers who have disagreed with the establishment view cannot, and should not, be dismissed as "traitors" to their race. As Du Bois wrote almost century ago in defense of himself and other black dissenters of his day: "The hushing of the criticism of honest opponents is a dangerous thing." Free and open debate is, as John Stuart Mill long ago pointed out, vital to progress and the search for truth. It is thus incumbent upon those who truly favor the advancement of blacks to condemn the intolerance of those who would silence Thomas and other black dissenters for something called "thinking white." American blacks have struggled too hard, and for too long, to surrender the precious right to read and to think for themselves—rights that were denied them in slavery—to any orthodoxy, black or white.

Besides, Thomas's conservative views are well within the black mainstream. Although only 8% of blacks surveyed consider themselves Republican, conservative views are, as a general matter, commonplace among blacks. According to a 1992 survey by the Joint Center for Political and Economic Studies, a black liberal think tank, more blacks today describe themselves as "conservative" (33%) than as "liberal" (29%). The Washington Post found, in a series of polls conducted in 1991, that 35% of blacks surveyed described themselves as "very conservative" or "conservative." Thomas's views are more representative still in light of the fact that "another 35% [of blacks] regard themselves as politically moderate." This means that 70% of blacks nationwide have lost faith in liberalism.

The instinctive conservatism of black Americans is also borne out in an array of issue-specific polls. According to a 1995 article in the Washington Post,

> Whether or not they accept the label, many blacks hold conservative views. On the death penalty, according to the Joint Center for Political Studies, blacks tilt 48 to 42 in favor. On denying increased welfare payments to welfare recipients who have more children, 5% of blacks approve. Roughly three-quarters back mandatory sentences for drug dealers, and 61% feel black leaders are too quick to cite racism as an excuse for black crime.

Recent Gallup pools report similar findings. For example, 85% of blacks polled support school choice, 53% disapprove of mandatory busing, and 77% oppose preferential treatment to make up for past discrimination. Moreover, an overwhelming 92% of blacks believe in God. With regard to the issue that drove much of the opposition to Thomas's nomination—abortion—polls find that 48% of blacks are pro-life, flatly opposing abortion under any circumstances.

It is thus inaccurate to characterize Thomas as holding views that no "true" black person could hold. In fact, Thomas's nomination was successful, in large part, due to blacks who rejected their leadership's opposition to his nomination and successfully pressured key southern Democrats to vote to confirm him. Blacks in the South favored the nomination by almost two to one. Some have suggested that blacks supported his nomination only because he is black and that blacks would support one of "their own" simply to maintain "black seat" on the Supreme Court. An alternative view, firmly supported by the survey data, is that blacks backed Thomas's nomination because they did not share their leaders' rabid opposition to his conservative opinions.

Now, five years later, the question is, have Thomas's conservative opinions on racial issues during his tenure on the Supreme Court been good for blacks? Retired U.S. Court of Appeals Judge A. Leon Higginbotham, whom some in the civil-rights community had hoped would succeed the late Justice Thurgood Marshall on the Supreme Court, thinks not. In a recent speech at New York University, Higginbotham argued that Thomas is paving the way to reinstituting "white supremacy" in this country. Thomas's conservative voting record, he surmised, was the result of a deep-seated psychological problem: "racial self-hatred." Higginbotham found it relevant in this regard that Thomas is married to a white woman, Virginia Lamp Thomas, which to Higginbotham is evidence that Thomas "hates black women." Thomas's psychological disorder, Higginbotham concluded, explained why he had constantly voted to "drag blacks to the oppression of the past."

A tell-tale sign of a weak argument on the merits is resort to ad hominen attacks. The Higginbotham diatribe is a case in point. If one considers what Thomas has actually written in his various opinions on affirmative action, redistricting, desegregation, and other issues of particular concern to blacks, it becomes clear that Higginbotham's charges are preposterous.

Foremost among the traditional civil-rights policies criticized by Thomas is affirmative action. Critics of affirmative action generally charge that it is a form of reverse discrimination that harms white males; in contrast, Thomas focuses on the deleterious effects such programs have on blacks. As he explained in the 1995 case *Adarand v. Pena,* race-based preference policies "stamp minorities with a badge of inferiority and may cause them to develop dependencies or to adopt an attitude that they are 'entitled' to preferences," which may lead them to fail or, even worse, not even to try to succeed. In fact, Thomas's important, but largely overlooked, 1995 speech to the Federalist Society excoriates "angry white males" who oppose affirmative action based on the same group-focused "victimology" that proponents of affirmative action exhibit.

He further explained his position in the speech:

> The culture of victimology—with its emphasis on the so-called "benevolent state"—delivers an additional (and perhaps worse) blow to dignity and self-worth. When the less fortunate do accomplish something, they are often denied the sense of achievement whic is so very important for strengthening and

empowering the human spirit. . . . They are just moving along with the "herd" of other victims. Such individuals also lack any incentive to be independent, because they know that as part of an oppressed group they will neither be singled out for the life choices they make nor capable of distinguishing themselves by their own efforts.

Thomas's message for black America is: It is a mistake to think that you cannot succeed without affirmative action; in fact, you cannot succeed with it.

Thomas's insistence on racial colorblindness in the redistricting and voting-rights cases, as in the affirmative-action cases, does not portend, as his critics claim, a new era of white supremacy. In making the contrary assertion, Higginbotham and other Thomas critics implicitly make two assumptions: (1) that citizens can be represented only by candidates of their own race, and (2) that black candidates will never garner enough support from whites to win in nonminority districts. Both assumptions are ill-founded. As for the first, it should be self-evident that what counts in determining whether a given candidate can represent a particular group of citizens is not his skin color but his position on the issues. When the candidate's positions on the issues accords with the voters', he can represent them—whether or not his skin color reflects a composite of their own. Anyone who doubts this need only ask himself who he would want to be his representative—someone of the same race who held different views or someone of a different race who holds the same views?

As for the claim that blacks cannot be elected except from "majority-minority" electoral districts—electoral districts that are racial safe havens for black candidates—the evidence indicates otherwise. In 1989, the voters of Virginia—the state that in earlier times had led the Confederacy and later the opposition to desegregation-elected L. Douglas Wilder, a black man, as their governor. Virginia is only 18% black. Wilder's election is no fluke, as the election to Congress of Carol Mosely Braun, Gary Franks, and J. C. Watts, all from majority-white jurisdictions, indicates, In fact, 83% of big-city black mayors over the past 30 years have won elections in majority-white cities. To be sure, racially polarized voting does occur occasionally, but that unfortunate phenomenon is the exception, not the rule.

There is an added dimension to the creation of majority-minority districts favored by the traditional civil-rights leadership. In his separate opinion in Holder v. Hall, the 1994 voting-rights case, Thomas argued that the so-called "black-preferred" candidates—that is, those who are elected from majority-minority districts—are, almost of necessity, ill-equipped to play any effective or meaningful role in the elected body at large. When such districts are created, "white-preferred candidates" need not be responsive to the concerns of blacks because the vast majority of black citizens are packed into compact districts represented by "their own" candidates. In a regime of majority-minority districts, then, the vast majority of the legislature—namely, white representatives elected from districts with comparatively trivial numbers of blacks—represent the interests of white citizens, and the interests of blacks are represented only by the handful of black representatives who are elected from majority-minority districts. The end result is that, to the extent that they have needs and policy desires that differ from those of white voters, black voters are denied meaningful, effective representation. The isolation of the black voter is worsened still by the fact that majority-minority districts, by virtue of the politics of racial militancy, inevitably elect candidates who are so liberal as to be out of the mainstream in the elected body.

As a consequence, in their zeal to ensure the election of a handful of liberal black officials in any given jurisdiction, the traditional black leadership unwittingly transformed the Voting Rights Act into an electoral boon for Republicans in the South. Although the leadership got what it wanted (a few friendly black faces in Congress), it is now clear that it also got far more than it bargained for—Speaker of the House Newt Gingrich and Senate Majority Leader Bob Dole. To the extent the black leadership is dissatisfied with the current Congress, the leadership has only itself to blame.

Another of Thomas's opinions, in *Missouri v. Jenkins* (1995), has been criticized by Higginbotham and others on the grounds that it would turn the clock back to the days before *Brown v. Board of Education* (1954). His opponents are correct to note that Thomas has criticized that landmark decision overturning school segregation, but they have ignored the fact that Thomas's criticism makes him a stauncher opponent of segregation than they. Thomas criticized the Brown Court not for what it did but for what it failed to do. The Court justified its rejection of *Plessy v. Ferguson's* (1896) "separate but equal" doctrine by citing faulty sociological studies that purported to show that legally sanctioned segregation "generates a feeling of inferiority" among blacks. As a result of this misguided focus on the emotional impact of segregation, the Court did not go far enough in protecting blacks (and others) against state-sponsored discrimination.

The case was, in Thomas's view, "a missed opportunity" because the Court did not unequivocally declare the Constitution color blind. As he explained in Jenkins:

> Brown I itself did not need to rely upon any psychological or social-science research in order to announce the simple, yet fundamental truth that the Government cannot discriminate among its citizens on the basis of race. . . . At the heart of this interpretation of the Equal Protection Clause lies the principle that the Government must treat citizens as individuals, and not as members of racial, ethnic or religious groups.

In short, Thomas criticized the Brown Court for not being emphatic enough about the evils and constitutional infirmities of "Jim Crow" and segregation. Indeed, Thomas's vie is precisely the position then-attorney Thurgood Marshall presented in his winning brief in the Brown case.

Finally, Thomas's opinion in the 1992 case *Dawson v. Delaware* illustrates the depth of his opposition to racism. In Dawson, the petitioner, a death-row inmate nicknamed "one of Satan's disciples," whose prison cell (and body) was adorned with swastikas, argued that he should be spared the death penalty (he had brutally murdered a woman) because he was of "good character" and had been a good prisoner. The state of Delaware attempted to rebut both claims by pointing to the undisputed fact that he was a member o the "Aryan Brotherhood," a racist prison gang that advocates violent retribution against minority inmates. The state courts upheld his resulting death sentence, but the Supreme Court vacated the sentence. The Supreme Court ruled not only that his membership in a white racist gang was "totally without relevance" to the character issue but that the First Amendment precluded the state from even telling the sentencing jury about Dawson's membership in the racist group.

Thomas, alone, dissented. He argued that Dawson's membership in a white supremacist prison gang, especially one that is as "vicious" and as "hostile to black inmates" as the Aryan Brotherhood, was, in fact, relevant at the sentencing phase. To him, just as membership in a church choir or the Boy Scouts can show good character and conduct, membership in a racist prison group that preaches race hatred can show that an inmate "has not been a 'well-behaved and well-adjusted prisoner'"and can "rebut [the inmate's! evidence of good character." Such evidentiary uses of constitutionally protected associations, Thomas argued, did not violate the First Amendment because "the Constitution permits courts and juries to consider character evidence in sentencing proceedings." Thomas's strong condemnation of white supremacy, which he reiterated last Term in *Capitol Square Review Board v. Pinette* (1995), a case involving the Ku Klux Klan, refutes the suggestion that he is blind to the problem of racism in America.

The long and short of it is this: Thomas's views are squarely within the mainstream of the black community. Unlike some of his critics, Thomas has remained true both to the Constitution and to the traditional civil-rights objective that the government must treat all of its citizens as individuals, without regard to their race. He has neither turned the clock back on black progress nor turned his back on the black community. Regrettably, the same cannot be said for Leon Higginbotham and most other traditional leaders of the black community.

STUDY QUESTIONS

1. What role have blacks played in presidential policy making in the post-civil rights era? What are the critical factors that determine black influence within presidential administrations? How viable is the presidency as a tool for civil rights advocacy?

2. How has race been a factor in presidential party politics in the last 20 years? Can the president lead an effectual public discourse on race relations? Can government be an engine for sustainable racial reform? If so, how?

3. Are majority-minority congressional districts a viable means to achieve black representation in the legislative process? Is the answer different depending on whether one is discussing voting for the candi-

date of one's choice or wielding institutional influence within the halls of Congress? Can whites meaningfully represent blacks and can blacks successfully represent whites?

4. What variables explain blacks' attitudes toward the Supreme Court? What is the empirical evidence? What are the implications of a lack of support for the Court in the African-American community?

5. Is the Supreme Court structured to defend majority as opposed to minority interests? Why? Why not? What is the significance of the doctrine of judicial review to the protection of minority interests? What are the constraints on using litigation as a strategy for achieving racial equality? Does it matter if blacks serve on the Court?

NOTES

1. Martha Riche, "The bean count is in," *The Washington Post*, 23 January 1994: c-2.

2. There is some disagreement over the impact of Jackson's candidacy on the black electorate. For example, Adolph Reed, Jr. *The Jesse Jackson phenomena: The crisis of purpose in Afro-American politics* (New Haven: Yale University Press) 1986; Katherine Tate *From protest to politics: The new black voters in American elections* (Cambridge: Harvard University Press) 1993.

3. See, for example, Carmines and Stimson *Issue evolution*; Kevin P. Phillips. *The politics of rich and poor: Wealth and the electorate in the Reagan aftermath.* (New York: Random House) 1990; Richard Viguerie. *The new right: We are ready to lead.* (Falls Church, VA: The Viguerie Co.) 1980.

4. See Randal Kennedy, "Is he a soul man?" *American Prospect* 10:43 1999:26–31; Armstrong Williams, "Do black voters have a good reason to support president Clinton?" *Insight on the News* 14:40, 1998: 22–26.

5. Carol M. Swain. *Black faces, black interests: The representation of African-Americans in Congress.* (Cambridge: Harvard University Press) 1993.

6. The vast majority of black members of Congress in the 20th century have been Democrats. The notable exceptions are DePriest, Edward Brooke (R-Mass.), Gary Franks (R-Conn.), and J.C. Watts (R-Oklahoma).

7. See David T. Canon, "Redistricting and the Congressional Black Caucus," *American Politics Quarterly* 23:2 1995: 159–189. William L. Clay. *Just permanent interests: Black Americans in Congress 1970–1991* (New York: Amistad Press) 1993; Charles E. Jones, "Testing a legislative strategy: the Congressional Black Caucus's Action-Alert Communications Network," *Legislative Studies Quarterly* (November 1987):521–537.

8. *A chronicle of the Congressional Black Caucus: The first twenty-five years* (Washington, D.C.: The Congressional Black Caucus) 1998.

9. The Caucus also helped to found the Joint Center for Political and Economic Studies as a research and service agency in support of legislative politicians and candidates.

10. David A. Bositis. *The Congressional Black Caucus in the 103rd Congress.* (Washington, D.C.: Joint Center for Political and Economic Studies; Lanham, Md.: Distributed by University Press of America).

11. See Chandler Davidson and Bernard Grofman (eds.), *Quiet revolution in the South: The impact of the Voting Rights Act, 1965–1990* (Princeton, NJ: Princeton University Press, 1994); David T. Canon *Race, redistricting, and representation: The unintended consequences*

of black majority districts (Chicago, IL: University of Chicago Press, 1999); David T. Canon, "Redistricting and the Congressional Black Caucus," *American Politics Quarterly* 23:2 April 1995:159–190; David T. Canon, "Electoral systems and the representation of minority interests in Legislatures," *Legislative Studies Quarterly* 24:3 Aug 1999; Lani Guinier *The tyranny of the majority: Fundamental fairness in representative democracy* (New York, NY: Free Press, 1994). Charles E. Jones, "Testing a legislative strategy: the Congressional Black Caucus's Action-Alert Communications Network," *Legislative Studies Quarterly* November 1987:521–537.

12. Chandler Davidson "The Voting Rights Act: a brief history," in Bernard Grofman and Chandler Davidson (eds.) *Controversies in minority voting: The Voting Rights Act in perspective* (Washington, D.C.: Brookings) 1992.

13. For instance, David Lublin. *The paradox of representation: Racial gerrymandering and minority interests in Congress* (Princeton: Princeton University Press) 1997.

14. See Edward Still, "Voluntary Constituencies: Modified at-large voting as a remedy for minority vote dilution in judicial elections, *Yale Law and Political Review* 1991; Delbert Taebel, Richard L. Engstrom, and Richard L. Cole, "Alternative electoral systems as remedies for minority vote dilution," *Hamline Journal of Public Law and Politics* 19, 1990:26–29.

15. See Kevin Hill, "Does the creation of majority black districts aid Republicans? An analysis of the 1992 congressional elections in eight southern states," *Journal of Politics* 57 (1995):384–401.

16. John R. Petrocik and Scott Despasato, "The partisan consequences of majority-minority redistricting in the south," *Journal of Politics* 60,3 (1998):613–633.

17. Kenny J. Whitby. *The color of representation: Congressional behavior and black interests.* (Ann Arbor, MI: University of Michigan Press) 1997.

18. See Lucius J. Barker, "The Supreme Court from Warren to Burger: Implications for black Americans and the political system," *Washington University Law Quarterly* 4, 1973: Twiley W. Barker and Michael Combs, "Civil rights and liberties in the first term of the Rehnquist Court: the quest for doctrines and values," *National Political Science Review* 1 1989: 31–57; Abraham L. Davis and Barbara Luck Graham. *The Supreme Court, race and civil rights.* (Thousand Oaks, CA: Russell Sage) 1995; John R. Howard. *The shifting wind: the Supreme Court and civil rights from Reconstruction to Brown* (Albany: State University of New York Press) 1999.

19. Norman C. Amaker. *Civil rights and the Reagan administration* (Washington, D.C.: the Urban Institute Press) 1988; Vincent Blasi. *The Burger Court: the counter revolution that wasn't* (New Haven: Yale University Press); Sheldon Goldman, "Reagan's judicial legacy: Completing the puzzle and summing up, *Judicature* April–May 1989; Michael Pertschuck and Wendy Schaetzel. *The people rising: the campaign against the Bork nomination* (New York: Thunder's Mouth Press) 1989.

20. See also James Thomas Tucker. "Tyranny of the judiciary: judicial dilution of consent under section 2 of the Voting Rights A." *William and Mary Bill of Rights Journal* 7, 3 (February 1999):443.

21. Kimberle Crenshaw. "Culture watch: Clarence Thomas, the law and the color-blind hustle." An Address to the National Bar Association, 1997; Leon A. Higginbotham, Jr. "Disinvitation: talking back to Supreme Court Justice Clarence Thomas." *National Law Journal* 20,49 (August 3, 1998):A23; Crenshaw and other on Hill-Thomas.

22. But see, Dawson *Behind the Mule.*

PUBLIC POLICY AND THE FUTURE OF RACIAL POLITICS IN AMERICA

Race is an enduring issue on the American policy agenda.[1] The examples are too many to list, but it is obvious that government activity associated with things like Radical Reconstruction, the rise of Jim Crow, and the civil rights movement, is indicative of the significance of race to the policy making process. That is, the process by which problems are identified, solutions are proposed, and policies are implemented.[2] Put differently, race is an important topic to which government officials and politicians devote considerable attention.

How the politics of race plays out in the policy process, however, turns on the interplay between political actors (e.g., policy advocates, government officials, and politicians), the environment (e.g., party balance in the Congress and White House, the national mood), and the presence or absence of external forces such as war and significant economic shocks (e.g., the Depression).[3] Thus, civil rights policy from the early 1950s to the mid-1960s is best understood as a case where a clear problem (racial inequality) had a viable set of solutions (e.g., Civil Rights Act, Voting Rights Act, *Brown*, etc.) in the context of a booming peacetime economy and a tolerant national mood. Likewise, the more conservative race policy agenda of the Reagan and Bush administrations was successful by pointing to a problem (e.g., violations of traditional American values by racial minorities; reverse discrimination), which had a clear solution (ending race-based policymaking), in an environment of economic recession and war (hot and cold).[4] In short, the race problem continues to be of central concern to American policymakers.

This chapter examines three of the more controversial public policy areas effecting racial minorities: poverty/welfare, crime, and affirmative action. Solving the problem of economic inequality between the races has been a cornerstone of 20th century American racial policy. The rise of the welfare state associated with the Great Society programs of the 1960s was as a direct result of racial differences in socio-economic status. Crime has long been associated with minority communities.[5] In the last 20 years or so, however, the link between race and crime has attracted significant attention from policymakers.[6] Finally, affirmative action is perhaps the most volatile racial issue on the policy agenda.[7] That is, race has been at the center of the debate over how education, jobs, and promotions are distributed in the society. Although these three policy areas are clearly significant, there are many others that one might (e.g., housing, education, health, and technology). Nonetheless, poverty/welfare, crime and criminal justice, and affirmative action represent three of the more salient racial policy arenas.

POVERTY AND WELFARE

Poverty has been a long-standing concern of the African-American community. It was not until the 1960s, however, that black poverty received systematic attention from government officials. The government's response to black poverty was to develop the Great Society welfare initiative. Aid to Families with Dependent Children (AFDC) was the most visible of the welfare programs.[8] While black participation in AFDC (and other welfare programs) increased dramatically during the 1970s, poverty remained a persistent social problem.[9]

Martin Gilens points to three factors that put black poverty on to the policy agenda in the 1960s.[10] The first has to do with the in-migration of the black population from the rural south to the urban north. The steady stream of blacks that relocated during the middle third of the 20th century produced a secular increase in the number of blacks receiving welfare benefits. The second reason is that black leaders politicized poverty during the civil rights movement. After all, Martin Luther King, Jr. was in Memphis to march for economic justice on the day he was assassinated. The third reason concerns the urban violence or riots of the mid-to-late 1960s. From this view, black poverty shot to the top of the policy agenda as a terrified nation watched black discontent spill out into the streets of the country's largest cities.

By the 1980s, however, persistent black poverty called the Great Society programs into serious question. In **Behind the Mule***, Michael C. Dawson concludes that, [P]ersistent large gaps between black and white economic fortunes are found across the range of the two races' economic strata." For example, Dawson reports United States Census Bureau data indicating that the ratio of black to white median family income rose through the mid-1970s but flattened out and even receded in the 1980s. More distressingly, the ratio of black to white unemployment has remained at roughly two to one since the Brown decision. Dawson also compares black/white poverty rates in the years since the civil rights movement and finds blacks are about three times as likely as whites to be poor. Finally, many people point to the growth in the size of the black middle class as evidence that economic disparities are improving. The evidence does not appear to support such assertions, as Dawson notes: "[T]he black middle class remains vulnerable to individual setbacks, changes in government economic policy, and swings in national and local economies."[11] All in all, the economic status of most African-Americans has not dramatically improved since the early 1970s.*

BEHIND THE MULE
—•—

Michael C. Dawson

Excerpt from Chapter 2: Race, Class, and African-American Economic Polarization

THE STRUCTURE OF THE AFRICAN-AMERICAN POLITICAL ECONOMY: A SHORT REVIEW

The structure of the American political economy has helped determine the shape and scope of life chances for African-Americans at any given moment. Further, since the 1960s this structure has undergone extensive changes that have had profound implications for African-American life chances. Specifically, the changing structure of the American economy and the distribution of life chances of African-Americans has had and continues to have a massive impact on the development of African-American class structure.

BLACK AND WHITE INCOME TRENDS

This section begins with an analysis of postwar income trends. Income inequality (particularly *net* inequality, which includes government transfer payments—the so-called safety net) declined throughout most of the postwar period until the 1970s (Dennis 1983; Moss and Tilly 1991). As Dennis has pointed out, disagreement over the distribution of income has been perhaps the most conflictual area of American politics—one could argue that racial conflict is another candidate (Dennis 1983). Tax policy, affirmative action, transfer and entitlement programs, and agricultural subsidies all fall under the rubric of income-enhancing or income-redistributing programs.

Figure 10-1 shows the relative ratio of black to white median income from 1947 to 1987. While there was an improvement in the ratio during most of the 1960s and the first half of the 1970s, the ratio was relatively flat throughout the 1980s. As Reich (1981) details, the ratio of black to white male incomes rose until the early 1970s, when black men were making approximately 75% of white men's income outside the South.

TRENDS IN UNEMPLOYMENT AND LABOR FORCE PARTICIPATION

Unemployment is the most dismal area of discussion in black political economy. Figure 10-2 shows trends in black and white unemployment rates between 1954 and 1990. By May of 1983, during the Reagan recession, official

■ **FIGURE 10-1**

RATIO OF BLACK TO WHITE MEDIAN FAMILY INCOME, **1947–1987**

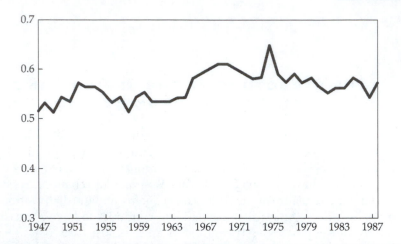

(SOURCES AND NOTES: The data for 1947–1974 come from *The Social and Economic Status of the Black Popluation in the U.S.: An Historical view, 1790–1978,* Current Population Reports, Special Studies, Series p-23, no. 80. The data for 1975–1987 are compiled from U.S. Bureau of the Census, *Statistical Abstract of the United States, 1990,* Table 727. The data for 1947–1954 are for black and "other" races; after 1954 the data are tabulated separately for blacks.)

■ **FIGURE 10-2**

QUARTERLY BLACK AND WHITE UNEMPLOYMENT RATES, **1954–1991**

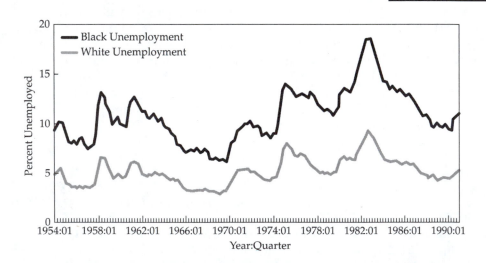

(SOURCE: Citibase Econometric Database.)

black unemployment rates had soared to 20.8% (*Black Enterprise Magazine* 1983). Black unemployment rates declined to the high teens during the Reagan recovery, but continue to be more than double white rates. By 1988, fourteen states still had black unemployment rates of greater than or equal to 15% (U.S. Department of Labor 1989). States with such high black unemployment rates are concentrated in the South and Midwest and include those with large black populations such as Illinois and Michigan. The gap between black and white unemployment, unlike that of income, shows no signs of narrowing. Farley (1984, 40) states that "there has been no racial convergence in unemployment rates. At all dates, the racial discrepancy was at least as large at the end of this period as at the beginning. In fact, a closer look at the data reveals that unemployment rates have risen more over time among nonwhites than among whites."

A combination of factors has led to the precipitous rise in African-American unemployment. Government action, spurred by black protest, opened up employment opportunities for blacks from the 1940s to the 1960s. These opportunities had narrowed owing to Jim Crow legislation and custom throughout the first forty years of the century (Farley 1984). The advent of war and massive pressure from black workers under the leadership of A. Philip Randolph led to "the greatest economic gains, in terms of both real advances and in relation to whites, since the Civil War" (Harris 1982). The pressure led to President Franklin D. Roosevelt's establishment of the Federal Employment Practices Committee (FEPC). Harris (1982) describes the effect of the establishment of the FEPC on the war industries and concludes that the structure of the labor market had been changed largely in favor of blacks. John F. Kennedy and Lyndon B. Johnson followed with a combination of executive orders and legislation in 1961 (Kennedy's executive order barring employment discrimination in federal employment) and 1964 (the 1964 Civil Rights Act) that broadly extended employment antidiscrimination law (Farley 1984).

However, structural changes in the American political economy were producing conditions that would eventually have a tragic impact on black labor force participation. Black labor force participation reached its height in the early 1950s (Farley 1984). As mentioned earlier, Pinkney reports that between 1945 and 1970 black labor force participation declined from 90% to 70%. By 1982 this rate had declined to below 60% (Pinkney 1984; Farley 1984). Farley comments that both white and black men's participation rates have declined, but that the decline for white men is almost entirely explained by the drop in participation of men in the over-55 age bracket. For blacks the decline in the participation of elderly workers accounts for only one third of the decline. Discouraged workers—workers unemployed for so long that they are no longer on the unemployment rolls—account for much of the difference between black and white rates. In 1979, for example, the National Urban League estimated that the true black unemployment rate, including discouraged workers, was 23.1%—twice the 11.3% official rate (Pinkney 1984). The difference in rates has widened from five points to twelve points between 1950 and 1982. The sea change that saw the rapid decline in labor participation occurred around 1970. The rate of discouraged workers was highest for black males aged 25 to 54 (Farley 1984). This cohort would ordinarily represent the primary income-earning group.

Wilson (1980) asserts that the changes that led to the 1954 doubling of the ratio of black to white unemployment rates, the rise in the number of discouraged black workers, massive minority teenage unemployment, and the reduction in hours for workers in manufacturing (especially blacks) were structural in nature. Among the underlying reasons he cites for these changes are the shift from a goods-based economy to a service-based economy; the migration of jobs from the cities to the suburbs and from the Northeast and the Midwest first to the South and Southwest and finally offshore; and the growth of corporate power in the economy.

Several forms of economic restructuring in addition to the deindustrialization described by Wilson have accelerated black losses in employment. Johnson and Oliver (1990) argue, "Among cities with high rates of deconcentration, black male unemployment rates, idleness, and total black male joblessness were significantly greater than in cities in which job deconcentration was low." Holzer (1989) summarizes several studies that show that greater transit times from central cities to suburban-based jobs, deindustrialization, and deconcentration are factors that lead to greater black joblessness. Further, Holzer points out that residential segregation and the propensity for manufacturing plants to locate away from concentrations of African-Americans are further barriers that make it more difficult for African-American workers to relocate to the suburbs or other regions when central-city factories and businesses move.

Among the most significant structural changes were the growth of the importance of corporate industries in the economy and the subsequent development of a surplus black labor force. Several factors are at work in these industries. They emphasize technology in order to maximize profits, thus making many black workers redundant. Wilson also argues that there is now a greater demand for well-educated, technologically oriented workers, technicians, managers, and professionals and a declining demand for unskilled and semiskilled labor. Wilson claims that black workers face a ceiling in occupational and wage levels in these industries. Entry-level jobs have become scarce, putting a particularly severe strain on minority youth seeking jobs (Wilson 1980).

BLACK POVERTY

All of the factors discussed in this section have led to a situation in which African-Americans are three times more likely to live below the poverty line than whites. Nearly 70% of these poor families are headed by women (Pinkney 1984). Poverty afflicted 55% of all blacks in 1959, 30% in 1974, and 36% in 1982 (Farley 1984). Even when we look at families below the poverty line, as opposed to individuals, in 1987, 30% of black families were below the

■ FIGURE 10-3

BLACK AND WHITE POVERTY RATES, 1959–1988

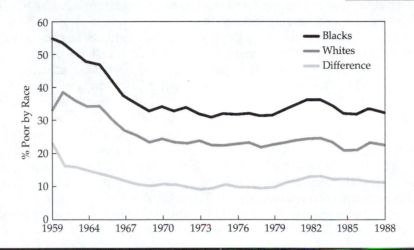

(SOURCES AND NOTES: The data are compiled by the author from U.S. Bureau of the Census, *Statistical Abstract of the United States. Abstracts* from the following years were used: 1964–1966, 1968–1971, 1973–1975, 1977–1982, 1984–1986, and 1990. Data for blacks were not available for 1959–1965 and 1967; the reported data for "nonwhites" appear here. There were reported changes in measurement in 1969, 1974, and 1987. For more details, see the notes in the cited *Abstracts*.)

poverty line. Despite enormous variation in poverty rates by family type, black poverty is greater than white poverty for all family types (Jaynes and Williams 1989). Figure 10-3 shows the trends in black and white poverty.

A few comments on poverty and African-Americans are appropriate at this juncture. Poverty is widespread among African-Americans. Black youth as well as the elderly suffer disproportionately. Both black youth and the black elderly are three times more likely to live in poor households than whites (Farley 1984). In 1987, 45% of black children age 14 and under lived in poor households, as opposed to 15% of white children (U.S. Bureau of the Census 1990). The percentage of African-American children living below the poverty line has fluctuated between 40% and 47% since 1979 (U.S. Bureau of the Census 1990).

The fact that nearly half of all black children grow up in poverty, coupled with the long-term erosion in black labor participation rates, portends the establishment of a permanent class of desperately poor African-Americans. This trend, if unchecked, will have enormous consequences not only for black progress, black politics, and American economic productivity, but for the stability of American society.

Those who argue that the economic status of African-Americans is improving and converging with that of whites often point to the explosion in the size of the black middle class.

THE VULNERABILITY OF THE BLACK MIDDLE CLASS

As pointed out in Chapter 1, the black middle class doubled in size in the period from approximately 1960 to 1980.

However, some features of this growing black middle class suggest that the black middle class is far from reaching parity with the white middle class and in fact is fairly vulnerable. First, according to 1989 Census Bureau figures, the black middle class comprises approximately 40% of African-American households. This is significantly less than the 70% of white households that have achieved middle-class status (Wilkerson 1990). African-American middle-class households are, on average, a third poorer than white middle-class households. Black middle-class status, unlike white middle-class status, is dependent on two paychecks (Wilkerson 1990). Finally, black businesses and middle-class occupations tend to be concentrated in fewer fields than their white counterparts (Jaynes and Williams 1989).

Another distinctive feature of the increase in the black middle class is the large size of the government sector. Pinkney (1984) documents the tremendous size of this sector, showing that 67% of all black professionals and managers (as opposed to 17% of this class in the general population) and 42% of all black administrators work for the government. (These were 1980 figures.) Part of the black job growth in the government sector was due to the enormous growth of the state itself as a result of the Great Society programs, what Dwight D. Eisenhower termed the military-industrial complex, and regulatory government (Wilson 1980). Furthermore, as of 1969 black women working for the state earned 93% of what white women did. They only made 74% of white women's earnings in the private sector. Black men earned 77% of white male government workers' earnings while earning only 65% of the wages of white men in the private sector (Reich 1981). Such earning differentials would tend to draw black wage earners into the government sector.

Smith and Welch (1989) argue that there has been a shift in the 1980s toward middle-class blacks leaving traditional middle-class occupations and joining the nation's economic elite in the private sector. They base much of their optimism on the future economic status of African-Americans who have recently entered the labor force in prime economic sectors but are just beginning to move up the occupational ladder. However, they offer little evidence in support of this observation, and many other observers underline the economic vulnerability of the black middle class (Landry 1987; Updegrave 1989).

The vulnerability of the black middle class is apparent along yet another dimension—the lack of wealth this class possesses. Oliver and Shapiro use the information in Tables 10-2 and 10-3 to show that household wealth is less for black families earning over $50,000 per year than for white households earning less than $10,000 per year. The net financial assets of white households with incomes of less than $10,000 per year total over $10,000. The only African-Americans with positive net financial assets belong to households with incomes of more than $50,000 per year.

▪ TABLE 10-2

PERCENTAGE SHARES OF AGGREGATE WEALTH HELD BY EACH FIFTH AND
BY THE TOP 10, 5, AND 1% OF HOUSEHOLDS, 1984

	Net Worth		Net Financial Assets	
	White	Black	White	Black
Lowest fifth	0	—	—	—
Second fifth	3	0	0	—
Third fifth	11	4	3	0
Fourth fifth	21	21	13	1
Top fifth	65	77	85	99
Top 10%	47	53	67	91
Top 5%	33	35	51	76
Top 1%	14	12	24	30

(SOURCE: Adapted from Oliver and Shapiro 1989, 16.)

▪ TABLE 10-3

WEALTH AND FAMILY STATUS OF HOUSEHOLDERS (IN DOLLARS), 1984

	Median Net Worth			Median Net Financial Assets	
	White	Black	B/W Ratio	White	Black
Married couple	54,499	13,848	.25	7,540	0
Woman, no children	29,575	3,675	.12	4,217	0
Woman, children	3,320	0	—	0	0
Man, no children	a	a	—	a	a
Man, children	11,825	3,100	.26	1,663	0
Married couple, two Workers	50,475	19,470	.39	5,600	(265)
Married couple, ages 24–35, two workers	18,617	4,000	.21	900	(450)

[a] Subsample too small to analyze (1% or less).

(SOURCE: Oliver and Shapiro 1989, 17.)

The disparities in wealth are due in part to the lack of return on the human and other capital that members of the black middle class possess. Black men with a bachelor's degree earn 26% less than their white counterparts while those with graduate training receive 15% less (Landry 1987; Updegrave 1989). Segregation in housing also retards the accumulation of black wealth. Real estate in black middle-class communities appreciates at a much slower rate than real estate in white middle-class communities.

SUMMARY

Large gaps between black and white economic status are still found in late-20th-century America. Evidence for the large gaps in unemployment, poverly, and even income confirm that the Kerner Commission's judgment that the United States was moving toward two societies—one black, one white—is clearly reflected in the American landscape. Further, many of the causes of the erosion of some African-Americans' absolute and relative economic status can be traced directly or indirectly to state policy or the lack thereof. The management of aggregate demand which plays a major role in both the erosion of black earnings and employment, enforcement of anti-discriminatory statutes, support for affirmative action remedies, etc., are all within the purview of the national government. These are all factors that affect black income which are responsive to government policy. The devastation caused by industrial deconcentration and deindustrialization has led African-Americans to support politicians such as Jesse Jackson in their demands that *public* control over private-sector decisions such as the closing of plants be significantly strengthened. All of these factors would tend to reinforce the political salience of race.

———————————————— ■ ————————————————

*The Joint Center for Political and Economic Studies is an African-American think-tank, located in Washington, D.C., that collects information and publishes reports on the overall status of the African-American community. The following economic data are from the Center's **Data Bank** fact sheets. These data carry the Dawson analysis forward through the late 1990s and basically confirm his core results. In terms of income, for instance, the data indicate that the black/white gap remains about the same for all types of families between 1988 and 1997. Although the relative size of the gap is smallest for black married couples with both spouses in the labor force, the fact remains the even among this most "ideal" black income group, black/white disparities are the same as they were in the late 1980s. The Joint Center data also show that black unemployment rates continued to be twice that of whites through the late 1990s.[12] Finally, two pieces of evidence shed light on the status of the black middle class. First, the surge in the number of middle class blacks is no doubt related to increases in educational attainment—the racial gap in high school graduation rates is virtually nonexistent by 1997. On the other hand, income inequality between equally educated whites and blacks remains significant in the modern period. In sum, despite some gains there are still persistent economic gaps between black and white Americans.*

Of most notable concern is the existence of a significant and persistent black underclass. That is, those African-Americans who more or less permanently reside at the bottom of the social and economic order. Underclass communities are typically characterized by high rates of joblessness, crime, family dysfunction, and drug abuse. In response, scholars and policy-makers have devoted a great deal of attention to understanding the causes of and solutions to the underclass problem.[13]

FAMILY INCOME

—■—

Joint Center for Political and Economic Studies, Family Income, Earnings, and Educational Attainment of African-Americans 1967–1997

- The real median income for all families, adjusted for inflation, grew nearly 9% from $41,051 in 1993 to $44,568 in 1997. One third of this increase occurred between 1996 and 1997. The gains restored median family income to its 1989 pre-recessionary level ($44,284).

- The median income of African-American families in 1997 was $28,602, an increase of 20% over the median in 1993 ($23,927) and a gain of 5% over the median in 1996 ($27,131). The median incomes in 1997 of

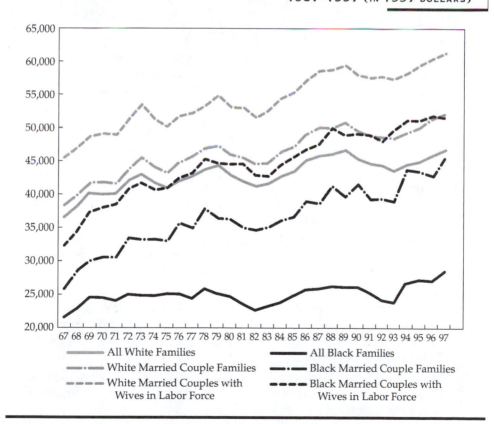

MEDIAN INCOME OF FAMILIES BY SELECTED FAMILY TYPES, 1967–1997 (IN 1997 DOLLARS)

Legend:
- All White Families
- All Black Families
- White Married Couple Families
- Black Married Couple Families
- White Married Couples with Wives in Labor Force
- Black Married Couples with Wives in Labor Force

(SOURCES: United States Census Bureau, http://www.census.gov/hhes/income/histinc/f07a.html and http://www./census.gov/hhes/income/histinc/f07b.html)

ANNUAL UNEMPLOYMENT RATES: 1988–1998, FOR PERSONS AGE 20 AND OLDER

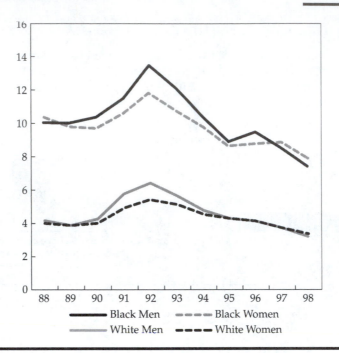

(SOURCE: Bureau of Labor Statistics.)

white families ($46,754) and of Hispanic families ($28,142) were both up 7% from their 1993 levels. Asian Pacific Islanders ($51,850) had the highest median family income among the race groups in 1997, a 5% increase over their 1993 median.

- The median income of black families ($28,602) in 1997 was only 61% of the median for white families. The gap in part reflects the much smaller percentage of black (47%) than of white (81%).

- Unemployment among workers ages 16 and over dropped from an annual rate of 7.8% in 1992 to 4.5% in 1998. Among blacks during this period, unemployment declined from 14.2% in 1992 to 8.2%, and among whites from 6.6% to 3.9%. Rates were slightly lower among workers age 20 and over (see graph).

- Of the 128.1 million persons who worked in 1997, 5.8% experienced some unemployment during the year. Of these, about 3 in 10 had two or more spells of joblessness.

- Higher percentages of blacks (16.5%) and Hispanics (14.1%) than whites (9.9%) were unemployed at some time in 1997. Among all

ANNUAL UNEMPLOYMENT RATES: 1988–1998, FOR PERSONS AGES 16 TO 19

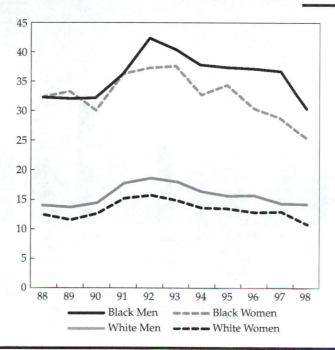

Black Men ▬▬▬ Black Women ▬ ▬ ▬

White Men ▬▬▬ White Women ▬ ▬ ▬

(SOURCE: Bureau of Labor Statistics.)

workers, the median[3] duration of unemployment fell 0.7 weeks to 13.1 weeks in 1997, but these spells were longer for black and Hispanic workers.

- Teenage unemployment is much higher among teens (ages 16–19) than among adults. Despite the improving economy, it remained very high for young black men (30%) and black women (25%) in 1998.

- These high rates reflect difficulties among blacks still enrolled in high school (31% unemployment in data for 16–24 year olds) rather than those enrolled in college (12%) or those not enrolled in school (17%).

- Unemployment among teens also peaked in 1992. For African-Americans, it reached 42% for men and 37% for women, and was 19% and 16%, respectively, for white men and women.

- Youth unemployment rates have also consistently remained at least twice as high for blacks as for whites.

- About 2.6 million 16-to-24-year-olds were employed in the summer of 1998. At 25%, black youths' unemployment rate was about 3 times higher than that for whites (8.4%).

MEDIAN ANNUAL EARNINGS BY EDUCATIONAL ATTAINMENT, 1998

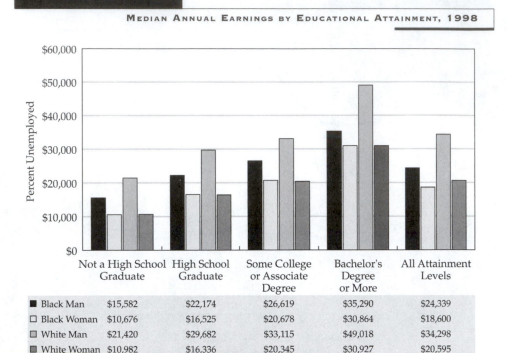

	Not a High School Graduate	High School Graduate	Some College or Associate Degree	Bachelor's Degree or More	All Attainment Levels
■ Black Man	$15,582	$22,174	$26,619	$35,290	$24,339
☐ Black Woman	$10,676	$16,525	$20,678	$30,864	$18,600
☐ White Man	$21,420	$29,682	$33,115	$49,018	$34,298
■ White Woman	$10,982	$16,336	$20,345	$30,927	$20,595

Persons 25 years of age and older.

(SOURCE: United States Census Bureau. http://www.census.gov/population/socdemo/race/black/tab98/tab12A.txt)

- Generally, additional education pays off equally well for black and white men and women. Black and white women who completed high school earned about 50% more in 1998 than those who did not; the comparable pay-off for black and white men was about 40%. Completing some college beyond high school increased annual earnings by 20% to 25% above those who stopped at high school, except among white men (only about 12% higher). Workers with bachelor's or advanced degrees earned about 50% more than those with only some college, except among black men, who earned about one-third more.

- Although education pays off in higher earnings, the inequalities in the annual earnings of comparably educated black and white men and women remained substantial. In 1998, black men earned, on average, 71 cents for every dollar earned by white men. Black male college graduates earned 72 cents for every dollar earned by comparable whites. The ratio among black men was better only for high school graduates (75 cents) and those with some college (80 cents).

PERCENT OF HIGH SCHOOL GRADUATES AMONG 25–29 YEARS OLDS, 1957–1997

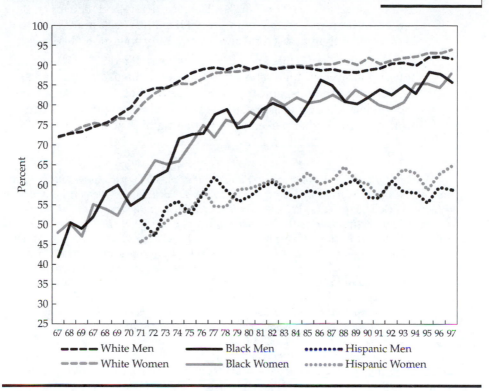

(SOURCES: 1957–1970 United States Census Bureau (Data for whites includes Hispanics), http://www.census.gov/population/socdemo/education/tablea-01.txt. 1971–1997 National Center for Education Statistics (Data is for non-Hispanic whites), http://nces.ed.gov/pubs98/condition98/c98p22.pdf)

Black women's median earnings were about 91% of white women's, primarily due to differences in educational attainments: comparably educated black and white women had virtually equal annual earnings.

HIGH SCHOOL COMPLETION

- The percentage of young (25- to 29-year-old) African-Americans and whites who have completed high school has risen dramatically since 1960. Among young African-Americans, the percentage of high school graduates rose from 39% in 1960 to 87% in 1997. During the same period, high school completion among young whites grew by nearly a third, from about 62% to 93%.

- High school completion rates for 25- to 29-year-old Hispanics have not risen as much as those for other groups over the past 30 years, and remained much lower in 1997 (62%). This, in part, reflects the much higher dropout rate among immigrant Hispanics (44% among 16- to 24-year-olds) than first- (17%) and later (22%) generation Hispanics.

- The percentages of white and Hispanic women aged 25- to 29-years-old who completed high school has equaled or surpassed the percentages of white and Hispanic men 1981. During that period, black men and women have reversed positions several times regarding which group had the higher percentage completing high school.

William Julius Wilson is the primary proponent of the view that changes in the structure of the American economy has perpetuated black poverty. In the following excerpt from **When Work Disappears,** *Wilson examines two broad categories identified with the structural perspective. Demand-side explanations argue that fluctuations in the labor market have disproportionately affected black (primarily male) workers. According to this view shifts in the type, location, and skill requirements of available jobs for low-skilled workers all contributed to the stagnation of black earnings. Supply-side explanations call attention to the ". . . decline in the relative supply of college graduates and the influx of poor immigrants." The demand for educated workers combined with competition from poor immigrants thus weakened the black labor market position. In short, a change away from an industrial, goods-producing economy to one based on services and technology placed less-skilled (black) workers in a highly marginal position.[14] Given that dysfunctional "ghetto behavior" is the byproduct of racial economic disparities not the cause, appropriate policy prescriptions reside with more thoughtful and creative social policy. Whether full employment or federal protections in the housing, banking, and insurance markets, the impetus for change lies with the public sector.*

WHEN WORK DISAPPEARS:
THE WORLD OF THE NEW URBAN POOR

William Julius Wilson

Excerpt from Chapter 2: Societal Changes and Vulnerable Neighborhoods

The disappearance of work in many inner-city neighborhoods is partly related to the nationwide decline in the fortunes of low-skilled workers. Although the growing wage inequality has hurt both low-skilled men and women, the problem of declining employment has been concentrated among low-skilled men. In 1987–89, a low-skilled male worker was jobless eight and a half weeks longer than he would have been in 1967–69. Moreover, the proportion of men who "permanently" dropped out of the labor force was more than twice as high in the late 1980s than it had been in the late 1960s. A precipitous drop in real wages—that is, wages adjusted for inflation—has accompanied the increases in joblessness among low-income workers. If you arrange all wages into five groups according to wage percentile (from highest to lowest), you see that men in the bottom fifth of this income distribution experienced more than a 30% drop in real wages between 1970 and 1989.

Even the low-skilled workers who are consistently employed face problems of economic advancement. Job ladders—opportunities for promotion within firms—have eroded, and many less-skilled workers stagnate in dead-end, low-paying positions. This suggests that the chances of improving one's earnings by changing jobs have declined: if jobs inside a firm have become less available to the experienced workers in that firm, they are probably even more difficult for outsiders to obtain.

But there is a paradox here. Despite the increasing economic marginality of low-wage workers, unemployment dipped below 6% in 1994 and early 1995, many workers are holding more than one job, and overtime work has reached a record high. Yet while tens of millions of new jobs have been created in the past two decades, men who are well below retirement age are working less than they did two decades ago—and a growing percentage are neither working nor looking for work. The proportion of male workers in the prime of their life (between the ages of 22 and 58) who worked in a given decade full-time, year-round, in at least eight out of ten years declined from 79% during the 1970s to 71% in the 1980s. While the American economy saw a rapid expansion in high technology and services, especially advanced services, growth in blue-collar factory, transportation, and construction jobs, traditionally held by men, has not kept pace with the rise in the working-age population. These men are working less as a result.

The growth of a nonworking class of prime-age males along with a larger number of those who are often unemployed, who work part-time, or who work in temporary jobs is concentrated among the poorly educated, the school dropouts, and minorities. In the 1970s, two-thirds of prime-age male workers with less than a high school education worked full-time, year-round, in eight out of ten years. During the 1980s, only half did so. Prime-age black men experienced a similar sharp decline. Seven out of ten of all black men worked full-time, year-round, in eight out of ten years in the 1970s, but only half did so in the 1980s. The figures for those who reside in the inner city are obviously even lower.

These changes are related to the decline of the mass production system in the United States. The traditional American economy featured rapid growth in productivity and living standards. The mass production system benefited from large quantities of cheap natural resources, economies of scale, and processes that generated higher uses of productivity through shifts in market forces from agriculture to manufacturing and that caused improvements in one industry (for example, reduced steel costs) to lead to advancements in others (for example, higher sales and greater economies of scale in the automobile industry). In this system plenty of blue-collar jobs were available to workers with little formal education. Today, most of the new jobs for workers with limited education and experience are in the service sector, which hires relatively more women. One study found that the U.S. created 27 clerical, sales, and service jobs per thousand of working-age population in the 1980s. During the same period, the country lost 16 production, transportation, and laborer jobs per thousand of working-age population. In another study the social scientists Robert Lerman and Martin Rein revealed that from 1989 to 1993, the period covering the economic downturn, social service industries (health, education, and welfare) added almost 3 million jobs, while 1.4 million jobs were lost in all other industries. The expanding job market in social services effect the recession-linked job loss in other industries.

The movement of lower-educated men into the growth sectors of the economy has been slow. For example, "the fraction of men who have moved into so-called pink-collar jobs like practical nursing or clerical work remains negligible." The large concentration of women in the expanding social service sector partly accounts for the striking gender differences in job growth. Unlike lower-educated men, lower-educated women are working more, not less, than in previous years. The employment patterns among lower-educated women, like those with higher education and training, reflect the dramatic expansion of social service industries. Between 1989 and 1993, jobs held by women increased by 1.3 million, while those held by men barely rose at all (by roughly 100,000).

Among the factors that have contributed to the growing gap in employment and wages between low-skilled and college-educated workers is the increased internationalization of the U.S. economy. As the economists Richard B. Freeman and Lawrence F. Katz point out:

> In the 1980s, trade imbalances implicitly acted to augment the nation's supply of less educated workers, particularly those with less than a high school education. Many production and routine clerical tasks could be more easily transferred abroad than in the past. The increased supply of less educated workers arising from trade deficits accounted for as much as 15% of the increase in college–high school wage differential from the 1970s to the mid-1980s. In contrast, a balanced expansion of international trade, in which growth in exports matches the growth of imports, appears to have fairly neutral effects on relative labor demand. Indeed, balanced growth of trade leads to an upgrading in jobs for workers without college degrees, since export-sector jobs tend to pay higher wages for "comparable" workers than do import-competing jobs.

The lowering of unionization rates, which accompanied the decline in the mass production system, has also contributed to shrinking wages and nonwage compensation for less skilled workers. As the economist Rebecca Blank has pointed out, "unionized workers typically receive not only higher wages, but also more nonwage benefits. As the availability of union jobs has declined for unskilled workers, nonwage benefits have also declined."

Finally, the wage and employment gap between skilled and unskilled workers is growing partly because education and training are considered more important than ever in the new global economy. At the same time that changes in technology are producing new jobs, they are making many others obsolete. The workplace has been revolutionized by technological changes that range from the development of robotics to information highways. While educated workers are benefiting from the pace of technological change, involving the increased use of computer-based technologies and microcomputers, more routine workers face the growing threat of job displacement in certain industries. For example, highly skilled designers, engineers, and operators are needed for the jobs associated with the creation of a new set of computer-operated machine tools; but these same exciting new opportunities eliminate jobs for those trained only for manual, assembly-line work. Also, in certain businesses, advances in word processing have increased the demand for those who not only know how to type but can operate specialized software as well; at the same time, these advances reduce the need for routine typists and secretaries. In the new global economy, highly educated and thoroughly trained men and women are in demand. This may be seen most dramatically in the sharp differences in employment experiences among men. Unlike men with lower education, college-educated men are working more, not less.

The shift in demand has been especially devastating for those low-skilled workers whose incorporation into the mainstream economy has been marginal or recent. Even before the economic restructuring of the nation's economy, low-skilled African-Americans were at the end of the employment queue. Their economic situation has been further weakened because they tend to reside in communities that not only have higher jobless rates and lower employment growth but lack access to areas of higher employment and employment growth as well. Moreover, as we shall see in Chapter 5, they are far more likely than other ethnic and racial groups to face negative employer attitudes.

Of the changes in the economy that have adversely affected low-skilled African-American workers, perhaps the most significant have been those in the manufacturing sector. One study revealed that in the 1970s "up to half of the huge employment declines for less-educated blacks might be explained by industrial shifts away from manufacturing toward other sectors." Another study reported that since the 1960s "deindustrialization" and the "erosion in job opportunities especially in the Midwest and Northeast . . . bear responsibility for the growth of the ranks of the 'truly disadvantaged." The manufacturing losses in some northern cities have been staggering. In the twenty-year period from 1967 to 1987, Philadelphia lost 64% of its manufacturing jobs; Chicago lost 60%; New York City, 58%; Detroit, 51%. In absolute numbers, these percentages represent the loss of 160,000 jobs in Philadelphia, 326,000 in Chicago, 520,000—over half a million—in New York, and 108,000 in Detroit.

Another study examined the effects of economic restructuring in the 1980s by highlighting the changes in both the variety and the quality of blue-collar employment in general. Jobs were grouped into a small number of relatively homogeneous clusters on the basis of job quality (which was measured in terms of earnings, benefits, union protection, and involuntary part-time employment). The authors found that both the relative earnings and employment rates among unskilled black workers were lower for two reasons: traditional jobs that provide a living wage (high-wage blue-collar cluster, of which roughly 50% were manufacturing jobs) declined, as did the quality of secondary jobs on which they increasingly had to rely, leading to lower relative earnings for the remaining workers in the labor market. As employment prospects worsened, rising proportions of low-skilled black workers dropped out of the legitimate labor market.

The factors contributing to the relative decline in the economic status of disadvantaged workers are not solely due to those on the demand side, such as economic restructuring. The growing wage differential in the 1980s is also a function of two supply-side factors—the decline in the relative supply of college graduates and the influx of poor immigrants. "In the 1970s the relative supply of college graduates grew rapidly, the result of the baby boomers who enrolled in college in the late 1960s and early 1970s in response to the high rewards for college degrees and the fear of being drafted for the Vietnam War," state Freeman and Katz. "The growth in supply overwhelmed the increase in demand for more educated workers, and the returns to college diminished." In the 1980s, the returns for college increased because of declining growth in the relative supply of college graduates.

Also in the 1980s, a large number of immigrants with little formal education arrived in the United States from developing countries, and affected the wages of poorly educated native workers, especially those who had dropped out of high school. According to one estimate, nearly one-third of the decline in earnings for male high school dropouts compared with other workers in the 1980s may be linked to immigration. However, although the increase in immigration contributed to the growing inequality, it is only one of several factors depressing the wages of low-skilled workers. As Sheldon Danziger and Peter Gottschalk point out in this connection, "Immigrants are heavily concentrated in a few states, such as California and Florida . . . inequality did rise in these states, but it rose in most areas, even those with very few immigrants."

The increasing suburbanization of employment has accompanied industrial restructuring and has further exacerbated the problems of inner-city joblessness and restricted access to jobs. "Metropolitan areas captured nearly 90% of the nation's employment growth; much of this growth occurred in booming 'edge cities' at the metropolitan periphery. By 1990, many of these 'edge cities' had more office space and retail sales than the metropolitan downtowns." Over the last two decades, 60% of the new jobs created in the Chicago metropolitan area have been located in the northwest suburbs of Cook and Du Page counties. African-Americans constitute less than 2% of the population in these areas.

Blacks living in central cities have less access to employment, as measured by the ratio of jobs to people and the average travel time to and from work, than do central-city whites. Moreover, unlike most other groups of workers across the urban/suburban divide, less educated central-city blacks receive lower wages than suburban blacks who have similar levels of education. And the decline in earnings of central-city blacks is related to the decentralization of employment—that is, the movement of jobs from the cities to the suburbs—in metropolitan areas.

The rise of conservative ideology associated with the Reagan-Bush years was, in part, built on an intellectual framework rejecting the idea that government intervention could solve social problems.[15] In fact, as argued below in the excerpt from Charles Murray's book **Losing Ground***, social programs instituted in the 1960s and 1970s actually contributed to racial inequality. From this view, social welfare programs foster a dysfunctional dependency on government "handouts" (e.g., food stamps, aid to families with dependent families and subsidized housing) among the black lower class. Far from providing opportunity, therefore, these programs enhance a "culture of poverty" and contribute to a general pattern of outcomes that are counterproductive and socially unacceptable. In essence, black inequality can be traced to government-induced value deficiency among large segments of the African-American community. Ultimately the onus for change is on the black community itself.*

LOSING GROUND

Charles Murray

Excerpt from Chapter 12: Incentives to Fail I: Maximizing Short-Term Gains

When large numbers of people begin to behave differently from ways they behaved before, my first assumption is that they do so for good reason. In this chapter and the one that follows, I will apply this assumption to the trends of the 1960s and 1970s and suggest that it fits the facts.

Specifically, I will suggest that changes in incentives that occurred between 1960 and 1970 may be used to explain many of the trends we have been discussing. It is not necessary to invoke the *Zeitgeist* of the 1960s, or changes in the work ethic, or racial differences, or the complexities of post-industrial economies, in order to explain increasing unemployment among the young, increased dropout from the labor force, or higher rates of illegitimacy and welfare dependency. All were results that could have been predicted (indeed, in some instances were predicted) from the changes that social policy made in the rewards and penalties, carrots and sticks, that govern human behavior. All were rational responses to changes in the rules of the game of surviving and getting ahead. I will not argue that the responses were the right ones, only that they were rational. Even of our mistakes, we say: It seemed like a good idea at the time.

I begin with the proposition that all, poor and not-poor alike, use the same general calculus in arriving at decisions; only the exigencies are different. Poor people play with fewer chips and cannot wait as long for results. Therefore they tend to reach decisions that a more affluent person would not reach. The reformers of the 1960s were especially myopic about this, tending not only to assume that the poor and not-poor were alike in trying to maximize the goods in their lives (with which I agree), but also that, given the same package of benefits, the decision that seems reasonable to one would seem reasonable to the other. They failed to recognize that the behaviors that are "rational" are different at different economic levels.

In the American setting, a racial overlay obscures this obvious point. The rational (albeit wrong) decisions we will be talking about are the ones that poor people (mostly black, it seems) made. The not-poor people (mostly white, it seems) made other, better decisions. The result of the overlay has often been embarrassed silence. Let us drop the racial baggage that goes with the American context and make the point first in a less emotional setting.

Imagine for a moment that you have been asked to explain the seemingly irrational behavior of a farmer in a developing country. This farmer, you are told, cultivates rice on land that is badly suited for rice but ideally suited for jute. An agriculture officer has explained this to the farmer and explained also that by growing jute he will have enough money to buy all the rice he needs and a large surplus as well. A benign government has offered to train the farmer in the art of jute cultivation, yet the farmer refuses to switch. Why is he so stubborn?

After some reflection, you arrive at a few reasonable hypotheses for explaining the farmer's behavior. For example, he knows he can eat the rice if he cannot sell it, whereas he cannot eat the jute. Also, he has no personal knowledge that the government is correct about next year's price for jute. He has no personal knowledge that jute will grow as well as promised under local conditions. He does know, however, with absolute certainty, that he cannot tolerate even a small chance that the new crop will fail. The penalty for being wrong can be starvation. Therefore, quite rationally, he refuses to take an unacceptable risk. Such might be your reasoning, and it would come down to this: *If I were in the farmer's position, I would make the same decision.*

Experts may disagree with your explanation. They may point out that you have not read the literature on this particular agrarian culture, that the farmer's behavior in fact reflects a complicated and ancient heritage. You listen and are impressed by the scholarship and the intricate tracings of causes and effects. But your earlier analysis is valid. On strictly economic grounds, it still makes sense not to switch to jute. The subtle anthropological explanation is interesting. It may even be true. But it is *not necessary* to explain the farmer's behavior.

Much the same applies to many of the commentaries about the intractability of American poverty and its associated problems despite the many programs that are supposed to help. Fascinating explanations are offered. Many of these explanations surely have an element of truth—they "explain some of the variance," as the statisticians put it. But surprisingly little has been made of the distinction between the behaviors that make sense when one is poor and the behaviors that make sense when one is not poor.

In the exercise we are about to conduct, it is important to suspend thoughts about how the world ought to work, about what the incentives should be. The objective is to establish what the incentives *are* (or were), and how they are likely to affect the calculations of a person who has few chips and little time. It is also important to put aside the distant view of long-term rewards that we, surveying the scene from above, know to be part of the ultimate truth of self-interest, and instead to examine the truth as it appears at ground level at the time decisions must be made.

DRAMATIS PERSONAE

Our guides are a young couple—call them Harold and Phyllis. I deliberately make them unremarkable except for the bare fact of being poor. They are not of a special lower-class culture. They have no socialized propensities for "serial monogamy." They are not people we think of as "the type who are on welfare." They have just graduated from an average public school in an average American city. Neither of them is particularly industrious or indolent, intelligent or dull. They are the children of low-income parents, are not motivated to go to college, and have no special vocational skills. Harold and Phyllis went together during their last year in high school and find themselves in a familiar predicament. She is pregnant.

They will have a child together. They will face the kinds of painful decisions that many young people have had to face. What will they decide? What will seem to them to be "rational" behavior?

We shall examine the options twice—first, as they were in 1960, then as they were only ten years later, in 1970. We shall ignore the turbulent social history of the intervening decade. We shall ignore our couple's whiteness or blackness. We simply shall ask: Given the extant system of rewards and punishments, what course of action makes sense?

OPTIONS IN 1960

Harold's Calculations, Pre-Reform

Harold's parents have no money. Phyllis has no money. If Harold remains within the law, he has two choices: He can get a job, or he can try to get Phyllis to help support him.

Getting Phyllis to support him is intrinsically more attractive, but the possibilities are not promising. If Phyllis has the baby, she will qualify for $23 a week in AFDC ($63 in 1980 purchasing power). This is not enough to support the three of them. And, under the rules of AFDC, Phyllis will not be able to contribute more to the budget. If she gets a job, she will lose benefits on a dollar-for-dollar basis. There is in 1960 no way to make the AFDC payment part of a larger package.

Also, Harold and Phyllis will not be able to live together. AFDC regulations in 1960 prohibit benefits if there is "a man in the house." Apart from its psychic and sexual disadvantages, this regulation also means that Harold cannot benefit from Phyllis's weekly check. The amount cannot possibly be stretched across two households.

It follows that, completely apart from the moral stance of Harold, his parents, or society, it is not possible to use Phyllis for support. Whether or not he decides to stay with her, he will have to find a job.

The only job he can find is working the presses in a dry cleaning shop. It pays the rock-bottom minimum wage—$40 for a forty-hour week, or about

$111 in the purchasing power of the 1980 dollar. It is not much of a living, not much of a job. There is no future in it, no career path. But it pays for food and shelter. And Harold has no choice.

The job turns out to be as tedious as he expected. It is hot in the laundry, and Harold is on his feet all day; he would much rather not stay there. But the consequences of leaving the job are intolerable. Unemployment Insurance will pay him only $20 ($56 in 1980 purchasing power). He stays at the laundry and vaguely hopes that something better will come along.

PHYLLIS'S CALCULATIONS, PRE-REFORM

Phyllis has three (legal) options: to support herself (either keeping the baby or giving it up for adoption); to go on AFDC (which means keeping the baby); or to marry Harold.

Other things being equal, supporting herself is the least attractive of these options. Like Harold, she can expect to find only menial minimum-wage employment. There is no intrinsic reason to take such a job.

The AFDC option is worth considering. The advantage is that it will enable her to keep the baby without having to work. The disadvantages are the ones that Harold perceives. The money is too little, and she is not permitted to supplement it. And Harold would not be permitted to be a live-in husband or father. If she tries to circumvent the rules and gets caught, she faces being cut off from any benefits for the foreseeable future.

If Phyllis thinks ahead, the economic attraction of AFDC might appear more enticing. The total benefits she will receive if she has several children may seem fairly large. If she were already on AFDC it might make sense to have more children. But, right now, setting up a household with Harold is by far the most sensible choice, even given the miserable wage he is making at the laundry.

Being married (as opposed to just living together) has no short-term economic implications.

The choice of whether to get married is dependent primarily on non-economic motivations, plus the economic advantages to Phyllis of having Harold legally responsible for the support of her and the baby.

Once the decision not to go on AFDC is made, a new option opens up. As long as Phyllis is not on AFDC, no penalty is attached to getting a part-time or full-time job.

OPTIONS IN 1970

Harold's and Phyllis's namesakes just ten years later find themselves in the identical situation. Their parents have no money; he doesn't want to go to school any longer; she is pregnant; the only job he can get is in the back room of a dry cleaners. That much is unchanged from 1960.

HAROLD'S CALCULATIONS, POST-REFORM

Harold's options have changed considerably. If he were more clever or less honest (or, perhaps, just more aggressive), he would have even more new options. But since he is none of those things, the major changes in his calculations are limited to these:

First, the AFDC option. In 1960, he had three objections to letting Phyllis go on welfare: too little money, no way to supplement it, and having to live separately from his family. By 1970, all three objections have been removed.

Economically, the total package of AFDC and other welfare benefits has become comparable to working. Phyllis will get about $50 a week in cash ($106 in 1980 dollars) and another $11 in Food Stamps ($23 in 1980 dollars). She is eligible for substantial rent subsidies under the many federal housing programs, but only a minority of AFDC recipients use them, so we will omit housing from the package. She will get Medicaid. We assume that a year's worth of doctor's bills and medication for a mother and infant is likely to be more than $250 (many times that if there is even one major illness), and we therefore add $5 a week (1980 dollars) onto the package. Without bending or even being imaginative about the new regulations, without tapping nearly all the possible sources of public support, and using conservative estimates in reaching a dollar total, the package of benefits available to Phyllis in a typical northern state has a purchasing power of about $134. This minimal package adds up to $23 more than the purchasing power of forty hours of work at a minimum-wage job ten years earlier, in 1960.

Also, the money can be supplemented. If Phyllis works, she can keep the first thirty dollars she makes. After that, her benefits are reduced by two dollars for every three additional dollars of income.

Harold has even greater flexibility. *As long as he is not legally responsible for the care of the child*—a crucial proviso—his income will not count against her eligibility for benefits. He is free to work when they need a little extra money to supplement their basic (welfare) income.

The third objection, being separated from Phyllis, has become irrelevant. By Supreme Court ruling, the presence of a man in the house of a single woman cannot be used as a reason to deny her benefits.

The old-fashioned solution of getting married and living off their earned income has become markedly inferior. Working a full forty-hour week in the dry-cleaning shop will pay Harold $64 ($136 in 1980 dollars) *before* Social Security and taxes are taken out. The bottom line is this: Harold can get married and work forty hours a week in a hot, tiresome job; or he can live with Phyllis and their baby without getting married, not work, and have more disposable income. From an economic point of view, getting married is dumb. From a noneconomic point of view, it involves him in a legal relationship that has no payoff for him. If he thinks he may sometime tire of Phyllis and fatherhood, the 1970 rules thus provide a further incentive for keeping the relationship off the books.

PHYLLIS'S CALCULATIONS, POST-REFORM

To keep the baby or give it up? To get married or not? What are the pros and cons?

Phyllis comes from a poor family. They want her out of the house, just as she wants to get out of the house. If she gives up the baby for adoption (or, in some states by 1970, has a legal abortion), she will be expected to support herself; and, as in 1960, the only job she will be able to find is likely to be unattractive, with no security and a paycheck no larger than her baby would provide. *The only circumstance under which giving up the baby is rational is if she prefers any sort of job to having and caring for a baby.* It is commonly written that poor teenaged girls have babies so they will have someone to love them. This may be true for some. But one *need* not look for psychological explanations. Under the rules of 1970, it was rational on grounds of dollars and cents for a poor, unmarried woman who found herself to be pregnant to have and keep the baby even if she did not particularly want a child.

In Phyllis's case, the balance favors having the baby. What about getting married?

If Phyllis and Harold marry and he is employed, she will lose her AFDC benefits. His minimum wage job at the laundry will produce no more income than she can make, and, not significantly, he, not she, will have control of the check. In exchange for giving up this degree of independence, she gains no real security. Harold's job is not nearly as stable as the welfare system. And, should her marriage break up, she will not be able to count on residual benefits. Enforcement of payment of child support has fallen to near-zero in poor communities. In sum, marriage buys Phyllis nothing—not companionship she couldn't have otherwise, not financial security, not even increased income. In 1970, her child provides her with the economic insurance that a husband used to represent.

Against these penalties for getting married is the powerful positive inducement to remain single: Any money that Harold makes is added to their income without affecting her benefits as long as they remain unmarried. It is difficult to think of a good economic reason from Phyllis's viewpoint why marriage might be attractive.

Harold and Phyllis take the economically logical step—she has the baby, they live together without getting married, and Harold looks for a job to make some extra money. He finds the job at the laundry. It is just as unpleasant a job as it was in 1960, but the implications of persevering are different. In 1970, unlike 1960, Harold's job is *not* his basic source of income. Thus, when the back room of the laundry has been too hot for too long, it becomes economically feasible and indeed reasonable to move in and out of the labor market. In 1980 dollars, Unemployment Insurance pays him $68 per week. As the sole means of support it is not an attractive sum. But added to Phyllis's package, the total is $202, which beats the heat of the presses. And, if it comes to it, Harold can survive even without the Unemployment payment. In 1970, Phyllis's welfare package is bringing in more real income than did a minimum-wage job in 1960.

Such is the story of Harold and Phyllis. They were put in a characteristically working-class situation. In 1960, the logic of their world led them to behave in traditional working-class ways. Ten years later, the logic of their world had changed and, lo and behold, they behaved indistinguishably from "welfare types." What if we had hypothesized a more typical example—or at least one that fits the stereotype? What if we had posited the lower-class and black cultural influences that are said to foster high illegitimacy rates and welfare dependency? The answer is that the same general logic would apply, but with even more power. When economic incentives are buttressed by social norms, the effects on behavior are multiplied. But the main point is that the social factors are not necessary to explain behavior. There is no "breakdown of the work ethic" in this account of rational choices among alternatives. There is no shiftless irresponsibility. It makes no difference whether Harold is white or black. There is no need to invoke the spectres of cultural pathologies or inferior upbringing. The choices may be seen much more simply, much more naturally, as the behavior of people responding to the reality of the world around them and making the decisions—the legal, approved, and even encouraged decisions—that maximize their quality of life.

WHAT ABOUT WORK INCENTIVES?

The stories of Harold and Phyllis were constructed to reflect four major changes in the administration of AFDC that took place in the 1960s. In 1961, federal law was changed to permit AFDC payments to families with an unemployed father. Eventually, twenty-five states adopted this option. In 1966, the Department of Health, Education and Welfare issued guidelines forbidding unannounced visits to the home to check eligibility. At about the same time, lawyers from the federal Legal Services program began filing cases challenging eligibility restrictions. The challenges had immediate effects on the practices of individual states. In 1968 these effects were generalized to the nation as a whole by the Supreme Court's decision in *King v. Smith*, which struck down the man-in-the-house eligibility restriction.

The other and most highly touted improvement (at the time, all of these changes were seen by a variety of sponsors as long-needed improvements) in the administration of AFDC occurred in 1967. The work disincentives associated with AFDC had been widely recognized for many years. To diminish these barriers to work, Congress passed what came to be known as the "thirty-and-a-third" rule, which permitted women on AFDC to keep the first $30 of earnings without losing their AFDC benefit and thereafter took only two of each three dollars of earnings. The intent was to provide a positive incentive for women on AFDC to get a job and eventually become self-sufficient. The political refrain at the time was that AFDC participants remained on welfare because they had no reason to get a job. Earnings were taxed at 100% until they amounted to more than the welfare check, and at exorbitantly high effective rates beyond that point. It was true that the thirty-and-a-third rule taxed income after $30 at a 67% rate. But, clearly, this was better than the 100% exacted by the earlier rules.

In the story of Harold and Phyllis, however, the thirty-and-a-third rule played a negative role in their calculations: It improved the total package available to them, and served as an added reason to choose the welfare option. This was not an idiosyncrasy of the situation in which we placed Harold and Phyllis. The legislation accomplished its purpose in a limited, technical sense. It provided an incentive to work for those women who were already on welfare. The problem is that the same rule provided a much stronger incentive for women who were not on welfare to get on it and then become trapped in it. The net effect was to raise the value of being eligible for AFDC and thereby, via a classic market response, increase the supply of eligible women.

This inherent quality of the thirty-and-a-third rule was first explicated by economist Frank Levy in an article in the *Journal of Human Resources*. His conclusions follow from an unembellished layout of the labor/leisure choice, translated from the way the reform was written. As Levy summarizes it:

> [A]ny AFDC parameter change which increases the program's break-even income will reduce expected labor supply in the population . . . But greater work incentives, including lower tax rates, greater disregards, and a more liberal deductions policy, will likewise lower expected hours of work. While these incentives may encourage increased work among women who previously worked very little, the increase will be more than offset by other women who are induced to cut back on work, including some women who were former nonrecipients. [Emphasis in the original]

The important point about the thirty-and-a-third rule (and the story of Harold and Phyllis) is that rules designed to have a certain narrow effect can in fact have a broad spectrum of unintended effects. They affect men as well as women, calculations about marriage and children as well as calculations about jobs and welfare. They interact with changes in divorce and abandonment law. They interact with changes in the Unemployment Insurance rules, minimum wage rates, the eligibility requirements for Food Stamps and subsidized housing and Disability Insurance. It is the total effect of well-intentioned changes in the incentive structure, not any one specific change, that is the key to comprehending what happened.

———————————————————■———————————————————

By the second Clinton term, it had become clear that critics of the Great Society welfare model had won. Welfare programs like AFDC were perceived as actually encouraging welfare dependency and out-of-wedlock births. The change in the national mood was in no small measure related to the perception that welfare recipients were disproportionately undeserving racial minorities who, due to lack of morals and values, were unwilling, not unable, to work.[16] Moreover, there is compelling evidence that the media's depiction of welfare as most problematic in the African-American community had as much to do with these changes in public opinion as to the actual contribution of blacks to the caseload of welfare programs.[17]

In his remarks at the signing of Public Law 104-193, or the Personal Responsibility and Work Opportunity Reconciliation Act (PRWORA) of 1996 President Clinton vowed to "make welfare what it was meant to be: a second chance, not a way of life." The basic premise of the Act is to move welfare recipients into the work force. Workfare, as it has been called, requires welfare recipients to work in exchange for public assistance. The most notable change is that the Temporary Assistance for Needy Families (TANF) Program has replaced AFDC as the major in-kind transfer mechanism. The TANF program provides block grants to individual states, who then tailor the program to their state's specific welfare needs.

*The following selection is a **"TANF Fact Sheet"** published by the Administration of Children and Families in the Department of Health and Human Services. The TANF program has several key provisions:*

1. *recipients to work after two years on assistance*
2. *recipients to work in subsidized or unsubsidized employment, on-site job training, vocational training, or the provision of child care services*
3. *a maximum of five cumulative years for cash aid*
4. *unmarried minor parents required to live with adults or under adult supervision*
5. *states can create jobs with existing funds now designated for welfare checks*

The jury is still out on the impact of welfare reform on the black community. As one might expect, the administration claims that welfare reform has been a resounding success.[18] On the other hand, critics maintain that the program has failed to make significant headway in moving poor black Americans, particularly single mothers, from welfare to work.[19] The results of the 2000 presidential elections, it would seem, will have a significant impact on the future of social welfare policy in the U.S.

TANF FACT SHEET

· ────

Administration for Children and Families

TEMPORARY ASSISTANCE FOR NEEDY FAMILIES (TANF)

On August 22, 1996, President Clinton signed into law "The Personal Responsibility and Work Opportunity Reconciliation Act of 1996," a comprehensive bipartisan welfare reform plan that dramatically changed the nation's welfare system into one that requires work in exchange for time-limited assistance. The Temporary Assistance for Needy Families (TANF) program replaces the former Aid to Families with Dependent Children (AFDC) and Job Opportunities and Basic Skills Training (JOBS) programs, ending the federal entitlement to assistance. In TANF, states and territories operate programs, and tribes have the option to run their own programs. States, territories, and tribes each receive a block grant allocation with a requirement on states to maintain a historical level of state spending known as maintenance of effort. The total federal block grant is $16.8 billion each year until fiscal year (FY) 2002. The block grant covers benefits, administrative expenses, and services. States, territories, and tribes determine eligibility and benefit levels and services provided to needy families.

The Personal Responsibility and Work Opportunity Reconciliation Act of 1996 (PRWORA) gives states enormous flexibility to design their TANF programs in ways that promote work, responsibility, and self-sufficiency, and strengthen families. Except as expressly provided under the statute, the federal government may not regulate the conduct of states.

States may use TANF funding in any manner "reasonably calculated to accomplish the purposes of TANF." These purposes are: to provide assistance to needy families so that children can be cared for in their own homes; to reduce dependency by promoting job preparation, work and marriage; to prevent out-of-wedlock pregnancies; and to encourage the formation and maintenance of two-parent families.

HIGHLIGHTS OF TANF

WORK REQUIREMENTS

With few exceptions, recipients must work after two years on assistance. Twenty-five percent of all families in each state must be engaged in work activities or have left the rolls in fiscal year FY 1997, rising to 50% in FY 2002. Single parents must participate for at least 20 hours per week the first year, increasing to at least 30 hours per week by FY 2000. Two-parent families must work 35 hours per week by July 1, 1997. Unless a state opts out, non-exempt adult recipients who are not working must participate in community service two months after they start receiving benefits. Single parents with a child under 6 who cannot find child care cannot be penalized for failure to meet the work requirements. States can exempt from the work requirement single parents with children under age one and disregard these individuals in the calculation of participation rates for up to 12 months. Failure to participate in work requirements can result in either a reduction or termination of benefits to the family.

WORK ACTIVITIES

To count toward state work requirements, recipients will be required to participate in unsubsidized or subsidized employment, on-the-job training, work experience, community service, 12 months of vocational training, or they must provide child care services to individuals who are participating in community service. Up to 6 weeks of job search (no more than 4 consecutive weeks) would count toward the work requirement. However, no more than

25% of those meeting the participation rates of each state's caseload may count toward the work requirement solely by participating in vocational training or by being a teen parent in secondary school. The teen parent limitation is phased in over several years.

A Five-Year Time Limit

Families who have received assistance for five cumulative years (or less at state option) will be ineligible for cash aid under the new welfare law. States will be permitted to exempt up to 20% of their caseload from the time limit, and states will have the option to provide non-cash assistance and vouchers to families that reach the time limit using Social Services Block Grant or state funds.

State Maintenance of Effort Requirements

States must maintain their own spending on welfare at 80% or more of FY 1994 levels. States must also maintain spending at 100% of FY 1994 levels to access a $2 billion contingency fund designed to assist states affected by high population growth or economic downturn. In addition, states must maintain 100% of FY 1994 or FY 1995 spending on child care (whichever is greater) to access additional child care funds beyond their initial allotment. To receive their full allocation, states must demonstrate they are spending on activities related to TANF 80% of the amount of non-federal funds they spent in FY 1994 on AFDC and related programs. If they meet minimum work requirements, their mandatory state effort is reduced to 75%.

ADDITIONAL FUNDING

- Performance bonus to reward work and reductions in out-of-wedlock births. Through FY 2003, $1 billion will be available for performance bonuses to reward states for moving welfare recipients into jobs. There is also a $100 million annual appropriation for bonuses to states that reduce the number of out-of-wedlock births and abortions.
- Contingency fund and loans. A $2 billion (over 5 years) contingency fund is available for states experiencing economic downturns, comprised of an $800 million (over 4 years) fund to provide supplemental grants for states with high population growth and low welfare spending, and a $1.7 billion federal loan fund.

Penalties

States can incur reductions in their block grant allocations for failure to:

- Satisfy work requirements, a penalty of 5% in the first year, increasing by 2% per year for each consecutive failure with a cap of 21%

- Comply with five-year limit on assistance, a 5% penalty
- Meet state maintenance of effort requirements under either TANF or the contingency fund, based on amount of state underspending
- Reduce recipient grants for refusing without good cause to participate in work activities, a penalty of between 1% and 5%, based on the degree of noncompliance and imposed in the succeeding fiscal year
- Maintain assistance when parents cannot find child care for child under age 6, a penalty of 5%
- Submit required reports, a penalty of 4%
- Comply with paternity establishment and child support enforcement requirements, up to a 5% penalty
- Participate in the Income and Eligibility Verification System, up to a 2% penalty
- Repay a federal loan on time, based on amount unpaid
- In addition, for the misuse of funds states can be penalized for the amount misused and, if found intentionally misused, an additional penalty of 5%
- States must expend additional state funds to replace federal penalty reductions. States can seek exceptions under limited conditions and develop a corrective compliance plan before they are penalized. The total penalty assessed in a given year may not exceed 25% of a state's block grant allotment.

PERSONAL EMPLOYABILITY PLANS

States are required to make an initial assessment of recipients' skills. States can also develop personal responsibility plans for recipients which identify the education, training, and job placement services needed to move into the workforce.

TEEN PARENT LIVE AT HOME AND STAY IN SCHOOL REQUIREMENTS

Unmarried minor parents will be required to live with a responsible adult or in an adult-supervised setting and participate in educational and training activities in order to receive assistance. States will be responsible for locating or assisting in locating adult-supervised settings for teens.

STATE PLANS

The Department of Health and Human Services (HHS) reviews the plans only for completeness. States must allow for a 45-day comment period on the state plan by local governments and private organizations and consult with them. The state plan must have "objective criteria" which are "fair" and "equitable" for eligibility and benefits and must explain appeal rights.

JOB SUBSIDIES

The law also allows states to create jobs by taking money now used for welfare checks and using it to create community service jobs or to provide income subsidies or hiring incentives for potential employers.

STATE FLEXIBILITY

States which received approval for welfare reform waivers before July 1, 1997 have the option to operate their cash assistance program under some or all of these waivers until their expiration.

EFFECTIVE DATES

States had until July 1, 1997 to submit their state plans and begin implementing TANF, although they could opt to implement earlier.

TRIBAL PROVISION

Federally-recognized Indian tribes may apply to operate a TANF block grant program. TANF allotments for Indian tribes are based upon previous state expenditures of federal dollars in AFDC, Emergency Assistance (EA), and JOBS in fiscal year 1994. Tribal TANF programs could be implemented as early as July 1, 1997. Like states, Indian tribes may use their TANF funding in any manner reasonably calculated to accomplish the purposes of TANF, and they have broad flexibility to determine eligibility, method of assistance, and benefit levels. Unlike state plans, tribal plans are approved by HHS. Also, HHS and tribes reach agreement on time limits, work requirements, and minimum participation rates.

REGULATION

Final regulations of the welfare reform bill, published by HHS on April 12, 1999, are intended to help all welfare recipients who can work go to work, and to encourage states to work with all families. They provide states with a basic framework for implementing the new welfare program, reinforce the importance of work requirements, promote positive outcomes for needy children and families, and fulfill the new federal role of supporting state flexibility, innovation, and success. The regulations incorporate the core TANF accountability provisions, including work requirements, time limits, state penalties, and data collection and reporting requirements. In general, they reflect a limited and restrained federal role. Since Congress specifically limited the authority of the federal government to regulate the new TANF program, the regulations cover only areas where Congress specifically directed the Secretary to regulate or where the Secretary is regulating her own actions.

———————————————————— ■ ————————————————————

CRIME AND CRIMINAL JUSTICE

The final decade of the 20th century saw crime climb to the top of the nation's policy agenda. It has captured the attention of policymakers, politicians, and the mass public. Increasingly, states are spending larger percentages of their annual budgets on crime control policies. Likewise, politicians are proposing more and tougher policies aimed at reducing crime (e.g., "three strikes and you're out legislation). Of course, much of this activity is driven by the fact that the public believes crime is rampant. Although down from its high water mark in the early 1990s, crime continues to rank in the top three of the nation's most important problems among the American public. For example, a March 2000 Gallup poll shows crime closely trailing education, and morals but well ahead of the economy, healthcare, the environment, and race relations as issues deserving of public attention.[20] In short, crime is one of the nation's most pressing policy dilemmas.

The link between crime and race is in no small measure related to the longstanding stereotype of blacks as aggressive and lawless.[21] In a recent study of white stereotypes, for instance, Peffley and Hurwitz found that from one-third to one-half of their sample viewed African-Americans as violent.[22] Crime and race are also connected empirically. That is, there has been a noticeable upsurge in the number of blacks (most notably men)[23] arrested and incarcerated.[24] There are three common explanations for the relatively high incidence of black crime: racism in the criminal justice system,[25] a blocked opportunity structure,[26] and the moral failure of individuals and communities.[27]

In his chapter **"African-Americans and the Criminal Justice System,"** *Marc Mauer argues that black/white differences in incarceration rates are explained either directly or indirectly by racial bias in the criminal justice system. Mauer points to five critical factors. Whereas higher black arrest rates surely account for a portion of the disproportionate rates of incarceration, he urges caution in interpreting these data. For example, higher black arrest rates may be a function of the disproportionate number of drug arrests among blacks, which, in turn, are out of line with actual black drug usage. Second, prior criminal histories are clearly important to explaining racial differences in the prison population. Here Mauer notes that the acquisition of a criminal record can be simply based on the color of one's skin (e.g., DWB—Driving While Black) as opposed to higher rates of commission. A third reason has to do with racial bias in prosecution and sentencing. Racial differences in the application of the death penalty are but one example he cites. Fourth, public perceptions about the appropriate policy response are related to race in the way that policy is conceived and formulated. In other words, how the problem is framed dictates the nature of the response. For example, Mauer compares the intensity of the war on drugs to the more tepid response to drunk driving. Finally, Mauer points to recent policy changes that have had an adverse effect on the African-American community (e.g., indeterminate sentencing). The end result is a disproportionately high number of African-Americans behind bars.*

RACE TO INCARCERATE

———————————— ■ ————————————

Marc Mauer

Excerpt from Chapter 7: African-Americans and the Criminal Justice System

I f we are to understand the means by which the disparities in imprisonment have developed, three areas of inquiry are most relevant: crime
rates; criminal histories; racial bias in prosecution and sentencing.

CRIME RATES

All things being equal, the most relevant factors that determine whether an offender will be sentenced to prison are the severity of the offense for which he
or she is convicted and the offender's prior record. Thus, if African-Americans
exhibit higher rates of violent offending and/or have lengthier criminal histories than other groups, we would expect this to be reflected in the composition
of the prison population.

For property crimes, African-Americans constituted 32% of arrests in 1996,
disproportionate to their share of the overall population. For violent crimes,
though, black offending rates are considerably higher than for other groups,
accounting for 43% of these arrests in 1996. As noted, arrest rates do not always correlate with crime rates (particularly for drug offenses), but they do
provide a benchmark by which to assess criminal activity. While these arrest
ratios are disturbing, they have remained stable for twenty years; the black
proportion has fluctuated in a narrow range of 43–47%.[1] (This is clearly a
very different picture than one would gather from watching only the eleven-
o'clock news on television. Even during the upsurge of black juvenile homi-
cides in the late 1980s, a declining rate of homicide among black adults
resulted in a stable rate overall for African-Americans.)

In another examination of the impact of arrest rates on incarceration in the
1980s, sociologists Robert Crutchfield, George Bridges, and Susan Pitchford
found that at a national level, higher black arrest rates accounted for 89.5% of
racial disparity in imprisonment. As in the Blumstein studies, these authors
used arrests as a proxy for crime rates. At the state level, though, the amount
of disparity that could be explained by arrests varied significantly. In the
northeast states, only 69% of racial disparity was accounted for by arrest,
while in the north central states, fewer blacks were actually incarcerated than
one would have predicted by just using arrest data.[2] Overall, this suggests
that a variety of factors, which may include crime rates, law enforcement pri-
orities, and sentencing legislation, may play a role in the degree of racial disparity in incarceration.

CRIMINAL HISTORIES

Prior criminal history is generally considered to be another explanation for
some of the disparity in rates of imprisonment. Of course, whether one

acquires a criminal record is itself very much a function of race, geographical location, and other factors.

For example, in recent years, many African-Americans have become acquainted with the crime known as "Driving While Black." In different parts of the country, there is strong evidence regarding the propensity of police to stop black males while driving for alleged traffic violations. Often, the justification offered for these actions, based on supposed drug courier "profiles," is that they are necessary for apprehending drug traffickers. In Volusia County in central Florida, for example, researchers documented traffic stops made by local police in the late 1980s. More than 70% of all drivers stopped were either African-American or Hispanic. For the state as a whole, blacks constituted 12% of the driving age population and 15% of drivers convicted of traffic violations. Blacks and Hispanics were also stopped for longer periods of time than whites, and represented 80% of the cars that were searched following a stop.[3] To the extent that some drivers of all races may possess drugs or other illegal goods, traffic stops that disproportionately affect minorities will also detect a disproportionate number of minority offenders.

RACIAL BIAS IN PROSECUTION AND SENTENCING

Few honest observers of the criminal justice system would contend that race never played a role in determining rates of conviction and incarceration. Nonetheless, some observers do suggest that in the modern era, racially biased decision-making has effectively been removed from the criminal justice system or at least does not play a significant role. Thus, we see academic texts with titles such as *The Myth of a Racist Criminal Justice System*, citing statistical evidence to argue that race plays no significant factor in how offenders are treated in the system.[4] These presentations generally fail to consider how the criminal justice system has come to operate in such an unbiased manner when bias is still frequently encountered in other institutions.

In fact, the influence of race can be seen very clearly in some areas of the criminal justice system. Death penalty sentences provide the most compelling evidence. A series of studies demonstrates that, controlling for a wide range of variables, the race of both victim and offender has a significant impact on the determination of a sentence of death as opposed to life in prison. David Baldus and colleagues, for example, found that murder defendants charged with killing whites faced a 4.3 times greater chance of receiving death than those charged with killing blacks.[5]

A close look at the federal sentencing guidelines themselves also suggests the difficulty of eliminating nonracial forms of bias in the system. One of the original justifications for the guidelines was the intent to eliminate favored treatment for wealthier defendants. A doctor convicted of Medicaid fraud, for example, would no longer be able to offer to domate his medical services to the community as a means of escaping a stay in prison.

NOTES

1. Michael Tonry, *Malign Neglect: Race, Crime, and Punishment in America* (New York: Oxford University Press, 1995), p. 64.

2. Robert D. Crutchfield, George S. Bridges, and Susan R. Pitchford, "Analytical and Aggregation Biases in Analyses of Imprisonment: Reconciling Discrepancies in Studies of Racial Disparity," *Journal of Research in Crime and Delinquency* 31 (May 1994).

3. David A. Harris, "'Driving While Black' and All Other Traffic Offenses: The Supreme Court and Pretextual Traffic Stops," *Journal of Criminal Law and Criminology* 87 (Summer 1997), p. 562.

4. William Wilbanks, *The Myth of a Racist Criminal Justice System* (Monterey, Calif.: Brooks/Cole, 1987).

5. David C. Baldus, Charles Pulaski, and George Woodworth, "Comparative Review of Death Sentences: An Empirical Study of the Georgia Experience," *Journal of Criminal Law and Criminology* 74 (Fall 1983), pp. 661–753.

A second school of thought maintains that group differences in crime rates are rooted in economic deprivation, thus, indirectly related to race. In other words, poverty compels people to commit crime in order to meet basic life requirements. In their article **"Industrial Restructuring and Violence: the Link Between Entry-level Jobs, Economic Deprivation, and Black and White Homicide,"** *Shihadeh and Ousey evaluate the literature on blocked opportunity structures and offer an alternative conceptualization. Their basic claim is that standard materialist theories that posit an economic motive to crime underappreciate the impact that poverty and unemployment have on the "organization and normative structure of communities." The disappearance of jobs in the inner city, on this line of reasoning, has a direct effect on the social disintegration of the community. Their empirical findings show that joblessness creates economic deprivation that, in turn, raises homicide rates. Moreover, the predictors of murder rates are similar between whites and blacks. As the authors note, "race differences in urban violence may derive from race differences in the structural impediments within major cities."*

INDUSTRIAL RESTRUCTURING AND VIOLENCE: THE LINK BETWEEN ENTRY-LEVEL JOBS, ECONOMIC DEPRIVATION, AND BLACK AND WHITE HOMICIDE

Edward S. Shihadeh and Graham C. Ousey

ECONOMIC DEPRIVATION AND CRIME

The idea that economic deprivation contributes to crime is an old and widely held view in sociology. Several of the classic theories of crime, including Marxist, strain, and utilitarian, rely heavily on economic factors such as poverty and unemployment to account for variations in crime rates. Researchers since the 19th century have suggested a positive association between poverty and crime in urban areas. While most studies support this view (Bailey 1984; Decker 1980; Harries 1976; Loftin & Parker 1985; Messner & Tardiff 1986; Patterson 1991), some research finds evidence to the contrary (Blau & Blau 1982; Crutchfield et al. 1982; Messner 1983). This may be due to the fact that the relationship between poverty and crime is contingent upon the specific crime category under consideration (Crutchfield et al. 1982; Patterson 1991).

Some have also suggested that crime is partially explained by poor employment prospects, as reflected in unemployment rates (Allan & Steffensmeier 1989). But despite the intuitive appeal and theoretical support of an unemployment and crime relationship (U-C), a few studies actually report a negative unemployment-crime relationship. Such findings contribute to what Chiricos (1987) terms the "consensus of doubt" regarding the relationship between unemployment and crime. But according to his review, the vast majority of studies find a positive relationship between unemployment and crime. And of the city and county level studies that find a statistically significant U-C relationship, virtually all of them report a positive association. So despite some evidence to the contrary, readers of the review are left doubting not the U-C relationship, but the "consensus of doubt" itself.

The link between crime and poverty or unemployment has received considerable attention in both historic and contemporary research. But only a handful of macro crime studies specifically examine the relationship with racially disaggregated data. For instance, of the cross-sectional studies that use racially disaggregated crime rates (Huff-Corzine et al. 1986; Sampson 1985, 1987; South & Felson 1990; Harer & Steffensmeier 1992; Messner & Golden 1992; Peterson & Krivo 1993; Smith et al. 1992; Shihadeh & Steffensmeier 1994; Shihadeh & Flynn 1996; Shihadeh & Ousey 1996) less than half included black unemployment (or some derivation thereof) as a distinct predictor. And of those, only Sampson (1985), using 1970 data, finds a negative association between unemployment and crime. The rest, using more recent data, report the more expected positive association (Sampson 1987; Smith, Devine & Shelley 1992; Shihadeh & Steffensmeier 1994; Shihadeh & Flynn 1996). Thus, the handful of evidence from racially disaggregated studies strongly indicates that economic deprivation creates an upward pressure on crime rates.

The theoretical foundation of the deprivation-crime link relies on the notion that deprivation creates economically motivated offenders who are compelled to commit crime in order to satisfy basic needs (e.g., Bonger 1916; Cantor & Land 1985; Land et al. 1994). While economic motivation likely makes a nontrivial contribution to high crime rates, particularly for property crimes, as a stand-alone guiding principle it is limited in a number of respects. First, motivationally based explanations of crime suffer from what Sampson and Wilson (1995) term the "'materialist fallacy'—that economic (or materialist) causes necessarily produce economic motivations" (45). They point out that strain or materialist theories have not fared well empirically and "the image of the offender stealing to survive flourishes only as a straw man." (45). The modern welfare state buffers the full effect of poverty and joblessness through unemployment compensation, welfare, and other government programs (Allan & Steffensmeier 1989).

Second, such theories rely on the troubling presupposition that macro-level relationships reflect the sum of a series of individual-level social-psychological processes. Consider Blau and Blau's (1982) prominent statement that highly stratified environments generate feelings of hostility and frustration in individuals. When inequality is based on ascriptive characteristics, such as race, these sentiments can be highly pronounced and can find expression in the form of violence. The reductionist nature of the Blau's explanation is clearly evident and makes it impossible to distinguish between individual and aggregate social processes. If macro-level studies fail to make that distinction, it begs the larger question—why examine this relationship at the aggregate level? Yet, as the research on family structure and crime has shown, it is possible for the the-oretical relationship between variables to be distinct at various levels of analysis. Much of the extant research has generally failed to yield evidence of a significant individual-level relationship—that single-parent households are more likely to produce juvenile delinquents (Ensminger et al. 1983; LaFree et al. 1992; Ross & Sawhill 1975; but see Matsueda & Heimer 1987). Yet at the aggregate level, Sampson (1987) and Shihadeh and Steffensmier (1994) find extremely strong associations between the rates of family disruption and the rates of juvenile violence. They argue that widespread family disruption weakens the formal and informal capacity of communities to control their members—regardless of the type of family those members are from—which in turn may lead to higher rates of offending.

Our point is that aggregate-level explanations of crime should not have to assume that individual offenders necessarily possess the characteristics of the aggregate predictors. Just as macrotheoretical links between crime and family structure should not require that perpetrators themselves are products of single-parent households, likewise, economic deprivation—crime explanations need not adhere to the restriction that perpetrators are poor or unemployed. Yet this is precisely the implication of motivationally based theories which posit that the aggregate link is an additive function of a set of economically motivated individuals. The challenge for macrosocial research on crime—indeed, its raison d'etre—is to identify the macrosocial contexts that are conducive to crime rather than to reproduce individual-level analogs at a higher level.

With that in mind, we view economic deprivation exemplified by high rates of unemployment and poverty as having profoundly negative consequences on both the organization and normative structure of communities, consequences that are far more devastating to community life than the creation of economically motivated offenders. Widespread deprivation is an embedded structural condition that can delegitimize conventional norms and weaken the capacity of communities to cultivate allegiance to mainstream institutions (Shihadeh & Steffensmeier 1994; Messner 1988).

The implications of this for minority communities are potentially serious considering that more than one-half of all black men in central cities between the ages of 18 and 29 are either unemployed, underemployed, or out of the labor force altogether (Lichter 1988). Conditions this extreme exacerbate the sense of exclusion in many low-income communities and weaken the social attachment to mainstream institutions among large segments of center-city residents.

Because joblessness and poverty are daily experiences in the harsh reality of ghetto life, certain value and normative responses may arise which further isolate ghetto residents. Rather than reiterating the culture of poverty perspective (see Lewis 1961, 1968; Gastil 1971), we emphasize that oppositional ghetto practices—which can distance members from the wider society—are proximate outcomes to the structural impediments faced by a significant number of urban blacks. Elijah Anderson (1993, 1994) notes that impoverished young black males have little hope of acquiring meaningful employment and are therefore deprived of the primary means by which males in our society prove their worth. They instead strive for achievable goals, by seeking out peer support and fostering an image based on violence, shored up with clothing, jewelry, hair styles, facial expressions and gait (Anderson 1994). His research reveals that even young males with otherwise nonviolent predispositions feel compelled to take on a street-oriented demeanor and demonstrate the ready willingness to use force. Thus structural impediments, such as deleterious labor force conditions, can generate milieu effects that are conducive to crime. In this sense, our focus is not the characteristics of individual offenders, but on the social conditions that have criminogenic consequences.

On the basis of this review, our general heuristic framework is that the structural link between economic restructuring and crime involves two macrosocial paths. First, the mass exodus of entry level jobs created by urban industrial restructuring contributes to economic deprivation in the form of high rates of poverty and joblessness. Second, economic deprivation then creates an upward pressure on the rates of serious crime. However, some recent research has revealed important race differences in the correlates of crime (Harer & Steffensmeier 1992; Sampson 1987; Smith, Devine & Shelley 1992; Shihadeh & Steffensmeier 1994; Shihadeh & Ousey 1996). This may be clue to the vivid contrasts between black and white urban life. Given the objective harshness of many black communities in urban areas, one might expect to see an effect only for them. But from our vantage point, the relationship between low skill jobs, economic deprivation and violent crime is essentially structural—one that should exist based upon the contextual features of urban systems and should transcend the race composition of communities. So despite the fact that black communities are worse off, white communities should also have high crime rates given a similar set of circumstances. There is little basis to conclude, therefore, that the relationship between the key theoretical variables ought to differ between blacks and whites.

From a research perspective, these links are theoretically important but have not been explored systematically. The present study adds to our knowledge about the structural predictors of crime in several respects. From a theoretical standpoint, we introduce the notion that economic deprivation is a mediating variable between urban restructuring and violence in center-cities. We also estimate models using racially disaggregated data in order to examine any race differences in this macro-social relationship. Finally, because these are dynamic and processual forces, we estimate models that include the change in our key indicators over the last several decades.

DISCUSSION AND CONCLUSION

The relationship between low skill jobs, economic deprivation, and the rates of violence, appears to transcend racial lines. A reduction in the availability of low skill jobs has detrimental consequences for both black and white urban communities. The decline of industries dominated by entry-level employment is associated with an increase in economic deprivation and, indirectly, elevated rates of murder. The implications of this are important for macro-crime research on the race differences in the correlates of crime. Our analysis suggests that there are similarities between blacks and whites in the structural predictors of homicide—at least for the predictors used in our models. This supports the view that race differences in urban violence may derive from race differences in the structural impediments within major cities. To be sure, the contrast between black and white urban life are often vivid. And many black communities are heavily laden with structural factors that are crime-producing. Nonetheless, the basic link between jobs, economic conditions and serious crime is the same for both race groups.

But despite the black-while similarity in how industrial restructuring translates into violence, there are some notable differences. Not only is there a major race-gap in homicide rates, but our models explain a lower proportion of variance among blacks than among white. Clearly, there are other factors that create an upward pressure on violence rates in black communities. Rather than fully accounting for all aspects of black urban life, our models examine closely only one of many potential problems in urban areas. Wilson (1987, 1993), Massey and Denton (1993) and others document a broad range of pathologies that have transformed black inner-cities. Black ghettos are subject to an historical legacy of intense and long term deprivation, where a number of major social problems intersect. Of particular note is the flight of the black middle class away from traditionally black areas in the center city. This out-migration removed the vertical integration of old black neighborhoods and transformed them into areas of concentrated poverty (Wilson 1987). Those who remained were left isolated from social and economic opportunities, and isolated from mainstream role models who can legitimize the idea of a successful middle-class adulthood. So we are skeptical of any effort to reduce the race differences in violence to a single factor or process. On the contrary, the long term legacy of black deprivation has yielded a multitude of factors that are, today, conductive to violence.

One of the more vexing crime policy problems concerns the disproportionately high rates of violent crime among inner-city minority youth. In **"The Root Cause of Crime: Moral Poverty,"** *Bennett et al., warn that juvenile violent crime is a "ticking time bomb" given the* *large youth cohort and their propensity for murder and mayhem. Youth "superpredators," the authors contend, are the "youngest, biggest, baddest generation any society has ever known." They are remorseless, slack-jawed, cold-blooded killers who have neither respect nor fear of adult authority. Bennett et al., discount structural and racial predictors of crime in favor of an expla-nation based on moral poverty. From this perspective youth crime is related to the absence of adult supervision, mentoring, and role models. Moral poverty has two consequences for youth crime—the lack of impulse control and the lack of empathy. The empirical evidence for their the-ory is based on research findings that indicate the key explanatory variables for youth violent crime are the extent of a mother's supervision, family substance abuse, and child abuse. In short, Bennett et al. place the blame for moral poverty on the shoulders of inner city adult communities.*

BODY COUNT:
MORAL POVERTY . . . AND HOW TO WIN
AMERICA'S WAR AGAINST CRIME AND DRUGS

William J. Bennett, John J. DiIulio, Jr., and John P. Walters

THE TICKING CRIME BOMB

To better understand the criminal landscape in America, here are some impor-tant facts you need to know: most of the street crimes that concern and frighten us are committed by men under the age of 25. Over the next decade or so, the number of young men in the population will increase substantially. And a large fraction of boys are likely to be raised in circumstances that put them at risk of becoming street predators. In short, America is a ticking crime bomb.

The evidence is overwhelming. It shows that since 1985 the rate of homicide committed by adults age 25 and older has dropped by 25% (from 6.3 to 4.7 per 100,000). Over the same period, however, the homicide rate among 18- to 24-year-olds increased by 61% (from 15.7 to 25.3 per 100,000). And over the last decade, the rate of homicide committed by teenagers ages 14 to 17 more than doubled (from 7 to 19.1 per 100,000). Thus, as Fox concludes, "although the percentage of 18- to 24-year-olds has declined in recent years, younger teens have become more involved in serious violent crime, including homicide, thereby expanding the limits of the violence-prone group to as young as 14."

Males ages 14 to 24 are now about 8% of the population but they constitute 27% of all homicide victims and 48% of all murderers. Between 1985 and 1992 the rate at which males ages 14 to 17 committed murder increased by about 50% for whites and over 300% for blacks. By the early 1990s the homicide of-fending rate per 100,000 among black males ages 14 to 17 hovered around 150 (versus 15 for whites), while the homicide offending rate for black males ages 18 to 24 hovered around 200 (versus 20 for whites). Ominously, white males ages 14 to 17 "have diminished in relative size to less than 7% [of the popula-tion], but have remained 10% of homicide victims and 17% of the perpetra-tors. More striking, however, is that over the past decade, black males ages 14–24 have remained just above 1% of the population yet have expanded from 9 to 17% of the victims and from 17 to 30% of the offenders."

The trends are also ominous for nonfatal acts of criminal violence and rates of weapons offenses among young males. For example, between 1973 and 1992, the rate of violent victimizations of black males ages 12 to 24 increased about 25%; black males ages 16 to 19 sustained one violent crime for every eleven persons in 1973 versus one for every six in 1992. From 1987 to 1992, the average annual rate of handgun victimization per 1,000 young black males was three to four times higher than for young white males.

As we will explain later in this chapter, black-white differences in rates of criminal offending reflect the fact that, on average, black children are more likely than white children to grow up without two parents or other adults who supervise, nurture, and provide for them. As Professor Glenn Loury has eloquently written, crime is a problem of "sin, not skin." So, as you read these data, do keep in mind that race is, in effect, a proxy for the density of stable, consistent adult supervision in the lives of at-risk children. Give black children, on average, the level of positive adult social support enjoyed by white children, and the rates would reverse themselves.

THE SUPERPREDATORS

To reiterate a point we have already made: as high as America's body count is today, a rising tide of youth crime and violence is about to lift it even higher. A new generation of street criminals is upon us—the youngest, biggest, and baddest generation any society has ever known.

Today, for example, America is home to roughly 7.5 million boys ages 14 to 17. UCLA Professor James Q. Wilson has estimated that by the year 2000, "there will be a million more people" in that age bracket than there were in 1995, half of them male. Based on well-replicated longitudinal studies, he predicts that 6% of these boys "will become high rate, repeat offenders—thirty thousand more young muggers, killers, and thieves than we have now. Get ready," he warns.

The problem, however, is not just that a growing population of boys means more bad boys. The problem is that today's bad boys are far worse than yesteryear's, and tomorrow's will be even worse than today's. As Wilson has observed, there are

> two restraints on behavior—morality, enforced by individual conscience or social rebuke, and law, enforced by police and courts. . . . As the costs of crime decline or the benefits increase, as drugs and guns become more available, as the glorification of violence becomes more commonplace, as families and neighborhoods lose some of their restraining power—as all of these things happen, almost all of us will change our behavior to some degree. For the most law-abiding among us, the change will be modest. . . . For the least law-abiding among us, the change will be dramatic. . . .

Based on all that we have witnessed, researched, and heard from people who are close to the action, here is what we believe: America is now home to thickening ranks of juvenile "superpredators"—radically impulsive, brutally remorseless youngsters, including ever more preteenage boys, who murder, assault, rape, rob, burglarize, deal deadly drugs, join gun-toting gangs, and create serious communal disorders. They do not fear the stigma of arrest, the pains of imprisonment, or the pangs of conscience. They perceive hardly any relationship between doing right (or wrong) now and being rewarded (or punished) for it later. To these mean-street youngsters, the words "right" and "wrong" have no fixed moral meaning.

Virtually everyone we know who is close to the nation's crime problem, from big-city police officers to inner-city preachers, from juvenile probation officers to public school teachers, agrees that more and more of today's crime-prone kids are sheer terrors. The exceptions are certain crime "experts" and pundits—the same ones who denied or trivialized the crack and crime epidemic of the 1980s until it was too late for anything but eulogies to its victims. We have yet to meet anyone who seriously doubts that today' troubled teens are more troubled than those of the 1950s. Common sense alone should be sufficient to prove that the one-drive-by-shooting-a-night street gangs of the late 1980s and early 1990s represent a far greater physical and moral menace than the one-knife-fight-a-year street gangs of earlier decades.

THE USUAL SUSPECTS: SOME LIBERAL FALLACIES

Whatever the degree of factual consensus about the drug and crime body count and the rise in youth violence, when it comes to explaining why so many Americans are exposed to so much criminal victimization, liberals and conservatives generally part company, often quickly, and sometimes completely.

Some liberals insist that the problem stems from a lack of meaningful programs; some conservatives insist that it stems from a lack of no-frills prisons. Liberals argue that criminals kill because there are too many guns; conservatives respond that criminals kill because there are too few executions. Liberals assert that the justice system is shot through with procedural racism; conservatives assert that the justice system is shot through with technical loopholes. And while both liberals and conservatives may agree that adverse economic conditions breed crime, the former are more inclined to lament the lack of well-paying jobs, the latter to lament the lack of well-motivated job-seekers.

These are the usual explanatory suspects—programs, prisons, guns, executions, racism, loopholes, and economic circumstances. Each of them, we believe, explains a little. But none of them, either alone or in combination with the others, explains crime and disorder, rampaging youth violence, or the ever-deadly drug-crime nexus.

THE TRUE CULPRIT

What is the fundamental cause of predatory street crime?

Moral poverty.

Moral poverty mocks well-intentioned programs and fills no-frills prisons. Moral poverty makes some young men pull triggers the way some old men fire off angry letters. Moral poverty unleashes more murderers in a single year than America has executed in this century. Moral poverty makes both racism and legal loopholes mere backdrops in a crime drama featuring family disintegration, child abuse, and child neglect. And moral poverty, not economic poverty, is what marks some disadvantaged youngsters for a life of drugs and crime while passing over others in equal or greater material distress.

To repeat what we mentioned in Chapter 1: moral poverty is the poverty of being without loving, capable, responsible adults who teach you right from wrong; the poverty of being without parents and other authorities who habituate you to feel joy at others' joy, pain at others' pain, satisfaction when you do right, remorse when you do wrong; the poverty of growing up in the virtual absence of people who teach morality by their own everyday example and who insist that you follow suit. In the extreme, moral poverty is the poverty of growing up severely abused and neglected at the hands of deviant, delinquent, or criminal adults.

Whatever their material circumstances, kids of whatever creed, color, demographic description, socioeconomic status, region, or zip code are far more likely to become (*pace West Side Story*) criminally depraved when they are morally deprived. The abject moral poverty that produces superpredators most often begins very early in life in settings where deep and abiding love is nowhere but unmerciful abuse is the norm. An extremely morally impoverished beginning early in life makes children vicious who are by nature merely aggressive, makes children remorseless who are disposed to be uncaring, and makes children radically impulsive who have difficulty sitting still, concentrating, and thinking ahead. In general, we believe, today's juvenile superpredators are children who, in order to be civilized and socialized into adulthood, would have needed a maximum dosage of moral tutelage from parents, teachers, coaches, clergy, and other responsible adults, but instead received either no such moral education, or were persistently exposed to its opposite by adults who severely abused and neglected them, encouraged them to act out, and rewarded their antisocial words and deeds.

The twin character scars left by moral poverty—lack of impulse control and lack of empathy—reinforce each other and make it far more likely that the individual will succumb to either the temptations of crime, or the blandishments of drugs, or, as so often happens, both. Once a morally impoverished individual has mixed crime with drugs, he is far more likely to go right on mixing them, and, in turn, pursuing whatever instant gratifications he desires (sex, money, laughs, "respect"), and at whatever human and financial cost to others (up to and including the sudden loss of their lives) it may entail.

Below we will flesh out some of the empirical evidence that we believe supports our theory of moral poverty, and justifies our confidence that its explanatory reach far exceeds the explanatory grasp of any and all of the usual suspects.

The flip side of moral poverty is moral health. Being born healthy to or raised by loving biological or adoptive parents or guardians of whatever race, creed, color, socioeconomic status, or demographic description is perhaps the luckiest fate that can befall a human being. To be born into or raised by such a family, and to grow up surrounded by loving, caring, responsible adults—parents or guardians, neighbors, teachers, coaches, clergy—is to be raised in moral wealth.

Children need the love, attention, and guiding discipline of loving, caring, responsible adults who are there to hug and scold, encourage and restrain, reward and punish in accordance with basic social norms governing how people should relate to one another—speak respectfully to peers and authorities; use physical force against others only in self-defense; never simply to express anger for "the fun" of it; and so on. To become civilized and socialized, let alone to be made cooperative and good-natured, all children need to be taught right from wrong by adults who, most if not all of the time, teach it by their own, everyday example.

As every parent of more than one child knows, children differ in their personalities, temperaments, and sociability. Before they're out of diapers, some children seem to listen and cooperate almost without being told; others seem naturally disposed to go their own way; and a few behave like "untamed terrors." Generally speaking, and other things being equal, boys are a harder-to-tame, harder-to-socialize lot than girls, and some boys are naturally more irritable, more impulsive, and harder to control than others.

Thus, some children require more, and more persistent, adult guidance and supervision than others if they are to become good adults (at the outside) and refrain from wantonly harming other people or stealing their property (at a minimum). In any functional society, even most "untamed terrors" and "troubled teens" become good people. Most never even come close to being totally self-centered liars, thieves, domestic abusers, or violent predators. The reason is that along the way—in homes, in schools, on playing fields, in churches, and elsewhere—most receive the necessary doses of loving, caring, responsible adult guidance and supervision they need.

The empirical evidence to support our moral poverty theory of crime and delinquency is diverse, pervasive, and, we think, common-sensical. Our theory is that, *ceteris paribus*, the probability that a child will become a superpredator or adult career criminal varies inversely with the number and quality of positive and persistent adult influences in a child's life (parents, teachers, coaches, clergy, and others). Moral wealth breeds social health; moral poverty breeds crime and social decay.

AFFIRMATIVE ACTION

Affirmative action policy is one of the most controversial issues on the public agenda.[28] During the 1960s, civil rights advocates concluded that simply removing legal barriers to equal opportunity was insufficient as a means to integrate American society. In response, they pushed for a policy agenda that sought to remedy racial segregation affirmatively. Put differently, race conscious remedies were necessary even if it meant granting preferential treatment to racial minorities.[29] As early as 1961, for example, federally sponsored contractors prodded President Kennedy to sign Executive order 10925 prohibiting racial discrimination. Similarly, President Johnson signed executive orders in 1965 and 1967 to create the administrative apparatus to oversee federal enforcement of equal opportunity policy (i.e., the Equal Employment Opportunity Commission and the Office of Federal Contract Compliance).

Affirmative action policy took center stage in 1967 with the introduction of the *Philadelphia Plan*.[30] Equal opportunity advocates had been complaining for some time that labor unions discriminated against black workers in the skilled trades. In particular, the unions restricted admission to the coveted apprenticeship programs by reserving new slots for friends and relatives.[31] Moreover, a shortage of skilled laborers resulted in spiraling housing costs. The Department of Labor responded by directing the Office of Federal Contract Compliance (OFCC) to require bidders on federal projects to submit "manning tables" for minority employment. Although the OFCC guidelines did not explicitly specify numerical quotas, they did place a premium on goals, timetables, and targets.

The most serious challenge to affirmative action policy came in the form of the **Regents of the University of California v. Bakke** *(1978). The Bakke case involved the admission of Alan Bakke, a white male, to the medical school at the University of California, Davis. The Davis campus had earlier instituted a special admissions program for "economically and/or educationally disadvantaged applicants and members of a minority group." Bakke's core claim was that Davis officials had denied him admission because of the color of his skin. Bakke's attorneys revealed that he had scored higher on the relevant entrance exams than many of the minorities admitted under the special program. Moreover, no disadvantaged whites had been admitted to the special program even though a nontrivial number had applied. In short, Bakke argued that the Davis admissions program violated his rights under the equal protection clause of the 14th amendment. In a 5–4 decision, the Supreme Court ruled that Bakke's rights had been violated and ordered his admission to the program. The Court also stipulated, however, that race could be used as a factor in admission decisions.*

REGENTS OF THE UNIVERSITY OF CALIFORNIA V. BAKKE

Certiorari to the Supreme Court of California No. 76–811.
Argued October 21, 1977—Decided June 28, 1978

The Medical School of the University of California at Davis (hereinafter Davis) had *two admissions* programs for the entering class of 100 students—the regular admissions program and the special admissions program. Under the regular procedure, candidates whose overall undergraduate grade point averages fell below 2.5 on a scale of 4.0 were summarily rejected. About one out of six applicants was then given an interview, following which he was rated on a scale of 1 to 100 by each of the committee members (five in 1973 and six in 1974), his rating being based on the interviewers' summaries, his overall grade point average, his science courses grade point average, and his Medical College Admissions Test (MCAT) scores, letters of recommendation, extracurricular activities, and other biographical data, all of which resulted in a total "benchmark score." The full admissions committee then made offers of admission on the basis of their review of the applicant's file and his score, considering and acting upon applications as they were received. The committee chairman was responsible for placing names on the waiting list and had discretion to include persons with "special skills." A separate committee, a majority of whom were members of minority groups, operated the special admissions program. The 1973 and 1974 application forms, respectively, asked candidates whether they wished to be considered as "economically and/or educationally disadvantaged" applicants and members of a "minority group" (blacks, Chicanos, Asians, American Indians). If an applicant of a minority group was found to be "disadvantaged," he would be rated in a manner similar to the one employed by the general admissions committee. Special candidates, however, did not have to meet the 2.5 grade point cut-off and were not ranked against candidates in the general admissions process. About one-fifth of the special applicants were invited for interviews in 1973 and 1974, following which they were given benchmark scores, and the top choices were then given to the general admissions committee, which could reject special candidates for failure to meet course requirements or other specific deficiencies.

The special committee continued to recommend candidates until 16 special admission selections had been made. During a four-year period 63 minority students were admitted to Davis under the special program and 44 under the general program. No disadantaged whites were admitted under the special program, though many applied. (Respondent, a white male, applied to Davis in 1973 and 1974, in both years being considered only under the general admissions program.) Though he had a 468 out of 500 score in 1973, he was rejected since no general applicants with scores less than 470 were being accepted after respondent's application, which was filed late in the year, had been processed and completed. At that time four special admission slots were still unfilled. In 1974 respondent applied early, and though he had a total score of 549 out of 600, he was again rejected. In neither year was his name placed on the discretionary waiting list. In both years special applicants were admitted with significantly lower scores than respondent's (After his second rejection, respondent filed this action in state court for mandatory injunctive and declaratory relief to compel his admission to Davis, alleging that the special admissions program operated to exclude him on the basis of his race in violation of the Equal Protection Clause of the 14th Amendment a provision of the California Constitution, and §SC 601 of Title VI of the Civil Rights Act of 1964, which provides, *inter alia*, that no person shall on the ground of race or color be excluded from participating in any program receiving federal financial assistance.) Petitoner cross-claimed for a declaration that its special admissions program was lawful. The trial court found that the special program operated as a racial quota, because minority applicants in that program were rated only against one another, and 16 places in the class of 100 were reserved for them. Declaring that petitioner could not take race into account in making admissions decisions, the program was held to violate the Federal and State Constitutions and Title VI. Respondent's admission was not ordered, however, for lack of proof that he would have been admitted but for the special program. The California Supreme Court, applying a strict-scrutiny standard, concluded that the special admissions program was not the least intrusive means of achieving the goals of the admittedly compelling state interests of integrating the medical profession and increasing the number of doctors willing to serve minority patients. Without passing on the state constitutional or federal statutory grounds the court held that petitioner's special admissions program violated the Equal Protection Clause. Since petitioner could not satisfy its burden of demonstrating that respondent, absent the special program, would not have been admitted, the court ordered his admission to Davis.

Held: The judgment below is affirmed insofar as it orders respondent's admission to Davis and invalidates petitioner's special admissions program, but is reversed insofar as it prohibits petitioner from taking race into account as a factor in its future admissions decisions.

Cal. 3d 34, 553 P. 2d 1152, affirmed in part and reversed in part.

Mr. Justice Powell concluded:

1. Title VI proscribes only those racial classifications that would violate the Equal Protection Clause if employed by a State or its agencies. Pp. 12–18.

2. Racial and ethnic classifications of any sort are inherently suspect and call for the most exacting judicial scrutiny. While the goal of achieving a diverse student body is sufficiently compelling to justify consideration of race in admissions decisions under some circumstances, petitioner's special admissions program, which forecloses consideration to persons like respondent, is unnecessary to the achievement of this compelling goal and therefore invalid under the Equal Protection Clause. Pp. 18–49.

3. Since petitioner could not satisfy its burden of proving that respondent would not have been admitted even if there had been no special admissions program, he must be admitted. P. 49.

Mr. Justice Brennan, Mr. Justice White, Mr. Justice Marshall, and Mr. Justice Blackmun concluded:

1. Title VI proscribes only those racial classifications that would violate the Equal Protection Clause if employed by a State or its agencies. Pp. 4–31.

2. Racial classifications call for strict judicial scrutiny. Nonetheless, *the purpose of overcoming substantial, chronic minority underrepresentation in the medical profession is sufficiently important to justify petitioner's remedial use of race.* Thus, the judgment below must be reversed in that it prohibits race from being used as a factor in university admissions. Pp. 31–55.

Mr. Justice Stevens, joined by The Chief Justice, Mr. Justice Stewart, and Mr. Justice Rehnquist, being of the view that whether race can ever be a factor in an admissions policy is not an issue here; that Title VI applies; and that respondent was excluded from Davis in violation of Title VI, concurs in the Court's judgment insofar as it affirms the judgment of the court below ordering respondent admitted to Davis. Pp. 1–14.

In his chapter "The Law of Affirmative Action," Girardeau Spann reviews affirmative action law from the mid-1970s to the late 1990s.[32] He argues that the direction of affirmative action law has been a function of the ideological composition of the Supreme Court. For example, early affirmative action law was dominated by a majority bloc of liberal justices who routinely voted in favor of affirmative action programs. In more recent times, on the other hand, a conservative majority bloc has cast pro-affirmative action votes in only seven of the fifty-eight cases it heard. Spann goes on to identify the three most salient legal issues in affirmative action law: standard of review, justiciability, and stigmas/stereotypes. With regard to standard of review, Spann argues that the "strict scrutiny" test may, in fact, be dispositive. That is, "strict scrutiny will remain "fatal in fact" because a majority of the Court will never find an affirmative action program adequate to meet strict scrutiny standards that are theoretically capable of being satisfied." As for justiciability, Spann maintains that it is "unclear what justifications for affirmative action the Court will recognize as legitimate." Thus, for these two issues, Spann concludes that disposition will ultimately be determined by the incoming president's future appointments to the Court. Finally, Spann considers the question of whether or not affirmative action programs stigmatize recipients as well as "innocent whites." He concludes that the Court is willing to accept "a relatively high level of stereotyping" although "the degree of burden that an affirmative action plan places on innocent whites is likely to be a significant factor."

THE LAW OF AFFIRMATIVE ACTION: TWENTY-FIVE YEARS OF SUPREME COURT DECISIONS ON RACE AND REMEDIES

Giradeau A. Spann

Excerpt from Chapter 5: The Law of Affirmative Action

T he Supreme Court's first twenty-five years of affirmative action decisions have generated a body of case law that has fluctuated over time, but now disfavors racial affirmative action. That body of law has identified a number of subsidiary issues that are relevant to the constitutionality of affirmative action, and it has offered tentative resolutions to some of those issues while leaving other issues largely unresolved. The law that has developed over the course of the Court's first twenty-five-year engagement with affirmative action is not doctrinally stable. Rather, the Supreme Court's law of affirmative action seems highly dependent upon the political preferences of the justices who happened to be sitting on the Court when particular cases were decided. Moreover, because many of the Supreme Court's affirmative action cases have been decided by a bare 5–4 majority of the Court, subsequent Supreme Court appointments are likely to have a significant effect on the direction of future developments in the Supreme Court's law of affirmative action. Nevertheless, it is possible to make certain statistical observations about the Court's affirmative action cases, and about the voting behavior of individual justices with respect to many of the subsidiary issues that the Court has identified as relevant to the constitutionality of affirmative action. At the moment, the affirmative action voting blocs on the Supreme Court appear to be relatively stable. This suggests that most *de jure* affirmative action programs—programs making explicit use of racial classifications—will continue to be invalidated by the Supreme Court as long as the Court's personnel remains the same. However, the manner in which the unresolved doctrinal issues relevant to affirmative action will ultimately be resolved remains uncertain. It is also uncertain how receptive the Court will be to the substitution of *de facto* affirmative action—affirmative action making use of nonracial classifications that correlate with race—for the *de jure* affirmative action that the current Court disfavors. Predictions about the future law of affirmative action can best be made through the time-horored tradition of analyzing how particular justices feel about particular affirmative action issues, and then by counting votes on the Court.

AFFIRMATIVE ACTION VOTING BLOCS

The views of most Supreme Court justices on the issue of affirmative action have been very consistent. Individual justices have tended to vote in affirmative action cases in ways that correlate with their overall political views. Accordingly, conservative justices have typically voted against affirmative action claims, and liberal justices have typically voted in favor of affirmative action. A five-justice conservative voting bloc has formed on the present Court consisting of justices who have almost never voted to uphold an affirmative action plan in a constitutional case. The members of this conservative bloc are Chief Justice Rehnquist, and Justices O'Connor, Scalia, Kennedy, and Thomas. All five members of the conservative bloc voted to uphold the redistricting plan at issue in one case—*Hunt v. Cromartie*—but the plan eliminated rather than created a majority-minority district, and the approval was provisional in that the Court merely held that disputed issues of fact precluded the entry of summary judgment. The five conservative-bloc justices did not indicate how they would vote on the basis of a fuller record developed after discovery and trial. Chief Justice Rehnquist was the only conservative-bloc member to vote in favor of an affirmative action plan in any other case. Of the fifty-eight votes cast by members of this conservative bloc in the sixteen constitutional cases considered by a member of the bloc, only seven votes were cast in favor of any affirmative action program.

Similarly, an initial three-justice liberal voting bloc existed for many years, consisting of justices who had always voted to uphold the affirmative action plans at issue in cases that the Court resolved on constitutional grounds. The members of this liberal bloc were Justices Brennan, Marshall, and Blackmun. Of the twenty-four votes cast by members of this initial liberal bloc in the nine constitutional affirmative action cases considered by a member of the bloc, all twenty-four votes were cast in favor of the affirmative action programs at issue.

The three justices in the initial liberal bloc have now left the Court. All five justices in the conservative bloc, however, are currently serving on the Court. In addition to these five conservative-bloc justices, the four remaining justices sitting on the Supreme Court today are Justices Stevens, Souter,

Ginsburg, and Breyer. These four justices have now come to constitute a new liberal voting bloc on the issue of affirmative action. Of the thirty-eight votes cast by members of the Court's present liberal bloc in the sixteen constitutional affirmative action cases considered by a member of the bloc, only three votes have been cast against the affirmative action programs at issue. All three of these votes were cast by Justice Stevens. The affirmative action votes of Justice Stevens have varied over time, but since 1990, Justice Stevens has always voted to uphold the affirmative action claims in the constitutional cases that he has considered. Accordingly, of the thirty-one votes cast by members of the Court's present liberal bloc in the nine constitutional affirmative action cases that have been decided since 1990, all thirty-one of those votes have been cast in favor of the affirmative action claims at issue. The more consistent voting pattern exhibited by Justice Stevens since 1990 may have come from a desire on the part of Justice Stevens to distance himself from the conservative voting bloc that has emerged on the present Court. In addition to Justice Stevens, the other three justices who make up the present Court's liberal bloc on affirmative action—Justices Souter, Ginsburg, and Breyer—have voted to uphold each affirmative action program that they considered in a constitutional case. Although Justices Stevens and Souter always vote together in constitutional cases, they tend not to sign each other's opinions. In sum, the present Supreme Court contains a solid five-justice conservative majority that has opposed affirmative action on constitutional grounds with an extremely high degree of consistency, and a four-justice liberal minority that has rejected constitutional challenges to affirmative action with an extremely high degree of consistency.

STANDARD OF REVIEW

The issue that has captured most of the Court's attention in its affirmative action cases has been the appropriate standard of review. Because racial affirmative action programs employ race-based classifications to make resource allocation decisions, they are arguably subject to strict judicial scrutiny under *Korematsu v. United States*, which holds that racial classifications are "immediately suspect" and subjects them to "the most rigid scrutiny." The legal test traditionally applied under the strict-scrutiny standard is that, in order to be valid, the racial classification under review must advance a compelling state interest, and must be narrowly tailored or even "necessary" to the advancement of that interest. However, application of this strict-scrutiny test to affirmative action classifications is controversial. To the extent that affirmative action programs are benign rather than invidious in nature—to the extent that they are intended to *promote* rather than undermine equality by neutralizing the effects of prior discrimination—affirmative action classifications should arguably be exempt from the strict scrutiny to which racial classifications that burden racial minorities are subject. The reason that the standard-of-review issue has received so much attention is that the standard-of-review issue may well be dispositive in affirmative action cases. Since the Supreme

Court issued its *Korematsu* decision in 1944, no racial classification has withstood strict scrutiny by the Supreme Court.

The Court began considering the affirmative action issue in 1974, but was unable to achieve majority agreement on an appropriate standard of review until its 1989 decision in *City of Richmond v. J.A. Croson Co.* In an opinion by Justice O'Connor, the Court held that strict scrutiny applied to a municipal affirmative action program that set aside 30% of the municipality's government contracting funds for minority construction contractors. Four justices believed that it was inappropriate to apply strict scrutiny to benign affirmative action programs. Justice O'Connor limited her opinion to state and local affirmative action programs because a 1980 Supreme Court decision in the case of *Fullilove v. Klutznick* had previously upheld the constitutionality of a virtually identical federal set-aside program. Justice O'Connor's Croson opinion distinguished Fullilove on the grounds that Congress possessed special powers under section 5 of the 14th Amendment, that state and local legislatures did not possess, to remedy racial discrimination.

Notwithstanding *Croson*, the Court's 1990 decision in *Metro Broadcasting v. FCC* upheld the constitutionality of two FCC minority preference plans that had been designed to increase broadcast diversity. One plan gave a preference to minority-owned broadcasters in the award of FCC broadcast licenses, and the other plan provided certain tax advantages to marginal licensees who sold their stations to minority-owned broadcasters. *Metro Broadcasting* held that only intermediate scrutiny applied to federal affirmative action programs—or more specifically, to affirmative action plans authorized by Congress in the exercise of its power to remedy discrimination under section 5 of the 14th Amendment. Intermediate scrutiny is typically viewed as requiring that a classification be substantially related to an *important* governmental interest, rather than necessary to advance a *compelling* state interest, as is required under strict scrutiny. Justice Brennan's majority opinion distinguished *Croson* as involving a local rather than a congressional affirmative action program—just as Justice O'Connor's Croson opinion had invoked that factor as a basis for distinguishing *Fullilove*. Realistically, the justices seem simply to have been voting in accordance with their political views about affirmative action. Only Justice White—who has often favored federal regulation under circumstances in which he disfavored analogous state regulation—appears actually to have believed that the distinction between congressional and local affirmative action programs was important. Justice White was one of the swing votes in the *Croson and Metro Broadcasting* cases. The other swing vote was Justice Stevens, who tended to focus on the presence or absence of legislative findings of prospective benefit in determining the validity of an affirmative action plan.

Adarand overruled *Metro Broadcasting* and established a single strict-scrutiny standard of review for all affirmative action programs, whether congressional or local in nature. Justice O'Connor wrote a majority opinion for the present Court's conservative voting bloc—Justices O'Connor, Rehnquist, Scalia, Kennedy, and Thomas—that simply extended the reasoning that Justice O'Connor had adopted in *Croson*. Although this seems at least superficially to have settled the standard-of-review issue, four justices dissented in *Adarand*, arguing that congressional affirmative action plans are entitled to greater deference than local plans. The four dissenters in *Adarand* were the members of the present Court's liberal voting bloc—Justices Stevens, Souter, Ginsburg, and Breyer. Ironically, now that Metro Broadcasting has been overruled, the four dissenters may have *actually* come to believe in the importance of a distinction between federal and local affirmative action programs.

In addition to the fact that four justices dissented from the strict-scrutiny holding of *Adarand*, the *Adarand* decision has left it unclear whether the strict scrutiny that the majority envisions is fatal scrutiny. All nine of the justices who participated in the *Adarand* decision appear formally to view strict scrutiny as permitting some forms of affirmative action. Justice O'Connor's majority opinion—joined by Justices Rehnquist, Scalia, Kennedy, and Thomas—expressly states that strict scrutiny is not "fatal in fact," but is intended merely to insure that affirmative action programs are benign rather than invidious. Justice O'Connor reiterated this point in *Missouri v. Jenkins*, a school desegregation case that was decided the same day as *Adarand*. In addition, Justice Stevens pointed out that the majority purported to adopt the concept of strict scrutiny articulated by Justice Powell in *Regents of the University of California v. Bakke*—a case invalidating a racial preference in a medical school admissions program—which Justice Powell found to have been satisfied in *Fullilove*. Justice Souter believed that the affirmative action program at issue in *Adarand* was adequate to survive the majority's strict scrutiny on remand. Justice Ginsburg believed that strict scrutiny was fatal for invidious racial classifications, but not for benign classifications in affirmative action programs. Justice Breyer joined the dissents of both Justices Souter and Ginsburg.

Although the five justices in the *Adarand* majority signed Justice O'Connor's majority opinion stating that strict scrutiny was not necessarily fatal scrutiny, there is some reason to be skeptical about the degree of commitment that those five justices have to this principle. Justice Scalia seems to have rejected the suggestion that an affirmative action program could ever survive strict scrutiny. He expressly limited the degree to which he was joining the majority opinion by including the unusual proviso that he was willing to "join the opinion of the Court . . . except insofar as it may be inconsistent with" the views expressed in his concurrence. His concurrence goes on to assert that the desire to remedy the effects of past discrimination could never constitute a compelling governmental interest. In addition, Justice Scalia has in the past favored limiting affirmative action to the actual victims of discrimination. This limitation does not seem to recognize the legitimacy of race-based affirmative action at all, but rather applies the "race neutral" principle that the state can compensate the victims of the state's own prior misconduct. Justice Kennedy has also been receptive to the actual-victim limitation, and Chief Justice Rehnquist has endorsed this limitation in Title VII cases. Justice Thomas forcefully asserted in *Adarand* that all racial classifications were immoral, whether invidious or benign, terming affirmative action "racial paternalism." However, in *Missouri v. Jenkins*, which was decided the same day as *Adarand*, Justice Thomas expressed a certain fondness for historically black schools. This might cause him to view strict scrutiny as less than fatal if necessary to permit the voluntary maintenance of historically black schools in black neighborhoods.

It may turn out that after *Adarand*, strict scrutiny will remain "fatal in fact" because a majority of the Court will never find an affirmative action program adequate to meet the strict-scrutiny standards that are theoretically capable of being satisfied. This would be consistent with the history of the Court's equal protection jurisprudence since *Korematsu*, and it would satisfy the draconian pronouncements of Justices Scalia and Thomas. Because the program at issue in *Adarand* is a mild one, ultimately consisting of only a rebuttable presumption that minority contractors are disadvantaged, the fate of *Adarand* on remand may be telling. After remand, the district court entered summary judgment for the plaintiff, holding that the *Adarand* affirmative action plan did not survive strict scrutiny because it was not narrowly tailored. The court of appeals then vacated the district court decision, finding that the case had become moot. Nevertheless, the district court invalidation of the *Adarand* presumption may be an indication that the Supreme Court's *Adarand* holding is indeed sweeping, and that Justice O'Connor is mistaken in her assertion that strict scrutiny will not always be fatal scrutiny.

JUSTIFICATIONS, FINDINGS, AND QUOTAS

If *Adarand* is ultimately interpreted to permit some affirmative action programs to survive strict scrutiny, it remains unclear what justifications for affirmative action the Court will recognize as legitimate. In the past, the Court has distinguished between two types of justifications and has treated them differently. The Court held in *Croson* that when strict scrutiny applies, permissible affirmative action is limited to that which is necessary to remedy particularized acts of past discrimination, and is not available merely to remedy the effects of general societal discrimination that has caused the underrepresentation of racial minorities in particular occupations or social roles. However, in *Metro Broadcasting*, the Court held that the pursuit of prospective diversity was a permissible goal for a congressional affirmative action program. The prospective-diversity justification upheld in *Metro Broadcasting* is very similar to the general-societal-discrimination justification that the Court rejected in *Croson*, in that it de-emphasizes the importance of particularized acts of past discrimination and permits affirmative action addressed to the underrepresentation of minorities in particular aspects of the culture. But, *Metro Broadcasting* was decided under the relatively more tolerant standard of intermediate scrutiny that the Court expressly rejected in *Adarand*.

Closely related to the issue of what goals constitute legitimate justifications for affirmative action is the issue of what findings are required for an affirmative action plan to be valid. If affirmative action is to be limited to the provision of narrow remedies for identifiable acts of prior discrimination, the Court must know both that there were such acts of prior discrimination and how widespread the prior discrimination was in order to ensure that a remedy is sufficiently narrow. The Supreme Court has frequently addressed the need for formal findings of past discrimination, but the actual importance of formal findings is difficult to assess. In *Croson*, the Court relied heavily on both the absence of reliable findings of past discrimination and the absence of narrow tailoring in invalidating the Richmond set-aside plan. Moreover, the *Metro Broadcasting* case stressed the presence of congressional findings in upholding the FCC affirmative action plans at issue in that case. This suggests that the presence or absence of reliable findings may continue to be dispositive. However, the Court was unreceptive to the evidence of extensive congressional deliberations that was before it in *Adarand*, but was quite deferential to the cursory congressional consideration that occurred in *Fullilove*.

Notwithstanding the Court's stated aversion to quotas, the Court has been willing to uphold racial quotas on several occasions. The Court upheld the "distress sale" program in *Metro Broadcasting*, which the dissent characterized as a rigid quota and a 100% set-aside, although the majority rejected that characterization. In addition, the Court upheld quotas in *Paradise, Sheet Metal Workers,* and *Fullilove*. The Court also upheld the percentage targets used as the basis for the reapportionment plan in *United Jewish Organizations*. It may be that *United Jewish Organizations* was tacitly overruled in *Miller*, which reached the opposite result under very similar facts. But whether this seems true or not depends upon how seriously one takes Justice Kennedy's efforts in Miller to distinguish *United Jewish Organizations*. And despite the Court's contrary assurances, the "distress sale" set-aside that the Court upheld in *Metro Broadcasting* appears to have been a quota in every meaningful sense of the term.

The Supreme Court's sometime aversion to quotas is traceable to Justice Powell's opinion in *Regents of the University of California v. Bakke*, where the Court invalidated a 16% minority preference in a medical school admissions program, but nevertheless upheld the use of race as a permissible basis for affirmative action in appropriate cases. Justice Powell opposed rigid quotas but approved of the consideration of race as a factor, favorably citing the Harvard College admissions criteria. Presumably, such opposition to quotas is based upon their mechanistic inflexibility and their potential to generate divisive resentment, both of which may decrease as the consideration of race becomes less visible. Nevertheless, both proponents and targets of affirmative action may well secretly favor quotas because they are administratively convenient. Quotas clearly convey the degree of minority representation that is appropriate in particular circumstances, and they provide a safe harbor from potential liability for racial discrimination. However, quotas also constitute a blatant admission that race is an important social category, thereby belying the aspirational claim that the United States is a color-blind nation. Once again, characterization of an affirmative action program as involving a disfavored quota or a permissible guideline that treats race as a factor is likely to be determined by how a justice otherwise feels about the desirability of the particular affirmative action program at issue.

STIGMAS, STEREOTYPES, AND BURDENS

The question of whether an affirmative action plan stigmatizes or stereotypes either its intended beneficiaries or the innocent whites who are forced to bear the burden of the plan is a question that the Supreme Court discusses in virtually all of its affirmative action decisions. Nevertheless, this too appears to be an issue that is of rhetorical rather than operative importance. The general stigmatization argument is that affirmative action will ultimately backfire: it will brand the intended beneficiaries of an affirmative action plan as inferior because of their inability to compete successfully on the merits; and it will fuel latent racial tensions as innocent whites come to resent having to bear the burdens of affirmative action. A version of this argument was first articulated by Justice Douglas in *DeFunis v. Odegaard,* and then reasserted by Justice Brennan in *United Jewish Organizations v. Carey,* and by Justice Powell in *Bakke.* However, the argument has not been asserted in a case in which it appears to have been dispositive. For example, Justice O'Connor referred to— but the Court did not rely upon—the general stigmatization argument in her opinion invalidating the Richmond set-aside plan in *Croson.* She also unsuccessfully asserted the general stigmatization argument in her dissent from the Court's opinion upholding the FCC plans in *Metro Broadcasting.* Moreover, Justice Stevens—who is sensitive to the stigmatization argument— chose not to accept that argument as a basis for invalidating the preferential teacher layoff plan in *Wygant.* In *Adarand,* Justice O'Connor argued that strict scrutiny was necessary to distinguish legitimate affirmative action programs from illegitimate racial stereotyping, but she did not place any particular stress on the danger of stigmatization. To the extent that stigmatization is deemed to be synonymous with racial stereotyping, the *Metro Broadcasting* Court's acceptance of both the proffered broadcast diversity rationale and the asserted nexus that exists between station ownership and broadcast diversity seems to have constituted acceptance of a relatively high degree of racial stereotyping.

In theory, an affirmative action plan can also be invalidated because of the manner in which it stigmatizes whites. The argument appears to be that, to the extent that affirmative action is used to remedy the effects of past discrimination, affirmative action stigmatize whites by charging them with having engaged in past racial discrimination. Sometimes, the issue of stigmatization or stereotyping that adversely affects whites seems to be conflated with the issue of burden on whites. Again, however, no plan has actually been found invalid because of the imposition of such a stigma. In *United Jewish Organizations,* the reapportionment plan at issue benefited black voters by diluting the voting strength of white Hasidic Jews. Although that plan presented perhaps the strongest case for invalidating an affirmative action plan because of the stigma that it imposed on whites, the Court nevertheless chose to uphold the plan.

The degree of burden that an affirmative action plan places on innocent whites is likely to be a significant factor. The Court almost always discusses the burden imposed on innocent whites by an affirmative action plan that it is reviewing—although the majority opinion in *Croson* curiously did not contain any explicit discussion of the burden imposed on innocent whites. *Metro Broadcasting* upheld a plan that interfered only with the prospective expectations of innocent whites and did not burden whites with any change in the status quo, while *Wygant* invalidated a plan that called for the layoff of white teachers rather than minority teachers with less seniority. In fact, four of the five justices who voted to invalidate the *Wygant* plan focused on the burden that the plan imposed on white teachers. The distinction between frustrated expectations and reduction of the status quo may not ultimately have much meaning. Nevertheless, some justices have treated the distinction as outcome-determinative, and have stressed their opposition to the use of layoffs—as opposed to prospective hiring goals—in affirmative action plans. Among currently sitting justices, Chief Justice Rehnquist has viewed the distinction as dispositive, and Justice O'Connor has endorsed the distinction without endorsing its dispositive character. In addition, the Court's Title VII affirmative action cases indicate that the Court is quite attentive to both the nature and scope of the burden imposed upon innocent whites, including whether the burden is voluntarily assumed or court-imposed.

It is unclear whether the Court will ultimately prove more receptive to voluntary or court-ordered affirmative action plans. The Court's Title VII cases state that, for statutory purposes, voluntary affirmative action plans can be implemented free from restrictions that would apply to court-ordered plans. The issue is most likely to be relevant with respect to the burden borne by innocent whites. If a burden has been voluntarily assumed, it may be acceptable without evidence of prior discrimination or narrow tailoring even though a court could not have imposed that burden as part of a remedial order in the absence of such a voluntary assumption.

The voluntary affirmative action issue is directly related to the often-imposed requirement that the affirmative action plan be justifiable as a remedy for past discrimination. If it turns out that acceptable affirmative action in particular contexts is limited to plans that seek to remedy the effects of past discrimination, evidence of past discrimination may be required before voluntary affirmative action is permitted. This view was rejected by the Court in *United Steelworkers of America v. Weber*, which permitted voluntary affirmative action plans even in the absence of a showing of prior unlawful discrimination. Nevertheless, the holding of *Weber* is rather fragile. Four justices—Justices Rehnquist, White, O'Connor, and Scalia—have expressed the view that *Weber* was incorrectly decided, and that voluntary affirmative action should not be permitted in the absence of grounds for court-ordered affirmative action. In addition, Justices Kennedy and Thomas, who were not on the Court when *Weber* was decided, have almost never voted in favor of an affirmative action program. This creates a five-justice majority—consisting of Justices Rehnquist, O'Connor, Scalia, Kennedy, and Thomas—who may be willing to disallow the voluntary affirmative action that the Supreme Court authorized in *Weber*. Moreover, these conservative-bloc justices are the same five justices who comprised the majority in *Adarand*, and their willingness to overrule *Metro Broadcasting* indicates that they may also be willing to overrule *Weber*.

It may be that *Adarand* itself renders unconstitutional any reading of Title VII that does not insist on demonstrable prior discrimination as a prerequisite to voluntary affirmative action. The financial incentive at issue in *Adarand* encouraged private parties to consider race in the selection of subcontractors. If such official encouragement of private race consciousness in the absence of a demonstrated need to remedy prior discrimination violates the equal protection clause in the *Adarand* bidding context, it may be that the similar official encouragement to engage in race-conscious employment decisions in order to avoid a potential Title VII violation would also violate the equal protection clause—at least in the absence of a showing that such race consciousness was a narrowly tailored remedy for past discrimination. This is an issue that the Supreme Court did not address in *Weber*. In addition, to the extent that *Weber* was rooted in the belief that affirmative action is subject to less demanding scrutiny because of its benign nature, *Weber* seems to be in direct conflict with the *Adarand* holding that the benign nature of affirmative action does not provide immunity from strict scrutiny.

Finally, it is interesting to note that the Court first flirted with and then rejected the notion that no race-conscious burden could *ever* be imposed upon innocent whites unless necessary to provide a remedy to an actual victim of discrimination. An actual-victim limitation would constitute a rejection of the concept of affirmative action. It would rely solely on tort-type remedies to compensate victims of discrimination, without any effort to overcome the limitations of the tort system in dealing with widespread undifferentiated injuries. Nevertheless, the current Court appears to contain at least two justices who approve of the actual-victim limitation—Justices Rehnquist and Scalia. In addition, up to three other justices—Justices O'Connor, Kennedy, and Thomas—may come to adopt the actual-victim view, as evidenced by the fact that they almost always vote against affirmative action.

The California Civil Rights Initiative of 1996, or Proposition 209, served as a lightning rod for the debate over affirmative action. It prohibits "government instrumentalities" from "discriminating against" or "granting preferential treatment to" people on the basis of race, sex, color, ethnicity, or national origin. The proposition does not prohibit compliance with federal affirmative actions laws nor does it prohibit compliance with guidelines that would prevent the state from receiving money from federal government. The following selection is taken from the **"California Ballot Pamphlet"** *published by the Secretary of State before the 1996 elections. The goal of the Pamphlet is to provide voters with an analysis of the proposal by the state's Legislative Analyst, as well as arguments for and against the ballot measure. For example, the Legislative Analyst calls attention to the fiscal impact of the proposal noting that the elimination of state affirmative action plans would "result in savings to state and local governments." The Analyst's summary also spells out the impact of the proposition on voluntary school desegregation programs as well as university admissions.*

CALIFORNIA BALLOT PAMPHLET, PROPOSITION 209

■

*Prohibition Against Discrimination or Preferential Treatment
by State and Other Public Entities. Initiative Constitutional Amendment*

OFFICIAL TITLE AND SUMMARY PREPARED BY THE ATTORNEY GENERAL

- Prohibits the state, local governments, districts, public universities, colleges, and schools, and other government instrumentalities from discriminating against or giving preferential treatment to any individual or group in public employment, public education, or public contracting on the basis of race, sex, color, ethnicity, or national origin.

- Does not prohibit reasonably necessary, bona fide qualifications based on sex and actions necessary for receipt of federal funds.

- Mandates enforcement to extent permitted by federal law.

- Requires uniform remedies for violations. Provides for severability of provisions if invalid.

SUMMARY OF LEGISLATIVE ANALYST'S ESTIMATE OF NET STATE AND LOCAL GOVERNMENT FISCAL IMPACT:

- The measure could affect state and local programs that currently cost well in excess of $125 million annually.

- Actual savings to the state and local governments would depend on various factors (such as future court decisions and implementation actions by government entities).

ANALYSIS BY THE LEGISLATIVE ANALYST

BACKGROUND

The federal, state, and local governments run many programs intended to increase opportunities for various groups—including women and racial and ethnic minority groups. These programs are commonly called "affirmative action" programs. For example, state law identifies specific goals for the participation of women-owned and minority-owned companies on work involved with state contracts. State departments are expected, but not required, to meet these goals, which include that at least 15% of the value of contract work should be done by minority-owned companies and at least 5% should be done by women-owned companies. The law requires departments, however, to reject bids from companies that have not made sufficient "good faith efforts" to meet these goals.

Other examples of affirmative action programs include:

- Public college and university programs such as scholarship, tutoring, and outreach that are targeted toward minority or women students.
- Goals and timetables to encourage the hiring of members of "under-represented" groups for state government jobs.
- State and local programs required by the federal government as a condition of receiving federal funds (such as requirements for minority-owned business participation in state highway construction projects funded in part with federal money).

Proposal

This measure would eliminate state and local government affirmative action programs in the areas of public employment, public education, and public contracting to the extent these programs involve "preferential treatment" based on race, sex, color, ethnicity, or national origin. The specific programs affected by the measure, however, would depend on such factors as (1) court rulings on what types of activities are considered "preferential treatment" and (2) whether federal law requires the continuation of certain programs.

The measure provides exceptions to the ban on preferential treatment when necessary for any of the following reasons:

- To keep the state or local governments eligible to receive money from the federal government.
- To comply with a court order in force as of the effective date of this measure (the day after the election).
- To comply with federal law or the United States Constitution.
- To meet privacy and other considerations based on sex that are reasonably necessary to the normal operation of public employment, public education, or public contracting.

Fiscal Effect

If this measure is approved by the voters, it could affect a variety of state and local programs. These are discussed in more detail below.

PUBLIC EMPLOYMENT AND CONTRACTING. The measure would eliminate affirmative action programs used to increase hiring and promotion opportunities for state or local government jobs, where sex, race, or ethnicity are preferential factors in hiring, promotion, training, or recruitment decisions. In addition, the measure would eliminate programs that give preference to women-owned or minority-owned companies on public contracts. Contracts affected by the measure would include contracts for construction projects, purchases of computer equipment, and the hiring of consultants. These pro-hibitions would not apply to those government agencies that receive money under federal programs that require such affirmative action.

The elimination of these programs would result in savings to the state and local governments. These savings would occur for two reasons. First, gov-ernment agencies no longer would incur costs to administer the programs. Second, the prices paid on some government contracts would decrease. This would happen because bidders on contracts no longer would need to show "good faith efforts" to use minority-owned or women-owned subcontractors. Thus, state and local governments would save money to the extent they oth-erwise would have rejected a low bidder—because the bidder did not make a "good faith effort"—and awarded the contract to a higher bidder.

Based on available information, we estimate that the measure would result in savings in employment and contracting programs that could total tens of millions of dollars each year.

PUBLIC SCHOOLS AND COMMUNITY COLLEGES. The measure also could affect funding for public schools (kindergarten through grade 12) and community college programs. For instance, the measure could eliminate, or cause funda-mental changes to, *voluntary* desegregation programs run by school districts. (It would not, however, affect *court-ordered* desegregation programs.) Exam-ples of desegregation spending that could be affected by the measure include the special funding given to (1) "magnet" schools (in those cases where race or ethnicity are preferential factors in the admission of students to the schools) and (2) designated "racially isolated minority schools" that are lo-cated in areas with high proportions of racial or ethnic minorities. We esti-mate that up to $60 million of state and local funds spent each year on voluntary desegregation programs may be affected by the measure.

In addition, the measure would affect a variety of public school and com-munity college programs such as counseling, tutoring, outreach, student fi-nancial aid, and financial aid to selected school districts in those cases where the programs provide preferences to individuals or schools based on race, sex, ethnicity, or national origin. Funds spent on these programs total at least $15 million each year.

Thus, the measure could affect up to $75 million in state spending in pub-lic schools and community colleges.

The State Constitution requires the state to spend a certain amount each year on public schools and community colleges. As a result, under most situ-ations, the Constitution would require that funds that cannot be spent on programs because of this measure instead would have to be spent for *other* public school and community college programs.

UNIVERSITY OF CALIFORNIA AND CALIFORNIA STATE UNIVERSITY. The meas-ure would affect admissions and other programs at the state's public univer-sities. For example, the California State University (CSU) uses race and ethnicity as factors in some of its admissions decisions. If this initiative is passed by the voters, it could no longer do so. In 1995, the Regents of the University of California (UC) changed the UC's admissions policies, effective for the 1997–98 academic year, to eliminate all consideration of race or ethnicity. Passage of this initiative by the voters might require the UC to implement its new admissions policies somewhat sooner.

Both university systems also run a variety of assistance programs for students, faculty, and staff that are targeted to individuals based on sex, race, or ethnicity. These include programs such as outreach, counseling, tutoring, and financial aid. The two systems spend over $50 million each year on programs that probably would be affected by passage of this measure.

SUMMARY. As described above, this measure could affect state and local programs that currently cost well in excess of $125 million annually. The actual amount of this spending that might be saved as a result of this measure could be considerably less, for various reasons:

- The amount of spending affected by this measure could be less depending on (1) court rulings on what types of activities are considered "preferential treatment" and (2) whether federal law requires continuation of certain programs.

- In most cases, any funds that could not be spent for existing programs in public schools and community colleges would have to be spent on other programs in the schools and colleges.

- In addition, the amount affected as a result of *this* measure would be less if any existing affirmative action programs were declared unconstitutional under the United States Constitution. For example, five state affirmative action programs are currently the subject of a lawsuit. If any of these programs are found to be unlawful, then the state could no longer spend money on them—regardless of whether this measure is in effect.

- Finally, some programs we have identified as being affected might be changed to use factors other than those prohibited by the measure. For example, a high school outreach program operated by the UC or the CSU that currently uses a factor such as ethnicity to target spending could be changed to target instead high schools with low percentages of UC or CSU applications.

PROHIBITION AGAINST DISCRIMINATION OR PREFERENTIAL TREATMENT BY STATE AND OTHER PUBLIC ENTITIES. INITIATIVE CONSTITUTIONAL AMENDMENT.

ARGUMENT IN FAVOR OF PROPOSITION 209

THE RIGHT THING TO DO! A generation age, we did it right. We passed civil rights laws to prohibit discrimination. But special interests hijacked the civil rights movement. Instead of equality, governments imposed quotas, preferences, and set-asides.

Proposition 209 is called the California Civil Rights Initiative because it restates the historic Civil Rights Act and proclaims simply and clearly: "The state shall not discriminate against, or grant preferential treatment to, any individual or group, on the basis of race, sex, color, ethnicity or national origin in the operation of public employment, public education, or public contracting."

"REVERSE DISCRIMINATION" BASED ON RACE OR GENDER IS PLAIN WRONG! And two wrongs don't make a right! Today, students are being rejected from public universities because of their RACE. Job applicants are turned away because their RACE does not meet some "goal" or "timetable." Contracts are awarded to high bidders because they are of the preferred RACE.

That's just plain wrong and unjust. Government should not discriminate. It must not give a job, a university admission, or a contract based on race or sex. Government must judge all people equally, without discrimination!

And, remember, Proposition 209 keeps in place all federal and state protections against discrimination!

BRING US TOGETHER! Government cannot work against discrimination if government itself discriminates. Proposition 209 will stop the terrible programs which are dividing our people and tearing us apart. People naturally feel resentment when the less qualified are preferred. We are all Americans. It's time to bring us together under a single standard of equal treatment under the law.

STOP THE GIVEAWAYS! Discrimination is costly in other ways. Government agencies throughout California spend millions of your tax dollars for costly bureaucracies to administer racial and gender discrimination that masquerade as "affirmative action." They waste much more of your money awarding high-bid contracts and sweetheart deals based not on the low bid, but on unfair set-asides and preferences. This money could be used for police and fire protection, better education and other programs—for everyone.

THE BETTER CHOICE: HELP ONLY THOSE WHO NEED HELP! We are individuals! Not every white person is advantaged. And not every "minority" is disadvantaged. Real "affirmative action" originally meant no discrimination and sought to provide opportunity. That's why Proposition 209 prohibits discrimination and preferences and allows any program that does not discriminate, or prefer, because of race or sex, to continue.

The only honest and effective way to address inequality of opportunity is by making sure that *all* California children are provided with the tools to compete in our society. And then let them succeed on a fair, color-blind, race-blind, gender-blind basis.

Let's not perpetuate the myth that "minorities" and women cannot compete without special preferences. Let's instead move forward by returning to the fundamentals of our democracy: individual achievement, equal opportunity and *zero tolerance for discrimination against—or for—any individual.*

Vote for FAIRNESS . . . not favoritism!

Reject preferences by voting YES on Proposition 209.

PETE WILSON
Governor, State of California
WARD CONNERLY
Chairman, California Civil Rights Initiative
PAMELA A. LEWIS
Co-Chair, California Civil Rights Initiative

REBUTTAL TO ARGUMENT IN FAVOR OF PROPOSITION 209

THE WRONG THING TO DO! A generation ago, Rosa Parks launched the Civil Rights movement, which opened the door to equal opportunity for women and minorities in this country. Parks is against this deceptive initiative. Proposition 209 highjacks civil rights language and uses legal lingo to gut protections against discrimination.

Proposition 209 says it eliminates quotas, but in fact, the U.S. Supreme Court already decided—twice—that they are illegal. Proposition 209's real purpose is to eliminate affirmative action equal opportunity programs for qualified women and minorities including tutoring, outreach, and mentoring.

PROPOSITION 209 PERMITS DISCRIMINATION AGAINST WOMEN. 209 changes the California Constitution to permit state and local governments to discriminate against women, excluding them from job categories.

STOP THE POLITICS OF DIVISION. Newt Gingrich, Pete Wilson, and Pat Buchanan support 209. Why? They are playing the politics of division for their own political gain. We should not allow their ambitions to sacrifice equal opportunity for political opportunism.

209 MEANS OPPORTUNITY BASED SOLELY ON FAVORITISM. Ward Connerly has already used his influence to get children of his rich and powerful friends into the University of California. 209 reinforces the "who you know" system that favors cronies of the powerful.

"There are those who say, we can stop now, America is a color-blind society. But it isn't yet, there are those who say we have a level playing field, but we don't yet." Retired General Colin Powell [5/25/96].

VOTE NO ON 209!!!

PREMA MATHAI-DAVIS
National Executive Director, YWCA of the U.S.A.
KAREN MANELIS
*President, California American Association
of University Women*
WADE HENDERSON
Executive Director, Leadership Conference on Civil Rights

ARGUMENT AGAINST PROPOSITION 209

VOTE NO ON PROPOSITION 209

HARMS EQUAL OPPORTUNITY FOR WOMEN AND MINORITIES. California law currently allows tutoring, mentoring, outreach, recruitment, and counseling to help ensure equal opportunity for women and minorities. Proposition 209 will eliminate affirmative action programs like these that help achieve equal opportunity for women and minorities in public employment, education and contracting. Instead of reforming affirmative action to make it fair for everyone, Proposition 209 makes the current problems worse.

PROPOSITION 209 GOES TOO FAR. The initiative's language is so broad and misleading that it eliminates equal opportunity programs including:

- tutoring and mentoring for minority and women students;
- affirmative action that encourages the hiring and promotion of qualified women and minorities;
- outreach and recruitment programs to encourage applicants for government jobs and contracts; and
- programs designed to encourage girls to study and pursue careers in math and science.

The independent, non-partisan California Legislative Analyst gave the following report on the effects of Proposition 209:

> "[T]he measure would eliminate a variety of public school (kindergarten through grade 12) and community college programs such as counseling, tutoring, student financial aid, and financial aid to selected school districts, where these programs are targeted based on race, sex, ethnicity or national origin." [*Opinion Letter to the Attorney General*, 10/15/95].

PROPOSITION 209 CREATES A LOOPHOLE THAT ALLOWS DISCRIMINATION AGAINST WOMEN. Currently, California women have one of the strongest state constitutional protections against sex discrimination in the country. Now it is difficult for state and local government to discriminate against women in public employment, education, and the awarding of state contracts because of their gender.

Proposition 209's loophole will undo this vital state constitutional protection.

PROPOSITION 209 LOOPHOLE PERMITS STATE GOVERNMENT TO DENY WOMEN OPPORTUNITIES IN PUBLIC EMPLOYMENT, EDUCATION, AND CONTRACTING, SOLELY BASED ON THEIR GENDER. PROPOSITION 209 CREATES MORE DIVISION IN OUR COMMUNITIES. It is time to put an end to politicians trying to divide our communities for their own political gain. "The initiative is a misguided effort that takes California down the road of division. Whether intentional or not, it pits communities against communities and individuals against each other."

Reverend Kathy Cooper-Ledesma
President, California Council of Churches.

GENERAL COLIN POWELL'S POSITION ON PROPOSITION 209: "Efforts such as the California Civil Rights Initiative which poses as an equal opportunities initiative, but which puts at risk every outreach program, sets back the gains made by women and puts the brakes on expanding opportunities for people in need."

Retired General Colin Powell, 5/25/96.

GENERAL COLIN POWELL IS RIGHT.
VOTE "NO" ON PROPOSITION 209—EQUAL OPPORTUNITY MATTERS
FRAN PACKARD
President, League of Women Voters of California
ROSA PARKS
Civil Rights Leader
MAXINE BLACKWELL
Vice President, Congress of California Seniors,
Affiliate of the National Council of Senior Citizens

REBUTTAL TO ARGUMENT AGAINST PROPOSITION 209

Don't let them change the subject. Proposition 209 bans discrimination and preferential treatment—period. Affirmative action programs that don't discriminate or grant preferential treatment will be UNCHANGED. Programs designed to ensure that all persons—regardless of race or gender—are informed of opportunities and treated with equal dignity and respect will continue as before.

Note that Proposition 209 doesn't prohibit consideration of economic disadvantage. Under the existing racial-preference system, a wealthy doctor's son may receive a preference for college admission over a dishwasher's daughter simply because he's from an "underrepresented" race. THAT'S UNJUST. The state must remain free to help the economically disadvantaged, but not on the basis of race or sex.

Opponents mislead when they claim that Proposition 209 will legalize sex discrimination. Distinguished legal scholars, liberals and conservatives, have rejected that argument as ERRONEOUS. Proposition 209 adds NEW PROTECTION against sex discrimination on top of existing ones, which remain in full force and effect. It does NOTHING to any existing constitutional provisions.

Clause c is in the text for good reason. It uses the legally-tested language of original 1964 Civil Rights Act in allowing sex to be considered only if it's a "bona fide" qualification. Without that narrow exception, Proposition 209 would require unisex bathrooms and the hiring of prison guards who strip-search inmates without regard to sex. Anyone opposed to Proposition 209 is opposed to the 1964 Civil Rights Act.

Join the millions of voters who support Proposition 209. Vote YES.

DANIEL E. LUNGREN
Attorney General, State of California
QUENTIN L. KOPP
State Senator
GAIL L. HERIOT
Professor of Law

The impact of Proposition 209 is a matter of some disagreement. Critics maintain that one significant result is the significant decline of African-American and Latino students to the elite campuses of the University of California system.[33] Others contend that Proposition 209 has not hurt minority student's chances for university admission but has actually enhanced the status of minority students on campus.[34] A third perspective concludes that the results of Proposition 209 are decidedly mixed due to ambiguity in recent court interpretations of the amendment.[35] In short, affirmative action policy is at a crossroads.

STUDY QUESTIONS

1. What are the competing theories about the persistence of black poverty? Have social welfare policies such as AFDC failed to ameliorate black poverty (and indeed, made matters worse) or is the answer found in the structure of the American political economy? What are the main assumptions of movement to reform welfare? How should one understand welfare reform in the context of the theoretical models? How has the media influenced the public's perception of the nexus between race, poverty, and welfare?

2. What causes crime? Why is violent crime concentrated in inner-city neighborhoods? In other words, to what extent is crime directly, or indirectly, related to race? Do you favor punishment or rehabilitation as the appropriate policy response to the crime problem? Has the media influenced the public debate about crime policy?

3. What factors gave rise to affirmative action as a major focus of the policy agenda in the United States? What accounts for the change from policies based on wide-spread racial remedies in the 1960s and 1970s, to one that more narrowly delineates the conditions under which race-based policies are acceptable? How does the federal nature of the U.S. government effect the design and application of affirmative action policy? Do you support measures such as California's Proposition 209? Why? Why not?

NOTES

1. See, for instance, Richard F. America, "Reparations and Public Policy," *Review of Black Political Economy* 26, 3 (Winter, 1999):77; Cedric Herring (ed.) *African-Americans and the*

public agenda: The paradoxes of Public Policy. (New York: Russell Sage) 1997; James Jennings (ed.) *Race, politics, and economic development.* (London: Verso Press) 1992; Glenn C. Loury, "Color-blinded" *New Republic* 219, 7–8 (August 17, 1998): 12; Paula D. McClain (ed.) *Minority group influence: agenda setting, formulation, and public policy* (Westport, Conn.: Greenwood Press) 1993; Mitchell F. Rice and Woodrow Jones, Jr. (eds.) *Contemporary public policy perspectives and black Americans: Issues in an era of retrenchment* (Westport, Conn.: Greenwood Press) 1984; Paul R. Sniderman and Edward G. Carmines. *Reaching beyond race.* (Cambridge: Harvard University Press) 1997.

2. See, John W. Kingdon, "How do issues get on public policy agendas," in W.J. Wilson. (ed.) *Sociology and the Public Agenda.* (Russell Sage: Newbury Park).

3. This discussion draws on John W. Kingdon. *Agendas, alternatives, and public policies.* (Boston: Little, Brown) 1984.

4. The Clinton record on racial policy is rather mixed. On the one hand, the president has appointed African-Americans to high offices, commissioned a blue-ribbon panel on race, and perhaps been more connected to the black community than any other American president. On the other, he has failed to support some of his black appointees, has supported a generally punitive crime and social welfare agenda, and has not followed through on the race initiative.

5. James Q. Wilson, *Thinking about crime.* (New York: Vintage Books) 1984.

6. Jon Hurwitz and Mark Peffley. "Public perceptions of crime and race: The role of racial stereotypes," *American Journal of Political Science.* 4 (1997): 375–401; Stuart Scheingold, "Politics, public policy, and street crime." *Annals of the American Academy of Political and Social Science.* 539 (1995): 155–68.

7. George Stephanopoulos and Christopher Edley, Jr. *Affirmative action review: Report to the President.* (Washington, D.C.: Executive Office of the President) 1995.

8. Dona Cooper Hamilton and Charles V. Hamilton. *The dual agenda: Race and social welfare policies of civil rights organizations.* (New York: Columbia University Press) 1997.

9. Michael B Katz. "Race, poverty, and welfare: Du Bois's legacy for policy." *Annals of the American Academy of Political and Social Science* 568 (March, 2000):111; Alex Waddan. *The politics of social welfare.* (Cheltenham, UK: Edward Elgar) 1997.

10. Martin Gilens. "How the poor became black: the racialization of American poverty in the mass media."

11. Elise Cose, *Race of a Privileged Class.* (New York: Harper, Row) 1993; Melvin L. Oliver and Thomas Shapiro, *Black Wealth, White Wealth: a New Perspective on Racial Inequality.* (New York: Routledge) 1995.

12. In addition, the Joint Center data on poverty indicate that black (and Hispanic) children are more than twice as likely to be poor than are white children.

13. See, for example, Sheldon Danziger and Peter Gottschalk (eds.) *Uneven tides: Rising inequality in America* (New York: Russell Sage Foundation) 1993; Neil Gilbert, "The size and influence of the underclass: An exaggerated view. *Society* 37,1 Nov, 1999:42, Christopher Jencks and Paul E. Peterson (eds.) *The urban underclass.* (Washington, D.C.: Brookings) 1991; John D. Kasarda, "Urban industrial transition and the underclass," *Annals of the American Academy of Political and Social Science* 501 (1990): 26–47; Charles Murray, "And now for the bad news: the underclass *Society* 37,1 (Nov, 1999):13; William J. Wilson. *The truly disadvantaged: the inner city, the underclass, and public policy* (Chicago: University of Chicago Press) 1987.

14. The concentration of black poverty in "ghetto" areas has led scholars to study the impact of residential segregation on black economic fortunes. This school of thought is perhaps best represented in Massey and Denton's book *American Apartheid.* Their core

claim is that "[T]he coincidence of rising poverty and high levels of segregation guarantees that blacks will be exposed to a social and economic environment that is far harsher than anything experienced by any other racial or ethnic group." As the authors demonstrate, exogenous economic shocks (e.g., economic restructuring, and globalization) to urban black communities trigger a "spiral of neighborhood decline." An increase in the number of dilapidated buildings, for instance, is quickly followed by a process of social disorganization marked by violent crime, drug use, and a general ". . . isolation from the mainstream of American society." Thus, when a geographically segregated group experiences relatively high rates of poverty, the impact is concentrated in a unique and detrimental fashion.

15. See, for example, Irving Kristol, "American conservatism 1945–1995," *Public Interest* 121 Fall 1995:80–92.

16. David Zucchino. *The myth of the welfare queen*. (New York: Simon and Schuster) 1997

17. Martin Gilens. ""Race Coding" and white opposition to welfare. "*American Political Science Review* 90,3 (1996): 593 and "Racial attitudes and opposition to welfare." *Journal of Politics* (1995): 994.

18. See, for example, *TANF Annual Report to Congress, 1997* (www.acf.dhhs.gov/new/welfare).

19. Children's Defense Fund. *Welfare to what? Early findings on family hardship and well-being* (www.childrensdefense.org/fairstart_welfare2what.html) December 1998.

20. See, www.gallup.com/poll

21. There is a growing literature that suggests the persistent of racial stereotypes is related to media images of African-Americans. See, Robert Entman and Andrew Rojecki. The black image in the white mind: Media and race in America. (Chicago: University of Chicago Press) 2000; Franklin D. Gilliam, Jr and Shanto Iyengar. "Prime Suspects: The Influence of Local Television News on the Viewing Public," *American Journal of Political Science* 44,3 (July 2000): 560; Franklin D. Gilliam, Jr., Shanto Iyengar, Adam Simon and Oliver Wright. "Crime in black and white: The violent, scary world of local news," *Harvard International Journal of Press/Politics* 1 (1996): 6; Darnel Hunt. *Screening the Los Angeles "Riots": Race, seeing, and resistance*. (New York: Cambridge University Press) 1997; Mark Peffley, Todd Shields and Brian Williams. "The intersection of race and crime in television news stories: An experimental study," *Political Communication* 13 (1996): 309–328.

22. Mark Peffley and Jon Hurwitz. "Whites' stereotypes of blacks: Sources and consequences." In Jon Hurwitz and Mark Peffley (eds.) *Perception and prejudice*. (New Haven: Yale University press) 1998.

23. For research on race, crime, and gender see, Kimberle Williams Crenshaw. "Mapping the margins: intersectionality, identity politics, and violence against women of color." *Stanford Law Review* 43, 6 (July, 1991): 1241; Enid Logan. "The wrong race, committing crime, doing drugs, and maladjusted for motherhood: the nation's fury over "crack babies." *Social Justice* 26,1 (Spring, 1999): 115

24. See, for example, Franklin D., Gilliam, Jr. "Race, crime, and public policy in California," in Michael B. Preston and Bruce Cain (eds.) *Racial and ethnic politics in California*. (Berkeley: IGS Press) 1998; Coramae Richey Mann, *Unequal justice: A question of color* (Bloomington, IN: Indiana University Press) 1993; ; Jerome G. Miller. *Search and destroy : African-American males in the criminal justice system*. (New York: Cambridge University Press) 1996; The Urban League. *The State of Black America 1999* (New York: Urban League) 1999.

25. See, for instance, Samuel R. Gross and Robert Mauro. *Death and discrimination: Racial disparities in capital sentencing* (Boston, MA: Northeastern University Press) 1989; NAACP, *Beyond The Rodney King Story: An Investigation of Police Conduct in Minority Communities* (Boston, MA: Northeastern University Press) 1995; Katheryn K. Russell.

The color of crime: Racial hoaxes, white fear, black protectionism, police harassment, and other macroaggressions (New York: New York University Press) 1997; David A. Sklansky. "Traffic stops, minority motorists, and the future of the Fourth Amendment." *Supreme Court Review* (1997): 271.

26. See, Robert J. Bursik, Jr. and Harold G. Grasmik. "Economic deprivation and neighborhood crime rates, 1960–1980." *Law & Society Review* 27, 2 (May, 1993):263; Lance Hannon and James Defronzo. "The truly disadvantaged, public assistance, and crime." *Social Problems* 45, 3 (August, 1998): 383; Gary LaFree, Kriss A. Drass, and Patrick O'Day. "Race and crime in postwar America: Determinants of African-American and white rates, 1957–1988." *Criminology* 30 (1992): 157; James F. Short Jr. 1997. *Poverty, ethnicity, and violent crime.* (Boulder, Colo.: Westview Press) 1997; William J. Stuntz. "Race, class, and drugs." *Columbia Law Review* 98, 7 (Nov, 1998): 1794.

27. See, Patrick A. Langan. "No racism in the justice system." *Public Interest.* (Fall 1994): 51; Randall Kennedy. *Race, crime, and the law.* (New York: Pantheon Books) 1997; Ralph Slovenko "Criminals by choice." *International Journal of Offender Therapy & Comparative Criminology* 43, 2 (June, 1999): 248; James Q. Wilson. *Thinking about crime.* (New York: Vintage Books) 1984; James Q. Wilson and Richard J. Hernstein. *Crime and human nature.* (New York: Simon and Schuster) 1985.

28. The following is just a sampling of the voluminous literature on affirmative action: William G Bowen and Derek Bok. *The shape of the river : long-term consequences of considering race in college and university admissions.* (Princeton, N.J.: Princeton University Press) 1998; Kimberle Crenshaw. "Playing race cards: constructing a proactive defense of affirmative action." *National Black Law Journal* 16, 2 (Spring, 1998): 196; Luke Charles Harris and Uma Narayan. "Affirmative action as equalizing opportunity: challenging the myth of "preferential treatment." *National Black Law Journal* 16,2 (Spring, 1998): 127; Albert G. Mosley and Nicholas Capaldi, *Affirmative action: Social justice or unfair preference?* (Lanham, MD: Rowmann & Littlefield) 1996; Sunita Parikh. *The politics of preference democratic institutions and affirmative action in the United States and India* (Ann Arbor: University of Michigan Press) 1997; Abigail M. Thernstrom. *Whose votes count? : affirmative action and minority voting rights* (Cambridge, Mass. : Harvard University Press) 1987; Richard F. Tomasson, Faye J. Crosby, and Sharon D. Herzberger. *Affirmative action: the pros and cons of policy and practice* (Lanham, Md.: American University Press) 1996.

29. Michael Rosenfeld. *Affirmative action and justice: a philosophical and constitutional inquiry.* (New Haven: Yale University Press).

30. The Plan actually covered employment in several cities. Its genesis was based on Executive Order 11246 (the establishment of OFCC) and the controlling federal statute—Title VII of the 1964 Civil Rights Act. See, James E. Jones, Jr. "The bugaboo of employment quotas." *Wisconsin Law Review* (1970): 41–403; and "The genesis and present status of affirmative action in employment: economic, legal and political realities." *University of Iowa Law Review* 70 (1985):901.

31. Dean J Kotlowski,."Richard Nixon and the origins of affirmative action. *Historian* 60, 3 (Spring, 1998): 523.

32. Girardeau A. Spann. *The law of affirmative action: twenty-five years of Supreme Court decisions on race and remedies* (New York: New York University Press) 2000.

33. See, for example, Gregory Rodriguez, and Ronald Takaki. "California's big squeeze." *Nation* 267, 10 (Oct 5, 1998): 21.

34. See, for example, Martin Trow. "California after racial preferences." *Public Interest* 135 (Spring, 1999): 64.

35. For instance, see Lance T. Izumi. "Judging preferences: Proposition 209's implementation is hindered by state judge's decision." *California Journal* 30, 1 (Jan. 1999): 42.

CITATIONS

Part One: The Political History of Race
Chapter 1: The Pre-Civil War Period: 1787–1862

1. *The Constitution of the United States: Article I section 3, Article II section 9, Article IV section 2.*
2. John Hope Franklin, and Moss, Alfred A. Jr. *From Slavery to Freedom*. New York: Knopf (1968).
3. *Dred Scott v. Sanford 393 US. 60 (1856).*

Chapter 2: The Civil War, Reconstruction, and Jim Crow (1863–1953)

4. *The Emancipation Proclamation (1863).*
5. *The Constitution of the United States: 13th Amendment (1865) 14th Amendment (1868) 15th Amendment (1870).*
6. Eric Foner. *Reconstruction: America's Unfinished Revolution, 1863–1877.* New York: Harper and Row (1988).
7. *Plessy v. Ferguson 163 US. 537 (1896).*
8. I. A. Newby, *Jim Crow's Defense*. Baton Rouge: Louisiana State University (1965).

Part Two: The Civil Rights Movement
Chapter 3: Legalism (1950–1958)

9. *Sweatt v. Painter et al, 339 US. 629 (1950).*
10. *Brown v. Board of Education of Topeka 503 US. 978 (1954).*
11. *Bolling et al v. Sharpe et al. 347 US. 497 (1954).*
12. *Brown v. Board of Education of Topeka 349 US. 294 (1955).*
13. *Cooper v. Aaron 358 US. 1 (1958).*

Chapter 4: Nonviolent Direct Action (1955–1965)

14. Taylor Branch, "First Trombone," *Brooking Review* 17(2) (Spring 1999).
15. Aldon Morris. *The Origins of the Modern Civil Rights Movement*. New York: Free Press (1984).

16. Malcolm X. *Malcolm X Speaks: Selected Speeches*. George Breitman (ed.) New York: Grove Weidenfeld (1990).
17. Harvard Sitkoff. *The Struggle for Black Equality*. New York: Hill and Wang (1981).
18. Martin Luther King, Jr. "Letter from a Birmingham Jail [1963]" in *Why We Can't Wait*. New York: Harper Collins (1964).
19. *Martin Luther King Jr., "I Have a Dream" (1963).*
20. *Civil Rights Act, P.L. 88–352 (1964).*
21. *Voting Rights Act, P.L. 89–110 (1965).*

Chapter 5: Black Power (1961–1972)

22. *McCone Commission Report on the Los Angeles Riots (1965).*
23. *Student Nonviolent Coordinating Committee, "The Basis of Black Power" (1965).*
24. *The Black Panther Party Platform (1966)* G. Louis. Heath (ed.) The Scarecrow Press, Inc: Lanham, Maryland (1976).
25. David Hilliard and Lewis Cole. *This Side of Glory: The Autobiography of David Hilliard and the Story of the Black Panther Party*. Boston: Little Brown (1993).
26. Elaine Brown. *A Taste of Power: A Black Woman's Story*. New York: Pantheon (1992).

Part Three: The Contemporary Consequences of the Struggle for African-American Liberation
Chapter 6: Whither Racism?

27. Donald R. Kinder and Lynn M. Sanders. *Divided by Color: Racial Politics and Democratic Ideals*. Chicago: University of Chicago Press (1996).
28. Jody David Armour. *Negrophobia and Reasonable Racism: The Hidden Costs of Being Black in America*. New York: New York University Press (1997).

29. Ellis Cose. *Color Blind: Seeing Beyond Race in a Race-Obsessed World*. New York: Harper Collins (1997).

30. Derek Bell. *Faces at the Bottom of the Well*. New York: Free Press (1987).

Chapter 7: Ideology, Identity, and Black Political Thought

31. Marcus Garvey, "Declaration of Rights of the Negro Peoples of the World [1920]" in *Philosophy and Opinions of Marcus Garvey*, Amy Jacques Garvey (ed.) New York: Atheneum (1974).

32. Molefi Asante, "The Afrocentric Idea in Education," *Journal of Negro Education* (Spring 1991).

33. W.E.B. Du Bois, Burghardt, "The Talented Tenth [1903]," in *The Souls of Black Folk*, Nathan Huggins (ed.) New York: Literary Classics (1986).

34. Booker T. Washington, "The Atlanta Exposition Address [1895]," *Up from Slavery*. New York: Penguin (1986).

35. Shelby Steele. *The Content of Our Character*. New York: St. Martin's Press (1990).

36. Cornell West. *Race Matters*. Boston: Beacon Press (1993).

37. Patricia Hill Collins. *Black Feminist Thought: Knowledge, Consciousness, and the Politics of Empowerment*. (New York: Routledge) 1991.

Chapter 8: Racial Politics in Urban America

38. Richard Hatcher, "Inaugural Address [1967]," *Black Power Gary Style*. Alex Poinsett (ed.) Chicago: Johnson Publishing Company, Inc. (1970).

39. Lawrence D. Bobo and Franklin D. Gilliam, Jr. "Race, Socio-Political Participation, and Black Empowerment," *American Political Science Review* 84 (1990:377–393).

40. Aldon Morris, "The Future of Black Politics: Substance versus Process and Formality," *The National Political Science Review*, 3 (1993:168–174).

41. Jim Sleeper, "The End of the Rainbow" *The New Republic* (November 1993).

42. Raphael J. Sonenshein. "The Battle Over Liquor Stores in South Central Los Angeles: The Management of an Interminority Conflict." *Urban Affairs Review* 31,6 (July 1996): 710.

Chapter 9: Racial Politics at the National Level: The Presidency, the Congress, and the Supreme Court

The Presidency

43. Robert C. Smith. *We Have No Leaders: African-Americans in the Post-Civil Rights Era*. Albany: State University of New York Press (1996).

44. Jesse Jackson, *"Address Before the 1984 Democratic National Convention."*

45. Thomas Byrne Edsall with Mary D. Edsall. *Chain Reaction: The Impact of Race, Rights, and Taxes on American Politics*. (New York: W. W. Norton) 1992.

46. Renee M. Smith. "The Public Presidency Hits the Wall: Clinton's Presidential Initiative on Race." *Presidential Studies Quarterly* 28,4 (1998): 780.

Congress

47. Carol M. Swain. "The Future of Black Representation." *The American Prospect* (Fall 1995): 78.

48. Lani Guinier. "The Representation of Minority Interests." In *Classifying By Race*. Paul E. Peterson (ed.) (Princeton: Princeton University Press) 1995.

49. Kenny J. Whitby and Franklin D. Gilliam, Jr., "Representation in Congress: Line Drawing and Minorities," *Great Theater: The American Congress in the 1990s*. Herbert F. Weisberg and Samuel C. Patterson (eds.) Cambridge: Cambridge University Press (1998).

The Supreme Court

50. James L. Gibson and Gregory A. Caldeira. "Blacks and the Supreme Court: Models of Diffuse Support." *Journal of Politics* 54,4 (1992): 1120.

51. Girardeau A. Spann. *Race Against the Court: the Supreme Court and Minorities in Contemporary America*. (New York: New York University Press) 1993.

52. Stephen F. Smith. "On Justice Clarence Thomas." *Public Interest* 124 (Summer 1996): 72.

Chapter 10: Public Policy and the Future of Racial Politics in America

Poverty and Welfare

53. Michael C. Dawson. *Behind the Mule*. Princeton: Princeton University Press. (1994).

54. "Family Income, Earnings and Educational Attainment of African Americans 1967–1997," *Joint Center for Political and*

Economic Studies. (Washington D.C.: Joint Center for Political and Economic Studies) 1998.

55. William Julius Wilson. *When Work Disappears: The World of the New Urban Poor.* New York: Knopf (1997).

56. Charles Murray. *Losing Ground.* New York: Basic Books (1984).

57. Administration for Children and Families. *TANF Fact Sheet.* (Washington, D.C.: Department of Health and Human Services) 1998.

Crime and Criminal Justice

58. Marc Mauer. *Race to Incarcerate.* (New York: The New Press) 1999.

59. Edward S. Shihadeh and Graham C. Ousey. "Industrial Restructuring and Violence: The Link Between entry-level Jobs, Economic Deprivation, and Black and White Homicide." *Social Forces 77,* 1 (September 1998): 185.

60. William J. Bennett, John J. DiIulio, Jr., and John P. Walters. *Body Count: Moral Poverty . . . And How to Win America's War Against Crime and Drugs.* (New York: Simon and Schuster) 1996.

Affirmative Action

61. *Regents of the University of California v. Bakke 76 US 811 (1978).*

62. Girardeau A. Spann. *The Law of Affirmative Action : Twenty-Five Years of Supreme Court Decisions on Race and Remedies.* (New York: New York University Press) 2000.

63. California Ballot Pamphlet. *Proposition 209.* (Sacramento: California Secretary of State) 1996.

CREDITS

The American Prospect: "The Future of Black Representation" by Carol Swain from *The American Prospect*, Issue 23, Fall 1995. Reprinted with permission from The American Prospect, Copyright © 1995. The American Prospect, PO Box 383080. Cambridge, MA 02138. All rights reserved.

Beacon Press: "The Pitfalls of Racial Reasoning" pages 23–32 from *Race Matters* by Cornel West. Copyright © 1993 by Cornel West. Reprinted by permission of Beacon Press, Boston.

Cambridge University Press: "Representation in Congress: Line Drawing and Minorites" by Kenny J. Whitby and Franklin D. Gilliam, Jr., in *Great Theatre: The American Congress in the 1990s,* edited by Herbert F. Weisberg and Samuel C. Patterson. Reprinted with the permission of Cambridge University Press.

Center for the Study of Presidency: Excerpts from "The Public Policy Hits the Wall: Clinton's Presidential Initiative on Race" by R. M. Smith in *Presidential Studies Quarterly*. Copyright © 1998. Reprinted by permission.

Dover Publications: "The Atlanta Exposition Address" from *Up From Slavery* by Booker T. Washington (1919). Dover Publications, 1986.

Farrar, Straus and Giroux, LLC: Excerpts from "We Shall Overcome" from *The Struggle for Black Equality* by Harvard Sitkoff. Copyright © 1981 by Harvard Sitkoff. Reprinted by permissions of Hill and Wang, a division of Farrar, Straus and Giroux, LLC.1.

HarperCollins: Pages 214–228–242 from *Color Blind* by Ellis Cose. Copyright © 1996 by Ellis Cose. Reprinted by permission of HarperCollins Publishers, Inc. Pages 77–84, 88–9, 95–6, 102, 110, 113, 118–19, 121 from *Reconstruction: America's Unfinished Revolution 1863–1877* by Eric Foner. Copyright © 1988 by Eric Foner. Reprinted by permissions of HarperCollins Publishers, Inc.

Howard University: "The Afrocentric Idea in Education" by Molefi K. Asante in *The Journal of Negro Education*, 60(2), pages 170–180. Copyright © 1991. Reprinted by permission.

Johnson Publishing Company, Inc: Excerpt of "Inaugural Address [1967]" by R. Hatcher in *Black Power Gary Style* edited by A. Poinsett. Copyright © 1970. Reprinted by permission.

Journal of Politics: Excerpt from "Blacks and the Supreme Court: Models of Diffuse Support by J. L. Gibson and G.A. Caldeira in *Journal of Politics*. Copyright © 1992. Reprinted by permission.

Little, Brown and Company: Pages 113, 114, 115–26 from *This Side of Glory* by David Hilliard and Lewis Cole. Copyright © by David Hilliard and Lewis Cole. By permission of Little, Brown and Company (Inc.).

Louisiana State University Press: Reprinted by permissions of Louisiana State University Press from *Jim Crow's Defense: Anti-Negro Thought in America, 1900–1930,* by I.A. Newby. Copyright © 1965 by Louisiana State University Press.

McGraw-Hill: J. Franklin, *From Slavery to Freedom,* (pp. 122–26, 143–47). Copyright © 1994 by J.H. Franklin. Reprinted by permissions of The McGraw-Hill Companies.

The New Republic: "The End of the Rainbow" by Jim Sleeper, *The New Republic*, November 1, 1993. Reprinted by permission of The New Republic, Copyright © 1993, The New Republic, Inc.

New York University Press: Excerpt from *Negrophobia and Reasonable Racism* by Jody David Armour. Copyright © 1997 by New York University Press. Reprinted by permission. Pages 161, 163–71 from *Race Against the Court: the Supreme Court and Minorities in Contemporary America* by Girardeau A. Spann. Copyright © 1993 by New York University Press. Reprinted by permission.

Pathfinder Press: Selection from *Malcolm X Speaks* by Malcolm X. Copyright © 1965, 1989 by Betty Shabazz and Pathfinder Press. Reprinted by permission.

Perseus Books Group: Chapter 3 (pages 47–64) from *Faces at the Bottom of the Well* by Derrick Bell. Copyright © by BasicBooks, Inc. Reprinted by permission of Basic-Books, a member of Perseus Books, LLC. Pages 154–167 from *Losing Ground: American Social Policy 1950–1980* by Charles Murray. Copyright © 1984 by Charles Murray. Reprinted by permission of Basic-Books, a member of Perseus Books, LLC.

Princeton University Press: Pages 15–18, 21–25, 28–30, and 32–34 from *Behind the Mule* by Michael C. Dawson. Copyright © 1994 by Princeton University Press. Reprinted by permission of Princeton University Press. Pages 21, 22, 33–42 from "The Representation of Minority Interests" by Lani Guiner in *Classifying by Race* edited by Paul E. Peterson. Copyright © 1995 by Princeton University Press. Reprinted by permission of Princeton University Press.

Public Interest: Selection from "On Justice Clarence Thomas" by S.F. Smith in *Public Interest*. Copyright © 1996. Reprinted by permssion.

Random House, Inc.: Excerpts from "A Woman's Revolution" in *A Taste of Power: A Black Woman's Story* by Elaine Brown. Copyright © 1992 by Elaine Brown. Reprinted by permission of Pantheon, a Division of Random House, Inc. Excerpts from *When Work Disappears* by William Julius Wilson. Copyright © 1996 by William Julius Wilson. Reprinted by permission of Alfred A. Knopf, a Division of Random House, Inc.

Routledge, Inc: Excerpt pages 19–22 and 33–39, copyright © 1991 from *Black Feminist Thought: Knowledge, Consciousness, and The Politics of Empowerment* by Patricia Collins. Reproduced by permission of Taylor & Francis, Inc./Routledge, Inc., http://www.routledge-ny.com.

Rutgers University: "The Future of Black Politics: Substance Versus Process and Formality" by Aldon Morris in *The National Political Science Review*, issue 3, pages 168–74. Copyright © 1993. Reprinted by permission of Transaction Publishers, Rutgers University.

The Scarecrow Press: Excerpt from *The Black Panther Party Platform* by G. L. Heath, Copyright © 1966. Reprinted by permission.

Simon & Schuster: Reprinted with the permission of Simon & Schuster from *Parting the Waters*, by Taylor Branch. Copyright © by Taylor Branch. Reprinted with the permission of Simon & Schuster from "Declaration of Rights of the Negro Peoples of the World" in *Philosophy and Opinions of Marcus Garvey* by Marcus Garvey. Copyright © 1986 by Antheneum. Reprinted with the permission of The Free Press, a Division of Simon & Schuster, Inc., from *The Origins of the Civil Rights Movement: Black Communities Organizing for Change* by Aldon D. Morris. Copyright © 1984 by The Free Press.

Social Forces: "Industrial Restructuring and Violence: The Link Between Entry-Level Jobs, Economic Deprivation, and Black and White Homicide" by E. Shihadeh. Reprinted from *Social Forces*, Vol. 77, 1998. Copyright © The University of North Carolina Press.

State University of New York Press: Excerpt from *We Have No Leaders: African-Americans in the Post-Civil Rights Era* by Robert C. Smith by permission of the State University of New York Press. Copyright © 1996 State University of New York. All rights reserved.

Student Non-violent Coordinating Committee: "The Basis of Black Power" Copyright © 1965. Reprinted by permission.